BETTY CROCKER'S
COOKING
AMERICAN STYLE
A Sampler Of Heritage Recipes

Betty Crocker's
4 IN 1 COOKBOOK COLLECTION

1
Betty Crocker's
COOKING AMERICAN STYLE

2
Betty Crocker's
SALADS

3
Betty Crocker's
HAMBURGER COOKBOOK

4
Betty Crocker's
DO-AHEAD COOKBOOK

 **GOLDEN PRESS • NEW YORK**
Western Publishing Company, Inc.
Racine, Wisconsin

BETTY CROCKER'S
COOKING
AMERICAN STYLE
A Sampler Of Heritage Recipes

®️ **Golden Press/New York**
Western Publishing Company, Inc.
Racine, Wisconsin

Photo credits appear on page 160.

Printed in the U.S.A. by Western Publishing Company, Inc.
Published by Golden Press, New York, New York.
Library of Congress Catalog Card Number: 75-34817

CONTENTS

INTRODUCTION

A collection of American recipes is a little like the friendship quilts women all over the country used to sew. Each friend gave something of her own, so that the finished quilt was full of personal memories stitched into a colorful design.

This book, too, is filled with memories. Good cooking from many places and backgrounds has contributed to the great variety in our culinary heritage. Region by region it is perhaps impossible to define American cooking, but when favorite recipes are gathered in one book, many overall characteristics do begin to emerge, like the pattern in a quilt. Side by side we find catfish cooked in a small farmhouse in Georgia and Cioppino assembled in a San Francisco apartment. We find Hasty Pudding from New England and Corn Oysters from the Midwest. Even a glance through this group of American recipes is proof of the two outstanding qualities of American cooking: the legendary American ingenuity and the diversity of influences. From this wide array we've chosen a sampler of American favorites, as appealing today as they were in the region or time they originated.

The people from all over the world who settled America brought their own food customs and, often, seeds in their pockets or sewn into their clothes. Somewhere in this huge new country they found a climate or a landscape that reminded them of home. They planted their native produce and reproduced their favorite recipes. With inventive substitutions for what was not available, the recipes gradually accommodated themselves to the new land. Children and grandchildren raised on the American versions of their parents' traditional ethnic foods are usually surprised when they travel to their ancestors' homeland. The well-loved breads, pastas or desserts are not the same there. Like the people, the recipes became naturalized Americans.

Ethnic and regional specialties are still a strong part of our evolving style, but now the variety of foods available throughout the country makes it possible for us to reproduce any recipe we desire. The continuing thread in our patchwork is the lucky abundance of vegetables, dairy products, meats and grains throughout our history. This abundance, as much as the diversity of the settlers, has influenced the extensive variety we continue to enjoy.

Almost anything can be grown in at least one of the fifty states, and with our shipping network, North Dakotans enjoy fresh artichokes from California, New Yorkers appreciate the tender Carolina okra and spring asparagus arrives in still-frozen Michigan almost as fresh as when it left Florida. Modern growing and storage techniques have made the limitations of season and place almost obsolete. Alaskan crab is very much at home in Missouri, and some of the most ephemeral berries travel all over the country both in and out of season.

The abundance and choice we take for granted today actually began after 1840. Until then fruits and vegetables were limited to their short growing seasons and were available only in their special locales. Since all food was thought to have the same nutritional value, there was no widespread interest in elusive vegetables. Nourishment meant one thing: quantity! But suddenly in the 1840s a new and important word, *iceman*, came into general use. Along with the icebox in the kitchen came the railroad cars bringing fresh produce, seafood and meat to the cities. One of the first such systems ran along the "pea shore" of New Jersey and picked up seasonal vegetables and fruits for New York City.

The perfection of the canning process at about the same time also helped revolutionize the American diet. By the end of the Civil War the soldiers, who had first tasted canned seafood, corned beef and vegetables in army camps, spread the word all over the country. From then on, ships, Conestoga wagons and households were stocked with rows of "tins." The era of convenience had begun.

More than anything else, the expansion of the railroad in the West sped this era of variety in foods on its way. After the 1880s the refrigerated railroad cars that crisscrossed the country supplied Americans with still more fresh beef and pork. Later, irrigation of the great valleys of California made a perpetual growing season for many fruits and vegetables.

These changes were rapid. The rural household stocked with root vegetables, salted meat and a barrel of cider evolved in little more than a few decades into our demanding kitchens that take for granted foods from all over the country and the electric appliances that help us prepare them.

Today, cooking demonstrations on television, more leisure time, easier world travel and fine cooking equipment give American cooks their sophisticated approach to food.

One result of this new sophistication is a renewed appreciation for our own heritage, a rediscovery of the best eating traditions of American households. We've begun to value the unique aspects of our cooking history, especially the experimental and adaptive attitudes American cooks always have had.

That was so of necessity. The very first transactions between the Indians and the English settlers seem to have involved food—the corn, squashes and beans native to America. These versatile vegetables and the game and seafood plentiful along the New England coast became the foundation of American cooking. Over 350 years later, the most definite culinary heritage we feel is for the foods that carried the English settlers through those first few winters. A pungent pot of baked beans, a pumpkin pie fragrant with spices, creamy clam chowder, the colorful mixture of limas and corn—these still are rich in our memories.

We are a long way from the frugal cupboards of colonial days. Far enough in fact that many cooks are reviving the old skills of preserving fruits, baking breads and making sausage. Often in our nostalgia for the time when food was "natural," when pickles lined the kitchen shelves and the house was filled with the warm smell of freshly baked loaves, we forget the long hours of drudgery our great-grandmothers put in to produce those foods. Even a quick look at antique cookbooks, with their advice about various agues and chills and their herbal cures and purges, reminds us of the different household skills involved at that backbreaking time. It's not hard to imagine that any great-grandmother, given the choice, would opt for easier cooking methods.

Our rediscovery of American culinary traditions, then, is from the long viewpoint of progress. With our modern appliances and supermarkets, we are free to enjoy fully the preparation of early American dishes and to continue to experiment with food in the best tradition of American cooking. Perhaps it is from this point on, now that the flow of immigration has slowed, that American cooking will take new directions. After all, our history is very short, and it took hundreds of years for other cuisines to develop.

The development of American cooking thus far has been well documented. In 1796 Amelia Simmons wrote *American Cookery*, the first book to include native foods. Ever since then cookbooks have been flourishing publications both nationally and locally. Women's organizations always have made and sold collections of recipes, not only as a way to raise funds, but from a desire to share good food. *Betty Crocker's Cooking American Style* continues in that tradition of sharing. We have simply selected good food from American kitchens past and present. The ingredients and instructions for the recipes had to be updated for modern kitchens, and, of course, every recipe was tested thoroughly by the staff at the Betty Crocker Kitchens. Not surprisingly, the recipes evoked an enthusiastic response from both our staff and the home testers throughout the country who were delighted to rediscover these traditional favorites.

Many recipes we've included keep to the basic simplicity and naturalness of the early settlers' food. Breads, corn, seafood and relishes, particularly, hearken back to those thrifty cooks who took advantage of what was naturally available. In our own time we can learn a lot about economizing by adapting their principles. Also well represented in our collection is the hearty food of the farmlands, where cooks continued in that early habit of integrity of ingredients, bounty and wholesomeness.

From these foundations we've collected a group of America's best-loved foods. Many of the recipes are traditional, and a real effort has been made to preserve the essence of the original "receipts." Many are authentic regional specialties and some are more recent recipes that have become popular all across the country.

These recipes testify to the fact that American cooking is still innovative and adaptive. From our diverse beginnings and our rich heritage, we continue to reap an abundant harvest.

Pictured opposite.
An array of bakings from all across the country. Clockwise from top: Georgia Raised Biscuits (page 10), Midwest Chocolate Cake (page 23), Sourdough Bread (page 16), Rhubarb and Strawberry Pie (page 49) and Yellow Fruitcake (page 28).

BAKING DAY

BAKING DAY

One marvel of American cooking is the large number of baking recipes that survive from a time when the circumstances and ingredients made baking a difficult and rigorous task fraught with chance. Until 1890, cup and spoon sizes were variable, and recipes usually were no more specific than "add a teacup" or "a wine glass" or, most mysteriously, "a lump." In addition, there were no regulated ovens and often no leavening. As these baking recipes were handed down, many a cake must have emerged from the oven as heavy as lead. Before the invention of baking powder, the determination to produce a light cake often went to great lengths. One early pound cake recipe from Virginia instructs that the eggs be beaten for *five* hours before adding them to the batter. About the fate of the unfortunate cook no record remains!

In early New England, baking day centered on breads made with cornmeal or with dried pumpkin that was ground into a flour. The simplest loaf was actually a flat cake made of cornmeal, water and salt, which came to be known as "johnnycake." Cornmeal was the baker's staple, North and South. Hoecake and ashcake, similar to johnnycake, were common, and in the South spoon bread was—and still is—a popular dish made with cornmeal. All corn grown in America is of five basic kinds, and these different varieties of corn produce different meals when ground. Boone County white, a type of dent corn, produced the fine white meal Southerners preferred in their baking, while Northerners tended to use flint corn, which produced the yellow, slightly heavier meal. Early Americans always were fond of hot breads with meals.

The Dutch settlers in New York were more progressive in bread making than their New England neighbors, whose wheat crops failed in the Massachusetts soil. Missing their native breads—waffles, crullers and doughnuts—the Dutch quickly planted fields of wheat, barley and rye, then built windmills to grind the grains. Soon the New Netherlands wheat was sold to the colonies in the North and South, but the breads made from wheat continued to be special until the great wheat farms of the Midwest began pouring out their bounty in the middle of the nineteenth century.

In the West, the pioneer women, the prospectors and the chuckwagon cooks who baked breads along the trail were cooking under the most adverse circumstances. Sourdough is a bread that became so identified with the early prospectors that they even were called "sourdoughs." Crocks of "starter" for sourdough biscuits, pancakes and loaves were kept going for years. Each time the cook used a little starter, more flour, water and salt were added to the crock and the fermentation continued. When temperatures dropped, the trail cook sometimes took the crock to bed so the cold wouldn't kill the starter.

If bread baking was tricky, fine baking was even more hazardous. The easily available coarse grains were heavy. Later perlash, a leavener derived from burned wood, was introduced for

Wheat fields seem to stretch forever across the American prairie.

baking, but many cooks refused to use it because it had a bitter taste. Finally, in the last half of the nineteenth century, there were two major breakthroughs. One was the commercial production of baking powder, which started in the 1850s. After a large advertising campaign and the publication of cookbooks by the manufacturer, suspicious housewives finally were convinced of the safety of the product, which for years had been rumored to be poisonous.

Then came the development of the milling industry in the Midwest. From early beginnings, two men, Washburn and Crosby, established the Washburn Crosby Company, which later with other interests formed General Mills.

Many cakes that were popular over a century ago are still being made today. Of course we have standardized the measurements and carefully adapted every recipe to modern kitchens. Many of the old recipes were known as "great" cakes for a reason: the enormous quantities of ingredients they called for. The recipes in this chapter keep all that was "great" except the size and effort. One of these famous cakes, perhaps the glory of the Southern kitchen, is Lane Cake, which with its strong competitor Lady Baltimore, is still a traditional holiday treat. Maple-Nut Chiffon Cake, Midwest Chocolate Cake and Boston Cream Pie are also representative of the rich legacy we've inherited from determined bakers.

Though pastry desserts are common all over the world, pies somehow seem peculiarly American. Probably this is because so many of our favorites developed here. Pumpkin pie is, of course, a native. English main-dish "pyes" of minced meats evolved in America into desserts sweetened with molasses. The abundance of fruits inspired cobblers, pandowdies, deep dish pies, tarts, dumplings—all guises for simple fruit pies. In this section we've gathered a pie-safe full of the great favorites: Apple Pandowdy, Fresh Blueberry Tart, Apple Dumplings. Our Rhubarb and Strawberry Pie and Mincemeat-Pumpkin Pie are marvelous variations on old standbys. Superb Black Bottom, Chess and Shoofly Pies are so tempting they'll make you want to revive the old farm custom of pie for breakfast.

Also in this section are cookies: Jumbles, Hermits, Joe Froggers and icebox cookies—now updated and called Refrigerator Nut Cookies. These and others are great nibbles for a lunch box or for that one thing that hasn't changed in the American kitchen—the cookie jar.

Happily, most of the rigors of baking have long since disappeared. Aided not only by ovens with thermostats, but by dependable yeast, baking powder, timers and standardized recipes, even a novice can enjoy baking. Surely there is no greater example of the heritage of the American cook than this legacy of fine breads, cakes, cookies and pies.

BREADS

DIXIE BISCUITS

2 cups cake flour or 1¾
   cups all-purpose flour*
2½ teaspoons baking powder
¾ teaspoon salt**

⅓ cup shortening or firm
   butter or margarine
¾ cup milk

Heat oven to 425°. Mix flour, baking powder and salt. Cut in shortening until mixture looks like fine crumbs. Stir in almost all the milk. Stir in just enough additional milk to make a soft, puffy, easy-to-roll dough. (Too much milk makes dough sticky, not enough makes biscuits dry.)

Round up dough on lightly floured cloth-covered board. (If using all-purpose flour, knead about 10 times.) Pat into circle about ½ inch thick with floured hands. Fold into thirds; pat again into circle about ½ inch thick. Cut with floured 1¾-inch biscuit cutter.

Place on ungreased baking sheet 1 inch apart for crusty sides, close together for soft sides. Prick biscuits several times with fork. Brush biscuits with light corn syrup, evaporated milk, slightly beaten egg or egg white if desired.

Bake until golden brown, 12 to 15 minutes. Serve hot. ABOUT 16 BISCUITS.

*If using self-rising flour, omit baking powder and salt.
**If using butter or margarine, reduce salt to ½ teaspoon.

GEORGIA RAISED BISCUITS

1 package active dry yeast
2 cups warm water (105 to
   115°)
4½ cups all-purpose flour*

1 tablespoon sugar
2 teaspoons salt
½ cup shortening
Butter or margarine, softened

Dissolve yeast in warm water; reserve. Mix flour, sugar and salt. Cut in shortening until mixture looks like fine crumbs. Stir in reserved yeast mixture to make a soft, puffy, easy-to-roll dough.

Round up dough on lightly floured cloth-covered board. Knead 20 to 25 times. Divide in half; roll each half ¼ inch thick. Cut with floured 2-inch biscuit cutter. Spread tops of biscuits with butter. Place half of the biscuits buttered sides up 1 inch apart on ungreased baking sheet. Top with remaining biscuits, buttered sides up. Cover; let rise until almost double, about 45 minutes.

Heat oven to 400°. Bake until golden brown, 15 to 20 minutes. Serve hot.   ABOUT 2½ DOZEN BISCUITS.

*If using self-rising flour, omit salt.

Many of America's hot breads originated in the South, where breakfast still is not complete without ham and biscuits. On the opposite page, Crusty Dixie Biscuits with slivers of Smithfield ham make a delicate sandwich, and the soft, puffy Georgia Raised Biscuits layered with slices of ham are good for Sunday supper.

The light, sugar-crusted Yam Muffins that follow are especially good with pork dishes, as Louisiana families have enjoyed them for generations. But all of these biscuits and muffins can be thoroughly enjoyed with your favorite spread, preserve or honey.

YAM MUFFINS

1½ cups all-purpose flour*
½ cup sugar
2 teaspoons baking powder
½ teaspoon salt
½ teaspoon ground cinnamon
½ teaspoon ground nutmeg
½ cup milk
½ cup mashed cooked yams or
   sweet potatoes

¼ cup butter or margarine,
   melted
1 egg
½ cup chopped pecans or
   walnuts (optional)
1 tablespoon sugar

Heat oven to 400°. Grease bottoms of 12 medium muffin cups (2¾ inches in diameter). Mix all ingredients except 1 tablespoon sugar just until all flour is moistened. Batter should be lumpy. Fill muffin cups ⅔ full. Sprinkle ¼ teaspoon sugar over batter in each cup.

Bake 18 to 20 minutes. Immediately remove from pan.   1 DOZEN MUFFINS.

*If using self-rising flour, omit baking powder and salt.

BLUEBERRY MUFFINS

1 egg
1 cup milk
¼ cup vegetable oil
2 cups all-purpose flour*

¼ cup sugar
3 teaspoons baking powder
1 teaspoon salt
1 cup blueberries

Heat oven to 400°. Grease bottoms of 12 medium muffin cups (2¾ inches in diameter). Beat egg; stir in milk and oil. Stir in flour, sugar, baking powder and salt just until all flour is moistened. Batter should be lumpy. Fold in blueberries. Fill muffin cups ⅔ full.

Bake until golden brown, 20 to 25 minutes. Immediately remove from pan.   1 DOZEN MUFFINS.

*If using self-rising flour, omit baking powder and salt.

The early settlers learned to cook with cranberries from the Indians of the Cape Cod area, who added cranberries and nuts to their corn breads. Cakes of dried venison and cranberries, called pemmican, were a mainstay of the Indian diet.

CRANBERRY-ORANGE NUT BREAD

2 cups all-purpose flour*
¾ cup sugar
1½ teaspoons baking powder
¾ teaspoon salt
½ teaspoon baking soda
¼ cup butter or margarine,
  softened

1 tablespoon grated orange peel
¾ cup orange juice
1 egg
1 cup cranberries, chopped
½ cup chopped nuts

Heat oven to 350°. Grease bottom of loaf pan, 9x5x3 inches. Mix flour, sugar, baking powder, salt and baking soda. Stir in butter until mixture is crumbly. Stir in orange peel, juice and egg just until all flour is moistened. Stir in cranberries and nuts. Spread in pan.

Bake until wooden pick inserted in center comes out clean, 55 to 65 minutes. Loosen edges of loaf with spatula; remove from pan. Let stand at least 8 hours before slicing.

*If using self-rising flour, omit baking powder and salt. Reduce baking soda to ¼ teaspoon.

BOSTON BROWN BREAD

1 cup all-purpose flour* or rye flour
1 cup whole wheat flour
1 cup cornmeal
2 teaspoons baking soda
1 teaspoon salt

2 cups buttermilk
¾ cup molasses
1 cup raisins (optional)
Butter or margarine

Grease four 4¼x3-inch cans (16-ounce vegetable cans). Beat all ingredients except butter 30 seconds on low speed in large mixer bowl, scraping bowl constantly. Pour into cans, filling each about ⅔ full. Cover each tightly with aluminum foil.

Place cans on rack in Dutch oven or steamer; pour boiling water into pan to level of rack. Cover pan. Keep water boiling over low heat until wooden pick inserted in center of bread comes out clean, about 3 hours. (Add boiling water, if necessary, during steaming.)

Remove cans from pan; immediately unmold breads. Serve warm with butter.

*If using self-rising flour, reduce baking soda to 1 teaspoon and omit salt.

We're probably fortunate in our culinary heritage that white flour wasn't readily available in early America. If it had been, perhaps we might not have developed the wide range of recipes in our baking tradition that the use of other grains gave us.

One of these grains was buckwheat, which was immortalized in the song "Dixie": "There's buckwheat cakes and Injun batter . . ." but is even more popular in the Northwest. Another grain, rye, was also available early on. It was mixed with cornmeal to make Rye 'n' Injun, a dark bread flavored with molasses. The perfection of that rough loaf became our steamed Boston Brown Bread.

Many corn breads were named for their shapes or the way they were cooked, and these simple names are often quaint to modern ears. Ashcakes, corn pone, scratch back, hasty pudding, hoecakes, spider bread, johnnycakes and slappers are a few of the breads that were familiar to the early settlers. Another, baked grits, is made from coarse cornmeal ground from hulled corn. Traditionally, Baked Grits with Garlic Cheese accompanies turkey, quail or other game birds.

BUCKWHEAT CAKES

1 package active dry yeast
¼ cup warm water (105 to 115°)
1¾ cups lukewarm milk
  (scalded, then cooled)
2 tablespoons packed brown
  sugar
1 teaspoon salt
3 eggs
¼ cup butter or margarine,
  softened
1 cup all-purpose flour*
1 cup buckwheat flour

Dissolve yeast in warm water in 3-quart bowl. Stir in remaining ingredients. Beat until smooth. Cover; let rise in warm place 1½ hours. Stir down batter. Cover; refrigerate at least 8 hours. (Batter can be kept up to 12 hours in refrigerator.)

Stir down batter. Grease heated griddle if necessary. Pour batter from ¼-cup measuring cup or tip of large spoon onto griddle. Turn cakes as soon as they are puffed and full of bubbles but before bubbles break. Bake other side until golden brown. ABOUT SIXTEEN 4-INCH CAKES.

*If using self-rising flour, omit salt.

NOTE: Unbleached flour can be substituted for all-purpose flour in this recipe.

Buckwheat Waffles: Pour batter from cup or pitcher onto center of hot waffle iron. Bake until steaming stops, about 5 minutes. Remove waffle carefully. ABOUT EIGHT 7-INCH WAFFLES.

Whole Wheat Cakes and Waffles: Substitute stone-ground whole wheat flour for the buckwheat flour.

FLUFFY SPOON BREAD

1½ cups boiling water
1 cup cornmeal
1 tablespoon butter or
    margarine, softened
3 eggs, separated
1 cup buttermilk

1 teaspoon salt
1 teaspoon sugar
1 teaspoon baking powder
¼ teaspoon baking soda
Butter or margarine

Heat oven to 375°. Grease 2-quart casserole. Stir boiling water into cornmeal; continue stirring to prevent lumping until mixture is cool. Blend in 1 tablespoon butter and the egg yolks. Stir in buttermilk, salt, sugar, baking powder and baking soda. Beat egg whites just until soft peaks form; fold into batter. Pour into casserole.

Bake until puffed and golden brown, 45 to 50 minutes. Serve hot with butter.

JOHNNYCAKES

1 cup cornmeal
1 tablespoon sugar (optional)
1 teaspoon salt

1 cup boiling water
1 cup milk
Bacon fat

Heat cornmeal in 2-quart ovenproof bowl in 375° oven, stirring twice, 5 minutes. Stir in sugar and salt. Pour in boiling water gradually, stirring vigorously with fork until all lumps are removed. Stir in enough milk to make a smooth, slightly thick batter. Grease heated griddle with bacon fat. Pour batter from ¼-cup measuring cup onto griddle, spreading to ¼-inch thickness.

Bake on both sides until brown. Stir enough milk into batter, if necessary, to make batter easy to spread.   ABOUT 8 JOHNNYCAKES.

BROILED CORNMEAL ROUNDS

1 cup dairy sour cream
¼ teaspoon salt
¼ teaspoon baking soda

1 egg, slightly beaten
⅔ cup white cornmeal
⅓ cup bacon fat, melted

Set oven control to broil and/or 550°. Mix sour cream, salt, baking soda and egg. Beat in cornmeal gradually until smooth. Stir in 3 tablespoons of the bacon fat. Divide remaining bacon fat among 12 medium muffin cups (2¾ inches in diameter); spread up sides of cups. Place muffin pan so top is 6 inches from heat; heat until bacon fat is hot, about 2 minutes. Pour about 2 tablespoons batter into each cup. Broil until tops are brown, 6 to 8 minutes.   12 ROUNDS.

Pictured opposite.
Cornmeal is the common starting point for these three American favorites. Left: Fluffy Spoon Bread. Right: Broiled Cornmeal Rounds. Bottom: Johnnycakes.

SQUASH ROLLS

1 cup milk
2 tablespoons butter or
   margarine
½ cup sugar
1 teaspoon salt

1 package active dry yeast
¼ cup warm water (105 to 115°)
1 cup mashed cooked winter
   squash
4½ to 5 cups all-purpose flour*

Heat milk, butter, sugar and salt until butter is melted. Cool to lukewarm. Dissolve yeast in warm water in 3-quart bowl. Stir in milk mixture, squash and 2 cups of the flour. Beat until smooth. Mix in enough remaining flour to make dough easy to handle.

Turn dough onto lightly floured surface; knead until smooth and elastic, about 5 minutes. Place in greased bowl; turn greased side up. Cover; let rise in warm place until double, about 1½ hours. (Dough is ready if an indentation remains when touched.)

Punch down dough. Shape into 1-inch balls. Place 3 balls in each of 24 greased medium muffin cups (2¾ inches in diameter). Let rise until double, 30 to 45 minutes.

Heat oven to 400°. Bake until light brown, 15 to 20 minutes. 2 DOZEN ROLLS.

*If using self-rising flour, omit salt.

Tortillas, breads with a Mexican heritage, are eagerly enjoyed at this San Antonio fiesta.

On the unsettled American frontier, every traveler carried a crock of sourdough starter for bread and flapjacks. Today, however, Sourdough Bread is almost synonymous with San Francisco. Booths at the airport sell the long paper-wrapped loaves to departing travelers much as stations at the edge of the desert sell gas.

As our recipe proves, it *is* possible to bake a good loaf at home, though without a humidity-controlled oven it's impossible to duplicate exactly the crusty loaves sold along the wharf.

SOURDOUGH BREAD

1 cup Sourdough Starter
   (page 17)
2½ cups all-purpose flour*
2 cups warm water (105 to 115°)
3¾ to 4¼ cups all-purpose flour*

3 tablespoons sugar
1 teaspoon salt
¼ teaspoon baking soda
3 tablespoons vegetable oil
Cold water

Mix Sourdough Starter, 2½ cups flour and 2 cups warm water in 3-quart glass bowl with wooden spoon until smooth. Cover; let stand in warm, draft-free place 8 hours.

Add 3¾ cups of the flour, the sugar, salt, baking soda and oil to mixture in bowl. Stir with wooden spoon until dough is smooth and flour is completely absorbed. (Dough should be just firm enough to gather into a ball. If necessary, add remaining ½ cup flour gradually, stirring until all flour is absorbed.)

Turn dough onto heavily floured surface; knead until smooth and elastic, about 10 minutes. Place in greased bowl; turn greased side up. Cover; let rise in warm place until dough is double, about 1½ hours. (Dough is ready if an indentation remains when touched lightly.)

Punch down dough; divide in half. Shape each half into a round, slightly flat loaf. Do not tear dough. Place loaves in opposite corners of greased baking sheet. Make three ¼-inch slashes in each loaf. Let rise until double, about 45 minutes.

Heat oven to 375°. Brush loaves with cold water. Place in middle of oven. Bake until loaves sound hollow when tapped, about 50 minutes, brushing occasionally with water. Remove from baking sheet; cool on wire racks.   2 LOAVES.

*Do not use self-rising flour in this recipe.

SOURDOUGH STARTER

1 teaspoon active dry yeast
¼ cup warm water (105 to 115°)
¾ cup milk
1 cup all-purpose flour*

Dissolve yeast in warm water in 3-quart glass bowl. Stir in milk. Stir in flour gradually. Beat until smooth. Cover with towel or cheesecloth; let stand in warm, draft-free place (80 to 85°) until starter begins to ferment, about 24 hours (bubbles will appear on surface of starter). If starter has not begun fermentation after 24 hours, discard and begin again. If fermentation has begun, stir well; cover tightly with plastic wrap and return to warm, draft-free place. Let starter stand until foamy, 2 to 3 days.

When starter has become foamy, stir well; pour into 1-quart crock or glass jar with tight fitting cover. Store in refrigerator. Starter is ready to use when a clear liquid has risen to top. Stir before using. Use 1 cup starter in recipe; reserve remaining starter. To remaining starter, add ¾ cup milk and ¾ cup flour. Store covered at room temperature until bubbles appear, about 12 hours; refrigerate.

Use starter regularly, every week or so. If the volume of the breads you bake begins to decrease, dissolve 1 teaspoon active dry yeast in ¼ cup warm water. Stir in ½ cup milk, ¾ cup flour and the remaining starter.

*Do not use self-rising flour in this recipe.

POTATO DOUGHNUTS

1 package active dry yeast
1½ cups warm water (105 to
   115°)
⅔ cup sugar
1½ teaspoons salt
⅔ cup shortening

2 eggs
1 cup lukewarm mashed
   cooked potatoes
6 to 7 cups all-purpose flour*
Glaze (below)

Dissolve yeast in warm water in 3-quart bowl. Stir in sugar, salt, shortening, eggs, potatoes and 3 cups of the flour. Beat until smooth. Mix in enough remaining flour to make dough easy to handle.

Turn dough onto well-floured surface; knead until smooth and elastic, about 5 minutes. Place in greased bowl; turn greased side up. Cover tightly; refrigerate at least 8 hours.

Punch down dough. Pat ¾ inch thick on lightly floured surface. Cut with floured 2½-inch doughnut cutter. Cover; let rise in warm place until indentation remains when touched, 45 to 60 minutes.

Heat vegetable oil or shortening (3 to 4 inches) to 375° in deep fat fryer or heavy saucepan. Fry doughnuts, turning once, until golden brown, 2 to 4 minutes; drain on paper. While warm, dip doughnuts in Glaze.   ABOUT 2½ DOZEN DOUGHNUTS.

*If using self-rising flour, omit salt.

GLAZE
Mix 3 cups powdered sugar and ½ cup boiling water until smooth.

BAKED GRITS WITH GARLIC CHEESE

2 cups milk
2 cups water
1 cup quick grits
1 teaspoon salt
¼ teaspoon pepper
1 package (6 ounces)
   garlic-flavored pasteurized
   process cheese spread

2 eggs, slightly beaten
1 tablespoon butter or
   margarine

Heat oven to 350°. Mix milk, water, grits, salt and pepper in 2-quart saucepan. Heat to boiling, stirring occasionally; reduce heat. Simmer uncovered, stirring frequently, until thick, about 5 minutes. Blend in cheese spread. Stir ¼ of the hot mixture into eggs; stir into remaining hot mixture in saucepan. Pour into greased 1½-quart casserole. Dot with butter. Bake uncovered 40 minutes. 6 TO 8 SERVINGS.

Pictured opposite.
A legacy of caring: Potato Doughnuts—and their holes—still warm and delicately glazed. Perhaps even better than those Great-grandma used to make!

Sticky buns, honey buns, pecan rolls—whatever they're called in your part of the country, these gooey-rich sweet rolls are an anytime natural with coffee, tea or milk.

STICKY BUNS

1 package active dry yeast
¼ cup warm water (105 to 115°)
¾ cup lukewarm milk (scalded, then cooled)
¼ cup granulated sugar
1 teaspoon salt
1 egg
½ cup butter or margarine, softened

3 to 3½ cups all-purpose flour*
Caramel Sauce (below)
1½ to 2 cups pecan halves
¼ cup butter or margarine, softened
½ cup granulated sugar
½ cup packed brown sugar
1½ teaspoons ground cinnamon

Dissolve yeast in warm water in 3-quart bowl. Stir in milk, ¼ cup granulated sugar, the salt, egg, ½ cup butter and 1½ cups of the flour. Beat until smooth. Mix in enough remaining flour to make dough easy to handle.

Turn dough onto lightly floured surface; knead until smooth and elastic, about 5 minutes. Place in greased bowl; turn greased side up. Cover; let rise in warm place until double, about 1½ hours. (Dough is ready if an indentation remains when touched.)

Pour about 1 tablespoon Caramel Sauce into each of 36 greased medium muffin cups (2¾ inches in diameter). Place 3 or 4 pecan halves flat sides up in sauce in each muffin cup.

Punch down dough; divide in half. Roll each half into rectangle, 18x9 inches, on lightly floured surface. Spread with 2 tablespoons butter. Mix ½ cup granulated sugar, the brown sugar and cinnamon. Sprinkle half of the sugar-cinnamon mixture evenly over each rectangle. Roll up tightly, beginning at one of the long sides. Pinch edge of dough into roll to seal. Stretch and shape until even. Cut each roll into 18 slices about 1 inch wide. Place 1 slice cut side down in each muffin cup. Let rise until double, about 45 minutes.

Heat oven to 375°. Bake until golden brown, 15 to 20 minutes. Immediately invert on large trays or baking sheets. Let pans remain a minute so caramel will drizzle down.   3 DOZEN BUNS.

*If using self-rising flour, omit salt.

CARAMEL SAUCE
Heat 1 cup packed brown sugar, 1 cup dark corn syrup and ¼ cup butter or margarine to boiling; reduce heat. Simmer uncovered 1 minute; cool.

SUNSHINE CAKE

8 egg whites
½ teaspoon cream of tartar
½ teaspoon salt
1½ cups sugar
5 egg yolks

1 cup all-purpose flour*
2 tablespoons water
½ teaspoon almond extract
½ teaspoon lemon extract
½ teaspoon vanilla

Heat oven to 325°. Beat egg whites, cream of tartar and salt in large mixer bowl until foamy. Beat in 1 cup of the sugar, 1 tablespoon at a time; continue beating until stiff and glossy. Reserve meringue.

Beat egg yolks in small mixer bowl until very thick and lemon colored, about 5 minutes. Beat in remaining ½ cup sugar gradually. Beat in flour alternately with water and flavorings on low speed. Fold egg yolk mixture into reserved meringue. Spread in ungreased tube pan, 10x4 inches. Cut through batter gently with spatula.

Bake until top springs back when touched lightly in center, 1 hour to 1 hour 5 minutes. Immediately invert pan on funnel; let hang until completely cool.

*If using self-rising flour, omit salt.

It seems that pound cakes, with their virtues of lasting well and not requiring a frosting, have always been a teatime standby. Old recipes call for a pound each of flour, eggs, butter and sugar, mixed and then baked in one-pound loaves. Here's an updated version that keeps the name but skips the pounds.

POUND CAKE

2¾ cups sugar
1¼ cups butter or margarine,
   softened
5 eggs
1 teaspoon vanilla

3 cups all-purpose flour*
1 teaspoon baking powder
½ teaspoon ground mace
¼ teaspoon salt
1 cup evaporated milk

Heat oven to 350°. Grease and flour tube pan, 10x4 inches, or 12-cup bundt cake pan. Beat sugar, butter, eggs and vanilla 30 seconds on low speed in large mixer bowl, scraping bowl constantly. Beat 5 minutes on high speed, scraping bowl occasionally. Beat in flour, baking powder, mace and salt alternately with milk on low speed. Spread in pan.

Bake until wooden pick inserted in center comes out clean, 1 hour 10 minutes to 1 hour 20 minutes. Cool 20 minutes; remove from pan. Cool completely.

*Do not use self-rising flour in this recipe.

HARD TIMES CAKE

1 cup packed brown sugar
2 teaspoons ground cinnamon
½ teaspoon ground nutmeg
½ teaspoon ground cloves
1¼ cups water
⅓ cup shortening

2 cups raisins
2 cups all-purpose flour*
1 teaspoon baking powder
1 teaspoon baking soda
1 teaspoon salt

Mix sugar, cinnamon, nutmeg, cloves, water, shortening and raisins in 2-quart saucepan. Heat to boiling. Boil uncovered 3 minutes; cool.

Heat oven to 325°. Grease and flour loaf pan, 9x5x3 inches, or baking pan, 9x9x2 inches. Mix flour, baking powder, baking soda and salt. Stir into raisin mixture. Pour into pan.

Bake until wooden pick inserted in center comes out clean, loaf about 1¼ hours, square about 55 minutes. Cool 10 minutes; remove from pan. Cool completely.

*Do not use self-rising flour in this recipe.

Of all the cakes baked in America, probably none are more loved than the chocolate ones. German Chocolate Cake and Midwest Chocolate Cake are two of the finest. A version of German Chocolate was brought to Texas in the early 1800s, and below is the grass-roots recipe that swept the country to become a classic. Midwest Chocolate Cake is a down-home favorite that is as rich as chocolate can be.

GERMAN CHOCOLATE CAKE

½ cup boiling water
1 bar (4 ounces) sweet cooking
    chocolate
2 cups sugar
1 cup butter or margarine,
    softened
4 egg yolks
1 teaspoon vanilla

2½ cups cake flour
1 teaspoon baking soda
1 teaspoon salt
1 cup buttermilk
4 egg whites, stiffly beaten
Coconut-Pecan Frosting
    (page 23)

Heat oven to 350°. Grease 3 round layer pans, 8 or 9x1½ inches, or 2 baking pans, 8x8x2 or 9x9x2 inches. Line bottoms of pans with waxed paper. Pour boiling water over chocolate, stirring until chocolate is melted; cool.

Beat sugar and butter in large mixer bowl until light and fluffy. Beat in egg yolks, 1 at a time. Blend in chocolate and vanilla on low speed. Mix in flour, baking soda and salt alternately with buttermilk; continue beating after each addition until batter is smooth. Fold in egg whites. Divide among pans.

Bake until top springs back when touched lightly in center, 8-inch rounds 35 to 40 minutes, 9-inch rounds 30 to 35 minutes, 8-inch squares 45 to 50 minutes, 9-inch squares 40 to 45 minutes. Cool 10 minutes; remove from pans. Cool completely. Fill layers and frost top of cake with Coconut-Pecan Frosting.

COCONUT-PECAN FROSTING

1 cup sugar
1 cup evaporated milk
½ cup butter or margarine
3 egg yolks

1 teaspoon vanilla
1⅓ cups flaked coconut
1 cup chopped pecans

Mix sugar, milk, butter, egg yolks and vanilla in 1-quart saucepan. Cook over medium heat, stirring frequently, until thick, about 12 minutes. Remove from heat; stir in coconut and pecans. Beat until of spreading consistency.

MIDWEST CHOCOLATE CAKE

2 cups all-purpose flour*
2 cups sugar
1 cup water
¾ cup dairy sour cream
¼ cup shortening
1¼ teaspoons baking soda
1 teaspoon salt

½ teaspoon baking powder
2 eggs
1 teaspoon vanilla
4 ounces melted unsweetened chocolate (cool)
Chocolaty Chocolate Frosting (below)

Heat oven to 350°. Grease and flour two 9-inch or three 8-inch round layer pans. Beat all ingredients except frosting 30 seconds on low speed in large mixer bowl, scraping bowl constantly. Beat 3 minutes on high speed, scraping bowl occasionally. Pour into pans.

Bake until top springs back when touched lightly in center, 30 to 35 minutes. Cool 10 minutes; remove from pans. Cool completely. Fill layers and frost cake with Chocolaty Chocolate Frosting; refrigerate.

*If using self-rising flour, reduce baking soda to ¼ teaspoon, omit salt and baking powder.

CHOCOLATY CHOCOLATE FROSTING

5 ounces melted unsweetened chocolate (cool)
2½ cups powdered sugar
¼ cup hot water

4 egg yolks
⅓ cup butter or margarine, softened

Mix chocolate, 1½ cups of the sugar and the hot water until smooth; stir in remaining sugar. Beat in egg yolks, 1 at a time, until smooth. Beat in butter.

$\mathbf{A}$ cake from the grand tradition —just as perfect for a conclusion to a holiday feast now as it was when it waited on the polished sideboards of colonial Williamsburg or bluegrass Kentucky.

Whenever a recipe begins with caramelized sugar, you can be sure of a sumptuous sweetness. Our Burnt Sugar Cake is further endowed with a delicious Caramel Frosting.

BURNT SUGAR CAKE

1½ cups sugar
½ cup boiling water
2 eggs, separated
½ cup butter or margarine, softened
1 teaspoon vanilla

2¼ cups all-purpose flour*
3 teaspoons baking powder
1 teaspoon salt
1 cup milk
Caramel Frosting (below)

Heat ½ cup of the sugar in heavy 8-inch skillet, stirring constantly, until sugar is melted and golden brown. Remove from heat; stir in boiling water slowly. Cook over low heat, stirring constantly, until sugar lumps are dissolved. Add enough water to syrup, if necessary, to measure ½ cup; cool.

Heat oven to 375°. Grease and flour two 9-inch or three 8-inch round layer pans. Beat egg whites in small mixer bowl until foamy. Beat in ½ cup of the sugar, 1 tablespoon at a time; continue beating until very stiff and glossy. Reserve meringue.

Beat butter, remaining ½ cup sugar, the egg yolks and vanilla 30 seconds on low speed in large mixer bowl, scraping bowl constantly. Beat 5 minutes on high speed, scraping bowl occasionally. Beat in syrup. Beat in flour, baking powder and salt alternately with milk. Fold in reserved meringue. Pour into pans.

Bake until wooden pick inserted in center comes out clean, 20 to 25 minutes. Cool 10 minutes; remove from pans. Cool completely. Fill layers and frost cake with Caramel Frosting. Arrange pecan or walnut halves around top edge of cake if desired.

*If using self-rising flour, omit baking powder and salt.

CARAMEL FROSTING

2 tablespoons butter or margarine
⅔ cup packed dark brown sugar
⅛ teaspoon salt

⅓ cup whipping cream or evaporated milk
2⅓ to 2½ cups powdered sugar
½ teaspoon vanilla

Heat butter in 2-quart saucepan until melted. Stir in brown sugar, salt and cream. Heat to boiling, stirring constantly. Remove from heat; cool to lukewarm. Stir in enough powdered sugar gradually until of spreading consistency. Stir in vanilla.

Pictured opposite.
Burnt Sugar Cake with Caramel Frosting—a flavorful cake from yesterday, every bit as delicious today.

LANE CAKE

8 egg whites
2 cups sugar
1 cup butter or margarine,
    softened
1 teaspoon vanilla

3¼ cups all-purpose flour*
3½ teaspoons baking powder
¾ teaspoon salt
1 cup milk
Lane Frosting (below)

Heat oven to 350°. Grease and flour 2 round layer pans, 9x1½ inches. Beat egg whites in large mixer bowl until foamy. Beat in 1 cup of the sugar, 1 tablespoon at a time; continue beating until stiff and glossy. Reserve meringue.

Beat remaining 1 cup sugar, the butter and vanilla 30 seconds on low speed in large mixer bowl, scraping bowl constantly. Beat 5 minutes on high speed, scraping bowl occasionally. Beat' in flour, baking powder and salt alternately with milk (batter will be stiff). Stir ¼ of the reserved meringue into flour mixture. Fold in remaining meringue. Spread about 2 cups evenly in each pan. Refrigerate remaining batter.

Bake until wooden pick inserted in center comes out clean, 25 to 30 minutes. Cool 10 minutes; remove from pans. Repeat with remaining batter; cool. Fill layers and frost top of cake with Lane Frosting, allowing some to drizzle down side. To store cake, wrap in plastic wrap or aluminum foil and refrigerate. Cake can be refrigerated up to 3 weeks or frozen up to 2 months (flavor mellows with storage).   20 SERVINGS.

*If using self-rising flour, omit baking powder and salt.

NOTE: All the batter can be baked at once in 2 round layer pans, 9x1½ inches, 40 to 45 minutes. Cool; split layers horizontally in half.

LANE FROSTING

¾ cup butter or margarine
12 egg yolks, slightly beaten
2 cups minus 2 tablespoons
    sugar
¾ teaspoon salt
1½ cups chopped pecans

1½ cups chopped raisins
1½ cups shredded coconut
1½ cups red candied cherries,
    cut into fourths
⅓ cup bourbon

Heat butter in 3-quart saucepan over low heat until melted. Stir in egg yolks, sugar and salt. Cook over low heat, stirring constantly, until mixture is slightly thickened, about 10 minutes (do not boil). Remove from heat; stir in remaining ingredients. Cool. If necessary, stir in additional bourbon until of spreading consistency.

NOTE: Leftover egg whites can be refrigerated up to 10 days in tightly covered container, or they can be frozen.

LADY BALTIMORE CAKE

½ cup raisins, chopped
6 dried figs, cut up
3 tablespoons cognac or brandy
½ cup chopped pecans

Seven-Minute Frosting (below)
8- or 9-inch two-layer white
    cake

Mix raisins, figs and cognac; let stand until cognac is absorbed, about 1 hour. Stir in pecans. Stir raisin mixture into 1 cup of the frosting; fill layers. Frost cake with remaining frosting.

SEVEN-MINUTE FROSTING

1½ cups sugar
¼ teaspoon cream of tartar or 1
    tablespoon light corn syrup

⅓ cup water
2 egg whites
1 teaspoon vanilla

Mix sugar, cream of tartar, water and egg whites in top of double boiler. Beat 1 minute on high speed. Place over boiling water (water should not touch bottom of pan). Beat 7 minutes on high speed. Remove pan from water; add vanilla. Beat 2 minutes on high speed.

OLD-FASHIONED FRUITCAKE

3 cups all-purpose flour*
1⅓ cups sugar
2 teaspoons salt
1 teaspoon baking powder
2 teaspoons ground cinnamon
1 teaspoon ground nutmeg
1 cup orange juice
1 cup vegetable oil
¼ cup dark corn syrup

4 eggs
2 cups raisins
1 pound mixed candied fruits
    (2 cups)
1 package (8 ounces) pitted
    dates, cut up (1½ cups)
½ pound pecan halves (about 2
    cups)

Heat oven to 275°. Line 2 loaf pans, 9x5x3 or 8½x4½x2½ inches, with aluminum foil; grease. Beat all ingredients except fruits and nuts 30 seconds on low speed in large mixer bowl, scraping bowl constantly. Beat 3 minutes on high speed, scraping bowl occasionally. Stir in fruits and nuts. Spread evenly in pans.

Bake until wooden pick inserted in center comes out clean, 2½ to 3 hours. Cover with aluminum foil during last hour of baking, if necessary, to prevent excessive browning. Remove from pans; cool. Wrap in plastic wrap or aluminum foil and store in refrigerator or cool place.

*Do not use self-rising flour in this recipe.

NOTE: Best made 3 or 4 weeks in advance. Can be wrapped in wine- or brandy-dampened cloth.

YELLOW FRUITCAKE

3 cups all-purpose flour*
1½ cups sugar
1½ teaspoons baking powder
¾ teaspoon salt
¾ cup shortening
¾ cup butter or margarine,
    softened
⅔ cup orange juice
9 eggs
1 package (15 ounces) golden
    raisins (about 3 cups)
1 pound candied cherries, cut
    in halves (about 2½ cups)

¾ pound candied pineapple,
    cut up (about 2 cups)
¼ pound candied citron, cut up
    (about ⅔ cup)
¼ pound candied orange peel,
    cut up (about ⅔ cup)
½ pound pecan halves (about 2
    cups)
½ pound blanched whole
    almonds (1½ cups)
1 can (3½ ounces) flaked
    coconut

Heat oven to 275°. Line 2 loaf pans, 9x5x3 inches, with aluminum foil; grease. Beat all ingredients except fruits and nuts 30 seconds on low speed in large mixer bowl, scraping bowl constantly. Beat 3 minutes on high speed, scraping bowl occasionally. Stir in fruits and nuts. Spread evenly in pans.

Bake until wooden pick inserted in center comes out clean, 2½ to 3 hours. Cover with aluminum foil during last hour of baking, if necessary, to prevent excessive browning. Remove from pans; cool. Wrap in plastic wrap or aluminum foil and store in refrigerator or cool place.

*Do not use self-rising flour in this recipe.

SNOWBALLS

1 cup all-purpose flour*
¾ cup sugar
1¾ teaspoons baking powder
½ teaspoon salt
½ cup milk
¼ cup shortening

½ teaspoon vanilla
2 egg whites
Sweetened whipped cream
Crushed sweetened peaches or
    strawberries

Grease eight 6-ounce custard cups generously. Beat all ingredients except egg whites, whipped cream and peaches 30 seconds on low speed in small mixer bowl, scraping bowl constantly. Beat 1 minute on high speed, scraping bowl occasionally. Add egg whites; beat 2 minutes on high speed, scraping bowl occasionally. Pour into custard cups, filling each about ½ full. Cover each loosely with aluminum foil.

Place custard cups on rack in Dutch oven or roasting pan; pour boiling water into pan to depth of 1½ inches. Cover pan. Keep water boiling over low heat until wooden pick inserted in center of cake comes out clean, about 40 minutes.

Remove custard cups from pan and let stand 10 minutes; unmold. Serve warm with whipped cream and peaches.   8 CAKES.

*Do not use self-rising flour in this recipe.

Coconut Snowballs: Cool cakes. Prepare your favorite fluffy white frosting. Roll each cake in frosting, using 2 spoons to turn; smooth off excess frosting with knife. Place on dessert plates and sprinkle generously with grated or shredded coconut. Serve with chocolate, caramel or strawberry sauce if desired.

NOTE: If all cups do not fit in pan, steam as many as possible; refrigerate others and steam later.

PINEAPPLE UPSIDE-DOWN CAKE

¼ cup butter or margarine
1 can (20 ounces) sliced
    pineapple in heavy syrup
⅔ cup packed brown sugar
Maraschino cherries (optional)
1½ cups cake flour or 1¼ cups
    all-purpose flour*
1 cup granulated sugar

1½ teaspoons baking powder
½ teaspoon salt
¾ cup milk
⅓ cup shortening
1 egg
1 teaspoon vanilla
Sweetened whipped cream

Heat oven to 350°. Heat butter in oven in 9-inch ovenproof skillet or baking pan, 9x9x2 inches, until melted. Drain pineapple, reserving 2 tablespoons syrup. Stir syrup into butter; sprinkle evenly with brown sugar. Arrange pineapple slices in butter mixture. Place cherry in center of each pineapple slice.

Beat remaining ingredients except cream 30 seconds on low speed in large mixer bowl, scraping bowl constantly. Beat 3 minutes on high speed, scraping bowl occasionally. Pour evenly over pineapple slices.

Bake until wooden pick inserted in center comes out clean, 40 to 45 minutes. Invert on heatproof platter. Leave skillet over cake a few minutes. Serve warm with whipped cream.   9 SERVINGS.

*If using self-rising flour, omit baking powder and salt.

Apricot Upside-down Cake: Substitute 1 can (about 17 ounces) apricot halves for the pineapple slices.

Peach Upside-down Cake: Substitute 1 can (about 16 ounces) sliced peaches for the pineapple slices.

Plum Upside-down Cake: Substitute 1 can (about 17 ounces) Greengage or purple plums, cut in halves and pitted, for the pineapple slices.

MAPLE-NUT CHIFFON CAKE

2 cups all-purpose flour*
¾ cup granulated sugar
¾ cup packed brown sugar
3 teaspoons baking powder
1 teaspoon salt
½ cup vegetable oil
7 egg yolks

¾ cup cold water
2 teaspoons maple flavoring
1 cup egg whites (7 or 8)
½ teaspoon cream of tartar
1 cup very finely chopped nuts
Browned Butter Glaze (below)

Heat oven to 325°. Mix flour, granulated sugar, brown sugar, baking powder and salt. Make a "well" and add in order: oil, egg yolks, water and maple flavoring. Beat with spoon until smooth. Beat egg whites and cream of tartar in large mixer bowl until stiff peaks form. Pour egg yolk mixture gradually over egg whites, folding just until blended. Sprinkle nuts over batter; fold in with a few strokes. Pour into ungreased tube pan, 10x4 inches. Cut through batter gently with spatula.

Bake until top springs back when touched lightly in center, 60 to 70 minutes. Immediately invert pan on funnel; let hang until completely cool. Spread cake with Browned Butter Glaze, allowing some to drizzle down side.

*If using self-rising flour, omit baking powder and salt.

BROWNED BUTTER GLAZE
⅓ cup butter
2 cups powdered sugar

1½ teaspoons vanilla
2 to 4 tablespoons hot water

Heat butter in 2-quart saucepan over medium heat until light brown; cool slightly. Blend in sugar and vanilla. Stir in water, 1 tablespoon at a time, until of spreading consistency.

HOT WATER SPONGE CAKE

3 eggs
¾ cup sugar
⅓ cup hot water or hot milk
1 teaspoon vanilla

½ teaspoon lemon extract
1¼ cups cake flour
1½ teaspoons baking powder
½ teaspoon salt

Heat oven to 350°. Grease and flour baking pan, 8x8x2 or 9x9x2 inches. Beat eggs in small mixer bowl on high speed 5 minutes; pour into large mixer bowl. Beat in sugar gradually. Beat in water, vanilla and lemon extract on low speed. Beat in flour, baking powder and salt on low speed; continue beating just until batter is smooth. Pour into pan.

Bake until top springs back when touched lightly in center, 25 to 30 minutes; cool. Nice served with sweetened sliced strawberries.

Pictured opposite.
A delectable demonstration of the versatility of nuts. From top: Maple-Nut Chiffon Cake (this page), Pecan Pie (page 47) and Filbert Bars (page 40).

Not a true pie, not quite a cake or custard, Boston Cream Pie has good qualities from each. Martha Washington's version is said to have had jam, and sometimes cream filling, sandwiched between layers with powdered sugar sprinkled on top, but Americans have long since opted for custard and chocolate.

Boston Cream Pie is always a pleasing combination of textures and subtle flavors. Because of the custard filling, this pie must be stored in the refrigerator.

BOSTON CREAM PIE

1½ cups cake flour or 1¼ cups
   all-purpose flour*
1 cup sugar
1½ teaspoons baking powder
½ teaspoon salt
¾ cup milk

⅓ cup shortening
1 egg
1 teaspoon vanilla
Cream Filling (below)
Chocolate Glaze (below)

Heat oven to 350°. Grease and flour round layer pan, 9x1½ inches. Beat all ingredients except filling and glaze 30 seconds on low speed in large mixer bowl, scraping bowl constantly. Beat 3 minutes on high speed, scraping bowl occasionally. Pour into pan.

Bake until wooden pick inserted in center comes out clean, about 35 minutes. Cool 10 minutes; remove from pan. Cool completely. Split cake horizontally in half. Fill layers with Cream Filling. Spread top of cake with Chocolate Glaze; refrigerate.

*If using self-rising flour, omit baking powder and salt.

CREAM FILLING
⅓ cup sugar
2 tablespoons cornstarch
⅛ teaspoon salt

1½ cups milk
2 egg yolks, slightly beaten
2 teaspoons vanilla

Mix sugar, cornstarch and salt in 2-quart saucepan. Mix milk and egg yolks; stir gradually into sugar mixture. Cook over medium heat, stirring constantly, until mixture thickens and boils. Boil and stir 1 minute. Remove from heat. Stir in vanilla; cool.

CHOCOLATE GLAZE
3 tablespoons butter or
   margarine
2 squares (1 ounce each)
   unsweetened chocolate

1 cup powdered sugar
¾ teaspoon vanilla
About 2 tablespoons hot water

Heat butter and chocolate in 1-quart saucepan over low heat, stirring constantly, until chocolate is melted. Remove from heat; stir in sugar and vanilla. Stir in water, 1 teaspoon at a time, until smooth and of spreading consistency.

ORANGE-LEMON REFRIGERATOR CAKE

1 cup plus 2 tablespoons
   all-purpose flour*
1 cup granulated sugar
2 teaspoons baking powder
¾ teaspoon salt
½ cup cold water
⅓ cup vegetable oil

3 egg yolks
5 or 6 egg whites (⅔ cup)
½ teaspoon cream of tartar
Orange-Lemon Filling (below)
1 cup chilled whipping cream
¼ cup powdered sugar

Heat oven to 350°. Mix flour, granulated sugar, baking powder and salt. Stir in water, oil and egg yolks until smooth. Beat egg whites and cream of tartar in large mixer bowl until stiff peaks form. Pour egg yolk mixture gradually over egg whites, folding just until blended. Pour into 2 ungreased round layer pans, 8 or 9x1½ inches.

Bake until top springs back when touched lightly in center, 30 to 35 minutes. Immediately invert pans with edges on 2 other pans; let hang until layers are completely cool. Loosen edges from pans with spatula. Turn pans over; hit edges sharply to loosen completely.

Split cake layers horizontally in half. Stack layers, spreading ½ cup of the Orange-Lemon Filling between layers. Frost top and side of cake with remaining filling. Wrap in plastic wrap or aluminum foil and refrigerate at least 12 hours.

Just before serving, beat whipping cream and powdered sugar in chilled bowl until stiff; frost cake. Garnish with grated orange or lemon peel if desired; refrigerate.

*If using self-rising flour, omit baking powder and salt.

ORANGE-LEMON FILLING

½ cup sugar
2 tablespoons cornstarch
⅛ teaspoon salt
1 cup orange juice
½ cup water
2 egg yolks, slightly beaten
2 tablespoons lemon juice

1 tablespoon grated orange
   peel
1 tablespoon butter or
   margarine
2 egg whites
¼ cup sugar

Mix ½ cup sugar, the cornstarch and salt in 2-quart saucepan. Stir in orange juice and water gradually. Cook over medium heat, stirring constantly, until mixture thickens and boils. Boil and stir 1 minute. Stir at least half of the hot mixture slowly into egg yolks. Blend egg yolk mixture into hot mixture in saucepan. Boil 1 minute, stirring constantly. Remove from heat. Stir in juice, peel and butter; cool.

Beat egg whites until foamy. Beat in ¼ cup sugar, 1 tablespoon at a time; continue beating until stiff and glossy. Fold orange mixture into egg whites.

COOKIES

A special treat for good girls and boys always has been, and still is, cookies. Hermits, Joe Froggers, Jumbles and Chocolate Crinkles come from a long line of cookies with whimsical names. There were Petticoat Tails, Snickerdoodles, Brambles, Tangle Breeches, Wasps' Nests—names that give away the nature of all these cookies, which is that they're for fun, both to say and to eat.

HERMITS

2 cups packed brown sugar
1 teaspoon baking soda
1 teaspoon salt
1 teaspoon ground cinnamon
1 teaspoon ground nutmeg
½ cup shortening
½ cup butter or margarine, softened

½ cup cold coffee
2 eggs
3½ cups all-purpose flour*
2½ cups raisins
1½ cups chopped nuts

Heat oven to 375°. Mix sugar, baking soda, salt, cinnamon, nutmeg, shortening, butter, coffee and eggs. Stir in flour, raisins and nuts. Drop dough by rounded teaspoonfuls 2 inches apart onto ungreased baking sheet.

Bake until almost no imprint remains when touched lightly in center, 8 to 10 minutes.   ABOUT 8 DOZEN COOKIES.

*If using self-rising flour, omit baking soda and salt.

SOFT PUMPKIN COOKIES

1 cup sugar
1 cup canned pumpkin
½ cup shortening
1 tablespoon grated orange peel
2 cups all-purpose flour*
1 teaspoon baking powder

1 teaspoon baking soda
1 teaspoon ground cinnamon
¼ teaspoon salt
½ cup raisins
½ cup chopped nuts

Heat oven to 375°. Mix sugar, pumpkin, shortening and orange peel. Stir in flour, baking powder, baking soda, cinnamon and salt. Stir in raisins and nuts. Drop dough by teaspoonfuls onto ungreased baking sheet. Bake until light brown, 8 to 10 minutes.   ABOUT 4 DOZEN COOKIES.

*If using self-rising flour, omit baking powder, baking soda and salt.

Chocolate Chip-Pumpkin Cookies: Substitute ½ cup semisweet chocolate chips for the raisins or nuts.

Known as sesame seeds in most of the country, "benne" is the name Southerners learned to call these seeds, which were brought from Africa by slaves. Toasting benne seeds develops their flavor and also gives these cookies a slightly crunchy texture.

BENNE SEED COOKIES

1 cup benne (sesame) seed
1½ cups packed brown sugar
1 cup all-purpose flour*
¼ teaspoon baking powder
¼ teaspoon salt

¾ cup butter or margarine,
  melted
1 egg
1 teaspoon vanilla

Heat oven to 375°. Toast benne seed on ungreased baking sheet until brown, 10 to 12 minutes. Mix all ingredients. Drop dough by ½ teaspoonfuls 1½ inches apart onto greased baking sheet.

Bake until brown, 4 to 6 minutes. Cool about 30 seconds before removing from baking sheet. ABOUT 6 DOZEN COOKIES.

*If using self-rising flour, omit baking powder and salt.

JUMBLES

2¾ cups all-purpose flour*
1½ cups packed brown sugar
1 teaspoon salt
½ teaspoon baking soda
1 cup dairy sour cream

½ cup shortening
2 eggs
1 teaspoon vanilla
1 cup chopped nuts (optional)
Browned Butter Glaze (page 30)

Mix all ingredients except glaze. Cover and refrigerate if soft.

Heat oven to 375°. Drop dough by level tablespoonfuls 2 inches apart onto ungreased baking sheet.

Bake until almost no imprint remains when touched lightly in center, about 10 minutes. Immediately remove from baking sheet; cool. Spread with Browned Butter Glaze. ABOUT 4½ DOZEN COOKIES.

*If using self-rising flour, omit salt and baking soda.

Applesauce Jumbles: Omit sour cream and stir in ¾ cup applesauce, 1 teaspoon ground cinnamon, ¼ teaspoon ground cloves and 1 cup raisins.

Fruit Jumbles: Omit nuts and stir in 2 cups candied cherries, cut in halves, 2 cups cut-up dates and 1½ cups chopped pecans. Drop dough by rounded teaspoonfuls onto ungreased baking sheet. Place a pecan half on each cookie. Omit glaze. ABOUT 7 DOZEN COOKIES.

CHOCOLATE CRINKLES

½ cup vegetable oil
4 ounces melted unsweetened
    chocolate (cool)
2 cups granulated sugar
2 teaspoons vanilla

4 eggs
2 cups all-purpose flour*
2 teaspoons baking powder
½ teaspoon salt
1 cup powdered sugar

Mix oil, chocolate, granulated sugar and vanilla. Blend in eggs, 1 at a time. Stir in flour, baking powder and salt. Cover and refrigerate at least 3 hours.

Heat oven to 350°. Drop dough by teaspoonfuls into powdered sugar; roll in sugar. Shape into balls. Place about 2 inches apart on greased baking sheet. Bake until almost no imprint remains when touched lightly in center, 10 to 12 minutes.   ABOUT 6 DOZEN COOKIES.

*If using self-rising flour, omit baking powder and salt.

Ginger was one of the prize spices settlers could obtain from the ships that plied the West Indies. Among their earliest desserts were heavy ginger cakes sweetened with dark molasses. Later, German and Dutch settlers in New York and Pennsylvania baked light gingerbread, large cookies shaped like people and crisp gingersnaps. Virtually every generation of American children since has favored goodies spiced with ginger.

These spicy Gingersnaps and hot chocolate make a perfect welcome-home snack on a blustery day.

GINGERSNAPS

1 cup sugar
¾ cup shortening
¼ cup dark molasses
1 egg
2¼ cups all-purpose flour*

1½ teaspoons baking soda
1 tablespoon ground ginger
1 teaspoon ground cinnamon
¼ teaspoon salt
Sugar

Mix 1 cup sugar, the shortening, molasses and egg. Stir in remaining ingredients except sugar. Cover and refrigerate 1 hour.

Heat oven to 375°. Shape dough by rounded teaspoonfuls into balls; dip tops in sugar. Place sugared sides up 3 inches apart on lightly greased baking sheet.

Bake until edges of cookies are set (centers will be soft), 10 to 12 minutes. Immediately remove from baking sheet.   ABOUT 4 DOZEN COOKIES.

*If using self-rising flour, omit baking soda and salt.

FARM-STYLE OATMEAL COOKIES

2 cups packed brown sugar
1 cup lard or 1 cup plus 2
   tablespoons shortening,
   melted
½ cup buttermilk

1 teaspoon vanilla
4 cups quick-cooking oats
1¾ cups all-purpose flour*
1 teaspoon baking soda
¾ teaspoon salt

Heat oven to 375°. Mix sugar, lard, buttermilk and vanilla. Stir in remaining ingredients. Shape dough into 1-inch balls. Place 3 inches apart on ungreased baking sheet. Flatten cookies with glass dipped in water to 2½ inches in diameter.

Bake until golden brown, 8 to 10 minutes. Immediately remove from baking sheet. Store in tightly covered container. ABOUT 7 DOZEN COOKIES.

*If using self-rising flour, omit baking soda and salt.

REFRIGERATOR NUT COOKIES

1 cup sugar
1 cup butter or margarine,
   softened
2 eggs
1½ teaspoons vanilla

3 cups all-purpose flour*
1 teaspoon salt
½ teaspoon baking soda
½ cup finely chopped nuts

Mix sugar, butter, eggs and vanilla. Stir in flour, salt, baking soda and nuts. Divide dough into 3 parts. Shape each part into roll 1½ inches in diameter and about 7 inches long. Wrap in waxed paper or plastic wrap and refrigerate at least 4 hours.

Heat oven to 400°. Cut dough into ⅛-inch slices. Place 1 inch apart on ungreased baking sheet.

Bake until light brown, 8 to 10 minutes. Immediately remove from baking sheet. ABOUT 7 DOZEN COOKIES.

*If using self-rising flour, omit salt.

Butterscotch Slices: Substitute 1 cup packed brown sugar for the sugar; omit nuts.
Cinnamon Slices: Substitute ½ cup granulated sugar and ½ cup packed brown sugar for the sugar and 1 tablespoon ground cinnamon for the vanilla; omit nuts.
Orange-Almond Slices: Stir in 1 tablespoon grated orange peel with the sugar and substitute ½ cup finely chopped blanched almonds for the nuts.

America's settlers prepared all their meals in kitchens like this one at the Pilgrim Village restoration in Plymouth, Massachusetts.

Sour cream adds a special touch to many foods, including these delicious cookies. And nowadays you don't sour your own cream, as your ancestors did.

OLD-FASHIONED SOUR CREAM COOKIES

1 cup sugar	1 teaspoon baking powder
¼ cup shortening	½ teaspoon baking soda
¼ cup butter or margarine, softened	½ teaspoon salt
	¼ teaspoon ground nutmeg
1 egg	½ cup dairy sour cream
1 teaspoon vanilla	Sugar
2⅔ cups all-purpose flour*	

Heat oven to 425°. Mix 1 cup sugar, the shortening, butter, egg and vanilla. Stir in remaining ingredients except sugar. Divide dough into 3 parts. Roll each part ¼ inch thick on lightly floured cloth-covered board. Cut with 2-inch cookie cutter; sprinkle with sugar. Place on ungreased baking sheet.

Bake until almost no imprint remains when touched lightly in center, 6 to 8 minutes.   ABOUT 4½ DOZEN COOKIES.

*If using self-rising flour, omit baking powder, baking soda and salt.

NOTE: Dough can be shaped by tablespoonfuls into balls, then flattened on baking sheet with greased bottom of glass dipped in sugar.

JOE FROGGERS

1 cup sugar	1 teaspoon baking soda
½ cup shortening	1½ teaspoons ground ginger
1 cup dark molasses	½ teaspoon ground cloves
½ cup water	½ teaspoon ground nutmeg
4 cups all-purpose flour*	¼ teaspoon ground allspice
1½ teaspoons salt	Sugar

Mix 1 cup sugar and the shortening. Stir in remaining ingredients except sugar. Cover and refrigerate at least 3 hours.

Heat oven to 375°. Roll dough ¼ inch thick on lightly floured cloth-covered board. Cut into 3-inch circles; sprinkle with sugar. Place on well-greased baking sheet.

Bake until almost no imprint remains when touched lightly in center, 10 to 12 minutes. Cool about 2 minutes before removing from baking sheet.   ABOUT 3½ DOZEN COOKIES.

*If using self-rising flour, omit salt and baking soda.

Pictured opposite.
Milk and cookies—then as now, the perfect anytime treat: sugar-dusted Joe Froggers (bottom) and Old-fashioned Sour Cream Cookies (top).

FILLED DATE BARS

Date Filling (below)
1 cup packed brown sugar
½ cup butter or margarine,
    softened
¼ cup shortening

1¾ cups all-purpose flour*
1 teaspoon salt
½ teaspoon baking soda
1½ cups quick-cooking oats

Prepare Date Filling; cool.

Heat oven to 400°. Mix sugar, butter and shortening. Stir in remaining ingredients. Press half of the sugar mixture evenly in greased baking pan, 13x9x2 inches. Spread with filling. Sprinkle remaining sugar mixture over filling, pressing lightly.

Bake until light brown, 25 to 30 minutes. Cool slightly. Cut into bars, about 2x1½ inches.   3 DOZEN COOKIES.

*If using self-rising flour, omit salt and baking soda.

DATE FILLING
Mix 3 cups cut-up dates (1 pound), ¼ cup sugar and 1½ cups water. Cook over low heat, stirring constantly, until thickened, about 10 minutes.

Bar cookies weren't invented in America, but so many developed here that they have become an integral part of our baking heritage. The preeminent bar cookie is, of course, the brownie. More unusual are Filled Date Bars and Filbert Bars. A late variation on the many dried fruit bar cookies, Filled Date Bars became popular in the twentieth century when the California date crops began to flourish. Filberts, or hazelnuts, make a bar cookie with a nice crunch.

FILBERT BARS

1 cup sugar
1 cup butter or margarine,
    softened
1 egg, separated

1½ cups all-purpose flour*
¼ teaspoon salt
1 cup finely chopped filberts

Heat oven to 275°. Mix sugar, butter and egg yolk. Stir in flour and salt. Spread in ungreased jelly roll pan, 15½x10½x1 inch. Beat egg white slightly; brush over dough. Sprinkle filberts evenly over top, pressing lightly.

Bake until golden brown, about 1 hour. Immediately cut into bars, about 2x1 inch. Cool and store in tightly covered container. 75 COOKIES.

*If using self-rising flour, omit salt.

The American passion for chocolate started early and shows no signs of abating. Although chocolate originated in the Americas, it made a circuitous entrance into North American cooking. Explorers took cacao beans, from which chocolate is made, back to Spain from Mexico and South America, where the Indians used them extensively. It is said they even had their own version of an ice-cream drink: liquefied cacao poured over mountain snow.

When the English came to America, chocolate came back with them. By 1765 there already was a chocolate processing factory in New England. Americans were turning out cookies, cakes, pies and candies whenever they could afford chocolate and sugar. Hot chocolate became a favorite drink after the British tea tax was imposed. Later, when the cost of refining was reduced, chocolate was produced in quantity. The following recipe for Double-frosted Brownies is after the true chocolate-lover's heart.

DOUBLE-FROSTED BROWNIES

½ cup butter or margarine
2 squares (1 ounce each)
   unsweetened chocolate
1 cup granulated sugar
2 eggs
1 teaspoon vanilla
½ cup all-purpose flour*
¼ teaspoon salt

½ cup chopped walnuts
1½ cups powdered sugar
½ cup whipping cream
⅓ cup butter or margarine
1 teaspoon vanilla
3 squares (1 ounce each)
   unsweetened chocolate

Heat oven to 350°. Heat ½ cup butter and 2 squares chocolate in 2-quart saucepan over low heat, stirring constantly, until melted. Remove from heat; stir in granulated sugar, eggs and 1 teaspoon vanilla. Stir in flour, salt and walnuts. Spread dough in greased baking pan, 9x9x2 inches, or baking dish, 11¾ x7½ x1¾ inches.

Bake until brownies begin to pull away from sides of pan, 20 to 25 minutes; cool.

Heat powdered sugar, cream and ⅓ cup butter to boiling in 2-quart saucepan over medium heat, stirring constantly. Boil, without stirring, until candy thermometer registers 234° (or until small amount of mixture dropped into very cold water forms a soft ball that flattens when removed from water). Cool slightly. Beat in 1 teaspoon vanilla until smooth and of spreading consistency; spread topping over cooled brownies.

Heat 3 squares chocolate over low heat until melted; cool. Spread over topping. Refrigerate until chocolate is set. (Refrigerate until 1 hour before serving in warm weather.)   5 DOZEN COOKIES.

*If using self-rising flour, omit salt.

PIES

Pies were baked early in the morning on farms, and pie for breakfast seemed perfectly natural. Fresh Blueberry Tart and other glorious fruit pies swimming in bright juice were summer favorites, but winter brought out the pie baker's inventiveness with nuts, dried fruits and root vegetables such as carrots and sweet potatoes. At times even those were gone. This happened often enough to give the last weeks of winter the poignant name "the six weeks want." It must have been at such a time that someone with an intense taste for apple pie spotted the cider vinegar and, with true ingenuity, created Vinegar Pie, with its tart hint of apples.

Every farmhouse used to have a pie safe, a large cabinet with pierced tin or screened doors. Inside, safe from insects, cooled the day's pies. Modern pies, whether latticed, double crust or deep dish, use a flaky tried-and-true pastry like the one below.

PASTRY

8- OR 9-INCH ONE-CRUST PIE OR BAKED PIE SHELL
1 cup all-purpose flour*
½ teaspoon salt
⅓ cup plus 1 tablespoon shortening or ⅓ cup lard
2 to 3 tablespoons cold water

8- OR 9-INCH TWO-CRUST PIE
2 cups all-purpose flour*
1 teaspoon salt
⅔ cup plus 2 tablespoons shortening or ⅔ cup lard
4 to 5 tablespoons cold water

Mix flour and salt. Cut in shortening. Sprinkle in water, 1 tablespoon at a time, mixing until all flour is moistened and pastry almost cleans side of bowl (1 to 2 teaspoons water can be added).

Gather pastry into ball; shape into flattened round on lightly floured cloth-covered board. (For Two-Crust Pie, divide pastry in half and shape into 2 flattened rounds.) Roll 2 inches larger than inverted pie plate with floured stockinet-covered rolling pin. Fold pastry into quarters; unfold and ease into pie plate.

For One-Crust Pie: Trim overhanging edge of pastry 1 inch from rim of pie plate. Fold and roll pastry even with pie plate; flute.

For Baked Pie Shell: Heat oven to 475°. Prick bottom and side of pastry thoroughly with fork. Bake 8 to 10 minutes.

For Two-Crust Pie: Turn filling into pastry-lined pie plate. Trim overhanging edge of pastry ½ inch from rim of pie plate. Roll other round of pastry. Fold into quarters; cut slits so steam can escape. Place over filling and unfold. Trim overhanging edge of pastry 1 inch from rim of pie plate. Fold and roll top edge under lower edge, pressing on rim to seal; flute.

*If using self-rising flour, omit salt. Pie crusts made with self-rising flour differ in flavor and texture from those made with plain flour.

FRESH BLUEBERRY TART

1 cup all-purpose flour
2 tablespoons granulated sugar
⅛ teaspoon salt
½ cup butter or margarine,
    softened
1 tablespoon white vinegar

1 cup granulated sugar
2 tablespoons flour
¼ teaspoon ground cinnamon
3 cups blueberries
2 tablespoons powdered sugar

Mix 1 cup flour, 2 tablespoons granulated sugar, the salt and butter with hands. Stir in vinegar. Press dough evenly on bottom and 1 inch up side of ungreased 9-inch loose-bottom layer pan or 9-inch springform pan. Be sure no thin areas appear at bottom seam of pan. Refrigerate at least 15 minutes.

Heat oven to 400°. Mix 1 cup granulated sugar, 2 tablespoons flour and the cinnamon. Stir in 2 cups of the blueberries gently, reserving 1 cup of the largest berries. Spread filling evenly over crust.

Bake until crust is golden brown, 50 to 60 minutes. Sprinkle with reserved berries and powdered sugar. Cool and remove pan rim. 6 TO 8 SERVINGS.

NOTE: Tart can be baked in baking pan, 8x8x2 inches.

CARROT PIE

4 cups sliced uncooked carrots
    (about 1 pound)
Pastry for 9-inch One-Crust Pie
    (page 42)
2 eggs
¾ cup packed light brown
    sugar

½ teaspoon salt
½ teaspoon ground cinnamon
½ teaspoon ground nutmeg
¼ teaspoon ground cloves
¼ teaspoon ground allspice
1 cup evaporated milk
2 tablespoons honey

Heat 1 inch water to boiling in 2-quart saucepan. Add carrots. Cover and heat to boiling; reduce heat. Cook until carrot slices are very tender, 15 to 20 minutes; drain. Press carrot slices through sieve to measure 2 cups pulp. (Or place in blender container. Cover and blend until uniform consistency.) Cool.

Heat oven to 400°. Prepare pastry. Beat eggs slightly; beat in carrot pulp and remaining ingredients. Pour into pastry-lined pie plate. Cover edge with 3-inch strip of aluminum foil to prevent excessive browning.

Bake 30 minutes; remove foil. Bake until filling is set, 10 to 15 minutes. Cool slightly. Serve warm or refrigerate. Nice served with sweetened whipped cream.

APPLE PANDOWDY

6 medium tart apples, pared and thinly sliced (about 6 cups)
½ cup sugar
½ teaspoon ground cinnamon
¼ teaspoon salt
¼ teaspoon ground nutmeg
½ cup maple-flavored syrup or light molasses
3 tablespoons water

2 tablespoons butter or margarine, melted
1¼ cups all-purpose flour
¼ teaspoon salt
⅓ cup shortening
3 tablespoons milk
3 tablespoons butter or margarine, melted
Cream

Heat oven to 350°. Mix apples, sugar, cinnamon, ¼ teaspoon salt and the nutmeg. Turn into ungreased 2-quart casserole. Mix syrup, water and 2 tablespoons butter; pour over apple mixture.

Mix flour and ¼ teaspoon salt. Cut in shortening. Sprinkle in milk, 1 tablespoon at a time, mixing until all flour is moistened and pastry almost cleans side of bowl.

Gather pastry into ball; shape into flattened round on lightly floured cloth-covered board. Roll round to fit top of casserole with floured stockinet-covered rolling pin. Place over apples in casserole; brush with 3 tablespoons melted butter.

Bake 30 minutes; remove from oven. Cut crust into small pieces with sharp knife, mixing pieces into apple filling. Bake until apples are tender and pieces of crust are golden, about 30 minutes. Serve hot with cream.   6 SERVINGS.

APPLE DEEP DISH PIE

Pastry for 9-inch One-Crust Pie (page 42)
1½ cups sugar
½ cup all-purpose flour*
1 teaspoon ground nutmeg
1 teaspoon ground cinnamon

¼ teaspoon salt
12 cups thinly sliced pared apples (about 12 medium)
2 tablespoons butter or margarine

Heat oven to 425°. Prepare pastry as directed except—roll into 10-inch square. Fold in half; cut slits near center. Mix sugar, flour, nutmeg, cinnamon and salt; toss with apples. Turn into ungreased square pan, 9x9x2 inches. Dot with butter. Cover with crust that has slits cut in it; fold edges under just inside edges of pan. Bake until juice begins to bubble through slits in crust, about 1 hour. Serve warm.   9 SERVINGS.

*If using self-rising flour, omit salt.

Pictured opposite.
Apples in abundance—and in a variety of delicious guises. From left: Apple Pandowdy (this page), Candy Apples on Sticks (page 152), Apple Butter (page 120) and Apple Dumplings (page 46).

APPLE DUMPLINGS

2 cups all-purpose flour*
2 teaspoons baking powder
1 teaspoon salt
¾ cup shortening
½ cup milk
6 baking apples (each about 3
    inches in diameter), pared
    and cut into quarters

6 tablespoons sugar
Ground cinnamon
Ground nutmeg
Syrup (below)
Whipping cream

Heat oven to 375°. Mix flour, baking powder and salt. Cut in shortening. Stir in milk until all flour is moistened. Gather pastry into ball. Roll ⅔ of the pastry into 14-inch square on generously floured cloth-covered board with floured stockinet-covered rolling pin; cut into 4 squares. Roll remaining pastry into rectangle, 14x7 inches; cut into 2 squares.

Place 4 apple quarters on each pastry square. Sprinkle each with 1 tablespoon sugar, the cinnamon and nutmeg. Bring corners of pastry up over apple and press together. Place dumplings in ungreased baking pan, 13x9x2 inches. Pour Syrup over dumplings.

Bake until crust is golden and apples are tender, about 45 minutes. Spoon Syrup over dumplings. Serve warm with cream.   6 SERVINGS.

*If using self-rising flour, omit baking powder and salt.

SYRUP

2 cups sugar
¼ teaspoon ground cinnamon
¼ teaspoon ground nutmeg

2 cups water
¼ cup butter or margarine

Heat sugar, cinnamon, nutmeg and water to boiling. Remove from heat; stir in butter until melted.

MINCEMEAT-PUMPKIN PIE

Pastry for 9-inch One-Crust Pie
    (page 42)
½ cup sugar
½ teaspoon ground cinnamon
¼ teaspoon salt

¼ teaspoon ground nutmeg
1½ cups prepared mincemeat
1 cup canned pumpkin
½ cup milk
2 eggs, beaten

Heat oven to 425°. Prepare pastry. Mix sugar, cinnamon, salt, nutmeg, mincemeat and pumpkin. Stir in milk and eggs. Pour into pastry-lined pie plate. Cover edge with 3-inch strip of aluminum foil to prevent excessive browning.

Bake 25 minutes; remove foil. Bake until top is golden brown, 10 to 15 minutes. Cool slightly. Serve warm or refrigerate.

To someone from the South, nothing compares with a luscious peach pie—except perhaps Pecan Pie when the short season for local peaches is over. Both of these pies can be served in the traditional way—with a liberal dollop of whipped cream. But try them also in that all-American fashion, a la mode, with a scoop of your favorite ice cream on top.

PEACH CRUMBLE PIE

Pastry for 9-inch One-Crust Pie
   (page 42)
4 cups quartered peeled
   peaches (8 to 10 medium)
½ cup granulated sugar
½ teaspoon ground nutmeg
2 tablespoons cream

1 egg
½ cup all-purpose flour
¼ cup packed brown sugar
¼ teaspoon ground cinnamon
¼ teaspoon ground nutmeg
¼ cup butter or margarine,
   softened

Heat oven to 425°. Prepare pastry. Arrange peaches in pastry-lined pie plate. Mix granulated sugar and ½ teaspoon nutmeg; sprinkle over peaches. Beat cream and egg; pour over peaches. Mix flour, brown sugar, cinnamon, ¼ teaspoon nutmeg and the butter until crumbly; sprinkle over peaches. Cover edge with 3-inch strip of aluminum foil to prevent excessive browning.

Bake 30 minutes; remove foil. Bake until top is golden brown, 5 to 10 minutes. Cool slightly. Serve warm.

PECAN PIE

Pastry for 9-inch One-Crust Pie
   (page 42)
½ cup packed dark brown
   sugar*
1 tablespoon flour
¼ teaspoon salt
1 cup light corn syrup

1 tablespoon butter or
   margarine, melted
2 eggs
1 teaspoon vanilla
1½ cups pecan halves (5½
   ounces)

Heat oven to 350°. Prepare pastry. Beat sugar, flour, salt, corn syrup, butter, eggs and vanilla with hand beater. Stir in pecans. Pour into pastry-lined pie plate.

Bake until filling is set, 45 to 55 minutes. Cool slightly. Serve warm or refrigerate.

*½ cup granulated sugar and 1 cup dark corn syrup can be substituted for the dark brown sugar and light corn syrup.

Chocolate Pecan Pie: Melt 2 squares (1 ounce each) unsweetened chocolate with the butter.

Arizona, Florida and California grow most of our year-round citrus crops. A large portion of the lime crop grows in Florida, and one variety favored for pies only grows down in the humid Florida Keys. Their famous Key Lime Pie that swept the country in the late nineteenth century was invented soon after condensed milk, one of its main ingredients, began to be canned in 1858. Since then lime pies of all types—and lemon, too—have become American classics.

DOUBLE-CRUST LEMON PIE

2 large lemons
2 cups sugar
1 teaspoon salt

Pastry for 9-inch Two-Crust
Pie (page 42)
4 eggs

Grate 2 teaspoons peel from lemons. Peel lemons, removing all white membrane. Cut lemons into very thin slices; place in bowl. Stir in lemon peel, sugar and salt.

Heat oven to 425°. Prepare pastry. Beat eggs thoroughly; pour over lemon slice mixture and mix well. Pour into pastry-lined pie plate. Cover with top crust that has slits cut in it; seal and flute. Cover edge with 3-inch strip of aluminum foil to prevent excessive browning.

Bake 35 minutes; remove foil. Bake until knife inserted near edge of pie comes out clean, 10 to 15 minutes. Cool slightly and refrigerate.

LIME CHIFFON PIE

9-inch Baked Pie Shell (page 42)
½ cup sugar
1 envelope unflavored gelatin
4 eggs, separated
⅔ cup water
⅓ cup lime juice (about 2
    limes)

1 tablespoon grated lime peel
Few drops green food color
    (optional)
½ teaspoon cream of tartar
½ cup sugar

Bake pie shell; cool. Mix ½ cup sugar and the gelatin in 1-quart saucepan. Mix egg yolks, water and lime juice; stir into sugar mixture. Cook over medium heat, stirring constantly, just until mixture boils. Stir in lime peel and food color. Chill in bowl of ice and water or in refrigerator, stirring occasionally, until mixture mounds slightly when dropped from spoon.

Beat egg whites and cream of tartar until foamy. Beat in ½ cup sugar, 1 tablespoon at a time; continue beating until stiff and glossy. Do not underbeat. Fold lime mixture into meringue; pile into pie shell. Refrigerate until set, at least 3 hours.

RHUBARB AND STRAWBERRY PIE

Pastry for 9-inch Two-Crust
   Pie (page 42)
1½ cups sugar
2 tablespoons quick-cooking
   tapioca

¼ teaspoon salt
2 cups ½-inch pieces rhubarb
2 cups strawberries
1 egg yolk, slightly beaten

Heat oven to 425°. Prepare pastry. Mix sugar, tapioca and salt; toss with rhubarb and strawberries. Stir in egg yolk. Turn into pastry-lined pie plate. Cover with top crust that has slits cut in it; seal and flute. Cover edge with 3-inch strip of aluminum foil to prevent excessive browning.

Bake 30 minutes; remove foil. Bake until crust is golden brown and juice begins to bubble through slits in crust, 10 to 15 minutes.

The distant ancestors of Fried Pies were oilcakes—fried, fruit-stuffed sweet rolls often served at Mount Vernon. Since fritters and fried pies cook quickly, cooks long ago discovered how handy they are for last-minute desserts.

FRIED PIES

1 package (12 ounces) mixed
   dried fruit
2 to 3 tablespoons sugar
¾ teaspoon ground cinnamon
½ teaspoon ground nutmeg
2 cups all-purpose flour*

1 teaspoon baking powder
½ teaspoon salt
¼ cup shortening
½ cup milk
1 egg, slightly beaten

Remove prune pits; cut up fruit. Heat fruit and enough water to cover to boiling; reduce heat. Cover and simmer until pears are tender, 20 to 25 minutes; drain. Stir in sugar, cinnamon and nutmeg.

Mix flour, baking powder and salt. Cut in shortening. Mix milk and egg; stir into flour mixture until all flour is moistened and pastry almost cleans side of bowl. Gather pastry into ball; divide in half. Roll each half ⅛ to 1/16 inch thick on lightly floured cloth-covered board with floured stockinet-covered rolling pin. Cut each half into four 6-inch rounds. Place ¼ cup fruit mixture on each round. Moisten lower edge of round; fold pastry over. Press edges firmly with fork to seal securely.

Heat vegetable oil or shortening (3 to 4 inches) to 375° in deep fat fryer or heavy saucepan. Fry pies in hot oil until golden brown on both sides, 3 to 4 minutes; drain on paper towels.   8 PIES.

*If using self-rising flour, omit baking powder and salt.

CHESS PIE

Pastry for 8-inch One-Crust Pie
  (page 42)
1 cup sugar
1 tablespoon flour
¼ cup butter or margarine,
  softened

5 egg yolks
½ cup light cream (20%)
⅛ teaspoon salt

Heat oven to 400°. Prepare pastry. Beat sugar, flour, butter and egg yolks until smooth. Stir in cream and salt. Pour into pastry-lined pie plate.

Bake 10 minutes. Reduce oven temperature to 325°. Bake until top is golden and center is set, about 30 minutes. Cool slightly. Serve warm or refrigerate.

SOUTHERN PEANUT BUTTER PIE

Pastry for 9-inch One-Crust Pie
  (page 42)
⅔ cup sugar
½ teaspoon salt

1 cup dark corn syrup
⅓ cup creamy peanut butter
3 eggs
1 cup salted peanuts

Heat oven to 375°. Prepare pastry. Beat sugar, salt, corn syrup, peanut butter and eggs; stir in peanuts. Pour into pastry-lined pie plate.

Bake until pastry is golden brown, 40 to 50 minutes. (Center of filling may be slightly soft but will become firm as pie cools.) Cool slightly and refrigerate. Nice served with sweetened whipped cream or ice cream.

VINEGAR PIE

8-inch Baked Pie Shell (page 42)
1 cup sugar
2 tablespoons flour
2 tablespoons cider vinegar
2 eggs, beaten

1 tablespoon butter or
  margarine
½ teaspoon lemon extract
Sweetened whipped cream

Bake pie shell; cool. Mix sugar and flour in 2-quart saucepan. Add enough water to vinegar to measure 1 cup; blend into eggs. Stir egg mixture gradually into sugar mixture. Cook over medium heat, stirring constantly, until mixture thickens and boils. Boil and stir 1 minute. Remove from heat; stir in butter and lemon extract. Cool slightly. Pour into pie shell; refrigerate. Serve with whipped cream.

Pictured opposite.
Each of these pies reflects the character and charm of the South. From top: Southern Peanut Butter Pie (this page), Lime Chiffon Pie (page 48) and Chess Pie (this page).

BLACK BOTTOM PIE

9-inch Baked Pie Shell (page 42)
½ cup sugar
2 tablespoons cornstarch
½ teaspoon salt
2 cups milk
2 eggs, separated
2 teaspoons unflavored gelatin

3 tablespoons cold water
2 tablespoons rum or 2
    teaspoons rum flavoring
1 ounce melted unsweetened
    chocolate (cool)
¼ teaspoon cream of tartar
⅓ cup sugar

Bake pie shell; cool. Mix ½ cup sugar, the cornstarch and salt in 2-quart saucepan. Mix milk and egg yolks; stir gradually into sugar mixture. Cook over medium heat, stirring constantly, until mixture thickens and boils. Boil and stir 1 minute. Reserve 1 cup of the custard mixture. Sprinkle gelatin on cold water to soften; stir into remaining hot mixture in saucepan. Stir in rum. Chill in bowl of ice and water or in refrigerator, stirring occasionally, until mixture mounds slightly when dropped from spoon. Mix chocolate and the reserved custard mixture; pour into baked pie shell.

Beat egg whites and cream of tartar until foamy. Beat in ⅓ cup sugar, 1 tablespoon at a time; continue beating until stiff and glossy. Do not underbeat. Fold gelatin mixture into meringue. Spread over chocolate mixture. Refrigerate until set, at least 3 hours. Spread sweetened whipped cream over pie and sprinkle with shaved chocolate if desired.

SHOOFLY PIE

Pastry for 9-inch One-Crust Pie
    (page 42)
¾ cup all-purpose flour*
½ cup packed brown sugar
½ teaspoon salt
½ teaspoon ground cinnamon
¼ teaspoon ground ginger

⅛ teaspoon ground nutmeg
3 tablespoons butter or
    margarine
¾ cup hot water
½ teaspoon baking soda
½ cup dark molasses
1 egg yolk, well beaten

Heat oven to 400°. Prepare pastry. Mix flour, sugar, salt, cinnamon, ginger, nutmeg and butter with hands until crumbly. Mix water and baking soda in 1-quart bowl. Stir in molasses and egg yolk. Pour into pastry-lined pie plate. Sprinkle crumbly mixture over molasses mixture. Bake 15 minutes. Reduce oven temperature to 325°. Bake until crust and crumbs are brown, about 20 minutes. Serve warm.

*If using self-rising flour, omit salt.

Pictured opposite.
Five mainstays of American cooking, each with a heritage all its own. From top: Stuffed Green Peppers (page 66), Country Captain (page 75), Barbecued Spareribs (page 67), Manhattan Clam Chowder (page 57) and Yankee Pot Roast of Beef (page 65).

MAINSTAYS

MAINSTAYS

In Mainstays, American cooking is at its most originally American. What could be more native than Red Flannel Hash, Barbecued Spareribs or Maryland Crab Cakes? It is in Mainstays, too, that regional cookery is most evident. The Codfish Cakes and Clam Chowder of New England, Chili Con Carne from the Southwest, Jambalaya and Brunswick Stew from the South, the West's Beef Pot Roast, Western Style, and Cioppino—each region's main courses transplant easily to dinner tables all over the country. The center of attraction is not, of course, always meat or fish. Slow-baking bean dishes and soups, with their indescribable aura of comfort, have long been nourishing American Mainstays, too.

Early Americans enjoyed an abundance of game, freshwater fish and seafood. Maine lobster, which is such a treat for us today, was once ordinary enough that residents along the coast were almost embarrassed to serve it to guests. Certain West Coast clams, which now are rare, used to be so common that they were loaded onto carts to be fed to chickens and pigs. Bear, squirrel, buffalo, seal, opossum, venison and dozens of game birds are some of the robust meats that were considered standard fare in different parts of the country. In Europe, throughout history, meat was scarce for all but the wealthy. When colonists came to America they encountered a greater variety and quantity of meat than they'd ever dreamed possible. Even more than either fruits and vegetables, it is the availability of meat that contributes to the garden of paradise tone in the early descriptions of American food.

The most famous beef in this country grew from the few head of cattle Spanish explorers brought over for their missions. From the cows that wandered away from the mission lands, the huge roving herds of the West developed. Later replaced by meatier breeds, the longhorn is an almost legendary creature said to once have had a horn span up to seven feet and the ability to smell water miles away. Nothing in the history of our westward expansion, not even the gold rush, compares with the lore of the cowboys and the raw cowtowns where cattle were loaded onto trains and taken to city stockyards.

Before the railroads began transporting beef all over the country, the most plentiful meat was pork. Pigs were easy for farm families to raise and almost every part was useful. After the hams and chops came spareribs, bacon, sausage, headcheese, scrapple and cracklings. Chicken, at that time, was grown commercially only on a small scale. Families valued their hens and served chicken as a special Sunday dinner or for guests. Poultry, cows and sheep were valuable for eggs, milk or wool, but pigs were raised exclusively for food.

Fish were even more plentiful than meat. In the early years along the Atlantic coast, survival often depended on fishing and on digging clams. The Massachusetts and Chesapeake Bays teemed with fish when settlers first arrived on their shores. Cod, particularly, was the staple of New Englanders. It has been known, then and now, as "The Sacred Cod" for several reasons. Traditionally it was believed by the Pilgrims to be the miracle fish that Christ used when he fed the

The cowboy is still a necessary link in today's streamlined beef-processing chain.

multitudes. The indentations on the fish's body were said to be Christ's thumb and finger marks. More practically, the cod was sacred because it was the source of life and livelihood for so many settlers.

Another plentiful saltwater fish was the native American shad. Writers of the time claimed that such large schools traveled up the Hudson River it was hard to catch anything other than shad. Like lobster, the shad wasn't appreciated until its numbers began to decline. By the end of the Revolutionary War, fishermen noticed that the quantity of seafood was declining. Some thought the booms of cannon fire drove the fish away, but it is more likely that the effects of overfishing had begun.

Until refrigeration became common, whatever fish or meats were available had to be prepared immediately or smoked, pickled or salted for storage. Fish usually were salted or dried, as they had been for hundreds of years, but meats were treated in many ways. The hickory-smoked taste we still esteem was developed as a way to delay spoilage. The pungent flavor of corned beef is from the preservation method of pickling with spices. From the Indians, settlers learned to make jerky, dried beef or buffalo strips.

Thanks to refrigeration, meat and fish cookery are simple today. We can buy the exact quantity we need any time of year. The challenge now, in preparation of main courses, is cost. Meat is the highest priced item on the food budget. Fish, especially shellfish, are becoming scarce, and therefore more costly. With this in mind, our selection of Mainstays emphasizes ways of stretching the budget. Soups, stews and dried bean dishes are traditional ways of doing this, with recipes such as Boston Baked Beans or Pennsylvania Dutch Chicken and Corn Soup. Thrifty American cooks also can rely on Family Meat Loaf, Yankee Pot Roast of Beef, Tuna-Cheese Burgers and Hot Chicken Salad. Not that we've forgotten the glories of the American table—the Broiled Marinated Leg of Lamb, Publick House Lobster Pie, Stuffed Pork Chops and many others.

We have chosen not to include those great national favorites, the hot dog and the hamburger, in their classic forms. So completely are they a part of everyday menus that we felt anyone old enough to turn on the stove must know several ways of preparing them! But we have included Corn Dogs and Sloppy Joes, both perfect for children's parties because they're different ways of serving what is sure to be popular.

Our Mainstays are divided by the method of cooking: slow-cooking Soups and Stews that used to simmer on the back burners of the old wood-fired stoves; Oven Features, which are easy for the cook and often help you save energy by cooking more than one dish at a time; and Skillet Specialties and Deep Fries, both usually speedy preparations.

Whether delicate or hearty, simple or festive, all these great Mainstays that have been handed down to us still will hold the center of attention on any table.

SOUPS

If dried beans have ever been underestimated in American cooking, now is certainly the time for their rediscovery. Famed in the dining hall of the U.S. Senate, Senate Bean Soup is a sustaining and economical patriotic favorite, just the thing for a tailgate picnic on a brisk autumn day. Bean soup can be elegant, too. Black Bean Soup with its colorful garnishes dispels any lingering aura of the ordinary.

SENATE BEAN SOUP

1 pound dried navy beans
   (about 2 cups)
12 cups water
1 ham bone
1 cup chopped onion
1 cup chopped celery

1 clove garlic, finely chopped
2½ cups mashed cooked
   potatoes
2 teaspoons salt
¼ teaspoon pepper

Heat beans and water to boiling in 5-quart Dutch oven; boil 2 minutes. Remove from heat; cover and let stand 1 hour.

Add ham bone. Heat to boiling; reduce heat. Cover and simmer until beans are tender, about 2 hours. Stir in remaining ingredients. Cover and simmer 1 hour. Remove ham bone; trim ham from bone and stir into soup.   12 TO 14 SERVINGS.

BLACK BEAN SOUP

1 package (7.5 ounces) dried
   black beans
6 cups water
1 ham bone *
2 carrots, sliced
1 cup chopped celery
1 cup chopped onion
2 cloves garlic, finely chopped

1 small dried hot pepper,
   crumbled
1 bay leaf
1 teaspoon salt
6 lemon slices
1 hard-cooked egg, shredded
¼ cup chopped red onion
Dry white wine (optional)

Heat beans and water to boiling in 4-quart Dutch oven; boil 2 minutes. Remove from heat; cover and let stand 1 hour.

Add ham bone. Heat to boiling; reduce heat. Cover and simmer until beans are tender, about 2 hours. Stir in carrots, celery, 1 cup chopped onion, the garlic, pepper, bay leaf and salt. Cover and simmer 1 hour. Remove ham bone and bay leaf. Soup can be pressed through food mill. (Or place in blender container. Cover and blend until uniform consistency.) Trim ham from bone and stir into soup. Serve with lemon slices, shredded egg, ¼ cup chopped red onion and the wine.   6 SERVINGS.

* 1 pound smoked pork hocks or ham shank can be substituted for the ham bone.

CHEESE-POTATO SOUP

3 medium potatoes, pared and
    chopped (about 2 cups)
1 large onion, chopped (about 1
    cup)
2 teaspoons instant chicken
    bouillon

1½ cups water
8 ounces pasteurized process
    cheese spread loaf, cut up

Heat potatoes, onion, bouillon and water to boiling in 2-quart saucepan. Cover and cook until potatoes are tender, about 10 minutes. Place in blender container; add cheese. Cover and blend until uniform consistency.   4 SERVINGS.

CRAB BISQUE

1 can (11½ ounces) condensed
    green pea soup
1 can (10¾ ounces) condensed
    tomato soup
2 cups milk

1 can (6½ ounces) crabmeat,
    drained and cartilage
    removed
2 tablespoons dry white wine
Thin lemon slices

Mix soups in 2-quart saucepan. Stir in milk gradually. Stir in crabmeat and wine; heat over low heat, stirring occasionally, but do not boil. Serve with lemon slices. 5 SERVINGS.

MANHATTAN CLAM CHOWDER

¼ cup finely chopped onion
¼ cup finely cut-up lean salt
    pork
2 cans (6½ ounces each)
    minced or whole clams,*
    drained (reserve liquid)
2 cups finely chopped pared
    uncooked potatoes

⅓ cup chopped celery
1 cup water
1 can (16 ounces) tomatoes
2 teaspoons snipped parsley
1 teaspoon salt
¼ teaspoon dried thyme leaves
⅛ teaspoon pepper

Cook and stir onion and pork until onion is tender and pork is crisp. Stir clam liquid, potatoes, celery and water into onion mixture. Heat to boiling. Cover and cook until potatoes are tender, about 10 minutes. Stir in clams, tomatoes (with liquid), parsley, salt, thyme leaves and pepper. Heat to boiling, stirring occasionally.   4 TO 6 SERVINGS.

*1 pint shucked fresh clams can be substituted for the canned clams. Drain clams, reserving liquid. Chop clams and add with potatoes.

LANDLUBBER'S NEW ENGLAND CLAM CHOWDER

½ cup chopped onion
¼ cup cut-up bacon or lean salt
  pork
2 cans (8 ounces each) minced
  clams, drained (reserve
  liquid)

1 cup finely chopped pared
  uncooked potato
½ teaspoon salt
Dash of pepper
2 cups milk

Cook and stir onion and bacon in 2-quart saucepan until onion is tender and bacon is crisp. Add enough water, if necessary, to reserved clam liquid to measure 1 cup. Stir clams, liquid, potato, salt and pepper into onion mixture. Heat to boiling. Cover and cook until potato is tender, about 15 minutes. Stir in milk; heat until hot, stirring occasionally.   6 SERVINGS.

The essence of one kind of colonial cooking remains intact in the Pennsylvania Dutch countryside of southeastern Pennsylvania. There, the home of Shoofly Pie, scrapple, Apple Butter and pretzels, market day is as colorful as the brightly painted hex signs on the old barns. Shelves of homemade bread and preserves are baked and put up the same way they have been by generations of Pennsylvania Dutch. Their proud, traditional ways of cooking and living endure with virtually no change.

At the end of market day, when the tourists speed back to the cities, the buggies turn toward home and, perhaps, a dinner of scrapple or Chicken and Corn Soup. Our soup has the shortcut of canned corn, but it preserves the Pennsylvania Dutch spirit of combining simple ingredients in a surprising and delicious way.

PENNSYLVANIA DUTCH CHICKEN AND CORN SOUP

4- to 4½-pound stewing
  chicken, cut up
12 cups water
1 medium onion, cut into
  fourths
2 teaspoons salt
1 teaspoon whole mixed
  pickling spice

2 cans (17 ounces each) whole
  kernel corn
1½ cups finely chopped celery
  (with leaves)
2 hard-cooked eggs, chopped
2 teaspoons salt
⅛ teaspoon pepper
Rivels (page 59)

Remove any excess fat from chicken. Heat chicken, giblets, neck, water, onion, 2 teaspoons salt and the pickling spice to boiling; reduce heat. Cover and simmer until thickest pieces of chicken are tender, 2½ to 3 hours. Strain broth. Refrigerate chicken and broth separately.

Remove chicken from bones; remove skin if desired. Cut chicken into small pieces. Remove fat from broth. Heat broth, chicken, corn (with liquid) and celery to boiling; reduce heat. Simmer uncovered 10 minutes. Stir in eggs, 2 teaspoons salt and the pepper. Stir in Rivels. Cover and simmer 7 minutes.   10 TO 12 SERVINGS.

RIVELS
Mix 1 cup all-purpose flour, ¼ teaspoon salt and 1 egg, beaten, until crumbly.

STEWS

Georgia, North Carolina and Virginia all claim to be the birthplace of Brunswick Stew. Since there's no way to settle the dispute, we'll say this is indubitably a Southern specialty and a long-time favorite for church cookouts, political rallies, family reunions and other outdoor gatherings. Squirrel, sometimes a main ingredient, gradually has been replaced with chicken, but Brunswick Stew, like Jambalaya, may vary from place to place and season to season. Long simmering gives Brunswick Stew its memorable flavor.

BRUNSWICK STEW

3- to 3½-pound stewing
    chicken, cut up
4 cups water
1½ teaspoons salt
2 cans (16 ounces each)
    tomatoes
1 can (17 ounces) whole
    kernel corn
1 can (14 ounces) lima beans
1 medium potato, pared and
    cubed (about 1 cup)

1 medium onion, chopped
¼ pound lean salt pork, cut
    into 1-inch pieces
1 teaspoon salt
¼ teaspoon pepper
Dash of cayenne red pepper
½ cup water
2 tablespoons flour

Remove any excess fat from chicken. Heat chicken, giblets, neck, 4 cups water and 1½ teaspoons salt to boiling in 5-quart Dutch oven; reduce heat. Cover and simmer until thickest pieces of chicken are tender, about 1 hour.

Skim fat from broth. Remove chicken from bones if desired. Stir in tomatoes (with liquid), corn (with liquid), beans (with liquid), potato, onion, pork, 1 teaspoon salt, the pepper and red pepper. Heat to boiling; reduce heat. Simmer uncovered 1 hour. Shake ½ cup water and the flour in covered jar. Stir into stew. Heat to boiling, stirring constantly. Boil and stir 1 minute.   8 TO 10 SERVINGS.

When the local ingredients include turtles, crayfish, okra, redfish, sassafras, pecans, lake shrimp, red pepper, chicory and yams and the local residents are Spanish, French, African and a sprinkling of Italian, German and English, an unusual cuisine is bound to evolve.

Creole and Acadian cookery, two strains of native Louisiana cooking, are similar. The city Creoles were families descended from the early Spanish and French; Acadians, commonly called Cajuns, were those French exiles from Acadia (now Nova Scotia) who made their homes in the bayou country.

Even the word *jambalaya* evokes the rhythmic language that the Cajuns still speak, while just a glance at the recipe for Chicken Gumbo reveals something of the lineage of this cuisine. *Gumbo* is an African word for the okra that was brought to America by slaves. Filé powder, added just before serving, is made from dried sassafras leaves. It was originally used as a seasoning by the Choctaws and is used as a thickener and seasoning in many Creole recipes.

CHICKEN GUMBO

3- to 4-pound broiler-fryer
   chicken, cut up
1 cup chopped celery tops
1 medium onion, sliced
1 clove garlic, crushed
   (optional)
1 large bay leaf, crumbled
2 teaspoons salt
2 cups water or chicken broth
2 tablespoons butter or
   margarine

⅔ cup chopped onion
½ cup chopped green pepper
1 can (28 ounces) tomatoes
¼ cup snipped parsley
½ teaspoon red pepper sauce
1½ cups fresh or frozen okra
⅓ cup uncooked long-grain rice
Dash of pepper
1½ teaspoons filé powder

Remove any excess fat from chicken. Heat chicken, giblets, neck, celery tops, sliced onion, garlic, bay leaf, salt and water to boiling; reduce heat. Cover and simmer until thickest pieces of chicken are done, about 45 minutes. Strain broth. Refrigerate chicken and broth separately.

Remove chicken from bones; remove skin if desired. Cut chicken into pieces. Remove fat from broth. Place broth and chicken pieces in saucepan.

Cook and stir butter, chopped onion and green pepper until onion is tender but not brown. Stir green pepper mixture, tomatoes (with liquid), parsley and pepper sauce into chicken and broth. Heat to boiling; reduce heat. Simmer uncovered 15 minutes. Stir in okra, rice and pepper; simmer 20 minutes. Remove from heat; stir in filé powder. (Soup can be prepared ahead; stir in filé powder after reheating.)　4 TO 6 SERVINGS.

Pictured opposite.
Two hearty main dishes from the Louisiana bayou country. From top: Chicken Gumbo (this page) and Jambalaya (page 84).

Mainstays　**61**

OLD-FASHIONED BEEF STEW

¼ cup all-purpose flour
1½ teaspoons salt
⅛ teaspoon pepper
1½ pounds beef stew meat, cut into 1½-inch pieces
2 tablespoons shortening
⅓ cup chopped onion
3 cups hot water
1 can (8½ ounces) small white whole onions, drained, or 2 medium onions, cut into fourths

3 medium potatoes, pared and cut into fourths
2 carrots, cut into 1-inch slices
½ cup fresh, frozen or canned green peas
1 beef bouillon cube
Snipped parsley

Mix flour, salt and pepper. Coat beef with flour mixture. Heat shortening in 4-quart Dutch oven until melted; brown beef. Stir in chopped onion. Cook 5 minutes, stirring frequently; drain off fat.

Add hot water. Heat to boiling; reduce heat. Cover and simmer 2 hours. Stir in remaining ingredients except parsley.

Cover and simmer until vegetables are tender, about 30 minutes. Thicken stew if desired: Shake ½ cup cold water and 1 to 2 tablespoons flour in tightly covered jar. Stir into stew. Heat to boiling, stirring constantly. Boil and stir 1 minute. Sprinkle with parsley. 4 TO 6 SERVINGS.

A pot of lima beans with ham is reminiscent of a time when there was always a pot simmering on the back burner. Pork hock, a cut from the foreleg, is flavorful and inexpensive.

LIMA BEANS WITH PORK HOCKS

2 pounds smoked pork hocks
6 cups water
1 pound dried lima beans (about 2 cups)
1 large onion, chopped

1½ teaspoons dry mustard
1 to 3 dried hot peppers
1 clove garlic, finely chopped
Salt
Pepper

Heat pork hocks and water to boiling in 4-quart Dutch oven; reduce heat. Cover and simmer 30 minutes. Add beans. Heat to boiling; boil 2 minutes. Add onion, mustard, hot peppers and garlic. Heat to boiling; reduce heat. Cover and simmer until beans are tender, 1 to 1¼ hours. Add enough water, if necessary, to keep beans covered while simmering. Remove hocks; trim pork from bones and stir into beans. Season with salt and pepper.   6 SERVINGS.

Although most people assume chili is a Mexican import, the fact is that it is a product of the Southwest. It has been avidly discussed and devoured there for over a hundred years. Today, there is even a large organization for chili lovers in Texas, the state where everyone knows what you mean when you order "a bowl of red." No self-respecting Texan would add beans to his *chili con carne* (chili with meat), but if you're not a purist, it certainly is a good way to stretch the protein.

CHILI CON CARNE

2 pounds dried pinto beans
   (about 4 cups)
12 cups water
1 tablespoon plus 2 teaspoons
   salt
2 cloves garlic, finely chopped

1 large bay leaf
2 pounds lean ground beef
2 medium onions, sliced
1 cup tomato juice
3 tablespoons chili powder
1½ teaspoons ground cumin

Heat beans and water to boiling in 6-quart Dutch oven; boil 2 minutes. Remove from heat; cover and let stand 1 hour.

Stir in salt, garlic and bay leaf. Heat to boiling; reduce heat. Cover and simmer until beans are tender, 1 to 1½ hours. Discard bay leaf.

Cook and stir ground beef and onions until beef is brown. Stir beef mixture, tomato juice, chili powder and cumin into beans. Heat to boiling; reduce heat. Cover and simmer 1 hour.   10 SERVINGS.

OYSTER STEW

¼ cup butter or margarine
1 pint oysters, drained*
2 cups milk
½ cup light cream (20%)
½ cup fresh or bottled clam
   liquid

1 teaspoon salt
Dash of cayenne red pepper
Dash of Worcestershire sauce
Paprika
Oyster crackers (optional)

Heat butter in 8-inch skillet until melted. Add oysters. Cook and stir over low heat just until edges curl. Heat milk, cream and clam liquid in 2-quart saucepan. Stir in salt, red pepper, Worcestershire sauce and oysters. Sprinkle with paprika. Serve with crackers.   4 SERVINGS.

*The oyster liquid can be substituted for the clam liquid.

Fisherman's Wharf in San Francisco, where tourists stroll along the water eating sourdough bread and feasting on fresh crab and shrimp from paper cups, is lined with seafood restaurants that serve a more sophisticated fare. Cioppino, for example, is a California invention that varies with the day's catch or the fish-market specials. A feast for the eye as well as the palate, Cioppino exhibits several unique attributes of California cooking. Because of the olive groves and vineyards, olive oil and wine are staples of cooking in most of the Far West. Herbs and spices are used generously, perhaps a heritage from the Mexicans, Spanish, Russians and Chinese.

The Mexican and Spanish cooking of the early Western settlers was enhanced by the Russian seal hunters who were attracted to the coast. After the waves of pioneers began to infiltrate the West, thousands of Chinese laborers were brought in to help finish the transcontinental railroad. Thus, an astonishing melting pot occurred in the West, and experimentation in cooking developed as a norm rather than as an exception. The addition, for instance, of prunes and olives in Beef Pot Roast, Western Style, is the kind of imaginative flair that Westerners typically bring to day-to-day fare.

Trawlers ply the seas in every kind of weather to bring back the fixin's for delicious dishes like Cioppino (this page).

CIOPPINO

3 pounds dressed firm saltwater fish (sea bass, halibut, haddock, turbot)
1 live Dungeness crab
1 pound large raw shrimp
12 clams, oysters or mussels (or combination)
2 large onions, chopped (about 2 cups)
1 large green pepper, chopped (about 1 cup)
¼ cup olive oil
1 can (28 ounces) tomatoes
2 cups tomato juice
1 to 2 teaspoons salt
½ teaspoon dried basil leaves
⅛ teaspoon pepper
2 cloves garlic, finely chopped
1 bay leaf
2 cups dry red wine
Snipped parsley

Cut fish into serving pieces. Crack crab. Peel and devein shrimp. Steam clams to open; remove top shells and reserve liquid. Place fish and crab in 8-quart Dutch oven; reserve shrimp and clams.

Cook and stir onions, green pepper and oil in 3-quart saucepan until onions are tender. Stir in reserved clam liquid, tomatoes (with liquid), tomato juice, salt, basil, pepper, garlic and bay leaf. Heat to boiling; reduce heat. Simmer uncovered 10 minutes. Stir in wine; pour over fish and crab. Heat to boiling; reduce heat. Cover and simmer 20 minutes. Add shrimp. Cover and simmer 5 minutes. Arrange clams on the half shells on top. Cover and simmer 3 minutes. Sprinkle with parsley.   6 TO 10 SERVINGS.

YANKEE POT ROAST OF BEEF

¼ cup all-purpose flour
2 teaspoons salt
½ teaspoon pepper
4- to 5-pound boneless beef
    shoulder pot roast
1 tablespoon shortening
½ cup water
2 cups sliced celery

3 medium potatoes, pared and
    cut into ½-inch cubes
    (about 2 cups)
2 cups diced carrots
2 cups ½-inch cubes rutabaga
    or yellow turnips
1 cup chopped onion

Mix flour, salt and pepper; rub over beef roast. Heat shortening in skillet or Dutch oven until melted; brown beef on all sides. Drain off fat; add water. Heat to boiling; reduce heat. Cover tightly and simmer on top of range or in 325° oven 2 hours.

Add vegetables. Add ¼ cup water if necessary. Cover and simmer until beef and vegetables are tender, 45 to 60 minutes. 12 TO 16 SERVINGS.

Across the country, the variations on pot roast are as distinctive as local accents. Chances are you have your own idea of the way pot roast should be prepared. For a change, however, try it with these Yankee or Western overtones.

BEEF POT ROAST, WESTERN STYLE

1 cup water
1 cup pitted prunes
    (about ½ pound)*
2 teaspoons salt
½ teaspoon ground ginger
¼ teaspoon pepper
4- to 5-pound boneless
    beef shoulder pot roast
1 tablespoon shortening

1½ cups chopped onion
2 cloves garlic, finely
    chopped
½ cup water or dry red
    wine
1 can (6 ounces) pitted
    ripe olives, drained
5 ounces mushrooms, sliced
    (about 2 cups)

Pour 1 cup water over prunes; reserve. Mix salt, ginger and pepper; rub over beef roast. Heat shortening in skillet or Dutch oven until melted; brown beef on all sides. Drain off fat; add onion, garlic and water. Heat to boiling; reduce heat. Cover tightly and simmer on top of range or in 325° oven 2 hours.

Add prunes, olives and mushrooms. Cover and cook until beef is tender, about 1 hour. 12 TO 16 SERVINGS.

*1 cup dried apricots, cut in halves, can be substituted for the prunes.

OVEN FEATURES

FAMILY MEAT LOAF

1 can (16 ounces) tomatoes
2 pounds ground beef
2 eggs
1 cup old-fashioned oats

2 teaspoons salt
¼ teaspoon pepper
¼ teaspoon ground nutmeg

Place tomatoes (with liquid) in blender container. Cover and blend 5 seconds on low speed. Mix all ingredients; spread evenly in ungreased loaf pan, 9x5x3 inches. Bake uncovered in 350° oven until done, about 1½ hours. Drain off fat once during baking.   8 SERVINGS.

STUFFED GREEN PEPPERS

6 large green peppers
1 pound ground beef
2 tablespoons chopped
   onion
1 teaspoon salt

⅛ teaspoon garlic salt
1 cup cooked rice
1 can (15 ounces) tomato
   sauce

Heat oven to 350°. Cut thin slice from stem end of each pepper. Remove all seeds and membranes. Cook peppers in boiling salted water (½ teaspoon salt to 1 cup water) 5 minutes; drain. Cook and stir ground beef and onion in 10-inch skillet until beef is brown and onion is tender; drain off fat. Stir in salt, garlic salt, rice and 1 cup of the tomato sauce; heat until rice is hot. Stuff each pepper lightly with ½ cup beef mixture. Stand peppers upright in baking dish, 8x8x2 inches. Pour on remaining tomato sauce. Cover with foil and bake 45 minutes. Remove foil and bake 15 minutes.   6 SERVINGS.

SPICY CORNED BEEF

4-pound beef corned brisket
1 tablespoon whole mixed
   pickling spice
1 medium onion, cut into
   fourths
1 carrot, cut in half

1 stalk celery, cut in half
⅓ cup packed brown sugar
1 tablespoon prepared brown
   mustard
½ cup sweet pickle juice

Cover beef corned brisket with cold water. Add pickling spice, onion, carrot and celery. Heat to boiling; reduce heat. Cover and simmer until beef is tender, about 4 hours. Cool beef in broth. Place beef fat side up in ungreased baking pan, 13x9x2 inches. Score fat surface lightly. Mix sugar and mustard; spread over fat. Pour pickle juice into pan. Bake uncovered in 300° oven 1 hour, basting occasionally with pan juices.   8 TO 10 SERVINGS.

Like many culinary terms, the word *barbecue* derives from a description of a method of cooking. In Spanish, *barbacoa* means an elevated framework of sticks, one of the oldest cooking methods and the one most suited to the slow cooking of whole game.

By now the enormous barbecues of the Southwest have been adapted to almost every backyard in America. Is it the ancient appeal of sitting around a campfire, or does food really taste better outdoors?

BARBECUED SPARERIBS

4½ pounds pork spareribs,
   cut into serving pieces

Tomato, Mustard or
   Spicy Barbecue Sauce (below)

Place pork spareribs meaty sides up on rack in shallow roasting pan. Do not add water. Do not cover. Roast in 325° oven 1 hour. Brush spareribs with Tomato Barbecue Sauce. Bake, turning and brushing frequently with sauce, until spareribs are tender, about 45 minutes. 5 OR 6 SERVINGS.

TOMATO BARBECUE SAUCE

1 tablespoon dry mustard
1½ teaspoons onion salt
½ teaspoon garlic powder
⅔ cup catsup
⅓ cup water

¼ cup butter or margarine
2 tablespoons Worcestershire
   sauce
¼ teaspoon red pepper
   sauce

Heat all ingredients, stirring frequently, until butter is melted.

MUSTARD BARBECUE SAUCE

⅓ cup prepared brown
   mustard

⅓ cup molasses
⅓ cup cider vinegar

Mix mustard and molasses; stir in vinegar.

SPICY BARBECUE SAUCE

1 teaspoon sugar
1 teaspoon onion salt
½ teaspoon garlic powder
½ teaspoon pepper
Dash of cayenne red pepper

⅓ cup butter or margarine
2 tablespoons water
2 tablespoons vinegar
1 tablespoon Worcestershire
   sauce

Heat all ingredients, stirring frequently, until butter is melted.

Barbecued Chicken: Cut two 2½- to 3-pound broiler-fryer chickens into serving pieces. Place skin sides up on rack in shallow roasting pan; brush with vegetable oil. Roast in 325° oven 45 minutes. Brush chicken with Tomato Barbecue Sauce. Bake, turning and brushing frequently with sauce, until thickest pieces are done, about 30 minutes. 6 TO 8 SERVINGS.

ROAST PORK LOIN WITH SAGEY ONIONS

4-pound boneless pork top loin
   roast (double)
Salt
Pepper
2 pounds yellow onions

1¼ teaspoons ground sage
1 teaspoon salt
¼ teaspoon pepper
Gravy (below)

Place pork roast fat side up on rack in shallow roasting pan. Sprinkle with salt and pepper. Insert meat thermometer so tip is in center of thickest part of pork and does not rest in fat. Do not add water. Do not cover. Roast in 325° oven 1½ hours.

Heat 2 inches water to boiling. Add onions. Cover and heat to boiling. Cook until tender, 15 to 20 minutes; drain. Chop onions coarsely; stir in sage, 1 teaspoon salt and ¼ teaspoon pepper. Remove pork and rack from pan; pour off drippings, reserving ¼ cup. Mound onion mixture in center of pan; place pork on top. Roast until meat thermometer registers 170°, about 1 hour.   8 SERVINGS.

GRAVY
Mix reserved ¼ cup drippings and ¼ cup all-purpose flour. Cook over low heat, stirring constantly, until mixture is smooth and bubbly. Remove from heat; stir in 2 cups water. Heat to boiling, stirring constantly. Boil and stir 1 minute. Season with salt and pepper.

STUFFED PORK CHOPS

1 jar (14 ounces)
   cranberry-orange relish
2 tablespoons packed brown
   sugar
½ teaspoon salt
4 pork loin chops, 1 inch thick
   (with pockets for stuffing)
2 tablespoons flour

2 teaspoons salt
¼ teaspoon pepper
1 tablespoon shortening
1 large rutabaga (about 2
   pounds), pared and cut into
   ½-inch slices
Salt
¼ cup water

Heat oven to 350°. Mix relish, sugar and ½ teaspoon salt. Spoon 2 tablespoons of the relish mixture into each pork chop pocket; secure opening with wooden picks. Mix flour, 2 teaspoons salt and the pepper; rub over chops. Heat shortening in 10-inch skillet until melted; brown chops on both sides.

Place chops in corners of ungreased baking dish, 13½x8¾x1¾ inches. Layer rutabaga slices in center of baking dish; sprinkle each layer with salt. Pour water into skillet. Stir and scrape brown particles from skillet; pour over chops and rutabaga. Cover baking dish with aluminum foil. Bake until rutabaga is tender and chops are done, about 1½ hours. Serve with remaining relish.   4 SERVINGS.

Pictured opposite.
The farmlands of the Midwest inspired this Sunday dinner specialty—Roast Pork Loin with Sagey Onions.

SCALLOPED POTATOES AND HAM

The regional smokehouse, fragrant with hams, is now mainly a part of our past.

6 medium potatoes, pared
  and thinly sliced (about
  4 cups)
3 tablespoons flour
1 teaspoon salt

¼ teaspoon pepper
1½ cups cubed cooked ham
¼ cup finely chopped onion
¼ cup butter or margarine
2½ cups milk

Heat oven to 350°. Layer ¼ of the potato slices in greased 2-quart casserole; sprinkle each of the first 3 layers with 1 tablespoon flour, ¼ teaspoon salt, dash of pepper, ½ cup ham and 1 tablespoon onion. Dot each layer with 1 tablespoon butter. Sprinkle top with remaining salt, pepper and onion. Dot with remaining butter. Heat milk just to scalding; pour over potato mixture. Cover and bake 30 minutes. Uncover and bake until potatoes are tender, 60 to 70 minutes. Let stand 5 to 10 minutes before serving.   4 TO 6 SERVINGS.

As everyone who grew up on cowboy movies knows, sheep were not welcome in Western grazing lands. Miles of film recorded the shoot-outs between the sheep herders and the cowboys. Today, Colorado and other Western states raise both beef and lamb, so despite the Saturday movies, the dispute was settled.

And lucky for us, for lamb has become an American favorite. Most often it is simply roasted—and a roast leg of lamb is frequently the choice for a spring or Easter feast. In fact, lamb is so delicious in its unadorned preparation that relatively few elaborate variations have developed. Americans have cultivated such a taste for lamb that recipes for mutton are almost unknown here.

In the three selections that follow, lamb proves itself to be a very adaptable meat. Whether barbecued in a spicy sauce, marinated in wine and then broiled, or ground and made into tasty patties, lamb accommodates itself equally well.

BARBECUED BREAST OF LAMB

4 pounds breast of lamb,
  cut into serving pieces
2 medium onions, sliced
2 cloves garlic, finely
  chopped
2 teaspoons salt
2 teaspoons chili powder
¾ cup catsup

¾ cup water
¼ cup plus 1 tablespoon
  cider vinegar
1 tablespoon plus 1 teaspoon
  Worcestershire sauce
¼ teaspoon red pepper
  sauce

Brown lamb in 4-quart Dutch oven; drain off fat. Mix remaining ingredients; pour over lamb. Cover and bake in 350° oven 1¼ hours. Uncover and bake 15 minutes; drain off fat.   6 SERVINGS.

BROILED MARINATED LEG OF LAMB

5- to 8-pound leg of lamb,
    boned and butterflied
2 cups dry red wine
¼ cup vegetable oil
2 teaspoons salt

2 teaspoons dried rosemary
    leaves, crushed
2 cloves garlic, crushed
¼ teaspoon pepper

Place lamb in plastic bag or shallow baking dish. Mix remaining ingredients; pour over lamb. Fasten bag securely or cover dish with plastic wrap. Refrigerate at least 48 hours but no longer than 96 hours, turning lamb occasionally.

Drain lamb, reserving marinade. Slash outer edge of any fat on lamb at 1-inch intervals to prevent curling (do not cut into lamb). Set oven control to broil and/or 550°. Place lamb on rack in broiler pan. Place broiler pan so top of lamb is 5 to 6 inches from heat.

Broil until brown, about 25 minutes, brushing occasionally with reserved marinade. Turn lamb; broil until desired doneness, 20 to 30 minutes, brushing occasionally. Cut lamb across grain into thin slices.   ABOUT 8 SERVINGS.

Broiled Butterflied Leg of Lamb: Omit marinade. Rub lamb with 1 clove garlic; brush with vegetable oil. Slash outer edge of any fat at 1-inch intervals (do not cut into lamb). Broil as directed above.

BEST BROILED LAMB PATTIES

1 pound ground lamb
2 tablespoons dry bread crumbs
1 tablespoon snipped parsley
½ teaspoon salt
¼ teaspoon dill weed

1 egg
1 clove garlic, minced
4 slices bacon
Apricot-Mint Sauce (below)

Mix meat, bread crumbs, parsley, salt, dill weed, egg and garlic. Shape mixture into 4 patties, 1 inch thick and about 3 inches in diameter. Wrap slice of bacon around edge of each patty and secure with wooden picks.

Set oven control at broil and/or 550°. Broil patties 3 inches from heat about 15 minutes, turning once.   4 SERVINGS.

APRICOT-MINT SAUCE
Mix 2 jars (4¾ ounces each) strained apricots (baby food), ¼ cup mint-flavored apple jelly and 1 drop green food color.

BAKED CATFISH

1 dressed catfish (3 to 4
    pounds)*
½ teaspoon salt
⅛ teaspoon pepper
2 cups soft bread cubes
2 tablespoons snipped parsley
1 tablespoon pickle relish
1 small onion, finely chopped

1 egg, beaten
½ teaspoon salt
¼ teaspoon pepper
2 tablespoons butter or
    margarine, melted
6 slices lean salt pork
Broth (below)

Heat oven to 350°. Wash catfish in cold water; pat dry with paper towels. Rub cavity with ½ teaspoon salt and ⅛ teaspoon pepper. Mix bread cubes, parsley, relish, onion, egg, ½ teaspoon salt and ¼ teaspoon pepper; spoon lightly into cavity. Close opening with skewers; lace with string. Brush fish with butter. Cut 3 slits in each side; place a slice of salt pork in each slit. Place fish in greased shallow baking dish. Bake uncovered, spooning Broth over fish occasionally, until fish flakes easily with fork, 45 to 60 minutes. 6 SERVINGS.

*Other large fish such as lake trout, bass, haddock, salmon, whitefish, cod or red snapper can be substituted for the catfish.

BROTH
Heat 1½ cups water, 4 lemon slices, 1 onion slice, 1 bay leaf, crumbled, ½ cup chopped celery tops and 4 peppercorns to boiling; reduce heat. Cover and simmer 20 minutes; strain.

SALMON CASSEROLES

1 can (16 ounces) salmon,
    drained and flaked
½ teaspoon salt
Dash of pepper
2 tablespoons milk
1 egg, slightly beaten
⅔ cup chopped celery

2 tablespoons chopped onion
3 tablespoons shortening
½ teaspoon salt
½ teaspoon ground sage
⅓ cup milk
2 cups soft bread crumbs
4 green pepper rings

Heat oven to 350°. Mix salmon, ½ teaspoon salt, dash of pepper, 2 tablespoons milk and the egg. Press lightly on bottoms and about halfway up sides of 4 greased 10-ounce baking dishes.

Cook and stir celery, onion and shortening in 2-quart saucepan until celery is tender. Stir in ½ teaspoon salt, the sage, ⅓ cup milk and the bread crumbs. Spoon into center of each baking dish, pressing lightly to make celery mixture level with salmon mixture. Bake uncovered 25 minutes. Top each with pepper ring; bake 5 minutes. Nice served with a cheese sauce. 4 SERVINGS.

TUNA-CHEESE BURGERS

1 can (6½ ounces) tuna,
    drained
1 cup chopped celery
½ cup cut-up process
    American cheese
¼ cup finely chopped onion

¼ teaspoon salt
⅛ teaspoon pepper
¼ cup mayonnaise or salad
    dressing
6 hamburger buns
Butter or margarine, softened

Heat oven to 350°. Mix all ingredients except buns and butter. Spread buns with butter. Fill with tuna mixture. Place each sandwich on square of aluminum foil; fold edges securely. Place on baking sheet. Bake until tuna mixture is hot, about 20 minutes. 6 SANDWICHES.

TUNA-NOODLE CASSEROLE

8 ounces uncooked egg noodles
2 cans (6½ ounces each) tuna,
    well drained
1½ cups dairy sour cream
¾ cup milk
1 can (3 ounces) sliced
    mushrooms, drained

1½ teaspoons salt
¼ teaspoon pepper
¼ cup dry bread crumbs
¼ cup grated Parmesan cheese
2 tablespoons butter or
    margarine, melted

Heat oven to 350°. Cook noodles as directed on package; drain. Return noodles to saucepan; stir in tuna, sour cream, milk, mushrooms, salt and pepper. Pour into ungreased 2-quart casserole. Mix bread crumbs, cheese and butter; sprinkle evenly over tuna mixture. Bake uncovered until hot and bubbly, 35 to 40 minutes. 6 TO 8 SERVINGS.

SCALLOPED OYSTERS

2 cups crushed soda crackers
    (about 40 squares)
½ teaspoon salt
⅛ teaspoon pepper
Dash of ground mace

¼ cup butter or margarine,
    melted
1 pint oysters, cut in halves
½ cup half-and-half

Heat oven to 400°. Mix crackers, salt, pepper, mace and butter. Pat half of the cracker mixture evenly in buttered baking dish, 8x8x2 inches. Arrange oysters on cracker mixture. Sprinkle remaining cracker mixture over oysters. Pour half-and-half over top. Bake uncovered until hot, about 20 minutes. 4 OR 5 SERVINGS.

Think of Maine and what comes to mind? Some might say blueberries or the charming scenery of the rocky coast, but for most of us, Maine is synonymous with lobster. The cold water off that state is the ideal home for the awkward and unlikely looking creature that has become America's most luxurious seafood.

Are we to believe the many records about the quantities and sizes of the lobsters our ancestors first hauled out of the Maine waters? Apparently lobsters, which are long-lived creatures, had been undisturbed before the European settlement in America. Many had lived a hundred years and had grown to prodigious lengths. But to imagine a six-foot lobster is to find oneself in the realm of tall tales!

Lobsters, as prices tell us, are the victims of over-demand. Occasionally someone pulls in a twenty-five-pounder, but these days lobsters usually aren't in the water long enough to grow so large. It takes about seven years for a lobster to reach the smallest legal size for catching.

If you've ever noticed that one claw on a lobster is larger than the other, there's a reason: lobsters are either left- or right-handed, and the claw they use becomes more developed.

Although live lobsters are seasonal and not always easy to find, here is an interesting recipe that uses canned lobster meat, available all year long.

PUBLICK HOUSE LOBSTER PIE

¼ cup butter or margarine
2 tablespoons flour
½ teaspoon salt
2 cups half-and-half
2 eggs, slightly beaten
2 cans (5 ounces each) lobster, drained and cut up (2 cups)
½ cup dry white wine

½ cup cracker crumbs
¼ cup crushed potato chips
2 tablespoons grated Parmesan cheese
1 teaspoon paprika
¼ cup butter or margarine, melted

Heat oven to 300°. Heat ¼ cup butter in 2-quart saucepan over low heat until melted. Stir in flour and salt. Cook over low heat, stirring constantly, until mixture is smooth and bubbly. Remove from heat; stir in half-and-half gradually. Heat to boiling, stirring constantly. Boil and stir 1 minute.

Stir at least half of the hot mixture into eggs. Blend egg mixture into hot mixture in saucepan. Cook over medium heat, stirring constantly, 3 minutes. Remove from heat; stir in lobster and wine. Pour into ungreased baking dish, 11¾ x 7½ x 1¾ inches. Mix cracker crumbs, potato chips, cheese, paprika and ¼ cup butter; sprinkle over lobster mixture. Bake uncovered until lobster is hot, about 15 minutes. 4 SERVINGS.

HOT CHICKEN SALAD

2 cups cut-up cooked chicken
   or turkey
2 cups thinly sliced celery
¾ cup mayonnaise or salad
   dressing
2 tablespoons finely chopped
   onion

2 tablespoons capers
1 teaspoon curry powder
½ teaspoon salt
½ cup toasted slivered almonds

Heat oven to 350°. Mix chicken, celery, mayonnaise, onion, capers, curry powder and salt. Spoon into ungreased 1-quart casserole or six 1-cup baking dishes. Sprinkle with almonds. Bake uncovered until chicken mixture is hot, about 20 minutes.   6 SERVINGS.

Was this dish brought to the port of Savannah by a mysterious captain of the spice trade, as Georgians claim, or was it the wild invention of a local cook desperately tired of fried chicken? No one knows the true originator of Country Captain, but many cooks know this bold and pungent dish's appeal for an exciting menu.

COUNTRY CAPTAIN

½ cup all-purpose flour
1 teaspoon salt
¼ teaspoon pepper
2½- to 3-pound broiler-
   fryer chicken, cut up
¼ cup vegetable oil
1 large onion, chopped
1 green pepper, chopped
1 clove garlic, finely
   chopped, or ⅛ teaspoon
   garlic powder

1 can (16 ounces) tomatoes
1½ teaspoons curry
   powder
½ teaspoon dried thyme
   leaves
¼ teaspoon salt
¼ cup currants or raisins
⅓ cup toasted slivered
   blanched almonds
3 cups hot cooked rice

Chicken is a traditional mainstay at crowd-size cookouts like this one in Mount Morris, Illinois.

Heat oven to 350°. Mix flour, 1 teaspoon salt and the pepper. Coat chicken with flour mixture. Heat oil in 10-inch skillet. Cook chicken in oil over medium heat until light brown, 15 to 20 minutes. Place chicken in ungreased 2½-quart casserole. Drain oil from skillet.

Add onion, green pepper, garlic, tomatoes (with liquid), curry powder, thyme and ¼ teaspoon salt to skillet. Heat to boiling, stirring frequently to loosen brown particles from skillet. Pour over chicken. Cover and bake until thickest pieces are done, about 40 minutes. Skim fat from liquid if necessary; add currants. Bake 5 minutes. Sprinkle with almonds. Serve with rice. Accompany with grated fresh coconut and chutney if desired.   4 SERVINGS.

The politician who promises a chicken in every pot probably gets the votes, for chicken always has been an unequivocal winner. Although it once was scarce enough to be reserved for Sunday dinner, now, fortunately, it is usually one of the best bargains at the meat counter. From Juneau to Miami, there are innumerable recipes for preparing this talented bird.

Hot Chicken Salad (page 75) with its touch of curry, gives interest to a light dinner out of doors on a summer evening. Chicken in Cream shares those two attributes busy cooks appreciate: it is both elegant and requires no watching. And what could be more American than Crunchy Oven-fried Chicken?

CHICKEN IN CREAM

½ cup all-purpose flour*
1 teaspoon salt
¼ teaspoon pepper
2½- to 3-pound broiler-
    fryer chicken, cut up

2 cups light cream (20%)
Paprika

Heat oven to 325°. Mix flour, salt and pepper. Coat chicken with flour mixture. Place skin sides down in ungreased baking dish, 13½x8¾x1¾ inches. Pour cream over chicken. Bake uncovered 45 minutes; turn. Bake until thickest pieces are done, 30 to 45 minutes (do not overbake). Place chicken on warm platter. Stir enough hot water or milk into baking dish, if necessary, to give sauce desired consistency; pour over chicken. Sprinkle with paprika. 4 OR 5 SERVINGS.

*If using self-rising flour, decrease salt to ½ teaspoon.

CRUNCHY OVEN-FRIED CHICKEN

1 cup corn flake cereal
    crumbs
1 teaspoon onion salt
⅛ teaspoon pepper

2½- to 3-pound broiler-
    fryer chicken, cut up
½ cup butter or
    margarine, melted*

Heat oven to 350°. Mix cereal crumbs, onion salt and pepper. Dip chicken in butter; roll in cereal crumb mixture. Place skin sides up in ungreased baking pan, 13x9x2 inches. Pour remaining butter over chicken. Bake uncovered until thickest pieces are done, 1¼ to 1½ hours. 4 SERVINGS.

*½ cup evaporated milk can be substituted for the butter; use greased pan.

Herbed Chicken: Stir 1 teaspoon crushed dried rosemary, marjoram, tarragon or sage leaves into the melted butter.

Pictured opposite.
Chicken is a traditional choice for American picnics. Complement Crunchy Oven-fried Chicken (this page) with Sunshine Cake (page 21), Fresh Mushroom and Spinach Salad (page 108), Dilled Beans (page 126) and Squash Rolls (page 16).

Mainstays 77

How did America's most famous bird ever get its un-American name? Early sixteenth-century explorers took the birds, domesticated by the Indians, back to Spain from Mexico long before America was settled. As the popularity of the new bird spread over Europe, most people assumed it had come from the exotic East. The French named it "dinde" (d'Inde), meaning "from India." The Germans thought it was a chicken from Calicut, on the coast of Malabar, and called it "KaleKuttisch Hün." It was the English who decided the strange bird must be from Turkey, possibly as a misunderstanding of the Indian name, "furkee."

Our domestic turkeys are easy to roast and have become a symbol of American holidays. After preparing the turkey and stuffing it just before roasting, heat oven to 325°. Place turkey breast side up on rack in open shallow roasting pan. Brush with shortening, oil or butter. Insert meat thermometer so tip is in thickest part of inside thigh muscle or thickest part of breast meat and does not touch bone. Do not add water. Do not cover. Approximate cooking time for an 8- to 12-pound turkey is 3½ to 4½ hours, for a 12- to 16-pound turkey, 4½ to 5½ hours. Meat thermometer should register 185°. When turkey is done, remove from oven and allow to stand about 20 minutes for easiest carving. As soon as possible after serving, remove every bit of stuffing from turkey. Cool stuffing, meat and any gravy promptly; refrigerate and use within two days.

CHESTNUT STUFFING FOR TURKEY

1 pound chestnuts	7 cups soft bread cubes
1½ cups chopped celery (with leaves)	2 teaspoons salt
	1½ teaspoons dried sage leaves
¾ cup finely chopped onion	1 teaspoon dried thyme leaves
1 cup butter or margarine	½ teaspoon pepper

Cut an X on rounded side of each chestnut. Heat chestnuts and enough water to cover to boiling. Boil uncovered 10 minutes; drain. Remove shells and skins. Heat chestnuts and enough water to cover to boiling. Boil uncovered 10 minutes; drain and chop.

Cook and stir celery, onion and butter in 10-inch skillet until onion is tender. Stir in about ⅓ of the bread cubes. Turn mixture into deep bowl. Add remaining bread cubes, the salt, sage, thyme, pepper and chestnuts; toss lightly. Stuff and roast turkey as described above.
9 CUPS STUFFING (ENOUGH FOR 12-POUND TURKEY).

Corn Bread Stuffing: Omit chestnuts. Substitute 9 cups corn bread cubes for the soft bread cubes.

Oyster Stuffing: Omit chestnuts. Increase soft bread cubes to 8 cups and add 2 cans (8 ounces each) oysters, drained and chopped.

PHEASANT WITH WINE SAUCE

1 teaspoon salt
¼ teaspoon ground cloves
¼ teaspoon ground nutmeg
¼ teaspoon ground thyme
¼ teaspoon pepper
2 pheasants
4 slices bacon
1 teaspoon instant chicken
    bouillon

½ cup boiling water
1 cup dry red wine
2 tablespoons finely chopped
    onion
2 tablespoons snipped parsley
⅓ cup currant jelly

Heat oven to 350°. Mix salt, cloves, nutmeg, thyme and pepper; rub over outsides and in cavities of pheasants. Tie legs of each pheasant. Place breast sides up on rack in jelly roll pan, 15½ x 10½ x 1 inch; place bacon slices over pheasant breasts. Stir bouillon into boiling water. Mix chicken bouillon, wine, onion and parsley; pour into pan. Bake uncovered until pheasants are tender, 1 to 1½ hours. Place pheasants on warm platter. Strain liquid into saucepan; add jelly. Heat until jelly is melted, stirring constantly. Cut pheasants into serving pieces; top with sauce. Nice served with wild rice.   4 TO 6 SERVINGS.

To Americans, all the birds of the air have been fair game at one time or another. From the wild turkey of the Pilgrims' days to the domesticated duck of today, the distinctive flavor of game birds has always lent itself beautifully to our methods of cooking.

SAVORY DUCKLING

1 ready-to-cook duckling (4 to 5
    pounds)
2 teaspoons salt
1 small onion
3 sprigs parsley

½ cup dry vermouth
½ cup dark corn syrup
1 tablespoon lemon juice
1 teaspoon ground coriander

Sprinkle cavity of duckling with salt; place onion and parsley in cavity. Fasten neck skin to back with skewers. Lift wing tips up and over back for natural brace. Place duckling breast side up on rack in shallow roasting pan.

Heat vermouth, corn syrup, lemon juice and coriander to boiling; reduce heat. Simmer uncovered, stirring occasionally, until reduced to ½ cup. Spoon ¼ cup of the sauce into cavity of duckling. Do not cover. Roast in 325° oven, pricking skin with fork and brushing occasionally with remaining sauce, until drumstick meat feels very soft, about 2½ hours. Place a piece of aluminum foil loosely over breast if duckling becomes too brown.   2 OR 3 SERVINGS.

BOSTON BAKED BEANS

2 pounds dried navy or pea
   beans (about 4 cups)
8 cups water
1 medium onion
½-pound piece salt pork (with
   rind)

1 cup molasses
3 tablespoons packed brown
   sugar
2 teaspoons salt
1½ teaspoons dry mustard
¼ teaspoon pepper

Heat beans and water to boiling in 3- to 4-quart Dutch oven; boil 2 minutes. Remove from heat; cover and let stand 1 hour.

Add enough water, if necessary, to cover beans. Heat to boiling; reduce heat. Cover and simmer until tender, 1 to 1½ hours. (To test, blow on a few beans in a spoon; skins will burst and peel back if done.) Drain beans, reserving liquid.

Heat oven to 300°. Place onion in ungreased 3- to 4-quart bean pot, casserole or Dutch oven; cover with beans. Cover pork with boiling water; let stand 5 minutes. Drain pork; cut through rind in crisscross pattern to depth of 1 inch. Bury pork rind side up in beans so that only rind shows. Mix molasses, sugar, salt, mustard, pepper and reserved bean liquid; pour over beans. Cover and bake 2½ to 3 hours. Uncover and bake 30 minutes. Add enough hot water during baking, if necessary, to keep beans moist.   12 TO 15 SERVINGS.

SOUTHERN BAKED BEANS

1 pound dried white marrow or
   navy beans (about 2 cups)
6 cups water
¾ pound lean salt pork or
   smoked pork, sliced
½ cup chopped onion
2 cloves garlic, finely chopped
½ teaspoon red pepper sauce
1 bay leaf, crumbled

¼ cup catsup
¼ cup molasses
1½ teaspoons dry mustard
½ teaspoon salt
½ teaspoon ground ginger
1½ teaspoons Worcestershire
   sauce
⅓ cup packed dark brown sugar

Heat beans and water to boiling; boil 2 minutes. Remove from heat; cover and let stand 1 hour. Stir in pork, onion, garlic, pepper sauce and bay leaf. Heat to boiling; reduce heat. Cover and simmer until beans are tender, 1½ to 2 hours. (Do not boil or beans will burst.)

Heat oven to 400°. Drain beans, reserving liquid. Add enough water, if necessary, to measure 2 cups. Stir catsup, molasses, mustard, salt, ginger and Worcestershire sauce into bean liquid. Place beans in ungreased shallow 2-quart casserole; pour reserved bean liquid over beans. Arrange pork slices on top; sprinkle with sugar. Bake uncovered 1 hour.   6 SERVINGS.

Pictured opposite.
Try an old New England twosome for a Saturday night menu: Boston Baked Beans (this page) and Boston Brown Bread (page 12).

80   Mainstays

SKILLET SPECIALTIES

RED FLANNEL HASH

1½ cups chopped cooked beef
  corned brisket*
1½ cups chopped cooked
  potatoes
1 can (16 ounces) diced beets,
  drained (1½ cups)
⅓ cup chopped onion
½ teaspoon salt
¼ teaspoon pepper
¼ cup shortening
Snipped parsley

Mix all ingredients except shortening and parsley. Heat shortening in 10-inch skillet over medium heat until melted. Spread beef mixture in skillet. Brown, turning occasionally with wide spatula, 10 to 15 minutes. Sprinkle with parsley.   4 SERVINGS.

*1 can (12 ounces) corned beef yields approximately 2 cups.

SLOPPY JOES

1 pound ground beef
½ cup chopped onion
⅓ cup chopped celery
⅓ cup chopped green pepper
⅓ cup catsup
¼ cup water
1 tablespoon Worcestershire
  sauce
⅛ teaspoon red pepper sauce
1 teaspoon salt
6 hamburger buns, split and
  toasted

Cook and stir ground beef and onion in 10-inch skillet until beef is brown and onion is tender; drain off fat. Stir in remaining ingredients except buns. Cover and cook over low heat just until vegetables are tender, 10 to 15 minutes. Fill buns with beef mixture. 6 SANDWICHES.

NOTE: For saucier Sloppy Joes, increase catsup to ½ cup.

For early settlers and present-day campers and outdoorsmen alike, the skillet has been an essential cooking tool.

LIVER AND ONIONS

2 medium onions, thinly sliced
3 tablespoons butter or
  margarine
1 pound beef liver, ½ to ¾ inch
  thick
½ cup all-purpose flour
¼ cup shortening
Salt
Pepper

Cook and stir onions and butter in 10-inch skillet until tender. Remove from skillet; keep warm. Coat liver with flour. Heat shortening in skillet. Cook liver in hot shortening over medium heat on each side until brown, 2 to 3 minutes. Add onions; heat until hot. Sprinkle with salt and pepper.   4 SERVINGS.

LAMB AND RED NOODLES

2 pounds lamb arm or blade chops or neck slices, ¾ inch thick
2 tablespoons water
3 cups water
1 can (6 ounces) tomato paste
1½ teaspoons salt
⅛ teaspoon pepper
Dash of cayenne red pepper
1 bay leaf, crumbled
1 large clove garlic, finely chopped
4 ounces uncooked wide egg noodles
½ cup shredded Cheddar cheese

Brown lamb chops in 10-inch skillet; drain off fat. Add 2 tablespoons water. Cover and simmer until lamb is tender, about 1 hour. Cool; remove lamb from bones.

Return lamb to skillet. Stir in 3 cups water, the tomato paste, salt, pepper, red pepper, bay leaf and garlic. Heat to boiling; reduce heat. Cover and simmer 30 minutes.

Stir in noodles. Cover and cook until noodles are tender, about 12 minutes. Sprinkle with cheese.   4 SERVINGS.

SPICY BRAISED VENISON

3- to 3½-pound venison chuck roast
2 onions, sliced
12 peppercorns
12 juniper berries (optional)
6 whole cloves
2 bay leaves
2 teaspoons salt
1½ cups red wine vinegar
1 cup boiling water
2 tablespoons shortening
½ cup cold water
¼ cup all-purpose flour
2 teaspoons sugar

Place venison roast, onions, peppercorns, juniper berries, cloves, bay leaves, salt, vinegar and 1 cup boiling water in earthenware bowl or glass baking dish. Cover with plastic wrap. Refrigerate at least 3 days, turning venison twice a day with 2 wooden spoons. (Never pierce venison with fork.)

Drain venison, reserving vinegar mixture. Heat shortening in 12-inch skillet or 4-quart Dutch oven; brown venison. Add vinegar mixture. Cover and simmer until venison is tender, 3 to 3½ hours. Remove venison and onions from skillet; keep warm. Strain and measure liquid in skillet. Add water, if necessary, to measure 2 cups; pour into skillet. Cover and simmer 10 minutes. Shake ½ cup cold water, the flour and sugar in tightly covered jar. Stir slowly into liquid in skillet. Heat to boiling, stirring constantly. Boil and stir 1 minute. Serve with venison and onions.   6 SERVINGS.

SMOTHERED RABBIT

2 domestic rabbits (2 to 2½
    pounds each) or 4 wild
    rabbits, cut up
1½ cups cider vinegar
½ cup chopped onion
2 tablespoons packed light
    brown sugar
1 tablespoon dry mustard
2 teaspoons salt

1 cup all-purpose flour
1 tablespoon granulated sugar
½ teaspoon pepper
¼ teaspoon grated nutmeg
Vegetable oil, lard, shortening
    or bacon fat
½ cup all-purpose flour
3 cups water

Place rabbit in shallow glass dish. Mix vinegar, onion, brown sugar, mustard and salt; pour over rabbit. Cover and refrigerate at least 12 hours but no longer than 24 hours, turning rabbit occasionally.

Drain rabbit and pat dry. Mix 1 cup flour, the granulated sugar, pepper and nutmeg. Coat rabbit with flour mixture. Heat oil ¼ inch deep in heavy 12-inch skillet. Brown rabbit; remove from skillet. Drain oil, reserving ½ cup. Stir in ½ cup flour; stir in water slowly. Heat to boiling, stirring constantly. Boil and stir 1 minute. Place rabbit in gravy; reduce heat. Cover and simmer until tender, 1 to 1½ hours. Stir in additional water if necessary.   4 TO 6 SERVINGS.

JAMBALAYA

2 medium onions, chopped
½ medium green pepper,
    chopped
1 clove garlic, finely chopped
3 tablespoons olive or vegetable
    oil
1 pound fresh or frozen raw
    shrimp, peeled and deveined
1 cup uncooked regular rice

2 cups chicken broth
1 can (16 ounces) tomatoes
1 teaspoon salt
⅛ teaspoon pepper
⅛ teaspoon ground thyme
⅛ teaspoon red pepper sauce
1 bay leaf, crumbled
½ pound cubed cooked ham
    (about 1½ cups)

Cook and stir onions, green pepper, garlic and 2 tablespoons of the oil in 4-quart Dutch oven over low heat 3 minutes. Add shrimp. Cook, stirring frequently, until shrimp are pink, about 5 minutes. Turn shrimp mixture into bowl; reserve.

Cook remaining 1 tablespoon oil and the rice in Dutch oven over medium-high heat, stirring frequently, until rice is light brown, about 10 minutes. Stir in chicken broth, tomatoes (with liquid), salt, pepper, thyme, pepper sauce and bay leaf. Heat to boiling; reduce heat. Cover and simmer until rice is tender, about 15 minutes. Stir in reserved shrimp mixture and the ham. Cover and cook just until shrimp and ham are hot.   6 SERVINGS.

BACON-FRIED CHICKEN

½ cup all-purpose flour
1 teaspoon salt
¼ teaspoon pepper
2½ - to 3-pound broiler-fryer
    chicken, cut up

¼ pound bacon, cut into small
    pieces

Mix flour, salt and pepper. Coat chicken with flour mixture. Fry bacon partially in 10-inch skillet. Cook chicken and bacon over medium heat until chicken is brown, 15 to 20 minutes; reduce heat.

Cover tightly and simmer, turning chicken once or twice, until thickest pieces are done, 20 to 30 minutes. (If skillet cannot be covered tightly, add 1 to 2 tablespoons water.) Uncover and cook 10 minutes.   4 SERVINGS.

PHILADELPHIA SCRAPPLE

1¼ pounds pork blade steaks
2½ cups water
1½ teaspoons salt
¼ teaspoon pepper
½ cup yellow cornmeal

¼ cup all-purpose flour
½ teaspoon rubbed sage
¼ teaspoon ground allspice
Flour
1 tablespoon shortening

Heat pork steaks, water, salt and pepper to boiling in 2-quart saucepan; reduce heat. Cover and simmer until pork falls off bones, about 1½ hours.

Strain broth; refrigerate until cold. Cut pork into small pieces. Remove fat from broth. Mix cornmeal, ¼ cup flour, the sage and allspice in 2-quart saucepan. Stir in 1 cup of the broth. Cook over medium heat, stirring constantly, until mixture thickens. Stir in pork. Add enough water to remaining broth to measure 1½ cups; stir gradually into cornmeal mixture. Heat to boiling; reduce heat. Simmer uncovered 30 minutes. Spread evenly in greased loaf pan, 9x5x3 inches. Cover and refrigerate until firm, at least 12 hours. (Scrapple can be refrigerated at this point up to 36 hours longer. Wrap securely in aluminum foil.)

Unmold scrapple; cut into ½-inch slices. Coat with flour. Heat shortening in skillet. Brown slices on both sides in hot shortening.   8 SERVINGS (2 SLICES EACH).

Pennsylvania Scrapple: Substitute 1¼ pounds pork liver, kidney, heart and pork scraps for the pork blade steaks. Stir in 1 medium onion, chopped, with the pork.

The country skill of raising and curing pork to have a specific flavor is an old one, highly developed in Poland, Germany and Italy, where the ability to control ham's flavor has long been practiced. In Italy, for example, the characteristic flavor of prosciutto comes from feeding the pigs on the whey from Parmesan cheese. Many aspects of American curing methods came from such Old World knowledge, but others were discovered by accident.

Near Smithfield, Virginia, farmers noticed that the meat from pigs that grazed on peanuts had a special taste. Gradually the farmers learned curing techniques that heightened that special flavor, and the name *Smithfield* on ham became an assurance of excellence. Only ham cured in or immediately around the town of Smithfield can bear that name. These noble hams, festooned with a string of cranberries, share the center of attraction with the turkey at Thanksgiving and other holiday feasts in the South.

For less auspicious occasions, country hams are popular in every nook and cranny of America. Because of the salt used in the curing process, Smithfield and country ham should be trimmed and soaked in warm water before cooking. In Tennessee, Kentucky and the Midwest, where country ham curing is still an art, Fried Ham and Red-Eye Gravy, a breakfast classic, has never gone out of style.

FRIED HAM AND RED-EYE GRAVY

2 packages (12 ounces each)
    country ham slices

1 cup hot coffee or water
Dixie Biscuits (page 10)

Trim excess fat from ham slices; reserve. Soak ham in warm water 15 minutes; drain. Heat reserved ham fat in 10-inch skillet over medium heat until melted. Brown ham on both sides over medium heat; remove to warm platter. Pour drippings from skillet. Pour hot coffee into skillet. Stir and scrape ham particles from skillet; pour over Dixie Biscuits. Serve with ham. 4 TO 6 SERVINGS.

CORN-EGG SCRAMBLE

½ pound bacon, cut into small
    pieces
4 eggs
1 can (16 ounces) whole kernel
    corn, drained

Salt
Pepper

Fry bacon in 10-inch skillet until crisp; drain off fat. Beat eggs; stir in corn. Pour over bacon pieces in skillet. Cook and stir until eggs are thickened throughout but still moist. Season with salt and pepper. 4 SERVINGS.

Pictured opposite.
Country ham is no stranger to a hearty farmland breakfast—shown here in Fried Ham and Red-Eye Gravy (this page). Serve it with Corn-Egg Scramble (this page), Dixie Biscuits (page 10) and Peach Honey (page 122).

Cod is a dreary name that hides this fish's virtuoso talents. In the Northeast, generations of Americans have been raised on Codfish Cakes, Codfish Puff and other salted-cod recipes. Most New England households kept a barrel of cod in the cellar, along with the root vegetables. And in Boston, there's even a plaque in the government chambers commemorating this favorite fish.

CODFISH PUFF

½ pound boneless salt cod
3 medium potatoes, pared and
    cut into ½-inch cubes (2½
    cups)
1½ cups hot water
4 eggs, beaten

1 tablespoon butter or
    margarine
⅛ teaspoon pepper
2 tablespoons shortening or
    bacon fat
Catsup or cheese sauce

Place cod in bowl; cover with cold water. Soak 1 to 2 hours; drain. Repeat process.

Place cod and potatoes in 3-quart saucepan; cover with hot water. Heat to boiling. Cover and cook until potatoes are tender, about 20 minutes. Mash or beat undrained cod and potatoes 1 to 2 minutes on medium speed in large mixer bowl until smooth. Beat in eggs, butter and pepper.

Heat shortening in 10-inch skillet until melted. Spread cod mixture evenly in skillet. Cover and cook over low heat until golden brown crust forms on bottom and side, about 10 minutes. Invert on heat-proof platter. Serve with catsup.   6 SERVINGS.

DEEP FRIES

CODFISH CAKES

4 ounces boneless salt cod
5 or 6 medium potatoes, pared
    and cut into ¼-inch cubes
    (about 4 cups)

⅓ cup finely chopped onion
2 tablespoons flour
⅛ teaspoon pepper
Catsup

Place cod in bowl; cover with cold water. Soak 1 to 2 hours; drain.

Place cod, potatoes and onion in 3-quart saucepan; cover with hot water. Heat to boiling. Cover and cook until potatoes are tender, about 20 minutes; drain. Mash or beat potato mixture about 1 minute on high speed in large mixer bowl until smooth. Stir in flour and pepper. Refrigerate until cold, about 1 hour.

Heat vegetable oil or shortening (3 to 4 inches) to 375° in deep fat fryer or heavy saucepan. Drop potato mixture by rounded tablespoonfuls, 4 or 5 at a time, into hot oil. Fry until golden brown, about 2 minutes; drain. Serve with catsup.   4 SERVINGS.

In American kitchens, "fried" has become a natural adjective for chicken. But the method of frying varies from cook to cook. Some prefer deep fat, others shallow fat. Some prefer a batter coating, others bread crumbs or flour.

When you fry chicken—or other fare—in deep fat, the temperature of the oil is the key to success. Use a deep-fat thermometer to determine exactly when the oil reaches the correct temperature.

CHICKEN WITH PUFFITS AND MILK GRAVY

2½ - to 3-pound broiler-fryer
    chicken, cut up
½ cup all-purpose flour*
1 teaspoon salt
¼ teaspoon pepper

Puffits (below)
2 tablespoons flour
½ teaspoon salt
1½ cups milk

Remove any excess fat from chicken. Place chicken in 3-quart saucepan. Add enough water to cover. Heat to boiling; reduce heat. Cover and simmer 20 minutes. Drain chicken and pat dry.

Heat vegetable oil or shortening (3 to 4 inches) to 360° in deep fat fryer or heavy saucepan. Mix ½ cup flour, 1 teaspoon salt and the pepper. Coat chicken with flour mixture. Fry in hot oil until golden, about 6 minutes; drain on paper towels.

Increase oil temperature to 375°. Slide Puffits carefully into hot oil, turning as they rise to surface. Fry until golden brown, about 8 minutes; drain on paper towels. Keep chicken and Puffits warm in oven while preparing gravy.

Blend 2 tablespoons of the hot cooking oil, 2 tablespoons flour and ½ teaspoon salt in 1-quart saucepan. Cook over low heat, stirring constantly, until mixture is smooth and bubbly. Remove from heat; stir in milk gradually. Heat to boiling, stirring constantly. Boil and stir 1 minute. Serve with chicken and Puffits.   4 SERVINGS.

*If using self-rising flour, decrease salt to ½ teaspoon.

PUFFITS
1½ cups all-purpose flour**
1½ teaspoons baking powder
1 teaspoon salt

¼ cup shortening
½ cup milk

Mix flour, baking powder and salt. Cut in shortening until mixture looks like fine crumbs. Stir in almost all the milk. Stir in just enough additional milk to make a soft, puffy, easy-to-roll dough. (Too much milk makes dough sticky, not enough makes Puffits dry.) Round up dough on lightly floured cloth-covered board. Roll ½ inch thick. Cut with floured 2-inch biscuit cutter.

**If using self-rising flour, omit baking powder and salt.

CORN DOGS

1 pound frankfurters
1 cup all-purpose flour*
2 tablespoons cornmeal
1½ teaspoons baking powder
½ teaspoon salt

3 tablespoons shortening
¾ cup milk
1 egg, beaten
1 medium onion, grated
   (optional)

Pat frankfurters dry with paper towels. Heat vegetable oil or shortening (3 to 4 inches) to 365° in deep fat fryer or heavy saucepan. Mix flour, cornmeal, baking powder and salt. Cut in shortening. Stir in milk, egg and onion. Dip frankfurters into batter, allowing excess batter to drip into bowl. Fry in hot oil, turning once, until brown, about 6 minutes; drain on paper towels. Insert wooden skewer in end of each frankfurter if desired.   5 SERVINGS.

*If using self-rising flour, omit baking powder and salt.

MARYLAND CRAB CAKES

1 pound Atlantic crabmeat,
   drained and cartilage
   removed
1½ cups soft white bread
   crumbs (no crusts)
1 teaspoon dry mustard

½ teaspoon salt
⅛ teaspoon pepper
2 tablespoons butter or
   margarine, melted
2 egg yolks, beaten

Mix all ingredients. Shape into 4 patties 3½ inches in diameter and about ¾ inch thick. Refrigerate until firm, about 1½ hours.

Heat vegetable oil or shortening (1 inch) to 375°. Fry patties until golden brown on both sides, 4 to 5 minutes; drain.   4 PATTIES.

CLAM FRITTERS

¾ cup all-purpose flour
1 teaspoon baking powder
½ teaspoon salt
¼ cup milk
1 egg

2 cans (8 ounces each) minced
   clams,* drained (reserve ¼
   cup liquid)
Cocktail sauce or tartar sauce

Heat vegetable oil or shortening (3 to 4 inches) to 375° in deep fat fryer or heavy saucepan. Beat flour, baking powder, salt, milk, egg and reserved clam liquid with hand beater until smooth. Stir in clams. Drop by level tablespoonfuls into hot oil. Fry until golden brown, about 5 minutes; drain on paper towels. Serve with cocktail sauce.   3 OR 4 SERVINGS.

*1 cup shucked fresh clams, finely chopped, can be substituted for the canned clams.

Pictured opposite.
Whether your produce is home-grown or store-bought, you'll enjoy these fresh ways to serve it. Clockwise from top: Stewed Plums (page 116), Pecan Eggplant (page 100), Broccoli with Easy Cheese Sauce (page 96), Mashed Potatoes and Rutabaga (page 104) and Caesar Salad (page 108).

KITCHEN GARDEN

KITCHEN GARDEN

Throngs of people stop at roadside fruit and vegetable stands on summer weekends. The sight of deep-red tomatoes, potatoes with dirt still on the skins, crisp peas and just-picked peaches is immensely satisfying, particularly if the stand happens to be on the edge of an orchard or a field of tall green corn.

So appealing are these fresh foods to Americans that in recent years more and more people are planting their own. This revival of kitchen gardens, or Victory gardens as they were called during World War II, may take form as a small plot in the backyard, a few flowerpots of cherry tomatoes or herbs on the windowsill or half an acre in the country. Whatever the circumstances, the impulse is the same: to return to a natural connection with the growing of our food.

Satisfying as it is to raise your own fruits and vegetables or to buy directly from farmers by the road, the supermarket produce available to most of us is, in fact, not only fresh but of an astonishing diversity. We are spoiled enough now to regard broccoli, beans, peppers, eggplant and many other vegetables as year-round crops. Fruits our ancestors would have stared at in amazement, such as pineapples, tangerines and dates, seem quite ordinary.

Many early settlers, however, survived on the native crops that they were able to store for the winter and plants that they could gather in the wilds. For them the first vegetable of spring was often the dandelion. Although most people now see dandelions only as the scourge of lawns, to our ancestors it was useful as a vegetable, salad, soup, tea and even as a wine. Many neglected plants that were eaten in early America are still abundant in the woods today.

It seems that practically everyone who ever immigrated to America felt compelled to describe its natural bounty in diaries and letters. Edmund Flagg, writing of Illinois in 1837, was amazed at the fruits: "Endless thickets of the wild plum and the blackberry, interlaced and matted together by the young grape-vines streaming with gorgeous clusters, were to be seen stretching for miles along the plain. . . . Vast groves of the ruby crab-apple, the golden persimmon, the black and white mulberry, and the wild cherry, were sprinkled with their rainbow hues in isolated masses over the prairie."

That wealth of fruit is still available, though now it is more apt to be from carefully controlled cultivation than from wild thickets and clusters stretching along the prairie. Seven thousand varieties of apples grow in the United States today. Some types are available all year, along with many citrus fruits. Even the perishable peaches, pears, grapes and plums are longer seasonal crops now. Until the turn of the century, grapefruit was almost unknown outside Florida, and there was no commercial cultivation of melons at all. Judging from the number of times watermelons are mentioned in connection with nineteenth-century picnics in old diaries, everyone must have had their own backyard patch. Mark Twain appreciated them so much that he insisted Eve never would have repented if she'd tasted a watermelon instead of an apple.

Choose among America's year-round diversity of produce for traditional or new recipes alike.

The widespread distribution of America's natural wealth of produce is, of course, quite recent. What was available to most cooks was the long-lasting produce they were able to winter over or dry: root vegetables, beans, apples and, primarily, corn. The storage of these was usually in the cellar of the house or in an outdoor root cellar dug out of the side of a hill and faced with stones. Even in the wake of the almost unlimited choice we enjoy all year, these winter vegetables retain their popularity in our cuisine. We've gathered recipes that treat these favorites imaginatively: our Maple Baked Acorn Squash is beautifully glazed with syrup, our Sweet Potato Chips are a variation of an all-time favorite. We've also included recipes for less familiar vegetables, such as Creamed Radishes and Parsnip Cakes, because they're so good they deserve a comeback.

Perhaps it is because American cooks were used to preparing root vegetables and reconstituting dried fruits that led them to overcook the more tender vegetables when they were available. In 1837, Eliza Leslie's cookbook advises us to boil a cabbage or cauliflower two hours! Today we prefer the crisp texture and peak flavor vegetables keep if cooking time is brief and the pot is taken immediately off the burner, not left on for the vegetables to wilt and lose their color and vitamins while being kept warm.

In addition to simplicity of basic preparation, a special plus for vegetable cookery in inflationary times is its economy. Many of us coping with the high prices of meat are discovering that entire dinners of vegetable combinations can be satisfying and creative.

Reading old cookbooks, one almost can hear the homilies of the last centuries: "Waste not, want not," and "A penny saved. . . ." The household art that did just that was preserving. "Putting up" fruits and vegetables was another important way to be thrifty and to outwit winter. Today, as in the last century, a bumper crop in the garden is likely to go straight to the pantry shelf, or its modern equivalent. The jewel-colored rows of tomatoes, peppers, peaches and berries were once counted on to brighten the table on drab January days. Now, long after that need is gone, preserving still is popular. Both improved techniques and more time to enjoy cooking have contributed to this new interest in the traditional art. Part of its pleasure might also be in fulfilling those early notions of thrift, such as making Watermelon Rind Pickles or gathering in all the still-green tomatoes before the first frost for a tangy Green Tomato Mincemeat. But the abiding interest, old and new, must come from the very particular satisfaction of serving or giving your own Spiced Pickled Peaches, Dilled Beans or Apple Butter. Despite the many excellent products available commercially, *your* brand of Bread-and-Butter Pickles somehow seems a little crisper, *your* Mincemeat a little more special.

This pantry shelf and our harvest of fruits and vegetables is the best of home-grown America, in touch with its past but authentically America today.

VEGETABLES

GREEN BEANS, CAPE COD STYLE

1 pound green beans, cut in
   halves lengthwise
2 tablespoons cream
¼ teaspoon salt

1 tablespoon butter or
   margarine
Dash of pepper

Heat beans and 1 inch salted water (½ teaspoon salt to 1 cup water) to boiling. Cook uncovered 5 minutes. Cover and cook until tender, 10 to 15 minutes; drain. Stir in remaining ingredients.   4 SERVINGS.

THREE-BEAN CASSEROLE

1 package (10 ounces) frozen
   lima beans
1 package (9 ounces) frozen cut
   green beans
1 package (9 ounces) frozen cut
   wax beans
2 tablespoons butter or
   margarine

2 tablespoons flour
¾ teaspoon salt
½ teaspoon monosodium
   glutamate
⅛ teaspoon pepper
1 cup milk
½ cup grated Parmesan or
   Romano cheese

Cook beans as directed on packages except—omit salt; drain. (If beans have the same cooking time, they can be cooked together.) Place in ungreased baking dish, 8x8x2 inches.

Heat oven to 375°. Heat butter in 2-quart saucepan over low heat until melted. Stir in flour, salt, monosodium glutamate and pepper. Cook, stirring constantly, until mixture is smooth and bubbly. Remove from heat; stir in milk. Heat to boiling, stirring constantly. Boil and stir 1 minute. Pour over beans. Sprinkle with cheese. Bake uncovered until bubbly and brown, about 20 minutes.   8 SERVINGS.

TEXAS PINTO BEANS

1 pound dried pinto beans
   (about 2 cups)
4 cups water
¼-pound piece salt pork (with
   rind)

2 teaspoons chili powder
¼ teaspoon red pepper sauce

Heat beans and water to boiling in 3-quart saucepan; boil 2 minutes. Remove from heat; cover and let stand 1 hour.

Stir in pork, chili powder and pepper sauce. Heat to boiling; reduce heat. Cover and simmer until beans are tender, about 1½ hours. Remove pork; slice and stir into beans.   12 SERVINGS.

RED BEANS AND RICE

1 pound dried red, pinto or
    kidney beans (about 2 cups)
4 cups water
¼ pound lean salt pork or
    smoked pork, cut up

1 cup chopped onion
1 tablespoon flour
1 teaspoon salt
½ teaspoon red pepper sauce
4 cups hot cooked rice

Heat beans and water to boiling in 3-quart saucepan; boil 2 minutes. Remove from heat; cover and let stand 1 hour.

Brown pork in 8-inch skillet. Add onion and flour; cook and stir until onion is tender. Stir pork mixture, salt and pepper sauce into beans. Heat to boiling; reduce heat. Cover and simmer, stirring occasionally, until beans are tender, 1½ to 2 hours. Add enough water, if necessary, to prevent sticking. Serve over rice.   8 SERVINGS.

In some parts of the South it is fervently believed that black-eyed peas for dinner on New Year's Day will bring good luck all year long. Consequently, black-eyed peas and hog jowl are often considered traditional fare on the first of January.

    Also dear to the Southern heart, but with no such guarantee of good fortune, are Hoppin' John and Red Beans and Rice, the latter a spicy Creole dish.

HOPPIN' JOHN

½ pound dried black-eyed peas
    (about 1 cup)
3½ cups water
¼ pound slab bacon, lean salt
    pork or smoked pork
1 onion, sliced
¼ to ½ teaspoon very finely
    chopped fresh hot pepper or
    ⅛ to ¼ teaspoon crushed
    dried hot pepper

½ cup uncooked long-grain rice
1 teaspoon salt
Pepper

Heat peas and water to boiling in 2-quart saucepan; boil 2 minutes. Remove from heat; cover and let stand 1 hour.

Cut bacon into 8 pieces. Stir bacon, onion and hot pepper into peas. Heat to boiling; reduce heat. Cover and simmer until peas are tender, 1 to 1½ hours.

Stir in rice, salt and pepper. Cover and simmer, stirring occasionally, until rice is tender, about 25 minutes. Stir in additional water, if necessary, to cook rice.   6 TO 8 SERVINGS.

Broccoli, cauliflower and cabbage, all from the same family tree, are hardy vegetables that travel well. The irrigated farmlands of the West now keep us stocked with a fresh supply all year. Although these are not native plants, even the earliest cookbooks describe how to prepare them. One advises that if care is taken in cooking, cabbage can retain its beauty. This, of course, is every bit as true today. Similarly, both broccoli and cauliflower can benefit from a little special care.

BROCCOLI WITH EASY CHEESE SAUCE

1½ pounds broccoli
6 ounces process American
    cheese, sliced
⅓ cup milk

¼ teaspoon onion salt
1 drop red pepper sauce
    (optional)

Heat 1 inch salted water (½ teaspoon salt to 1 cup water) to boiling. Add broccoli. Cover and heat to boiling. Cook until stems are tender, 12 to 15 minutes; drain.

Heat remaining ingredients over medium heat, stirring frequently, until cheese is melted and mixture is smooth, 6 to 8 minutes. Pour cheese sauce over broccoli.   4 SERVINGS.

Green or red cabbage, Savoy cabbage, Danish or Chinese cabbage—some of the several hundred varieties of this versatile vegetable grow in every state and every climate. In Alaska, the vegetable growing season is limited to a few weeks in summer when the sun shines for twenty hours a day. This short but intensive concentration causes cabbages there to grow up to sixty pounds each.

QUICK CRISPY CABBAGE

1 medium head green cabbage
    (about 1½ pounds), shredded
½ cup milk
1 tablespoon butter or
    margarine

½ teaspoon salt
Dash of pepper

Heat cabbage and milk to simmering in 10-inch skillet over medium heat, stirring frequently. Cover and simmer, stirring occasionally, until cabbage is crisp-tender, about 5 minutes. Stir in butter, salt and pepper.   4 SERVINGS.

FRIED CABBAGE, COUNTRY STYLE

2 tablespoons bacon fat
1 medium head green cabbage
   (about 1½ pounds),
   shredded
2 tablespoons cream

1½ teaspoons lemon juice or
   vinegar
Salt
Pepper

Heat bacon fat in 10-inch skillet. Add cabbage. Cook over low heat, stirring frequently, until light brown. Cover and cook, stirring occasionally, until crisp-tender, about 5 minutes. Stir in cream and lemon juice; heat until cream is hot. Sprinkle with salt and pepper. 4 SERVINGS.

Fried Red Cabbage: Substitute vegetable oil for the bacon fat and red cabbage for the green cabbage.

CREAMY CAULIFLOWER SOUP

2 cups water
1 medium head cauliflower
   (about 2 pounds), broken
   into flowerets, or 6 cups
   cauliflowerets
¾ cup thinly sliced celery
½ cup chopped onion
1 tablespoon lemon juice
2 tablespoons butter or
   margarine

2 tablespoons flour
2½ cups water
1 tablespoon instant chicken
   bouillon
¾ teaspoon salt
⅛ teaspoon pepper
Dash of ground nutmeg
½ cup whipping cream
Grated cheese (optional)

Heat 2 cups water to boiling in 3-quart saucepan. Add cauliflower, celery, onion and lemon juice. Cover and heat to boiling. Cook until tender, about 10 minutes; do not drain. Press cauliflower mixture through food mill. (Or place in blender container. Cover and blend until uniform consistency.)

Heat butter in 3-quart saucepan over low heat until melted. Stir in flour. Cook, stirring constantly, until mixture is smooth and bubbly. Remove from heat; stir in 2½ cups water. Heat to boiling, stirring constantly. Boil and stir 1 minute. Stir in cauliflower mixture, bouillon, salt, pepper and nutmeg. Heat just to boiling. Stir in cream; heat but do not boil. Serve with grated cheese. 8 SERVINGS.

Creamy Broccoli Soup: Substitute 1½ pounds broccoli, cut up, for the cauliflower; omit the lemon juice.

Creamy Cabbage Soup: Substitute 1 medium head cabbage (about 1½ pounds), shredded, for the cauliflower; cook only 5 minutes.

It's always fun to shop at outdoor market stalls like this one, near Boston's Faneuil Hall.

A nineteenth-century etiquette book cautions, "It is not elegant to *gnaw* Indian corn." In spite of that, corn-on-the-cob always has been an American institution.

Corn was the great resource of the New World. By the time the colonists arrived, it already was a highly cultivated plant. The Indians, who had refined it from a wild grass, depended on corn as the staple of their diet, a complete food used as a grain, a vegetable and even as tobacco. In all the Indian languages, *corn* translates to "our life."

One of the first history lessons American children learn is how the Indians taught the Pilgrims to cultivate corn by planting the kernels in the soil with a small fish, as fertilizer, in each mound. The Pilgrims—and every other group of settlers—quickly learned to use all parts of the corn plant.

Misickquatash, which sounded like "succotash" to English ears, could be made all year from dried kernels and beans simmered in bear, venison or other fat. Later, Corn Oysters with maple syrup became popular for breakfast or, served plain, for supper. Skillet Corn offers a more genteel mode of eating corn, for those who don't want "to gnaw Indian corn."

CORN OYSTERS

1 cup bacon fat	2 eggs, slightly beaten
1 cup vegetable oil	1 can (16 ounces) whole kernel
1 cup all-purpose flour	corn, drained (reserve ¼ cup
1 teaspoon baking powder	liquid)
1 teaspoon salt	

Heat fat and oil to 375° in 10-inch skillet. Mix flour, baking powder, salt, eggs and reserved corn liquid. Stir in corn. Drop by rounded tablespoonfuls into hot fat. Fry until golden brown on all sides, 4 to 5 minutes; drain on paper towels. 2 DOZEN CORN OYSTERS.

Nutmeg-Corn Oysters: Stir in 1 teaspoon ground nutmeg with the flour.

SKILLET CORN

4 ears corn	¼ teaspoon salt
2 tablespoons butter or	Dash of pepper
margarine	
2 tablespoons light cream or	
milk	

Cut enough kernels from corn to measure 2 cups (scrape ears with back of knife to extract all pulp and milk). Cook and stir all ingredients in 10-inch skillet over medium heat until butter is melted. Cover and cook over low heat until corn is tender, 10 to 15 minutes. 3 OR 4 SERVINGS.

Pictured opposite.
Regional variations on a truly native food—corn. Clockwise from top: The South contributes Brunswick Stew (page 59); Skillet Corn (this page) and Summer Succotash (page 100) come from New England; and the Midwest gives us Corn Oysters (this page) and Corn Relish (page 129).

After the most frugal years had passed, the colonists cooked a succotash with chicken and corned beef, which they served every year on December 21, the anniversary of the Pilgrims' landing at Plymouth Rock.

The Summer Succotash below adds a lavish dash of cream to the original succotash's ingredients.

SUMMER SUCCOTASH

4 ears corn
2 cups shelled fresh lima beans
(about 3 pounds unshelled)
⅓ cup cut-up lean salt pork or
bacon

¼ cup chopped onion
½ cup light cream (20%)
¼ teaspoon salt
⅛ teaspoon pepper

Cut enough kernels from corn to measure 2 cups. Mix beans, pork and onion in 3-quart saucepan; add enough water to cover. Heat to boiling; reduce heat. Cover and simmer until beans are tender, 20 to 25 minutes. Stir in corn. Heat to boiling; reduce heat. Cover and simmer until corn is tender, about 5 minutes; drain. Stir in cream, salt and pepper. Heat until cream is hot, stirring occasionally.   6 SERVINGS.

Although eggplant has been settled in this country for a long time, it still has something of an exotic air about it, as though it had determined to keep its foreign citizenship. Many popular recipes for eggplant can be traced to Turkish, Greek or Italian origins by the use of olive oil, Parmesan cheese and other ingredients not indigenous to America. Pecan Eggplant, however, with its use of butter and pecans, is a native son.

PECAN EGGPLANT

¼ cup butter or margarine
1 medium eggplant (about 1½
pounds), pared and cut into
½-inch slices
1 cup light cream (20%)

1 teaspoon salt
½ teaspoon paprika
⅛ teaspoon pepper
½ cup chopped pecans

Heat oven to 300°. Heat butter in 10-inch skillet over low heat until melted. Add eggplant. Cook, turning once, until golden brown. Place in ungreased baking dish, 13½x8¾x1¾ inches. Pour cream over eggplant. Sprinkle with salt, paprika, pepper and pecans. Bake uncovered until cream is absorbed, about 1 hour.   4 SERVINGS.

Okra and tomatoes have a natural affinity for each other. Both belong in burgoos, Brunswick stews and gumbos. Okra Skillet combines tomatoes, onion and corn with okra in a sort of vegetable gumbo, bounteous and colorful.

OKRA SKILLET

¼ cup finely cut-up lean salt
   pork (about ¼ pound)*
½ cup chopped onion
2 cups sliced okra (about ¾
   pound) or 1 package (10
   ounces) frozen cut okra,
   thawed

4 medium tomatoes, peeled
   and cut into eighths
1 cup fresh corn (2 to 3 ears)
Dash of pepper

Cook and stir pork and onion in 10-inch skillet until pork is golden; stir in okra. Cook over medium-high heat, stirring constantly, 3 minutes. Stir in tomatoes and corn. Cover and simmer until corn is tender, 10 to 15 minutes. Stir in pepper.   4 SERVINGS.

*2 tablespoons butter or margarine can be substituted for the pork; stir in 1 teaspoon salt with the pepper.

ORANGE BEETS

1¼ pounds beets (about 5
   medium)
6 cups water
1 tablespoon vinegar
1 teaspoon salt
1 tablespoon cornstarch
1 tablespoon packed brown
   sugar

¾ teaspoon salt
Dash of pepper
¾ cup orange juice
1 tablespoon vinegar
1 teaspoon finely shredded
   orange peel

Cut off all but 2 inches of beet tops; leave root ends attached. Heat water, 1 tablespoon vinegar and 1 teaspoon salt to boiling in 3-quart saucepan. Add beets. Cover and heat to boiling. Cook until beets are tender, 35 to 45 minutes; drain. Run cold water over beets; slip off skins and remove root ends. Cut beets into slices.

Mix cornstarch, sugar, ¾ teaspoon salt and the pepper in 1-quart saucepan. Stir orange juice and 1 tablespoon vinegar gradually into cornstarch mixture. Cook, stirring constantly, until mixture thickens and boils. Boil and stir 1 minute. Stir in beets and orange peel; heat until beets are hot.   4 SERVINGS.

FRIED PARSNIPS

1½ pounds parsnips (about 6
    medium)
2 tablespoons butter or
    margarine

Freshly ground pepper

Heat 1 inch salted water (½ teaspoon salt to 1 cup water) to boiling. Add parsnips. Cover and heat to boiling. Cook until tender, 20 to 30 minutes; drain. Cut into ½-inch slices. Heat butter in 10-inch skillet over low heat until melted. Add parsnips. Cook, stirring frequently, until golden brown. (Add butter if necessary.) Sprinkle with pepper. 4 SERVINGS.

Digging up the potato is the first step in bringing this popular and versatile root vegetable to the market place.

When village houses with root cellars began to give way to apartments with central heating housed in the cellar, we lost touch with several delicious vegetables that used to winter over nicely in dark corners, along with the barrels of cider, salted fish and maple sugar.

Many of us have never tasted rutabagas, parsnips or turnips. Only the potato's popularity escaped from the root cellar undiminished. Perhaps its place in the American menu is due, in no small part, to the many Irish-Americans who still recall stories of the devastating potato famine that impelled their forbears to come to this country.

Root vegetables have a particular strength of character, an earthiness readily apparent in Fried Parsnips but only hinted at in Parsnip Cakes and in Mashed Potatoes and Rutabaga.

PARSNIP CAKES

1¼ pounds parsnips (about 5
    medium)
2 tablespoons flour
½ teaspoon salt
Dash of pepper
2 tablespoons butter or
    margarine, softened

1 tablespoon chopped onion
1 egg, beaten
Dried bread crumbs or cracker
    crumbs
¼ cup shortening

Heat 1 inch salted water (½ teaspoon salt to 1 cup water) to boiling. Add parsnips. Cover and heat to boiling. Cook until tender, 20 to 30 minutes; drain and mash.

Mix parsnips, flour, salt, pepper, butter, onion and egg. Shape parsnip mixture into 8 patties; coat with crumbs. Heat shortening in 10-inch skillet over low heat. Add parsnip patties. Cook over medium heat, turning once, until golden brown, about 5 minutes. 4 SERVINGS.

The potato portion of today's meat-and-potato meals usually means "baked," "mashed" or "French fried." Good though these treatments are, the following recipes from yesteryear will add a welcome change of pace to that most American twosome.

OLD-TIMEY CREAMED POTATOES

5 or 6 medium potatoes, pared
    and cut into ¼-inch cubes
    (about 4 cups)
2 cups half-and-half

1 teaspoon salt
⅛ teaspoon pepper
Snipped parsley or chives

Heat potatoes, half-and-half, salt and pepper to simmering in heavy 10-inch skillet over low heat, stirring frequently. Cover and simmer, stirring frequently, until potatoes are tender, about 30 minutes. Sprinkle with parsley.   4 TO 6 SERVINGS.

PENNSYLVANIA POTATO FILLING

3 eggs
1½ cups mashed cooked
    potatoes
1½ cups milk
4 cups Italian or French bread
    cubes

½ cup chopped onion
¼ cup butter or margarine
1 teaspoon salt
⅛ teaspoon pepper

Heat oven to 375°. Beat eggs, potatoes and milk in large mixer bowl until smooth. Cook and stir bread cubes, onion and butter in 10-inch skillet until bread cubes are light brown and onion is tender. Stir bread cube mixture, salt and pepper into potato mixture. Turn into greased 1½-quart casserole. Bake uncovered until top is golden, about 1 hour.   6 TO 8 SERVINGS.

FARM-FRIED POTATOES

2 tablespoons shortening or
    vegetable oil
5 or 6 medium potatoes, pared
    and thinly sliced (about 4
    cups)

1 large onion, thinly sliced
1½ teaspoons salt
Pepper
2 tablespoons butter or
    margarine

Heat shortening in 10-inch skillet until melted. Layer ⅓ each of potato and onion slices in skillet; sprinkle each layer with ½ teaspoon salt and dash of pepper. Dot top layer with butter. Cover and cook over medium heat 20 minutes. Uncover and cook until potatoes are brown, turning once.   4 TO 6 SERVINGS.

MASHED POTATOES AND RUTABAGA

3 medium potatoes, pared and
cut up (about 2 cups)
1 large rutabaga (about 2
pounds), pared and cut into
½-inch cubes

1 teaspoon sugar
3 tablespoons butter or
margarine
1 teaspoon salt
⅛ teaspoon pepper

Heat 1 inch salted water (½ teaspoon salt to 1 cup water) to boiling
in each of 2 saucepans. Add potatoes to one saucepan and rutabaga
and sugar to the other saucepan. Cover and heat to boiling. Cook
until potatoes and rutabaga are tender, 20 to 25 minutes; drain.
Mash potatoes and rutabaga together until no lumps remain. Beat in
butter, salt and pepper until mixture is smooth and fluffy. (Beat in
enough hot milk, if necessary, to make mixture smooth and
fluffy.)   6 SERVINGS.

CREAMED RADISHES

1⅓ pounds red radishes, thinly
sliced (about 4 cups)
2 tablespoons butter or
margarine

2 tablespoons flour
1 teaspoon salt
⅛ teaspoon pepper
½ cup whipping cream

Place radishes in 3-quart saucepan; add enough water to cover. Heat
to boiling; reduce heat. Simmer uncovered until crisp-tender, 5 to 7
minutes; drain, reserving 1 cup liquid. Return radishes to saucepan.

Heat butter in 1-quart saucepan over low heat until melted. Stir in
flour, salt and pepper. Cook, stirring constantly, until mixture is
smooth and bubbly. Remove from heat; stir in cream and reserved
radish liquid. Heat to boiling, stirring constantly. Boil and stir 1
minute. Stir into radishes; heat until radishes are hot. Sprinkle with
snipped parsley or chives if desired.   6 TO 8 SERVINGS.

MAPLE BAKED ACORN SQUASH

2 acorn squash (1 to 1½ pounds
each)
4 tablespoons maple-flavored
or maple syrup

4 tablespoons cream

Heat oven to 350°. Cut each squash in half; remove seeds and fibers.
Place squash cut sides up in ungreased baking pan. Spoon 1 tablespoon syrup and 1 tablespoon cream into each half. Bake uncovered
until tender, about 1 hour.   4 SERVINGS.

Do you know the difference between yams and sweet potatoes? Although used interchangeably in cooking, they are not related botanically. Sweet potatoes are members of the morning glory family. Their skin and flesh are paler and somewhat drier than the darker orange yam's. Yams are noticeably sweeter than sweet potatoes.

Like pumpkin, both sweet potatoes and yams blend well with other flavors. Because of this they are prepared as muffins and sweet pies and as vegetables with many variations, such as the spice and fruit ones following Candied Sweet Potatoes or Yams. Deep-fried Sweet Potato Chips are a novel accompaniment for pork roasts and hams.

CANDIED SWEET POTATOES OR YAMS

2 pounds sweet potatoes or
   yams (about 6 medium) or 1
   can (23 ounces) sweet
   potatoes or yams, drained
½ cup packed brown sugar

3 tablespoons butter or
   margarine
3 tablespoons water
½ teaspoon salt

If using fresh sweet potatoes or yams, heat enough salted water to cover potatoes (½ teaspoon salt to 1 cup water) to boiling. Add potatoes. Cover and heat to boiling. Cook until tender, 30 to 35 minutes; drain. Slip off skins. Cut potatoes into ½-inch slices. If using canned potatoes, cut into ½-inch slices.

Heat sugar, butter, water and salt in 8-inch skillet over medium heat, stirring constantly, until smooth and bubbly. Add potato slices; stir gently until slices are glazed and hot.   4 TO 6 SERVINGS.

Orange Sweet Potatoes: Substitute 3 tablespoons orange juice for the water and add 1 tablespoon grated orange peel.

Pineapple Sweet Potatoes: Omit the water and add 1 can (8¼ ounces) crushed pineapple (with syrup).

Spicy Sweet Potatoes: Stir ½ teaspoon ground cinnamon or ¼ teaspoon ground allspice, cloves, mace or nutmeg into sugar mixture in skillet.

SWEET POTATO CHIPS

Cut 4 medium pared sweet potatoes or yams (about 1 pound) into $1/16$-inch slices. Soak in 2 quarts ice water 1 hour. Drain and pat dry. Heat vegetable oil or shortening (3 inches) to 360° in deep fat fryer or heavy saucepan. Fry potato slices until light brown around edges, 1 to 2 minutes; drain on paper towels. Sprinkle with salt. Keep warm in oven.   4 SERVINGS.

SPINACH WITH BACON AND ONION

1 slice bacon, cut up	¼ teaspoon salt
1 small onion, thinly sliced	Dash of pepper
1 pound spinach	

Cook and stir bacon and onion in 10-inch skillet until bacon is crisp. Add about half of the spinach, the salt and pepper. Cover and cook over medium heat 2 minutes. Add remaining spinach. Cover and cook, stirring occasionally, until spinach is tender, 3 to 10 minutes.   3 OR 4 SERVINGS.

The seasonal pleasure of tomatoes is still a distinct one, for despite all the modern agricultural and transportation wonders, no greenhouse has succeeded in duplicating the taste and texture of a locally grown, sun-ripened tomato.

Although native to the Western Hemisphere, the tomato came to our land by a circuitous route. It is thought that the conquistadors brought it to Europe from Mexico; but not until the late 1700s did it appear here — and then, the "love apple" was considered an aphrodisiac or, worse, poisonous. By the mid-1900s the tomato finally gained wide acceptance as a food.

In most home vegetable gardens, growers often find themselves with a sudden abundance and begin looking up recipes for Tomato Mincemeat, pickles and sauces. Fried Tomatoes and Cream Gravy is another excellent use for that summer excess.

FRIED TOMATOES AND CREAM GRAVY

½ cup cornmeal*	⅓ cup butter, margarine or bacon fat
3 tablespoons flour	1 cup whipping cream
2 teaspoons sugar	½ teaspoon salt
2 teaspoons salt	Snipped parsley or green onion tops
¼ teaspoon pepper	Crisply fried bacon, lean salt pork or sausage
4 firm ripe or green large tomatoes, cut into ¾-inch slices	

Mix cornmeal, flour, sugar, 2 teaspoons salt and the pepper. Coat tomato slices with cornmeal mixture. Heat butter in 10-inch skillet until melted. Add tomato slices. Cook, turning once, until golden brown. Place in shallow baking dish or on platter; keep warm. Heat cream and ½ teaspoon salt to boiling in same skillet; pour over tomato slices. Sprinkle with parsley. Serve with bacon.   4 TO 6 SERVINGS.

*½ cup all-purpose flour can be substituted for the cornmeal and flour.

Pictured opposite.
Your kitchen garden takes on new taste with these American classics. Clockwise from top: Wilted Lettuce Salad (page 109), Spinach with Bacon and Onion (this page), Creamed Radishes (page 104), Green Beans, Cape Cod Style (page 94) and Orange Beets (page 101).

SALADS

Despite its name, Caesar (or California) Salad is said to have been created in Tijuana, Mexico, during the twenties. Whatever its beginnings, the original salad of romaine lettuce mixed with grated cheese, coddled eggs and bread cubes fried in olive oil started a no-end-in-sight trend. Caesar Salad quickly crossed the border and became the last word in sophisticated American restaurants. Diners managed to extricate the secret of the coddled eggs from chefs and, finally, Caesar Salad became a classic of the American home kitchen.

CAESAR SALAD

2 cloves garlic, cut in halves
4 slices white bread
⅔ cup olive oil
1 teaspoon salt
½ teaspoon pepper
2 large bunches romaine

Coddled Eggs (below)
1 lemon
½ cup grated Parmesan or
  Romano cheese
1 can (2 ounces) anchovy fillets,
  chopped

Rub large salad bowl with garlic. Trim crusts from bread; cut bread into cubes. Heat ⅓ cup of the oil in 10-inch skillet. Add garlic and bread cubes. Cook over medium heat, stirring constantly, until bread cubes are brown. Remove from heat; discard garlic.

Mix remaining ⅓ cup oil, the salt and pepper in salad bowl. Tear romaine into bite-size pieces into salad bowl. Toss until leaves glisten. Break Coddled Eggs onto romaine; squeeze juice from lemon over romaine. Toss until leaves are well coated. Add cheese, anchovies and bread cubes; toss.   8 SERVINGS.

CODDLED EGGS
Place 2 eggs in warm water. Heat enough water to completely cover eggs to boiling in saucepan. Immerse eggs in boiling water. Remove from heat; cover and let stand 30 seconds. Immediately cool eggs in cold water.

FRESH MUSHROOM AND SPINACH SALAD

2 tablespoons tarragon or wine
  vinegar
¾ teaspoon salt
¼ teaspoon monosodium
  glutamate
1 small clove garlic, crushed

Generous dash of freshly
  ground pepper
8 ounces mushrooms, sliced
16 ounces spinach, torn into
  bite-size pieces
¼ cup vegetable oil

Mix vinegar, salt, monosodium glutamate, garlic and pepper; toss with mushrooms and let stand 15 minutes. Toss spinach and oil until leaves glisten. Toss mushroom mixture with spinach.   4 TO 6 SERVINGS.

Three generations of this American family enjoy a hearty outdoor picnic.

WILTED LETTUCE SALAD

4 slices bacon, cut up
¼ cup vinegar
2 bunches leaf lettuce,
    shredded (about 4 cups)
⅓ cup chopped green onions
2 teaspoons sugar
¼ teaspoon salt
⅛ teaspoon pepper

Fry bacon until crisp in 10-inch skillet. Stir in vinegar; heat until hot. Remove skillet from heat; add lettuce and onions. Sprinkle with sugar, salt and pepper; toss 1 to 2 minutes until lettuce is wilted.   4 SERVINGS.

Dill Wilted Lettuce: Add ½ teaspoon dried dill weed and ½ teaspoon dry mustard with the vinegar.

ORANGE-AVOCADO SALAD

2 oranges, pared and sliced
2 avocados, peeled, pitted and
    cut into wedges
2 small onions, sliced and
    separated into rings
Crisp salad greens
Orange Dressing (below)

Arrange oranges, avocados and onions on salad greens on salad plates. Drizzle Orange Dressing over salads.   4 SERVINGS.

ORANGE DRESSING
¼ cup vegetable oil
1 tablespoon lemon juice
½ teaspoon grated orange peel
2 tablespoons orange juice
1 tablespoon sugar
⅛ teaspoon salt
⅛ teaspoon dry mustard

Shake all ingredients in tightly covered jar.

PICKLED EGGS ON GREENS

6 hard-cooked eggs, peeled
1 cup cider vinegar
1 cup beet liquid
⅓ cup granulated or packed
    brown sugar
½ teaspoon salt
1 small onion, chopped
4 whole cloves
Shredded greens

Place eggs in bowl or jar. Mix remaining ingredients except greens; pour over eggs. Cover and refrigerate at least 2 days. Slice eggs; serve on greens.   6 SERVINGS.

Spiced Pickled Eggs: Substitute 2 cups white vinegar for the cider vinegar and beet liquid.

The Waldorf Astoria Hotel on Park Avenue in New York was the original home of this unpretentious salad, but the walnuts were a later addition. Made with good, crisp apples and tossed together quickly, refreshing Waldorf Salad combines the three crunch textures of apples, celery and nuts. The ready availability of canned fruits and fresh fruits in season makes fruit salads year-round fare. They go well as an accompaniment to any meat.

WALDORF SALAD

2 cups diced unpared apple
1 cup diced celery
⅓ cup coarsely chopped nuts
½ cup mayonnaise or salad
 dressing

Lettuce cups
Maraschino cherries (optional)

Mix apple, celery, nuts and mayonnaise. Serve in lettuce cups and garnish with maraschino cherries.   4 TO 6 SERVINGS.

HEAVENLY HASH SALAD

1 package (6¼ ounces)
 miniature marshmallows
 (3½ cups) or 40 large
 marshmallows, quartered
1 can (20 ounces) pineapple
 chunks, drained and
 quartered (reserve syrup)

2 cups seedless green grapes
½ cup slivered blanched
 almonds
Crisp lettuce
Whipped Cream Dressing
 (below)

Mix marshmallows and reserved pineapple syrup in 3-quart bowl. Cover and refrigerate 12 to 18 hours.

Stir pineapple, grapes and almonds into marshmallow mixture. Cover and refrigerate 2 to 3 hours. Serve over lettuce with Whipped Cream Dressing.   8 TO 10 SERVINGS.

WHIPPED CREAM DRESSING

2 egg yolks, slightly beaten
2 tablespoons sugar
2 tablespoons water
2 tablespoons vinegar or lemon
 juice

¼ teaspoon dry mustard
¼ teaspoon salt
Dash of pepper
½ cup chilled whipping cream

Cook all ingredients except cream in 1-quart saucepan over medium heat, stirring constantly, until mixture thickens and boils. Boil and stir 1 minute. Remove from heat; cool. Beat cream in chilled bowl until stiff. Fold into dressing.

FRUIT SALAD WITH LIME-HONEY DRESSING

Banana
Lemon juice
Pineapple slices
Orange slices or sections

Seedless green grapes
Melon balls or slices
Crisp lettuce cups
Lime-Honey Dressing (below)

Slice banana; dip slices into lemon juice to prevent darkening. Arrange fruits in lettuce cups on salad plates. Drizzle Lime-Honey Dressing over salads.

LIME-HONEY DRESSING

¾ cup vegetable oil
½ teaspoon grated lime peel
⅓ cup fresh lime juice (about 2 limes)
⅓ cup honey

1 teaspoon dry mustard
¾ teaspoon seasoned salt
½ teaspoon paprika
⅛ teaspoon white pepper

Shake all ingredients in tightly covered jar. Refrigerate until 30 minutes before serving time. Shake before serving.

A touch of citrus does wonders for many casseroles, cakes and vegetables; it does the same for other fruits. As in the recipe above, mellow sweet fruits seem to come into their own with the piquant Lime-Honey Dressing. The same complementary sweet and sour taste is achieved in Triple-Orange Molded Salad by filling the center of a slightly tart orange ring with sweet marshmallows, coconut and pineapple. Of the hundreds of gelatin salads in American cooking, this is one of the most impressive.

TRIPLE-ORANGE MOLDED SALAD

2 cups boiling liquid (water or fruit syrup)
1 package (6 ounces) orange-flavored gelatin
1 pint orange sherbet
2 cans (11 ounces each) mandarin orange segments, drained

1 can (13¼ ounces) pineapple chunks, drained
1 cup flaked coconut
1 cup miniature marshmallows
1 cup dairy sour cream or ½ cup whipping cream, whipped

Pour boiling liquid on gelatin in bowl; stir until gelatin is dissolved. Add sherbet; stir until melted. Stir in 1 can of the orange segments (1 cup). Pour into 6-cup ring mold. Refrigerate until firm.

Mix remaining orange segments, the pineapple, coconut and marshmallows. Fold in sour cream. Refrigerate at least 3 hours. Unmold gelatin; fill center with fruit mixture.   10 TO 12 SERVINGS.

GARBANZO-KIDNEY BEAN SALAD

1 can (20 ounces) white kidney
  beans, drained
1 can (15 ounces) garbanzo
  beans, drained
1 can (15 ounces) red kidney
  beans, drained
1½ cups diced peeled tomatoes
  (about 3 medium)
1 fresh hot pepper, seeded and
  finely chopped

¾ cup chopped red or sweet
  white onion
⅔ cup chopped green or red
  pepper
⅓ cup sliced green onions
1 bottle (8 ounces) herb and
  garlic French dressing
½ teaspoon salt
2 or 3 drops red pepper sauce
Lettuce

Mix all ingredients except lettuce. Cover and refrigerate at least 3
hours, stirring occasionally. Remove bean mixture with slotted
spoon to lettuce-lined salad bowl just before serving.   10 TO 12
SERVINGS.

If a picture is worth a thousand words, a taste must be worth even
more—at least in the case of the avocado. Its taste has a unique
quality about it that has been described as smooth, nutty and buttery. But avocado has something undefinable about it that is only
avocado. Although native to Mexico, avocados were latecomers to
North American cuisine and did not become popular until the thir-
ties, when they were known as alligator pears.

Our avocados were first grown in Florida during the last century
and in California at the Spanish missions, and are still grown only in
those two states. The fame of the avocado, however, has spread all
across the country. Many cooks are skillful with stuffed or baked
avocados, chilled avocado soups and salads. Guacamole (pronounced
as if the u were a w) has several uses. Great as it is as a salad, it is
equally good as a cocktail dip or spread. The recipe for Orange-
Avocado Salad (page 109) shows the Western and Southwestern tal-
ent for the element of surprise that characterized their cooking.
A sensational contrast in taste and color.

GUACAMOLE SALAD

2 ripe avocados, peeled and
  pitted
3 tablespoons grated onion
1 tablespoon lemon or lime
  juice
1 teaspoon salt

1 canned green hot pepper,
  finely chopped
1 medium tomato, peeled,
  seeded and chopped
Shredded lettuce

Mash avocados. Add onion, lemon juice, salt and hot pepper; beat
until creamy. Fold in tomato. Cover and refrigerate no longer than 3
hours. Serve on lettuce.   5 OR 6 SERVINGS.

Pictured opposite.
Zesty flavor favorites of the
Southwest are combined in the
colorful Garbanzo-Kidney Bean
Salad. Be sure to make it ahead
of time so the flavors can blend
and mellow.

FRUITS

RAW APPLESAUCE

3 medium eating apples, pared
  and cut up
¼ cup light corn syrup

2 tablespoons lemon juice
2 teaspoons sugar
Dash of salt

Place half of the apples and the remaining ingredients in blender container. Cover and blend 1 to 2 minutes on high speed until smooth. Add remaining apples; repeat.   ABOUT 2 CUPS APPLESAUCE.

NOTE: For variety in texture and color, use unpared apples.

Making apple butter today the old-fashioned way: in a large kettle over an open fire, with a heavy wooden paddle for stirring.

In the early years, everyone drank several mugs of cider a day—not our grocery store variety, but an alelike fermented cider with plenty of punch. This boon from the orchards was one pleasure not banned by the strict religious sects that settled America.

Johnny Appleseed, who actually existed and wandered about Ohio, Indiana and Illinois dressed in a coffee sack scattering seeds he gathered at cider mills, is not the only benefactor in the history of apple growing. Pioneers planted the orchards of Washington State with tiny plants they nurtured all the way across the country.

Of the hundreds of varieties grown, a few are marketed nationally. The Red Delicious, easily identifiable by its bumpy bottom and deep red color, is one of the best-known eating apples. It is not good for cooking. Stayman and Newtown Pippin are all-purpose apples. Golden Delicious, Winesap, Jonathan and McIntosh are excellent for eating. The tart, firm apples ideal for applesauce, apple butter and baking are Rome Beauty, York Imperial and Rhode Island Greening. Still others may be sold in your area.

Whole books on apple cookery attest to their diversity, from plain to fancy, but as with many fruits, the unadorned methods of preparation are often the most popular. Raw Applesauce and Glazed Baked Apples are two such recipes.

GLAZED BAKED APPLES

4 large baking apples
½ cup sugar

¼ teaspoon red food color

Heat oven to 400°. Core apples; pare upper half of each apple. Place apples in ungreased baking dish, 8x8x2 inches. Pour boiling water (¼ inch deep) into baking dish. Cover with aluminum foil.

Bake 25 minutes. Sprinkle 1 tablespoon sugar over each apple. Stir food color into syrup in baking dish; spoon over apples. Bake uncovered, spooning syrup over apples occasionally, until apples are tender when pierced with fork, 20 to 25 minutes. Sprinkle 1 tablespoon sugar over each apple; spoon syrup over apples.   4 SERVINGS.

A visitor offered flummery, grunt, fool, sippit or slump for dessert probably would be inclined to refuse, which would be a pity since these odd names belong to a group of homespun desserts that are the glory of American fruit cookery.

Various crisps, pandowdies, brown Bettys, deep dish pies, cobblers and summer puddings share with them the generous use of a certain fruit gathered in season. Though battered tin berry pails no longer hang on hooks on the back porch and the word "berrying" has almost dropped from most of our vocabularies, wild berries and fruits are still abundant in the countryside. Blueberries in Maine, beach plums on Cape Cod, scuppernong grapes in North Carolina, raspberries in New Jersey and many other fruits and berries grow in tangles along out-of-the-way roadsides.

All the American fruit desserts have a delightful honesty about them, like the simple charm of a calico dress or a country garden of hollyhocks and climbing roses.

BLUEBERRY CRISP

1 package (16 ounces) frozen
    unsweetened blueberries or
    3 cups blueberries
2 tablespoons lemon juice
⅔ cup packed brown sugar
½ cup all-purpose flour

½ cup quick-cooking oats
¾ teaspoon ground cinnamon
¼ teaspoon salt
⅓ cup butter or margarine,
    softened
Cream or ice cream

Heat oven to 375°. Place blueberries in ungreased baking dish, 8x8x2 inches. Sprinkle with lemon juice. Mix remaining ingredients except cream; sprinkle over blueberries. Bake uncovered until topping is golden brown and blueberries are hot, about 30 minutes. Serve with cream. 4 TO 6 SERVINGS.

CRANBERRY-ORANGE RELISH

4 cups cranberries (1 pound)
1 unpeeled orange, cut up

1½ to 2 cups sugar

Chop cranberries and orange pieces in food grinder, using fine blade. Stir in sugar. Cover and refrigerate at least 24 hours before serving. 3½ CUPS RELISH.

Cranberry-Apple Relish: Reduce cranberries to 3 cups. Chop 6 unpared medium red apples, cut up, with the cranberries and orange pieces.

NOTE: Cranberries and orange pieces can be chopped in blender following manufacturer's directions.

BROILED HONEY GRAPEFRUIT

2 grapefruit, cut in halves
¼ cup honey

8 drops aromatic bitters
(optional)

Remove seeds from grapefruit halves. Cut around edges and sections to loosen; remove centers. Mix honey and bitters; drizzle about 1 tablespoon over each grapefruit half. Set oven control to broil and/or 550°. Broil grapefruit halves with tops 5 inches from heat about 5 minutes.   4 SERVINGS.

The delicate flavor of rose water was highly prized in the nineteenth century, particularly as an accent for fruits. Although this flavoring is not common today, it is available at many drugstores and gourmet shops.

SHAKER PEACHES

3 tablespoons butter or
   margarine
2 tablespoons water
6 large firm ripe peaches,
   peeled, halved and pitted

Rose water
¼ cup packed brown sugar
Sweetened whipped cream or
   ice cream (optional)

Heat butter in heavy 10-inch skillet until melted. Add water; place peach halves hollow sides up in skillet. Place a drop of rose water and 1 teaspoon sugar in each hollow. Cover and simmer until peaches are tender, about 20 minutes. Serve with syrup from skillet and whipped cream.   6 SERVINGS.

NOTE: Peaches can be served as a meat or poultry accompaniment.

STEWED PLUMS

2 cups water
¾ to 1 cup sugar
2 tablespoons lemon juice
⅛ teaspoon salt

Dash of ground allspice
2 cinnamon sticks
2 pounds ripe plums

Heat water, sugar, lemon juice, salt, allspice and cinnamon sticks to boiling in 3-quart saucepan. Add plums. Cook uncovered over medium heat just until plums are tender, about 15 minutes. Cool and refrigerate. Serve as a breakfast fruit, dessert or meat accompaniment.   8 SERVINGS.

NOTE: Italian prune, Santa Rosa, Greengage or Damson plums can be used in this recipe.

PRUNES IN PORT

Heat 1 pound prunes, 2 cups port or other sweet red wine and ½ cup water to boiling in 2-quart saucepan; reduce heat. Cover and simmer until tender, 10 to 15 minutes. Cool and refrigerate. Serve as a relish or dessert.

Prunes in Claret: Substitute 2 cups claret or other dry red wine for the port; stir ⅓ cup sugar into prune mixture after simmering.

NOTE: If pitted prunes are used, reduce prunes to 12 ounces. Simmer 5 minutes.

STEWED RHUBARB

¾ to 1 cup sugar
½ cup water
4 cups 1-inch pieces rhubarb

Few drops red food color
(optional)

Heat sugar and water to boiling, stirring occasionally. Add rhubarb; reduce heat. Simmer uncovered until rhubarb is tender and slightly transparent, about 10 minutes. Stir in food color.   5 SERVINGS.

FONDANT-DIPPED STRAWBERRIES

2 cups sugar
1¼ cups water
2 tablespoons light corn syrup

½ teaspoon almond extract
1 quart whole strawberries

Heat sugar, water and corn syrup to boiling in 2-quart saucepan over medium heat, stirring constantly, until sugar is dissolved. Boil, without stirring, until candy thermometer registers 240° (or until small amount of mixture dropped into very cold water forms a soft ball that flattens when removed from water). Pour onto moistened baking sheet, heatproof platter or marble slab without scraping saucepan. Cool just until lukewarm. Scrape mixture toward center of baking sheet, using broad, stiff spatula or wooden spoon. Spread mixture out again, using long, firm strokes; continue spreading until mixture is firm and white. Knead until smooth and creamy. Cover and refrigerate at least 12 hours.

Wash and thoroughly dry strawberries. Heat fondant over hot (not boiling) water until melted. Stir in almond extract and enough hot water (1 to 2 tablespoons) to make fondant dipping consistency. Dip strawberries into fondant, leaving stem ends visible. Place strawberries stem ends down on wire rack; let harden. Refrigerate no longer than 6 hours.   4 TO 5 DOZEN STRAWBERRIES.

BROILED FRESH FRUIT

Halve and pit 1 peach, nectarine or apricot or halve and core 1 pear. Make a few partial cuts through fruit. Brush each half with ¼ to ½ teaspoon butter or margarine, softened. Top halves in one of the following ways:

☐ Brush with soy sauce; sprinkle with ground ginger. Serve with pork, beef or poultry.

☐ Sprinkle with seasoned salt and pepper. Serve with lamb, veal or pork.

☐ Drizzle with lemon or lime juice; sprinkle with ½ teaspoon brown sugar and dash of ground nutmeg. Serve with smoked pork or vegetables.

☐ Drizzle with honey or maple-flavored syrup; sprinkle with ground cinnamon. Serve with ham, pork or corned beef.

☐ Spread with mixture of 2 tablespoons orange marmalade and ¼ teaspoon dry mustard. Serve with pork, beef or poultry.

☐ Drizzle with sherry or brandy; sprinkle with grated orange peel. Serve with pork, beef or poultry.

Set oven control to broil and/or 550°. Broil fruit halves with tops about 5 inches from heat until bubbly, 4 to 6 minutes.

BRANDY FRUITS

Pour 2 cups brandy into sterilized large pottery or clear glass container. Add 4 cups assorted fresh fruits* and 4 cups sugar; stir gently until sugar is dissolved. Cover tightly and let stand in cool place 3 days, then refrigerate 4 days.

Add assorted fruits (no more than 4 cups) and an equal amount of sugar at a minimum of 1-week intervals; stir gently. Cover tightly and let stand in cool place 3 days, then refrigerate at least 4 days.

Fruits can be served 1 week after the second addition of fruits and sugar or additional fruits and sugar can be added as directed above. Serve 1 week after last addition of fruits and sugar.

Serve over ice cream, sherbet, cake, custard, pudding or cut-up fruits. Or pack in jars and refrigerate indefinitely.

*Use firm ripe fruits; do not use bruised fruits. Fruits should be clean and dry. Peel, pit and cut into large slices peaches, apricots, nectarines and plums; pare, core and slice pears; remove rind, eyes and core from pineapple and cut pineapple into chunks; cut grapes in halves, removing seeds if necessary; pit cherries. Strawberries, blackberries, raspberries, currants and orange or tangerine sections can also be used. Do not use fresh apples or bananas. Unsweetened frozen fruits can be used.

Pictured opposite.
Start Brandy Fruits just as soon as fresh fruits are abundant so you can use the widest assortment possible. It makes an excellent hostess gift!

PUT-UPS

Process fruits, tomatoes and pickled vegetables in a boiling-water-bath canner. Process all common vegetables (low acid foods) in a steam-pressure canner. Wash all fruits and vegetables thoroughly whether or not they are to be pared. (Dirt contains some of the bacteria hardest to kill.)

Examine tops and edges of standard jars and lids. Discard any with cracks, chips, dents or rust. Wash jars in hot, soapy water; rinse well. Cover jars with hot water until used; invert on folded towel to drain just before filling. Prepare lids as directed by the manufacturer.

Fill water-bath canner containing a wire or wooden rack half full with hot water; heat. (Water should be hot but not boiling when jars are placed in canner.) Pack hot mixture in hot jars leaving headspace specified in each recipe. Wipe tops and screw-threads of jars with damp cloth; seal immediately as directed by manufacturer.

Place each jar, as it is filled, on rack in water bath; allow enough space for water to circulate. (Jars should not touch each other or fall against side of canner.) Add boiling water to cover jars to depth of 1 to 2 inches. (Do not pour boiling water directly on jars.) Cover canner. Heat water to boiling; reduce heat to hold water at a steady gentle boil. Start counting processing time, using time specified in each recipe. Remove jars from canner; complete seals as directed by manufacturer.

Place jars upright and several inches apart on rack or folded cloth; keep out of drafts but do not cover. Test for seal after about 12 hours (metal caps or lids will be depressed in center; lids with wire clamps and rubber seals will not leak when inverted). If seal is incomplete, empty jar, repack and reprocess food as if fresh or refrigerate for *immediate* use. Remove screw bands carefully. Store in cool, dry area.

APPLE BUTTER

4 quarts sweet apple cider	2 cups sugar
3 quarts pared and quartered cooking apples (about 4 pounds)	1 teaspoon ground cinnamon
	1 teaspoon ground ginger
	½ teaspoon ground cloves

Heat cider to boiling in 5-quart Dutch oven. Boil uncovered until cider measures 2 quarts, about 1¼ hours. Add apples. Heat to boiling; reduce heat. Simmer uncovered, stirring frequently, until apples are soft and can be broken apart with spoon, about 1 hour. (Apples can be pressed through sieve or food mill at this point if smooth apple butter is desired.)

Stir in sugar, cinnamon, ginger and cloves. Heat to boiling; reduce heat. Simmer uncovered, stirring frequently, until no liquid separates from pulp, about 2 hours. Heat to boiling. Pour into hot jars, leaving ¼-inch headspace; seal. Process 10 minutes in boiling water bath.   ABOUT 3½ PINTS.

If you've never canned, you might start with this recipe anytime at all. Apricot and Pineapple Preserves are especially easy because the fruits already are prepared. It's a particularly good choice in mid-winter, when some fresh fruits might be unavailable.

APRICOT AND PINEAPPLE PRESERVES

1 package (12 ounces) dried
    apricots, cut in halves
2 cans (13¼ ounces each)
    pineapple chunks, cut
    in halves
1 jar (8 ounces) maraschino
    cherries, drained and cut
    into fourths (reserve syrup)

3 cups water
5 cups sugar
2 tablespoons lemon juice

Mix apricots, pineapple (with syrup), reserved cherry syrup and the water in 4-quart Dutch oven. Let stand 1 hour.

Stir in sugar. Heat to boiling; boil rapidly 10 minutes. Stir in lemon juice. Boil, stirring occasionally, until thickened, about 35 minutes. Stir in cherries. Pour boiling mixture into hot jars, leaving ¼-inch headspace; seal. Process 15 minutes in boiling water bath.   ABOUT 6 HALF-PINTS.

SPICED PICKLED CHERRIES

4 cans (16 ounces each) pitted
    tart water pack red cherries,
    drained, or 6 cups pitted red
    sour cherries
3 cups cider vinegar

6 cups sugar
6 whole cinnamon sticks
1 teaspoon whole allspice
1 teaspoon whole cloves

Mix cherries and vinegar in nonmetal container. Cover and refrigerate 24 hours.

Drain cherries, reserving liquid. Mix reserved cherry liquid, the sugar and spices. Heat to boiling; boil 1 minute. Pour over cherries; cool. Cover and refrigerate 24 hours.

Drain cherries, reserving syrup. Heat syrup to boiling. Pour over cherries; cool. Cover and refrigerate 24 hours. Repeat process.

Drain cherries, reserving syrup. Pack cherries in hot jars, leaving ½-inch headspace. Heat syrup to boiling. Pour over cherries, leaving ½-inch headspace; seal. Process 25 minutes in boiling water bath. Store 1 month before serving as a relish with game, poultry or meat.   4 OR 5 PINTS.

PEACH HONEY

4 pounds fully ripe medium peaches, peeled and coarsely chopped

¼ cup water
6 cups sugar

Cook peaches in water until soft. Press peaches through sieve or food mill to measure 6 cups pulp. (Or place in blender container. Cover and blend until uniform consistency.)

Mix peach pulp and sugar in 3-quart saucepan. Heat to boiling. Boil gently, stirring frequently, until mixture thickens, 20 to 25 minutes. Pour boiling mixture into hot jars, leaving ¼-inch headspace; seal. Process 10 minutes in boiling water bath.   7 OR 8 HALF-PINTS.

Spiced Peach Honey: Stir in 1 teaspoon ground cinnamon and ¼ teaspoon ground cloves with the peach pulp and sugar.

PEACH PRESERVES

4 pounds ripe peaches, peeled and sliced (about 8 cups)

6 cups sugar
¼ cup lemon juice

Toss peaches with sugar. Cover and refrigerate 12 to 24 hours.

Heat peach mixture to boiling, stirring constantly. Boil rapidly 20 minutes. Stir in lemon juice. Boil 10 minutes. Pour boiling mixture into hot jars, leaving ¼-inch headspace; seal. Process 15 minutes in boiling water bath.   ABOUT 6 HALF-PINTS.

Spiced Peach Preserves: Tie 8 whole cloves, 5 whole allspice, 2 cinnamon sticks, 2 blades mace and 1½ teaspoons ground coriander in cheesecloth bag; add to peach mixture before boiling. Remove spice bag before pouring mixture into jars.

Peaches have a limited growing season, so be sure to catch them while they are available, between May and October. As with other fruits for preserving, peaches should be ripe and firm—just at the peak of perfection, because, naturally, the preserve will be only as good as its ingredients. The skin color between the red areas should be yellow. The deeper and more uniform the yellow color, the riper the peach. A fully ripened peach will also yield slightly to gentle hand pressure.

A quick way to peel peaches is to dip them in boiling water for 20 to 30 seconds, then plunge them immediately into ice water. A cup of tea and a slice of warm homemade bread spread with peach preserves or peach honey is an old remedy for many small troubles.

SPICED PICKLED PEACHES

1 piece gingerroot
1 tablespoon whole allspice
1 tablespoon whole cloves
8 cups sugar

4 cups water
4 cups cider vinegar
6 pounds firm ripe small
    peaches, peeled (20 to 24)

Tie spices in cheesecloth bag. Mix spice bag, sugar, water and vinegar. Heat to boiling. Add half of the peaches. Cook just until tender, 10 to 15 minutes. Pack peaches in hot jars, leaving ¼-inch headspace. Cook remaining peaches and pack in hot jars. Remove spice bag. Heat syrup to boiling. Pour over peaches, leaving ¼-inch headspace; seal. Process 15 minutes in boiling water bath. ABOUT 5 QUARTS.

PEAR BUTTER

5 pounds pears, pared and
    sliced (about 10 cups)
¼ cup water

3 cups packed brown sugar
2 tablespoons lemon juice
½ teaspoon ground nutmeg

Cook pears in water until soft. Press through sieve or food mill to measure 6 cups pulp. (Or place in blender container. Cover and blend until uniform consistency.)

Mix pear pulp, sugar, lemon juice and nutmeg in 4-quart Dutch oven. Heat to boiling. Boil gently, stirring frequently, until mixture thickens, about 30 minutes. Pour boiling mixture into hot jars, leaving ¼-inch headspace; seal. Process 10 minutes in boiling water bath. 5 OR 6 HALF-PINTS.

PEAR CONSERVE

3 pounds winter pears, pared
    and sliced (about 8 cups)
4 cups sugar
¾ cup raisins

1 tablespoon grated orange peel
2 teaspoons grated lemon peel
¼ cup lemon juice
1 cup broken walnuts

Mix all ingredients except walnuts in 4-quart Dutch oven. Heat to boiling, stirring frequently. Boil, stirring occasionally, until mixture thickens slightly, 25 to 30 minutes. Stir in walnuts. Pour boiling mixture into hot jars, leaving ¼-inch headspace; seal. Process 15 minutes in boiling water bath. 4 OR 5 HALF-PINTS.

OLD-TIME STRAWBERRY PRESERVES

1 quart strawberries   2 tablespoons vinegar
4 cups sugar

Toss strawberries with sugar. Let stand 3 to 4 hours.

Heat strawberry mixture to boiling, stirring constantly. Boil rapidly 10 minutes. Stir in vinegar. Boil, skimming off foam, 10 minutes. Pour boiling mixture into hot jars, leaving ¼-inch headspace; seal. Process 15 minutes in boiling water bath.   ABOUT 4 HALF-PINTS.

NOTE: Be sure strawberries do not have hollow cores.

SPICED PINEAPPLE CHUNKS

2 ripe pineapples   16 whole cloves
3 cups sugar   Grated peel of 2 lemons
½ cup vinegar

Remove rind and core from pineapples; cut pineapple into chunks. Heat sugar, vinegar, cloves and lemon peel to boiling in 3-quart saucepan, stirring frequently. Add pineapple. Heat to boiling; reduce heat. Simmer uncovered, stirring occasionally, 10 minutes. Pack pineapple in hot jars, leaving ½-inch headspace. Heat syrup to boiling. Pour over pineapple, leaving ½-inch headspace; seal. Process 30 minutes in boiling water bath.   ABOUT 3 HALF-PINTS.

WATERMELON RIND PICKLES

¼ cup pickling or uniodized
    salt
8 cups cold water
4 quarts 1-inch cubes pared
    watermelon rind

1 piece gingerroot
3 sticks cinnamon, broken
2 tablespoons whole cloves
8 cups cider vinegar
9 cups sugar

Dissolve salt in cold water; pour over watermelon rind. Stir in additional water, if necessary, to cover rind. Let stand in cool place 8 hours.

Drain rind; cover with cold water. Heat to boiling. Cook just until tender, 10 to 15 minutes; drain. Tie spices in cheesecloth bag. Heat spice bag, vinegar and sugar to boiling; boil 5 minutes. Add rind; simmer 1 hour. Remove spice bag. Pack simmering mixture in hot jars, leaving ¼-inch headspace; seal. Process 10 minutes in boiling water bath.   7 OR 8 PINTS.

Pictured opposite.
"Put-by's"—a cupboard full of creative satisfaction. Some of those pictured include: Spiced Pickled Peaches (page 123), Watermelon Rind Pickles (this page), Pickled Beets and Onions (page 128) and Green Tomato Relish (page 132).

PRESERVED PUMPKIN STRIPS

1 medium pumpkin (about 7 pounds), pared
7 cups sugar

1 tablespoon plus 1 teaspoon grated lemon peel
1 cup lemon juice

Cut pumpkin into thin strips, about 2x½x⅛ inch (about 4 quarts). Place in nonmetal container. Mix with sugar. Cover and refrigerate 12 to 18 hours.

Mix pumpkin mixture, lemon peel and juice. Heat to boiling, stirring occasionally. Boil slowly until pumpkin is transparent and tender and syrup coats spoon, about 30 minutes. Pack boiling mixture in hot jars, leaving ¼-inch headspace; seal. Process 15 minutes in boiling water bath.   ABOUT 4 PINTS.

Dill has sparked the taste of pickles for hundreds of years. Among the earliest American users of dill were the Scandinavian immigrants in Wisconsin and Minnesota, who used it extensively.

Dilled Beans make a good accompaniment for picnic fried chicken. They're especially attractive when paired with bright Corn Relish or Garden Salad Pickles.

DILLED BEANS

4 quarts water
2 pounds green beans
2 cloves garlic
4 heads dill or 4 teaspoons dried dill weed
4 small dried hot peppers

2½ cups water
2 cups white vinegar
¼ cup pickling or uniodized salt

Heat 4 quarts water to boiling. Place 1 pound of the beans in wire basket; place in boiling water. Cover and boil 1 minute. Immediately plunge basket into cold water; cool 1 minute. Repeat with remaining 1 pound beans.

Pack beans vertically in hot jars, leaving ¼-inch headspace. Add ½ clove garlic, crushed, 1 head dill or 1 teaspoon dried dill weed and 1 pepper to each jar. Mix 2½ cups water, the vinegar and salt. Heat to boiling. Pour over beans, leaving ¼-inch headspace; seal. Process 10 minutes in boiling water bath. Store 2 weeks before serving. Serve chilled.   4 PINTS.

Dilled Okra: Substitute 2 pounds baby okra pods for the green beans. Blanch, pack and process as directed in recipe.

Candied Pickle Slices are put together rather than put up. Several head starts combine into a delicious, crisp pickle which tastes as though it should have been much more trouble than it is.

CANDIED PICKLE SLICES

1 quart whole sour or dill
    pickles, drained
3 cups sugar
¼ cup coarsely chopped
    pickled sweet cherry
    peppers

2 teaspoons instant minced
    onion
1 teaspoon celery seed
1 teaspoon mustard seed
½ teaspoon crushed dried hot
    peppers

Remove tips from pickles. Cut pickles into very thin slices or medium sticks; drain. Mix pickles and remaining ingredients in glass bowl. Cover and refrigerate at least 12 hours.

Stir pickle mixture until all sugar is dissolved. Pack pickles in pickle jar or several small jars. Pour syrup to rim of jar. Cover and refrigerate. Let stand at least 24 hours.   1 QUART.

NOTE: Do not use kosher-type dill pickles.

GARDEN SALAD PICKLES

3 pounds carrots, cut into strips
    1½ inches long and ⅜ inch
    wide (about 8 cups)
2 pounds wax beans, cut into
    1½-inch pieces (about 8
    cups)
8 cups water
2 teaspoons pickling or
    uniodized salt
4 medium onions, thinly sliced
    and separated into rings
    (about 4 cups)
3 medium red or green sweet
    peppers, coarsely chopped
    (about 3 cups)

3 fresh hot peppers, finely
    chopped (about 2
    tablespoons)
4 cups cider vinegar
3 cups sugar
2 tablespoons pickling or
    uniodized salt
2 tablespoons mustard seed
2 teaspoons ground turmeric
2 teaspoons paprika

Heat carrots, beans, water and 2 teaspoons salt to boiling in 8-quart Dutch oven over medium heat. Cook just until vegetables are tender, 8 to 10 minutes; drain. Stir in remaining ingredients. Heat to boiling; boil 5 minutes. Pack boiling mixture in hot jars, leaving ¼-inch headspace; seal. Process 10 minutes in boiling water bath.   8 OR 9 PINTS.

PICKLED BEETS AND ONIONS

7 pounds medium beets*
Vinegar
2½ cups sugar
2 tablespoons whole mixed
    pickling spice
2 teaspoons salt
3½ cups white vinegar
1½ cups water
2 pounds medium onions, cut
    into ¼-inch slices

Cut off all but 2 inches of beet tops; leave root ends attached. Heat enough water to cover beets to boiling. Add beets and 2 teaspoons vinegar for each quart water. Cover and heat to boiling. Cook until beets are tender, 35 to 45 minutes; drain. Run cold water over beets; slip off skins and remove root ends. Cut beets into slices.

Heat remaining ingredients to boiling in 6-quart Dutch oven; reduce heat. Simmer uncovered 10 minutes; stir in beets. Pack beets and onions in hot jars, leaving ½-inch headspace. Heat syrup to boiling. Pour over beets and onions, leaving ½-inch headspace; seal. Process 30 minutes in boiling water bath.   ABOUT 8 PINTS.

*7 cans (16 ounces each) sliced beets, drained, can be substituted for the beets.

Salt and vinegar are two basic ingredients in any pickles. Pure granulated, pickling or kosher salt are the best, if they're available. The materials that prevent caking in uniodized table salt can make the brine cloudy. The vinegar should be 40 to 60 grain with 4 to 6 percent acidity. Cider vinegar makes the flavors blend nicely but can darken light or white vegetables or fruits.

BREAD-AND-BUTTER PICKLES

3 quarts thinly sliced unpared
    cucumbers (about 4 pounds)
7 cups thinly sliced onions
    (about 2 pounds)
1 red sweet pepper, cut into
    strips
1 green pepper, cut into strips
½ cup pickling or uniodized
    salt
1 cup water
2½ cups cider or white vinegar
2½ cups sugar
2 tablespoons mustard seed
1 teaspoon celery seed
1 teaspoon ground turmeric

Mix cucumbers, onions and peppers. Dissolve salt in water; pour over vegetables. Place a solid layer of ice cubes or crushed ice over vegetables. Weight with a heavy object and let stand 3 hours.

Drain vegetables thoroughly. Mix vinegar, sugar and spices. Heat to boiling. Add vegetables; heat to boiling. Pack boiling mixture in hot jars, leaving ¼-inch headspace; seal. Process 10 minutes in boiling water bath.   ABOUT 6 PINTS.

CORN RELISH

9 ears corn	3 cups white vinegar
1½ cups sugar	3 medium onions, chopped
3 tablespoons flour	2 red sweet peppers, chopped
2 tablespoons pickling or uniodized salt	1 green pepper, chopped
2 teaspoons dry mustard	1 small head green cabbage, chopped
1 teaspoon ground turmeric	

Place corn in Dutch oven; add enough cold water to cover. Heat to boiling; boil uncovered 3 minutes. Cool; cut enough kernels from corn to measure 5 cups.

Mix sugar, flour, salt, mustard and turmeric; stir in vinegar. Heat to boiling. Add vegetables. Simmer uncovered 25 minutes. Pack simmering mixture in hot jars, leaving ¼-inch headspace; seal. Process 15 minutes in boiling water bath.   5 OR 6 PINTS.

NOTE: Onions, peppers and cabbage can be ground in food grinder, using coarse blade, or chopped in blender following manufacturer's directions.

Almost everything that grows has been put-by. In early America there were delicate conserves of red roses or rosemary flowers or leaves of wood sorrel. There were walnut catsups, pickled nasturtium buds and celery vinegars. The Northeast had its spiced crab apples, and the South its pickled peaches. The Southwest put up chili relishes and the Midwest favored corn relish and tomato preserves. Out West there were olives to be brined and fruits to make into jams.

One treasure in our ancestors' china closets was a cut-glass relish dish, often divided into three or four sections that attest to the number of preserves and relishes once served at a meal. The Pennsylvania Dutch exceeded, and indeed still exceed, even that. In their tradition, every important meal includes seven sweet dishes and seven sour dishes. The sweets might include peach honey or other fruit conserve, apple butter and spiced pears. Some of the favorite sours are pickled mushrooms, dilled beans, pickled beets and spicy relishes made of cabbage, corn or peppers. The plain and frugal aspect of the main-course fare in Pennsylvania Dutch cookery becomes much less severe when considered with the fourteen surrounding "sweets" and "sours."

At county fairs there is still fierce competition for the best dill pickles and strawberry jams. Many old skills belong to the past and have faded away. But the skills of preserving, and the pleasure of seeing a shelf lined with your own preserves, are still rewarding today.

It's Fair time! And a wealth of color delights visitors to the Bloomsburg Fair in Pennsylvania.

Kitchen Garden **129**

MINCEMEAT

1½ pounds lean beef chuck
1½ pounds tart cooking apples, pared and cut into fourths (about 1 quart)
½ pound beef suet
4 ounces candied orange peel
2 ounces candied citron
1 package (15 ounces) raisins
1 package (11 ounces) currants
1½ cups packed dark brown sugar
½ teaspoon salt
1 teaspoon ground cinnamon
½ teaspoon ground cloves
½ teaspoon ground allspice
¾ cup molasses
1 cup apple cider
Grated peel of 1 lemon

Place beef chuck in 4-quart Dutch oven; add enough water to cover. Heat to boiling; reduce heat. Cover and simmer until beef is tender, about 2 hours; drain, reserving ¾ cup of the broth. Cut beef into 1-inch pieces.

Grind beef, apples, suet, orange peel, citron and raisins in food grinder, using coarse blade. Mix in 4-quart Dutch oven. Stir in currants, sugar, salt, cinnamon, cloves, allspice, molasses and reserved broth. Heat to boiling; reduce heat. Simmer uncovered, stirring just enough to prevent sticking, 1 hour. Stir in cider and lemon peel. Simmer 5 minutes. Pack simmering mixture in hot jars, leaving 1-inch headspace; seal. (Mincemeat can be frozen at this point; cool quickly, pack in freezer containers, seal and freeze. Freeze no longer than 2 months.)

Place jars on rack in steam-pressure canner containing 2 to 3 inches hot water. Fasten canner cover according to manufacturer's directions. Place canner on high heat, leaving vent open until steam escapes steadily for 10 minutes. Close vent; heat to 10 pounds pressure. Cook 25 minutes.

Remove from heat. Let pressure return to normal, 20 to 25 minutes. (Do not run water over canner to speed cooling.) Open vent and remove cover. Place jars a few inches apart out of drafts to cool.

Test for seal after 12 hours (metal caps or lids will be depressed in center; lids with wire clamps and rubber seals will not leak when inverted). If seal is incomplete, either store jars in refrigerator for immediate use or heat mincemeat to boiling, pack in hot jars and process in canner. Store jars in cool, dark place.   ABOUT 5 PINTS.

NOTE: A 6-quart pressure cooker can be used to process pint jars. Vent 1 minute; close vent and heat to 10 pounds pressure. Process 45 minutes.

Minced meats of all kinds—buffalo, venison, beef, bear—began as a way of preserving meat by pickling it. When no fresh meat was to be had, the crocks of minced meat were ready for "pyes" and meat loaves. Gradually, mincemeat became long on vegetables, fruits and spices and short on meat. The result of that switch was the relishes and dessert pies we know today.

A jar of either Green Tomato Mincemeat or traditional Mincemeat makes a very personal gift to a hostess or to a friend before a holiday when cooking can become hectic. Because of the meat in mincemeats, it is necessary to use the steam-pressure method of processing.

GREEN TOMATO MINCEMEAT

2 quarts chopped green tomatoes (about 8 pounds), drained
2 quarts chopped pared tart cooking apples (about 3 pounds)
1 cup chopped beef suet (about ¼ pound)
1 pound raisins (about 3 cups)
2⅓ cups packed dark brown sugar
1 tablespoon pickling or uniodized salt
1 tablespoon ground cinnamon
½ teaspoon ground cloves
½ teaspoon ground allspice
½ cup cider vinegar
¼ cup light molasses

Place tomatoes in 6-quart Dutch oven; add enough boiling water to cover. Heat to boiling; boil 5 minutes. Drain; return tomatoes to Dutch oven. Add enough boiling water to cover. Heat to boiling; boil 5 minutes. Drain; return tomatoes to Dutch oven.

Stir in remaining ingredients. Heat to boiling; reduce heat. Simmer uncovered, stirring frequently to prevent sticking, until thickened, ½ to 1 hour. Pack simmering mixture in hot jars, leaving 1-inch headspace; seal.

Place jars on rack in steam-pressure canner containing 2 to 3 inches hot water. Fasten canner cover according to manufacturer's directions. Place canner on high heat, leaving vent open until steam escapes steadily 10 minutes. Close vent; heat to 10 pounds pressure. Cook 25 minutes.

Remove from heat. Let pressure return to normal, 20 to 25 minutes. (Do not run water over canner to speed cooling.) Open vent and remove cover. Place jars a few inches apart out of drafts to cool.

Test for seal after 12 hours (metal caps or lids will be depressed in center; lids with wire clamps and rubber seals will not leak when inverted). If seal is incomplete, either store jars in refrigerator for immediate use or heat mincemeat to boiling, pack in hot jars and process in canner. Store jars in cool, dark place.   5 OR 6 PINTS.

NOTE: A 6-quart pressure cooker can be used to process pint jars. Vent 1 minute; close vent and heat to 10 pounds pressure. Process 45 minutes.

GREEN TOMATO RELISH

2½ cups coarsely ground red
 sweet peppers (about 6
 peppers)
2 cups coarsely ground green
 tomatoes (about 2 pounds)
2 cups coarsely ground onions
 (about 2 pounds)
2 cups coarsely ground green
 cabbage (1 small head)
1½ cups coarsely ground green
 peppers (about 3 peppers)

¼ cup pickling or uniodized
 salt
3½ cups sugar
2 cups cider vinegar
1 cup water
1 tablespoon mustard seed
1 tablespoon ground turmeric
2 teaspoons celery seed

Mix vegetables and salt. Cover and let stand 12 to 18 hours.

Drain vegetables and rinse. Mix vegetables and remaining ingredients. Heat to boiling; reduce heat. Simmer uncovered 3 minutes. Pack simmering mixture in hot jars, leaving ⅛-inch headspace; seal. Process 10 minutes in boiling water bath.   5 OR 6 PINTS.

NOTE: Vegetables can be chopped if you prefer.

SWEET PEPPER RELISH

12 large red or green sweet
 peppers, finely chopped
1 tablespoon pickling or
 uniodized salt

3 cups sugar
2 cups white vinegar

Mix peppers and salt. Cover and let stand at least 12 hours.

Drain peppers, pressing out all liquid. Heat peppers, sugar and vinegar to boiling in 3-quart saucepan, stirring frequently; reduce heat. Simmer uncovered, stirring frequently, until thickened, about 45 minutes. Pour simmering mixture into hot jars, leaving ¼-inch headspace; seal. Process 10 minutes in boiling water bath.   ABOUT 6 HALF-PINTS.

NOTE: Peppers can be ground in food grinder, using medium blade.

Pictured opposite.
An array of sweets to tempt any palate. Clockwise from top: Lemon Snow Pudding with Stirred Custard (page 148), Old-fashioned Sponge Candy (page 154), Fudge Pudding Cake (page 144), Molasses Duff with Lemon Sauce (page 143) and Popcorn Balls (page 152).

SWEETS

Americans always have had an incredible appetite and determination for sweets. One of the events that led up to the Revolutionary War was the British imposition of a tax on molasses, which was commonly used as a sweetener at that time. "I know not why we should blush to confess that molasses was an essential ingredient in American independence," John Adams wrote. Probably no one did blush; the early Americans were far too fond of their puddings and candies for that.

The oldest truly American pudding is, of course, Indian Pudding. Though made in many ways, it is basically a dish of cornmeal, which the Indians sweetened with honey or maple sugar. In their search for sweeteners, it seems that the Indians tapped into almost every stalk and tree that grew. They made a kind of candy from the juice in the cornstalk and learned to tap the sweet sap of the birch as well as the maple trees. The New England colonists quickly learned these skills and depended on them for many years. Molasses wasn't imported from the West Indies in quantity until after 1700, and refined sugar remained a luxury for the very few. Even the sight of a little cane sugar in a bowl for Sunday visitors was considered a treat.

The sweets of early America are a real lesson in how frugality and inventiveness went hand in hand. The common denominator of these desserts was the economical use of ingredients. Leftover rice, cornmeal, sweet potatoes and stale bread were transformed out of necessity into the popular and hearty puddings we still enjoy today. For ordinary meals the puddings and custards usually were served plain. For guests or holidays there were often accompanying sauces or a pitcher of "pour cream." The most desired flavoring for these puddings was nutmeg, a spice so scarce that unscrupulous peddlers frequently sold unsuspecting buyers wooden nutmegs that had been doused with nutmeg extract. Connecticut must have been particularly prey to such tactics since it is still known as the "[Wooden] Nutmeg State."

Out on the frontier, spices were rare commodities indeed; and desserts were simple. In the early days of the westward move, fruit leather was a popular use of excess fruits around orchards. Apricots, peaches and other fruits were cooked, squeezed out and put on platters to dry. When they became leathery, they were rolled into layers or strung on threads and then hung in the kitchen. Another rather primitive sweet occasionally enjoyed in wagon trains or out on the range was unappetizingly named Spotted Pup, a mixture of sweetened rice "spotted" with a handful of raisins.

In this chapter we have Spotted Pup's more elegant relative, Creamy Rice Pudding, richer with sugar and spice than its frontier cousin. Many of our pudding recipes—Hasty Pudding, Bread Pudding and Indian Pudding—would have been right at home on an early American hearth. With their original virtues of economy and pleasing taste intact, they are still delightful family desserts. Other

Collecting maple syrup in Vermont. The Indians taught the early settlers how to use maple sugar as a sweetener.

more elaborate puddings, such as Molasses Duff with Brandy-Orange Sauce, Steamed Fig Pudding and Yam Pudding, also have nostalgic connections with our heritage and are interesting choices for special occasions.

During the eighteenth century, ice cream was the most desirable and the most unobtainable sweet Americans dreamed of. It was not only rare because sugar was so expensive, but the process of making it was tricky. Until the nineteenth century, ice was hard to come by. In winter, northern settlers could chip ice from frozen streams, but in the Deep South they had to wait for a hailstorm!

Considering the difficulties of making ice cream, a surprising amount of it was served. George Washington's ice-cream bill in the summer of 1790 was equivalent to two hundred dollars, quite a sum in those days. Thomas Jefferson brought back a French cook from a trip abroad and also brought hundreds of vanilla beans to flavor his favorite vanilla ice cream, which he usually served in a pastry crust to his guests.

After ice became readily available during the nineteenth century, ice-cream parlors began to open in the cities. In 1846, the popularity of ice cream turned into a national craze when Nancy Johnson invented the hand-cranked ice-cream maker. Every family wanted one. Recipes for dozens of flavors began to appear in cookbooks. Hokey-Pokey (slang for frozen dairy treats) carts began to ply the city streets. Ice cream became almost synonymous with dessert.

Along with ice cream, candy was becoming more accessible all during the last century. When cane and beet sugar became more easily available, Americans could indulge their fancies for sweets endlessly. Without thermometers, but undaunted by vague instructions to cook to a "hard crack" or to a "fine thread," cooks began to create peanut brittle, fudge and other fancy confections such as Fondant-dipped Strawberries and Pralines in their own homes. Pulling taffy and making popcorn balls were popular at parties, and many a batch of fudge was cooked over a gaslight in women's colleges around the country. The Soldier's Fudge, Molasses Taffy, Popcorn Balls and Candy Apples on Sticks in this chapter all are good introductions to the pleasures of candy making.

Though the popularity of making candy has abated somewhat in recent years, many cooks still have a few recipes they regularly make for holidays. The candies in this section are scrumptious gifts, and most are very simple to prepare. We've chosen several that have the added advantage of requiring no cooking. Sugarplums, Bourbon Balls and Brandied Stuffed Dates can be put together in a flash. Creole Kisses are baked with ease in the oven. Only the marvelous Fresh Coconut Candy takes much effort, and it is guaranteed to be worth every minute! A selection of these candies in a jar tied with ribbon makes the most welcome gift.

These confections, puddings and special treats Americans love are as sweet as ever!

PUDDINGS

BROWN PUDDING

1 cup all-purpose flour*
1 cup packed dark brown sugar
1 teaspoon baking powder
1 teaspoon ground cinnamon
¼ teaspoon salt
½ cup milk
2 tablespoons butter or
   margarine, softened

1 cup raisins
¾ cup chopped nuts
1¾ cups water
1 cup packed light brown sugar
2 tablespoons butter or
   margarine
⅛ teaspoon salt
Cream or ice cream

Heat oven to 350°. Mix flour, dark brown sugar, baking powder, cinnamon, ¼ teaspoon salt, the milk and 2 tablespoons butter. Stir in raisins and nuts. Pour into ungreased baking pan, 9x9x2 inches. Heat water, light brown sugar, 2 tablespoons butter and ⅛ teaspoon salt, stirring frequently, until butter is melted. Pour over batter. Bake 45 minutes. Serve with cream.   9 SERVINGS.

*If using self-rising flour, omit baking powder and salt.

CORNSTARCH PUDDING

⅓ cup sugar
3 tablespoons cornstarch
¼ teaspoon salt

2¼ cups milk
1½ teaspoons vanilla

Mix sugar, cornstarch and salt in 2-quart saucepan. Stir in milk gradually. Cook over medium heat, stirring constantly, until mixture thickens and boils. Boil and stir 1 minute. Remove from heat; stir in vanilla. Pour into dessert dishes. Cool slightly; refrigerate.   4 SERVINGS.

CREAMY RICE PUDDING

1 cup water
½ cup uncooked regular rice
½ teaspoon salt
2½ cups milk

¼ cup sugar
¼ teaspoon ground cinnamon
   or nutmeg
½ cup raisins (optional)

Heat oven to 350°. Heat water, rice and salt to boiling in 2-quart saucepan; reduce heat. Cover and simmer 10 minutes. Stir remaining ingredients into rice. Pour into ungreased 1½-quart casserole. Place casserole in pan of very hot water (1 inch deep).

Bake, stirring occasionally, until most of the milk is absorbed, 1½ to 1¾ hours.   6 TO 8 SERVINGS.

When oven temperatures were determined by the cook putting her fist in the oven and counting out "One potato, two potato . . ." or by tossing in a spoonful of flour and counting the seconds until it browned, it was only natural that the country's first desserts would not be too fussy. Often they were simply steamed over the fire, even outdoors if the family happened to be traveling.

America's heritage puddings, made with the most basic ingredients, illustrate the bird-in-hand necessity that launched American cooking. Their essence, too, embodies another early virtue—hospitality. There always was room for one more at the long harvest tables set with pewter tankards of cider and steaming bowls of Indian Pudding.

Today, many of these puddings seem especially appropriate for holiday meals. Or offer one as the final course at a friendly potluck party with each guest bringing an early American dish.

HASTY PUDDING

¾ cup cornmeal
¾ cup cold water
2½ cups boiling water
¾ teaspoon salt

Butter, margarine or light
   cream
Molasses or sugar

Mix cornmeal and cold water in 2-quart saucepan. Stir in boiling water and salt. Cook over medium heat, stirring constantly, until mixture thickens and boils; reduce heat. Cover and cook over low heat 10 minutes. Serve hot with butter and molasses as a cereal or dessert. 4 SERVINGS.

INDIAN PUDDING

½ cup cornmeal
4 cups milk, scalded
¼ cup molasses
3 eggs, well beaten

¼ cup sugar
¾ teaspoon salt
½ teaspoon ground ginger
Cream (optional)

Heat oven to 350°. Stir cornmeal into milk. Cook over low heat, stirring occasionally, until mixture coats metal spoon, about 10 minutes. Stir in molasses. Mix eggs, sugar, salt and ginger. Stir in hot cornmeal mixture gradually. Pour into ungreased 1½-quart casserole. Place casserole in pan of very hot water (1 inch deep).

Bake until knife inserted halfway between edge and center of pudding comes out clean and pudding is golden, about 1 hour. Serve hot with cream. 6 SERVINGS.

STEAMED FIG PUDDING

1 cup boiling water
1 cup finely cut-up dried figs
2 tablespoons shortening
1½ cups all-purpose flour*
1 cup sugar

1 teaspoon baking soda
1 teaspoon salt
1 cup chopped nuts
1 egg
Creamy Sauce (below)

Pour boiling water over figs; stir in shortening. Mix flour, sugar, baking soda, salt and nuts in 2-quart bowl. Stir in fig mixture and egg. Pour into well-greased 6-cup mold. Cover with aluminum foil.

Place mold on rack in Dutch oven or steamer; pour boiling water into pan halfway up mold. Cover pan. Keep water boiling over low heat until wooden pick inserted in center of pudding comes out clean, about 1½ hours.

Remove mold from pan and let stand 5 minutes; unmold. Serve warm with Creamy Sauce.   8 SERVINGS.

*Do not use self-rising flour in this recipe.

CREAMY SAUCE
Beat ¾ cup powdered sugar and ¾ cup butter or margarine, softened, in 1-quart saucepan until smooth and creamy. Stir in ¾ cup whipping cream. Heat to boiling, stirring occasionally. Serve immediately.

YAM PUDDING

3½ cups grated uncooked yams
    or sweet potatoes (about 2
    pounds)
1¼ cups milk
½ cup light corn syrup
3 eggs, beaten
2 tablespoons butter or
    margarine, softened

½ cup packed brown sugar
1 teaspoon ground cinnamon
½ teaspoon salt
½ teaspoon ground nutmeg
Cream or ice cream

Heat oven to 325°. Mix all ingredients except cream. Pour into greased baking dish, 8x8x2 inches.

Bake until knife inserted halfway between edge and center of pudding comes out clean, about 1 hour. Serve with cream.   6 TO 8 SERVINGS.

NOTE: To grate yams easily, use a blender following manufacturer's directions.

Pictured opposite.
Puddings hold a justifiably secure position in our culinary heritage. Left: Creamy Rice Pudding (page 136). Right: Date and Nut Pudding (page 140). Bottom: Steamed Fig Pudding with Creamy Sauce (this page).

DATE AND NUT PUDDING

3 eggs
¾ cup sugar
¾ cup all-purpose flour*
1½ teaspoons baking powder

½ teaspoon salt
1½ cups cut-up dates
¾ cup coarsely chopped nuts
Partially whipped cream

Heat oven to 325°. Beat eggs in small mixer bowl until light and fluffy, about 3 minutes. Beat in sugar gradually; continue beating until very thick. Stir in flour, baking powder and salt. Stir in dates and nuts. Pour into greased 9-inch pie plate or baking pan, 9x9x2 inches.

Bake until wooden pick inserted near center of pudding comes out clean, 45 to 55 minutes. Serve warm with whipped cream. 8 OR 9 SERVINGS.

*If using self-rising flour, omit baking powder and salt.

Prunes, dates, yams, figs and apples all make notable puddings, each somewhat regional in character. The origin of Ozark Pudding is obvious from its name, but it is a close kin to many puddings that are baked wherever there are apple orchards. Yam Pudding is Southern, but sweets made from carrots, pumpkins and other vegetables are characteristic of different areas. The dried fruit puddings—date, fig and prune—are only representative of the imaginative use of reconstituted fruits in our cookery. In most of these puddings the plentiful use of nuts indicates the abundance of wild nut trees in many areas of early America.

OZARK PUDDING

¾ cup sugar
⅓ cup all-purpose flour*
1½ teaspoons baking powder
⅛ teaspoon salt
1 egg
1 teaspoon vanilla

1 medium apple, pared and
    finely chopped (about 1 cup)
½ cup chopped nuts
Sweetened whipped cream, ice
    cream or hard sauce

Heat oven to 350°. Beat sugar, flour, baking powder, salt, egg and vanilla in small mixer bowl on medium speed until smooth, about 1 minute. Stir in apple and nuts. Pour into greased 8- or 9-inch pie plate.

Bake until golden brown, about 30 minutes. Cut into wedges. Serve warm with whipped cream. 6 SERVINGS.

*If using self-rising flour, reduce baking powder to 1 teaspoon and omit salt.

As much a part of the first kitchens as the iron skillet or the long white apron, bread pudding in its many artless guises endures as a useful and infinitely variable sweet. Perfectly plain, it is an appealing dessert after a spicy meal, but there are so many embellishments that the recipe below may be considered only a starting point for you. In the past, cooks served bread puddings with a berry puree, a lemon sauce or a sauce made from dried fruits. Sometimes the pudding was baked with layers of fruit or preserves, or perhaps with a handful of coconut or nuts.

Everyone, from adamant meat-and-potatoes fans to jaded gourmets, responds to the innocence of a well-made bread pudding.

OLD-FASHIONED BREAD PUDDING

2 cups milk
¼ cup butter or margarine
3 cups soft bread crumbs (3 to 4 slices bread)
½ cup sugar
1 teaspoon ground cinnamon or nutmeg
¼ teaspoon salt
2 eggs, slightly beaten
½ cup raisins (optional)

Heat oven to 350°. Heat milk and butter over medium heat until butter is melted and milk is scalded. Mix remaining ingredients in ungreased 1½-quart casserole; stir in milk mixture. Place casserole in pan of very hot water (1 inch deep).

Bake until knife inserted 1 inch from edge of pudding comes out clean, 40 to 45 minutes. Serve warm.   6 TO 8 SERVINGS.

OLD-FASHIONED TAPIOCA PUDDING

6 cups water
¾ cup pearl tapioca
2 cups milk
2 eggs, separated
½ cup sugar
¼ teaspoon salt
1 teaspoon vanilla

Pour water over tapioca; let stand about 12 hours.

Drain tapioca. Mix tapioca and milk in top of double boiler. Cover and cook over hot water, stirring occasionally, until tapioca is transparent, about 1 hour.

Beat egg yolks, ¼ cup of the sugar and the salt. Stir about half of the tapioca mixture gradually into egg yolk mixture; stir into hot tapioca mixture in pan. Cook over hot water, stirring frequently, 5 minutes. Remove from heat; stir in vanilla. Cool slightly. Beat egg whites until foamy. Beat in remaining ¼ cup sugar, 1 tablespoon at a time; continue beating until stiff and glossy. Fold tapioca mixture into egg whites.   8 TO 10 SERVINGS.

BAKED PRUNE WHIP

1 cup pitted prunes, cooked and
    cut up
⅓ cup sugar
¼ teaspoon salt

3 egg whites
1 tablespoon lemon juice
¼ cup chopped pecans
Sweetened whipped cream

Heat oven to 350°. Beat prunes, sugar, salt and egg whites in small mixer bowl until stiff. Fold in lemon juice and pecans. Spread in ungreased 1½-quart casserole. Place casserole in pan of very hot water (1 inch deep).

Bake until pudding is puffed and a thin film has formed on top, 30 to 35 minutes. Serve warm with whipped cream.   4 TO 6 SERVINGS.

Dumplings of all kinds were at one time a far more important part of the regular fare. Plain or mincemeat dumplings were economical and could be cooked quickly on the trail with whatever flour or grain was available. In dessert cookery, fruits often were cooked in the dumplings. These are unusual in that they are plain dumplings served for dessert.

DUMPLINGS IN CARAMEL SAUCE

Caramel Sauce (below)
1½ cups all-purpose flour* or
    1⅔ cups cake flour
½ cup sugar
1½ teaspoons baking powder
½ teaspoon salt

½ cup milk
1 tablespoon butter or
    margarine, melted
Cream or sweetened whipped
    cream

Prepare Caramel Sauce. Mix remaining ingredients except cream just until flour is moistened. Drop dough by 8 spoonfuls into boiling sauce. Cover and cook over low heat until dumplings are fluffy, about 15 minutes. Serve with cream.   8 SERVINGS.

*If using self-rising flour, omit baking powder and salt.

CARAMEL SAUCE

1½ cups sugar
2 cups boiling water
1½ teaspoons vanilla

2 tablespoons butter or
    margarine

Heat sugar in heavy 10-inch skillet, stirring constantly, until sugar is melted and golden. Remove from heat; stir in boiling water slowly. Cook over low heat, stirring constantly, until sugar lumps are dissolved. Stir in vanilla and butter. Heat to boiling; boil 2 minutes.

Sauces traditionally enhanced steamed puddings on festive occasions—and often they were laced with a bit of brandy. The pudding molds themselves were often as treasured as the pudding recipes.

MOLASSES DUFF

1 egg	1⅓ cups all-purpose flour*
½ cup molasses	1 teaspoon baking soda
2 tablespoons sugar	¼ teaspoon salt
2 tablespoons shortening	Brandy-Orange Sauce
½ cup boiling water	or Lemon Sauce (below)

Beat egg in small mixer bowl until thick. Beat in molasses and sugar on low speed. Melt shortening in boiling water; stir into molasses mixture. Beat in flour, baking soda and salt on low speed. Pour into well-greased 4-cup mold. Cover with aluminum foil.

Place mold on rack in Dutch oven or steamer; pour boiling water into pan halfway up mold. Cover pan. Keep water boiling over low heat until wooden pick inserted in center of pudding comes out clean, about 1½ hours.

Remove mold from pan and let stand 5 minutes; unmold. Serve warm with Brandy-Orange Sauce.   6 SERVINGS.

*Do not use self-rising flour in this recipe.

BRANDY-ORANGE SAUCE

3 tablespoons powdered sugar	2 tablespoons orange juice
2 egg yolks	1 to 2 tablespoons brandy
1 teaspoon grated orange peel	½ cup chilled whipping cream

Beat sugar, egg yolks and orange peel in small mixer bowl until thick. Beat in orange juice and brandy on low speed. Beat whipping cream in chilled bowl until stiff; fold in orange mixture. Serve immediately or refrigerate up to 1 hour.

LEMON SAUCE

½ cup sugar	2 tablespoons butter or
2 tablespoons cornstarch	margarine
¼ teaspoon salt	1 teaspoon grated lemon peel
1 cup water	2 tablespoons lemon juice

Mix sugar, cornstarch and salt in 1-quart saucepan. Stir in water gradually. Cook over medium heat, stirring constantly, until mixture thickens and boils. Boil and stir 1 minute. Remove from heat; stir in butter, lemon peel and juice. Serve warm.

NOTE: Sauce can be made ahead of time. Reheat over low heat, stirring constantly.

FUDGE PUDDING CAKE

1 cup all-purpose flour*
¾ cup granulated sugar
2 tablespoons cocoa
2 teaspoons baking powder
¼ teaspoon salt
½ cup milk
2 tablespoons vegetable oil

1 teaspoon vanilla
1 cup chopped nuts (optional)
1 cup packed brown sugar
¼ cup cocoa
1¾ cups hottest tap water
Ice cream

Heat oven to 350°. Mix flour, granulated sugar, 2 tablespoons cocoa, the baking powder and salt in ungreased baking pan, 9x9x2 inches. Stir in milk, oil and vanilla with fork until smooth. Stir in nuts. Spread evenly in pan. Sprinkle with brown sugar and ¼ cup cocoa. Pour *hot* water over batter.

Bake 40 minutes. Let stand 15 minutes. Spoon into dessert dishes or cut into squares and invert on dessert plates. Top with ice cream and spoon sauce over each serving.   9 SERVINGS.

*If using self-rising flour, omit baking powder and salt.

BAKED CUSTARD

3 eggs, slightly beaten
⅓ cup sugar
Dash of salt

1 teaspoon vanilla
2½ cups milk, scalded
Ground nutmeg

Heat oven to 350°. Mix eggs, sugar, salt and vanilla. Stir in milk gradually. Pour into 6 ungreased 6-ounce custard cups. Sprinkle with nutmeg. Place cups in baking pan, 13x9x2 inches; pour very hot water into pan to within ½ inch of tops of cups. Bake until knife inserted halfway between edge and center of custard comes out clean, about 45 minutes. Remove cups from pan; cool. Serve warm or cold.   6 SERVINGS.

Baked Caramel Custard: Heat ½ cup sugar in small heavy pan over low heat, stirring constantly, until sugar melts and becomes a golden brown syrup. Divide syrup among custard cups; tilt each cup so that syrup coats bottom. Allow syrup to harden in cups, about 10 minutes. Prepare custard; pour into cups. Bake as directed. Remove cups from pan; unmold. Serve warm or cold.

When Prohibitionists succeeded in outlawing the demon rum, the popularity of ice cream soared. The soda fountain became a social center in every town, and the soda jerk a local hero who concocted enormous banana splits, sundaes and sodas. When the zealous days of

Prohibition ended, manufacturers feared ice-cream sales would decline, but they need not have worried. Ice cream is more in demand than ever!

To make these ice creams you'll need an electric or hand-crank ice-cream freezer. If you use an electric freezer, be sure to follow the manufacturer's directions carefully.

PHILADELPHIA ICE CREAM

1 quart whipping cream   2 tablespoons vanilla
¾ cup sugar   ⅛ teaspoon salt

Mix all ingredients. Pour into freezer can; put dasher in place. Cover can and adjust crank. Place can in freezer tub. Fill freezer tub ⅓ full of ice; add remaining ice alternately with layers of rock salt (6 parts ice to 1 part rock salt). Turn crank until it turns with difficulty. Draw off water. Remove lid; take out dasher. Pack mixture down; replace lid. Repack in ice and rock salt. Let ripen several hours.   1½ QUARTS ICE CREAM.

STRAWBERRY ICE CREAM

1 pint strawberries   2 cups whipping cream
1 cup sugar   1 teaspoon vanilla
¼ teaspoon salt   Few drops red food color
1 cup milk   (optional)
3 egg yolks, beaten

Mash strawberries with ½ cup of the sugar; reserve. Mix remaining ½ cup sugar, the salt, milk and egg yolks in 3-quart saucepan. Cook over medium heat, stirring constantly, just until bubbles appear around edge. Cool to room temperature. Stir in cream, vanilla, strawberries and food color.

Pour into freezer can; put dasher in place. Cover can and adjust crank. Place can in freezer tub. Fill freezer tub ⅓ full of ice; add remaining ice alternately with layers of rock salt (6 parts ice to 1 part rock salt). Turn crank until it turns with difficulty. Draw off water. Remove lid; take out dasher. Pack mixture down; replace lid. Repack in ice and rock salt. Let ripen several hours.   ABOUT 1 QUART ICE CREAM.

Peach Ice Cream: Substitute 4 or 5 peeled ripe peaches for the strawberries (mashed peaches should measure 2 cups). Stir ½ cup of the sugar into peaches.

The old-time ice-cream parlor has delighted (and dismayed!) ice-cream lovers for decades.

Going to Lindy's for cheesecake used to be as much a part of a visit to New York as seeing the Statue of Liberty. New Yorkers, too, stopped in at Lindy's after the theater or a day of shopping. Even before Lindy's closed, its famous recipe became the standard by which all other cheesecakes were measured.

Originally, the German immigrants' *käse kuchen* had a zwieback crust, and some still prefer that to pastry. Cheesecake always has been popular as a Jewish dessert after dairy meals.

The large number of servings in a rich cheesecake makes it a perfect choice when you're feeding a crowd. Sliced peaches or strawberries often are served on top with the whipped cream, but purists would say this is gilding the lily.

LINDY'S CHEESECAKE

1 cup all-purpose flour
¼ cup sugar
½ cup butter or margarine, softened
1 egg yolk
1 tablespoon grated lemon peel
5 packages (8 ounces each) cream cheese, softened
1¾ cups sugar
3 tablespoons flour

¼ teaspoon salt
1 tablespoon grated orange peel
1 tablespoon grated lemon peel
5 eggs
2 egg yolks
¼ cup whipping cream
¾ cup chilled whipping cream
⅓ cup toasted slivered almonds (optional)

Heat oven to 400°. Grease 9-inch springform pan lightly; remove bottom. Mix 1 cup flour, ¼ cup sugar, the butter, 1 egg yolk and 1 tablespoon lemon peel with hands. Press ⅓ of the mixture evenly on bottom of pan; place on baking sheet.

Bake until golden, 8 to 10 minutes; cool. Assemble bottom and side of pan; secure side. Press remaining mixture all the way up side of pan.

Heat oven to 475°. Beat cream cheese, 1¾ cups sugar, 3 tablespoons flour, the salt, orange peel, 1 tablespoon lemon peel and 2 of the eggs in large mixer bowl until smooth. Continue beating, adding remaining eggs and 2 egg yolks, 1 at a time. Beat in ¼ cup whipping cream on low speed. Pour into pan.

Bake 15 minutes. Reduce oven temperature to 200°. Bake 1 hour. Turn off oven; leave cheesecake in oven 15 minutes. Cool ½ hour. Refrigerate at least 12 hours.

Loosen cheesecake from side of pan; remove side, leaving cake on bottom of pan. Beat ¾ cup whipping cream in chilled bowl until stiff. Spread whipped cream over top of cheesecake and decorate with almonds.   20 TO 22 SERVINGS.

Pictured opposite.
Lindy's Cheesecake is not only distinguished by its origin but also by its unique pastry crust. It's delicious!

MAPLE FRANGO

4 egg yolks
½ cup maple-flavored syrup

1 cup chilled whipping cream
½ teaspoon vanilla

Beat egg yolks in small mixer bowl until thick and lemon colored, about 5 minutes. Heat syrup just to boiling. Pour about half of the hot syrup very slowly in thin stream into egg yolks, beating constantly on medium speed. Stir egg yolk mixture into hot syrup in saucepan. Cook over low heat, stirring constantly, until slightly thickened; cool.

Beat whipping cream in chilled bowl until stiff. Fold in vanilla and egg yolk mixture. Pour into ice cube tray. Freeze until firm, at least 4 hours.   6 SERVINGS.

LEMON SNOW PUDDING

1 cup sugar
1 envelope unflavored gelatin
1¼ cups water
1 teaspoon grated lemon peel

¼ cup lemon juice
3 egg whites
Dash of salt
Stirred Custard (below)

Mix sugar and gelatin in 3-quart saucepan; stir in water. Cook over medium heat, stirring constantly, just until mixture boils. Remove from heat; stir in lemon peel and juice. Chill in bowl of ice and water or refrigerate until mixture mounds slightly when dropped from spoon.

Beat egg whites and salt in small mixer bowl until soft peaks form. Beat gradually into gelatin mixture in saucepan; continue beating on high speed until mixture begins to hold its shape, about 4 minutes.

Pour into ungreased 5-cup mold or into 6 to 8 individual molds. Refrigerate until set, at least 2 hours. Unmold and serve with Stirred Custard.   6 TO 8 SERVINGS.

STIRRED CUSTARD
3 tablespoons sugar
Dash of salt
2 eggs, slightly beaten

1⅔ cups milk
½ teaspoon vanilla

Mix sugar, salt and eggs in top of double boiler. Stir in milk gradually. Place over simmering water (water should not touch bottom of pan). Cook, stirring constantly, until mixture coats metal spoon, about 20 minutes. Remove pan from simmering water; stir in vanilla. Place top of double boiler in bowl of cold water until custard is cool; refrigerate.

Until the advent of the home candy thermometer, after World War I, candy making was often a matter of know-how and good timing. But that didn't stop adventuresome American cooks from developing regional candy favorites—including some that need no cooking.

CANDIES

Cotton candy, Candy Apples on Sticks (page 152) and Corn Dogs (page 90) are part of the fun at a fair—or anywhere.

BOURBON BALLS

2 cups finely crushed vanilla
    wafers (about 50)
2 cups finely chopped pecans or
    walnuts (about 8 ounces)
2 cups powdered sugar

¼ cup cocoa
½ cup bourbon
¼ cup light corn syrup
Granulated sugar or chocolate
    shot

Mix crushed wafers, pecans, powdered sugar and cocoa. Stir in bourbon and corn syrup. Shape mixture into 1-inch balls. Roll in granulated sugar. Refrigerate in tightly covered container several days before serving.   ABOUT 5 DOZEN CANDIES.

Brandy Balls: Substitute ½ cup brandy for the bourbon.

Rum Balls: Substitute ½ cup light rum for the bourbon.

Because 60 to 65 percent of a date is natural sugar, it is known as the candy that grows on trees. And the brandy and pecans in this confection enhance the date's naturally sweet talents.

Date trees were first brought to the Western world by Spanish missionaries. Virtually all the dates that are sold in America come from the arid valley around Indio, California. There, a vast oasis of palms springs up from the desert, and unwary travelers arriving there might imagine they've come upon the set for an exotic movie. Actually, Indio is a lively town that revolves around the cultivation of this unique fruit. After the harvest each February, a festival is held and a Queen Scheherazade is crowned. In literature, Scheherazade told tales for 1001 nights, but Indio's Scheherazade could probably recite 1001 uses for the versatile date.

BRANDIED STUFFED DATES

1 pound pitted dates
1 cup brandy

1 cup pecan halves
Sugar (optional)

Soak dates in brandy, turning occasionally, until most of the brandy is absorbed, about 24 hours. Stuff a pecan half in each date; press to close. Roll in sugar. Refrigerate in tightly covered container.   ABOUT 1 POUND CANDIES.

FRESH COCONUT CANDY

1 coconut
2 cups sugar
¼ cup light corn syrup

½ teaspoon vanilla
10 to 12 candied cherries, cut in
    halves (optional)

Heat oven to 350°. Pierce eyes at 1 end of coconut with ice pick or
screwdriver; drain liquid. Add enough water, if necessary, to measure ¾ cup liquid; refrigerate. Place coconut in shallow pan.

Bake until coconut cracks in several places, about 30 minutes. Reduce oven temperature to 250°. Remove coconut shell (tapping
lightly, if necessary, with a hammer to break open) and pare brown
skin. Grate enough coconut to measure 1 cup, packed. (Use grater or
blender; do not shred.) Spread grated coconut on baking sheet. Dry
in oven 15 minutes; cool.

Heat sugar, corn syrup and coconut liquid to boiling in 2-quart
saucepan over medium heat, stirring constantly, until sugar is dissolved. Boil, without stirring, until candy thermometer registers 240°
(or until small amount of mixture dropped into very cold water
forms a soft ball that flattens when removed from water).

Pour onto moistened baking sheet, heatproof platter or marble slab
without scraping saucepan. Cool just until lukewarm. Scrape mixture toward center of baking sheet, using broad, stiff spatula or
wooden spoon. Spread mixture out again with spatula, using long,
firm strokes; continue spreading until mixture is firm and white.
Knead until smooth and creamy, working vanilla and grated coconut
into mixture.

Heat mixture over hot (not boiling) water until melted. Drop by
teaspoonfuls onto waxed paper. Top each candy with cherry half. Let
stand until dry. Wrap individually in plastic wrap or waxed paper.   20 TO 24 CANDIES.

CREOLE KISSES

2 egg whites
¾ cup sugar

1 teaspoon vanilla
¾ cup finely chopped pecans

Heat oven to 300°. Beat egg whites in small mixer bowl until foamy.
Beat in sugar, 1 tablespoon at a time; continue beating until very
stiff and glossy. Stir in vanilla and pecans. Drop mixture by rounded
teaspoonfuls 2 inches apart onto greased baking sheet.

Bake until dry, about 20 minutes (do not let candies brown). Immediately remove from baking sheet.   ABOUT 2 DOZEN CANDIES.

Pictured opposite.
Candy has always played an important role in satisfying America's sweet tooth. From top: Fresh
Coconut Candy and Creole Kisses
(both this page), Candied Orange
Peel (page 156), Bourbon Balls
(page 149) and Soldier's Fudge
(page 155).

Candy apples go with the memory of circus music and the first glimpse of the sword swallower. Those huge trays of brightly enameled apples are still irresistible to anyone under twelve. Making them at home for a Halloween or birthday party is fun even for the adults who assist.

Decorating a Christmas tree with gingerbread men, strings of cranberries and popcorn goes along naturally with making popcorn balls. Any of the balls not devoured on the spot can be wrapped and also hung as ornaments.

Though we tend to associate popcorn balls with Christmas, popcorn originally was eaten at Thanksgiving. At the first Thanksgiving feast, Chief Massasoit's brother went into the woods and came back with bowls of popped corn, which the Pilgrims had never seen before. It's been a popular American snack food ever since.

CANDY APPLES ON STICKS

8 to 10 medium red apples	1 teaspoon red food color
2 cups sugar	Few drops oil of cloves
¾ cup water	(optional)
½ cup light corn syrup	

Insert wooden skewer in blossom end of each apple. Mix sugar, water, corn syrup and food color in top of double boiler. Heat to boiling. Boil over direct heat, without stirring, until candy thermometer registers 280° (or until a few drops of syrup dropped into very cold water separate into threads that are hard but not brittle). Stir in oil of cloves. Immediately place over boiling water in bottom of double boiler. Dip apples quickly in syrup, twirling until completely coated. Place on well-greased baking sheet; cool.   8 TO 10 CANDY APPLES.

POPCORN BALLS

½ cup sugar	Few drops food color
½ cup light corn syrup	8 cups popped corn (about ½
¼ cup butter or margarine	cup unpopped)
½ teaspoon salt	Butter or margarine

Heat sugar, corn syrup, ¼ cup butter, the salt and food color to simmering in 4-quart Dutch oven over medium-high heat, stirring constantly. Add popped corn. Cook and stir until corn is well coated, about 3 minutes. Cool slightly.

Shape mixture into 2-inch balls with hands dipped in cold water. Place on waxed paper; cool. Wrap individually in plastic wrap or place in plastic bags and tie.   1 DOZEN POPCORN BALLS.

MOLASSES NUT BRITTLE

1 cup dark corn syrup
½ cup sugar
½ cup light molasses

¼ cup butter or margarine
2 cups salted peanuts
¼ teaspoon baking soda

Butter jelly roll pan, 15½x10½x1 inch. Heat corn syrup, sugar, molasses and butter to boiling in 2-quart saucepan, stirring constantly. Stir in peanuts; heat to boiling. Boil, stirring frequently, until candy thermometer registers 280° (or until small amount of mixture dropped into very cold water separates into threads that are hard but not brittle). Watch carefully so mixture does not burn. Immediately remove from heat; stir in baking soda. Pour into pan and quickly spread evenly. Cool; break candy into pieces.   ABOUT 1 POUND CANDY.

Great-grandmother's memories of taffy pulls were as treasured as her old dance cards and the thin flowers pressed in the family Bible. Perhaps she met her favorite beau while pulling the long strands of taffy at her best friend's house. Moreover, if taffy pulls were as common as the literature indicates, she probably consumed far too much candy over the course of her adolescence. Today, for a Scout troop or a slumber party, taffy pulls are a novel entertainment, and the candy is as delicious as ever.

Molasses Taffy is the long-standing American favorite, but others have their advocates. Butterscotch was a late nineteenth-century fancy, and the saltwater taffy sold along the boardwalk in Atlantic City, New Jersey, is still shipped home by visitors from all over the world. With each piece wrapped in a twist of pastel waxed paper, that easily recognizable candy has become a hallmark of its native city.

MOLASSES TAFFY

1½ cups sugar
1½ cups light molasses
½ cup water

3 tablespoons butter or
    margarine
1 tablespoon vinegar

Butter baking pan, 13x9x2 inches. Heat all ingredients to boiling in 3-quart saucepan over medium heat, stirring constantly. Boil, stirring constantly, until candy thermometer registers 256° (or until small amount of mixture dropped into very cold water forms a hard ball). Pour into pan; cool.

When just cool enough to handle, pull taffy until satiny, light in color and stiff. Butter hands lightly if taffy becomes sticky. Pull into long strips ½ inch wide. Cut with scissors into 1-inch pieces. ABOUT 1½ POUNDS CANDY.

OLD-FASHIONED SPONGE CANDY

1 cup sugar
1 cup dark corn syrup

1 tablespoon cider vinegar
1 tablespoon baking soda

Heat sugar, corn syrup and vinegar to boiling in 2-quart saucepan over medium heat, stirring constantly, until sugar is dissolved. Boil, without stirring, until candy thermometer registers 300° (or until small amount of mixture dropped into very cold water separates into threads that are hard and brittle). Remove from heat; stir in baking soda quickly and thoroughly. Pour mixture into ungreased baking pan, 13x9x2 inches. Do not spread. Cool; break candy into pieces. Serve as candy or crush and sprinkle over ice cream, pudding or fruit.   1 POUND CANDY (5 CUPS CRUSHED).

The origin of pralines is traced to a French diplomat named Plessis-Praslin, whose butler prepared special sugar-coated almonds to cure his master's indigestion. Whether they succeeded or not isn't known, but his recipe came to America with the French settlers in New Orleans. Using the native pecans and brown sugar, the Creoles' adaptation of that cure became their most famous confection, perhaps the sweetest of all sweets.

PRALINES

2 cups packed light brown
  sugar
1 cup granulated sugar
1¼ cups milk
¼ cup light corn syrup

⅛ teaspoon salt
1 teaspoon vanilla
1½ cups pecan halves (5½
  ounces)

Heat brown sugar, granulated sugar, milk, corn syrup and salt to boiling in 3-quart saucepan, stirring constantly. Boil, without stirring, until candy thermometer registers 236° (or until small amount of mixture dropped into very cold water forms a soft ball that flattens when removed from water). Immediately remove thermometer. Cool, without stirring, until saucepan is cool to the touch, about 1½ hours.

Add vanilla and pecans. Beat with spoon until mixture is slightly thickened and just coats pecans but does not lose its gloss, about 1 minute. Drop by spoonfuls onto waxed paper. (Try to divide pecans equally.) Cool until candies are firm and no longer glossy, 12 to 18 hours.

Wrap individually in plastic wrap or waxed paper and store in tightly covered container.   ABOUT 1½ DOZEN CANDIES.

Fudge and penuche are luscious tempters, fun to make and fun to eat. Both keep well if stored between layers of waxed paper in an airtight container. Over the years tons of these candies have traveled through the U.S. mails to homesick campers, students and servicemen and women.

Candy lovers everywhere savor the special attractions of holiday candies. This is the window of a Boston sweet shop at Eastertime.

SOLDIER'S FUDGE

1 can (14 ounces) sweetened
    condensed milk
1 package (12 ounces)
    semisweet chocolate chips
1 square (1 ounce) unsweetened
    chocolate (optional)

1 teaspoon vanilla
1½ cups chopped nuts
    (optional)

Butter baking pan, 8x8x2 inches. Heat milk, chocolate chips and unsweetened chocolate in 2-quart saucepan over low heat, stirring constantly, until chocolate is melted and mixture is smooth. Remove from heat; stir in vanilla and nuts. Spread mixture evenly in pan. Refrigerate until firm. Cut into 1-inch squares. 2 POUNDS CANDY (64 SQUARES).

PENUCHE

1 cup granulated sugar
1 cup packed brown sugar
⅔ cup milk
2 tablespoons corn syrup
¼ teaspoon salt

2 tablespoons butter or
    margarine
1 teaspoon vanilla
½ cup coarsely chopped
    nuts (optional)

Butter loaf pan, 9x5x3 inches. Heat granulated sugar, brown sugar, milk, corn syrup and salt to boiling in 2-quart saucepan over medium heat, stirring constantly, until sugars are dissolved. Boil, stirring occasionally, until candy thermometer registers 234° (or until small amount of mixture dropped into very cold water forms a soft ball that flattens when removed from water). Remove from heat; stir in butter. Cool, without stirring, to 120° or until bottom of saucepan is lukewarm.

Add vanilla. Beat with wooden spoon until mixture is thick and no longer glossy, 5 to 10 minutes. (Mixture will hold its shape when dropped from spoon.) Stir in nuts quickly. Spread mixture evenly in pan. Cool until firm. Cut into 1-inch squares. 1 POUND CANDY (32 SQUARES).

SUGARPLUMS

1 package (15 ounces) raisins
8 ounces dried apricots (about
    1½ cups)
8 ounces dried figs (about 1⅓
    cups)

8 ounces pitted prunes (about
    1⅓ cups)
1 cup pecans or walnuts
    (optional)
Sugar (optional)

Chop all ingredients except sugar in food grinder, using coarse blade; mix thoroughly. Shape mixture by rounded teaspoonfuls into balls. Roll in sugar. Let stand uncovered until dry, about 4 hours. Refrigerate in tightly covered container.   ABOUT 7 DOZEN CANDIES.

Fruit Bars: Press mixture evenly in buttered baking pan, 13x9x2 inches. Cut into bars, about 3x1 inch. Wrap in plastic wrap or waxed paper.   32 CANDIES.

CANDIED GRAPEFRUIT PEEL

2 large grapefruit
Water

About 2½ cups sugar

Score grapefruit peel into sixths with sharp knife. Remove peel carefully with fingers. Scrape white membrane from peel with spoon (back of peel will appear porous when membrane is removed). Cut peel into strips ¼ inch wide. Heat peel and 8 cups water to boiling in 3-quart saucepan; reduce heat. Simmer uncovered 30 minutes; drain. Repeat process 3 times.

Heat 2 cups of the sugar and 1 cup water to boiling in 2-quart saucepan, stirring until sugar is dissolved. Add peel. Simmer uncovered, stirring occasionally, 45 minutes. Drain thoroughly in strainer. Roll peel in remaining sugar; spread on waxed paper to dry.   ABOUT ⅓ POUND CANDY.

Candied Orange Peel: Substitute 3 large oranges for the grapefruit. Simmer in water twice.

Food photography director: George Ancona

Other photographs: Title page — Len Weiss (left), Subli/Photo Trends (center), R. T. Cook/Contemporary Color (right); page 8 — Grant Heilman; page 16 — Brian Seed/Black Star; page 37 — Bob McNerling/Taurus Photos; page 54 — Grant Heilman; page 64 — Harry Gruyaert/Woodfin Camp Assoc.; page 70 — Brian Seed/Black Star; page 75 — Todd Tarbox/EPA; page 82 — George Ancona; page 92 — Brian Seed/Black Star; page 97 — Ted Spiegel/Black Star; page 102 — John Running/Stock Boston; page 108 — George Ancona; page 114 — Michael Philip Manheim; page 129 — Grant Heilman; page 134 — Grant Heilman; page 145 — Gordon Baer/Black Star; page 149 — Dunn/DPI; page 155 — George Ancona.

BETTY CROCKER'S
SALADS

BETTY CROCKER'S
SALADS

Golden Press • New York
Western Publishing Company, Inc.
Racine, Wisconsin

Photography Director: Len Weiss
Illustrator: Helen Federico

CONTENTS

TOSSED GREEN SALADS

A collection with character — featuring Great Caesar Salad,
Flaming Spinach Salad and many more. With combos like these, you'll
find there's no such thing as a "plain" green salad.

5

FRUIT SALADS

Fresh, canned or frozen — fruits from all over the
world star in top-billed salads for every season of the year.
Serve as a first course, on the side or even as dessert.

21

VEGETABLE SALADS

For family fare or company occasions, vegetables take on
a new look and a new importance. In salads — artfully arranged,
gracefully molded or gently tossed. Take your choice.

41

MAIN-DISH SALADS

Menu-making made easy! Start with Marinated Beef and
Mushrooms, Oriental Chicken Salad or any of these full-size salads.
Just add a bread and a beverage to round out the meal.

53

Index
71

Dear Friend—

When you stop to think about it, salads just may be one of America's biggest contributions to the world's fare. Over the years we've reached into our gardens, cupboards and freezers to create an almost infinite variety of salads.

With their color, zest and contrast, salads are welcome anytime, anywhere—at buffet suppers, casual picnics, elegant luncheons, family meals. Particularly good choices for a party buffet are Cucumber Salad Mold or Chef's Smorgasbord Salad; picnics become *picniques* with Picnic Tomatoes or Lentil-Ham Salad; luncheon guests will dote on Crab-Shrimp-Avocado Salad or Tuna-Cantaloupe Salads.

Regular mealtime salads should be just as interesting as those served on special occasions. Why not enjoy different ones at different times? You can serve a salad at the start of the meal, with the meal, at the end of the meal, even as the meal.

An appetizer salad should be just that. Its intent is to stimulate the appetite, not satisfy it. As such, choose a salad that's light, with a delicate dressing. Tossed green or simple fruit or vegetable salads are first-course favorites.

A "go-along" salad should complement the main course as well as provide a contrast in color, texture and flavor—such as Eggplant Salad with roast lamb, Watercress and Asparagus Toss with chicken or Spinach and Sprouts Salad with baked ham.

An end-of-meal salad is usually on the sweet side, refreshing the taste buds and replacing the dessert course. Strawberry Freeze, 24-Hour Salad or any molded fruit salad will fill the bill.

Main-dish salads are, of course, heartier. They usually include meat, fish, poultry, cheese or eggs—singly or in combination.

On the following pages you'll find all of the salads mentioned here, as well as many other inviting, intriguing ideas and recipes. Included throughout, too, are coordinated dressings and helpful information—adding up to a complete guide for salads from start to serve.

Betty Crocker

TOSSED GREEN SALADS

Spectacular Ways to Bring on the Smiles

Turn over a new leaf with these crisp, light, health-full salads.
When you're fixing and mixing greens, what goes together, when, if
and how are all-important. So our directions are precise and our
dressings are just right. But allowing for personal preferences,
we've also included a wide-ranging make-your-own-salad chart.
You'll find that these salads, particularly, seem to bloom
with the little extra touch only you can toss in.

TOSSED SALAD CRISSCROSS

(for 6 to 8 servings)
Find your own favorites, then mix and match to suit the occasion.

Basic Salad Greens
Choose 1 or more to total 12 cups.

Iceberg lettuce	Leaf lettuce	Escarole	Endive (French
Boston lettuce	Red leaf lettuce	Spinach	or Belgian)
Bibb lettuce	Romaine	Watercress	Curly endive

Add Salad Sparkers
Choose 1 or more to total 1½ cups.

Fresh vegetables:	Radishes, sliced	Fruit:	Meat, fish and poultry:
Carrots, thinly	Tomato wedges	Apples, cut into	Ham, tongue or
sliced	Zucchini, sliced	wedges or sliced	cold cuts, cut into
Cauliflowerets	Cooked vegetables:	Avocados, sliced	strips or cubes
Celery, sliced or		Orange sections	Shrimp, crabmeat
chopped	Artichoke hearts or	Cheese:	or lobster, cut up
Cucumbers, sliced	bottoms, plain or		Turkey or chicken,
or cubed	marinated	Parmesan, grated	cut up
Green peppers,	Dilled green beans	Swiss or Cheddar,	
chopped or sliced	Green peas, beans	cut into strips	
Mushrooms, sliced	or sliced carrots,	or cubes	
Onions, sliced or	marinated		
chopped			

Toss with . . .
Shake to mix.

¼ cup vegetable oil,	2 tablespoons cider,	¾ teaspoon salt	1 small clove
olive oil or	wine or tarragon	⅛ to ¼ teaspoon	garlic, crushed
combination	vinegar	pepper	

Garnish with . . .
Choose 1 or 2.

Bacon, crisply fried,	Carrot curls	Croutons	Hard-cooked eggs,
crumbled	Cherry tomatoes	French fried onions	sliced
Blue cheese,	Cocktail onions	Gherkins, sliced	Olives, sliced
crumbled			Salted nuts

GREAT CAESAR SALAD

Garlic Croutons (below)
Coddled Egg (below)
1 clove garlic, cut into halves
8 anchovy fillets, cut up
⅓ cup olive oil
1 teaspoon Worcestershire sauce
½ teaspoon salt
¼ teaspoon dry mustard
Freshly ground pepper
1 large or 2 small bunches romaine, torn into bite-size pieces
1 lemon
⅓ cup grated Parmesan cheese

Prepare Garlic Croutons and Coddled Egg. Rub large wooden salad bowl with cut clove of garlic. Allow a few small pieces of garlic to remain in bowl if desired. Mix anchovies, oil, Worcestershire sauce, salt, mustard and pepper in bowl; toss with romaine until leaves glisten. Break egg onto salad. Squeeze lemon over salad; toss. Sprinkle croutons and cheese over salad; toss.

6 servings.

Garlic Croutons
Heat oven to 400°. Trim crusts from 4 slices white bread. Butter both sides of bread slices generously; sprinkle slices with ¼ teaspoon garlic powder. Cut into ½-inch cubes. Bake in ungreased baking pan, 13x9x2 inches, stirring occasionally, until golden brown and crisp, 10 to 15 minutes.

Coddled Egg
Place cold egg in warm water. Heat enough water to boiling to cover egg completely. Immerse egg in boiling water with spoon; remove from heat. Cover and let stand 30 seconds. Immediately cool egg in cold water to prevent further cooking.

CREAMY LETTUCE TOSS

Sour Cream Dressing (below)
12 slices bacon
1 medium head iceberg lettuce, torn into bite-size pieces
3 green onions (with tops), finely chopped

Prepare Sour Cream Dressing. Fry bacon until crisp; drain, reserving 2 tablespoons bacon fat. Crumble bacon. Toss lettuce, onions, bacon and reserved bacon fat; toss with dressing.

6 servings.

Sour Cream Dressing
½ cup dairy sour cream or unflavored yogurt
1 tablespoon sugar
1 tablespoon vinegar
½ teaspoon salt

Mix all ingredients. *½ cup dressing.*

SALADE PROVENÇALE

2 large heads iceberg lettuce, torn into bite-size pieces
8 ounces spinach, torn into bite-size pieces
2 jars (about 7 ounces each) marinated artichoke hearts
2 cans (3⅞ ounces each) pitted ripe olives, drained
1 bottle (8 ounces) herb salad dressing

Divide lettuce and spinach between 2 large plastic bags; refrigerate. Just before serving, add 1 jar artichoke hearts (with liquid), 1 can olives and half of the salad dressing to each bag. Close bags tightly; shake vigorously. Serve in large bowl.

12 servings.

TOSSED GREEN SALADS   **7**

GOURMET TOSSED GREEN SALAD

1 medium head iceberg lettuce, torn
  into bite-size pieces
4 ounces mushrooms, sliced
1 small cauliflower, separated into
  tiny flowerets
1 small Bermuda onion, thinly sliced
  and separated into rings
1 medium green pepper, chopped
½ cup sliced pimiento-stuffed olives
½ cup crumbled blue cheese
  Classic French Dressing (below)

Toss lettuce, mushrooms, cauliflowerets,
onion, green pepper, olives and cheese. Cover
and refrigerate at least 1 hour. Just before
serving, toss with Classic French Dressing.

8 to 10 servings.

Classic French Dressing
¼ cup olive oil, vegetable oil or
  combination
2 tablespoons wine or tarragon
  vinegar
¾ teaspoon salt
¼ teaspoon freshly ground pepper
¼ teaspoon monosodium glutamate
1 small clove garlic, finely chopped
  or crushed

Toss salad with oil until leaves glisten. Mix
remaining ingredients; toss with salad.

FANTASTIC GREEN SALAD
Pictured on page 17.

9 cups bite-size pieces mixed salad
  greens (romaine, red leaf lettuce,
  leaf lettuce)
1 cup crumbled Gorgonzola cheese
  (about 4 ounces)°
  Generous dash of pepper
¼ cup vegetable oil
¼ cup tarragon vinegar

Place salad greens and cheese in bowl;
sprinkle with pepper. Toss salad with oil
until leaves glisten. Pour vinegar on salad;
toss.

8 servings.

° Your favorite crumbly cheese (such as
blue or feta) can be substituted for the
Gorgonzola cheese. Or use 1 cup diced
Gruyère or sharp Cheddar cheese.

MIXED GREENS WITH GARLIC DRESSING

Garlic Dressing (below)
8 cups bite-size pieces mixed salad greens (lettuce, curly endive, spinach)
1 cup cheese-and-garlic croutons

Prepare Garlic Dressing; toss with salad greens. Sprinkle with croutons.

4 servings.

Garlic Dressing
2 tablespoons vegetable oil
1 tablespoon plus 1½ teaspoons vinegar
1 teaspoon salt
¼ teaspoon prepared mustard
¼ teaspoon Worcestershire sauce
1 small clove garlic, crushed
Dash of pepper

Shake all ingredients in tightly covered jar.
About ¼ cup dressing.

FLAMING SPINACH SALAD
Pictured on page 18.

12 ounces spinach, torn into bite-size pieces
¼ cup sliced celery
2 tablespoons sliced green onions
4 slices bacon, cut into ½-inch pieces
2 tablespoons packed brown sugar
2 tablespoons vinegar
¼ teaspoon salt
⅛ teaspoon dried tarragon leaves
Dash of pepper
2 tablespoons brandy

Place spinach, celery and onions in serving dish. Fry bacon until crisp; drain on paper towels and reserve. Remove all but 1 tablespoon bacon fat from skillet. Stir brown sugar, vinegar, salt, tarragon and pepper into fat in skillet. Heat just to boiling; stir in bacon. Heat until bacon is hot; pour on spinach, celery and onions. Heat brandy just until warm; ignite and pour on salad. Toss and serve immediately.

4 servings.

iceberg

French endive

Boston

red leaf

curly endive

GREENS AND TOMATO-TOMATO

Pumpernickel Croutons (below)
Tomato Dressing (below)
10 cups bite-size pieces mixed salad greens (iceberg lettuce, curly endive)
2 tomatoes, chopped

Prepare Pumpernickel Croutons and Tomato Dressing. Toss salad greens, tomatoes and dressing; sprinkle with croutons.

8 servings.

Pumpernickel Croutons
Heat oven to 400°. Trim crusts from 4 slices pumpernickel or dark rye bread. Brush both sides of bread slices generously with vegetable oil or butter or margarine, softened; sprinkle slices with salt and 1 teaspoon dried dill weed or about 1 tablespoon snipped fresh dill weed. Cut into ½-inch cubes. Bake in ungreased baking pan, 13x 9x2 inches, stirring occasionally, until golden brown and crisp, 10 to 15 minutes.

Tomato Dressing
½ can (10¾-ounce size) condensed tomato soup (about ½ cup)
⅓ cup vegetable oil
¼ cup packed brown sugar
¼ cup vinegar
1 tablespoon snipped chives
1 teaspoon onion salt
1 teaspoon paprika
½ teaspoon dry mustard

Mix all ingredients. *About 1¼ cups dressing.*

TOSSED GODDESS BEAN SPROUTS

Green Goddess Dressing (below)
8 cups bite-size pieces Bibb lettuce
1 can (16 ounces) bean sprouts, rinsed and drained

Prepare Green Goddess Dressing; toss with lettuce and bean sprouts.

8 servings.

Green Goddess Dressing
¾ cup mayonnaise or salad dressing
2 tablespoons finely snipped parsley
1 tablespoon finely chopped onion
2 or 3 anchovy fillets, finely chopped, or 2 to 3 teaspoons anchovy paste
2 teaspoons tarragon wine vinegar
1 clove garlic, crushed

Mix all ingredients. *About 1 cup dressing.*

WATERCRESS AND ASPARAGUS TOSS
Pictured on page 17.

Lime Dressing (below)
3 bunches watercress, torn into bite-size pieces
1 pound asparagus, cut diagonally into thin slices

Prepare Lime Dressing; toss with watercress and asparagus.

6 servings.

Lime Dressing
¼ cup vegetable oil
Juice of 1 lime (about 1 tablespoon plus 1½ teaspoons)
½ teaspoon salt

Shake all ingredients in tightly covered jar. *About ⅓ cup dressing.*

KNOW YOUR SALAD GREENS

*There's a wide world of greens out there. Get to know them—
they're the basics for a prize-winning salad bowl.*

☐ Take lettuce for starters. Four main groups of its many varieties are commonly available: crisphead (notably iceberg); butterhead (including Boston and Bibb), with soft, pliable leaves; romaine (also called cos), with crisp, elongated dark leaves; and leaf lettuce (red or green), with tender "leafy" leaves that do not form heads.

☐ Then there's the endive family. It includes curly endive (sometimes miscalled chicory), a frilly, narrow-leaved, "bushy" type; escarole, a less frilly, broader-leaved variety; and Belgian or French endive, a type with narrow, blanched leaves that grow in compact, upright clusters.

☐ Now add watercress, spinach, mustard greens, celery leaves, beet tops, Chinese cabbage, nasturtium leaves and . . . and . . . and. . . .

☐ Whatever the green, it should look fresh and perky when purchased. Iceberg lettuce should be firm but resilient, "giving" slightly when squeezed. When buying butterhead and leaf lettuce, look for a bright green color (the deeper the green, the greater the vitamin A content).

☐ Store all greens in the refrigerator—in a covered container, a plastic bag or the crisper section. Watercress, parsley and fresh herbs, however, should be refrigerated in large screwtop jars. These and iceberg lettuce and romaine will keep up to a week; most other greens will droop within a few days.

☐ Wash greens several hours before using—they need time to get crisp. Wash well under running cold water, then shake off the excess moisture. To remove remaining moisture, toss in a kitchen towel or pat dry with paper towels. Return to the refrigerator.

☐ If you plan to use iceberg lettuce within a day or so, remove the core before washing. Strike the core end against a flat surface, then twist and lift out the core with your fingers. Hold the head, cored end up, under running cold water to separate and clean the leaves. Turn right side up to drain well; refrigerate in a plastic bag or in a bowl with an airtight lid.

☐ Tear (do not cut) salad greens into bite-size pieces. Exceptions? Serve iceberg lettuce cut into slices or wedges; cut Belgian endive lengthwise into quarters, crosswise into slices or simply strip off the leaves. With easily bruised butterheads, try to use the whole leaves; save the outer ones for lettuce "beds," use the small inner ones for salad.

☐ Try to use a variety of greens in tossed salads. Mix the light with the dark, the crisp with the tender. Team pale iceberg with dark-green spinach, romaine and/or curly endive. Red leaf lettuce adds color and delicate flavor. Accent with beet greens, red cabbage, fresh herbs and other "sparkers."

☐ Pour on dressing *just* before serving—using only enough to coat the leaves lightly. Toss.

GARBANZO
AND ZUCCHINI TOSS

1 bunch leaf lettuce, torn into
   bite-size pieces
1 bunch romaine, torn into
   bite-size pieces
1 can (15 ounces) garbanzo beans,
   drained
2 medium zucchini, sliced
⅓ cup bottled Italian salad dressing
   Freshly ground pepper

Toss lettuce, romaine, beans, zucchini and
salad dressing. Sprinkle with pepper.

10 to 12 servings.

ZUCCHINI SALAD

1 medium head iceberg lettuce, torn
   into bite-size pieces
1 small bunch romaine, torn into
   bite-size pieces
¼ cup olive oil or vegetable oil
2 medium zucchini, sliced
3 green onions, sliced
1 cup sliced radishes
3 tablespoons crumbled blue cheese
   (optional)
2 tablespoons tarragon or wine
   vinegar
¾ teaspoon salt
¼ teaspoon monosodium glutamate
1 small clove garlic, crushed
   Generous dash of pepper

Toss lettuce and romaine with oil until
leaves glisten. Add zucchini, onions, radishes
and cheese. Mix vinegar, salt, monosodium
glutamate, garlic and pepper; toss with salad.

6 to 8 servings.

SPINACH
AND SPROUTS SALAD

   Vinegar-Oil Dressing (below)
1 package (10 ounces) frozen
   Brussels sprouts
2 cups cauliflower pieces
10 ounces spinach, torn into bite-size
   pieces

Prepare Vinegar-Oil Dressing. Rinse frozen
Brussels sprouts under running cold water to
separate; drain. Toss Brussels sprouts and
cauliflower. Pour dressing on Brussels sprouts
and cauliflower. Cover and refrigerate at
least 4 hours, stirring occasionally. Just before serving, toss with spinach.

6 to 8 servings.

Vinegar-Oil Dressing
⅓ cup red wine vinegar
¼ cup vegetable oil
1 tablespoon lemon juice
½ teaspoon salt
¼ teaspoon dry mustard
¼ teaspoon pepper

Shake all ingredients in tightly covered jar.
About ⅔ cup dressing.

COLOR TOSS

¾ cup mayonnaise or salad dressing
½ cup dairy sour cream
1 small head iceberg lettuce, torn
   into bite-size pieces
1 package (10 ounces) frozen green
   peas
½ cup shredded Cheddar cheese
   (about 2 ounces)
½ cup grated carrot
3 tablespoons imitation bacon
2 tablespoons chopped green onions
½ teaspoon salt

Mix mayonnaise and sour cream; toss with
remaining ingredients.

8 servings.

PICKLE-CHEESE TOSS

  Pickle Dressing (below)
12 cups bite-size pieces mixed
   salad greens
 4 medium dill pickles, cut diagonally
   into slices
 8 ounces mozzarella cheese, cut
   into ⅜-inch pieces
 1 cup salted peanuts

Prepare Pickle Dressing; toss with salad
greens, pickles and cheese. Sprinkle with
peanuts.

12 servings.

Pickle Dressing
⅓ cup vegetable oil
3 tablespoons dill pickle juice
1 teaspoon salt
¼ teaspoon pepper

Shake all ingredients in tightly covered jar.
About ½ cup dressing.

SPINACH-AVOCADO SALAD

  Avocado Dressing (below)
10 ounces spinach, torn into bite-size
   pieces
¼ cup toasted sesame seed (see note)
 2 hard-cooked eggs, chopped
 1 small onion, thinly sliced and
   separated into rings
½ avocado, cut into ½-inch pieces
 1 hard-cooked egg, sliced

Prepare Avocado Dressing; toss with spinach, sesame seed, chopped eggs, onion and
avocado. Garnish with egg slices.

6 to 8 servings.

Note: To toast sesame seed, heat oven to
350°. Bake in ungreased baking pan, stirring
occasionally, until golden, 8 to 10 minutes.

Avocado Dressing
½ avocado
 2 to 3 tablespoons lemon juice
¼ cup vegetable oil
½ teaspoon salt
   Dash of pepper

Mash avocado with lemon juice; stir in remaining ingredients. *About ⅔ cup dressing.*

HEAD-START SALAD DRESSINGS

Take full advantage of prepared dressings but give them a hint of "homemade." You can add that personal touch with any of the following combinations:

For Vegetable Salads

☐ ¼ cup oil-and-vinegar salad dressing and ¼ teaspoon chili powder

☐ ¼ cup oil-and-vinegar salad dressing and ¼ teaspoon dried oregano leaves

☐ ¼ cup oil-and-vinegar salad dressing and ¼ teaspoon ground savory

☐ ¼ cup oil-and-vinegar salad dressing and ¼ teaspoon dried thyme leaves

☐ ½ cup mayonnaise or salad dressing and ¼ cup catsup

☐ ½ cup mayonnaise or salad dressing, ¼ cup chili sauce, 1 drop red pepper sauce and dash of chili powder

☐ ½ cup mayonnaise or salad dressing and ¼ cup frozen whipped topping (thawed)

For Fruit Salads

☐ ¼ cup creamy blue cheese salad dressing and 1 tablespoon apricot preserves

☐ ¼ cup creamy blue cheese salad dressing and 2 tablespoons creamy French salad dressing

☐ ¼ cup creamy blue cheese salad dressing and ⅛ teaspoon curry powder

☐ ¼ cup fruit salad dressing and ¼ teaspoon sesame seed

☐ ¼ cup French salad dressing and ⅛ teaspoon celery seed

☐ ½ cup mayonnaise or salad dressing, 2 tablespoons cranberry juice cocktail and ¼ teaspoon poppy seed

BANANA-SPINACH TOSS

2 tablespoons butter or margarine, softened
2 firm medium bananas, thinly sliced
  Salt
  Banana–Poppy Seed Dressing (below)
5 ounces spinach, torn into bite-size pieces

Heat oven to 350°. Brush bottom of jelly roll pan, 15½x10½x1 inch, with butter. Spread banana slices in single layer in pan; sprinkle with salt. Bake uncovered until golden brown and crisp, 25 to 30 minutes. Immediately remove from pan; drain on paper towels.

Prepare Banana–Poppy Seed Dressing; toss with spinach and bananas.

4 servings.

Banana–Poppy Seed Dressing
½ medium banana, mashed
2 tablespoons vegetable oil
1 tablespoon lemon juice
1½ teaspoons sugar
¼ teaspoon dry mustard
⅛ teaspoon salt
1½ teaspoons poppy seed

Mix banana, oil, lemon juice, sugar, mustard and salt. Stir in poppy seed. *About ½ cup dressing.*

ENDIVE-FRUIT SALAD

  Mallow Dressing (below)
½ bunch curly endive, torn into bite-size pieces
1 package (about 10 ounces) frozen melon balls, partially thawed and drained, or 1 cup fresh melon balls
2 apples, chopped

Prepare Mallow Dressing; toss with remaining ingredients.

8 servings.

Mallow Dressing
½ cup marshmallow crème
1 tablespoon plus 1½ teaspoons orange juice
2 tablespoons mayonnaise or salad dressing
⅛ teaspoon salt

Beat marshmallow crème and orange juice. Stir in mayonnaise and salt. *About ½ cup dressing.*

MANDARIN SALAD

¼ cup sliced almonds
1 tablespoon plus 1 teaspoon sugar
  Mandarin Dressing (below)
¼ medium head iceberg lettuce
¼ medium bunch romaine
2 medium stalks celery, chopped
2 green onions (with tops), thinly
  sliced
1 can (11 ounces) mandarin orange
  segments, drained

Cook almonds and sugar over low heat, stirring constantly, until sugar is melted and almonds are coated. Cool and break apart.

Prepare Mandarin Dressing. Tear lettuce and romaine into bite-size pieces; toss with dressing, celery, onions, orange segments and almonds.

4 to 6 servings.

Mandarin Dressing
¼ cup vegetable oil
2 tablespoons sugar
2 tablespoons vinegar
1 tablespoon snipped parsley
½ teaspoon salt
  Dash of pepper
  Dash of red pepper sauce

Shake all ingredients in tightly covered jar.
About ⅓ cup dressing.

SUNNY CITRUS SALAD

  Blue Cheese–Lemon Dressing
  (below)
1 small clove garlic, cut into halves
2 medium grapefruit, pared and
  sectioned
1 small head iceberg lettuce, torn
  into bite-size pieces
1 small bunch curly endive, romaine
  or chicory, torn into bite-size pieces
1 can (11 ounces) mandarin orange
  segments, drained
1 jar (2 ounces) sliced pimiento,
  drained
¼ teaspoon salt
  Freshly ground pepper

Prepare Blue Cheese–Lemon Dressing. Rub large salad bowl with cut clove of garlic. Place grapefruit sections, lettuce, endive, orange segments and pimiento in bowl; sprinkle with salt. Toss with dressing; sprinkle with pepper.

8 to 10 servings.

Blue Cheese-Lemon Dressing
¼ cup crumbled blue cheese (about
  1 ounce)
¼ cup vegetable oil
⅓ cup dairy sour cream
1 tablespoon lemon juice
¼ teaspoon grated lemon peel
¼ teaspoon garlic salt
¼ teaspoon salt
  Dash of monosodium glutamate

Mash cheese with fork. Stir in oil; beat until mixture is smooth. Stir in remaining ingredients. Cover and refrigerate at least 1 hour. *About ¾ cup dressing.*

Tossed greens — but with a difference. Clockwise from top left: Antipasto Toss (page 20), Fantastic Green Salad (page 8), Watercress and Asparagus Toss (page 10).

Flaming Spinach Salad (page 9) — sure to impress. Ignite the brandy and toss the salad at the table.

GRAPE-PEA SALAD

Creamy Oil Dressing (below)
½ head iceberg lettuce, torn into
   bite-size pieces
½ medium head red or green
   cabbage, coarsely shredded
1 cup fresh green peas or frozen
   green peas, thawed and drained
1 cup seedless green grapes

Prepare Creamy Oil Dressing; toss with remaining ingredients.

5 or 6 servings.

Creamy Oil Dressing
2 tablespoons vegetable oil
1 tablespoon red wine vinegar
1 teaspoon mayonnaise or salad
   dressing
¼ teaspoon salt
⅛ teaspoon lemon pepper
   Dash of paprika

Shake all ingredients in tightly covered jar.
¼ cup dressing.

ORANGE TOSS

2 cans (11 ounces each) mandarin
   orange segments, drained
½ small head iceberg lettuce,
   coarsely shredded
2 green onions, thinly sliced
   Bottled sweet-and-sour salad dressing

Reserve 4 orange segments. Toss remaining segments with lettuce. Divide lettuce mixture among 4 salad bowls; sprinkle with sliced onions. Garnish each salad with reserved orange segment; drizzle small amount salad dressing over each salad.

4 servings.

MINTED PINEAPPLE TOSS

Citrus Dressing (below)
½ head iceberg lettuce, torn into
   bite-size pieces
¼ bunch curly endive, torn into
   bite-size pieces
1 can (13¼ ounces) pineapple chunks,
   drained
½ medium green pepper, chopped
1 large stalk celery, chopped
¼ cup toasted broken walnuts
   (see note)
2 teaspoons snipped mint leaves

Prepare Citrus Dressing; toss with lettuce, endive, pineapple, green pepper, celery and walnuts. Garnish with mint leaves.

6 servings.

Note: To toast walnuts, heat oven to 350°. Bake in ungreased baking pan, stirring occasionally, until golden, about 10 minutes.

Citrus Dressing
¼ cup vegetable oil
2 tablespoons orange marmalade
2 tablespoons lemon juice
¾ teaspoon salt
   Dash of pepper
   Dash of red pepper sauce

Shake all ingredients in tightly covered jar.
½ cup dressing.

TOSSED GREEN SALADS **19**

ANTIPASTO TOSS

Pictured on page 17.

1 can (15 ounces) garbanzo beans,
  drained
1 jar (about 7 ounces) marinated
  artichoke hearts
¼ cup pitted ripe olives, drained
  and sliced
½ cup bottled herb-and-garlic or
  Italian salad dressing
2 bunches romaine, torn into bite-size
  pieces
1 bunch leaf lettuce, torn into
  bite-size pieces
2 hard-cooked eggs, sliced
½ cup sliced pepperoni
  Freshly ground pepper

Toss beans, artichoke hearts (with liquid), olives and salad dressing. Top with romaine and lettuce. Arrange eggs and pepperoni on salad greens; sprinkle with pepper. Cover and refrigerate no longer than 4 hours. Toss just before serving.

8 servings.

GLOSSY RED, WHITE AND GREEN SALAD

  Cocktail Sauce (below)
4 ounces spinach, torn into bite-size
  pieces
1 can (4½ ounces) small shrimp,
  drained
4 ounces mushrooms, sliced
1 cup cauliflowerets, cut into ½-inch
  pieces

Prepare Cocktail Sauce; toss with remaining ingredients.

6 servings.

Cocktail Sauce
½ cup chili sauce
1 teaspoon prepared horseradish
1 teaspoon lemon juice
¼ teaspoon Worcestershire sauce
  Dash of salt
  Dash of pepper

Shake all ingredients in tightly covered jar.
½ cup dressing.

SHRIMP COCKTAIL TOSS

Toss about 6 ounces spinach, torn into bite-size pieces, with 1 jar (about 4 ounces) shrimp cocktail.°

6 servings.

°1 can (4½ ounces) small shrimp, drained, and ¼ cup cocktail sauce can be substituted for the shrimp cocktail.

Note: For a two-tone salad, use half Bibb lettuce and half spinach.

FRUIT SALADS

Stand-out Attractions to Brighten Your Table

Splashy reds, glistening yellows and oranges,
soft colors, bold colors — almost reason enough to serve these salads.
But pretty as they are, fruit salads offer a wealth of other good things:
texture contrasts, from juicy lushness to solid crunchiness;
taste contrasts, from sweet to tart. And, naturally, literally an
orchard of vitamins and minerals. For you and others,
there are hardly any salads more rewarding than
these appetite teasers and pleasers.

APPLE-CHEESE WEDGES

⅓ cup pasteurized process smoky-flavored cheese spread
1 tablespoon finely chopped walnuts
2 apples, cut into wedges
   Salad greens

Mix cheese and walnuts. Spread 1 side of each apple wedge with cheese mixture. Put wedges together to make 4 apple halves. Serve each apple half rounded side up on salad greens.

4 servings.

WALDORF SALADS

2 medium apples, coarsely chopped
2 stalks celery, chopped
⅓ cup coarsely chopped walnuts
½ cup mayonnaise or salad dressing
4 to 6 lettuce cups
   Apple slices

Mix chopped apples, celery, walnuts and mayonnaise. Spoon salad into lettuce cups. Garnish with apple slices.

4 to 6 servings.

VARIATIONS

Curried Waldorf Salads: Stir ½ teaspoon curry powder into the mayonnaise.

Maple Nut Waldorf Salads: Stir ½ teaspoon maple flavoring and ¼ teaspoon ground cinnamon into the mayonnaise.

Molasses Waldorf Salads: Stir 1 tablespoon molasses into the mayonnaise.

Peanut Butter Waldorf Salads: Decrease mayonnaise to ⅓ cup and stir in ¼ cup crunchy peanut butter. Substitute peanuts for the walnuts.

MOONGLOW APRICOT SALAD

1 can (17 ounces) apricot halves, drained (reserve 1 teaspoon syrup)
1 package (3 ounces) cream cheese, softened
¼ cup cut-up dates
⅛ teaspoon ground ginger
⅓ cup finely chopped pecans
   Lettuce leaves

Mix reserved apricot syrup, the cream cheese, dates and ginger. Drop mixture by teaspoonfuls into pecans; roll around to coat completely. Shape into about 1-inch balls. Place 1 ball in each apricot half; arrange on lettuce.

4 servings.

CHERRY-GRAPE SALADS

1 can (16 ounces) pitted dark sweet cherries, drained
1 can (8¾ ounces) seedless green grapes, drained
1 carton (8 ounces) unflavored yogurt
1 cup flaked coconut
1 cup miniature marshmallows
6 lettuce cups

Mix cherries, grapes, yogurt, coconut and marshmallows. Cover and refrigerate at least 4 hours. Spoon salad into lettuce cups.

6 servings.

ORANGE-ONION SALADS

Ruby Blue Cheese Dressing (below)
3 medium oranges, pared and sliced
½ medium Bermuda onion, thinly sliced
Curly endive

Prepare Ruby Blue Cheese Dressing. Arrange 3 orange slices and 1 onion slice on endive on each of 6 salad plates; drizzle 2 to 3 tablespoons dressing over each salad.

6 servings.

Ruby Blue Cheese Dressing
⅔ cup crumbled blue cheese (about 3 ounces)
½ cup vegetable oil
⅓ cup catsup
3 tablespoons vinegar
1 tablespoon finely chopped onion
½ teaspoon salt
½ teaspoon pepper
½ teaspoon dry mustard
½ teaspoon paprika

Shake all ingredients in tightly covered jar. Refrigerate at least 3 hours. Shake before serving. *About 1 cup dressing.*

GRAPEFRUIT-ORANGE SALADS

1 grapefruit, pared and sectioned
1 can (11 ounces) mandarin orange segments, drained
1 cup bite-size pieces lettuce
¼ cup chopped celery
¼ cup mayonnaise or salad dressing
½ teaspoon instant minced onion
½ teaspoon lemon juice or vinegar
¼ teaspoon celery seed
Dash of salt
5 lettuce cups
Pomegranate seeds or chopped pimiento

Cut grapefruit sections into halves. Toss with orange segments, lettuce, celery, mayonnaise, onion, lemon juice, celery seed and salt. Spoon salad into lettuce cups; sprinkle with pomegranate seeds.

5 servings.

FRUIT SALADS 23

SHADY GLADE SALAD

No-Oil Dressing (below)
3 medium oranges, pared, sliced
  and cut into halves
5 medium radishes, sliced
2 stalks celery, cut diagonally
  into slices
3 green onions, sliced
1 medium green pepper, cut into
  1-inch strips
1 medium cucumber, sliced

Prepare No-Oil Dressing; pour on remaining ingredients in shallow glass or plastic dish. Cover and refrigerate at least 1 hour. Drain salad before serving.

8 servings.

No-Oil Dressing
⅔ cup water
½ cup sugar
⅓ cup vinegar
½ teaspoon salt
¼ teaspoon pepper

Shake all ingredients in tightly covered jar. *About 1⅓ cups dressing.*

PEACH SALADS

⅓ cup cut-up dried prunes
6 peach halves
  Salad greens
3 tablespoons slivered almonds
1 teaspoon grated lemon peel
1 cup frozen whipped topping, thawed
1 tablespoon slivered almonds

Place prunes in jar. Pour enough boiling water on prunes to cover. Cover and refrigerate at least 24 hours.

Arrange peach halves on salad greens. Stir prunes, 3 tablespoons almonds and the lemon peel into whipped topping. Spoon topping mixture onto peach halves. Garnish with 1 tablespoon almonds.

6 servings.

FRESH PEACH AND PEAR SALADS

1 package (3¾ ounces) vanilla instant
  pudding and pie filling
½ cup milk
⅓ cup dairy sour cream
1 package (10 ounces) frozen
  raspberries, thawed and drained
  (reserve syrup)
6 peaches, sliced
6 pears, sliced
  Leaf lettuce

Beat pudding and pie filling (dry), milk, sour cream and reserved raspberry syrup until smooth. Reserve 8 raspberries; fold remaining raspberries into pudding mixture. Refrigerate at least 1 hour.

Fold peaches and pears into raspberry mixture. Spoon salad onto lettuce and garnish with reserved raspberries.

8 servings.

PEACH SALADS
WITH MOLASSES CREAM

   Molasses Cream (below)
6 peaches, cut into halves°
   Leaf lettuce
3 tablespoons chopped nuts

Prepare Molasses Cream. Place peach halves cut sides up on lettuce; sprinkle with nuts. Top with Molasses Cream.

6 servings.

°12 canned peach halves, well drained, can be substituted for the fresh peaches.

Molasses Cream
Mix ½ cup frozen whipped topping, thawed, and 1 teaspoon molasses. *About ½ cup dressing.*

HULA SALADS

1 cup creamed cottage cheese
3 tablespoons raisins, nuts or cut-up
   dates
   Salad greens
1 can (8¼ ounces) sliced pineapple,
   drained
   Flaked or shredded coconut
4 maraschino cherries

Mix cottage cheese and raisins. Spoon ¼ cup of the cottage cheese–raisin mixture onto salad greens on each of 4 salad plates. Top with pineapple slice; sprinkle with coconut. Place cherry in center of each pineapple slice.

4 servings.

BURMESE
RICE-FRUIT SALAD

1 can (13¼ ounces) crushed pineapple,
   drained
1 cup chilled cooked rice
½ cup flaked coconut
¼ cup golden raisins
½ cup chilled whipping cream
2 tablespoons sugar
½ teaspoon vanilla
½ teaspoon almond extract
¼ teaspoon ground ginger
   Dash of salt
3 tablespoons slivered almonds
   Salad greens
1 tablespoon slivered almonds

Mix pineapple, rice, coconut and raisins. Beat cream, sugar, vanilla, almond extract, ginger and salt in chilled small mixer bowl until stiff; fold into rice mixture. Stir in 3 tablespoons slivered almonds. Spoon salad onto salad greens and garnish with 1 tablespoon slivered almonds.

4 to 6 servings.

PINEAPPLE FRUIT SALAD

1 pineapple
1 cup pitted dark sweet cherries
1 cup cantaloupe or other melon balls
  Fluffy Coconut Mayonnaise (below)

Cut pineapple lengthwise into halves through green top. Cut out pineapple, leaving ½-inch walls. Cut pineapple into bite-size pieces, removing any eyes and fibrous core. Mix pineapple pieces, cherries and cantaloupe balls; spoon into pineapple shells. Cover and refrigerate at least 1 hour.

Prepare Fluffy Coconut Mayonnaise; serve with salad.

4 to 6 servings.

Fluffy Coconut Mayonnaise
Mix 1½ cups frozen whipped topping, thawed, and ⅓ cup mayonnaise or salad dressing. Top with ¼ cup toasted flaked coconut (see note). *About 1⅓ cups dressing.*

Note: To toast coconut, heat oven to 350°. Bake in ungreased baking pan, stirring occasionally, until golden, 5 to 7 minutes.

PINK PINEAPPLE-BEET SALADS

1 jar (16 ounces) pickled beets,
  drained and chopped
1 can (13¼ ounces) pineapple chunks,
  drained
1 cup flaked coconut
1 cup miniature marshmallows
1 cup dairy sour cream
6 lettuce cups

Mix beets, pineapple, coconut, marshmallows and sour cream. Cover and refrigerate at least 4 hours. Spoon salad into lettuce cups.

6 servings.

MACARONI-PINEAPPLE TOSS

1 package (7 ounces) elbow macaroni
2 cans (20 ounces each) crushed
  pineapple, drained
1 cup shredded Cheddar cheese
  (about 4 ounces)
1 large stalk celery, chopped
¾ cup mayonnaise or salad dressing
⅓ cup quartered maraschino cherries

Cook macaroni as directed on package; drain. Rinse with cold water. Toss with remaining ingredients. Cover and refrigerate at least 1 hour.

6 servings.

24-HOUR SALAD

Old-fashioned Fruit Dressing (below)
1 can (17 ounces) dark sweet cherries, drained
2 cans (13¼ ounces each) pineapple chunks, drained (reserve 2 tablespoons syrup)
3 oranges, pared, sectioned and cut up
1 cup miniature marshmallows

Prepare Old-fashioned Fruit Dressing. Mix fruits and marshmallows; toss with dressing. Cover and refrigerate at least 12 hours.

8 to 10 servings.

Old-fashioned Fruit Dressing
2 eggs, beaten
2 tablespoons sugar
2 tablespoons vinegar or lemon juice
2 tablespoons reserved pineapple syrup
1 tablespoon butter or margarine
   Dash of salt
¾ cup chilled whipping cream

Heat eggs, sugar, vinegar, pineapple syrup, butter and salt just to boiling, stirring constantly. Remove from heat; cool. Beat cream in chilled small mixer bowl until stiff. Fold egg mixture into whipped cream. *About 2 cups dressing.*

WINTER FRUIT SALAD
Pictured on page 35.

Honey-Lime Dressing (below) or lime-flavored yogurt
1 avocado, cut into ¼-inch slices
   Lemon juice
   Salt
1 grapefruit, pared and sectioned°
1 apple, cut into ¼-inch slices°
   Spinach leaves
½ cup whole cranberry sauce

Prepare Honey-Lime Dressing. Sprinkle avocado slices with lemon juice and salt. Arrange avocado slices, grapefruit sections and apple slices in circle on spinach leaves. Spoon cranberry sauce into center. Serve with dressing.

4 servings.

°2 oranges and 2 bananas can be substituted for the grapefruit and apple.

Honey-Lime Dressing
2 tablespoons honey
2 tablespoons vegetable oil
2 tablespoons frozen limeade concentrate, thawed
¼ teaspoon celery seed

Mix all ingredients until smooth. *About ⅓ cup dressing.*

FRUIT SALADS **27**

TROPICAL AND EXOTIC FRUITS

Add a touch of the tropics to your fruit bowls and salads—no matter where you live. In today's markets, the world is virtually at your fingertips. But how and what to buy?

☐ Avocados will be unblemished if you anticipate their use by several days and buy firm ones. Let ripen at room temperature; when they yield to gentle pressure, they're ready to eat or to store in the refrigerator, where they'll keep for several days. Halved lengthwise and pitted, avocados serve as edible salad bowls; pared and sliced or cut up, they are added to the salad. To prepare an avocado, cut lengthwise, right around the hard center seed. Rotate the halves in opposite directions to help separate. If the seed won't dislodge, whack it with a sharp knife, twist the knife and lift out the seed. Strip off the avocado skin or, if necessary, pare. Sprinkle cut avocados with lemon or lime juice—the flesh discolors easily. Store an unused half, with the pit still in, closely wrapped in a plastic bag. To mash avocados, use a fork, sieve, blender or food mill.

☐ Bananas ripen better off the plant than on it. Select slightly green fruit and allow to mature as a cheerful centerpiece. When you think the ripening has gone far enough, ignore that popular jingle and refrigerate. The skins may blacken, but the flesh will keep for several days.

☐ The egg-shaped kiwi fruit of New Zealand hides a luscious green under its drab brown exterior. Let ripen at room temperature until soft, then refrigerate. Once peeled, the whole fruit is edible.

☐ Mangoes vary in size and shape. Allow to ripen at room temperature until the flesh yields to gentle pressure and any green is largely background color, then refrigerate. To prepare, score the tough skin in 4 to 6 sections, piercing it with a paring knife; strip the skin away and cut the fruit into slices.

☐ Papayas look like pear-shaped melons, but they grow on trees, not vines. If purchased when green, let ripen at room temperature for 3 to 5 days. When yellow-orange, refrigerate for use within 1 week. Prepare and serve just as you would cantaloupe.

☐ Pineapples don't ripen after picking. Try for one that has an aroma, no soft spots and a spirited green crown. Refrigerate if not using immediately. To prepare a pineapple for use, carefully twist out the green top; cut pineapple into halves, then quarters. Slice the fruit from the rind. Cut off the core and remove any "eyes."

☐ You don't eat pomegranates; you eat their fleshy red seeds, which may be frozen almost indefinitely. Select large red to purple fruits, heavy for their size, with tough skins. To prepare, cut lengthwise and remove the seeds with a spoon. Or score lengthwise in several places and soak in cold water 5 minutes; then break apart under water, separating the seeds from the pulp. Skim off the pulp and drain seeds. Scatter a few on a fruit salad to dazzle the diners.

TROPICAL FRUIT SALAD

Pictured on page 36.

   Almond Dressing (below)
3 bananas, sliced
2 avocados, sliced
2 kiwi fruit, sliced
1 mango, cut up
1 papaya, sliced
¼ cup toasted flaked coconut

Prepare Almond Dressing. Mix bananas, avocados, kiwi, mango and papaya; sprinkle with coconut. Serve with dressing.

8 servings.

Almond Dressing

⅓ cup toasted chopped almonds
⅓ cup orange juice
⅓ cup vegetable oil
3 tablespoons packed brown sugar
2 tablespoons light rum
¼ teaspoon salt
¼ teaspoon paprika

Shake all ingredients in tightly covered jar. Refrigerate at least 1 hour. *About 1 cup dressing.*

STARBURST FRUIT SALAD

   Peanut Dressing (right)
6 medium romaine leaves
3 small bananas
¼ cup chopped salted peanuts
1 can (13¼ ounces) pineapple chunks, drained
1 can (11 ounces) mandarin orange segments, drained
1 cup strawberries

Prepare Peanut Dressing. Arrange romaine leaves in starburst pattern on large serving plate. Cut bananas lengthwise into halves. Place 1 banana half, cut side down, in center of each romaine leaf; sprinkle with peanuts. Arrange pineapple chunks and orange segments alternately between banana halves. Place strawberries in center of starburst. Serve salad with dressing.

6 servings.

Peanut Dressing

¼ cup honey
¼ cup creamy peanut butter
1 tablespoon lemon juice

Mix all ingredients. *½ cup dressing.*

CANNED FRUIT SALAD PLATE

   Cheese Dressing (below)
1 can (16 ounces) pitted dark sweet cherries, chilled and drained
1 can (14 ounces) spiced red apple rings, chilled and drained
1 can (11 ounces) mandarin orange segments, chilled and drained
1 can (8¾ ounces) sliced pears, chilled and drained
1 cup pecan halves
   Salad greens

Prepare Cheese Dressing. Arrange cherries, apple rings, orange segments, pear slices and pecan halves on salad greens around bowl of dressing.

6 servings.

Cheese Dressing

1 cup shredded Cheddar cheese (about 4 ounces)
½ cup mayonnaise or salad dressing
½ cup dairy sour cream
¼ teaspoon red pepper sauce

Mix all ingredients. *About 1½ cups dressing.*

SUMMER FRUIT BOWL

Pictured on page 35.

2 peaches, cut up
1 cup blueberries
1 cup melon balls
1 cup sliced strawberries
1 cup seedless green grapes
3 tablespoons orange-flavored
   liqueur or orange juice
⅔ cup dairy sour cream
3 tablespoons packed brown sugar
   Brown sugar

Toss peaches, blueberries, melon balls, straw-berries, grapes and liqueur. Mix sour cream and 3 tablespoons brown sugar; sprinkle with additional brown sugar. Serve fruit mixture with sour cream dressing.

6 servings.

FRESH FRUIT ON CRISPY NOODLES

   Curry Dressing (below)
3 bananas, sliced
2 pears, cut up
2 peaches, sliced
2 cups pitted dark sweet cherries
1 can (8 ounces) crushed pineapple in
   juice, drained (reserve 2
   tablespoons juice)
2 cups chow mein noodles

Prepare Curry Dressing. Toss bananas, pears, peaches, cherries and pineapple. Arrange ⅓ cup chow mein noodles on each of 6 salad plates; top with fruit mixture. Serve with dressing.

6 servings.

Curry Dressing
½ cup dairy sour cream
2 tablespoons reserved pineapple
   juice
1 tablespoon honey
½ teaspoon curry powder

Mix all ingredients. *About ⅔ cup dressing.*

STRAWBERRY-RHUBARB MOLD

1 package (20 ounces) frozen
  unsweetened rhubarb
1 package (3 ounces) strawberry-
  flavored gelatin
1 or 2 drops red food color
  (optional)
1 can (8 ounces) crushed pineapple in
  juice
¼ cup chopped nuts
  Crushed Pineapple Dressing (below)
  Salad greens

Prepare Rhubarb Sauce as directed on package of frozen rhubarb; remove from heat. Stir in gelatin and food color. Refrigerate until very thick, about 1½ hours.

Reserve 2 tablespoons pineapple for Crushed Pineapple Dressing. Stir remaining pineapple (with juice) and nuts into gelatin mixture; pour into 4-cup mold. Refrigerate until firm, at least 4 hours.

Prepare Crushed Pineapple Dressing. Unmold salad on salad greens and serve with dressing.

6 servings.

Crushed Pineapple Dressing
½ cup frozen whipped topping,
  thawed
¼ cup mayonnaise or salad dressing
2 tablespoons reserved crushed
  pineapple

Mix all ingredients. *About ⅔ cup dressing.*

CHERRY-BERRY SALADS

1 cup boiling water
1 package (6 ounces) orange-flavored
  gelatin
2 cups strawberries, sliced
1 banana, sliced
1 can (21 ounces) cherry pie filling
1 teaspoon lemon juice
  Orange Topping (below)

Pour boiling water on gelatin in bowl; stir until gelatin is dissolved. Stir in strawberries, banana, pie filling and lemon juice. Pour into baking pan, 9x9x2 inches. Refrigerate until firm. Prepare Orange Topping; serve with salad.

8 or 9 servings.

Orange Topping
Mix 1 carton (8 ounces) dairy sour cream and 3 tablespoons orange marmalade. *About 1 cup topping.*

BERRY-WINE SALAD

1 cup boiling water
1 package (3 ounces) strawberry-
  flavored gelatin
1 package (10 ounces) frozen sliced
  strawberries, partially thawed
1 cup seedless green grapes
⅔ cup sweet white wine
  Salad greens
1 carton (8 ounces) strawberry-flavored
  yogurt

Pour boiling water on gelatin in bowl; stir until gelatin is dissolved. Stir in strawberries; break apart with fork. Stir in 1 cup grapes and the wine. Pour into 4-cup mold. Refrigerate until firm. Unmold on salad greens and serve with yogurt.

6 to 8 servings.

MOLDED SALADS

All-American beauties—these remarkably versatile salads may be made 2 to 3 days in advance. Perfect for do-aheaders.

☐ Almost anything that doesn't leak can be used as a salad mold, but the gelatin will thicken and firm more quickly in containers of thin metal, such as ice cube trays or stainless steel bowls. (Salads will unmold more easily, too.) A collection of pretty copper molds in varying sizes, however, leads to spectacular salads . . . and handsomely decorated kitchen walls.

☐ If you don't know the size of your mold, fill it with water and then measure the contents. If you want to use a 4-cup mold but have a 6-cup recipe, use the recipe as is. Don't try to adapt a gelatin recipe with partial amounts. The extra gelatin can be poured into individual molds or custard cups and used to accent other meals or for between-meal snacks.

☐ Follow recipe directions exactly when dissolving gelatin. Flavored and unflavored gelatins are dissolved by different methods.

☐ When adding solids, first thicken the gelatin mixture until it mounds slightly when dropped from a spoon. If you're in a hurry, place the mixture in a bowl of ice and water or in the freezer compartment instead of the refrigerator. If the gelatin becomes too firm, soften over hot water. When the mixture has thickened, fold in the solids. (Drain fruits and vegetables thoroughly to avoid diluting the gelatin.)

☐ To design a patterned mold, either arrange the solids in the bottom of your mold and carefully spoon the thickened gelatin over them, or first spoon a little thickened gelatin into the bottom of the mold and then arrange your solids in an attractive pattern. Allow each layer to become firm before proceeding with the next. For a dramatic effect, make each layer a different jewel-like color.

☐ To unmold, dip the mold in warm, not hot, water to the depth of its contents; carefully loosen the edge of the salad with the tip of a paring knife. Place a chilled serving plate on top of the mold and, holding tightly, invert both plate and mold as a unit. Shake— and plop, your salad is unmolded. If there is no plop, repeat the process. And again, if necessary. With large and multi-grooved molds, you may find it easier to first invert the mold on a chilled plate. Then press a well-wrung-out hot kitchen towel all over the mold and into the depressions until you hear the plop. Repeat if necessary.

STRAWBERRY FREEZE

1 quart strawberry ice cream
1 can (13¼ ounces) crushed
  pineapple, drained
1 carton (4½ ounces) frozen whipped
  topping, thawed
1 jar (4 ounces) maraschino cherries,
  drained and cut into halves
1 package (3 ounces) cream cheese,
  cut into ½-inch cubes
1 banana, sliced

Soften ice cream until consistency of whipped cream. Fold pineapple, whipped topping, cherries, cream cheese and banana into ice cream. Spread in ungreased baking pan, 13x9x2 inches. Freeze until firm, at least 3 hours.

15 servings.

RASPBERRY-PEACH SALADS

1 cup boiling water
1 package (6 ounces) raspberry-
  flavored gelatin
1 package (12 ounces) frozen
  raspberries
1 can (21 ounces) peach pie filling
1 teaspoon lemon juice
  Peach Topping (below)

Pour boiling water on gelatin in bowl; stir until gelatin is dissolved. Stir in frozen raspberries, pie filling and lemon juice. Pour into baking pan, 9x9x2 inches. Refrigerate until firm. Prepare Peach Topping; serve with salads.

8 or 9 servings.

Peach Topping
Mix 1 carton (8 ounces) unflavored yogurt and 3 tablespoons peach preserves. *About 1 cup topping.*

PASTEL FRUIT RING MOLD

2½ cups boiling water
1 package (6 ounces) cherry-flavored
  gelatin°
1 can (6 ounces) frozen lemonade
  concentrate
1 carton (9 ounces) frozen whipped
  topping, thawed
  Salad greens
1 pint raspberries°

Pour boiling water on gelatin in bowl; stir until gelatin is dissolved. Stir in frozen concentrate. Refrigerate until slightly thickened, about 1 hour 15 minutes.

Stir whipped topping into gelatin mixture; beat on low speed until light and fluffy, about 1 minute. Pour into 8-cup ring mold. Refrigerate until firm, at least 4 hours. Unmold on salad greens and fill center of salad with raspberries.

12 servings.

°Your favorite flavor gelatin and fruit can be substituted for the cherry-flavored gelatin and the raspberries.

FROSTED APRICOT SALAD

2 cups boiling water
1 package (6 ounces) orange-flavored gelatin
1 can (17 ounces) apricot halves
1 can (8¼ ounces) crushed pineapple
⅔ cup chopped pecans
2 large bananas
1 cup chilled whipping cream
1 package (3 ounces) cream cheese, softened
2 tablespoons powdered sugar
½ teaspoon almond extract
2 tablespoons flaked coconut

Pour boiling water on gelatin in bowl; stir until gelatin is dissolved. Stir in apricots (with syrup), pineapple (with syrup) and pecans. Refrigerate until slightly thickened, about 1½ hours.

Slice bananas; stir into gelatin mixture. Pour into baking dish or pan, 9x9x2 inches. Refrigerate until firm, at least 4 hours.

Beat cream in chilled small mixer bowl until stiff; beat in cream cheese, sugar and extract until mixture is smooth. Spread over gelatin; sprinkle with coconut.

8 or 9 servings.

WATERMELON MOLD

2 envelopes unflavored gelatin
3½ cups watermelon puree (see note)
¼ cup sugar
¼ cup fresh lemon juice
¼ teaspoon salt
½ package (8-ounce size) cream cheese, softened
⅓ cup mayonnaise or salad dressing
1 tablespoon milk
    Few drops green food color
    Mint leaves
    Watermelon balls

Sprinkle gelatin on 1 cup of the watermelon puree in saucepan to soften; stir in sugar. Stir over low heat until gelatin is dissolved. Remove from heat; stir remaining puree into gelatin mixture. Stir in lemon juice and salt; pour into 1-quart bowl. Refrigerate until firm, at least 8 hours. Stir gently during first hour to prevent separation.

Unmold watermelon on serving plate. Beat cream cheese, mayonnaise and milk until smooth; stir in food color. Frost mold with cream cheese mixture. Garnish with mint leaves and watermelon balls.

8 servings.

Note: To make puree, cut watermelon into pieces; remove seeds and rind. Place 3 cups melon pieces in blender container. Cover and blend until pureed, about 15 seconds. Repeat until desired amount of puree is obtained. Four pounds watermelon will yield about 3½ cups puree.

Fruit salads for any season: Winter Fruit Salad (page 27) in back, Summer Fruit Bowl (page 30) in front.

Tropical Fruit Salad (page 29). This exotic conversation-maker calls for avocados, bananas, papayas, mangoes and kiwis, a sprinkling of toasted coconut and a zesty Almond Dressing.

A salad on the side? Here are four excellent suggestions. Clockwise from top left: Picnic Tomatoes (page 46), Corny Coleslaw (page 43), Eight-Vegetable Marinade (page 47), Potato-Broccoli Salad (page 48).

Shapely do-ahead salads: Confetti Soufflé (page 52) in back, Avocado Molded Crown (page 50) in front.

CHERRY-PINEAPPLE SALAD

1 cup boiling water
1 package (3 ounces) cherry-flavored gelatin
¾ cup dairy sour cream
½ cup mayonnaise or salad dressing
2 teaspoons prepared horseradish
1 can (8¼ ounces) crushed pineapple, drained (reserve syrup)
½ cup chopped nuts
   Salad greens
   Black cherries or raspberries

Pour boiling water on gelatin in blender container. Cover and blend on low speed until gelatin is dissolved, about 10 seconds. Add sour cream, mayonnaise, horseradish and reserved pineapple syrup. Cover and blend on low speed 20 seconds. Stir in pineapple and nuts; pour into 4-cup mold. Refrigerate until firm, at least 4 hours. Unmold on salad greens and garnish with cherries.

6 servings.

VARIATION

Orange-Apricot Salad: Substitute orange-flavored gelatin for the cherry-flavored gelatin and 1 can (8¾ ounces) apricot halves for the pineapple. Do not stir apricot halves into gelatin mixture. Refrigerate gelatin mixture in bowl until slightly thickened. Arrange apricot halves cut sides up in mold. Pour gelatin mixture on apricots. Refrigerate until firm, at least 4 hours.

BLACK CHERRY MOLD

1 can (16 ounces) pitted dark sweet cherries, drained (reserve ¾ cup syrup)
¾ cup water or dry red wine
1 package (6 ounces) black cherry–flavored gelatin
1¾ cups ginger ale
1 package (3 ounces) slivered almonds (optional)
   Salad greens
1 carton (8 ounces) black cherry–flavored yogurt

Heat reserved cherry syrup and water to boiling; pour on gelatin in bowl. Stir until gelatin is dissolved. Stir in ginger ale. Refrigerate until slightly thickened.

Stir cherries and almonds into gelatin mixture; pour into 6-cup mold. Refrigerate until firm, at least 2 hours. Unmold on salad greens and serve with yogurt.

8 to 10 servings.

PINEAPPLE-BLUEBERRY SQUARES

2 cups boiling water
1 package (6 ounces) raspberry-flavored gelatin
1 can (16 ounces) blueberries, drained (reserve ⅔ cup syrup)
1 can (8¼ ounces) crushed pineapple
1 package (8 ounces) cream cheese, softened
½ cup dairy sour cream
¼ cup sugar
    Chopped nuts

Pour boiling water on gelatin in bowl; stir until gelatin is dissolved. Stir in blueberries, reserved blueberry syrup and the pineapple (with syrup). Pour into baking dish or pan, 8x8x2 inches. Refrigerate until firm, at least 4 hours.

Mix cream cheese, sour cream and sugar. Spread over gelatin; sprinkle with nuts. Cut into squares.

9 servings.

ORANGE-BUTTERMILK SALAD

1 cup boiling water
1 package (6 ounces) orange-flavored gelatin
1 cup vanilla ice cream
1 cup buttermilk
1 can (11 ounces) mandarin orange segments, drained
    Lemon–Sour Cream Dressing (below)
    Curly endive

Pour boiling water on gelatin in bowl; stir until gelatin is dissolved. Stir in ice cream until mixture is smooth. Stir in buttermilk and orange segments; pour into 5-cup mold. Refrigerate until firm, at least 4 hours.

Prepare Lemon–Sour Cream Dressing. Unmold salad on endive; serve with dressing.

8 to 10 servings.

Lemon–Sour Cream Dressing
½ cup dairy sour cream
1 tablespoon packed brown sugar
1 tablespoon sunflower nuts
1 teaspoon grated lemon peel

Mix all ingredients. *About ½ cup dressing.*

VEGETABLE SALADS

Sprightly Besides to Balance Your Menu

Seasonings and such can make a vegetable do perk-ups.
Then again, in combinations of twos, threes, fours and mores, they
can make you forget that vegetables were ever supposed to be dull.
These garden friends are in the best of company with special
dressings that add the just-right flavor. When you think of
mealtime vegetables, why not think of salads? They're a wonderful
change-of-pace way to insure your family the vitamins and
minerals only vegetables can provide.

FOUR-BEAN SALADS

Spicy Herb Dressing (below)
1 can (16 ounces) cut green beans,
   drained
1 can (15½ ounces) wax beans,
   drained
1 can (15½ ounces) kidney beans,
   drained
1 can (15 ounces) garbanzo beans,
   drained
½ cup finely chopped green pepper
½ cup sliced pitted ripe olives
¼ cup sliced green onions
¼ cup snipped parsley
1 jar (2 ounces) sliced pimiento,
   drained and finely chopped
6 lettuce cups

Prepare Spicy Herb Dressing. Place remaining ingredients except lettuce cups in large bowl; toss with dressing. Cover and refrigerate at least 4 hours.

Drain salad, reserving dressing; spoon into lettuce cups. (Dressing can be refrigerated and used again within 1 week.)

6 servings.

Spicy Herb Dressing
½ cup sugar
½ cup wine vinegar
½ cup vegetable oil
1½ teaspoons salt
½ teaspoon dry mustard
½ teaspoon pepper
½ teaspoon red pepper sauce
¼ teaspoon dried basil leaves
¼ teaspoon garlic powder

Shake all ingredients in tightly covered jar.
About 1½ cups dressing.

BEAN SALADS, MEXICAN STYLE

1 can (16 ounces) whole green beans,
   drained
1 can (12 ounces) Mexican-style corn,
   drained
2 tablespoons finely chopped onion
½ cup bottled red French salad
   dressing
   Dash of chili powder
½ cup shredded taco-seasoned or
   jalapeño pepper cheese (about
   2 ounces)
6 lettuce cups
½ small onion, thinly sliced and
   separated into rings
   Tortilla chips

Toss beans, corn and chopped onion with salad dressing. Cover and refrigerate at least 1 hour.

Sprinkle salad with chili powder; stir in cheese. Spoon salad into lettuce cups. Garnish with onion rings and serve with tortilla chips.

6 servings.

LEMON-LIMA SALADS

1 package (10 ounces) frozen green
   lima beans, cooked, drained and
   chilled
1 medium apple, coarsely chopped
2 tablespoons frozen lemonade
   concentrate, thawed
2 teaspoons vegetable oil
1 teaspoon prepared horseradish
4 lettuce cups
   Pomegranate seeds (optional)

Mix beans, apple, lemonade concentrate,
oil and horseradish. Spoon salad into lettuce
cups; sprinkle with pomegranate seeds.

4 servings.

FRUITED COLESLAW
FOR A CROWD

1 medium head green cabbage
   (about 1½ pounds), coarsely
   shredded
4 medium carrots, grated
1 cup golden raisins
1 can (15½ ounces) crushed pineapple,
   drained (reserve 1 tablespoon syrup)
3 cups miniature marshmallows
¾ cup mayonnaise or salad dressing
3 tablespoons lemon juice
½ teaspoon salt

Reserve ½ cup of the cabbage, ¼ cup of
the carrots and 1 tablespoon of the raisins.
Mix remaining cabbage, carrots and raisins,
the pineapple, reserved pineapple syrup,
marshmallows, mayonnaise, lemon juice and
salt. Cover and refrigerate at least 1 hour.

To serve, arrange reserved cabbage, carrots
and raisins in shape of large flower in center of coleslaw.

12 servings.

ORANGE-CABBAGE SLAW

1 can (8 ounces) crushed pineapple in
   juice, drained
½ cup dairy sour cream
½ cup orange marmalade
2 tablespoons vinegar
¾ teaspoon salt
6 cups finely shredded green cabbage
   (about 1½ pounds)

Mix pineapple, sour cream, marmalade,
vinegar and salt; toss with cabbage. Cover
and refrigerate at least 2 hours.

10 servings.

RED CABBAGE SALAD

½ small head red cabbage, finely
   shredded or chopped
⅔ cup applesauce
½ cup golden raisins or chopped
   apple
2 to 3 teaspoons prepared horseradish
¼ teaspoon salt

Mix all ingredients. Cover and refrigerate
at least 1 hour.

4 servings.

CORNY COLESLAW
Pictured on page 37.

4 cups finely shredded green cabbage
   (about 1 pound)
1 jar (about 9 ounces) corn relish
⅓ cup sliced green onions
¼ teaspoon salt

Mix all ingredients. Cover and refrigerate at
least 1 hour.

4 servings.

VEGETABLE SALADS   **43**

CREAMY COLESLAW

Creamy Dressing (below)
6 cups finely shredded green cabbage
 (about 1½ pounds)
⅓ cup chopped onion
⅓ cup chopped cucumber

Prepare Creamy Dressing; toss with remaining ingredients.

6 servings.

Creamy Dressing
⅔ cup mayonnaise or salad dressing
2 tablespoons sugar
2 tablespoons vinegar
1 tablespoon milk
½ teaspoon salt
⅛ teaspoon paprika

Mix all ingredients; refrigerate at least 1 hour. *About 1 cup dressing.*

CUCUMBER SALAD

1 medium cucumber
½ cup vinegar
½ cup water
2 tablespoons sugar
¼ teaspoon salt
1 small onion, thinly sliced
 Salad greens

Run tines of fork lengthwise down side of unpared cucumber; cut into thin slices. Mix vinegar, water, sugar and salt; pour on cucumber and onion. Cover and refrigerate at least 2 hours. Just before serving, drain and serve on salad greens.

4 to 6 servings.

EGGPLANT SALAD

1 medium eggplant
¼ cup snipped parsley
3 tablespoons snipped chives
½ teaspoon salt
 Dash of pepper
1 tablespoon lemon juice
1 cup shredded Cheddar cheese
 (about 4 ounces)
¼ cup mayonnaise or salad dressing
 Parsley
 Thin tomato wedges

Cut a large lengthwise slice from 1 side of eggplant. Cut thin layer from opposite side to prevent tipping if necessary. Scoop out eggplant, leaving ½-inch wall. Cut eggplant into ½-inch pieces. Cover and refrigerate eggplant shell.

Cook and stir eggplant pieces, snipped parsley, chives, salt and pepper until eggplant is crisp-tender, about 5 minutes. Stir in lemon juice. Refrigerate until chilled, about 1½ hours.

Stir cheese and mayonnaise into eggplant mixture; spoon into eggplant shell. Serve salad on bed of parsley and garnish with tomato wedges.

4 servings.

LETTUCE WEDGES WITH CREAMY TOPPING

1 medium head iceberg lettuce
1 package (3 ounces) cream cheese, softened
½ cup dairy sour cream
1 small carrot, grated
2 tablespoons finely chopped green pepper
2 tablespoons shredded Cheddar cheese
1 teaspoon lemon juice
½ teaspoon salt
¼ teaspoon onion salt
  Paprika

Cut lettuce into 6 wedges. Place a lettuce wedge on each of 6 salad plates. Make 3 or 4 vertical cuts almost to bottom of each wedge. Mix remaining ingredients except paprika; spoon onto wedges. Sprinkle with paprika.

6 servings.

BROILED SALADS

1 large head iceberg lettuce
⅓ cup bottled French salad dressing
3 tablespoons mayonnaise or salad dressing
6 tablespoons grated Parmesan cheese
4 slices bacon, crisply fried and crumbled

Set oven control to broil and/or 550°. Cut lettuce into 6 wedges; place on ungreased baking sheet. Mix salad dressing and mayonnaise; brush onto surfaces of lettuce wedges. Sprinkle with cheese. Broil with tops 2 to 3 inches from heat just until dressing and cheese bubble, about 2½ minutes. Sprinkle with bacon.

6 servings.

MUSHROOMS ITALIAN

½ cup olive or vegetable oil
2 tablespoons vinegar
2 tablespoons lemon juice
1 teaspoon salt
½ teaspoon dried basil leaves
¼ teaspoon dry mustard
⅛ teaspoon pepper
1 clove garlic, crushed (optional)
8 ounces mushrooms, sliced
  Snipped parsley

Shake all ingredients except mushrooms and parsley in tightly covered jar; pour on mushrooms. Cover and refrigerate no longer than 2 hours. Drain mushrooms and sprinkle with snipped parsley.

4 servings.

DILLED CHEESE AND PEA SALADS

1 package (10 ounces) frozen green peas
1 cup diced mild Cheddar cheese (about 4 ounces)
2 large stalks celery, chopped
¼ cup chopped dill pickle
½ cup mayonnaise or salad dressing
½ teaspoon dried dill weed or 1½ teaspoons snipped fresh dill weed
¼ teaspoon salt
8 lettuce cups

Rinse frozen peas under running cold water to separate; drain. Toss peas, cheese, celery, pickle, mayonnaise, dill weed and salt. Spoon salad into lettuce cups.

8 servings.

TOMATO-MUSHROOM SALADS

  Oil-Lemon Dressing (below)
4 small tomatoes, cut into wedges
4 ounces mushrooms, thinly sliced
½ cup pitted ripe olives
¼ cup snipped parsley
4 or 5 Bibb or Boston lettuce cups

Prepare Oil-Lemon Dressing; toss with tomatoes, mushrooms, olives and parsley. Cover and refrigerate until chilled. Spoon salad into lettuce cups.

4 or 5 servings.

Oil-Lemon Dressing
¼ cup vegetable oil
2 tablespoons lemon juice
¼ teaspoon salt
   Dash of pepper

Shake all ingredients in tightly covered jar. *About ⅓ cup dressing.*

TOMATO-CAULIFLOWER SALAD

⅓ cup bottled Italian salad dressing
¼ teaspoon salt
   Dash of pepper
4 small tomatoes, cut into wedges
2 cups cauliflowerets, cut into
   ¼- to ½-inch pieces
2 cups bite-size pieces curly endive
½ cup pimiento-stuffed olives
2 tablespoons snipped parsley
   Lettuce leaves

Mix salad dressing, salt and pepper; toss with tomatoes, cauliflower, endive, olives and parsley. Serve salad on lettuce.

6 to 8 servings.

PICNIC TOMATOES
Pictured on page 37.

3 hard-cooked eggs
1 tablespoon plus 1½ teaspoons
   mayonnaise, salad dressing or
   vinegar
¼ teaspoon dry mustard
⅛ teaspoon salt
⅛ teaspoon pepper
6 medium tomatoes
   Salt
   Pepper
6 parsley sprigs

Cut eggs lengthwise into halves. Slip out yolks; mash with fork. Stir in mayonnaise, mustard, ⅛ teaspoon salt and ⅛ teaspoon pepper. Fill egg whites with egg yolk mixture, heaping it up lightly.

Core tomatoes. Cut thin slice from stem end of each tomato; reserve slices. Remove pulp and juice from tomatoes; reserve for future use. Drain tomatoes cut sides down on paper towels 5 minutes. Sprinkle insides with salt and pepper. Press deviled egg half, yolk side up, into each tomato; top with tomato slice. Place parsley sprig on each tomato slice. Wrap tomatoes in plastic wrap; refrigerate at least 1 hour.

6 servings.

BULGUR AND TOMATO SALAD

2 cups boiling water
1 cup bulgur wheat
2 cups cherry tomatoes, cut into halves
3 tablespoons lemon juice
2 tablespoons snipped fresh mint leaves or 1 teaspoon dried mint leaves
2 tablespoons snipped chives
2 tablespoons snipped parsley
1 teaspoon salt
¼ teaspoon lemon pepper
Cherry tomatoes
Parsley

Pour water on bulgur; let stand 15 minutes. Drain. Mix bulgur, 2 cups tomatoes, the lemon juice, mint leaves, chives, 2 tablespoons parsley, the salt and lemon pepper. Cover and refrigerate 2 hours. Garnish with tomatoes and parsley.

6 to 8 servings.

EIGHT-VEGETABLE MARINADE

Pictured on page 37.

1 jar (about 7 ounces) marinated artichoke hearts
1⅓ cups bottled Italian salad dressing
¼ cup snipped parsley
1 package (10 ounces) frozen baby Brussels sprouts, thawed and drained
2 carrots, cut diagonally into slices
1 green pepper, cut into strips
1 cup cauliflower pieces
1 cup broccoli pieces
5 ounces mushrooms, cut into halves
1 medium cucumber, cut into ½-inch pieces

Mix artichoke hearts (with liquid), salad dressing and parsley. Toss remaining ingredients in large bowl; pour artichoke hearts and marinade on vegetables. Toss to coat all vegetables. Cover and refrigerate at least 2 hours.

Drain salad, reserving marinade. (Marinade can be refrigerated and used again within 1 week.)

10 servings.

VEGETABLE SALADS   **47**

VEGETABLES VINAIGRETTE

Vinaigrette Dressing (below)
1 can (8 ounces) cut green beans, drained
1 can (8 ounces) stewed tomatoes, drained
1 can (4 ounces) button mushrooms, drained
1 small onion, thinly sliced and separated into rings
5 lettuce cups

Prepare Vinaigrette Dressing; toss with beans, tomatoes, mushrooms and onion. Cover and refrigerate at least 8 hours. Spoon salad into lettuce cups.

5 servings.

Vinaigrette Dressing
¼ cup vegetable oil
2 tablespoons vinegar
1 teaspoon celery salt
1 teaspoon dry mustard
½ teaspoon salt
1 clove garlic, finely chopped

Shake all ingredients in tightly covered jar.
About ⅓ cup dressing.

MACARONI-BEET SALAD

1 cup uncooked macaroni
1 cup chopped cooked beets
½ cup chopped sweet gherkin pickle
¼ cup chopped onion
3 tablespoons bottled French salad dressing
½ teaspoon salt
Romaine leaves
Dairy sour cream

Cook macaroni as directed on package; drain. Rinse with cold water. Mix macaroni, beets, pickle and onion. Toss with salad dressing and salt. Cover and refrigerate at least 2 hours.

Line salad bowl with romaine leaves. Spoon salad into bowl and garnish with dollops of sour cream.

4 servings.

POTATO-BROCCOLI SALAD
Pictured on page 37.

1 package (10 ounces) frozen chopped broccoli
½ teaspoon salt
½ cup boiling water
1 cup cubed hot cooked potatoes
½ cup bottled oil-and-vinegar salad dressing
2 medium stalks celery, cut diagonally into slices
2 hard-cooked eggs, cut into fourths
⅓ medium head iceberg lettuce, torn into bite-size pieces
¾ teaspoon seasoned salt
¼ teaspoon lemon pepper

Sprinkle frozen broccoli with ½ teaspoon salt. Pour boiling water on broccoli in large bowl. Cover and let stand 3 minutes; drain. Stir in potatoes. Pour salad dressing on broccoli and potatoes. Cover and refrigerate at least 2 hours. Add remaining ingredients; toss.

8 servings.

NO-FUSS POTATO SALAD

1¾ cups boiling water
1 package (6 ounces) hash brown potatoes with onions
3 or 4 large stalks celery, chopped
¼ medium green pepper, finely chopped
1 jar (2 ounces) sliced pimiento, drained
1 cup shredded Cheddar cheese (about 4 ounces)
½ cup mayonnaise or salad dressing
1 teaspoon salt
½ teaspoon dry mustard
1 hard-cooked egg, sliced
2 tablespoons snipped parsley

Pour boiling water on potatoes. Let stand, stirring occasionally, until water is absorbed, about 30 minutes.

Stir celery, green pepper, pimiento, cheese, mayonnaise, salt and mustard into potatoes. Cover and refrigerate at least 1 hour. Garnish with egg slices and parsley.

6 to 8 servings.

POTATO SALAD

2 pounds potatoes (about 6 medium)
¼ cup finely chopped onion
¼ cup bottled Italian salad dressing
1 teaspoon salt
⅛ teaspoon pepper
½ cup mayonnaise or salad dressing
½ cup chopped celery
2 hard-cooked eggs, cut up

Heat 1 inch salted water (½ teaspoon salt to 1 cup water) to boiling. Add potatoes. Heat to boiling; reduce heat. Cover and cook until tender, 30 to 35 minutes. Drain potatoes; cool. Cut potatoes into cubes; stir in onion, salad dressing, salt and pepper. Cover and refrigerate at least 2 hours.

Just before serving, toss with mayonnaise until potatoes are well coated. Stir in celery and eggs.

4 to 6 servings.

HOT GERMAN POTATO SALAD

3 pounds potatoes (about 9 medium)
6 slices bacon
¾ cup chopped onion
2 tablespoons flour
2 tablespoons sugar
2 teaspoons salt
½ teaspoon celery seed
    Dash of pepper
¾ cup water
⅓ cup vinegar

Heat 1 inch salted water (½ teaspoon salt to 1 cup water) to boiling. Add potatoes. Heat to boiling; reduce heat. Cover and cook until tender, 30 to 35 minutes. Drain potatoes; cool.

Fry bacon in 10-inch skillet until crisp; remove from skillet and drain on paper towels. Cook and stir onion in bacon fat until tender and golden brown. Stir in flour, sugar, salt, celery seed and pepper. Cook over low heat, stirring constantly, until bubbly. Remove from heat; stir in water and vinegar. Heat to boiling, stirring constantly. Boil and stir 1 minute.

Crumble bacon. Cut potatoes into thin slices. Stir bacon and potatoes gently into hot mixture. Heat, stirring gently, until potatoes are coated and mixture is hot.

5 or 6 servings.

CUCUMBER SALAD MOLD

1 cup boiling water
1 package (3 ounces) lime-flavored
  gelatin
1 cup dairy sour cream
1 cup unsweetened pineapple juice
1 package (3 ounces) lime-flavored
  gelatin
½ cup lemon juice
1 teaspoon salt
4 medium cucumbers, shredded and
  drained (about 2 cups)°
  Salad greens
  Cucumber slices

Pour boiling water on 1 package gelatin in bowl; stir until gelatin is dissolved. Beat in sour cream with hand beater until smooth. Pour into 6-cup mold. Refrigerate just until set, about 2 hours.

Heat pineapple juice to boiling. Pour boiling pineapple juice on 1 package gelatin in bowl; stir until gelatin is dissolved. Stir in lemon juice and salt. Refrigerate until very thick, about 1½ hours.

Stir shredded cucumbers into gelatin mixture in bowl; pour on gelatin mixture in mold. Refrigerate until firm, at least 4 hours. Unmold on salad greens and garnish with cucumber slices.

10 to 12 servings.

°Cucumbers can be finely chopped in food grinder and drained.

AVOCADO MOLDED CROWN
Pictured on page 38.

2 envelopes unflavored gelatin
1 cup cold water
1 can (13¾ ounces) chicken broth
½ cup bottled green goddess salad
  dressing
¼ cup mayonnaise or salad dressing
2 medium avocados, cut up
¼ cup lemon juice
½ cup mayonnaise or salad dressing
1 small onion
¼ teaspoon salt
¼ teaspoon pepper
⅛ teaspoon red pepper sauce
9 drops green food color
3 drops yellow food color
  Lemon slices
  Watercress

Sprinkle gelatin on cold water in saucepan to soften; stir over low heat until gelatin is dissolved. Remove from heat. Stir in broth. Measure ½ cup of the gelatin mixture; reserve remaining gelatin mixture. Beat green goddess dressing and ¼ cup mayonnaise into the ½ cup gelatin mixture; pour into 6-cup mold. Refrigerate just until set, about 40 minutes.

Place avocado pieces in blender container; pour lemon juice on avocado pieces. Add reserved gelatin mixture, ½ cup mayonnaise, the onion, salt, pepper, pepper sauce and food colors. Cover and blend until smooth, about 10 seconds. Refrigerate until slightly thickened, about 30 minutes.

Pour avocado mixture gently on gelatin in mold. Refrigerate until firm, at least 6 hours. Unmold salad on serving plate and garnish with lemon slices and watercress.

8 servings.

VEGETABLE RING

4 envelopes unflavored gelatin
1 can (10½ ounces) condensed beef broth
1 can (46 ounces) cocktail vegetable juice
1 can (16 ounces) mixed vegetables, drained
4 large stalks celery, coarsely chopped
1 medium zucchini, chopped (about 1 cup)
1 tablespoon lemon juice
¼ teaspoon salt
4 drops red pepper sauce
   Yogurt Dressing (below)
   Parsley

Sprinkle gelatin on broth in 3-quart saucepan to soften; stir over low heat until gelatin is dissolved, about 3 minutes. Remove from heat; stir in vegetable juice, mixed vegetables, celery, zucchini, lemon juice, salt and pepper sauce. Pour into 12-cup ring mold. Refrigerate until firm, at least 8 hours. (Some vegetables may sink to the bottom; some may rise to the top. Stir when slightly thickened to distribute vegetables evenly.)

Prepare Yogurt Dressing. Unmold salad on serving plate. Garnish with parsley and serve with dressing.

12 to 16 servings.

Yogurt Dressing
1 carton (8 ounces) unflavored yogurt
¼ cup mayonnaise or salad dressing
¼ teaspoon salt
   Paprika

Mix yogurt, mayonnaise and salt; sprinkle with paprika. *About 1 cup dressing.*

INDIVIDUAL TOMATO ASPICS

1 envelope unflavored gelatin
2 cups tomato juice
1 tablespoon lemon juice
2 teaspoons vinegar
½ teaspoon salt
⅛ teaspoon onion juice
3 drops red pepper sauce
½ cup chopped celery
¼ cup chopped cucumber
   Bibb lettuce
   Mayonnaise or salad dressing

Sprinkle gelatin on ½ cup of the tomato juice in saucepan to soften; stir over low heat until gelatin is dissolved. Stir into remaining tomato juice; stir in lemon juice, vinegar, salt, onion juice and pepper sauce. Refrigerate until slightly thickened, about 25 minutes.

Stir celery and cucumber into gelatin mixture; pour into individual molds. Refrigerate until firm, at least 3 hours. Unmold on lettuce and serve with mayonnaise.

4 servings.

CONFETTI SOUFFLE

Pictured on page 38.

2 envelopes unflavored gelatin
¾ cup cold water
⅔ cup mayonnaise or salad dressing
2 tablespoons vinegar
1 tablespoon prepared mustard
¼ teaspoon salt
⅛ teaspoon pepper
1 cup cut-up green cabbage
1 medium carrot, cut into 1-inch pieces
⅓ medium cucumber, cut into 1-inch pieces
½ small onion, cut into halves
6 radishes, cut into halves
1 jar (2 ounces) diced pimiento, drained
3 egg whites
¼ teaspoon cream of tartar
    Cucumber slices
    Radish slices
    Mayonnaise or salad dressing

Make a 4-inch-wide band of triple thickness aluminum foil 2 inches longer than circumference of 4-cup soufflé dish. Extend depth of dish by securing foil band around top of dish.

Sprinkle gelatin on cold water in 2-quart saucepan to soften; stir over low heat until gelatin is dissolved. Remove from heat; stir in ⅔ cup mayonnaise, the vinegar, mustard, salt and pepper. Refrigerate until mixture mounds slightly when dropped from a spoon, 20 to 30 minutes.

Place cabbage, carrot, cucumber pieces, onion and radish halves in blender container; pour enough water on vegetables to cover. Cover and blend on medium to high speed until vegetables are chopped,

7 or 8 seconds. Drain thoroughly. Fold chopped vegetables and pimiento into gelatin mixture.

Beat egg whites and cream of tartar in small mixer bowl until stiff but not dry. Fold gelatin mixture into egg whites in large bowl. Turn mixture into soufflé dish. Refrigerate until firm, at least 4 hours. Remove band and garnish with cucumber and radish slices; serve with mayonnaise.

6 servings.

JELLIED BORSCH

1 can (16 ounces) shoestring beets, drained (reserve liquid)
2 envelopes unflavored gelatin
1½ teaspoons instant beef bouillon
2 cups finely shredded green or red cabbage
2 tablespoons snipped chives
1 tablespoon lemon juice
½ teaspoon salt
½ cup dairy sour cream
1 tablespoon snipped parsley
    Leaf lettuce

Add enough water to reserved beet liquid to measure 2 cups. Sprinkle gelatin on liquid in 1½-quart saucepan to soften; stir in instant bouillon. Stir over low heat until gelatin and bouillon are dissolved. Remove from heat; cool 5 minutes. Stir in beets, cabbage, chives, lemon juice and salt. Pour into baking pan, 8x8x2 or 9x9x2 inches. Refrigerate until mixture mounds slightly when dropped from a spoon, about 30 minutes.

Mix sour cream and parsley; swirl through beet mixture. Refrigerate until firm, at least 2 hours. Serve on lettuce.

8 or 9 servings.

MAIN-DISH SALADS

Satisfying Combinations That Make Almost a Meal

Here come the big taste-budding ones! Salads
bringing protein-rich, hunger-stopping meat, poultry, fish and eggs
blissfully together with delicious counterpoint basics. Virtually
brimming with vim and vigor, these salads are ready to carry
the meal. And to complete the feast, you'll find a tasty array of
salad-enhancing breads. All that's needed is a beverage.
Brunch, lunch and supper need never be quite the same again . . .
with all hands happier and better off for it!

CHEF'S SMORGASBORD SALAD
Pictured on the cover.

　Clear French Dressing (below)
3 cups bite-size pieces leaf lettuce
3 cups bite-size pieces spinach
3 cups bite-size pieces iceberg lettuce
3 cups bite-size pieces red leaf lettuce
8 slices bacon, crisply fried and crumbled
1 jar (about 7 ounces) marinated artichoke hearts, drained
1 cup croutons
2 hard-cooked eggs, chopped
2 to 3 cups ¼-inch strips fully cooked ham or turkey (8 to 12 ounces)
1 cup shredded Cheddar cheese (about 4 ounces)
½ cup chopped peanuts or cashews
½ cup sliced pitted ripe olives
½ cup sliced cucumbers
¼ cup sliced green onions
2 to 3 tablespoons chopped anchovies

Prepare Clear French Dressing. Arrange leaf lettuce, spinach, iceberg lettuce and red leaf lettuce in separate sections in large salad bowl. Place remaining ingredients in small containers around salad bowl. Serve with dressing.

6 to 8 servings.

Clear French Dressing
¾ cup olive oil, vegetable oil or combination
⅓ cup wine or tarragon vinegar
2¼ teaspoons salt
2 or 3 cloves garlic, crushed
¾ teaspoon monosodium glutamate
⅛ teaspoon pepper

Shake all ingredients in tightly covered jar. *About 1 cup dressing.*

HAM, RED BEAN AND RICE SALAD

1⅓ cups water
⅔ cup uncooked regular rice
½ teaspoon salt
1 bay leaf
　Snappy Dressing (below)
1 can (15½ ounces) red kidney beans, chilled and drained°
3 tablespoons finely chopped onion
½ large stalk celery, chopped
¼ teaspoon garlic salt
½ medium green pepper, chopped
2 cups ½-inch cubes fully cooked ham, chilled
　Celery leaves

Heat water, rice, salt and bay leaf to boiling, stirring once or twice; reduce heat. Cover and simmer 14 minutes. (Do not lift cover or stir.) Remove from heat; fluff lightly with fork. Cover and let steam 5 to 10 minutes. Refrigerate until chilled.

Prepare Snappy Dressing. Mix beans, onion, celery and garlic salt. Mix rice and green pepper. Arrange bean mixture, rice mixture and ham cubes in separate sections on platter. Garnish with celery leaves and serve with dressing.

5 servings.

°1½ cups cooked black beans can be substituted for the kidney beans.

Snappy Dressing
½ cup mayonnaise or salad dressing
¼ cup catsup
¼ teaspoon ground cumin
¼ teaspoon aromatic bitters

Mix all ingredients. *¾ cup dressing.*

Salade Niçoise (page 68) — a stylishly simple choice. Perfect for a luncheon or light supper.

Salads to serve as the main course. Clockwise from top left: Salad Lovers' Lasagne (page 58), Triple Decker Club Salad (page 63), Oriental Chicken Salad (page 66), Crab-Shrimp-Avocado Salad (page 67).

HAM-SESAME SEED SALAD

Oil-and-Vinegar Dressing (below)
2 cups cubed fully cooked ham
½ medium head iceberg lettuce, torn into bite-size pieces
½ medium cucumber, thinly sliced
2 green onions, thinly sliced lengthwise and cut into 1½-inch pieces
1 medium tomato, cut into thin wedges
2 tablespoons toasted sesame seed (see note)
Monterey Jack cheese, cut into ¼-inch strips (optional)

Prepare Oil-and-Vinegar Dressing. Toss with ham, lettuce, cucumber, onions, tomato and sesame seed. Garnish with cheese.

6 to 8 servings.

Note: To toast sesame seed, heat oven to 350°. Bake in ungreased baking pan, stirring occasionally, until golden, 8 to 10 minutes.

Oil-and-Vinegar Dressing
1 tablespoon vegetable oil
1 tablespoon vinegar
1½ teaspoons sugar
¾ teaspoon salt
½ teaspoon monosodium glutamate
1 small clove garlic, crushed

Shake all ingredients in tightly covered jar.
About ⅛ cup dressing.

HAM SALADS HAWAIIAN

Potato Nests (below)
1½ cups finely chopped fully cooked ham
⅓ cup mayonnaise or salad dressing
1 can (13¼ ounces) pineapple chunks, drained
1 large stalk celery, chopped
2 teaspoons finely chopped onion
¼ teaspoon prepared mustard
Dash of garlic powder (optional)

Prepare Potato Nests. Mix remaining ingredients; refrigerate at least 1 hour. Fill Potato Nests with salad.

5 servings.

Potato Nests
Heat oven to 400°. Empty 1 package (6 ounces) hash brown potatoes with onions into bowl. Pour enough very hot water on potatoes to cover; let stand 10 minutes. Drain completely. Toss potatoes with 1 egg, beaten, and 1 teaspoon salt. Press about ¼ cup potato mixture firmly and evenly against bottom and side of each of 10 greased 6-ounce custard cups. Place on baking sheet. Bake until edges are brown and crisp, 35 to 40 minutes. Remove from cups, loosening edges with knife if necessary. Cool on wire rack.

LENTIL-HAM SALAD

6 cups water
1 cup lentils
2 cups chopped fully cooked ham
½ cup bottled oil-and-vinegar salad dressing with herbs
¼ cup sliced green onions
¼ cup sliced pitted ripe olives
1 teaspoon salt
½ teaspoon pepper
  Lettuce leaves
  Parsley

Heat water and lentils to boiling; reduce heat. Cover and simmer 3 minutes; remove from heat. Let stand 1 to 2 hours.

Drain lentils; stir in ham, salad dressing, onions, olives, salt and pepper. Cover and refrigerate at least 1 hour.

Line salad bowl with lettuce leaves. Spoon salad into bowl and garnish with parsley.

4 servings.

PICNIC ROLL-UPS

6 slices salami or boiled ham
6 large lettuce leaves
  Mayonnaise or salad dressing
6 thin slices mozzarella cheese
  Lettuce leaves
  Tomato wedges

Place 1 salami slice on each of 6 lettuce leaves; spread mayonnaise over salami. Top each salami slice with cheese slice; roll up lettuce leaves. Cut roll-ups into bite-size pieces; secure with wooden picks. Serve roll-ups on lettuce. Garnish with tomato wedges.

6 servings.

SALAD LOVERS' LASAGNE
Pictured on page 56.

  Lasagne Dressing (below)
1 package (7 ounces) macaroni shells
1 cup shredded pizza cheese (about 4 ounces)
4 medium zucchini, chopped
½ cup sliced pitted ripe olives
  Salad greens
1 can (8 ounces) tomato sauce (optional)
8 slices salami
  Grated Parmesan cheese

Prepare Lasagne Dressing. Cook macaroni as directed on package; drain. Rinse with cold water. Toss macaroni, pizza cheese, zucchini and olives with dressing. Cover and refrigerate at least 3 hours.

Place salad greens on 8 salad plates. Spoon salad onto greens; drizzle each salad with about 2 tablespoons tomato sauce. Cut each salami slice into a spiral, about ¼ inch wide; arrange 1 slice on each salad. Serve with Parmesan cheese.

8 servings.

Lasagne Dressing
1 can (8 ounces) tomato sauce
½ cup mayonnaise or salad dressing
1 teaspoon salt
½ teaspoon garlic salt
½ teaspoon dried oregano leaves

Place all ingredients in blender container. Cover and blend on medium speed until smooth, about 10 seconds. *1½ cups dressing.*

SALAD-SIDE BREADS

Spreads, shakings and special touches that help to make all sorts of breads sensational salad partners.

French Mustard Slices
1 package (10 ounces) brown-and-serve French bread
¼ cup butter or margarine, softened
2 tablespoons snipped parsley
1 tablespoon prepared mustard
1 teaspoon instant minced onion
1 teaspoon lemon juice

Heat oven to 400°. Cut loaf diagonally into 1-inch slices. Mix remaining ingredients; spread on slices. Reassemble loaf; place on ungreased baking sheet. Bake about 15 minutes. *About 24 slices.*

Hickory French Bread
1 loaf (1 pound) French bread
½ cup butter or margarine, softened
1 cup shredded natural sharp Cheddar cheese (about 4 ounces)
1 tablespoon snipped parsley
½ teaspoon hickory-smoked salt
2 teaspoons Worcestershire sauce

Cut loaf diagonally into 1-inch slices. Mix remaining ingredients; spread on slices. Reassemble loaf; wrap in piece of heavy-duty aluminum foil, 28 × 18 inches, and seal securely. Heat in 350° oven 20 minutes. *About 24 slices.*

Hot Chili French Bread: Omit parsley and hickory-smoked salt. Decrease Worcestershire sauce to 1 teaspoon and mix in 1 to 2 teaspoons chopped hot chili peppers.

Spicy English Muffins
½ cup butter or margarine, softened
1 teaspoon chili powder
½ teaspoon onion salt
4 English muffins, split into halves

Set oven control to broil and/or 550°. Mix butter, chili powder and onion salt; spread on cut surfaces of muffin halves. Broil with tops about 3 inches from heat until golden brown, 2 to 3 minutes. *4 servings.*

Hot Bread in Foil
Cut 1 loaf (1 pound) French bread into 1-inch slices or cut Vienna, rye or pumpernickel bread into ½-inch slices. Spread generously with ½ cup butter or margarine, softened, or with 1 of the Butter Spreads (below). Reassemble loaf; wrap in piece of heavy-duty aluminum foil, about 28 × 18 inches, and seal securely. Heat in 400° oven 15 to 20 minutes. *About 24 slices.*

Butter Spreads: Mix ½ cup butter or margarine, softened, with 1 of the following:
☐ *Garlic*—1 medium clove garlic, finely chopped, or ⅛ teaspoon garlic powder
☐ *Onion*—2 tablespoons finely chopped onion or snipped chives
☐ *Seeded*—1 to 2 teaspoons celery, poppy, dill or sesame seed
☐ *Tarragon*—1 teaspoon dried tarragon leaves and ¼ teaspoon paprika

BRAUNSCHWEIGER LOAF

½ cup tomato juice
¼ cup cold water
 1 envelope unflavored gelatin
¾ pound Braunschweiger
 1 cup tomato juice
¾ cup finely chopped celery
½ cup mayonnaise or salad dressing
¼ cup chopped green pepper
¼ cup chopped pimiento-stuffed
    olives
¼ cup finely chopped green onions
 2 tablespoons lemon juice
 2 teaspoons sugar
½ teaspoon salt
½ teaspoon dry mustard
⅛ teaspoon pepper
⅛ teaspoon ground cloves
    Salad greens
 1 package (10 ounces) frozen asparagus
    spears, cooked, drained and chilled
 1 tomato, sliced
 2 hard-cooked eggs, sliced

Mix ½ cup tomato juice and the water. Sprinkle gelatin on juice mixture in 2-quart saucepan to soften; stir over low heat until gelatin is dissolved. Refrigerate until slightly thickened.

Soften Braunschweiger by mashing with spoon. Stir Braunschweiger, 1 cup tomato juice, the celery, mayonnaise, green pepper, olives, onions, lemon juice, sugar, salt, mustard, pepper and cloves into gelatin mixture. Pour into loaf pan, 9x5x3 inches. Refrigerate until firm. Unmold on salad greens; arrange asparagus and tomato and egg slices around loaf.

6 to 8 servings.

MARINATED BEEF AND MUSHROOMS

1½-pound beef sirloin steak,
    1½ inches thick
 1 jar (4½ ounces) sliced mushrooms,
    drained
 1 medium green pepper, sliced into
    thin rings
⅓ cup red wine vinegar
¼ cup vegetable oil
 1 teaspoon salt
½ teaspoon onion salt
½ teaspoon Worcestershire sauce
¼ teaspoon pepper
¼ teaspoon dried tarragon leaves,
    crushed
 2 cloves garlic, crushed
 4 lettuce cups
    Cherry tomatoes

Set oven control to broil and/or 550°. Broil steak with top 2 inches from heat until medium, about 13 minutes on each side. Cool; cut into ⅜-inch strips. Arrange strips in ungreased baking dish, 13½x8¾x1¾ inches. Place mushrooms on steak; top with green pepper rings. Mix vinegar, oil, salt, onion salt, Worcestershire sauce, pepper, tarragon and garlic; pour on steak and vegetables. Cover and refrigerate at least 3 hours, spooning vinegar mixture over vegetables occasionally.

Remove vegetables to lettuce cups with slotted spoon. Place steak next to vegetables and garnish with tomatoes.

4 servings.

TOSTADA SALADS

Guacamole Dressing (below)
1 pound ground beef
¾ cup water
1 package (1¼ ounces) taco seasoning mix
1 can (15½ ounces) red kidney beans, drained
¾ teaspoon salt
¼ teaspoon chili powder
6 tostadas
Six ½-inch slices iceberg lettuce
½ cup shredded taco-seasoned or jalapeño pepper cheese (about 2 ounces)
3 tomatoes, cut into thin wedges

Prepare Guacamole Dressing. Cook and stir ground beef in 10-inch skillet over medium-high heat until brown; drain. Stir in water, seasoning mix, beans, salt and chili powder. Heat to boiling; reduce heat. Cover and simmer 10 minutes.

Place 1 tostada on each of 6 salad plates; top with lettuce slice. Cut each lettuce slice about ¼ inch deep in crisscross pattern. Spoon ½ cup beef mixture onto each lettuce slice; sprinkle with cheese. Garnish with tomato wedges and serve with dressing.

6 servings.

Guacamole Dressing
1 avocado
1 small onion, finely chopped
2 canned green chili peppers, seeded and chopped (about 2 teaspoons)
1½ teaspoons lemon juice
½ teaspoon salt
¼ teaspoon pepper
Mayonnaise or salad dressing

Mash avocado; beat in onion, chili peppers, lemon juice, salt and pepper until creamy. Spoon dressing into dish. Spread with thin layer of mayonnaise to prevent discoloration. Cover and refrigerate. Stir gently just before serving. *About ¾ cup dressing.*

LIVER-TOMATO-ONION SALADS

1 cup biscuit baking mix
½ teaspoon salt
1 pound beef liver, cut into 4x¾-inch strips
½ cup buttermilk
2 tablespoons shortening
Lettuce leaves
2 medium tomatoes, thinly sliced
½ to 1 medium Bermuda onion, thinly sliced
¼ cup imitation bacon
Bottled Thousand Island or blue cheese salad dressing

Mix baking mix and salt; dip liver strips into baking mix, then into buttermilk and again into baking mix. Heat shortening in 10-inch skillet over medium heat until melted. Cook liver strips in shortening until brown, about 5 minutes on each side.

Place lettuce leaves on 4 salad plates. Arrange tomato and onion slices alternately down centers of leaves; sprinkle with imitation bacon. Arrange liver strips around tomato and onion slices. Serve salads with salad dressing.

4 servings.

GOURMET PLATTER

1 package (6½ ounces) wild-and-white rice mix
1 cup shredded Swiss cheese (about 4 ounces)
½ cup mayonnaise or salad dressing
¼ cup half-and-half
1 teaspoon dry mustard
½ teaspoon salt
¼ to ½ teaspoon dried rosemary leaves
12 strips Swiss cheese, 3x½x½ inch
12 thin slices smoked tongue
   Leaf lettuce
   Cherry tomatoes
   Parsley

Cook rice as directed on package; cool slightly. Stir in 1 cup cheese, the mayonnaise, half-and-half, mustard, salt and rosemary. Cover and refrigerate at least 2 hours.

Place 1 cheese strip on each tongue slice; roll up. Arrange rice mixture and tongue rolls on lettuce. Garnish with tomatoes and parsley.

6 servings.

CHILLED VEAL AND FRUIT SALAD

2 cups cut-up cooked veal
1 cup halved seeded Tokay grapes
1 medium green pepper, cut into strips
1 tablespoon lemon juice
½ teaspoon salt
2 bananas
2 tablespoons mayonnaise or salad dressing
2 tablespoons instant nonfat dry milk
1 tablespoon water
   Leaf lettuce
¼ cup toasted chopped pecans

Mix veal, grapes, green pepper, lemon juice and salt. Cover and refrigerate at least 2 hours.

Mash half of 1 banana; stir in mayonnaise, dry milk and water. Slice remaining bananas; add to veal mixture. Toss with banana-mayonnaise mixture. Serve on lettuce; sprinkle with pecans.

6 servings.

CRUNCHY DEVILED EGG SALADS

5 hard-cooked eggs, coarsely chopped
1 large stalk celery, chopped
1 tablespoon chopped onion
1 cup shoestring potatoes
⅓ cup mayonnaise or salad dressing
¾ teaspoon dry mustard
½ teaspoon salt
  Dash of ground marjoram (optional)
4 lettuce cups
  Parsley
1 hard-cooked egg, sliced

Toss chopped eggs, celery, onion, potatoes, mayonnaise, mustard, salt and marjoram. Spoon salad into lettuce cups. Garnish with parsley and egg slices.

4 servings.

CHOW MEIN CHICKEN SALADS

3 cups cut-up cooked chicken, chilled
1 cup chopped watermelon pickles
2 tablespoons chopped onion
2 large stalks celery, coarsely chopped
¾ cup mayonnaise or salad dressing
1 teaspoon salt
½ teaspoon curry powder
  Dash of pepper
1 cup chow mein noodles
6 lettuce cups
  Chow mein noodles

Mix chicken, pickles, onion, celery, mayonnaise, salt, curry powder and pepper. Stir in 1 cup chow mein noodles. Spoon salad into lettuce cups and garnish with chow mein noodles.

6 servings.

TRIPLE DECKER CLUB SALADS

Pictured on page 56.

  Thousand Island Dressing (below)
2 heads Bibb or Boston lettuce, torn
  into bite-size pieces
4 medium tomatoes or 2 beefsteak
  tomatoes, peeled and sliced
2 cups ¼-inch strips cooked chicken
  or turkey (about 8 ounces), chilled
4 slices bacon, cut into 1-inch
  pieces and crisply fried

Prepare Thousand Island Dressing. Divide lettuce among 4 individual salad plates; top with tomatoes, chicken and bacon. Serve with dressing.

4 servings.

Thousand Island Dressing
½ cup mayonnaise or salad dressing
1 hard-cooked egg, chopped
1 tablespoon chili sauce
1 tablespoon chopped pimiento-stuffed
  olives
¼ teaspoon paprika
  Dash of salt
  Dash of pepper

Mix all ingredients. Cover and refrigerate at least 24 hours. *About ¾ cup dressing.*

"YOUR BRAND" SALAD DRESSINGS

"Personal caring"—it's the only ingredient the production line can't handle. Here are a few old-time basic dressings to try when you'd rather do it yourself.

Mayonnaise
1 egg yolk
1 teaspoon dry mustard
1 teaspoon sugar
¼ teaspoon salt
  Dash of cayenne red pepper
2 tablespoons lemon juice
1 cup vegetable oil

Beat egg yolk, mustard, sugar, salt, red pepper and 1 tablespoon lemon juice in small mixer bowl on medium speed until blended. Beat in vegetable oil, 1 drop at a time; increase rate of addition as mixture thickens. Beat in remaining lemon juice; refrigerate. *About 1 cup dressing.*

Russian Dressing: Mix ½ cup Mayonnaise, ¼ cup chili sauce and a few drops onion juice. *About ¾ cup dressing.*

Red French Dressing
1 cup vegetable oil
⅔ cup catsup
½ cup vinegar
½ cup sugar
2 tablespoons minced onion
1 tablespoon lemon juice
1 teaspoon salt
1 teaspoon pepper
1 teaspoon dry mustard
1 teaspoon paprika

Shake all ingredients in tightly covered jar. Refrigerate at least 3 hours. *2⅔ cups dressing.*

Cooked Salad Dressing
¼ cup all-purpose flour
2 tablespoons sugar
1 teaspoon salt
1 teaspoon dry mustard
1½ cups milk
2 egg yolks, slightly beaten
⅓ cup vinegar
1 tablespoon butter or margarine

Mix flour, sugar, salt and mustard in 2-quart saucepan. Stir milk gradually into egg yolks; slowly stir into flour mixture. Heat to boiling over medium heat, stirring constantly. Boil and stir 1 minute. Remove from heat; stir in vinegar and butter. Cool slightly; refrigerate. *About 2 cups dressing.*

Italian Salad Dressing
1 cup vegetable oil
¼ cup lemon juice
¼ cup white vinegar
1 teaspoon salt
1 teaspoon sugar
½ teaspoon dried oregano leaves
½ teaspoon dry mustard
½ teaspoon onion salt
½ teaspoon paprika
⅛ teaspoon ground thyme
2 cloves garlic, crushed

Shake all ingredients in tightly covered jar. Refrigerate at least 2 hours. *1½ cups dressing.*

DOUBLE-LAYER CHICKEN MOLD

2 hard-cooked eggs, sliced
  Pimiento-stuffed olive halves
4 cups cut-up cooked chicken (see note)
2 cups chicken broth
3 tablespoons water
1 tablespoon lemon juice
¾ teaspoon salt
1½ envelopes unflavored gelatin
  (1 tablespoon plus 1½ teaspoons)
¾ cup chopped pimiento-stuffed
  olives
1 cup boiling water
1 package (3 ounces) lemon-flavored
  gelatin
½ cup cold water
½ cup mayonnaise or salad dressing
3 tablespoons vinegar or lemon juice
¼ teaspoon salt
2 large stalks celery, finely chopped
¼ cup snipped parsley
1 tablespoon plus 1½ teaspoons
  finely chopped onion
  Salad greens

Arrange egg slices and olive halves alternately in 8-cup ring mold; cover with 2 cups of the chicken. Mix broth, 3 tablespoons water, the lemon juice and ¾ teaspoon salt in saucepan. Sprinkle unflavored gelatin on broth mixture to soften; stir over low heat until gelatin is dissolved. Remove from heat; cool slightly. Stir in chopped olives. Pour broth mixture on chicken. Refrigerate until mixture mounds slightly when dropped from a spoon, about 2 hours.

Pour boiling water on flavored gelatin in bowl; stir until gelatin is dissolved. Stir in ½ cup water, the mayonnaise, vinegar and ¼ teaspoon salt; pour into ice cube tray. Freeze until firm around edges but soft in center, 15 to 20 minutes. Pour into bowl; beat with hand beater until fluffy. Stir in remaining chicken, the celery, parsley and onion; pour on mixture in mold. Refrigerate until firm, at least 4 hours. Unmold on salad greens.

12 servings.

Note: A 3- to 4-pound broiler-fryer chicken yields 3 to 4 cups cut-up cooked chicken.

CHICKEN-SPINACH SALAD WITH BACON

  Piquant Dressing (below)
2 cups cut-up cooked chicken or turkey
5 ounces spinach, torn into bite-size
  pieces
2 cups broccoli flowerets, cut into
  ¼-inch pieces
1 can (8½ ounces) water chestnuts,
  drained and sliced
4 slices bacon, crisply fried and
  crumbled
  Grated Parmesan cheese (optional)

Prepare Piquant Dressing; pour on chicken. Cover and refrigerate at least 15 minutes. Toss chicken with spinach, broccoli and water chestnuts; sprinkle with bacon. Serve with cheese.

6 servings.

Piquant Dressing
2 tablespoons soy sauce
1 tablespoon vinegar
1 tablespoon vegetable oil
½ teaspoon instant minced onion
¼ teaspoon sugar
⅛ teaspoon pepper

Shake all ingredients in tightly covered jar.
¼ cup dressing.

ORIENTAL CHICKEN SALAD

Pictured on page 56.

2 ounces uncooked maifun (rice stick) noodles°
  Ginger Dressing (below)
½ bunch romaine, torn into bite-size pieces
2 cups cut-up cooked chicken or turkey, chilled
¼ cup sliced green onions

Prepare noodles as directed on package for crispy noodles; drain. Prepare Ginger Dressing; toss with noodles and the remaining ingredients.

6 servings.

°6 cups chow mein noodles can be substituted for the maifun noodles; toss with Ginger Dressing and remaining ingredients.

Ginger Dressing
¼ cup vegetable oil
3 tablespoons vinegar
2 teaspoons sugar
1 teaspoon soy sauce
¾ teaspoon salt
½ teaspoon pepper
½ teaspoon monosodium glutamate
¼ teaspoon ground ginger

Shake all ingredients in tightly covered jar.
½ cup dressing.

HOT CHICKEN SALAD IN AVOCADO SHELLS

1 can (about 7 ounces) marinated artichoke hearts, drained and sliced
1 can (5 ounces) boned chicken, drained (about ½ cup)
1 jar (2 ounces) sliced pimiento, drained
⅓ cup mayonnaise or salad dressing
½ large stalk celery, chopped
½ teaspoon salt
½ teaspoon chili powder
3 avocados
½ cup shredded taco-seasoned or jalapeño pepper cheese (about 2 ounces)

Heat oven to 400°. Mix artichoke hearts, chicken, pimiento, mayonnaise, celery, salt and chili powder. Cut each avocado lengthwise into halves; remove pit. Cut thin layer from bottom of each half to prevent tipping if necessary. Place avocado halves cut sides up in ungreased baking pan, 9x9x2 inches. Spoon about ¼ cup chicken mixture onto each half, spreading to cover entire cut surface; sprinkle with cheese. Bake uncovered until chicken mixture is hot and cheese is melted, about 20 minutes.

6 servings.

CRAB-SHRIMP-AVOCADO SALAD

Pictured on page 56.

Creamy Dill Dressing (below)
1 can (8½ ounces) water chestnuts,
    drained and sliced
1 package (6 ounces) frozen crabmeat,
    thawed, drained and cartilage
    removed
2 cans (4½ ounces each) large
    shrimp, drained
1 medium cucumber, chopped
¼ cup sliced green onions
2 avocados, sliced
2 medium tomatoes, cut into wedges
    Lettuce leaves or cups

Prepare Creamy Dill Dressing; toss with water chestnuts, crabmeat, shrimp, cucumber and onions. Cover and refrigerate at least 1 hour.

Arrange avocados and tomatoes on lettuce. Top with crabmeat mixture.

4 or 5 servings.

Creamy Dill Dressing
½ cup mayonnaise or salad dressing
¼ cup dairy sour cream
2 tablespoons lemon juice
¼ teaspoon salt
¼ teaspoon dried dill weed

Mix all ingredients. *About ¾ cup dressing.*

MEDITERRANEAN SALADS

1 cup cauliflowerets, cut into
    1-inch pieces
1 small onion, sliced and separated
    into rings
½ medium green pepper, coarsely
    chopped
1 medium carrot, thinly sliced
1 stalk celery, coarsely chopped
½ cup dry red or white wine
¼ cup tarragon vinegar
1 small clove garlic, crushed
1 bay leaf
1 can (8 ounces) tomato sauce
1 can (6½ ounces) tuna, drained
1 can (4 ounces) mushroom stems and
    pieces, drained
8 small pimiento-stuffed olives
6 romaine leaves
6 anchovy fillets
6 celery leaves

Mix cauliflowerets, onion, green pepper, carrot, celery, wine, vinegar, garlic and bay leaf in 3-quart saucepan. Heat to boiling; reduce heat. Cover and simmer 3 minutes; stir in tomato sauce. Heat to boiling; reduce heat. Cover and simmer 3 minutes longer. Remove from heat; stir in tuna, mushrooms and olives. Cover and refrigerate at least 2 hours.

Spoon about 1 cup wine mixture onto each romaine leaf with slotted spoon. Garnish each salad with rolled-up anchovy fillet and celery leaf.

6 servings.

SALADE NIÇOISE

Pictured on page 55.

1 package (10 ounces) frozen
  French-style green beans
  French Dressing (below)
2 heads Bibb or Boston lettuce,
  torn into bite-size pieces
2 tomatoes, cut into sixths
2 hard-cooked eggs, cut into
  fourths
1 can (about 7 ounces) tuna, drained
2 tablespoons sliced pitted ripe
  olives, drained
6 anchovies
  Snipped parsley

Cook beans as directed on package; drain. Refrigerate until chilled. Prepare French Dressing. Place lettuce in salad bowl. Arrange beans, tomatoes and eggs around edge of salad. Mound tuna in center; sprinkle with olives. Garnish with anchovies and sprinkle with parsley; serve with dressing.

4 servings.

French Dressing
½ cup olive oil, vegetable oil or
  combination
2 tablespoons vinegar
2 tablespoons lemon juice
½ teaspoon salt
¼ teaspoon dry mustard
¼ teaspoon paprika

Shake all ingredients in tightly covered jar.
¾ cup dressing.

TUNA ON A SHOESTRING

1 can (6½ ounces) tuna, drained
1 cup shredded carrots
1 cup chopped celery
¼ cup finely chopped onion
¾ to 1 cup mayonnaise or salad
  dressing
1 can (4 ounces) shoestring potatoes
  Carrot curls (optional)

Toss tuna, carrots, celery, onion and mayonnaise until tuna is well coated with mayonnaise. Cover and refrigerate at least 1 hour.

Just before serving, fold in potatoes. Garnish with carrot curls.

4 to 6 servings.

TUNA-BEAN TOSS

1 can (16 ounces) cut green beans,
  drained
1 can (15 ounces) garbanzo beans,
  drained
1 can (8 ounces) green lima beans,
  drained
1 can (9¼ ounces) tuna, drained
2 large stalks celery, chopped
¾ cup mayonnaise or salad dressing
¼ cup lemon juice
1 tablespoon instant minced onion
½ teaspoon lemon pepper
¼ teaspoon garlic salt
¼ teaspoon salt
2 hard-cooked eggs, sliced
3 tablespoons snipped parsley

Mix beans, tuna, celery, mayonnaise, lemon juice, onion, lemon pepper, garlic salt and salt. Cover and refrigerate at least 1 hour. Garnish with egg slices and parsley.

8 servings.

FAMILY FAVORITE TUNA SALADS

1 package (7 ounces) macaroni shells or rings
2 cans (6½ ounces each) tuna, drained
1 jar (4½ ounces) pimiento-stuffed olives, drained and cut into halves
5 large stalks celery, chopped
½ to ¾ cup mayonnaise or salad dressing
2 teaspoons lemon juice
1 teaspoon onion salt
½ teaspoon celery salt
½ teaspoon salt
9 lettuce cups
Tomato wedges or sliced hard-cooked eggs
Parsley sprigs

Cook macaroni as directed on package; drain. Rinse with cold water. Toss macaroni, tuna, olives, celery, mayonnaise, lemon juice, onion salt, celery salt and salt. Cover and refrigerate at least 1 hour. Spoon salad into lettuce cups and garnish with tomato wedges and parsley sprigs.

9 servings.

TUNA-CANTALOUPE SALADS

1 package (6 ounces) frozen Chinese pea pods
3 cups cooked rice
2 cans (6½ ounces each) tuna, drained
⅓ cup mayonnaise or salad dressing
1 teaspoon instant chicken bouillon
¼ teaspoon ground ginger
3 small cantaloupes
⅓ cup cashews or salted peanuts, coarsely chopped

Rinse frozen pea pods under running cold water to separate; drain. Mix pea pods, rice, tuna, mayonnaise, instant bouillon and ginger. Cover and refrigerate at least 2 hours.

Cut cantaloupes crosswise into halves, using zigzag or scalloped cut; scoop out seeds. Cut thin layer from bottom of each half to prevent tipping if necessary. Spoon 1 cup rice mixture into each half; sprinkle with cashews.

6 servings.

TUNA-BROCCOLI MOLD

1 package (10 ounces) frozen chopped broccoli
10 pimiento-stuffed olives, cut into halves
2 cans (6½ ounces each) tuna, drained
2 tablespoons finely chopped onion
1 envelope unflavored gelatin
1½ cups chicken broth
3 tablespoons lemon juice
½ teaspoon salt
Pale salad greens
Mayonnaise or salad dressing

Cook broccoli as directed on package; drain. Arrange olive halves cut sides down in 4-cup mold; spread broccoli evenly over olive halves. Mix tuna and onion; press evenly over broccoli.

Sprinkle gelatin on broth in saucepan to soften; stir over low heat until gelatin is dissolved. Remove from heat; stir in lemon juice and salt. Pour gelatin mixture carefully on tuna mixture. Refrigerate until firm. Unmold on salad greens and serve with mayonnaise.

4 or 5 servings.

VARIATIONS

Chicken-Broccoli Mold: Substitute 2 cans (5 ounces each) boned chicken, drained, for the tuna and omit salt.

Salmon-Broccoli Mold: Substitute 1 can (16 ounces) red salmon, drained and flaked, for the tuna.

FESTIVE TUNA MOLD

1 can (10¾ ounces) condensed chicken broth
½ cup water
1 envelope unflavored gelatin
2 cans (9¼ ounces each) tuna, drained
2 jars (2 ounces each) diced pimiento, drained
6 hard-cooked eggs, chopped
4 large stalks celery, finely chopped
1 medium avocado, sliced
2 teaspoons grated lemon peel
2 teaspoons salt
¼ teaspoon pepper
1 cup chilled whipping cream
Salad greens

Mix broth and water in 3-quart saucepan. Sprinkle gelatin on broth mixture to soften; stir over low heat until gelatin is dissolved. Refrigerate until slightly thickened, about 50 minutes.

Stir tuna, pimiento, eggs, celery, avocado, lemon peel, salt and pepper into gelatin mixture. Beat cream in chilled small mixer bowl until stiff; fold into tuna mixture. Pour into baking pan, 9x9x2 inches. Refrigerate until firm, at least 4 hours. Serve on salad greens.

8 servings.

INDEX

BETTY CROCKER'S
HAMBURGER
COOKBOOK

BETTY CROCKER'S
Hamburger Cookbook

Photography Director: George Ancona
Illustrator: Barbara Bascove

 **GOLDEN PRESS / NEW YORK**
Western Publishing Company, Inc.
Racine, Wisconsin

Dear Meal Planner—

Have you noticed what's been happening to hamburger? From a humble economy food, reserved for family only, it has flowered into a great American tradition.

Today hamburger can be anything the occasion calls for: a nutritious meal-in-minutes for toddlers . . . a noon, night or wee-hours staple for teen-agers . . . a swift-and-simple or gourmet-grand entrée for adults. You can serve it solo, backed only by a bun, or you can mingle it richly with vegetables, cheeses, pastas or sauces. Change its shape and you change its name. It's a meat loaf! It's a meatball! It's a superdish! Yet with all this, hamburger is still a thrift food, pound for protein-packed pound, one of the best buys on the meat market.

So this book is dedicated to bringing you up to date on hamburger in all its infinite variety, from basic recipes to fabulous flights of fancy. Have you ever tried sausage-centered burgers? Avocado-topped taco patties? Wine-marinated hamburger kabobs? Or a meat loaf filled with such exotica as bananas, green pepper and orange marmalade? No? Well . . . here's your chance.

And because hamburger is so eminently freezeable, we've created a collection of special "freezer mixes" and other dishes to stow away for future reference. Finally, for those of you lucky enough to have a microwave oven, we've adapted some typical recipes to use in this fascinating time-saving appliance.

We hope you'll sample liberally from the recipes on the following pages. We think they'll help you capture the spirit of hamburger as it is today.

Cordially,

Betty Crocker

P.S. All these recipes were tested in the Betty Crocker Kitchens and in the homes of hamburger-lovers all across the country. So you can be sure that they'll work for you too.

Contents

All About Hamburger

Few cuts of meat have as much going for them—or for you—as hamburger. And its number-one virtue is versatility. You can use it as the basis for a snack, sandwich or main dish. You can keep it family-frank or dress it up for company. In fact, hamburger can put on just about any face a good cook wants it to. But even a can't-go-wrong meat like this has its finer points. And once you know these few ifs, ands and buts, you'll be that much farther ahead in the cooking game.

What's in a Name?

As far as most of us are concerned, "hamburger" is just another word for ground beef. There is, however, a distinction. And it's one that you should know about when it comes to the shopping scene. Federal laws specify the amount of fat permitted in the various types of ground beef; so it is really the amount of fat (or conversely, the amount of lean*) that determines the label. Here, then, are all those names you should know about:

_____

* Note that we express the fat-lean levels in the various types of ground beef in terms of the fat. There may be some sections of the country that use the percentage of lean instead; therefore, a 30 percent fat level would be expressed as 70 percent lean.

HAMBURGER: Any ground beef bearing this label can legally contain up to 30 percent fat. And this fat may consist of the natural fat attached to the beef plus "loose" beef fat.

GROUND BEEF: Here the amount of fat allowed under the law may also be 30 percent. The big difference between the _ground beef_ and _hamburger_ labels is that _ground beef_ can contain _only_ the fat attached to the beef. No other fat may be added to reach the 30 percent level. Thus, the fat content in meat labeled _ground beef_ is usually less than 30 percent.

LEAN GROUND BEEF (GROUND CHUCK): The fat level in ground beef bearing this label is usually about 20 percent.

EXTRA LEAN GROUND BEEF (GROUND ROUND): This type of ground beef usually contains about 15 percent fat.

Keep an eye out too for ground beef supplemented with vegetable protein sources—it's now available in some parts of the country. The labels for this type of beef mixture vary, but it is usually a bargain.

Most of the recipes in this book were tested with _ground beef_—a few call for a leaner cut, and they so specify.

Which One's for You?

It all depends. On your recipe and your budget. For a juicy broiled or grilled burger, your choice should be *ground beef* or *ground chuck*. The amount of fat in both types allows the burgers to baste themselves. If you prefer a leaner type, you will probably have a less juicy patty. But remember, the more fat, the more shrinkage.

Ground round and *ground chuck* are ideal for casseroles and other main dishes, though the fattier cuts will work just as well if you can drain off the excess fat after the meat has been browned.

And then there's the cost. The more fat, the lower the cost—that only stands to reason. Demand is another factor that affects the price tag. *Ground round* and *ground chuck* are more expensive because of all the other (and more costly) uses the butcher has for them. So here you must pay for your preferences.

No matter which label you head for, all types of ground beef should have a nice bright color. Fresh ground beef crumbles easily and smells good; a slick feel and an "off" odor are signs of age.

How to Store

Ground beef is far more perishable than other beef cuts. The grinding, quite naturally, exposes more of the meat to the air—hence, to bacteria. Therefore, a certain amount of care is called for.

If you're planning to use ground beef *within* 24 hours of purchase, you can store it in the meat keeper or the coldest part of your refrigerator. Prepackaged ground beef should be refrigerated right in its package, unopened. Beef ground to order, however, should be rewrapped loosely in waxed paper or aluminum foil and then refrigerated.

If you plan to store the ground beef for a while—and that means longer than 24 hours—then freeze you must. To maintain the meat's quality, first wrap it in an airtight, moisture-proof wrap. If burgers are part of your future plans, you can shape the meat into patties and stack them with a double layer of foil or freezer wrap between; then overwrap. Do not freeze ground beef longer than 3 to 4 months.

It's best to thaw ground beef still in its wrap in the refrigerator. If time is tight, you can use your microwave oven for speedy thawing (follow the manufacturer's instructions), or you can cook it from the frozen state—providing no handling is necessary and no additions are to be made before the meat is browned.

Season-ups

Below you will find a list of herbs and spices that are all compatible with hamburger. Be cautious, particularly when using fresh herbs and spices— they are usually stronger than the dried varieties. Start with a small amount and increase until you find the just-right flavor level.

allspice	mace
basil	marjoram
cayenne red	mustard
pepper	nutmeg
celery seed	oregano
chili powder	paprika
cumin seed	parsley
curry powder	sage
garlic	savory
ginger	sesame seed
lemon-pepper	thyme
marinade	

Patties & Sandwiches

Basic Hamburgers

1½ pounds ground beef
1 small onion, finely chopped (about ¼ cup)
¼ cup water or evaporated milk
1 teaspoon salt
1 teaspoon Worcestershire sauce
¼ teaspoon pepper

Mix all ingredients. Shape mixture into 6 patties, about ¾ inch thick. Broil or grill patties 4 inches from heat, turning once, to desired doneness, 10 to 15 minutes. Nice served on toasted buns with favorite topping.

6 patties.

VARIATIONS

Before mixing ingredients, add one or more of the following:
1 tablespoon horseradish
1 tablespoon prepared mustard
1 tablespoon snipped chives
1 to 2 tablespoons crumbled blue cheese
2 tablespoons sesame seed
¼ cup chopped ripe olives
¼ cup chopped dill pickle or pickle relish
¼ cup chopped nuts

Have a freezer? See page 68 for Freezer Burgers.

Hamburger Toppings

Broiled Onion Topping

1 tablespoon butter or margarine
2 medium onions, chopped (about
  1 cup)
⅛ teaspoon nutmeg
2 tablespoons dairy sour cream

Melt butter in small skillet. Add onions;
cook and stir until tender. Stir in remaining ingredients; spread on cooked patties.
Broil 2 inches from heat until hot, about
1 minute.

Enough for 6 patties.

Mushroom-Onion Topper

1 tablespoon butter or margarine
1 medium onion, thinly sliced
1 can (4 ounces) mushroom stems
  and pieces, drained
½ teaspoon Worcestershire sauce
⅛ teaspoon pepper

Melt butter in small skillet. Add onion;
cook and stir until tender. Stir in remaining ingredients and heat. Serve hot over
patties.

Enough for 6 patties.

Mustard Butter

¼ cup butter or margarine, softened
1 tablespoon snipped parsley
2 tablespoons prepared mustard
¼ teaspoon onion salt

Mix all ingredients. Spoon onto hot patties.

Enough for 6 patties.

Sesame Butter

¼ cup butter or margarine, softened
1 teaspoon Worcestershire sauce
½ teaspoon garlic salt
1 tablespoon toasted sesame seed
  (see note)

Mix all ingredients. Spoon onto hot patties.

Enough for 4 patties.

NOTE: To toast sesame seed, spread in ungreased shallow baking pan; bake in 350°
oven until golden brown, 5 to 10 minutes.

Zippy Tomato Sauce

2 tablespoons butter or margarine
½ cup chopped green pepper
1 small onion, thinly sliced
1 can (8 ounces) tomato sauce
1 cup chili sauce
1 teaspoon Worcestershire sauce
¼ teaspoon chili powder

Melt butter in small saucepan. Add green
pepper and onion; cook and stir until
onion is tender. Stir in remaining ingredients. Heat to boiling, stirring occasionally.
Serve hot over patties.

Enough for 8 patties.

Filled Hamburgers

1½ pounds ground beef
¼ cup dry bread crumbs
1 small onion, finely chopped
  (about ¼ cup)
1 egg
1 teaspoon salt
1 teaspoon Worcestershire sauce
¼ teaspoon pepper
  Fillings (below)

Mix all ingredients except fillings. Shape mixture into 12 thin patties, about 3½ inches in diameter. Top each of 6 patties with a filling, spreading to within ½ inch of edge. Cover wih a remaining patty, sealing edges firmly. Broil or grill patties 4 inches from heat, turning once, to desired doneness, about 10 minutes.

6 patties.

MIX-AND-MATCH FILLINGS

Use one or more of the following:

Dill pickle slices or pickle relish
Prepared mustard
Catsup
Horseradish
Onion slices or finely chopped onion
Tomato slices
Process American or Cheddar cheese
  slices

PEPPY CHEESE FILLING

½ cup shredded process American or
  Cheddar cheese
2 tablespoons mayonnaise or salad
  dressing
1 teaspoon Worcestershire sauce
½ teaspoon salt
½ teaspoon prepared mustard
¼ teaspoon pepper

Mix all ingredients.

Burgundy Burgers

1½ pounds ground beef
¼ cup Burgundy or other red wine
1 small onion, finely chopped
  (about ¼ cup)
1 tablespoon Worcestershire sauce
1 teaspoon seasoned salt
¼ teaspoon pepper
⅛ teaspoon garlic salt

Mix all ingredients. Shape mixture into 6 patties, about ¾ inch thick. Broil or grill patties 4 inches from heat, turning once, to desired doneness, 10 to 15 minutes. Nice served on toasted buns with a favorite topping (see page 7).

6 patties.

VARIATION

Blue Cheese Burgundy Burgers: Shape meat mixture into 12 thin patties, about 3½ inches in diameter. Place 1 tablespoon crumbled blue cheese on each of 6 patties. Top with a remaining patty, sealing edges firmly.

Supreme Burgers

2 pounds ground beef
1 envelope (about 1½ ounces) onion
  soup mix
½ cup dry bread crumbs
1 cup dairy sour cream
⅛ teaspoon pepper

Mix all ingredients. Shape mixture into 8 patties, about ¾ inch thick. Broil or grill 4 inches from heat, turning once, to desired doneness, 10 to 15 minutes.

8 patties.

Family Favorite Burgers

1½ pounds ground beef
 2 slices bread, torn into small
    pieces
⅓ cup milk
¼ cup catsup
 1 small onion, finely chopped
    (about ¼ cup)
 1 teaspoon salt
 2 teaspoons horseradish
 2 teaspoons Worcestershire sauce
 1 tablespoon prepared mustard

Mix all ingredients. Shape mixture into
6 patties, about ¾ inch thick. Broil or
grill 4 inches from heat, turning once, to
desired doneness, 10 to 15 minutes.

6 patties.

Zesty Burgers

1 pound ground beef
⅓ cup dry bread crumbs
½ cup water
1 teaspoon instant beef bouillon
1 teaspoon grated lemon peel
1 teaspoon lemon juice
½ teaspoon salt
½ teaspoon sage
½ teaspoon ginger
¼ teaspoon pepper

Mix all ingredients. Shape mixture into
4 patties, about ¾ inch thick. Broil or
grill 4 inches from heat, turning once, to
desired doneness, 10 to 15 minutes.

4 patties.

Keep the Secret

If you fill a burger, don't spoil the
surprise inside. Be sure to keep the
filling in the center of the patty and
press the outer edges together firmly.
The egg and bread crumbs in the
Filled Hamburgers recipe keep the
patties moist and there is no danger
of shrinking or pulling apart as the
patties cook. Best of all, what's inside
remains a secret.

Nifty Hamburgers on a Bun

8 small hamburger buns, split, or
   6 slices bread
   Prepared mustard or catsup
1 pound lean ground beef (chuck)
1 small onion, chopped (about ¼
   cup)
1 teaspoon salt
¼ teaspoon pepper

Heat oven to 500°. Spread cut sides of
hamburger buns or one side of each bread
slice with mustard. Mix meat, onion, salt
and pepper. Spread mixture over mustard, being careful to bring it to edges of
buns. Place meat sides up on ungreased
baking sheet. Bake until of desired doneness, about 5 minutes.

4 to 6 servings.

NOTE: If you like, you can have these
burgers ready and waiting in the freezer
for last-minute cooking. After spreading
meat mixture over buns, wrap each securely in heavy-duty or double thickness
regular aluminum foil and label; freeze
no longer than 2 months. To serve, unwrap desired number of hamburgers and
bake about 10 minutes.

Beef Boulette Burgers

2 pounds ground beef
1 cup dairy sour cream
½ cup dry bread crumbs
1 can (4 ounces) mushroom stems
 and pieces, drained and chopped
2 tablespoons finely chopped onion
2 tablespoons snipped parsley
1½ teaspoons salt
¼ teaspoon pepper

Mix all ingredients. Shape mixture into 8 patties, about ¾ inch thick. Broil or grill 4 inches from heat, turning once, to desired doneness, 10 to 15 minutes. (Pictured on page 18.)

8 patties.

Chili Cheese Burgers

1½ pounds ground beef
1 small onion, finely chopped
 (about ¼ cup)
1 teaspoon chili powder
1 teaspoon Worcestershire sauce
¾ teaspoon salt
¼ teaspoon garlic salt
¼ teaspoon pepper
¼ teaspoon red pepper sauce
 Dash cayenne red pepper
6 slices Cheddar cheese, 2×2
 inches
2 tablespoons canned chopped
 green chilies

Mix all ingredients except cheese and chilies. Shape mixture into 12 thin patties, about 3½ inches in diameter. Place 1 cheese slice and 1 teaspoon chilies on each of 6 patties. Top with a remaining patty, sealing edges firmly. Broil or grill patties 4 inches from heat, turning once, to desired doneness, 10 to 15 minutes. (Pictured on page 18.)

6 patties.

Blue Ribbon Burgers

2 pounds ground beef
2 teaspoons Worcestershire sauce
½ teaspoon salt
¼ teaspoon garlic salt
¼ teaspoon pepper
1 package (3 ounces) cream cheese,
 softened
2 tablespoons crumbled blue cheese
1 can (4 ounces) mushroom stems
 and pieces, drained and chopped

Mix meat, Worcestershire sauce and seasonings. Shape mixture into 12 thin patties, about 4 inches in diameter.

Mix cream cheese and blue cheese. Top each of 6 patties with cheese mixture, spreading to within ½ inch of edge; press mushrooms into cheese. Cover each with a remaining patty, sealing edges firmly. Broil or grill patties 4 inches from heat, turning once, to desired doneness, 10 to 15 minutes.

6 large patties.

Braunburgers

1 pound ground beef
¼ pound Braunschweiger (liver)
 sausage
¼ cup dairy sour cream
2 tablespoons finely chopped onion

Mix all ingredients. Shape mixture into 5 patties, about ¾ inch thick. Broil or grill 4 inches from heat, turning once, to desired doneness, 10 to 15 minutes.

5 patties.

NOTE: Because of the zesty sausage, no additional seasonings are necessary.

Caraway Burgers

1½ pounds ground beef
  1 medium onion, finely chopped
    (about ½ cup)
  1 teaspoon salt
  1 teaspoon caraway seed
  1 teaspoon Worcestershire sauce
  ¼ teaspoon pepper
  1 cup beer

Mix all ingredients except beer. Shape mixture into 6 patties, about 1 inch thick. Place in ungreased baking dish, 10×6×1¾ inches. Pour beer over patties; cover and refrigerate at least 3 hours (the meat may turn gray).

Remove patties from marinade. Broil or grill 4 inches from heat, turning once, to desired doneness, 15 to 20 minutes.

6 patties.

NOTE: If you prefer to make thinner patties, use a larger dish for marinating and turn patties occasionally while marinating. Broil or grill 10 to 15 minutes.

Reuben Burgers

  1 pound ground beef
  1 can (4½ ounces) corned beef
    spread or deviled ham
  1 small onion, finely chopped
    (about ¼ cup)
  ¼ teaspoon salt
  ⅛ teaspoon garlic salt
  ⅛ teaspoon pepper
  1 can (8 ounces) sauerkraut, drained
  5 slices Swiss cheese, 3×3 inches

Mix all ingredients except sauerkraut and cheese. Shape mixture into 5 patties, about ¾ inch thick.

Set oven control at broil and/or 550°. Broil patties 4 inches from heat, turning once, to desired doneness, 10 to 15 minutes. Top each patty with sauerkraut and a cheese slice. Broil until cheese is light brown.

Nice served on toasted rye or pumpernickel buns. (Pictured on page 19.)

5 patties.

Crunchy Teriyaki Burgers

1½ pounds ground beef
  ½ cup finely chopped water
    chestnuts
  ¼ cup soy sauce
  ¼ cup dry sherry or orange juice
  1 clove garlic, minced
  1 teaspoon molasses or brown
    sugar
  ⅛ teaspoon ginger

Mix meat and water chestnuts. Shape mixture into 6 patties, about ¾ inch thick. Place patties in ungreased baking dish, 10×6×1¾ inches. Mix remaining ingredients; pour over patties. Cover and refrigerate at least 3 hours, turning patties once.

Remove patties from marinade. Broil or grill patties 4 inches from heat to desired doneness, 10 to 15 minutes. Brush frequently with marinade and turn once.

6 patties.

Taco Patties

1½ pounds ground beef
1 small onion, chopped (about
 ¼ cup)
1 teaspoon salt
1 teaspoon Worcestershire sauce
¼ teaspoon pepper
¾ cup water
1 envelope (about 1¼ ounces)
 taco seasoning mix
1 ripe small avocado*
1 cup shredded Cheddar cheese
 (4 ounces)

Mix meat, onion, salt, Worcestershire sauce and pepper. Shape mixture into 6 patties, about ¾ inch thick. Brown patties in large skillet over medium-high heat, turning once. Remove patties and set aside. Pour fat from skillet.

Mix water and seasoning mix in same skillet; heat to boiling, stirring constantly. Reduce heat; return patties to skillet and turn each to coat with sauce.

Peel avocado and cut into 6 rings. Top each patty with an avocado ring; cover and simmer 10 minutes. Sprinkle with

cheese; cover and heat until cheese is melted, about 2 minutes. Serve sauce over patties. (Pictured on the cover and on page 18.)

Serve with refried beans and corn chips for a Mexicali meal.

6 patties.

* You can substitute 1 medium tomato, sliced, for the avocado rings.

Devilish Potato Stacks

1 pound ground beef
1 can (2¼ ounces) deviled ham
1 teaspoon Worcestershire sauce
 Mashed potato puffs (enough
 for 4 servings)
½ cup creamed cottage cheese
1 can (3 ounces) French fried
 onions

Heat oven to 350°. Mix meat, deviled ham and Worcestershire sauce. Shape mixture into 4 patties. Place patties in ungreased baking pan, 8×8×2 inches.

Prepare potato puffs as directed on package except—decrease water to 1 cup. Stir cottage cheese and half the onions into potatoes. Top each patty with ¼ of the potato mixture. Sprinkle with remaining onions. Bake uncovered to desired doneness, 30 to 40 minutes. Remove patties to serving plate with a slotted spoon.

4 patties.

Triple Cheese Patties

1½ pounds ground beef
¼ cup dry bread crumbs
1 small onion, chopped
    (about ¼ cup)
1 egg
1 teaspoon salt
1 teaspoon Worcestershire sauce
½ teaspoon basil leaves
¼ teaspoon pepper
⅛ teaspoon garlic salt
6 tablespoons creamed cottage
    cheese
¼ cup grated Parmesan cheese
1 can (8 ounces) tomato sauce
6 slices mozzarella or Swiss
    cheese, 3×3 inches

Mix meat, bread crumbs, onion, egg and seasonings. Shape mixture into 12 thin patties, about 4 inches in diameter.

Top each of 6 patties with 1 tablespoon cottage cheese, spreading to within ½ inch of edge; sprinkle with 2 teaspoons Parmesan cheese. Cover each with a remaining patty, sealing edges firmly.

Brown patties in large skillet over medium-high heat, turning once. Drain off fat. Pour tomato sauce over patties; cover and simmer 15 minutes. Place a cheese slice on each patty; cover and heat until cheese is melted, about 2 minutes. Serve sauce over patties. (Pictured on page 19.)

6 patties.

Hamburgers au Poivre

1 pound ground beef
½ teaspoon salt
½ to 1 tablespoon freshly cracked
    black pepper
1 tablespoon cognac or brandy
    (optional)
3 tablespoons dry red wine
    (optional)

Mix meat and salt. Shape mixture into 4 patties, about ¾ inch thick. Press pepper into both sides of each patty. Cook patties in large skillet over medium-high heat, turning once, to desired doneness, about 8 minutes. Drain off fat.

Sprinkle cognac over patties; immediately ignite if desired. Remove patties to warm platter.

Stir wine into drippings in skillet; heat just to boiling, stirring constantly. Serve sauce over patties.

4 patties.

Patties Parmigiana

1½ pounds ground beef (see note)
 1 small onion, finely chopped
   (about ¼ cup)
 1 teaspoon salt
 1 teaspoon Worcestershire sauce
 ¼ teaspoon pepper
 ½ cup Parmesan cheese
 ¼ cup cornflake crumbs
 1 egg, slightly beaten
 1 can (8 ounces) tomato sauce
 1 teaspoon Italian seasoning
 6 slices mozzarella cheese,
   3×3 inches

Mix meat, onion, salt, Worcestershire sauce and pepper. Shape mixture into 6 patties, about ¾ inch thick. Mix Parmesan cheese and cornflake crumbs. Dip patties into egg, then coat with crumb mixture. Brown patties in large skillet over medium heat, turning once. Drain off fat.

Mix tomato sauce and Italian seasoning; pour over patties in skillet. Cover and simmer 15 minutes. Top each patty with a cheese slice; cover and heat until cheese is melted, about 2 minutes. Serve sauce over patties.

6 patties.

NOTE: If ground beef is lean, it may be necessary to add a small amount of shortening or salad oil to the skillet when browning patties.

A Future Investment

Take advantage of the fact that your hamburger patties adapt nicely to do-ahead shaping. In fact, the waiting time in the refrigerator gives the seasonings a better chance to mingle with the meat, actually improving the taste. And it gives you a chance to do the shaping when you've got the time, avoiding that predinner rush. Try it someday soon. You'll be ahead on time and up on flavor.

Hamburgers Diane

 2 tablespoons butter or margarine
 1 teaspoon Worcestershire sauce
 ¼ teaspoon lemon juice
 1 clove garlic, minced
 1 small onion, sliced
 1 cup washed, trimmed sliced
   mushrooms*
 1 pound lean ground beef (chuck)
 ½ teaspoon salt
 ¼ teaspoon pepper

Melt butter in large skillet. Add Worcestershire sauce, lemon juice, garlic, onion and mushrooms; cook and stir over medium heat 2 minutes. Remove from heat.

Mix meat, salt and pepper. Shape mixture into 4 patties, about ¾ inch thick. Push mushroom-onion mixture to side of skillet. Cook patties in same skillet over medium-high heat, turning once, to desired doneness, about 10 minutes. Serve mushroom-onion mixture over patties. (Pictured on page 19.)

4 patties.

* You can substitute ½ cup drained canned sliced mushrooms for the fresh mushrooms.

Barbecue Hamburger Patties

1½ pounds ground beef
 1 medium onion, chopped (about
    ½ cup)
 1 teaspoon salt
⅓ cup catsup
⅓ cup chili sauce
 2 tablespoons brown sugar
 1 tablespoon lemon juice

Mix meat, onion and salt. Shape mixture
into 6 patties, about ¾ inch thick. Brown
patties in large skillet over medium-high
heat, turning once. Cover and cook over
low heat 10 minutes. Drain off fat.

Mix catsup, chili sauce, brown sugar and
lemon juice; pour over patties. Cover and
simmer 15 minutes, spooning sauce onto
patties occasionally. Serve the sauce over
patties.

6 patties.

Bavarian Patties with Sauerkraut

1½ pounds ground beef
½ cup applesauce
⅓ cup dry bread crumbs
 1 small onion, finely chopped
    (about ¼ cup)
 1 egg
 1 teaspoon salt
½ teaspoon allspice
 1 can (16 ounces) sauerkraut,
    drained

Mix all ingredients except sauerkraut.
Shape mixture into 6 patties, about ¾ inch
thick. Brown patties in large skillet over
medium heat, turning once. Drain off fat.
Spoon sauerkraut onto patties; cover and
simmer 15 minutes.

6 patties.

Tacos

MEAT FILLING

 1 pound ground beef
 1 medium onion, chopped (about
    ½ cup)
 1 can (15 ounces) tomato sauce
 1 teaspoon garlic salt
½ to 1 teaspoon chili powder
    Dash pepper

SHELLS AND TOPPINGS

8 to 10 taco shells
 1 cup shredded Cheddar cheese
    (4 ounces)
 1 cup shredded lettuce
 1 large tomato, chopped

Cook and stir meat and onion in skillet
until meat is brown. Drain off fat. Stir in
tomato sauce, garlic salt, chili powder and
pepper; simmer uncovered 15 minutes.

While Meat Filling is simmering, heat taco
shells as directed on package. Spoon Meat
Filling into taco shells. Top filling with
cheese, lettuce and tomato. If desired,
serve with taco sauce.

8 to 10 tacos.

*You can get a head start on this recipe with
Beef-Tomato Freezer Mix (see page 63).*

Chow Mein on a Bun

1 pound ground beef
1 medium onion, thinly sliced
⅔ cup water
2 tablespoons cornstarch
3 tablespoons soy sauce
1 tablespoon molasses
¼ teaspoon ginger
1 can (16 ounces) bean sprouts,
   rinsed and drained
1 can (8 ounces) water chestnuts,
   drained and sliced
8 hamburger buns, split and toasted

Cook and stir meat and onion in large skillet until onion is tender. Drain off fat. Mix water, cornstarch, soy sauce, molasses and ginger; stir into meat mixture. Add bean sprouts and water chestnuts. Cook, stirring constantly, until mixture thickens and boils, about 5 minutes. Serve on buns and pass additional soy sauce. (Pictured on page 19.)

8 sandwiches.

VARIATION

Chow Mein: Omit buns. Serve mixture over hot cooked rice or chow mein noodles.

Beef and Cabbage Joes

1 pound ground beef
1 medium onion, chopped (about
   ½ cup)
½ cup thinly sliced celery
2 cups shredded cabbage
⅓ cup chopped green pepper
¾ cup catsup
¼ cup water
¼ teaspoon salt
1 tablespoon prepared mustard
8 hamburger buns, split and
   toasted

Cook and stir meat, onion and celery in large skillet until meat is brown. Drain off fat. Stir in cabbage, green pepper, catsup, water, salt and mustard; heat to boiling, stirring occasionally. Reduce heat; cover and simmer until vegetables are tender, about 25 minutes. Spoon mixture onto bottom halves of buns; top with remaining halves.

8 sandwiches.

NOTE: If you have a microwave oven, see page 71 for specific instructions.

VARIATION

Sloppy Joes: Omit cabbage and salt.

At right—Meat loaves to fit the fancy of any family. Clockwise from upper left: Meat-and-Potato Squares (page 31), Savory Stuffed Meat Loaf (page 33), Bacon-wrapped Little Loaves (page 35), Onion Meat Loaf (page 32).

On pages 18–19—Patties either burger-style or fancy-fashion. Top row: Beef Boulette Burgers (page 10), Chili Cheese Burgers (page 10), Chow Mein on a Bun (this page), Reuben Burgers (page 11). Bottom row: Taco Patties (page 12), Triple Cheese Patties (page 13), Hamburgers Diane (page 14).

Sausage-centered Hamburger Rolls

1½ pounds ground beef
1 cup finely chopped unpared apple
⅓ cup chopped green onion
   (with tops)
1 egg
1 teaspoon salt
¼ teaspoon pepper
¼ teaspoon cinnamon
   Dash cloves
1 package (8 ounces) brown and
   serve sausage links
2 tablespoons flour
1 teaspoon instant beef bouillon
1 cup water

Mix meat, apple, onion, egg and seasonings. Divide mixture into 10 equal parts. Mold each part around a sausage link, sealing ends. Brown meat rolls in large skillet over medium heat. Remove meat rolls.

Pour all but 2 tablespoons fat from skillet. Stir flour into fat remaining in skillet. Cook over low heat, stirring constantly, until mixture is smooth and bubbly. Stir in bouillon and water. Heat to boiling, stirring constantly. Reduce heat; return meat rolls to skillet. Cover skillet and simmer 15 minutes.

Buttered noodles are a good "go-with" for this zesty dish.

6 to 8 servings.

At left—Meatballs for any occasion. Clockwise from upper left: Saucy Meatballs (page 23), Batter-dipped Fondue Meatballs (page 28), Harvest-Time Meatballs (page 24), Sweet-Sour Kabobs (page 27).

Hamburger Pasties

1 pound ground beef
1 small onion, chopped (about
   ¼ cup)
1 can (8 ounces) peas or diced
   carrots, drained*
1 medium potato, pared and shredded
1 cup shredded process American
   or Cheddar cheese (4 ounces)
¼ cup catsup
½ teaspoon garlic salt
¼ teaspoon pepper
1 tablespoon prepared mustard
1 package (11 ounces) pie crust mix
   or sticks

Heat oven to 375°. Cook and stir meat and onion in large skillet until meat is brown. Drain off fat. Remove from heat; stir in remaining ingredients except pie crust mix and set aside.

Prepare pastry for Two-crust Pie as directed on package. Divide dough into 8 equal parts. Roll each part on floured surface into a 7-inch circle. On half of each circle, spread about ½ cup meat mixture (packed) to within ½ inch of edge. Moisten edge of pastry with water. Fold pastry over filling, sealing edges with fork. Place on ungreased baking sheet; prick tops with fork.

Bake 30 to 35 minutes. You can serve these as sandwiches or, if you prefer, place on plates and top with a favorite gravy or sauce.

8 pasties.

* You can substitute 1 cup of a favorite cooked vegetable for the canned peas or carrots.

Like to plan ahead? See page 69 for Freezer Pasties. Or get a head start with Browned 'n Seasoned Freezer Mix (see page 61).

Meatballs

Basic Meatballs

1 pound ground beef
1 egg
1 small onion, chopped (about ¼ cup)
⅓ cup dry bread crumbs
¼ cup milk
¾ teaspoon salt
⅛ teaspoon pepper
1 teaspoon Worcestershire sauce

Mix all ingredients. Shape mixture by tablespoonfuls into 1½-inch balls. (For ease in shaping meatballs, occasionally wet hands with cold water.)

TO COOK IN SKILLET: Heat 1 tablespoon salad oil in large skillet; cook meatballs over medium heat until brown, about 20 minutes. Drain off fat.

TO COOK IN OVEN: Place meatballs in lightly greased baking pan, 13×9×2 or 15½×10½×1 inch; bake uncovered in 400° oven until light brown, about 20 minutes. Drain off fat.

About 24 meatballs.

NOTE: If you have a microwave oven, see page 71 for specific instructions.

Have a freezer? See page 69 for Freezer Meatballs.

Saucy Meatballs

Basic Meatballs (page 22)
1 can (10¾ ounces) condensed cream of chicken soup
⅓ cup milk
⅛ teaspoon nutmeg
½ cup dairy sour cream
Snipped parsley

Prepare Basic Meatballs. Combine cooked meatballs, soup, milk and nutmeg in large skillet; heat to boiling, stirring occasionally. Reduce heat; cover and simmer 15 minutes. Stir in sour cream; cover and heat 2 to 3 minutes. Sprinkle with parsley. (Pictured on page 20.)

4 or 5 servings.

NOTE: If you have a microwave oven, see page 71 for specific instructions.

Sweet-and-Sour Meatballs

Basic Meatballs (page 22)
1 tablespoon cornstarch
½ cup brown sugar (packed)
1 can (13¼ ounces) pineapple chunks
1 tablespoon soy sauce
⅓ cup vinegar
½ cup coarsely chopped green pepper

Prepare Basic Meatballs and set aside. Mix cornstarch and sugar in large skillet. Stir in pineapple (with syrup), soy sauce and vinegar. Cook, stirring constantly, until mixture thickens and boils. Add cooked meatballs; cover and simmer 10 minutes, stirring occasionally. Stir in green pepper; cover and simmer until pepper is crisp-tender, about 5 minutes.

4 or 5 servings.

Pepper Beef Balls

Basic Meatballs (page 22)
1 tablespoon butter or margarine
1 medium onion, sliced
1½ cups water
1½ teaspoons instant beef bouillon
½ teaspoon garlic salt
½ teaspoon ginger
3 tablespoons soy sauce
2 medium green peppers, cut into strips
2 tablespoons cornstarch
2 tablespoons water
1 large tomato, cut into eighths

Prepare Basic Meatballs and set aside. Melt butter in large skillet. Add onion; cook and stir until tender. Add cooked meatballs, 1½ cups water, the bouillon, garlic salt, ginger and soy sauce; heat to boiling. Reduce heat; cover and simmer 10 minutes, stirring occasionally.

Add green pepper. Mix cornstarch and 2 tablespoons water; stir into sauce mixture. Cook, stirring carefully, until mixture thickens and boils. Cover and simmer until pepper is crisp-tender, about 3 minutes. Add tomato; cover and heat 2 to 3 minutes.

Hot cooked rice makes an ideal accompaniment for this zesty dish.

4 or 5 servings.

Harvest-Time Meatballs

Basic Meatballs (page 22)
2 tablespoons butter or margarine
⅛ teaspoon instant minced garlic*
½ teaspoon thyme leaves
½ pound mushrooms, washed, trimmed
and sliced
3 medium zucchini, thinly sliced
(about 4 cups)
½ teaspoon salt
⅓ cup grated Parmesan cheese
2 tomatoes, cut into eighths

Prepare Basic Meatballs and set aside. Melt butter in large skillet. Add garlic, thyme leaves, mushrooms and zucchini; cook over medium-high heat 5 minutes, stirring occasionally.

Add cooked meatballs; cover and simmer, stirring occasionally, until vegetables are tender, about 10 minutes. Sprinkle with salt and cheese. Add tomatoes; cover and heat 2 to 3 minutes. (Pictured on page 20.)

4 or 5 servings.

* You can substitute 1 clove garlic, minced, or ⅛ teaspoon garlic powder for the instant minced garlic.

Hungarian Meatballs

Basic Meatballs (page 22)
1 tablespoon salad oil
2 medium onions, thinly sliced
¾ cup water
¾ cup dry red wine*
1 teaspoon caraway seed
2 teaspoons paprika
½ teaspoon marjoram leaves
½ teaspoon salt
¼ cup water
2 tablespoons flour

Prepare Basic Meatballs and set aside. Heat oil in large skillet. Add onions; cook and stir until tender. Add cooked meatballs, ¾ cup water, the wine, caraway seed, paprika, marjoram leaves and salt; heat to boiling. Reduce heat; cover and simmer 30 minutes, stirring occasionally.

Mix ¼ cup water and the flour; stir into sauce mixture. Heat to boiling, stirring carefully. Boil and stir 1 minute.

Especially nice served with boiled potatoes or noodles.

4 or 5 servings.

* You can substitute a mixture of ¾ cup water, 1 teaspoon instant beef bouillon and 1 tablespoon vinegar for the wine.

Sauerbraten Meatballs

Basic Meatballs (page 22)
1 tablespoon brown sugar
1 teaspoon instant beef bouillon
¼ teaspoon ground cloves
⅛ teaspoon pepper
1 bay leaf
¼ cup vinegar
1½ cups water
⅓ cup raisins (optional)
6 gingersnaps, broken into pieces

Prepare Basic Meatballs. Combine cooked meatballs and remaining ingredients in large skillet; heat to boiling, stirring occasionally. Reduce heat; cover and simmer 20 minutes, stirring occasionally. Remove bay leaf.

Nice served with mashed potatoes.

4 or 5 servings.

Meatball Stew

Basic Meatballs (page 22)
4 medium carrots, cut into 1-inch pieces*
2 stalks celery, cut into 1-inch pieces*
3 medium potatoes, pared and cut into 1-inch cubes*
1 can (16 ounces) stewed tomatoes
1 teaspoon salt
1 teaspoon instant beef bouillon
⅛ teaspoon pepper
1 bay leaf
¾ cup water

Prepare Basic Meatballs except—cook in Dutch oven. Drain off fat.

Add remaining ingredients; heat to boiling. Reduce heat; cover and simmer, stirring occasionally, until vegetables are tender, about 40 minutes. Remove bay leaf.

4 or 5 servings.

* You can substitute 1 package (24 ounces) frozen vegetables for stew for the carrots, celery and potatoes.

Meatball Stew with Dumplings

Basic Meatballs (page 22)
1 can (10¾ ounces) condensed cream of celery soup
¼ cup dairy sour cream
1 can (16 ounces) peas, cut green beans or sliced carrots
1 can (15 ounces) potatoes, drained and sliced
Egg Dumplings (below) or Parsley Dumplings (below)

Prepare Basic Meatballs except—cook meatballs in Dutch oven. Drain off fat. Add soup, sour cream, peas (with liquid) and sliced potatoes; heat to boiling, stirring occasionally.

Prepare dumplings; drop dough by tablespoonfuls onto boiling mixture. Simmer uncovered 10 minutes. Cover and simmer 10 minutes longer.

4 or 5 servings.

EGG DUMPLINGS
2 cups biscuit baking mix
2 eggs
2 tablespoons milk

Mix all ingredients until a soft dough forms.

PARSLEY DUMPLINGS
2 cups biscuit baking mix
2 tablespoons parsley flakes
⅔ cup milk

Mix all ingredients until a soft dough forms.

Meatball Dinner

Basic Meatballs (page 22)
1 can (10¾ ounces) condensed
   cream of mushroom soup
¾ cup milk
1 package (10 ounces) frozen mixed
   vegetables

Prepare Basic Meatballs and set aside. Mix soup and milk in large skillet. Stir in vegetables; heat to boiling. Reduce heat; cover and simmer until vegetables are tender, about 10 minutes. Add cooked meatballs; heat through.

4 or 5 servings.

Swedish Meatballs

1 pound ground beef
½ pound ground lean pork
1 medium onion, finely chopped
   (about ½ cup)
¾ cup dry bread crumbs
1 tablespoon snipped parsley
2 teaspoons salt
⅛ teaspoon pepper
1 teaspoon Worcestershire sauce
1 egg
½ cup milk
¼ cup salad oil
¼ cup flour
1 teaspoon paprika
½ teaspoon salt
⅛ teaspoon pepper
2 cups water
¾ cup dairy sour cream

Mix meat, onion, bread crumbs, parsley, 2 teaspoons salt, ⅛ teaspoon pepper, the Worcestershire sauce, egg and milk. Refrigerate 2 hours.

Shape mixture by tablespoonfuls into balls. Heat oil in large skillet; slowly cook meat-balls until brown. Remove meatballs from skillet and set aside.

Mix flour, paprika, ½ teaspoon salt and ⅛ teaspoon pepper into oil in skillet. Cook over low heat, stirring constantly, until mixture is smooth and bubbly. Remove from heat; stir in water. Heat to boiling, stirring constantly. Boil and stir 1 minute.

Reduce heat; gradually stir in sour cream, mixing until smooth. Add cooked meat-balls; heat through.

6 to 8 servings.

Porcupines

1 pound ground beef
½ cup uncooked regular rice
½ cup water
1 small onion, chopped (about
   ¼ cup)
1 teaspoon salt
½ teaspoon celery salt
⅛ teaspoon garlic powder
⅛ teaspoon pepper
1 can (15 ounces) tomato sauce
1 cup water
2 teaspoons Worcestershire sauce

Mix meat, rice, ½ cup water, the onion and seasonings. Shape mixture by table-spoonfuls into 1½-inch balls.

TO COOK IN SKILLET: Cook meatballs in large skillet over medium heat until brown. Add remaining ingredients; heat to boiling. Reduce heat; cover and simmer 45 minutes.

TO COOK IN OVEN: Place meatballs in un-greased baking dish, 8×8×2 inches. Mix remaining ingredients and pour over meat-balls. Cover and bake in 350° oven 45 minutes. Uncover and bake 15 minutes longer.

4 or 5 servings.

Sweet-Sour Kabobs

1½ pounds ground beef
 1 tablespoon soy sauce
 1 can (14¼ ounces) sliced pineapple, drained (reserve syrup)
 2 tablespoons brown sugar
 2 tablespoons vinegar
 2 tablespoons soy sauce
 2 teaspoons cornstarch
 4 green onions, cut into 2-inch
   pieces
 1 small green pepper, cut into
   1-inch pieces
12 cherry tomatoes

Mix meat and 1 tablespoon soy sauce. Shape mixture by tablespoonfuls into 36 balls. Place in glass bowl or plastic bag.

Mix reserved pineapple syrup, the brown sugar, vinegar and 2 tablespoons soy sauce until sugar is dissolved. Pour over meatballs. Cover and refrigerate at least 3 hours.

Drain marinade from meatballs into small saucepan; stir in cornstarch. Cook, stirring constantly, until mixture thickens and boils. Boil and stir 1 minute. Remove sauce from heat and set aside.

Cut pineapple slices into quarters. On each of six 12-inch metal skewers, alternate 6 meatballs with pineapple pieces and vegetables. Brush kabobs with part of the sauce.

Set oven control at broil and/or 550°. Broil kabobs 4 inches from heat to desired doneness, 15 to 20 minutes. Brush occasionally with sauce and gently push with fork to turn. (Pictured on page 20.)

6 servings.

Wine-marinated Kabobs

 1 pound ground beef
 ½ pound large mushrooms, washed
   and trimmed
 ¼ cup salad oil
 ½ cup Burgundy or other red wine
 1 teaspoon marjoram leaves
 ½ teaspoon salt
 ⅛ teaspoon instant minced garlic
 1 teaspoon Worcestershire sauce
 2 tablespoons catsup

Shape meat by tablespoonfuls into 24 balls. Place in glass bowl or plastic bag in shallow glass dish; add mushrooms. Mix remaining ingredients; pour over meatballs and mushrooms. Cover and refrigerate at least 8 hours, turning meatballs and mushrooms occasionally.

On each of four 12-inch metal skewers, alternate 6 meatballs with mushrooms.

Set oven control at broil and/or 550°. Broil kabobs 4 inches from heat to desired doneness, 15 to 20 minutes. Brush occasionally with remaining marinade and gently push with fork to turn.

4 servings.

Batter-dipped Fondue Meatballs

1½ pounds lean ground beef (chuck)
1 egg
¼ cup dry bread crumbs
2 tablespoons beer or apple juice
1 teaspoon garlic salt
  Frothy Batter (below)
2 cups salad oil
½ cup butter* (do not use margarine)
  Two of the sauces (below and right)

Mix meat, egg, bread crumbs, beer and garlic salt. Shape mixture by teaspoonfuls into ¾-inch balls. Prepare Frothy Batter.

Heat oil and butter in metal fondue pot to 375°. Spear meatballs with fondue forks, dip into batter and cook in hot oil to desired doneness, about 2 minutes. Serve with sauces. (Pictured on page 20.)

About 7 dozen appetizer meatballs.

NOTE: These meatballs can also be cooked without the batter.

*You can omit the butter and increase salad oil to 2½ cups.

FROTHY BATTER
1 cup biscuit baking mix
½ cup beer or apple juice
1 egg

Mix all ingredients with fork. (Batter will be slightly lumpy.)

MUSTARD SAUCE
½ cup mayonnaise or salad dressing
2 tablespoons prepared mustard
1 tablespoon finely chopped onion

Mix all ingredients; refrigerate until serving time.

About ½ cup.

HORSERADISH SAUCE
½ cup dairy sour cream
1 tablespoon horseradish
⅛ teaspoon Worcestershire sauce

Mix all ingredients; refrigerate until serving time.

About ½ cup.

BLUE CHEESE SAUCE
½ cup butter or margarine, softened
2 tablespoons crumbled blue cheese
2 teaspoons prepared mustard
⅛ teaspoon garlic powder

Mix all ingredients; refrigerate until serving time.

About ½ cup.

MOCK BEARNAISE SAUCE
¼ cup dairy sour cream
¼ cup mayonnaise or salad dressing
1 tablespoon tarragon vinegar
½ teaspoon tarragon leaves
¼ teaspoon dried shredded green onion
¼ teaspoon salt

Mix all ingredients; refrigerate until serving time.

About ½ cup.

Appetizer Meatballs

Prepare Basic Meatballs (page 22) except—shape mixture by teaspoonfuls into ¾-inch balls and decrease cooking time to about 15 minutes. Serve with wooden or plastic picks.

48 appetizer meatballs.

Party-pleaser Meatballs

Basic Meatballs (page 22)
½ cup flaked coconut
¼ cup currant or grape jelly
¼ cup chopped chutney or chutney sauce
¼ cup dry red wine or orange juice
2 teaspoons dry mustard

Prepare Basic Meatballs except—add coconut before mixing ingredients. Shape mixture by teaspoonfuls into ¾-inch balls and bake in 400° oven 15 minutes. Drain off fat.

In large skillet, heat remaining ingredients to boiling. Add meatballs; cover and simmer, stirring occasionally, until sauce thickens and meatballs are glazed, about 20 minutes. Serve with wooden or plastic picks.

48 appetizer meatballs.

Cocktail Surprise Meatballs

Basic Meatballs (page 22)
1 jar (5⅛ ounces) cocktail onions, drained*
¾ cup catsup
⅓ cup grape or currant jelly
⅓ cup water

Prepare Basic Meatballs except—shape mixture by teaspoonfuls around onions into 1-inch balls and bake in 400° oven 15 minutes. Drain off fat.

Combine catsup, jelly and water in large skillet. Add meatballs; heat to boiling, stirring occasionally. Reduce heat; cover and simmer 20 minutes, stirring occasionally. The onion centers are very hot, so be sure to let the meatballs cool slightly before serving with wooden or plastic picks.

48 appetizer meatballs.

* You can substitute drained pineapple tidbits or slices of small dill or sweet pickles for the cocktail onions.

Keep the Heat on

When your party plans call for appetizer meatballs, make sure you keep them appetizing. And above all that means keep them warm. You can serve them from a chafing dish or from an electric skillet or saucepan. Be careful to regulate heat so that the sauce doesn't scorch or stick. An attractive casserole on a warming tray will also do the trick. If your server's on the small side, it's a good idea to keep some of the meatballs on the range (over hot water) and refill the serving dish as the need arises.

Meat Loaves

Basic Meat Loaf

1½ pounds ground beef
3 slices bread, torn into small pieces*
1 egg
1 cup milk
1 small onion, chopped (about ¼ cup)
1 tablespoon Worcestershire sauce
1 teaspoon salt
½ teaspoon dry mustard
¼ teaspoon pepper
¼ teaspoon sage
⅛ teaspoon garlic powder
½ cup catsup, chili sauce or barbecue
   sauce (optional)

Heat oven to 350°. Mix all ingredients except catsup. Spread mixture in ungreased loaf pan, 9×5×3 inches, or shape into loaf in ungreased baking pan. Spoon catsup onto loaf. Bake uncovered 1 to 1¼ hours. Drain off fat.

6 servings.

* You can substitute ½ cup dry bread crumbs, ½ cup wheat germ or ¾ cup quick-cooking oats for the bread pieces.

NOTE: If you have a microwave oven, see page 71 for specific instructions.

Have a freezer? See page 68 for Freezer Meat Loaf.

Cheese-Potato Meat Loaf

Basic Meat Loaf (page 30)
¼ cup crumbled blue cheese
Mashed potato puffs (enough
for 4 servings)
Crumbled crisply fried bacon

Prepare Basic Meat Loaf except—mix in
half the cheese; shape into loaf in ungreased pan, 13×9×2 inches. Omit catsup
and bake as directed. Drain off fat.

Prepare potato puffs as directed on package except—stir remaining cheese into
potatoes. Spread potatoes on sides and
top of meat loaf. Sprinkle with bacon
and bake 10 minutes.

6 servings.

Meat-and-Potato Squares

Basic Meat Loaf (page 30)
Mashed potato puffs (enough
for 4 servings)
½ cup shredded Cheddar cheese

Prepare Basic Meat Loaf except—spread
mixture in ungreased baking pan, 8×
8×2 or 9×9×2 inches. Omit catsup and
decrease baking time to 40 to 50 minutes. Drain off fat.

Prepare potato puffs as directed on package. Spread hot potatoes evenly over meat
in pan and sprinkle with cheese. Bake
until cheese is melted, 2 to 4 minutes.
(Pictured on page 17.)

6 servings.

Meat Loaf Leftovers

Barbecue Meat Loaf

For four ½-inch slices meat loaf, mix ½
cup barbecue sauce and 2 tablespoons
water in skillet. Place slices in skillet, turning to coat all sides with sauce. Heat to
boiling. Cover and cook over low heat,
brushing sauce on slices occasionally, until meat is hot, 10 to 15 minutes.

Potato-topped Meat Loaf

For four ½-inch slices meat loaf, prepare
mashed potato puffs as directed on package for 4 servings; set aside. Set oven control at broil and/or 550°. Broil slices with
tops 3 to 4 inches from heat 5 minutes.
Spread potatoes on slices and sprinkle
with shredded Cheddar cheese. Broil until
cheese is melted, about 2 minutes.

Souped-up Meat Loaf

For four ½-inch slices meat loaf, mix ½
to 1 can (10¾-ounce size) condensed cream
of celery soup or any favorite condensed
cream soup and ¼ to ½ cup milk in skillet. Heat to boiling, stirring frequently.
Reduce heat; place slices in skillet, turning to coat all sides with sauce. Cover and
simmer until meat slices are hot, 10 to 15
minutes.

Roast Meat Loaf

2 pounds ground beef
1 medium onion, chopped (about ½ cup)
1 egg
½ cup quick-cooking oats
½ cup milk
1 tablespoon snipped parsley
1½ teaspoons salt
½ teaspoon savory or thyme
¼ teaspoon pepper
½ cup catsup or chili sauce
2 tablespoons brown sugar

Heat oven to 350°. Mix all ingredients except catsup and brown sugar. Press mixture firmly in ungreased loaf pan, 8½ × 4½ × 2½ inches (see note). Loosen edges with spatula and unmold loaf in ungreased baking pan, 13 × 9 × 2 inches. Mix catsup and sugar; spoon onto loaf. Bake uncovered 1 to 1¼ hours. (Pictured on the cover.)

8 servings.

NOTE: If you don't have a pan this size, shape mixture into loaf in center of shallow baking pan.

VARIATION

Roast Meat Loaf Ring: Press meat mixture firmly in ungreased 5- to 6-cup ring mold. Unmold in baking pan by rapping mold against bottom of pan. Brush with catsup mixture. Bake 50 minutes. If you like, fill the ring with hot potato salad or creamed peas.

Onion Meat Loaf

2 pounds ground beef
1 envelope (about 1½ ounces) onion soup mix
⅔ cup milk
1 egg
3 tablespoons brown sugar
3 tablespoons catsup
1 tablespoon prepared mustard

Heat oven to 350°. Mix meat, onion soup mix, milk and egg. Press mixture firmly in ungreased loaf pan, 8½ × 4½ × 2½ inches (see note). Loosen edges with spatula and unmold loaf in ungreased baking pan, 13 × 9 × 2 inches.

Mix remaining ingredients; spoon onto loaf. Bake uncovered 1 hour. (Pictured on page 17.)

8 servings.

NOTE: If you don't have a pan this size, shape mixture into loaf in center of shallow baking pan.

Do Ahead and Coast Later

Want to stamp out that last-minute scurrying? You can make your meat loaf mixture several hours in advance (or even the night before); spread it in the loaf pan or shape in baking pan, cover and refrigerate. When the dinner hour draws near, just pop the pan in the oven . . . and relax. Remember that to compensate for the cold meat and the cold pan, you may have to add another 5 to 10 minutes to the baking time. (See page 68 for information on freezing your meat loaf mixture.) The bonus—waiting time in the refrigerator gives the seasonings a better chance to flavor the meat.

Savory Stuffed Meat Loaf

1½ pounds ground beef
2 slices bacon, cut up
½ cup milk
1 egg
¼ cup dry bread crumbs
2 tablespoons snipped parsley
1 tablespoon Worcestershire sauce
1 teaspoon salt
½ teaspoon dry mustard
¼ teaspoon pepper
⅛ teaspoon garlic powder
Meat Loaf Stuffing (below)

Heat oven to 350°. Mix all ingredients except stuffing. Spread ⅔ of the mixture in ungreased loaf pan, 9×5×3 inches, pressing mixture up sides of pan to within ¾ inch of top.

Spoon stuffing onto mixture in pan; then top with remaining meat mixture, covering stuffing completely. Bake uncovered 1 hour 10 minutes. Drain off fat. Let stuffed meat loaf stand 5 minutes before cutting into thick slices. (Pictured on page 17.)

6 servings.

MEAT LOAF STUFFING
¼ cup butter or margarine
1 small onion, chopped (about ¼ cup)
½ cup chopped celery (with leaves)
2 cups soft bread cubes
¼ teaspoon salt
¼ teaspoon sage
⅛ teaspoon thyme
Dash pepper

Melt butter in large skillet. Add onion and celery; cook and stir until onion is tender. Remove from heat; stir in remaining ingredients.

Zucchini-layered Meat Loaf

Basic Meat Loaf (page 30)
½ cup shredded Swiss cheese
½ cup thinly sliced zucchini
2 tablespoons chopped pimiento

Prepare Basic Meat Loaf except—spread ⅓ of the mixture evenly in ungreased loaf pan, 9×5×3 inches. Sprinkle half each of the cheese, zucchini and pimiento in layers on mixture to within ½ inch of sides of pan; repeat. Top with remaining meat mixture, covering layers completely and spreading mixture to sides of pan. Omit catsup and bake uncovered 1¼ hours. Drain off fat. Let stuffed meat loaf stand 5 minutes before cutting into thick slices.

6 servings.

Spooned-up Skillet Meat Loaf

2 pounds ground beef
1 envelope (about 1½ ounces) onion soup mix
½ cup quick-cooking oats
½ cup water
½ cup dairy sour cream
2 eggs, beaten
¼ cup grated Parmesan cheese

Cook and stir meat in large skillet until brown. Drain off fat. Stir in soup mix, oats and water. Cover and simmer about 5 minutes, stirring occasionally. Stir in sour cream and eggs. Spread meat mixture evenly in skillet; sprinkle cheese over top. Cover and simmer until set, about 5 minutes. If desired, serve with catsup.

6 to 8 servings.

Surprise Meat Loaf Squares

1½ pounds ground beef
 2 cups finely chopped pared
   eggplant
 1 medium onion, chopped
   (about ½ cup)
 1 egg
 ½ cup milk
 ¼ cup quick-cooking oats
1½ teaspoons salt
 ½ teaspoon basil leaves
 1 can (16 ounces) stewed tomatoes
 1 clove garlic, minced
 1 tablespoon cornstarch
 ¾ teaspoon salt

Heat oven to 350°. Mix meat, eggplant, onion, egg, milk, oats, 1½ teaspoons salt and the basil leaves. Spread mixture in ungreased baking pan, 8×8×2 or 9×9×2 inches. Bake uncovered 45 to 50 minutes. Drain off fat.

Mix tomatoes, garlic, cornstarch and ¾ teaspoon salt in small saucepan. Cook, stirring constantly, until mixture thickens and boils. Boil and stir 1 minute. Cut meat loaf into squares and top with tomato sauce.

6 servings.

Saucy Mini-Loaves

 1 pound ground beef (see note)
 ⅓ cup cracker crumbs
 1 can (10¾ ounces) condensed
   cream of mushroom soup
 ¼ cup milk
 1 egg
 1 small onion, chopped (about
   ¼ cup)
 ¾ teaspoon salt
 ⅛ teaspoon nutmeg
 ⅛ teaspoon pepper
 ½ cup chopped unpared cucumber
 3 tablespoons milk
 ⅓ cup chopped tomato
 ½ cup dairy sour cream

Heat oven to 350°. Mix meat, cracker crumbs, ½ cup of the soup, ¼ cup milk, the egg, onion and seasonings. Press mixture in 12 ungreased muffin cups. Bake 30 to 35 minutes.

In small saucepan, heat remaining soup, the cucumber and 3 tablespoons milk to boiling, stirring frequently. Reduce heat; stir in tomato and sour cream and heat just to boiling, stirring constantly. Serve sauce over mini-loaves.

4 to 6 servings.

NOTE: If ground beef is very fat, place muffin pan in a jelly roll pan to catch any juices that may cook over.

The meat loaf is done and it's a beauty! And you want to keep it that way. The simple trick is to use two wide spatulas to lift the loaf out of the pan. Simply sidle a spatula down each end of the pan and slip under the loaf. Then gently lift both ends—at the same time. Steady now.

Meat Loaf Tropicale

1½ pounds ground beef
1 egg
1 cup mashed ripe banana (about 2 large)
½ cup quick-cooking oats
½ cup chopped green pepper
2 tablespoons chopped onion
1 teaspoon salt
1 teaspoon prepared mustard
¼ teaspoon nutmeg
⅛ teaspoon allspice
2 slices bacon
3 tablespoons orange marmalade

Heat oven to 350°. Mix all ingredients except bacon and marmalade. Spread mixture in ungreased loaf pan, 9×5×3 inches. Crisscross bacon slices on loaf, then spread marmalade on top. Bake uncovered 1 to 1¼ hours. Drain off fat.

6 servings.

NOTE: The banana adds a unique, almost mysterious flavor and a special moistness to this elegant meat loaf.

Heidelberg Meat Loaf

1½ pounds ground beef
3 slices rye bread, torn into small pieces
1 cup beer or beef bouillon
1 egg
1 small onion, chopped (about ¼ cup)
1 teaspoon salt
1 teaspoon caraway seed (optional)
½ teaspoon celery seed
¼ teaspoon pepper

Heat oven to 350°. Mix all ingredients. Spread mixture in ungreased loaf pan, 9×5×3 inches. Bake uncovered 1 to 1¼ hours. Drain off fat.

6 servings.

Bacon-wrapped Little Loaves

1½ pounds ground beef
1 cup shredded Cheddar cheese (4 ounces)
1 egg
¼ cup dry bread crumbs
1 small onion, chopped (about ¼ cup)
¼ cup lemon juice
¼ cup chopped green pepper
½ cup water
½ teaspoon instant beef bouillon
1 teaspoon salt
6 slices thin-sliced bacon, cut into halves

Heat oven to 350°. Mix all ingredients except bacon. Shape mixture into 6 loaves. Crisscross 2 half-slices bacon on each loaf, tucking ends under loaf. Place loaves on rack in shallow baking pan; bake uncovered 50 minutes. (Pictured on page 17.)

6 servings.

Main Dishes

Hamburger Stroganoff

1 pound ground beef
1 medium onion, chopped (about ½ cup)
1 clove garlic, minced
3 tablespoons flour
1 teaspoon instant beef bouillon
¾ teaspoon salt
¼ teaspoon pepper
1 can (4 ounces) mushroom stems and pieces, drained
1 cup water
1 cup dairy sour cream
2 cups hot cooked noodles or rice

Cook and stir meat, onion and garlic in large skillet until meat is brown. Drain off fat. Mix in flour, bouillon, salt, pepper and mushrooms. Stir in water and heat to boiling, stirring constantly. Reduce heat; cover and simmer 10 minutes. Stir in sour cream and heat. Serve over noodles; if you wish, garnish with parsley.

4 servings.

You can get a head start on this recipe with Beef-Mushroom Freezer Mix (see page 59).

Skillet Goulash

1 pound ground beef
1 medium onion, chopped (about ½ cup)
1 can (16 ounces) tomatoes
½ cup chopped celery
½ cup water
1½ teaspoons salt
¼ teaspoon pepper
⅛ teaspoon basil leaves
⅛ teaspoon marjoram leaves
3 ounces uncooked fine noodles (about 1½ cups)

Cook and stir meat and onion in large skillet until meat is brown. Drain off fat. Stir in tomatoes (with liquid) and remaining ingredients; break up tomatoes.

Heat to boiling. Reduce heat; cover and simmer, stirring occasionally, until noodles are tender, about 20 minutes. (Add a small amount of water if necessary.)

5 servings (1 cup each).

You can get a head start on this recipe with Browned 'n Seasoned Freezer Mix (see page 61).

All-American Hot Dish

1 pound ground beef
1 medium onion, chopped (about
    ½ cup)
1 can (8 ounces) whole kernel corn
1 can (8 ounces) tomato sauce
¼ cup halved pitted ripe olives
4 ounces uncooked noodles (about
    2 cups)
2 cups water
1 teaspoon oregano leaves
½ teaspoon salt
¼ teaspoon pepper
1 cup shredded Cheddar cheese
    (4 ounces)

Cook and stir meat and onion in large
skillet until meat is brown. Drain off fat.
Stir in corn (with liquid) and remaining
ingredients.

TO COOK IN SKILLET: Heat mixture to boiling. Reduce heat and simmer uncovered,
stirring occasionally, until noodles are tender, about 20 minutes.

TO COOK IN OVEN: Pour mixture into ungreased 2-quart casserole. Cover and bake
in 375° oven 30 minutes, stirring occasionally. Uncover and bake until mixture
thickens, about 15 minutes.

6 servings (1 cup each).

*You can get a head start on this recipe with
the Browned 'n Seasoned Freezer Mix (see
page 61).*

Creamy Beef-Noodle Combo

1 pound ground beef
1 medium onion, chopped (about
    ½ cup)
1 can (4 ounces) mushroom stems
    and pieces
1 can (10¾ ounces) condensed
    cream of mushroom soup
2 stalks celery, sliced (about 1 cup)
½ cup chopped green pepper
¼ cup sliced pimiento
1 cup milk
1 tablespoon Worcestershire sauce
1 teaspoon salt
4 ounces uncooked noodles (about
    2 cups)

Cook and stir meat and onion in large
skillet until meat is brown. Drain off fat.
Stir in mushrooms (with liquid) and remaining ingredients; heat to boiling. Reduce heat; cover and simmer, stirring
occasionally, until noodles are tender,
about 25 minutes. A small amount of
water can be added if necessary. (Pictured on page 56.)

5 servings (1 cup each).

*You can get a head start on this recipe with
the Browned 'n Seasoned Freezer Mix (see
page 61).*

Pasta: How Much to Cook?

Macaroni, spaghetti or noodles—take
your pick. For 2 cups of cooked pasta,
start with:

1 cup macaroni (3 to 3½ ounces)
3½ to 4 ounces spaghetti
2 to 2½ cups noodles (4 ounces)

Double Cheese
Hamburger Casserole

4 ounces uncooked medium noodles
(about 2 cups)
1 pound ground beef
⅓ cup chopped onion
¼ cup chopped celery
1 can (8 ounces) tomato sauce
1 teaspoon salt
1 package (3 ounces) cream cheese,
softened
½ cup creamed cottage cheese
¼ cup dairy sour cream
1 medium tomato (optional)

Cook noodles as directed on package; drain. While noodles are cooking, cook and stir meat, onion and celery in large skillet until meat is brown. Drain off fat. Stir in noodles, tomato sauce, salt, cream cheese, cottage cheese and sour cream.

TO COOK IN SKILLET: Heat mixture to boiling. Reduce heat and simmer uncovered 5 minutes, stirring frequently. Remove from heat. Cut tomato into thin slices and arrange on meat mixture. Cover until tomato slices are warm, about 5 minutes.

TO COOK IN OVEN: Turn mixture into ungreased 1½-quart casserole. Cut tomato into thin slices and arrange on meat mixture. Cover and bake in 350° oven until hot, about 30 minutes.

5 servings (1 cup each).

Lasagne

MEAT SAUCE
1 pound ground beef
2 cloves garlic, minced
3 cans (8 ounces each) tomato
sauce*
½ teaspoon salt
¼ teaspoon pepper
½ teaspoon oregano leaves

NOODLES AND CHEESE
1 package (8 ounces) lasagne noodles
1 carton (12 ounces) creamed
cottage cheese (1½ cups)
2 cups shredded mozzarella or Swiss
cheese (8 ounces)
⅓ cup grated Parmesan cheese

Cook and stir meat and garlic in large skillet until meat is brown. Drain off fat. Stir in tomato sauce, salt, pepper and oregano leaves. Cover and simmer 20 minutes.

While Meat Sauce is simmering, cook noodles as directed on package; drain.

Heat oven to 350°. In ungreased baking pan, 13×9×2 inches, or baking dish, 11¾×7½×1¾ inches, layer half each of the noodles, meat sauce, cottage cheese and mozzarella cheese; repeat. Sprinkle Parmesan cheese over top. Bake uncovered until hot and bubbly, about 40 minutes.

6 servings.

* You can substitute 1 can (16 ounces) tomatoes and 1 can (6 ounces) tomato paste for the tomato sauce.

Like to plan ahead? See page 68 for Freezer Lasagne. Or get a head start with Beef-Tomato Freezer Mix (see page 63).

Italian Spaghetti

2 pounds ground beef
1 medium onion, chopped (about ½ cup)
2 cans (15 ounces each) tomato sauce
2 cans (12 ounces each) tomato paste
1 can (7½ ounces) pitted ripe olives, drained and sliced (½ cup)
2 envelopes (about 1½ ounces each) Italian-style spaghetti mix with mushrooms
1 cup chopped green pepper
3 cups water
1 tablespoon sugar
1 teaspoon oregano leaves
2 cloves garlic, minced
1 bay leaf
14 to 16 ounces uncooked long spaghetti
Grated Parmesan cheese

Cook and stir meat and onion in large skillet or Dutch oven until meat is brown. Drain off fat. Stir in remaining ingredients except spaghetti and cheese; heat to boiling. Reduce heat; cover and simmer 1½ hours, stirring occasionally. Remove bay leaf. Cook spaghetti as directed on package; drain. Serve sauce over spaghetti and sprinkle with Parmesan cheese.

8 servings.

One-Skillet Spaghetti

1 pound ground beef
2 medium onions, chopped (about 1 cup)
1 can (28 ounces) tomatoes
¾ cup chopped green pepper
½ cup water
1 can (4 ounces) mushroom stems and pieces, drained
2 teaspoons salt
1 teaspoon sugar
1 teaspoon chili powder
1 package (7 ounces) thin spaghetti, broken into pieces
1 cup shredded Cheddar cheese (4 ounces)

Cook and stir meat and onions in large skillet or Dutch oven until meat is brown. Drain off fat. Stir in tomatoes (with liquid) and remaining ingredients except Cheddar cheese; break up tomatoes.

TO COOK IN SKILLET: Heat mixture to boiling. Reduce heat; cover and simmer, stirring occasionally, until spaghetti is tender, about 30 minutes. (A small amount of water can be added if necessary.) Sprinkle with cheese. Cover and heat until cheese is melted.

TO COOK IN OVEN: Pour mixture into ungreased 2- or 2½-quart casserole. Cover and bake in 375° oven, stirring occasionally, until spaghetti is tender, about 45 minutes. Uncover; sprinkle with shredded Cheddar cheese and bake about 5 minutes.

7 servings (1 cup each).

You can get a head start on this recipe with Beef-Tomato Freezer Mix (see page 63).

Manicotti

MEAT FILLING

1 pound ground beef
¼ cup chopped onion (about
   1 small)
3 slices bread, torn into small
   pieces
1½ cups shredded mozzarella cheese
1 egg
½ cup milk
1 tablespoon snipped parsley
1 teaspoon salt
¼ teaspoon pepper

PASTA

1 package (8 ounces) manicotti shells

TOMATO SAUCE

1 can (4 ounces) mushroom stems
   and pieces
1 can (15 ounces) tomato sauce
1 can (12 ounces) tomato paste
¼ cup chopped onion (about 1 small)
1 clove garlic, minced
4 cups water
1 tablespoon Italian seasoning
½ teaspoon sugar
½ teaspoon salt
⅛ teaspoon pepper
⅓ cup grated Parmesan cheese

Cook and stir meat and ¼ cup onion in large skillet until meat is brown. Drain off fat. Remove from heat; stir in remaining ingredients for Meat Filling.

Fill uncooked manicotti shells, packing the filling into both ends. Place shells in ungreased baking pan, 13×9×2 inches.

Heat oven to 375°. Heat mushrooms (with liquid) and the remaining ingredients for Tomato Sauce except cheese to boiling, stirring occasionally. Reduce heat and simmer uncovered 5 minutes. Pour sauce over shells. Cover with aluminum foil and bake until shells are tender, 1½ to 1¾ hours. Sprinkle with cheese. Cool 5 to 10 minutes before serving.

6 to 8 servings.

Have a freezer? See page 69 for Freezer Manicotti.

Mexican Fiesta Casserole

1 pound ground beef
   Salt and pepper
1 cup shredded Cheddar cheese
   (4 ounces)
1 cup dairy sour cream
⅔ cup mayonnaise or salad dressing
2 tablespoons finely chopped onion
2 cups biscuit baking mix
½ cup water
2 to 3 medium tomatoes, thinly sliced
¾ cup chopped green pepper
   Paprika (optional)

Heat oven to 375°. Cook and stir meat in skillet until brown. Drain off fat. Season meat with salt and pepper; set aside. Mix cheese, sour cream, mayonnaise and onion; set aside.

Stir baking mix and water until a soft dough forms. With floured fingers, pat dough in greased baking pan, 13×9×2 inches, pressing dough ½ inch up sides of pan. Layer meat, tomato slices and green pepper on dough. Spoon sour cream mixture over top and sprinkle with paprika. Bake uncovered until edges of dough are light brown, 25 to 30 minutes. Cool 5 minutes, then cut into squares.

5 or 6 servings.

Enchiladas

MEAT FILLING

1 pound ground beef
1 medium onion, chopped (about ½ cup)
½ cup dairy sour cream
1 cup shredded Cheddar cheese (4 ounces)
2 tablespoons snipped parsley
1 teaspoon salt
¼ teaspoon pepper

TORTILLA BASE

Salad oil
8 tortillas

HOT TOMATO SAUCE

1 can (15 ounces) tomato sauce
⅓ cup chopped green pepper
1 clove garlic, minced
1½ to 2 teaspoons chili powder
½ teaspoon oregano leaves
¼ teaspoon ground cumin
⅔ cup water

Cook and stir meat in large skillet until brown. Drain off fat. Stir in remaining ingredients for Meat Filling. Remove from heat; cover and set aside.

Heat ¼ inch salad oil in skillet over medium heat. Dip each tortilla quickly into oil, turning once with tongs, just until limp; drain on paper towel.

In small saucepan, heat all ingredients for Hot Tomato Sauce except water to boiling, stirring occasionally. Reduce heat and simmer uncovered 5 minutes. Pour sauce into 8- or 9-inch shallow dish.

Heat oven to 350°. Dip each tortilla into sauce to coat both sides; place about ¼ cup Meat Filling on center and roll tortilla around filling. Arrange in ungreased baking dish, 11¾ × 7½ × 1¾ inches. Pour remaining sauce and the water over tortillas. Bake uncovered until bubbly, about 20 minutes. If you wish, garnish with slices of ripe olives, avocado, hard-cooked egg or shredded lettuce. (Pictured on page 53.)

4 or 5 servings.

Have a freezer? See page 69 for Freezer Enchiladas.

A Bit About Tortillas

The Mexicans know all about the care and handling of the tortilla, their traditional flat, unleavened bread. So take a tip from south of the border. When it comes to making Enchiladas, it's best to dip the tortillas in oil first—it makes them soft and easy to roll. Then drain off the excess oil so that the zesty sauce will cling to the surface. And this advice holds true whether you have chosen either corn or flour tortillas—canned, frozen or refrigerated.

The tortilla is also the basis for the taco shell, which you can purchase already crisply fried and folded into a half-moon shape—ready for its many fillings.

Company Beef Oriental

1½ pounds ground beef
 1 medium onion, sliced
 1 clove garlic, minced
 ¼ cup soy sauce
 2 tablespoons cornstarch
 1 tablespoon molasses
 1 teaspoon instant beef bouillon
 ¾ cup water
 1 package (6 ounces) frozen
    Chinese pea pods
 ½ can (8-ounce size) water
    chestnuts, drained and sliced
 1 can (5 ounces) bamboo shoots,
    drained
 1 can (11 ounces) mandarin orange
    segments, drained (reserve syrup)

Cook and stir meat, onion and garlic in large skillet until meat is brown. Drain off fat. Mix soy sauce, cornstarch and molasses; stir into meat mixture. Stir in bouillon, water, pea pods, water chestnuts, bamboo shoots and reserved mandarin orange syrup; heat to boiling.

Reduce heat; cover and simmer 10 minutes, stirring occasionally. Stir in mandarin orange segments; cover and heat about 2 minutes.

Nice served with hot cooked rice and additional soy sauce. (Pictured on the cover.)

6 servings (1 cup each).

Safari Supper

1½ pounds ground beef
 1 medium onion, sliced
 1 cup uncooked regular rice
2½ cups water
 2 teaspoons instant chicken bouillon
 1 teaspoon curry powder
 ½ teaspoon salt
 ¼ teaspoon ginger
 ¼ teaspoon cinnamon
 3 tablespoons chunky peanut butter
 1 tablespoon honey
 ½ cup raisins

Cook and stir meat and onion in large skillet until onion is tender. Drain off fat. Stir in remaining ingredients.

TO COOK IN SKILLET: Heat mixture to boiling. Reduce heat; cover and simmer, stirring occasionally, until rice is tender, about 35 minutes. (A small amount of water can be added if necessary.)

TO COOK IN OVEN: Turn mixture into ungreased 2-quart casserole. Cover and bake in 350° oven, stirring occasionally, until rice is tender, 50 to 60 minutes. (Add a small amount of water if necessary.)

8 servings (1 cup each).

Hearty Beef Supper

2 pounds ground beef
1 large onion, chopped (about 1 cup)
1 cup uncooked cracked wheat (see note)
2 cups chopped tomato (about 2 medium)
2 cups water
3 tablespoons snipped parsley
2 teaspoons instant beef bouillon
1½ teaspoons salt
½ teaspoon oregano leaves
¼ teaspoon instant minced garlic
¼ teaspoon pepper
½ cup grated Parmesan cheese

Cook and stir meat and onion in large skillet until meat is brown. Drain off fat. Stir in remaining ingredients except cheese; heat to boiling. Reduce heat; cover and simmer, stirring occasionally, until wheat is tender, about 30 minutes. (A small amount of water can be added if necessary.) Stir in cheese. Garnish with additional snipped parsley and Parmesan cheese.

7 servings (1 cup each).

NOTE: The nutlike texture of cracked wheat reminds one of brown rice; in fact, it is cooked and used in the same way too.

Rundown on Rice
Heed the following chart for the rice of your choice. For 2 cups cooked rice, start with:

⅔ cup regular white rice
½ cup processed rice
1 cup precooked (instant) rice
½ cup brown rice

Spanish Rice with Beef

1 pound ground beef
1 medium onion, chopped (about ½ cup)
1 cup uncooked regular rice
⅔ cup chopped green pepper
1 can (16 ounces) stewed tomatoes
5 slices bacon, crisply fried and crumbled
2 cups water
1 teaspoon chili powder
½ teaspoon oregano leaves
1¼ teaspoons salt
⅛ teaspoon pepper

Cook and stir meat and onion in large skillet until meat is brown. Drain off fat. Stir in remaining ingredients.

TO COOK IN SKILLET: Heat mixture to boiling. Reduce heat; cover and simmer, stirring occasionally, until rice is tender, about 30 minutes. (A small amount of water can be added if necessary.)

TO COOK IN OVEN: Pour mixture into ungreased 2-quart casserole. Cover and bake in 375° oven, stirring occasionally, until rice is tender, about 45 minutes.

6 servings (1 cup each).

You can get a head start on this recipe with Beef-Tomato Freezer Mix (see page 63).

South Seas Combo

2 pounds ground beef
1 medium onion, chopped (about ½ cup)
1 cup sliced celery
2½ cups coarsely chopped pared apple
2 to 3 teaspoons curry powder
2 tablespoons flour
2 teaspoons instant beef bouillon
1 cup water
1 can (4 ounces) mushroom stems and pieces, drained
2 tablespoons sherry (optional)
2 bananas, peeled and sliced*
4 cups hot cooked rice

Cook and stir meat and onion in large skillet until onion is tender. Drain off fat. Stir in celery, apple and curry powder; cook uncovered 5 minutes, stirring occasionally. Stir in remaining ingredients except bananas and rice; heat to boiling. Reduce heat and simmer uncovered about 30 minutes, stirring occasionally.

Stir in bananas; cover and cook over low heat 5 minutes. Serve over rice. If you wish, garnish with crumbled crisply fried bacon or chopped peanuts.

8 servings.

* You can substitute 1 can (13½ ounces) pineapple chunks, drained, for the sliced bananas.

Curry Delight

2 pounds ground beef
1 large onion, chopped (about 1 cup)
1 can (16 ounces) tomatoes
1 large apple, chopped (about 1¼ cups)
1 to 1½ tablespoons curry powder
2 tablespoons coconut (optional)
2 tablespoons raisins
1 tablespoon chopped chutney
2 teaspoons instant beef bouillon
1½ teaspoons salt
1 cup uncooked regular rice
2½ cups water
Chopped peanuts

Cook and stir meat and onion in Dutch oven until meat is brown. Drain off fat. Stir in tomatoes (with liquid) and remaining ingredients except peanuts; break up tomatoes.

TO COOK IN DUTCH OVEN: Heat mixture to boiling. Reduce heat; cover and simmer, stirring occasionally, until rice is tender, 30 to 45 minutes. (A small amount of water can be added if necessary.) Garnish with peanuts.

TO COOK IN OVEN: Turn mixture into ungreased 3-quart casserole. Cover and bake in 350° oven, stirring occasionally, until rice is tender, 45 to 55 minutes. Garnish with peanuts.

7 servings (1 cup each).

Souper Baked Sandwich

1½ pounds ground beef
 1 small onion, chopped (about
   ¼ cup)
 ½ cup chopped celery
 ½ teaspoon salt
 4 cups herb-seasoned stuffing cubes
1½ cups milk
 2 eggs
 1 can (10¾ ounces) condensed
   cream of mushroom soup
 1 teaspoon dry mustard
 1 cup shredded Cheddar cheese
   (4 ounces)

Heat oven to 350°. Cook and stir meat, onion and celery in large skillet until meat is brown. Drain off fat. Stir in salt.

Arrange stuffing cubes in greased baking pan, 9×9×2 or 11¾×7½×1¾ inches; top with meat mixture. Beat milk, eggs, soup and mustard; pour over meat and sprinkle with cheese. Bake uncovered until knife inserted in center comes out clean, 30 to 40 minutes. Cool 5 minutes, then cut into squares.

About 6 servings.

Mexicali Spoon Bread Casserole

MEAT MIXTURE

1½ pounds ground beef
 1 large onion, chopped (about
   1 cup)
 ¼ cup chopped green pepper
   (optional)
 1 clove garlic, minced
 1 can (15 ounces) tomato sauce
 1 can (12 ounces) vacuum-pack
   whole kernel corn
1½ teaspoons salt
 2 to 3 teaspoons chili powder
 ⅛ teaspoon pepper
 ½ cup sliced ripe olives

CORNMEAL TOPPING

1½ cups milk
 ½ cup yellow cornmeal
 ½ teaspoon salt
 ¾ cup shredded Cheddar cheese
 2 eggs, beaten

Heat oven to 375°. Cook and stir meat, onion, green pepper and garlic in large skillet until onion is tender. Drain off fat. Stir in tomato sauce, corn (with liquid), 1½ teaspoons salt, the chili powder, pepper and olives; heat to boiling. Reduce heat and simmer uncovered while preparing Cornmeal Topping.

Mix milk, cornmeal and ½ teaspoon salt in saucepan. Cook and stir over medium heat just until mixture boils. Remove from heat; stir in cheese and eggs.

Turn hot Meat Mixture into ungreased 2½- to 3-quart casserole. Immediately pour topping onto Meat Mixture. Bake uncovered until knife inserted in topping comes out clean, about 40 minutes.

6 to 8 servings.

Saucy Bean'n Beef Pie

1 pound ground beef
1 can (3 ounces) French fried
  onions
¼ cup dry bread crumbs
1 can (10¾ ounces) condensed
  cream of mushroom soup
1 egg
¼ teaspoon thyme leaves
¼ teaspoon salt
  Dash pepper
1 can (16 ounces) French-style green
  beans, drained

Heat oven to 350°. Mix meat, half the onions, the bread crumbs, ¼ cup of the soup, the egg, thyme leaves, salt and pepper. Press mixture evenly against bottom and side of ungreased 9-inch pie pan.

Turn beans into meat-lined pan; spread remaining soup over beans. Bake uncovered 35 minutes. Arrange remaining onions on top; bake 10 minutes. Cool 5 minutes, then cut into wedges.

4 or 5 servings.

Egg Size Know-how

Eggs have some sizable differences, ranging from extra large to large to medium to small. Be sure to check the prices carefully—if within the same grade there is less than a 7-cent difference per dozen between one size and the next larger size, then by all means buy the bigger. More than 7 cents—buy the smaller.

Cheeseburger Pie

CRUST
1 cup biscuit baking mix
¼ cup milk or light cream

MEAT FILLING
1 pound ground beef
1 medium onion, chopped (about
  ½ cup)
½ teaspoon salt
¼ teaspoon pepper
2 tablespoons biscuit baking mix
1 tablespoon Worcestershire sauce

TOPPING
2 medium tomatoes, sliced
2 eggs
1 cup shredded Cheddar cheese
  (4 ounces)

Heat oven to 375°. Mix 1 cup baking mix and the milk until a soft dough forms. Gently smooth dough into a ball on floured cloth-covered surface; knead 5 times. Roll dough 2 inches larger than inverted 9-inch pie pan. Ease into pan and flute edge of dough.

Cook and stir meat and onion in large skillet until meat is brown. Drain off fat. Stir in salt, pepper, 2 tablespoons baking mix and the Worcestershire sauce. Turn Meat Filling into pastry-lined pan.

Arrange tomato slices on filling. Beat eggs slightly; stir in cheese. Spoon onto tomatoes, spreading to cover completely. Bake about 30 minutes. Cut into wedges. Serve with chili sauce if you like.

6 servings.

You can get a head start on this recipe with the Browned 'n Seasoned Freezer Mix (see page 61).

Peppy Pizza Pie

1 pound ground beef
2 ounces pepperoni, chopped (about
⅓ cup)
⅓ cup dry bread crumbs
1 egg
½ teaspoon oregano leaves
¼ teaspoon salt
1 can (8 ounces) tomato sauce
1 can (8 ounces) mushroom stems
and pieces, drained*
¼ cup sliced pitted ripe olives
1 cup shredded mozzarella cheese
(4 ounces)

Heat oven to 400°. Mix meats, bread
crumbs, egg, oregano leaves, salt and half
the tomato sauce. Press mixture evenly
against bottom and side of ungreased 10-
inch pie pan (see note).

Sprinkle mushrooms and olives in meat-
lined pan; pour remaining tomato sauce
over vegetables. Bake uncovered 25 minutes. (The pepperoni gives a red-flecked
appearance to the meat.) Sprinkle pie with
cheese; bake 5 minutes. Cool 5 minutes,
then cut into 6 wedges.

6 servings.

* You can substitute 1 can (8 ounces) cut
green beans, drained, or 1 can (8 ounces)
whole kernel corn, drained, for the mushrooms.

NOTE: If you have to use a 9-inch pie pan,
place it in a shallow baking pan to catch
any juices that may cook over.

Potluck Surprise

1½ cups uncooked elbow macaroni
1½ pounds ground beef
1 medium onion, chopped (about
½ cup)
1½ teaspoons salt
1 teaspoon Italian seasoning
¼ teaspoon pepper
1 small eggplant, pared and cut into
½-inch cubes (about 4 cups)
1 cup dairy sour cream
¼ cup chopped pimiento*
2 cups shredded Cheddar cheese
(8 ounces)

Heat oven to 350°. Cook macaroni as directed on package; drain. While macaroni
is cooking, cook and stir meat and onion
in Dutch oven until meat is brown. Drain
off fat. Stir in salt, Italian seasoning, pepper, macaroni, eggplant, sour cream, pimiento and 1 cup of the cheese.

Turn into ungreased 3-quart casserole.
Sprinkle with remaining cheese. Bake uncovered until eggplant is tender, 45 to 50
minutes.

6 to 8 servings.

* You can substitute ½ cup sliced pimiento-
stuffed olives for the chopped pimiento.

Hamburger Pizza

CRUST

2½ cups biscuit baking mix
1 package active dry yeast
⅔ cup hot water

MEAT MIXTURE

1 pound ground beef
1 medium onion, chopped (about ½ cup)
1 can (15 ounces) tomato sauce
2 teaspoons oregano leaves
¼ teaspoon pepper

TOPPING

½ cup chopped green pepper (optional)
2 cups shredded Cheddar or mozzarella cheese (8 ounces)
1 cup grated Parmesan cheese

Heat oven to 425°. Mix baking mix and yeast; stir in water and beat vigorously. Turn dough onto well-floured surface; knead until smooth, about 20 times. Let dough rest a few minutes.

While dough is resting, cook and stir meat and onion in large skillet until onion is tender. Drain off fat. Stir in tomato sauce, oregano leaves and pepper; set aside.

Divide dough in half. Roll each half on ungreased baking sheet into rectangle, 13 × 10 inches, or on pizza pan into 12-inch circle. Pinch edges to make a slight rim. Spread Meat Mixture almost to edges. Top with green pepper and cheeses. Bake until crust is brown and filling is hot and bubbly, 15 to 20 minutes. Cut into squares or wedges.

2 pizzas.

You can get a head start on this recipe with Beef-Tomato Freezer Mix (see page 63).

Baked Pizza Sandwich

1 pound ground beef
1 can (15 ounces) tomato sauce
1 teaspoon oregano leaves
2 cups biscuit baking mix
1 egg
⅔ cup milk
1 package (8 ounces) sliced process American or mozzarella cheese
1 can (2 ounces) sliced mushrooms, drained
¼ cup grated Parmesan cheese

Heat oven to 400°. Cook and stir meat in large skillet until brown. Drain off fat. Stir half the tomato sauce and the oregano leaves into meat; heat to boiling. Reduce heat and simmer uncovered 10 minutes.

While meat mixture is simmering, mix baking mix, egg and milk. Measure ¾ cup of the batter and set aside. Spread remaining batter in greased baking pan, 9 × 9 × 2 inches. Pour remaining tomato sauce over batter, spreading it evenly. Layer 4 slices cheese, the meat mixture, mushrooms and remaining cheese slices on batter. Spoon reserved batter on top. Sprinkle with Parmesan cheese. Bake uncovered until golden brown, 20 to 25 minutes. Cool 5 minutes, then cut into squares.

5 or 6 servings.

Minnesota Minestrone

2 pounds ground beef
1 large onion, chopped (about
   1 cup)
1 clove garlic, minced
1 can (28 ounces) tomatoes
1 can (15 ounces) kidney beans
1 can (12 ounces) vacuum-pack
   whole kernel corn
2 stalks celery, sliced (about
   1 cup)
2 cups shredded cabbage (about
   ¼ head)
2 small zucchini, sliced (about
   2 cups)
1 cup uncooked elbow macaroni or
   broken spaghetti
2 cups water
½ cup red wine or water
2 teaspoons instant beef bouillon
1½ teaspoons salt
1½ teaspoons Italian seasoning
   Grated Parmesan cheese

Cook and stir meat, onion and garlic in Dutch oven until meat is brown. Drain off fat. Stir in tomatoes (with liquid), kidney beans (with liquid), corn (with liquid) and remaining ingredients except cheese; break up tomatoes.

Heat to boiling. Reduce heat; cover and simmer, stirring occasionally, until macaroni and vegetables are tender, about 30 minutes. Serve with Parmesan cheese. (Pictured on page 56.)

10 servings (1½ cups each).

Wipe Away Those Tears!

If you're one of those cooks who start to weep at the very thought of chopping onions, take heart. Here's a new trick to try. Cut the ends off the onions, peel and rinse under cold water; then wrap and refrigerate for at least an hour or two. When you are ready to use the onions, simply chop with a sharp knife.

Beef and Lentil Stew

1 pound ground beef
1 medium onion, chopped (about
   ½ cup)
1 clove garlic, minced
1 can (4 ounces) mushroom stems
   and pieces
1 can (16 ounces) stewed tomatoes
1 stalk celery, sliced
1 large carrot, sliced
1 cup uncooked lentils
3 cups water
¼ cup red wine (optional)
1 bay leaf
2 tablespoons snipped parsley
2 teaspoons salt
1 teaspoon instant beef bouillon
¼ teaspoon pepper

Cook and stir meat, onion and garlic in Dutch oven until meat is brown. Drain off fat. Stir in mushrooms (with liquid) and remaining ingredients; heat to boiling. Reduce heat; cover and simmer, stirring occasionally, until lentils are tender, about 40 minutes. Remove bay leaf.

6 servings (1⅓ cups each).

Beef Moussaka

1½ pounds ground beef
1 medium onion, chopped (about ½ cup)
2 tablespoons snipped parsley
1 teaspoon salt
¼ teaspoon pepper
⅛ teaspoon nutmeg
1 can (8 ounces) tomato sauce
¼ cup dry red wine or tomato juice
1 medium eggplant
6 eggs
¾ cup milk
½ teaspoon salt
⅓ cup grated Parmesan cheese

Heat oven to 375°. Cook and stir meat and onion in large skillet until meat is brown. Drain off fat. Stir in parsley, 1 teaspoon salt, the pepper, nutmeg, tomato sauce and wine; heat to boiling. Reduce heat and simmer uncovered 5 minutes.

Pare eggplant and cut into ½-inch slices. Arrange half the eggplant slices in ungreased baking dish, 11¾ × 7½ × 1¾ inches; top with half the meat mixture. Repeat with remaining eggplant slices and meat mixture. Cover with aluminum foil and bake until eggplant is tender, about 40 minutes.

Beat eggs, milk and ½ teaspoon salt; pour over hot casserole and sprinkle with cheese. Bake uncovered until custard is set, 10 to 15 minutes. Cool 10 minutes, then cut into squares. (Pictured on page 53.)

8 servings.

Hungry Boy's Casserole

1 pound ground beef
2 stalks celery, sliced (about 1 cup)
1 medium onion, chopped (about ½ cup)
1 clove garlic, minced
1 can (16 ounces) garbanzo or lima beans
1 can (16 ounces) pork and beans
½ cup chopped green pepper
1 teaspoon salt
1 can (6 ounces) tomato paste

Cook and stir meat, celery, onion and garlic in large skillet until meat is brown. Drain off fat. Stir in garbanzo beans (with liquid) and remaining ingredients.

TO COOK IN SKILLET: Heat mixture to boiling. Reduce heat; cover and simmer 10 minutes, stirring occasionally.

TO COOK IN OVEN: Pour mixture into ungreased 2-quart casserole. Cover and bake in 375° oven until hot and bubbly, about 45 minutes.

6 servings (1 cup each).

At right—Hamburger dishes to delight family or company. Clockwise from top: Apple-filled Squash Halves (page 45), Enchiladas (page 41), Beef Moussaka (this page).

On page 54—With Browned 'n Seasoned Freezer Mix: Freezer Mix Pizzawiches (page 62), Freezer Mix Cheeseburger Pie (page 62).

On page 55—With Beef-Tomato Freezer Mix: Freezer Mix Lentil Stew (page 65), Freezer Mix One-Dish Spaghetti (page 65).

Chili Macaroni

1 pound ground beef
2 medium onions, chopped (about 1 cup)
1 can (15½ ounces) kidney beans
1 can (28 ounces) tomatoes
1 can (8 ounces) tomato sauce
1 cup chopped green pepper (optional)
1 cup uncooked elbow macaroni
2 to 4 teaspoons chili powder
1 teaspoon salt
⅛ teaspoon cayenne red pepper
⅛ teaspoon paprika

Cook and stir meat and onions in large skillet or Dutch oven until meat is brown. Drain off fat. Stir in kidney beans (with liquid), tomatoes (with liquid) and remaining ingredients; break up tomatoes.

Heat to boiling. Reduce heat; cover and simmer, stirring occasionally, until macaroni is tender, 20 to 30 minutes. If you prefer a thinner consistency, add water or wine.

6 servings (1⅓ cups each).

VARIATION

Chili con Carne: Omit elbow macaroni and simmer uncovered until of desired consistency, about 30 minutes.

At left—Hearty and handsome casserole fare. Clockwise from top: Minnesota Minestrone (page 51), Muffin-topped Chili (this page), Creamy Beef-Noodle Combo (page 37).

Muffin-topped Chili

Chili con Carne (left)
1 cup biscuit baking mix
2 tablespoons cornmeal
1 egg
⅓ cup milk
1 tablespoon cornmeal

Prepare Chili con Carne except—decrease simmering time to 15 minutes.

Heat oven to 425°. Mix baking mix, 2 tablespoons cornmeal, the egg and milk; beat vigorously ½ minute. Pour hot Chili con Carne into ungreased 3-quart casserole. Drop batter by spoonfuls around edge of casserole; sprinkle batter with 1 tablespoon cornmeal. Bake uncovered 25 minutes. (Pictured on page 56.)

6 to 8 servings.

Vegetable Beef Noodle Dinner

1 package (10 ounces) frozen green peas
1 pound ground beef
2 cups hot water
1 can (10½ ounces) condensed beef broth (bouillon)
1 package (6.5 ounces) mix for beef noodle
2 tablespoons chopped pimiento

Rinse frozen peas with small amount of running cold water to separate and remove ice crystals; set aside. Cook and stir meat in large skillet until brown. Drain off fat. Stir in water, beef broth, Noodles, Sauce Mix, peas and pimiento; heat to boiling. Reduce heat; cover and simmer about 10 minutes, stirring occasionally. Uncover and cook to desired consistency.

4 or 5 servings.

Freezer Fare

To take full advantage of all that you're doing (or want to do), take full advantage of your freezer and of all the good foods that can be stored in it. Particularly hamburger. And that's what this chapter is all about. Here we show you how to make the most of the time you have—when you have it—with a special collection of hamburger recipes that will help you get a head start on the dinner hour.

Leading off, you will find a triple-threat attack on time with hamburger "freezer mixes," especially developed for savory spin-offs as sandwich, soup or casserole. And talk about variety. These mixes come in three very different flavor combinations: Beef-Mushroom Freezer Mix, Browned 'n Seasoned Freezer Mix and Beef-Tomato Freezer Mix. For added convenience and time saving, these frozen mixtures may be defrosted and heated in a microwave oven: Place freezer container in microwave oven and microwave 4 minutes just to loosen. Place frozen mix in 2-quart casserole; omit water but make any other ingredient additions as directed in the recipe. Cover and cook in microwave oven, stirring occasionally, until hot, 12 to 15 minutes. Add any remaining ingredients as directed and microwave until of desired doneness, 5 to 15 minutes. (The time will depend on the amount of added ingredients and whether the ingredients are just being heated or actually being cooked.)

Next, "Individual Dinners in Foil," some very special ideas for a family on the go. With these, you can make your dinner whenever the spirit strikes; then divvy it up in individual serving packets, label and freeze. These one-per-person dinner packets are sure to fit the comings and goings of today's life-styles. And they're perfect for double-quick heating in a microwave oven. (Timing tip: One or more packets can be heated in a conventional oven in the same amount of time. In a microwave oven, you must allow extra time for each extra packet.)

What about the all-time favorites? They're here too. "Favorite Fixin's" details the freezer treatment—including storage times and heating directions—for a number of recipes from other chapters. Take a tip and think about setting aside a few hours to "cook" for your freezer, and then relax in the knowledge that dinner will *always* be waiting, however busy the day and no matter what the unexpected brings.

Now stop and think about the way you use your freezer. Are you planning on it —and with it—to help free up your food time? We think it's the easy answer to how you can manage—in spite of, and because of, all you do in your busy days.

Beef-Mushroom Freezer Mix

4 pounds ground beef
2½ large onions, chopped (about 2½ cups)
2 cloves garlic, minced
3 cans (10¾ ounces each) condensed cream of mushroom soup
3 cans (4 ounces each) mushroom stems and pieces, drained
½ cup water or red wine
1 tablespoon instant beef bouillon
½ teaspoon pepper

Cook and stir meat in Dutch oven until brown. Drain off fat. Stir in remaining ingredients; heat to boiling. Reduce heat; cover and simmer 15 minutes, stirring occasionally. Divide mixture among four 1-quart freezer containers (about 3 cups in each). Cool quickly. Cover and label; freeze no longer than 3 months (see note). Use freezer mix in the recipes that follow.

About 12 cups.

NOTE: Mixture can be stored in refrigerator up to 3 days. When using in these recipes, add water and other ingredients as directed but decrease cooking time.

Freezer Mix Meat-and-Potato Favorite

1 container frozen Beef-Mushroom Freezer Mix
⅓ cup water
2 cups frozen fried shredded potato rounds

Dip container of frozen mix into hot water just to loosen. In 2-quart saucepan, heat frozen mix and water to boiling. Reduce heat; cover and simmer, stirring frequently, until mix is thawed, about 20 minutes.

Heat oven to 375°. Place half the potato rounds in ungreased 1½-quart casserole; pour meat mixture over potato rounds and top with remaining potato rounds. Cover and bake 25 minutes. Uncover and bake until potato rounds are brown, about 10 minutes longer.

4 servings.

Freezer Mix Romanoff

1 container frozen Beef-Mushroom
    Freezer Mix
⅓ cup water
1 package (5.5 ounces) noodles
    Romanoff

Dip container of frozen mix into hot water just to loosen. In 2-quart saucepan, heat frozen mix and water to boiling. Reduce heat; cover and simmer, stirring frequently, until mix is thawed, about 20 minutes.

Prepare noodles Romanoff as directed on package except—omit butter and milk; stir sour cream-cheese sauce mix and cooked noodles into meat mixture and heat to boiling. Reduce heat; cover and simmer 5 minutes.

4 or 5 servings.

Freezer Mix Chow Mein

1 container frozen Beef-Mushroom
    Freezer Mix
¼ cup water
1 tablespoon soy sauce
2 teaspoons cornstarch
2 teaspoons molasses
¼ teaspoon ginger
1 can (16 ounces) Chinese
    vegetables, drained
2 to 3 cups chow mein noodles or
    hot cooked rice

Dip container of frozen mix into hot water just to loosen. In 2-quart saucepan, heat frozen mix and water to boiling. Reduce heat; cover and simmer, stirring frequently, until mix is thawed, about 20 minutes.

Mix soy sauce, cornstarch, molasses and ginger; stir soy sauce mixture and Chinese vegetables into meat mixture. Cook, stirring constantly, until mixture thickens and boils. Boil and stir 1 minute. Serve over chow mein noodles and top with additional soy sauce.

4 servings.

Freezer Mix Barley Soup

1 container frozen Beef-Mushroom
    Freezer Mix
3 cups water
½ cup uncooked barley
1 cup sliced celery
1 cup sliced carrot
1 sprig parsley
1 bay leaf
¾ teaspoon salt

Dip container of frozen mix into hot water just to loosen. In Dutch oven, heat frozen mix and remaining ingredients to boiling. Reduce heat; cover and simmer, stirring frequently, until mix is thawed and barley and vegetables are tender, 30 to 40 minutes. Remove bay leaf.

4 servings (1½ cups each).

Freezer Mix Stroganoff

1 container frozen Beef-Mushroom
    Freezer Mix
¼ cup water
¾ cup dairy sour cream
2 cups hot cooked noodles or rice

Dip container of frozen mix into hot water just to loosen. In 2-quart saucepan, heat frozen mix and water to boiling. Reduce heat; cover and simmer, stirring frequently, until mix is thawed, about 20 minutes. Stir in sour cream and heat. Serve over noodles.

4 servings.

Browned 'n Seasoned Freezer Mix

4 pounds ground beef
1½ large onions, chopped (about 1½ cups)
3 cloves garlic, minced
2 teaspoons salt
¾ teaspoon pepper

Cook and stir meat, onions and garlic in Dutch oven until meat is brown. Drain off fat. Stir in seasonings. Spread meat mixture in 2 ungreased baking pans, 13×9×2 inches. Freeze 1 hour. (This partial freezing prevents the meat from freezing together solidly.)

Crumble meat mixture into small pieces; place in heavy plastic bag or freezer container. Seal securely and label; freeze no longer than 3 months. Use freezer mix in the recipes that follow.

About 14 cups.

NOTE: You can use this mix in any recipe for drained, seasoned browned ground beef. Each 3½ cups lightly packed frozen mix is the equivalent of 1 pound ground beef, ⅓ cup chopped onion, 1 small clove garlic, ½ teaspoon salt and dash of pepper. (If mixture is not frozen, allow 3 cups.)

Freezer Mix Dinner

Prepare 1 package (6.5 ounces) mix for beef noodle or 1 package (7.25 ounces) mix for chili tomato as directed except—substitute 3½ cups lightly packed frozen Browned 'n Seasoned Freezer Mix for the drained browned ground beef.

5 servings (1 cup each).

Freezer Mix Meat and Potatoes Au Gratin

Prepare 1 package (5.5 ounces) au gratin potatoes as directed except—use 2-quart casserole, omit butter and stir in 3½ cups lightly packed frozen Browned 'n Seasoned Freezer Mix with the water.

4 or 5 servings.

Freezer Mix Skillet Goulash

Prepare Skillet Goulash (page 36) except —substitute 3½ cups lightly packed frozen Browned 'n Seasoned Freezer Mix for the drained browned ground beef and onion; decrease salt to 1 teaspoon.

5 servings (1 cup each).

Freezer Mix All-American Hot Dish

Prepare All-American Hot Dish (page 37) except—substitute 3½ cups lightly packed frozen Browned 'n Seasoned Freezer Mix for the drained browned ground beef and onion; omit salt.

6 servings (1 cup each).

Freezer Mix Beef-Noodle Combo

Prepare Creamy Beef-Noodle Combo (page 37) except—substitute 3½ cups lightly packed frozen Browned 'n Seasoned Freezer Mix for the drained browned ground beef and onion; decrease salt to ½ teaspoon.

5 servings (1 cup each).

Freezer Mix Cheeseburger Pie

Prepare Cheeseburger Pie (page 48) except—substitute 3½ cups lightly packed frozen Browned 'n Seasoned Freezer Mix, 2 tablespoons biscuit baking mix and 1 tablespoon Worcestershire sauce for the Meat Filling. (Pictured on page 54.)

6 servings.

Freezer Mix Pasties

Prepare Hamburger Pasties (page 21) except—substitute 3½ cups lightly packed frozen Browned 'n Seasoned Freezer Mix for the drained browned ground beef and onion; omit garlic salt and pepper.

8 pasties.

Freezer Mix Pizzawiches

  1 can (6 ounces) tomato paste
  ¼ cup grated Parmesan cheese
3½ cups lightly packed frozen
     Browned 'n Seasoned Freezer
     Mix
  1 teaspoon Italian seasoning
     Dash red pepper sauce
  6 slices bread or 5 hamburger
     buns, split
     Shredded mozzarella or process
     American cheese

Heat oven to 500°. Mix tomato paste, Parmesan cheese, freezer mix and seasonings. Spread mixture on bread slices and place on ungreased baking sheet. Top each with a spoonful of shredded cheese. Bake until cheese is bubbly, 5 to 10 minutes. (Pictured on page 54.)

5 or 6 servings.

Beef-Tomato Freezer Mix

4 pounds ground beef
2½ large onions, chopped (about 2½ cups)
1 cup chopped green pepper
3 cloves garlic, minced
3 cans (15 ounces each) tomato sauce
1 can (12 ounces) tomato paste
2 teaspoons salt
¾ teaspoon pepper

Cook and stir meat in Dutch oven until brown. Drain off fat. Stir in remaining ingredients; heat to boiling. Reduce heat; cover and simmer 15 minutes, stirring occasionally. Divide mixture among four 1-quart freezer containers (about 3 cups in each). Cool quickly. Cover and label; freeze no longer than 3 months (see note). Use freezer mix in the recipes that follow.

About 12 cups.

NOTE: If you prefer, the mixture can be stored in the refrigerator up to 3 days. When using in the following recipes, add water and other ingredients as directed but decrease the cooking time.

Freezer Mix Pizza

Prepare Hamburger Pizza (page 50) except—omit green pepper in Topping and substitute the following mixture for the Meat Mixture:

1 container frozen Beef-Tomato
  Freezer Mix
¼ cup water
1 teaspoon Italian seasoning
  Dash red pepper sauce

Dip container of frozen mix into hot water just to loosen. In 2-quart saucepan, heat frozen mix and remaining ingredients to boiling. Reduce heat; cover and simmer, stirring frequently, until mix is thawed, about 20 minutes.

2 pizzas.

Freezer Mix Spanish Rice

1 container frozen Beef-Tomato
  Freezer Mix
5 slices bacon, crisply fried and
  crumbled
1 cup uncooked regular rice
2½ cups water
1 teaspoon chili powder
½ teaspoon oregano leaves

Dip container of frozen mix into hot water just to loosen. In large skillet, heat frozen mix and remaining ingredients to boiling. Reduce heat; cover and simmer, stirring occasionally, until mix is thawed and rice is tender, about 30 minutes. (Add a small amount of water if necessary.)

4 servings (1 cup each).

Freezer Mix Tacos

Prepare Tacos (page 15) except—substitute the following mixture for the Meat Filling:

1 container frozen Beef-Tomato
  Freezer Mix
1 to 2 teaspoons chili powder
⅛ teaspoon cayenne red pepper
  (optional)
  Dash red pepper sauce
¼ cup water

Dip container of frozen mix into hot water just to loosen. In 2-quart saucepan, heat frozen mix and remaining ingredients to boiling. Reduce heat; cover and simmer, stirring frequently, until mix is partially thawed, about 15 minutes. Uncover and simmer 15 minutes, stirring occasionally.

8 to 10 tacos.

Freezer Mix Sloppy Joes

1 container frozen Beef-Tomato
  Freezer Mix
¼ cup water
1 cup sliced celery
1 tablespoon catsup
1 teaspoon brown sugar (optional)
1 teaspoon Worcestershire sauce
6 to 8 hamburger buns, split and
  toasted

Dip container of frozen mix into hot water just to loosen. In 2-quart saucepan, heat frozen mix, water, celery, catsup, brown sugar and Worcestershire sauce to boiling. Reduce heat; cover and simmer, stirring frequently, until mix is partially thawed, about 15 minutes. Uncover and simmer, stirring occasionally, until of desired consistency, about 10 minutes. Spoon onto bottom halves of buns; top with remaining halves.

6 to 8 sandwiches.

Freezer Mix Enchilada Casserole

1 container frozen Beef-Tomato
  Freezer Mix
¼ cup water
1 can (2¼ ounces) sliced ripe olives,
  drained (½ cup)
1½ to 2 teaspoons chili powder
6 corn tortillas
1½ cups shredded Cheddar or
  Monterey Jack cheese

Dip container of frozen mix into hot water just to loosen. In 2-quart saucepan, heat frozen mix, water, olives and chili powder to boiling. Reduce heat; cover and simmer, stirring frequently, until mix is thawed, about 20 minutes.

Heat oven to 375°. Layer half each of the tortillas, meat mixture and cheese in ungreased baking dish, 11¾ × 7½ × 1¾ inches; repeat. Bake uncovered until bubbly, 30 to 40 minutes.

4 or 5 servings.

Freezer Mix Lasagne

Prepare Lasagne (page 38) except—substitute the following mixture for the Meat Sauce:

1 container frozen Beef-Tomato
  Freezer Mix
½ teaspoon oregano leaves
1 tablespoon snipped parsley
¼ cup water

Dip container of frozen mix into hot water just to loosen. In 2-quart saucepan, heat frozen mix, oregano leaves, parsley and water to boiling. Reduce heat; cover and simmer 15 minutes, stirring frequently. Uncover and simmer, stirring occasionally, until mix is thawed.

6 servings.

Freezer Mix
One-Dish Spaghetti

1 container frozen Beef-Tomato
   Freezer Mix
3 cups water
1 can (4 ounces) mushroom stems
   and pieces, drained
1 package (7 ounces) thin spaghetti,
   broken into pieces
1 teaspoon oregano leaves
1 teaspoon sugar
1 teaspoon chili powder
1 cup shredded Cheddar cheese
   (4 ounces)

Dip container of frozen mix into hot water just to loosen. In Dutch oven, heat frozen mix and remaining ingredients except cheese to boiling. Reduce heat; cover and simmer, stirring frequently, until mix is thawed and spaghetti is tender, about 30 minutes. (A small amount of water can be added if necessary.) Sprinkle with cheese; cover and heat until cheese is melted. (Pictured on page 55.)

6 servings (1 cup each).

Freezer Mix Goulash

1 container frozen Beef-Tomato
   Freezer Mix
¼ cup water
¼ cup catsup
1 cup sliced celery
1 can (4 ounces) mushroom stems
   and pieces, drained
1 teaspoon paprika
1 teaspoon brown sugar
1 teaspoon Worcestershire sauce
3 ounces noodles (about 1½ cups)

Dip container of frozen mix into hot water just to loosen. Place frozen mix and remaining ingredients except noodles in 2-quart saucepan; heat to boiling. Reduce heat; cover and simmer, stirring frequently, until mix is thawed and celery is tender, about 40 minutes.

While meat mixture is simmering, cook noodles as directed on package; drain. Stir noodles into meat mixture and simmer until hot.

4 servings.

Freezer Mix Lentil Stew

1 container frozen Beef-Tomato
   Freezer Mix
3 cups water
1 cup uncooked lentils
1 sprig parsley
1 bay leaf
1½ cups sliced fresh mushrooms
   (optional)
1 large carrot, sliced
1 large stalk celery, sliced
¼ cup red wine (optional)
½ teaspoon salt

Dip container of frozen mix into hot water just to loosen. In Dutch oven, heat frozen mix, water, lentils, parsley and bay leaf to boiling. Reduce heat; cover and simmer, stirring frequently, until mix is thawed, about 20 minutes.

Stir in remaining ingredients; heat to boiling. Reduce heat; cover and simmer until vegetables are tender, about 20 minutes. Remove bay leaf. (Pictured on page 55.)

5 servings (1⅓ cups each).

Individual Dinners in Foil

Here's a handy treatment to fit any family's catch-as-catch-can dinner schedule.

Cooking Guide for Individual Foil Dinners

TO SERVE FROM REGULAR OVEN: Place the desired number of frozen packets seam sides up on ungreased baking sheet. Bake on center rack of 450° oven until hot, 35 to 45 minutes.

TO SERVE FROM MICROWAVE OVEN: Unwrap *one* packet and place in a small glass dish; cover with dinner plate. Microwave, stirring once, until hot, 5 to 7 minutes. (Each serving can also be packaged and stored in paper or glass dishes or in plastic cooking bags, enabling it to go *directly* from freezer to microwave oven. Do not unwrap.)

Individual Meat-Macaroni Dinners

1 pound ground beef
1 small onion, chopped (about ¼ cup)
1 cup elbow macaroni, cooked and drained
1 can (11 ounces) condensed Cheddar cheese soup
1 can (16 ounces) mixed vegetables, drained
⅓ cup water
¼ teaspoon pepper

Cook and stir meat and onion in large skillet until onion is tender. Drain off fat. Remove from heat; stir in remaining ingredients. Divide mixture among four 12-inch squares of heavy-duty or double thickness regular aluminum foil. Wrap each securely and label; freeze no longer than 2 months.

When ready to serve, cook according to Cooking Guide (above).

4 servings.

Individual Beef-and-Bean Dinners

1 pound ground beef
1 small onion, chopped (about ¼ cup)
2 cans (16 ounces each) pork and beans in tomato sauce
⅓ cup chili sauce
1 tablespoon molasses or brown sugar
1 tablespoon prepared mustard
½ teaspoon salt

Cook and stir meat and onion in large skillet until onion is tender. Drain off fat. Remove from heat; stir in remaining ingredients. Divide mixture among five 12-inch squares of heavy-duty or double thickness regular aluminum foil. Wrap each securely and label; freeze no longer than 2 months.

When ready to serve, cook according to Cooking Guide (above).

5 servings.

Individual
Saucy Meat Patties in Foil

2 pounds ground beef
1 envelope (about 1½ ounces) onion
   soup mix
1 can (10¾ ounces) condensed
   cream of mushroom soup

Mix meat and onion soup mix. Shape mixture into 8 patties, about ¾ inch thick. Place each patty on 12-inch square of heavy-duty or double thickness regular aluminum foil. Spoon about 2½ tablespoons soup onto each patty. Wrap each securely and label; freeze no longer than 3 months.

When ready to serve, cook according to Cooking Guide (page 66) except—if using microwave oven, cover with waxed paper instead of dinner plate.

8 patties.

Individual
Tomato-Rice Dinners

1 pound ground beef
1 small onion, chopped (about
   ¼ cup)
1 can (10¾ ounces) condensed
   tomato soup
1½ cups uncooked instant rice
1 cup water
1 cup shredded Cheddar cheese
   (4 ounces)
½ cup chopped green pepper
   (optional)
½ teaspoon salt
½ teaspoon chili powder
¼ teaspoon basil leaves
⅛ teaspoon pepper

Cook and stir meat and onion in large skillet until onion is tender. Drain off fat. Remove from heat; stir in remaining in-

gredients. Divide mixture among five 12-inch squares of heavy-duty or double thickness regular aluminum foil. Wrap each securely and label; freeze no longer than 2 months.

When ready to serve, cook according to Cooking Guide (page 66).

5 servings.

Individual
Souper Beef Dinners

1 pound ground beef
1 small onion, chopped (about
   ¼ cup)
1 can (10¾ ounces) condensed
   cream of mushroom soup
1 can (16 ounces) cut green beans
   or whole kernel corn, drained
¼ cup water
1 can (3 ounces) French fried
   onions

Cook and stir meat and onion in large skillet until onion is tender. Drain off fat. Remove from heat; stir in remaining ingredients except French fried onions. Divide mixture among four 12-inch squares of heavy-duty or double thickness regular aluminum foil. Wrap each securely and label; freeze no longer than 2 months.

When ready to serve, cook according to Cooking Guide (page 66) except—open packets during the last 5 minutes of baking and sprinkle with French fried onions. If using microwave oven, sprinkle with onions after cooking.

4 servings.

Favorite Fixin's

A main dish waiting in the freezer. It's the answer to a busy cook's prayers—with a little help from the preplanning department. On these two pages you'll find a variety of hamburger recipes from the previous chapters, here for do-ahead fixing and no-fuss cooking. You can also use them as a guide for handling your own hamburger favorites. But if you do, here are a couple of tips to keep in mind:

☐ Be sure to avoid overcooking—it's the major pitfall of casseroles destined for the freezer. (A simple way out is to always undercook any pasta or rice; it will cook through when the casserole is reheated.) It's a good idea to soft-pedal spices too.

☐ Reheat frozen cooked casseroles in a 350° oven (usually 1 to 1½ hours), adding liquid if the food seems dry. Or empty the frozen dish into a saucepan (with a small amount of butter, margarine or water in the pan), cover tightly and place over medium heat.

Freezer Burgers

Prepare Basic Hamburgers (page 6) except —do not cook. Wrap each securely in heavy-duty or double thickness regular aluminum foil and label; freeze no longer than 3 months.

TO COOK IN SKILLET: Unwrap desired number of frozen patties and place in single layer in skillet. Cover and cook over medium-high heat 5 to 7 minutes. Turn patties; partially cover and cook over medium heat until of desired doneness, 5 to 7 minutes.

TO BROIL: Unwrap desired number of frozen patties and place on rack in broiler pan. Broil patties 6 inches from heat, turning once, to desired doneness, about 20 minutes.

6 patties.

Freezer Meat Loaf

Prepare Basic Meat Loaf (page 30) except —do not bake. Cover pan with aluminum foil and label; freeze no longer than 2 months.

TO SERVE: Bake frozen meat loaf uncovered in 350° oven 2 to 2¼ hours. Drain off fat.

6 servings.

Freezer Lasagne

Prepare Lasagne (page 38) except—do not bake. Cover with aluminum foil and label; freeze no longer than 2 months.

TO SERVE: Bake foil-covered frozen Lasagne in 350° oven 1¼ hours. Uncover and bake until golden brown, 15 to 30 minutes longer.

6 servings.

Freezer Meatballs

Meatballs can be frozen either before or after cooking. Prepare Basic Meatballs (page 22) except—after shaping or cooking, place in ungreased shallow baking pan and freeze uncovered 3 hours. (This prevents the meatballs from freezing together.) Remove from freezer and pack desired number of meatballs in heavy plastic bags or freezer containers or wrap in heavy-duty or double thickness regular aluminum foil; label. Freeze no longer than 3 months.

TO COOK FROZEN UNCOOKED MEATBALLS: Cook frozen meatballs in skillet or oven as directed in basic recipe except—increase baking time to 25 minutes.

TO REHEAT FROZEN COOKED MEATBALLS: Place frozen meatballs in ungreased baking pan and heat in 375° oven until hot, about 20 minutes. Or add frozen cooked meatballs to a sauce and simmer until hot, about 15 minutes.

About 24 meatballs.

Freezer Pasties

Prepare Hamburger Pasties (page 21) except—do not prick tops or bake. Wrap each pasty securely in heavy-duty or double thickness regular aluminum foil and label; freeze no longer than 2 months.

TO SERVE: Unwrap desired number of frozen pasties and place on ungreased baking sheet. Prick tops with fork and bake in 375° oven until hot, 40 to 45 minutes.

8 pasties.

Freezer Enchiladas

Prepare Enchiladas (page 41) except— place filled tortillas in ungreased baking pan, 13×9×2 inches; do not bake. Cover pan with aluminum foil and label; freeze no longer than 2 months.

TO SERVE: Pour ⅓ cup water over frozen Enchiladas; cover and bake in 350° oven 1 hour. Uncover and bake until golden brown and bubbly, about 15 minutes longer.

4 or 5 servings.

Freezer Manicotti

Prepare Manicotti (page 40) except—after filling shells, wrap securely in heavy-duty or double thickness regular aluminum foil and label; freeze no longer than 2 months. Do not prepare Tomato Sauce.

TO SERVE: Unwrap frozen shells and place in ungreased baking pan, 13×9×2 inches. Prepare Tomato Sauce and pour over shells. Cover and bake until shells are tender, 1¾ to 2 hours.

6 to 8 servings.

Freezer Stuffed Green Peppers

Prepare Stuffed Green Peppers (page 45) except—stir all the tomato sauce into the filling mixture; cover with aluminum foil but do not bake. Label; freeze no longer than 2 months.

TO SERVE: Bake foil-covered pan of frozen peppers in 350° oven until hot, 1 to 1¼ hours. Uncover; top peppers with Cheddar cheese slices, catsup or chili sauce and bake 5 minutes.

4 or 5 servings.

Microwave Specials

If you're the proud possessor of a microwave oven, you've no doubt discovered how its speed has added to the flexibility of your mealtime. But have you used it for your hamburger favorites? If not, you really ought to give it a try.

On the following page we bring you some basic recipes that appear in other sections of the book, this time adapted to microwave cooking. And although we have included only a sampling, the principles can be applied to many other hamburger-based recipes.

Notice, for example, that when meatballs are not accompanied by a sauce or gravy, we have suggested coating them with gravy mix to produce the appetizing brown color and flavor you're accustomed to.

Observe that we recommend shaping meat loaf in a shallower than usual form so that quick cooking will also mean even cooking.

If a hamburger casserole is the order of the day, the meat is first partially microwaved so that if there is excess fat, it can be drained off before any of the other ingredients are added.

Finally, when the recipe calls for covered cooking but your casserole lacks a fitting cover, try waxed paper or a dinner plate.

To help you make the most of your valuable time, we've applied the double-quick microwave method to some of the done-in-advance fare that you've stored in the freezer. All of the "freezer mixes" (see pages 58–65) can be defrosted *and* heated in a microwave oven, while an "individual dinner in foil" (see pages 66–67) can be taken from the freezer, popped into the microwave oven and ready to serve in less than 10 minutes.

Of course, there are certain variations in the performance of individual microwave ovens—just as there are in conventional ovens. The recipes in this chapter were tested in counter-top microwave ovens that plug into regular grounded 110- or 120-volt outlets, and a range of cooking times has been indicated to allow for individual differences in oven cooking patterns. Start with the minimum time and then increase the time if necessary to achieve the "doneness" described in the recipe. (For other types of microwave ovens, refer to the manufacturer's instruction book.)

Using these recipes as a starting point, you can perfect your technique of preparing a wide variety of hamburger dishes in your microwave oven. Success with these should encourage you to go on and adapt your own favorites.

Meat Loaf
in a Microwave Oven

Prepare Basic Meat Loaf (page 30) except —spread mixture in ungreased 10-inch glass pie pan and spoon catsup on top. Cover with inverted glass pie pan or dinner plate and microwave until meat is set in center, 18 to 20 minutes. Let stand covered 5 minutes before serving.

6 servings.

Browned Meatballs
in a Microwave Oven

Prepare Basic Meatballs (page 22) except —coat meatballs with 1 envelope (about 1 ounce) brown gravy mix and arrange in ungreased glass baking dish, 8×8×2 inches. Cover with waxed paper and microwave until done, 7 to 8 minutes. Drain off fat.

About 24 meatballs.

Saucy Meatballs
in a Microwave Oven

   Basic Meatballs (page 22)
1 can (10¾ ounces) condensed
   cream of chicken soup
⅓ cup milk
⅛ teaspoon nutmeg
½ cup dairy sour cream
   Snipped parsley

Prepare Basic Meatballs except—place meatballs in ungreased glass baking dish, 8×8×2 inches. Cover with waxed paper and microwave 5 to 6 minutes. Drain off fat.

Stir in soup, milk and nutmeg. Cover with waxed paper and microwave until mixture is bubbly, about 5 minutes. Stir

in sour cream and microwave 1 minute. Garnish with parsley.

4 or 5 servings.

NOTE: When the meatballs are served in a sauce, as is the case in this recipe, the gravy mix coating is not necessary because the sauce provides all the color and flavor needed.

Beef and Cabbage Joes
in a Microwave Oven

1 pound ground beef
1 medium onion, chopped (about
   ½ cup)
½ cup thinly sliced celery
2 cups shredded cabbage
⅓ cup chopped green pepper
¾ cup catsup
¼ teaspoon salt
1 tablespoon prepared mustard
8 hamburger buns, split and
   toasted

Crumble meat into ungreased 2-quart glass casserole; add onion and celery. Microwave uncovered, stirring once, until meat is set, about 5 minutes. Drain off fat. Stir in remaining ingredients except buns. Cover and microwave, stirring occasionally, until cabbage is desired doneness, about 14 minutes. Spoon onto bottom halves of buns; top with remaining halves.

8 sandwiches.

NOTE: By precooking the meat in the microwave oven before adding the sauce ingredients, it is possible to drain off the fat and keep the meat in small chunks, similar to those in conventional browning. When the precooking is omitted, the meat pieces will be very fine and the fat may need to be skimmed from the finished casserole.

Index

BETTY CROCKER'S
DO-AHEAD
COOKBOOK
Recipes for the Freezer and the Refrigerator

Betty Crocker's Do-Ahead Cookbook

Photography Director: GEORGE ANCONA

 GOLDEN PRESS • NEW YORK
Western Publishing Company, Inc.
Racine, Wisconsin

Library of Congress Catalog Number: 72-80848

To Busy Planners Everywhere—

Your life is crowded; you don't have the time to spend in the kitchen that you once did. And yet, wouldn't you like to put together real home-cooked meals in the limited time you have? Betty Crocker's Do-Ahead Cookbook was designed to help you do just that, by planning and doing ahead.

These recipes were developed because of today's life-style—hectic, informal, flexible, ever-changing. The idea behind the recipes is ahead-of-time; you prepare food at less-busy times, then store it in your freezer or refrigerator until it's needed.

For long-range planning, there are recipes for the freezer; for short-term planning, the refrigerator stores the food.

These foods-in-reserve can be thought of as a savings bank—not only for a rush-hour dinnertime, but throughout the day, or for spur-of-the-moment situations.

Main dishes, salads, vegetables, breads, desserts—they're all here, along with snack-type foods. Directions for preparing are ultra-clear, and we've made it especially easy for you to find the instructions for what-to-do when you're ready to serve the food.

A real boon to your plan-ahead cooking life is exact storage time—we give it with every recipe. Also detailed information on freezing—how to cool, wrap, label and freeze.

All of these recipes were tested in the Betty Crocker Kitchens, and then tested again by homemakers throughout the country. We're sure the recipes will pass the most crucial test of all—the on-the-spot cooking test conducted in the midst of your busy kitchen. Here's happy cooking and happy eating for all your family—from now on!

Cordially,

Betty Crocker

Contents

Your Freezer: Long-Range Planning

Your Freezer: Long-Range Planning

Without a doubt, one of the most valuable appliances you can own is a home freezer. It is responsible for a whole new world of food preparation and meal planning, and it really takes the burden out of day-to-day cooking.

If you use your freezer wisely, you will always be prepared for the expected as well as the unexpected situation. Use this do-ahead freezer section as a step-by-step workbook. With a freezer and the freezer recipes in this book, you'll be able to take advantage of your supermarket's food "specials," and use your time to best advantage.

Here are some of the special features in our freezer recipes:

1 The first item mentioned under the title of each recipe is its recommended storage time. This recommendation is the result of extensive storage tests made in the Betty Crocker Kitchens. It tells you how long this particular food will stay at its best while stored under the proper conditions (see pages 84-87). After that time, the food will not be spoiled, but it may lose some of its moisture or flavor.

2 The number of servings is indicated right after the storage time. You can, therefore, plan according to your needs.

3 After the cooking directions, the recipe will tell you to cool, wrap, label and freeze. This must be done correctly if your food is to maintain its high quality (see pages 84-87).

4 When you want to serve the food you have frozen, turn to the recipe once more for the post-freezing directions. These are listed below the cooking instructions. You'll find them quickly by looking for this symbol: ■—which is followed by **boldface type.** Read over all of the directions following the symbol when you're planning your meal—and be sure to see if there are other ingredients to be added. Note that most foods do not require thawing, but are heated immediately after they have been removed from the freezer.

Pictured on the preceding page:
Crêpes Suzette (page 63)

Meats and Main Dishes

FREEZER MEAT LOAF

Store no longer than 1 month. Makes enough for 2 meals—6 servings each.

  3 pounds ground beef
½ cup dry bread crumbs
3½ cups milk
  1 cup minced onion
  2 eggs
2½ to 3 teaspoons salt
  2 tablespoons Worcestershire sauce
¼ teaspoon pepper

Mix all ingredients. Divide in half; spread each half evenly in ungreased loaf pan, 9×5×3 inches. (To serve immediately, see below.) Wrap, label and freeze.

■ **2 hours 35 minutes before serving, remove Freezer Meat Loaf from freezer and unwrap.** Bake uncovered in 350° oven until done, about 2½ hours. Drain off fat once during baking. (1 loaf —6 servings.)

To Serve Immediately: Bake uncovered in 350° oven until done, about 1½ hours. Drain off fat once during baking. (1 loaf—6 servings.)

MEAT AND POTATO PIE

Store no longer than 2 months. Makes enough for 2 meals—4 or 5 servings each.

  2 pounds ground beef
2⅔ cups instant mashed potato puffs
  2 eggs
  2 teaspoons salt
¼ teaspoon pepper
  2 tablespoons instant minced onion
½ cup catsup
  2 cups milk

Mix all ingredients. Divide between 2 un-greased 9-inch pie pans; spread evenly. (To serve one immediately, see below.) Wrap, label and freeze.

■ **1 hour 15 minutes before serving, remove 1 pan Meat and Potato Pie from freezer and unwrap. Have ready:** instant mashed potato puffs (enough for 4 servings); ½ cup shredded sharp Cheddar cheese.

Bake pie uncovered in 375° oven 1 hour. After 50 minutes of baking, prepare potato puffs as directed on package. Mound potato around edge of meat; sprinkle cheese on potato. Bake until cheese is melted, 3 to 4 minutes. (4 or 5 servings.)

To Serve Immediately: Have ready: instant mashed potato puffs (enough for 4 servings); ½ cup shredded sharp Cheddar cheese.

Bake meat pie in 350° oven 40 to 45 minutes. After 30 minutes of baking, prepare potato puffs as directed on package. Mound potato around edge of meat; sprinkle cheese on potato. Bake until cheese is melted, 3 to 4 minutes. (4 or 5 servings.)

CHILI

Store no longer than 4 months. Makes enough for 4 meals—6 servings each.

   4 pounds ground beef
10 medium onions, chopped (about 5 cups)
   4 cans (28 ounces each) tomatoes
   1 can (15 ounces) tomato sauce
¼ cup chili powder
   2 tablespoons sugar
   1 tablespoon plus 1½ teaspoons salt

Cook and stir meat and onion in Dutch oven or large roasting pan until meat is brown and onion is tender. Spoon off fat. Stir in remaining ingredients. Heat tomato mixture until it boils. Reduce heat; simmer uncovered 1 hour 15 minutes. Spoon off fat if necessary.

Divide Chili among four 5- to 6-cup freezer containers. Cool quickly. Cover, label and freeze.

■ **45 minutes before serving, remove 1 container Chili from freezer; dip container into very hot water just to loosen. Have ready:** 1 can (15½ ounces) kidney beans, drained (reserve liquid).

Place reserved bean liquid and frozen block in saucepan. Cover tightly; cook over medium-high heat, turning occasionally, 25 minutes. Uncover; cook 20 minutes longer, stirring in kidney beans 5 minutes before Chili is done. Season with additional chili powder if desired. (6 servings.)

CHILI AND DUMPLINGS

Makes enough for 5 or 6 servings.

   Chili (above)
1 can (15 ounces) chili beans
1 package (14 ounces) corn muffin mix
½ cup shredded sharp Cheddar cheese

Six hours before serving, remove 1 container Chili from freezer; thaw at room temperature just until softened, not warm. Heat Chili and beans (with liquid) in large skillet until mixture boils. Reduce heat slightly.

Prepare muffin mix as directed on package except—decrease milk to ½ cup and stir in cheese. Drop dough by tablespoonfuls onto boiling chili. Cook uncovered over low heat 10 minutes. Cover tightly; cook 10 minutes.

CHUCKWAGON TURNOVERS

Store no longer than 3 months. Makes enough for 4 or 5 servings.

Meat Filling
   1 pound ground beef
½ cup chopped onion
⅔ cup shredded Swiss cheese
   1 egg, beaten
¼ teaspoon red pepper sauce
1½ teaspoons salt
   2 tablespoons snipped parsley

Pastry
   2 cups all-purpose flour*
   1 teaspoon salt
⅔ cup plus 2 tablespoons shortening
   4 to 5 tablespoons cold water

Cook and stir meat and onion until onion is tender. Remove from heat; cool slightly. Stir in remaining Meat Filling ingredients; set aside.

Prepare Pastry. Measure flour and salt into bowl; cut in shortening thoroughly. Sprinkle in water, 1 tablespoon at a time, mixing until all flour is moistened and dough almost cleans side of bowl (1 to 2 teaspoons water can be added if needed). Gather dough into a ball; divide in half.

Roll each half into 10-inch circle on lightly floured cloth-covered board. Place 1½ cups meat filling on half of each circle. Fold pastry over filling and press edges to seal securely. Prick tops of turnovers several times. Carefully place turnovers on ungreased baking sheet. (To serve immediately, see below.) Freeze uncovered until firm, about 2 hours. Remove turnovers from baking sheet. Wrap, label and return to freezer.

■ **35 minutes before serving, remove Chuckwagon Turnovers from freezer and unwrap; place on ungreased baking sheet.** Bake in 425° oven until brown, 25 to 30 minutes. Gravy or a tomato sauce is a nice addition.

To Serve Immediately: Bake in 425° oven until brown, 20 to 25 minutes. Gravy or a tomato sauce is a nice addition.

*If using self-rising flour, omit salt from Pastry. Pastry made with self-rising flour differs in flavor and texture.

ITALIAN SPAGHETTI SAUCE

Store no longer than 4 months. Makes enough for 24 servings—⅔ cup each.

Tomato-Meat Sauce
- **4 pounds ground beef**
- **¼ cup olive oil**
- **6 medium onions, finely chopped (about 3 cups)**
- **1 cup finely chopped green pepper**
- **8 cloves garlic, minced**
- **4 cans (16 ounces each) tomatoes**
- **4 cans (15 ounces each) tomato sauce**

Seasonings
- **3 tablespoons parsley flakes**
- **2 tablespoons sugar**
- **1½ to 2 tablespoons salt**
- **1 tablespoon oregano**
- **1 tablespoon basil**
- **1 teaspoon pepper**

Cook and stir meat in large skillet or Dutch oven until meat is brown. Spoon off fat; set meat aside.

Heat oil in 7- to 8-quart pan. Cook and stir onion, green pepper and garlic in oil until onion is tender. Stir in tomatoes, tomato sauce, Seasonings and the meat. Heat, stirring occasionally, until Tomato-Meat Sauce boils. Reduce heat; simmer uncovered 4 hours. (To serve immediately, see below.) Divide spaghetti sauce among four 1-quart freezer containers or three 6-cup freezer containers. Cool quickly. Cover, label and freeze.

■ **45 minutes before serving, remove 1 container Italian Spaghetti Sauce from freezer; dip container into very hot water just to loosen.** Place frozen block in 3-quart saucepan. Cover tightly; heat over medium heat, turning occasionally, 20 to 30 minutes. Reduce heat; uncover and simmer 10 minutes. While sauce heats, prepare hot cooked spaghetti for 6 or 9 servings. Serve sauce on hot cooked spaghetti; pass Parmesan cheese.

To Serve Immediately: Serve on hot cooked spaghetti; pass Parmesan cheese. [24 servings (⅔ cup meat sauce each).]

CHILI-MAC

Makes enough for 5 or 6 servings.

- **Italian Spaghetti Sauce (left)**
- **1 can (15½ ounces) kidney beans, drained (reserve liquid)**
- **1 tablespoon chili powder**
- **4 cups hot cooked macaroni**

Forty-five minutes before serving, remove one 1-quart container Italian Spaghetti Sauce from freezer; dip container into very hot water just to loosen. Place reserved bean liquid and frozen block in 3-quart saucepan. Cover tightly; heat over medium heat, turning occasionally, 20 to 30 minutes. Reduce heat; stir in beans and chili powder. Simmer uncovered 10 minutes. Serve on macaroni.

Storage Time for Beef at 0°

Most cuts	9 months
Ground	3 to 4 months
For stewing	4 months
Liver, heart, tongue	3 to 4 months
Cooked	2 months

To prepare for freezing: Place double layer of freezer wrap between steaks, chops, hamburger patties—to make them easy to separate. Using moisture-vapor-proof wrap, wrap closely to eliminate air. Do not season before freezing. You can freezer-store meat prepackaged, just as you bought it, for up to 2 weeks. Cook meat thawed or frozen.

To cook: Thaw wrapped meat in refrigerator or place frozen steaks and patties further than normal distance from broiler. In 300 to 325° oven, allow ⅓ to ½ more than the normal cooking time for frozen roasts.

MINI MEATBALLS

Store no longer than 2 months. Makes enough for 3 meals—4 or 5 servings each.

    3 pounds ground beef
    ⅓ cup minced onion
    1½ cups dry bread crumbs
    1 tablespoon salt
    ¼ teaspoon pepper
    1½ teaspoons Worcestershire sauce
    3 eggs
    ¾ cup milk

Mix all ingredients. Shape one-third of meat mixture by level tablespoonfuls into 1-inch balls. Place in ungreased jelly roll pan, 15½ × 10½ × 1 inch. Bake in 400° oven until done, about 10 minutes. (Can be served immediately. About 8 dozen meatballs.) Cool about 5 minutes. Freeze uncovered 15 minutes. Place partially frozen meatballs in 1-quart freezer container. Cover, label and return to freezer. Repeat 2 times. For variety and ease in preparation, use any of the recipes on this page for serving Mini Meatballs.

SWEET AND SOUR MEATBALLS

Makes enough for 4 or 5 servings.

    Mini Meatballs (above)
    1 cup sweet and sour sauce

Fifteen minutes before serving, remove 1 container Mini Meatballs from freezer. Heat sweet and sour sauce in large skillet until it boils. Place frozen meatballs in sauce. Reduce heat; cover tightly and simmer until meatballs are hot, about 10 minutes. Nice served on rice.

SPAGHETTI AND MEATBALLS

Makes enough for 4 or 5 servings.

    Mini Meatballs (left)
    1 jar (about 16 ounces) spaghetti sauce
    6 or 7 ounces spaghetti
    Parmesan cheese

Fifteen minutes before serving, remove 1 container Mini Meatballs from freezer. Heat spaghetti sauce in large skillet until it boils. Place frozen meatballs in sauce. Reduce heat; cover tightly and simmer until meatballs are hot, about 10 minutes.

While meatballs simmer, cook spaghetti as directed on package. Serve meatballs and sauce on spaghetti; pass Parmesan cheese.

MEATBALLS ROMANOFF

Makes enough for 4 or 5 servings.

    Mini Meatballs (left)
    2 tablespoons butter or margarine
    1 tablespoon flour
    1 package (5.5 ounces) noodles Romanoff
    1⅔ cups milk
    2 teaspoons parsley flakes
    2 tablespoons butter or margarine

Fifteen minutes before serving, remove 1 container Mini Meatballs from freezer. Melt 2 tablespoons butter in large skillet. Remove from heat; stir in flour and sauce mix from noodles Romanoff. Stir in milk slowly. Heat, stirring constantly, until sauce boils. Place frozen meatballs in sauce; heat until sauce boils. Reduce heat; cover tightly and simmer until meatballs are hot, about 10 minutes.

While meatballs simmer, cook noodles as directed on package except—stir parsley flakes and 2 tablespoons butter into cooked noodles. Serve meatballs and sauce on noodles.

Pictured at right, top to bottom: Spaghetti and Meatballs, Sweet and Sour Meatballs and Meatballs Romanoff

Arrange meat patties on a 10-inch pastry square and cover them with a 12-inch square.

With a fork, prick the pastry between and on top of the patties.

Hamburger-Onion Hoedown

HAMBURGER-ONION HOEDOWN

Store no longer than 3 months. Makes enough for 2 meals—4 to 6 servings each.

Meat Patties
- **2 pounds ground beef**
- **2 eggs, slightly beaten**
- **⅔ cup dry bread crumbs**
- **⅔ cup catsup**
- **½ cup chopped parsley**
- **1 envelope (about 1½ ounces) onion soup mix**
- **1⅓ cups warm water**

Pastry
- **4 cups all-purpose flour***
- **2 teaspoons salt**
- **1½ cups shortening**
- **½ to ⅔ cup cold water**

Mix Meat Patties ingredients; shape into 12 patties, ¾ inch thick.

Prepare Pastry. Measure flour and salt into bowl; cut in shortening thoroughly. Sprinkle in water, 2 tablespoons at a time, mixing until all flour is moistened and dough almost cleans side of bowl (1 to 2 teaspoons water can be added if needed). Gather dough into a ball; divide into 4 parts.

Roll 2 parts pastry into 10-inch squares for bottom crusts and 2 parts into 12-inch squares for top crusts. Place 10-inch squares on ungreased baking sheets; arrange 6 meat patties evenly on each square. Cover with 12-inch squares; seal edges. Press lightly between meat patties to mark servings. With fork, prick serving marks between patties and top of servings. Bake in 400° oven 40 to 45 minutes. (Can serve whole recipe immediately. 8 to 12 servings.) Cool quickly. Wrap, label and freeze.

■ **50 minutes before serving, remove 1 package Hamburger-Onion Hoedown from freezer and unwrap; place on ungreased baking sheet.** Heat in 400° oven until hot, about 45 minutes. If desired, serve with tomato sauce or beef gravy. (4 to 6 servings.)

*If using self-rising flour, omit salt. Pastry made with self-rising flour differs in taste and texture.

EASY POT-ROAST

Store no longer than 6 months. Makes enough for 6 to 8 servings.

3- pound beef chuck pot-roast (arm, blade, cross rib or boneless shoulder)*
2 teaspoons salt
¼ teaspoon pepper
2 medium onions, sliced
1 can (8 ounces) tomato sauce
1 tablespoon brown sugar
1 tablespoon horseradish
1 teaspoon prepared mustard

Place meat on 30×18-inch piece of heavy-duty aluminum foil. Season with salt and pepper; sprinkle onion on meat. Mix remaining ingredients; pour on meat. Fold foil over meat and seal securely. (To serve immediately, see below.) Label and freeze.

■ **4 hours 15 minutes before serving, remove Easy Pot-Roast from freezer and place wrapped meat in baking pan, 13×9×2 inches.** (If foil has torn during storage, overwrap with foil.) Cook in 350° oven until tender, about 4 hours. Place meat on warm platter; keep warm while making Gravy (below).

GRAVY

Spoon off fat from broth. Add enough water to broth to measure 2 cups; pour into pan. Shake ½ cup water and ¼ cup all-purpose flour in covered jar; stir slowly into broth. Heat, stirring constantly, until gravy boils. Boil and stir 1 minute. If desired, add few drops bottled brown bouquet sauce.

To Serve Immediately: Place wrapped meat in baking pan, 13×9×2 inches. Cook in 300° oven until tender, about 4 hours. Place meat on warm platter; keep warm while making Gravy (above).

*Rolled rump, bottom round or tip roast can be used in this recipe.

PEPPER STEAK

Store no longer than 4 months. Makes enough for 2 meals—4 or 5 servings each.

3 pounds beef round steak, 1 inch thick
½ cup soy sauce
1 cup water
¼ cup salad oil
¼ to ⅓ cup sugar
2 tablespoons cornstarch
½ teaspoon ginger
1 teaspoon garlic salt
2 medium onions, cut into ¼-inch slices

Trim fat carefully from meat; cut meat into strips, 2×1×¼ inch.* Place in baking dish, 11½×7½×1½ inches. Mix soy sauce and water; pour on meat. Refrigerate, turning meat occasionally, 2 hours. Remove meat from marinade; reserve marinade.

Heat oil in Dutch oven or large skillet. Cook meat in oil, turning frequently, until meat loses redness, about 15 minutes. Pour reserved marinade on meat. Mix sugar, cornstarch, ginger and garlic salt; stir into meat and marinade. Sprinkle onion on meat. Reduce heat; cover tightly and simmer 12 to 15 minutes. Divide meat and sauce between two 1-quart freezer containers. Cool quickly. Cover, label and freeze.

■ **30 minutes before serving, remove 1 container Pepper Steak from freezer. Have ready:** 2 medium green peppers, cut into strips (¾ inch wide); 2 medium tomatoes, peeled and cut into eighths; 3 to 4 cups hot cooked rice.

Dip container of meat and sauce into very hot water just to loosen. Place ½ cup water and frozen block in large skillet. Cover tightly; heat over medium-high heat, turning occasionally, until hot and bubbly, about 20 minutes. Stir in green pepper. Reduce heat; cover and simmer 5 minutes. Add tomato; cover and simmer 3 minutes. Serve on rice. (4 or 5 servings.)

*Meat is easier to cut when partially frozen.

HUNGARIAN GOULASH

Store no longer than 3 months. Makes enough for 6 to 8 servings.

- ¼ **cup shortening**
- 2 **pounds beef stew meat, cut into 1-inch cubes**
- 1 **cup sliced onion**
- ⅛ **teaspoon instant minced garlic**
- ¾ **cup catsup**
- 2 **tablespoons Worcestershire sauce**
- 1 **tablespoon brown sugar**
- 2 **teaspoons salt**
- 2 **teaspoons paprika**
- ½ **teaspoon dry mustard**
  Dash cayenne red pepper
- 1½ **cups water**

Melt shortening in large skillet. Cook and stir meat, onion and garlic in shortening until meat is brown and onion is tender. Drain off fat. Stir in remaining ingredients. Cover tightly; simmer 2 to 2½ hours. (To serve immediately, see below.) Pour into 1-quart freezer container. Cool quickly. Cover, label and freeze.

■ **45 minutes before serving, remove container Hungarian Goulash from freezer; dip container into very hot water just to loosen.** Place ½ cup water and frozen block in 3-quart saucepan. Cover tightly; heat over medium-low heat, turning occasionally, until hot and bubbly, about 30 minutes. While goulash heats, prepare hot cooked noodles for 6 to 8 servings. Serve goulash on noodles.

To Serve Immediately: Have ready: ¼ cup water; 2 tablespoons flour; hot cooked noodles for 6 to 8 servings.

Shake water and flour in tightly covered jar; stir slowly into meat mixture. Heat, stirring constantly, until gravy boils. Boil and stir 1 minute. Serve on noodles.

SWISS STEAK

Store no longer than 4 months. Makes enough for 2 meals—4 servings each.

Meat
- 2 **pounds beef round steak (top round, bottom round or sirloin), ½ inch thick**
- ¼ **cup all-purpose flour**
- ½ **teaspoon salt**
- ¼ **teaspoon pepper**
- 2 **tablespoons shortening**

Tomato Sauce
- ½ **cup minced green pepper**
- 1¼ **cups minced onion**
- 1 **can (16 ounces) tomatoes**
- 1 **teaspoon salt**
- ¼ **teaspoon pepper**

Lightly score surface of meat; cut meat into 8 serving pieces. Mix flour, ½ teaspoon salt and ¼ teaspoon pepper. Sprinkle half the flour mixture on one side of meat; pound in. Turn meat and pound in remaining flour mixture.

Melt shortening in large skillet. Brown meat in shortening over medium heat about 15 minutes. Reduce heat; cover tightly and simmer 1 hour. Add small amount of water if necessary.

Mix Tomato Sauce ingredients; pour on meat. (To serve whole recipe immediately, see below.) Cover; simmer 15 minutes. Divide meat between 2 ungreased baking pans, 8×8×2 inches. Spoon half the sauce on meat in each pan. Cool quickly. Wrap, label and freeze.

■ **45 minutes before serving, remove 1 pan Swiss Steak from freezer and unwrap.** Cook uncovered in 400° oven until tender, 30 to 40 minutes. (4 servings.)

To Serve Immediately: Cover tightly; simmer until tender, about 30 minutes. (8 servings.)

Pictured at right, top and bottom: Swiss Steak and Hungarian Goulash

Braised Beef on Rice. We show it here accompanied by Tomato Marinade (page 128).

Dividing meat and vegetables before freezing

BRAISED BEEF CUBES

Store no longer than 3 months. Makes enough for 2 meals—4 or 5 servings each.

Meat and Vegetables
- **¼ cup butter or margarine**
- **5 medium onions, sliced**
- **1 pound fresh mushrooms, sliced**
- **3 pounds beef stew meat, cut into 1-inch cubes**

Seasonings
- **1 clove garlic, minced**
- **2 teaspoons salt**
- **¼ teaspoon onion salt**
- **¼ teaspoon marjoram leaves**
- **¼ teaspoon thyme leaves**
- **⅛ teaspoon pepper**

Sauce
- **1 cup beef broth***
- **1 tablespoon plus 1½ teaspoons flour**
- **1½ cups red Burgundy**
- **2 or 3 drops red food color, if desired**

Melt butter in Dutch oven or large saucepan. Cook and stir onion and mushrooms in butter until onion is tender. Remove vegetables from pan; drain. Brown meat with garlic in same pan. Sprinkle remaining Seasonings on meat. Mix beef broth and flour; pour on meat. Heat, stirring constantly, until sauce boils. Boil and stir 1 minute. Stir in Burgundy. Cover tightly; simmer 1½ to 2 hours, stirring in onion and mushrooms 5 minutes before beef mixture is done.

Divide only the meat and vegetables between two 2-quart freezer containers. To 1 container, add ½ cup of the sauce in the pan. Cool quickly. Cover, label "Braised Beef" and freeze.

To other container, add remaining sauce and the red food color. Cool quickly. Cover, label "Beef Bourguignon" and freeze.

*Beef broth can be made by dissolving 1 beef bouillon cube or 1 teaspoon instant beef bouillon in 1 cup boiling water, or use canned beef broth (bouillon).

A hearty main dish à *la française,* Beef Bourguignon is perfectly complemented by crusty French bread.

BRAISED BEEF ON RICE

Makes enough for 4 or 5 servings.

- **1 container Braised Beef (page 16)**
- **2 tablespoons cornstarch**
- **2 tablespoons soy sauce**
- **1 can (10½ ounces) condensed beef broth* (bouillon)**
- **3 cups hot cooked rice**

Forty-five minutes before serving, remove container labeled "Braised Beef" from freezer. Dip container into very hot water just to loosen. Mix cornstarch, soy sauce and beef broth in medium saucepan. Place frozen block in broth. Heat uncovered over medium heat until hot, about 30 minutes. Serve on rice.

*Beef broth can be made by dissolving 2 beef bouillon cubes or 2 teaspoons instant beef bouillon in 1¼ cups boiling water.

BEEF BOURGUIGNON

Makes enough for 4 or 5 servings.

About 50 minutes before serving, remove container labeled "Beef Bourguignon" from freezer (see Braised Beef Cubes recipe on page 16).

Dip container into very hot water just to loosen. Place ½ cup water and frozen block in large saucepan. Heat uncovered over medium heat, turning occasionally, until hot, about 45 minutes. Traditionally served with French bread.

To Serve Immediately: Prepare Braised Beef Cubes (page 16) except—freeze only 1 container (for Braised Beef). Add remaining sauce and the red food color to remaining half of the meat mixture; serve.

Divide the ribs into serving pieces by cutting between bones with a sharp knife.

As they bake, brush the ribs 2 or 3 times with part of the sauce.

Pour the remaining sauce over the ribs.

BARBECUED RIBS

Store no longer than 4 months. Makes enough for 5 or 6 servings.

4½ pounds pork ribs (spareribs, back ribs or country-style ribs), cut into pieces

Sauce
¼ cup soy sauce
1 tablespoon cornstarch
1 bottle (18 ounces) barbecue sauce

Arrange meat meaty side up in open shallow roasting pan. Do not add water. Do not cover. Bake in 325° oven 1¾ hours.

Mix Sauce ingredients. (To serve immediately, see below.) Using ¾ cup of the sauce, baste ribs 2 or 3 times; bake 45 minutes longer.

Crisscross 2 pieces of heavy-duty aluminum foil, 28 × 18 inches; carefully mold to inside of Dutch oven. Arrange ribs in foil-lined Dutch oven. Pour the remaining sauce on ribs. Cool quickly. Wrap ribs securely in the foil, remove from Dutch oven, label and freeze.

■ **35 minutes before serving, remove Barbecued Ribs from freezer and unwrap.** Place ½ cup water and frozen block in Dutch oven. Cover tightly; heat over medium-high heat until it boils. Reduce heat; simmer covered until hot, about ½ hour.

To Serve Immediately: Using all of the sauce, baste meat 2 or 3 times while baking 45 minutes longer.

SWEET AND SOUR PORK

Store no longer than 1 week. Makes enough for 2 meals—5 or 6 servings each.

Meat
- **3 pounds lean pork Boston shoulder, cut into 1½-inch cubes**
- **2 cups water**
- **3 eggs**
- **1½ cups all-purpose flour***
- **3¾ teaspoons salt**
- **Salad oil**

Sauce
- **2 cans (20 ounces each) pineapple chunks, drained (reserve syrup)**
- **¾ cup catsup**
- **¼ cup plus 2 tablespoons water**
- **3 tablespoons cornstarch**
- **¼ cup plus 2 tablespoons vinegar**
- **1 tablespoon sugar**
- **1 tablespoon Worcestershire sauce**

Heat meat and water in tightly covered Dutch oven until water boils. Reduce heat; simmer 15 minutes and drain. Cool quickly.

Beat eggs slightly in large bowl; add meat. Toss meat with egg until pieces are well coated. Mix flour and salt. Sprinkle flour mixture on meat; toss until well coated. Heat oil (½ inch) in large skillet or electric frypan over medium-high heat. Brown meat in oil, ⅓ at a time, about 5 minutes; drain. Do not overcook. (One meal can be served immediately. Reserve half of the meat; keep warm while making Sauce.) Cool quickly. Divide meat in half. Wrap, label and freeze.

Prepare Sauce. Add enough water to reserved pineapple syrup to measure 1½ cups. Mix pineapple syrup, catsup, water, cornstarch, vinegar, sugar and Worcestershire sauce in medium saucepan. Cook over medium-high heat, stirring constantly, until mixture thickens and boils. Remove from heat; stir in pineapple chunks. (To serve 1 meal immediately, reserve half of sauce in saucepan; see right.) Divide sauce between two 1-quart freezer containers. Cool quickly. Cover, label and freeze.

■ **20 minutes before serving, remove 1 package Sweet and Sour Pork cubes and 1 container Sweet and Sour Pork sauce from freezer. Have ready:** 2 medium green peppers, cut into 1-inch pieces; 1 medium onion, cut into 1-inch pieces; 4 cups hot cooked rice.

Dip container of sauce into very hot water just to loosen. Place ¼ cup water and frozen block in large saucepan. Cover tightly; heat over medium-high heat until thawed, about 15 minutes.

While the sauce is thawing, heat oven to 400°. Unwrap pork cubes; place frozen meat on ungreased baking sheet. Heat in oven until hot, 10 to 12 minutes.

Stir green pepper and onion into sauce (they will remain crisp). Reduce heat; cover tightly and simmer 5 minutes. Stir pork cubes into sauce just before serving. Serve on rice. (5 or 6 servings.)

To Serve Immediately: Have ready: 2 medium green peppers, cut into 1-inch pieces; 1 medium onion, cut into 1-inch pieces; 4 cups hot cooked rice.

Boil and stir sauce 1 minute. Reduce heat; stir in green pepper and onion. (They will remain crisp.) Cover tightly; simmer 5 minutes. Just before serving, stir in reserved pork cubes. Serve on rice. (5 to 6 servings.)

*If using self-rising flour, decrease salt to 2 teaspoons.

Storage Time for Pork at 0°	
Most cuts	4 to 5 months
Ground	2 months
Sausage	2 months
Cooked	2 months
Ham (unsliced)	2 months

Note: Ham slices, bacon and frankfurters lose quality when frozen.

PIZZA

Store no longer than 4 months. Makes 4 pizzas.

Sauce

¾ **cup chopped onion**
⅛ **teaspoon instant minced garlic**
2 **cans (8 ounces each) tomato sauce or**
   2 **cups spaghetti sauce**
½ **teaspoon salt**
¼ **teaspoon pepper**

Dough

2 **packages active dry yeast**
1⅓ **cups warm water (105 to 115°)**
5 **cups buttermilk baking mix**

Topping

2 **cups sliced pepperoni (about 8 ounces)**
2½ **cups shredded mozzarella cheese**
3 **to 4 teaspoons oregano**

Mix Sauce ingredients; set aside. To make Dough, dissolve yeast in warm water. Stir in baking mix; beat vigorously. Turn dough onto well-floured board. Knead until smooth, about 20 times. Allow dough to rest a few minutes. Divide dough into 4 parts; roll each part into 10-inch circle. Place on greased baking sheets.

Heat oven to 425°. Spread about ½ cup sauce on each circle. Arrange pepperoni on sauce; sprinkle cheese and oregano on top. (To serve immediately, see below.) Bake 10 minutes. Remove Pizzas from baking sheets; cool on wire racks. Place each Pizza on cardboard circle. Wrap, label and freeze.

■ **15 minutes before serving, heat oven to 425°.** Remove Pizzas from freezer; unwrap and remove from cardboard circles. Place Pizzas on oven rack. Bake until hot, about 10 minutes.

VARIATIONS

Omit pepperoni and substitute one of the following:

1 **pound bulk Italian sausage, crumbled and browned**
1 **pound ground beef, browned and seasoned with 1 teaspoon salt and sprinkled with ½ cup chopped green pepper or 2 cups sliced pimiento-stuffed olives**

To Serve Immediately: Bake in 425° oven until crust is brown and filling is hot and bubbly, 15 to 20 minutes.

LASAGNE

Store no longer than 3 weeks. Makes enough for 8 to 10 servings.

Meat Sauce

1 **pound bulk Italian sausage or ground beef**
¾ **cup chopped onion**
1 **clove garlic, minced**
1 **can (16 ounces) tomatoes**
1 **can (15 ounces) tomato sauce**
2 **tablespoons parsley flakes**
2 **tablespoons sugar**
1 **teaspoon salt**
1 **teaspoon basil leaves**

Cheese Filling

3 **cups (two 12-ounce cartons) ricotta or creamed cottage cheese**
½ **cup grated Parmesan cheese**
1 **tablespoon parsley flakes**
1½ **teaspoons salt**
1½ **teaspoons oregano leaves**

Base and Topping

1 **package (8 ounces) lasagne noodles, cooked and drained**
¾ **pound mozzarella cheese, shredded**
½ **cup grated Parmesan cheese**

Cook and stir meat, onion and garlic in large saucepan or Dutch oven until meat is brown and onion is tender. Spoon off fat.

Add tomatoes and break up with fork. Stir in remaining Meat Sauce ingredients. Heat, stirring occasionally, until mixture boils. Reduce heat; simmer uncovered until mixture is the consistency of spaghetti sauce, about 1 hour. Mix Cheese Filling ingredients.

Heat oven to 350°. Reserve ½ cup meat sauce for thin top layer. In ungreased baking pan, 13×9×2 inches, layer ¼ each of the noodles, remaining sauce, mozzarella cheese and ricotta cheese mixture. Repeat 3 times. Spread reserved meat sauce on top; sprinkle ½ cup Parmesan cheese on meat sauce. Bake uncovered 45 minutes. (Can be served immediately.) Cool quickly. Wrap, label and freeze.

■ **1 hour 10 minutes before serving, remove Lasagne from freezer and unwrap.** Bake uncovered in 375° oven until bubbly, about 1 hour.

EGG FOO YONG

Store no longer than 1 month. Makes enough for 4 or 5 servings.

2 tablespoons salad oil
3 eggs
1 cup bean sprouts, rinsed and drained
½ cup chopped cooked pork
2 tablespoons chopped onion
1 tablespoon soy sauce

Heat oil in large skillet. Beat eggs; stir in remaining ingredients.

Pour ¼ cup mixture at a time into oil. With a wide spatula, push cooked egg up over meat to form a patty. When patties are set, turn and brown other side. [Can be served immediately with Sauce (below).] Place in ungreased 13×9× 1½-inch foil pan. Cool quickly. Wrap, label and freeze.

■ **20 minutes before serving, heat oven to 375°. Have ready:** Sauce (below).

Remove Egg Foo Yong from freezer and unwrap. Heat uncovered until hot, about 15 minutes. Serve with Sauce.

Note: If you prefer, recipe can be doubled so that half can be served immediately and half can be frozen.

SAUCE

1 tablespoon cornstarch
1 teaspoon sugar
1 teaspoon vinegar
2½ tablespoons soy sauce
½ cup water

Mix all ingredients in small saucepan. Cook over medium heat, stirring constantly, until mixture thickens and boils. Boil and stir 1 minute.

VEAL WITH TOMATO SAUCE

Store no longer than 3 months. Makes enough for 6 servings.

Meat
6 boneless veal cutlets (about
    4 ounces each)
¼ cup salad oil
2 cloves garlic, crushed

Tomato Sauce
1 cup thinly sliced onion
1 jar (3 ounces) sliced mushrooms, drained
2 tablespoons flour
1 teaspoon salt
¼ teaspoon pepper
1 can (8 ounces) tomato sauce
⅔ cup water

Pound meat until ¼ inch thick. Heat oil and garlic in large skillet over medium-high heat. Brown meat quickly in oil, about 5 minutes. Remove meat from skillet; set aside. Reduce heat to medium. Cook and stir onion and mushroom in skillet until onion is tender. Stir in flour, salt and pepper; pour tomato sauce and water on onion mixture. Heat, stirring constantly, until mixture boils. Boil and stir 1 minute.

Return meat to skillet. Cover tightly; simmer until done, about 30 minutes. (Can be served immediately.) Arrange meat and sauce in ungreased baking dish, 11½×7½×1½ inches, or foil container. Cool quickly. Wrap, label and freeze.

■ **1 hour before serving, remove Veal with Tomato Sauce from freezer and unwrap.** Heat uncovered in 375° oven until hot and bubbly, 50 to 55 minutes. If desired, serve with hot cooked spaghetti.

VEAL PARMESAN

Store no longer than 3 months. Makes enough for 4 servings.

Meat

4 boneless veal cutlets (4 ounces each)
½ cup dry bread crumbs
¼ cup grated Parmesan cheese
½ teaspoon salt
⅛ teaspoon pepper
⅛ teaspoon paprika
1 egg
⅓ cup salad oil

Sauce and Topping

3 tablespoons water
1 can (8 ounces) tomato sauce
½ teaspoon oregano, if desired
3 slices mozzarella cheese

Pound meat until ¼ inch thick. Mix crumbs, Parmesan cheese, salt, pepper and paprika. Beat egg slightly. Dip meat in egg, then coat with crumb mixture.

Heat oil in large skillet. Brown meat quickly in oil, about 6 minutes. (To serve immediately, see below.) Remove meat to ungreased baking dish, 11½×7½×1½ inches. Heat water, tomato sauce and oregano in skillet, stirring constantly, until mixture boils. Pour sauce on meat; arrange mozzarella cheese on sauce. Cool quickly. Wrap, label and freeze.

■ **55 minutes before serving, remove Veal Parmesan from freezer and unwrap.** Bake uncovered in 375° oven until done, 45 to 50 minutes.

Note: A 1-pound veal round steak, ½ inch thick, can be substituted for the veal cutlets. Cut into 4 serving pieces.

To Serve Immediately: Reduce heat; add water. Cover tightly; simmer until done, about 30 minutes. (Add small amount of water if necessary.) Remove meat from skillet; keep warm. Pour tomato sauce into skillet; stir in oregano. Heat sauce until it boils; pour on meat and arrange mozzarella cheese on top.

VEAL BIRDS

Store no longer than 3 weeks. Makes enough for 2 meals—4 servings each.

Meat

8 boneless veal cutlets (4 ounces each)

Stuffing

2 cups packaged herb-seasoned stuffing
1 pound bulk pork sausage, browned and drained
½ cup finely chopped celery
⅓ cup shortening

Sauce

2 cans (10¾ ounces each) condensed cream of mushroom soup
¾ cup milk

Pound meat until ¼ inch thick. Prepare stuffing as directed on package except—stir in sausage and celery. Press about ½ cup stuffing on each cutlet to within ½ inch of edge. Roll up, beginning at narrow end; secure with wooden picks.

Melt shortening in large skillet. Brown meat rolls in shortening. Remove meat from skillet; set aside. Pour off fat. Heat soup and milk in skillet, stirring constantly, until sauce is hot. Return meat to skillet. Cover tightly; simmer until done, about 45 minutes. (To serve whole recipe immediately, see below.) Divide rolls and sauce between 2 ungreased baking dishes, 8×8×2 inches. Cool quickly. Wrap, label and freeze.

■ **65 minutes before serving, remove 1 container Veal Birds from freezer and unwrap.** Cover tightly; heat in 400° oven 40 minutes. Uncover; heat 20 minutes. Place Veal Birds on warm platter and remove picks. Stir gravy; spoon on Veal Birds. (4 servings.)

To Serve Immediately: Place Veal Birds on warm platter and remove picks. Spoon gravy on Veal Birds. (8 servings.)

LAMB CURRY

Store no longer than 4 months. Makes enough for 4 to 6 servings.

¼ **cup butter or margarine**
1 **medium onion, chopped (about ½ cup)**
¼ **cup chopped green pepper**
¼ **cup chopped celery**
1 **apple, pared and thinly sliced**
1 **to 2 teaspoons curry powder**
¼ **to ½ teaspoon salt**
¼ **cup all-purpose flour**
2 **cups chicken broth***
2 **cups cubed cooked lamb**

Melt butter in large saucepan. Cook and stir onion, green pepper, celery and apple in butter until onion is tender. Stir in curry powder, salt and flour. Cook over low heat, stirring constantly, until mixture is hot. Remove from heat; stir in broth. Heat, stirring constantly, until broth boils. Boil and stir 1 minute. Stir in meat. Cook, stirring occasionally, until hot, about 10 minutes. (To serve immediately, see below.) Pour into 1-quart freezer container. Cool quickly. Cover, label and freeze.

■ **35 minutes before serving, remove Lamb Curry from freezer. Have ready:** 3 cups hot cooked rice; chopped peanuts; hard-cooked eggs and chutney for accompaniments.

Dip container of curry into very hot water just to loosen. Place ½ cup water and frozen block in 3-quart saucepan. Cover tightly; heat over medium heat, turning occasionally, until hot and bubbly, about 30 minutes. Serve on rice. Pass peanuts, hard-cooked eggs and chutney.

To Serve Immediately: Serve on 3 cups hot cooked rice. Pass chopped peanuts, hard-cooked eggs and chutney.

*Chicken broth can be made by dissolving 2 chicken bouillon cubes or 2 teaspoons instant chicken bouillon in 2 cups boiling water, or use canned chicken broth.

SHEPHERDS' PIE

Store no longer than 2 months. Makes enough for 2 meals—4 servings each.

4 **cups cubed cooked lamb, beef or veal**
¼ **cup chopped onion**
3 **cups cooked mixed vegetables (e.g., peas, carrots and/or corn)**
2 **cups gravy***

Mix all ingredients. Divide between 2 ungreased 1-quart casseroles. (To serve immediately, see below.) Wrap, label and freeze.

■ **65 minutes before serving, heat oven to 425°. Have ready:** instant mashed potato puffs (enough for 4 servings); 2 tablespoons snipped parsley.

Remove 1 casserole Shepherds' Pie from freezer and unwrap. Bake uncovered until hot and bubbly, about 1 hour. After casserole has baked 55 minutes, prepare potato puffs as directed on package. Mound potato on meat mixture; sprinkle parsley on potato. (4 servings.)

To Serve One Immediately: Have ready: instant mashed potato puffs (enough for 4 servings); 2 tablespoons snipped parsley.

Heat oven to 350°. Prepare potato puffs as directed on package. Mound potato on meat mixture; sprinkle parsley on potato. Bake uncovered until hot and bubbly, about 30 minutes. (4 servings.)

*Two cans (10¾ ounces each) gravy can be used.

Storage Time for Lamb and Veal at 0°	
Most cuts	6 to 9 months
Ground	3 to 4 months
Cooked	2 months

COOKED CHICKEN

Store no longer than 6 months. Makes enough for 2 meals—6 servings each.

3- to 3½-pound broiler-fryer chicken, cut up
1 sprig parsley
1 celery stalk with leaves, cut up
2 teaspoons salt
½ teaspoon pepper

Place all ingredients (with giblets) in large kettle. Add enough water to cover. Heat until water boils. Reduce heat; cover tightly and simmer until done, about 45 minutes.

Cool quickly. Remove skin and meat from pieces. Cut meat into large pieces. Divide meat between two 1-quart freezer containers (1½ to 2 cups in each). Strain broth (2 to 3½ cups). Divide broth between containers. Cover, label and freeze.

Use for Chicken Rice Casserole (right) and Chicken Tetrazzini (page 25).

Storage Time for Poultry at 0°	
Chicken and Turkey	9 months
Ducks and Geese	6 months
Giblets	3 months
Cooked Poultry	1 month
in broth or gravy	6 months

Note: Do not freeze any stuffing.

To Thaw Frozen Poultry

In the Refrigerator: Leave in its wrapping. Allow about 2 hours per pound. Cook immediately.

At Room Temperature: Leave wrapped; put into brown paper bag on a tray. Allow about 1 hour per pound. Refrigerate or cook immediately.

Under Running Water: Leave wrapped. Allow about ½ hour per pound. Refrigerate or cook immediately.

CHICKEN RICE CASSEROLE

Makes enough for 6 servings.

Cooked Chicken (left)

Sauce
¼ cup butter or margarine
⅓ cup all-purpose flour
1½ teaspoons salt
⅛ teaspoon pepper
1½ cups milk

Base
1½ cups cooked white or wild rice
1 can (3 ounces) sliced mushrooms, drained
⅓ cup chopped green pepper
2 tablespoons chopped pimiento
¼ cup slivered almonds

One hour before serving, remove 1 container Cooked Chicken from freezer. Dip container into very hot water just to loosen. Place frozen block in large saucepan. Cover tightly; heat, stirring occasionally, until thawed. Remove from heat.

Heat oven to 350°. Melt butter in large saucepan; stir in flour, salt and pepper. Cook over low heat, stirring constantly, until smooth and bubbly. Remove from heat; stir in 1 cup broth and the milk. Heat, stirring constantly, until sauce boils. Boil and stir 1 minute. Stir in Base ingredients.

Pour into ungreased baking dish, 10×6×1½ inches, or 1½-quart casserole. Bake uncovered 40 to 45 minutes. Sprinkle snipped parsley on top for added color.

CHICKEN TETRAZZINI

Makes enough for 6 servings.

Cooked Chicken (page 24)

Sauce
¼ cup butter or margarine
¼ cup all-purpose flour
½ teaspoon salt
¼ teaspoon pepper
1 cup whipping cream
2 tablespoons sherry, if desired

Base
7 ounces hot cooked spaghetti
1 can (3 ounces) sliced mushrooms, drained
½ cup grated Parmesan cheese

One hour before serving, remove 1 container Cooked Chicken from freezer. Dip container into very hot water just to loosen. Place frozen block in large saucepan. Cover tightly; heat, stirring occasionally, until thawed. Remove from heat.

Heat oven to 350°. Melt butter in large saucepan; stir in flour, salt and pepper. Cook over low heat, stirring constantly, until smooth and bubbly. Remove from heat; stir in 1 cup broth and the cream. Heat, stirring constantly, until sauce boils. Boil and stir 1 minute. Stir in sherry, spaghetti, chicken and mushrooms.

Pour into ungreased 2-quart casserole. Sprinkle cheese on top. Bake uncovered until bubbly, about 30 minutes. To brown, place briefly under broiler.

Cooking Time

A dish that you cook to freeze and use at a later date should be a little under-cooked; otherwise it may overcook as it reheats. When you prepare a double batch—one to eat and one to freeze—set the freezer batch aside a few minutes before it is fully cooked.

CHICKEN À LA KING

Store no longer than 3 months. Makes enough for 3 meals—4 or 5 servings each.

2 cans (6 ounces each) sliced mushrooms, drained (reserve ½ cup liquid)
1 cup diced green pepper
1 cup butter or margarine
1 cup all-purpose flour
2 teaspoons salt
½ teaspoon pepper
2 cups light cream
2½ cups chicken broth*
4 cups cut-up cooked chicken
2 jars (4 ounces each) pimiento, drained and chopped

In Dutch oven, cook and stir mushrooms and green pepper in butter 5 minutes. Stir in flour, salt and pepper. Cook over low heat, stirring constantly, until bubbly. Remove from heat; stir in cream, broth and reserved mushroom liquid. Heat, stirring constantly, until sauce boils. Boil and stir 1 minute. Stir in chicken and pimiento; heat until hot. (Can be served immediately on toast, hot rice or in patty shells. 12 to 14 servings.) Divide between three 1-quart freezer containers. Cool quickly. Cover, label and freeze.

■ **45 minutes before serving, remove 1 container Chicken à la King from freezer. Have ready:** toast, hot rice or patty shells.

Dip container of chicken into very hot water just to loosen. Place ½ cup water and frozen block in medium saucepan. Cover tightly; heat over medium-low heat, turning occasionally, until hot and bubbly. Serve on toast, hot rice or in patty shells. (4 or 5 servings.)

*Chicken broth can be made by dissolving 2 chicken bouillon cubes or 2 teaspoons instant chicken bouillon in 2½ cups boiling water.

3-IN-1 FREEZER CHICKEN

Store no longer than 4 months. Makes enough for 3 meals—4 to 6 servings each.

3 broiler-fryer chickens (2½ to 3 pounds each), cut up
1 sprig parsley
1 celery stalk with leaves, cut up
1 carrot, sliced
1 small onion, sliced
1 tablespoon salt
½ teaspoon pepper

Place all ingredients (with giblets) in large kettle. Add enough water to cover (about 3 quarts). Heat until water boils. Reduce heat; cover tightly and simmer until done, about 45 minutes.

Remove meat from broth. Cool quickly. Place pieces of 1 chicken in 2-quart freezer container; refrigerate. Remove skin and meat from remaining chickens. Cut meat into pieces (about 6 cups); refrigerate. Strain broth. Prepare Chicken Gravy (below).

CHICKEN GRAVY

8 cups chicken broth (reserve remaining broth for Egg Drop Soup)
2 cups water
1½ cups all-purpose flour
2 tablespoons salt
1 teaspoon pepper
⅛ teaspoon yellow food color

Spoon off fat from broth. Pour broth into 3-quart saucepan. Shake water and flour in covered jar; stir slowly into broth. Heat, stirring constantly, until gravy boils. Boil and stir 1 minute. Season with salt and pepper. Stir in food color. Cool quickly.

Prepare Chicken Almond Casserole (right), Chicken Pie and Chicken and Dumplings (page 28) as directed and freeze. Prepare Egg Drop Soup to serve today.

For Egg Drop Soup, have ready: remaining chicken broth (4 to 6 cups); ⅛ teaspoon salt; 1 egg, well beaten.

Heat chicken broth and salt until it boils; remove from heat. Stirring constantly, slowly pour egg in a thin stream into broth. If desired, sprinkle sliced green onion on soup. (4 to 6 servings.)

CHICKEN ALMOND CASSEROLE

Store no longer than 4 months. Makes enough for 6 to 8 servings.

4 cups cut-up cooked chicken (see 3-in-1 Freezer Chicken—left)
1 can (4 ounces) mushroom stems and pieces, drained
1 can (5 ounces) water chestnuts, drained and sliced
⅔ cup sliced almonds
1 tablespoon dried sweet bell peppers
2 teaspoons parsley flakes
½ teaspoon salt
2 cups Chicken Gravy (left)

Stir all ingredients into Chicken Gravy. Pour into 2-quart freezer container. Continue to cool quickly if necessary. Cover, label and freeze.

■ **24 hours before serving, remove Chicken Almond Casserole from freezer and place in refrigerator. About 20 minutes before serving, have ready:** ⅓ cup milk; 2 tablespoons sherry; Buttered Bread Crumbs (below).

Heat milk and chicken mixture in 2-quart saucepan over medium heat, stirring occasionally, until hot and bubbly, 10 to 12 minutes. Stir in sherry; heat slightly. Turn into serving dish; sprinkle Buttered Bread Crumbs on top. (Or, can be served on hot cooked rice.)

BUTTERED BREAD CRUMBS

Cook and stir 1 tablespoon butter or margarine and ¼ cup dry bread crumbs over medium heat until crumbs are golden brown, about 5 minutes.

Pictured at right, top to bottom: Chicken and Dumplings (page 28), Chicken Pie (page 28) and Chicken Almond Casserole

CHICKEN PIE

Store no longer than 4 months. Makes enough for 4 or 5 servings.

1 package (10 ounces) frozen
  peas and carrots
1 can (8 ounces) small whole onions,
  drained
1 can (4 ounces) mushroom stems and pieces
2 cups cut-up cooked chicken (see 3-in-1
  Freezer Chicken—page 26)
2 cups Chicken Gravy (page 26)
  Pastry for 9-inch One-crust Pie (page 77)

Rinse frozen peas and carrots with running cold water to remove ice crystals. Stir peas and carrots, onions, mushrooms (with liquid) and chicken into Chicken Gravy. Pour into ungreased 9-inch square foil pan.

Prepare Pastry; roll into 9-inch square. Fold in half; cut slits. Carefully place pastry on mixture; press edges of pastry onto rim of foil pan with fork. Freeze uncovered just until crust is firm, about 1 hour. Remove from freezer. Wrap, label and return to freezer.

■ **1 hour 30 minutes before serving, remove Chicken Pie from freezer and unwrap.** Loosely cover edges with 2- to 3-inch strip of aluminum foil to prevent excessive browning during baking. Bake in 450° oven until crust is brown and mixture is bubbly, about 1 hour 15 minutes. Let set 10 minutes before serving.

Storage Time for Cooked Dishes at 0°

Precooked foods	6 months
with sauce or gravy	3 months

If you want to use a special casserole, but not tie it up in the freezer, do this. Line the casserole with heavy foil and cook the food in it. Cool quickly; freeze till set. Remove dish in foil from casserole and wrap. To heat, unwrap and place in casserole.

CHICKEN AND DUMPLINGS

Store no longer than 4 months. Makes enough for 4 servings.

4 cups Chicken Gravy (page 26)
  Cooked pieces of 1 chicken (see 3-in-1
  Freezer Chicken—page 26)

Pour Chicken Gravy on chicken pieces in freezer container. Continue to cool quickly. Cover, label and freeze.

■ **24 hours before serving, remove chicken and gravy from freezer and place in refrigerator. Forty-five minutes before serving, have ready:** ½ cup milk and ingredients for Dumplings (below).

Heat chicken and gravy, milk and ½ cup water in large skillet over medium heat, stirring occasionally, until hot and bubbly, about 15 minutes.

Prepare dough for Dumplings; drop by tablespoonfuls onto chicken. Cook uncovered 10 minutes. Cover tightly; cook 20 minutes.

DUMPLINGS

1½ cups all-purpose flour*
 2 teaspoons baking powder
 ¾ teaspoon salt
 3 tablespoons shortening
 ¾ cup milk

Measure flour, baking powder and salt into bowl. Cut in shortening until mixture looks like meal. Stir in milk.

*If using self-rising flour, omit baking powder and salt.

CHICKEN-RICE ORANGE

Store no longer than 3 months. Makes enough for 2 meals—4 servings each.

Meat
¼ **cup shortening**
¼ **cup butter or margarine**
½ **cup all-purpose flour**
1 **teaspoon salt**
1 **teaspoon paprika**
¼ **teaspoon pepper**
2 **broiler-fryer chickens (2½ to 3 pounds each), cut up**

Sauce
2 **cups orange juice**
¼ **cup dry sherry or apple juice**
1 **tablespoon brown sugar**
2 **teaspoons salt**

Topping
1 **large onion, thinly sliced**
½ **cup chopped green pepper**
1 **can (6 ounces) sliced mushrooms, drained**

Heat oven to 425°. In oven, melt shortening and butter in 2 standard or foil baking pans, 13×9×2 inches. Mix flour, 1 teaspoon salt, the paprika and pepper. Coat chicken with flour mixture. Place 1 chicken in each baking pan; turn to coat with shortening. Turn skin side up. Bake uncovered 30 minutes. Mix Sauce ingredients in saucepan. Heat until mixture boils; remove from heat and set aside.

For Topping, sprinkle half the onion, the green pepper and mushrooms on each chicken. Pour half the orange sauce on each chicken. Bake uncovered until done, about 30 minutes. Cool quickly. Wrap, label and freeze.

■ **45 minutes before serving, remove 1 pan Chicken-Rice Orange from freezer and unwrap. Have ready:** ingredients for Orange Rice (right).
Heat chicken uncovered in 375° oven until hot, about 40 minutes. Prepare Orange Rice (right). Place rice and chicken on warm platter. Pour orange sauce into a small pitcher and spoon off fat; serve with chicken and rice. If desired, garnish with orange slices. (4 servings.)

ORANGE RICE

1½ **cups boiling water**
1 **cup uncooked regular rice**
⅔ **cup orange juice**
¼ **teaspoon allspice**
1 **teaspoon salt**

Heat oven to 375°. Mix all ingredients thoroughly in ungreased 1- or 1½-quart casserole or in baking dish, 10×6×1½ or 11½×7½×1½ inches. Cover tightly; bake until liquid is absorbed and rice is tender, 25 to 30 minutes.

FRIED CHICKEN

Store no longer than 4 weeks. Makes enough for 2 meals—4 servings each.

 Salad oil
2 **cups all-purpose flour**
2 **tablespoons salt**
2 **broiler-fryer chickens (2½ to 3 pounds each), cut up**
4 **eggs, slightly beaten**

Heat oil (¼ inch) in large skillet or electric frypan over medium-high heat. Mix flour and salt. Dip chicken in egg, then coat with flour mixture. Brown chicken, a few pieces at a time, in oil. Reduce heat. Layer chicken skin side down in skillet in the following order: breasts, thighs, drumsticks, backs and wings. Cover tightly; simmer, turning once or twice, until done, 30 to 40 minutes. (If skillet cannot be tightly covered, add 1 to 2 tablespoons water.) After chicken has simmered 25 minutes, uncover to crisp.

Remove chicken from skillet. (Can be served immediately. 8 servings.) Divide in half. Wrap in heavy-duty aluminum foil. Cool quickly. Label and freeze.

■ **50 minutes before serving, remove 1 package Fried Chicken from freezer and open foil wrap.** Place on oven rack. Heat in 375° oven until hot, 45 minutes. (4 servings.)

Note: Chicken normally can be stored for a longer period of time. Fried chicken is best, however, if used within 4 weeks of initial freezing.

BATTER-FRIED FISH

Store no longer than 2 weeks. Makes enough for 6 servings.

1 cup all-purpose flour*
1 teaspoon baking powder
½ teaspoon salt
1 egg
1 cup milk
¼ cup salad oil
2 pounds fish fillets, steaks or pan-dressed fish
   Flour

Prepare batter. Measure 1 cup flour, the baking powder, salt, egg, milk and salad oil into a bowl; beat with rotary beater until smooth. If fillets are large, cut into serving pieces. Coat fish with flour, then dip in batter to coat completely.

Heat oil (½ to 1 inch) in large pan or deep skillet. Cook fish in oil until golden brown, about 4 minutes on each side. Cool quickly. Wrap, label and freeze.

■ **About 25 minutes before serving, heat oven to 400°.** Heat Batter-fried Fish on ungreased baking sheet until hot, about 15 minutes.

*If using self-rising flour, omit baking powder and salt.

Storage Time for Fish at 0°

Cod, Yellow Perch, Bluefish, Haddock	9 months
Lake Bass, Flounder, Bluegill, Sunfish	7 to 8 months
Whitefish, Lake Trout, Catfish, Northern Pike, Shrimp	4 to 5 months

Note: Fish frozen in ice, glazed or kept in a freezer at −10° can be stored an additional 1 or 2 months.

SEAFOOD SALAD IN A PUFF BOWL

Store no longer than 3 months. Makes enough for 6 servings.

½ cup water
¼ cup butter or margarine
½ cup all-purpose flour*
⅛ teaspoon salt
2 eggs

Heat oven to 400°. Grease 9-inch glass pie pan. Heat water and butter until mixture boils vigorously. Stir in flour and salt. Beat over low heat until mixture leaves side of pan and forms a ball, about 1 minute. Remove from heat; cool slightly, about 10 minutes. Beat in eggs; beat until smooth and glossy. Spread batter evenly *just* to side of pan. Bake 45 to 55 minutes. Cool at room temperature. (To serve immediately, see below.) Remove from pan. Wrap, label and freeze.

■ **15 minutes before serving, heat oven to 400°. Have ready:** Seafood Salad (below); 2 hard-cooked eggs, sliced; watercress.

Remove puff bowl from freezer and unwrap; place on ungreased baking sheet. Heat in oven about 10 minutes. Cool. Fill with Seafood Salad. Garnish with egg slices and watercress.

*Self-rising flour can be used in this recipe.

SEAFOOD SALAD
2 to 2½ cups cooked shrimp, crabmeat or lobster
2 cups thinly sliced celery
½ to ⅔ cup mayonnaise or salad dressing
1 tablespoon minced green onion
½ teaspoon salt
   Dash pepper

Mix seafood and celery. Mix mayonnaise, onion, salt and pepper. Pour on seafood and celery; toss. Cover tightly; chill at least 2 hours.

To Serve Immediately: Have ready: Seafood Salad; 2 hard-cooked eggs, sliced; watercress.

Fill bowl with Seafood Salad. Garnish with egg slices and watercress.

CHEESE SOUFFLÉ

Store no longer than 2 months. Makes enough for 4 servings.

¼ **cup butter or margarine**
¼ **cup all-purpose flour**
½ **teaspoon salt**
¼ **teaspoon dry mustard**
   Dash cayenne red pepper
1 **cup milk**
1 **cup shredded process American cheese**
   (about 4 ounces)
3 **eggs, separated**
¼ **teaspoon cream of tartar**

Butter 4-cup soufflé dish. Melt butter in saucepan over low heat. Stir in flour and seasonings. Cook over low heat, stirring constantly, until mixture is smooth and bubbly. Remove from heat; stir in milk. Heat, stirring constantly, until sauce boils. Boil and stir 1 minute. Stir in cheese; heat until cheese is melted and sauce is smooth. Remove from heat.

Beat egg whites and cream of tartar until stiff but not dry; set aside. Beat egg yolks until very thick and lemon colored; stir into cheese mixture. Stir about ¼ of the egg whites into cheese mixture. Gently fold mixture into remaining egg whites.

Carefully pour into soufflé dish. Wrap, label and freeze.

■ **2 hours before serving, heat oven to 325°. Remove Cheese Soufflé from freezer and unwrap.** Make a 4-inch band of triple thickness aluminum foil 2 inches longer than the circumference of soufflé dish; butter one side. Extend depth of dish by securing foil band, buttered side in, around outside top of dish. Bake until knife inserted halfway between edge and center comes out clean, 1½ to 1¾ hours. Serve immediately. Carefully remove foil band and spoon soufflé onto serving plate.

Note: Recipe can be doubled. Pour soufflé into 2 buttered 4-cup soufflé dishes.

MACARONI AND CHEESE

Store no longer than 3 months. Makes enough for 6 to 8 servings.

6 **to 7 ounces elbow macaroni**
   (about 2 cups)
2 **tablespoons butter or margarine**
2 **tablespoons flour**
1¼ **teaspoons salt**
¼ **teaspoon pepper**
2 **cups milk**
2 **tablespoons grated onion**
3 **cups shredded process sharp American cheese (about 12 ounces)**
1 **tablespoon butter or margarine**

Cook macaroni as directed on package; place in ungreased 2-quart casserole. Melt 2 tablespoons butter in saucepan over low heat. Stir in flour, salt and pepper. Cook over low heat, stirring constantly, until mixture is smooth and bubbly. Remove from heat; stir in milk. Heat, stirring constantly, until sauce boils. Boil and stir 1 minute. Stir in onion and cheese; heat until cheese is melted and sauce is smooth. Pour sauce on macaroni; dot with 1 tablespoon butter. (To serve immediately, see below.) Cool quickly. Wrap, label and freeze.

■ **65 minutes before serving, remove Macaroni and Cheese from freezer and unwrap.** Bake uncovered in 425° oven until hot and bubbly throughout, about 1 hour.

To Serve Immediately: Heat oven to 375° Cover; bake 30 minutes. Uncover; bake 15 minutes.

Note: The Macaroni and Cheese can be divided between 2 ungreased 1-quart casseroles or foil pans, 8×8×2 inches. Cool quickly. Wrap, label and freeze. One hour before serving, heat oven to 425°. Remove 1 casserole Macaroni and Cheese from freezer and unwrap. Bake uncovered until hot and bubbly, about 45 minutes. (3 servings.)

Freezer Dinners

Cook's Night Out? Serve a piping hot dinner from freezer to oven to table in 25 to 35 minutes. We have designed our freezer dinners using leftover roasted meats and gravy; frozen, canned or leftover vegetables and a few special surprises that are sure to make your freezer dinners extra special!

Points to remember in preparing freezer dinners:

1. For ease and quick assembly, we recommend that you save the foil trays from commercially frozen dinners. If you don't have any, use foil broiler pans, cake or pie pans; shape divider compartments of foil to place in these pans. Fill the trays with the desired food, cover tightly with foil, label and freeze.

2. About 35 minutes before serving, heat oven to 450°. Heat frozen dinners in foil-covered commercial foil pans 25 minutes, in foil-covered homemade foil pans 35 minutes. (When heating 2 or more dinners in the same oven, allow 5 minutes longer.) When your dinner includes French fries or potato puffs, fold back foil to expose potatoes. Just before serving, stir gravy; spoon gravy on meat and season with salt.

3. Store no longer than 3 weeks.

4. Recommended portions for freezer dinners:

MEAT
3 ounces roast meats with ⅓ to ½ cup Gravy (page 33), or ½ cup sauce (page 33). (The meat without a gravy or sauce is dry and has a "reheated" taste.)

POTATOES OR RICE
½ cup Mashed Potatoes (below) with 1 teaspoon butter
½ cup frozen French fried potatoes or potato puffs
Instant Rice (below)

Mashed Potatoes
Prepare instant mashed potato puffs as directed on package for desired number of servings except—add 1 tablespoon additional milk for each serving. Cool.

Instant Rice
3 tablespoons uncooked instant rice
¼ cup water
⅛ teaspoon salt
½ teaspoon butter or margarine
Pinch of curry powder, if desired

Place all ingredients in foil pan. Freeze. When heating the frozen dinner, cook rice covered with foil.

VEGETABLES
½ cup frozen vegetables (mixed vegetables, corn, peas or green beans) with ½ teaspoon butter or margarine. Frozen carrots can also be used, if you add 2 tablespoons water.
⅓ to ½ cup canned or leftover vegetables with 2 tablespoons liquid and ½ teaspoon butter or margarine

ACCOMPANIMENTS
2 to 3 tablespoons cranberry sauce, Mustard Sauce (page 33), mint jelly, chutney, fruit pie filling with a pinch of cinnamon. (Place in separate compartment.)

Shape divider compartments of foil.

Arrange foods in compartments.

Mustard Sauce

1 tablespoon butter or margarine
1 tablespoon flour
½ teaspoon salt
¼ teaspoon pepper
1 cup milk
3 tablespoons prepared mustard
1 tablespoon horseradish

Melt butter in small saucepan over low heat. Stir in flour, salt and pepper. Cook over low heat, stirring constantly, until smooth and bubbly. Remove from heat; stir in milk. Heat, stirring constantly, until sauce boils. Boil and stir 1 minute. Stir in mustard and horseradish. Heat until hot. Cool.

About 1 cup.

GRAVY AND SAUCE FOR FROZEN DINNERS

To 1 packet (1¼ ounces) gravy mix, add 1½ cups water
To 1 can (10¾ ounces) gravy, add ¾ cup water
To 1 cup kettle or pan gravy, add ½ cup water
Cherry Sauce (below)

Cherry Sauce

½ cup cherry pie filling
¼ cup water
1 teaspoon lemon juice

Mix all ingredients. Pour on ham. Enough sauce for 2 frozen dinners.

Variations or Substitutions

If you are using large trays, you may have space to try some special treats or you may substitute them for potatoes or meat accompaniments. For a change of pace, try baked muffins, 2 teaspoons Double Chocolate Drops Dough (page 67) or ⅓ to ½ cup canned chocolate or vanilla pudding.

FREEZER DINNERS THAT WE RECOMMEND

Roast Turkey with Gravy
Cranberry Sauce
Buttered Sweet Potatoes
Buttered Green Beans
Blueberry Muffins
Vanilla Pudding

Roast Lamb with Gravy
Chutney or Mint Jelly
Instant Curried Rice
Buttered Mixed Vegetables

Roast Beef with Gravy
Sliced Peaches or Peach Pie Filling with Cinnamon
Twice Baked Potatoes
Buttered Peas

Baked Ham with Cherry Sauce (left)
Shredded Potato Patty
Asparagus
Carrots
Blueberry Muffins or Double Chocolate Drops Dough (page 67)

Roast Veal with Gravy
Buttered Green Beans
Mustard Sauce (left)
French Fried Potatoes

Roast Pork with Gravy
Spiced Crab Apple
Mexicali Corn
Broccoli Spears
Chocolate Pudding

Meat Loaf Slices with Gravy
Buttered Mashed Potatoes
Buttered Carrots
Orange Muffins

Roast Turkey freezer dinner

Roast Beef freezer dinner

Roast Pork freezer dinner

Appetizers and Snacks

INDIVIDUAL HOT SUB SANDWICHES

Store no longer than 1 month. Makes 8 sandwiches.

8 individual French rolls (about
   6 × 2½ inches each)
   Soft butter or margarine
8 slices salami or boiled ham
8 slices mozzarella cheese
8 slices cooked turkey or chicken
½ package (4-ounce size) blue cheese,
   crumbled

Cut rolls horizontally into 3 parts. Spread butter on all cut surfaces. Layer salami slice and cheese slice on bottom part of each roll. Place second part of roll on cheese; top with turkey slice and sprinkle blue cheese on turkey. Cover sandwich with third part of roll. Wrap each sandwich individually in heavy-duty aluminum foil. (To serve immediately, see below.) Label and freeze.

■ **35 minutes before serving, heat oven to 450°.** Remove Individual Hot Sub Sandwiches from freezer; heat wrapped sandwiches on oven rack 30 minutes.

To Serve Immediately: Heat oven to 425°. Heat wrapped sandwiches on oven rack 15 to 20 minutes.

TUNA SALAD SANDWICHES

Store no longer than 2 weeks. Makes 4 sandwiches.

1 can (6½ ounces) tuna, drained
¼ cup finely chopped sweet pickle
⅓ cup salad dressing* or dairy sour cream
¼ teaspoon salt
   Soft butter or margarine
8 slices bread

Mix all ingredients except butter and bread. Spread butter on bread, covering to edges. Spread filling on 4 slices; top each with a second slice. (Can be served immediately.) Place in sandwich bags; wrap each sandwich in heavy-duty aluminum foil, label and freeze.

■ **4 hours before serving, remove Tuna Salad Sandwich(es) from freezer and remove only foil wrap.** Thaw in sandwich bag(s) at room temperature.

*Do not use mayonnaise in this recipe.

VARIATIONS

Shrimp Salad Sandwiches: Substitute 1 can (4½ ounces) shrimp for tuna and use only 6 slices bread. Rinse shrimp; let stand in ice and water 20 minutes before mixing with other ingredients. (3 sandwiches.)

Crab Salad Sandwiches: Substitute 1 can (7½ ounces) crabmeat, drained and cartilage removed, for tuna.

Salmon Salad Sandwiches: Substitute 1 can (7¾ ounces) salmon, drained, for tuna.

For Pepped-up Sandwiches

Freezer-stored herbs or chopped onion add zip to sandwiches. To preserve herbs, wash and drain; wrap in foil or plastic bag. Put into carton or glass jar and store in freezer. Peel, wash and quarter onions; chop, then scald for 1½ minutes. Chill in iced water. Drain, package and freeze immediately.

SPICY RYE ROLLS

Store no longer than 2 weeks. Makes 6 sandwiches.

Butter Mixture
⅓ **cup soft butter**
 2 **tablespoons minced onion**
 2 **tablespoons prepared mustard**
 2 **teaspoons poppy seed**
 2 **teaspoons lemon juice**
   Dash cayenne red pepper

Rolls and Filling
 6 **rye rolls, split into halves**
 6 **slices Swiss cheese (about 6 ounces),**
   cut into halves
 6 **slices salami (about 4 ounces)**

Mix Butter Mixture ingredients. Spread Butter Mixture on cut surfaces of rolls. Layer cheese slice, salami slice and cheese slice on each bottom half. Place top half on cheese. Wrap each sandwich in heavy-duty aluminum foil. (To serve immediately, see below.) Label and freeze.

■ **40 minutes before serving, heat oven to 375°.** Remove Spicy Rye Rolls from freezer; heat wrapped rolls on oven rack 35 minutes.

To Serve Immediately: Heat oven to 350° before assembling rolls. Heat wrapped rolls on oven rack 25 minutes.

UNUSUAL SANDWICHES FOR THE FREEZER

Spread butter or margarine on bread slices. Spread one of the Fillings (below) on half of the slices; top with second slice. Cut sandwiches in half. Place in sandwich bags; wrap each in heavy-duty aluminum foil, label and freeze.

■ **4 hours before serving, remove sandwich(es) from freezer and remove only foil wrap.** Thaw in sandwich bag(s) at room temperature.

FILLINGS

CHIPPED BEEF-CREAM CHEESE
1 **package (3 ounces) cream cheese, softened**
1 **package (3 ounces) dried beef**

Spread cream cheese on buttered bread slice; top with dried beef. Store no longer than 3 weeks. Enough for 3 sandwiches.

DEVILED HAM-CHILI SAUCE
1 **can (2¼ ounces) deviled ham**
1 **tablespoon plus 1 teaspoon chili sauce**

Mix ingredients. Store no longer than 3 weeks. Enough for 2 sandwiches.

SARDINES, CAPERS AND CHILI SAUCE
1 **can (3¾ ounces) sardines, drained**
2 **tablespoons chili sauce**
2 **teaspoons capers, chopped**

Mix ingredients. Store no longer than 2 weeks. Enough for 2 sandwiches.

FRANKFURTER-APPLE BUTTER
1 **to 2 tablespoons apple butter**
1 **frankfurter, cut lengthwise into thirds**

Spread apple butter on buttered bread slice; top with frankfurter slices. Store no longer than 3 weeks. Enough for 1 sandwich.

SHRIMP-GREEN OLIVE-CREAM CHEESE
1 **can (4½ ounces) shrimp, rinsed,**
  drained and chopped
1 **package (3 ounces) cream cheese, softened**
2 **or 3 green olives, chopped**
  (2 tablespoons)

Mix ingredients. Store no longer than 2 weeks. Enough for 3 sandwiches.

PEANUT BUTTER-HONEY-DATE
2 **tablespoons peanut butter**
1 **teaspoon honey**
2 **or 3 dates, chopped (1 tablespoon)**

Mix ingredients. Store no longer than 2 weeks. Enough for 1 sandwich.

RIBBON CANAPÉS

Store no longer than 2 months. Makes 1 ribbon loaf (about 5½ dozen 4×1-inch canapés).

Trim crust from 1 unsliced loaf white and 1 unsliced loaf whole wheat sandwich bread. Cut each loaf horizontally into 1-inch slices.

For each ribbon loaf, spread softened butter or margarine on each of 2 slices white and 1 slice whole wheat bread. Prepare 3 Canapé Spreads (pages 36 to 39). Spread ¼ cup of one of the Canapé Spreads on each slice. Assemble loaf, alternating white and whole wheat slices; top with unspread whole wheat slice.

Place on baking sheet and freeze 1 hour. Cut loaf into ½-inch slices; cut each slice into 3 canapés.

VARIATION

Checkerboard Canapés: Cut 4-layer ribbon loaf (above) into ½-inch slices. Spread softened butter or margarine on 1 slice; top with a second slice with the dark strip on top of the light. Press together gently but firmly. Spread softened butter or margarine on second slice; top with a third slice with the light strip on top of the dark. Press together gently but firmly. Cut into 4 slices; cut each slice into 2 canapés.

About 5½ dozen 2×1½-inch canapés.

Do-Ahead Sandwiches

Freeze 1 to 3 weeks' supply of sandwiches. Spread bread slices to the edges with butter or margarine.

Sliced meat, poultry, cheese, cheese spread, peanut butter, salmon and tuna freeze well. Moisten with applesauce, fruit juice or dairy sour cream, not mayonnaise, salad dressing or jelly. Don't use fresh vegetables or boiled egg whites.

Freezer-wrap sandwiches individually. Place sandwich in lunchbox unthawed —it will defrost in 3 to 3½ hours.

FROZEN CANAPÉ TRAY

Store no longer than 2 months. Makes about 8 dozen 1-inch canapés per sandwich loaf.

Trim crust from day-old unsliced loaf white, whole wheat or rye sandwich bread. Cut loaf horizontally into ½-inch slices. Spread softened butter or margarine lightly on each slice; cut into desired shapes. Spread 1 level measuring teaspoonful of one of the canapé spreads (pages 36 to 39) to the edge of each canapé. Use two or more of the following canapé spreads for a tasty and attractive tray. (Can be served immediately.)

Place desired number of canapés on cardboard tray; cover with plastic wrap. Wrap with aluminum foil, label and freeze.

■ **45 minutes before serving, remove Frozen Canapé Tray from freezer and remove aluminum foil.** Let stand at room temperature covered with the plastic wrap.

CREAMY DEVILED HAM

1 can (4½ ounces) deviled ham
1 package (3 ounces) cream cheese, softened
1 tablespoon salad dressing*
1 teaspoon snipped chives
   Stuffed green olive slices

Mix deviled ham, cheese and salad dressing. Stir in chives. Garnish canapés with olive slices.

About 1 cup (enough for 4 dozen 1-inch canapés).

*Do not use mayonnaise in this recipe.

DEVILED HAM AND OLIVE SPREAD

1 can (4½ ounces) deviled ham
2 tablespoons chopped stuffed green olives
1 tablespoon chopped pickled onion
1 teaspoon snipped parsley

Mix all ingredients.

About ½ cup (enough for 2 dozen 1-inch canapés).

CHICKEN-HAM-CHEESE SPREAD

**1 can (5 ounces) boned chicken,
  rinsed and finely chopped
½ cup finely chopped ham
½ cup grated sharp Cheddar cheese
1 teaspoon salt
  Dash pepper
  Parsley leaves**

Mix all ingredients except parsley leaves. Garnish canapés with parsley leaves.

About 1¼ cups (enough for 5 dozen 1-inch canapés).

CHILI HAM SPREAD

**1 can (4½ ounces) deviled ham
1 tablespoon salad dressing*
¼ teaspoon onion juice
1 teaspoon minced chili peppers
  Green olive slices**

Mix all ingredients except olive slices. Garnish canapés with green olive slices.

About ½ cup (enough for 2 dozen 1-inch canapés).

*Do not use mayonnaise in this recipe.

CREAM CHEESE AND HORSERADISH SPREAD

**1 package (8 ounces) cream cheese,
  softened
2 tablespoons salad dressing*
1 teaspoon horseradish**

Mix cream cheese and salad dressing. Stir in horseradish.

About 1 cup (enough for 4 dozen 1-inch canapés).

*Do not use mayonnaise in this recipe.

CRABMEAT SPREAD

**1 can (7½ ounces) crabmeat, drained and
  cartilage removed
⅓ cup salad dressing*
1 tablespoon capers**

Mix all ingredients. Garnish canapés with additional capers.

About 1 cup (enough for 4 dozen 1-inch canapés).

*Do not use mayonnaise in this recipe.

To make Checkerboard Canapés (page 36), assemble a ribbon loaf from white and whole wheat breads and 3 Canapé Spreads, then slice it ½ inch thick.

Stack 3 ribbon slices, alternating light strips of bread over dark ones to make a checkerboard pattern. Slice again and cut slices in half.

Frozen Canapé Tray (page 36). Assorted canapés are featured here.

SHRIMP-DILL SPREAD

1 can (6¾ ounces) medium shrimp, rinsed,
   drained and finely chopped
⅓ cup salad dressing*
2 teaspoons lemon juice
½ teaspoon dill weed
¼ teaspoon salt
   Parsley leaves

Mix all ingredients except parsley leaves. Garnish canapés with parsley leaves.

About ¾ cup (enough for 3 dozen 1-inch canapés).

*Do not use mayonnaise in this recipe.

CLAM AND CREAM CHEESE SPREAD

1 package (8 ounces) cream cheese,
   softened
1 can (8 ounces) minced clams, rinsed and
   drained
½ teaspoon seasoned salt
¼ teaspoon Worcestershire sauce
¼ teaspoon onion juice
   Ripe olive slices

Mix cream cheese and clams. Stir in remaining ingredients except olive slices. Garnish canapés with ripe olive slices.

About 1¼ cups (enough for 5 dozen 1-inch canapés).

CRABMEAT AND MUSHROOM SPREAD

1 can (7½ ounces) crabmeat, drained
   and cartilage removed
1 can (4 ounces) mushroom stems and
   pieces, drained and finely chopped
3 tablespoons dairy sour cream
¼ teaspoon red pepper sauce
¼ teaspoon horseradish
½ teaspoon salt
   Parsley leaves
   Pimiento slices

Finely chop crabmeat. Mix all ingredients except parsley leaves and pimiento slices. Garnish canapés with parsley leaves and pimiento slices.

About 1¼ cups (enough for 5 dozen 1-inch canapés).

SAVORY SPREAD

1 package (3 ounces) cream cheese,
   softened
1 cup butter or margarine, softened
1 teaspoon prepared mustard
⅛ teaspoon curry powder
½ teaspoon horseradish
¼ teaspoon Worcestershire sauce
¼ teaspoon red pepper sauce
¼ teaspoon onion juice
   Ripe olives
   Pimiento

Mix cheese and butter. Stir in remaining ingredients except olives and pimiento. Garnish canapés with ripe olives and pimiento.

About 1⅓ cups (enough for about 5 dozen 1-inch canapés).

CHICKEN AND MUSHROOM SPREAD

1 can (5 ounces) boned chicken,
   rinsed and finely chopped
1 can (4 ounces) mushroom stems and
   pieces, drained and finely chopped
1½ teaspoons sherry
   Dash cayenne red pepper
   Cocktail onion halves

Mix all ingredients except onion halves. Garnish canapés with cocktail onion halves.

About 1 cup (enough for 4 dozen 1-inch canapés).

LIVERWURST AND MUSHROOM SPREAD

¼ pound liverwurst
1 can (4 ounces) mushroom stems and
   pieces, drained and finely chopped
1 teaspoon chili sauce
   Chopped hard-cooked egg yolk

Mash liverwurst with fork until smooth. Stir in mushrooms and chili sauce. Garnish canapés with chopped hard-cooked egg yolk.

About 1 cup (enough for 4 dozen 1-inch canapés).

KIPPERED HERRING SPREAD

1 can (3¼ ounces) kippered herring, drained
¼ teaspoon vinegar
¼ teaspoon red pepper sauce
Chopped hard-cooked egg yolk or pickle relish

Mix all ingredients except egg yolk. Garnish canapés with chopped hard-cooked egg yolk or pickle relish.

About ¼ cup (enough for 1 dozen 1-inch canapés).

CHEESE ROLLS

Store no longer than 10 months. Makes 2 dozen appetizers.

1 cup shredded natural Cheddar cheese
¼ cup grated or shredded Parmesan cheese
⅓ cup salad dressing
¼ teaspoon Worcestershire sauce
12 slices fresh soft bread
2 tablespoons butter, melted

Mix cheeses, salad dressing and Worcestershire sauce; set aside. Trim crusts from bread. Roll each slice lengthwise until thin and about 4½×4 inches. Cut slices crosswise in half; spread 1 rounded teaspoonful cheese mixture on each piece. Roll up, beginning at narrow end; secure with wooden picks. Brush rolls with melted butter. (To serve immediately, see below.) Freeze uncovered on ungreased baking sheet until firm, at least 2 hours. Divide rolls among freezer containers. Cover, label and return to freezer.

■ **15 minutes before serving, heat oven to 450°.** Remove Cheese Rolls from freezer; place on ungreased baking sheet. Bake until light brown, about 10 minutes.

To Serve Immediately: Heat oven to 400°. Place rolls on ungreased baking sheet. Bake until light brown, about 10 minutes.

OLIVE-CHEESE BALLS

Store no longer than 3 months. Makes 3 dozen appetizers.

2 cups shredded sharp natural Cheddar cheese
1¼ cups all-purpose flour*
½ cup butter or margarine, melted
36 pimiento-stuffed olives, drained

Mix cheese and flour. Stir in butter until mixture is smooth. (If dough seems dry, work with hands.) Shape dough by level teaspoonfuls around olives. (To serve immediately, see below.) Freeze uncovered on ungreased baking sheet until very firm, at least 2 hours. Place cheese balls in plastic freezer bags. Seal, label and return to freezer.

■ **25 minutes before serving, heat oven to 400°.** Remove Olive-Cheese Balls from freezer; place 2 inches apart on ungreased baking sheet. Bake until hot, about 20 minutes.

To Serve Immediately: Place 2 inches apart on ungreased baking sheet. Cover; chill at least 1 hour. Heat oven to 400°. Bake 15 to 20 minutes.

*Do not use self-rising flour in this recipe.

GUACAMOLE

Store no longer than 1 month. Makes about 2 cups.

2 ripe avocados, peeled and pitted
1 medium onion, finely chopped
1 or 2 small green chilies, finely chopped
1 teaspoon salt
½ teaspoon coarsely ground pepper
½ teaspoon ascorbic acid mixture

Mash avocados. Stir in remaining ingredients; beat until creamy. (To serve immediately, see below.) Pour Guacamole into 1-pint freezer container. Cover, label and freeze.

■ **3 hours before serving, remove Guacamole from freezer; thaw at room temperature. Have ready:** 1 medium tomato, peeled and finely chopped. Just before serving, stir in tomato.

To Serve Immediately: Stir in 1 medium tomato, peeled and finely chopped.

CRAB ROLLS

Store no longer than 6 weeks. Makes 2 dozen appetizers.

1 can (7½ ounces) crabmeat,
   drained and cartilage removed
¼ cup dairy sour cream
2 tablespoons chili sauce
¼ cup chopped green onion
½ teaspoon salt
½ teaspoon Worcestershire sauce
12 slices fresh soft bread
2 tablespoons butter, melted

Mix crabmeat, sour cream, chili sauce, onion, salt and Worcestershire sauce; set aside. Trim crusts from bread. Roll each slice lengthwise until thin and about 4½×4 inches. Cut slices crosswise in half; spread 1 rounded teaspoonful crab mixture on each piece. Roll up, beginning at narrow end; secure with wooden picks. Brush rolls with melted butter. (To serve immediately, see below.) Freeze uncovered on ungreased baking sheet until firm, at least 2 hours. Place rolls in freezer containers. Cover, label and return to freezer.

■ **15 minutes before serving, heat oven to 450°.** Remove Crab Rolls from freezer; place on ungreased baking sheet. Bake until light brown, about 10 minutes.

To Serve Immediately: Heat oven to 400°. Place rolls on ungreased baking sheet. Bake until light brown, about 10 minutes.

ORIENTAL-GLAZED CHICKEN WINGS

Store no longer than 3 weeks.

3 pounds chicken wings (17 or 18)
⅓ cup soy sauce
2 tablespoons salad oil
2 tablespoons chili sauce
¼ cup honey
1 teaspoon salt
½ teaspoon ginger
¼ teaspoon garlic powder
¼ teaspoon cayenne red pepper, if desired

For easier handling as finger food, separate chicken wings at joint before marinating. Mix remaining ingredients; pour on chicken. Cover; refrigerate, turning chicken occasionally, at least 1 hour.

Heat oven to 375°. Remove chicken from marinade; reserve marinade. Place chicken on rack in foil-lined broiler pan. Bake 30 minutes. Brush chicken with reserved marinade. Turn chicken and bake, brushing occasionally with marinade, until tender, about 30 minutes. (Can be served immediately.) Cool quickly. Wrap, label and freeze.

■ **15 minutes before serving, heat oven to 375°.** Remove Oriental-glazed Chicken Wings from freezer and unwrap; place on ungreased baking sheet. Heat until hot, about 10 minutes.

Note: Baked chicken wings can be covered and stored in refrigerator no longer than 24 hours. Heat in 375° oven about 7 minutes.

CHILI CHEESE FRIES

Store no longer than 6 months. Makes about 5 dozen appetizers.

Dough
- **4 cups all-purpose flour***
- **2 teaspoons salt**
- **2 teaspoons baking powder**
- **2 teaspoons chili powder**
- **1 cup milk**
- **2 eggs**
- **½ cup butter or margarine, melted**

Filling
- **¼ cup thinly sliced green onion tops**
- **¼ cup snipped parsley**
- **1 tablespoon butter or margarine**
- **¼ teaspoon salt**
- **¼ teaspoon pepper**
- **½ pound shredded Monterey (Jack) cheese**

Mix flour, 2 teaspoons salt, the baking powder and chili powder. Beat milk and eggs in small bowl; stir into flour mixture. Stir in melted butter. Turn dough onto lightly floured cloth-covered board; knead until smooth, about 4 minutes. Shape into ball. Cover with plastic wrap; set aside for 30 minutes.

Cook and stir onion and parsley in 1 tablespoon butter until onion is tender. Remove from heat; stir in ¼ teaspoon salt, the pepper and cheese.

Divide dough into 4 parts. Roll each part ⅛ inch thick; cut into 3-inch circles. Spoon filling by rounded ½ teaspoonful on center of each circle. Moisten edge of circle; fold dough over filling and press edges with fork to seal securely. (If seal does not hold, reseal on both sides with fork just before frying.)

Heat shortening or oil (1 inch) in large skillet to 400° Fry Chili Cheese Fries until golden brown on both sides, about 5 minutes; drain. Cool. Place desired number in freezer containers. Cover, label and freeze.

■ **15 minutes before serving, heat oven to 400°.** Remove Chili Cheese Fries from freezer; place on ungreased baking sheet. Heat until hot, about 10 minutes.

*If using self-rising flour, omit 2 teaspoons salt and the baking powder.

ESCARGOTS IN PETIT CHOUX (PUFF SHELLS)

Store no longer than 3 months. Makes 4 dozen puff shells.

- **1 cup water**
- **½ cup butter**
- **1 cup all-purpose flour**
- **4 eggs**

Heat oven to 400°. Heat water and butter until mixture boils vigorously. Stir in flour. Beat over low heat until mixture forms a ball, about 1 minute. Remove from heat. Beat in eggs; beat until smooth. Drop dough by slightly rounded teaspoonfuls onto ungreased baking sheet. Bake 25 to 30 minutes. (To serve half of recipe immediately, see below.) Cut puffs in half; cool. Place puffs on 2 pieces heavy-duty aluminum foil. Wrap, label and freeze.

■ **10 minutes before serving, heat oven to 400°. Have ready:** ingredients for Escargots (below).

Remove 1 package Puff Shells from freezer and open foil wrapper; place on ungreased baking sheet. Heat in oven until warm, about 5 minutes. Or, heat unwrapped frozen puff shells in electric bun warmer 25 minutes. Prepare Escargots. Guests spoon escargots and butter sauce into half of puff shell and top with other half. (2 dozen appetizers.)

ESCARGOTS

- **⅔ cup butter or margarine**
- **1 can (4½ ounces) escargots, rinsed and drained**
- **2 cloves garlic, crushed**
- **1 teaspoon parsley flakes**
- **1 teaspoon finely chopped green onion**
- **⅛ teaspoon pepper**
- **2 tablespoons dry white wine or, if desired, apple juice**

Melt butter in small saucepan. Stir in remaining ingredients; simmer 5 minutes. Serve in chafing dish.

To Serve Immediately: Cut 2 dozen puff shells in half; keep warm. Prepare Escargots (above). Guests spoon escargots and butter sauce into half of puff shell and top with other half. (2 dozen appetizers.)

Salads

FROZEN CHERRY-PINEAPPLE SALAD

Store no longer than 2 months. Makes enough for 12 servings.

1 can (12 ounces) pitted dark sweet
   cherries, drained (reserve syrup)
1 can (8¼ ounces) crushed pineapple,
   drained (reserve syrup)
2 tablespoons lemon juice
1 package (3 ounces) cherry-flavored gelatin
1 package (3 ounces) cream cheese
½ cup chopped pecans
1 bottle (6 ounces) carbonated cola beverage

Heat ½ cup of the combined reserved syrups and the lemon juice until mixture boils. Pour boiling syrup on gelatin in large bowl; stir until gelatin is dissolved. Cool to room temperature.

Cut cream cheese into small pieces. Stir cheese pieces, fruit, pecans and cola beverage into gelatin mixture. Chill until slightly thickened. Spoon mixture into 12 paper-lined muffin cups. Wrap, label and freeze. Freeze at least 24 hours.

■ **30 minutes before serving, remove Frozen Cherry-Pineapple Salad from freezer.** Remove salad from cups; serve on greens as a salad or, if you prefer, serve in sherbet glasses as a dessert.

FROZEN RASPBERRY SALAD

Store no longer than 2 months. Makes enough for 9 to 12 servings.

½ cup boiling water
1 package (3 ounces) raspberry-flavored
   gelatin
1 package (10 ounces) frozen
   raspberries, thawed
⅛ teaspoon salt
2 packages (3 ounces each)
   cream cheese, softened
1 cup dairy sour cream
1 can (16 ounces) whole cranberry sauce

Pour boiling water on gelatin in large bowl; stir until gelatin is dissolved. Stir in raspberries (with syrup). Mix remaining ingredients; stir into gelatin mixture. (Salad will be slightly lumpy.) Pour mixture into baking pan, 8×8×2 or 9×9×2 inches. Cover, label and freeze. Freeze at least 24 hours.

■ **20 minutes before serving, remove Frozen Raspberry Salad from freezer.** Let stand at room temperature 10 minutes. Cut salad into serving pieces.

FROZEN COCKTAIL SALAD

Store no longer than 4 weeks. Makes enough for 16 servings.

2 cups dairy sour cream
¾ cup sugar
1 tablespoon plus 1 teaspoon lemon juice
1 can (30 ounces) fruit cocktail, drained
2 medium bananas, cut into ¼-inch slices
½ cup coarsely chopped walnuts
1 jar (10 ounces) maraschino cherries
   (¾ cup), halved

Mix sour cream, sugar and lemon juice. Stir in fruit cocktail, bananas, walnuts and cherries. Pour mixture into 2 refrigerator trays. Cover, label and freeze. Freeze until firm, at least 24 hours. (Upright or chest freezers will freeze salad in about 2 hours.)

■ **15 minutes before serving, remove Frozen Cocktail Salad from freezer; place in refrigerator.** Cut each salad into 8 pieces, 2×2¼ inches. Stemmed red cherries make a bright garnish.

Vegetables

OVEN-FRIED EGGPLANT

Store no longer than 10 weeks. Makes enough for 4 servings.

½ cup seasoned bread crumbs
1 teaspoon salt
1 small eggplant (about 1 pound), pared
1 egg, slightly beaten

Heat oven to 375°. Grease jelly roll pan, 15½×10½×1 inch. Mix crumbs and salt. Cut eggplant into ½-inch slices; cut large slices into halves. Dip eggplant slices in egg, then coat with crumbs; arrange in pan. Bake uncovered 15 minutes; turn and bake 15 minutes longer. (Can be served immediately.) Cool thoroughly. Wrap, label and freeze.

■ **15 minutes before serving, heat oven to 450°.** Remove Oven-fried Eggplant from freezer and unwrap; arrange on ungreased jelly roll pan, 15½×10½×1 inch. Heat until hot, about 8 minutes.

FRENCH FRIED EGGPLANT

Store no longer than 1 month. Makes enough for 4 servings.

1 medium eggplant (about 1½ pounds), pared
⅔ cup milk
½ cup all-purpose flour*
¾ teaspoon baking powder
¼ teaspoon salt

Cut eggplant into ¼-inch slices; cut large slices into halves. Heat fat or oil (1 inch) in large skillet to 375°.

Beat remaining ingredients with rotary beater until smooth. Dip eggplant slices in batter, letting excess drip into bowl.

Fry a few slices at a time in hot fat, turning once, until golden brown; drain. (Can be served immediately.) Cool thoroughly. Wrap, label and freeze.

■ **15 minutes before serving, heat oven to 450°.** Remove French Fried Eggplant from freezer and unwrap; place on ungreased jelly roll pan, 15½×10½×1 inch. Heat until hot, about 8 minutes.

*If using self-rising flour, omit baking powder and salt.

Combine Frozen Vegetables

1 package artichoke hearts, 1 package green peas, 1 tablespoon lemon juice, 1 tablespoon butter.

1 package Chinese pea pods, 1 package carrot nuggets in butter sauce, 2 teaspoons lemon juice.

1 package chopped spinach, 1 package chopped broccoli, 1 tablespoon butter, 1 tablespoon lemon juice.

1 package cut green beans, 1 package cut wax beans, ½ teaspoon savory, 1 tablespoon butter.

Slice a large onion, then separate each slice into rings.

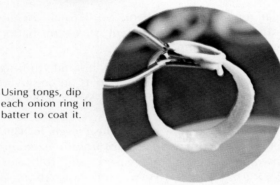

Using tongs, dip each onion ring in batter to coat it.

Drain the fried onion rings on paper towels.

FRENCH FRIED ONION RINGS

Store no longer than 3 months. Makes enough for 3 or 4 servings.

1 large Spanish or Bermuda onion
⅔ cup milk
½ cup all-purpose flour*
¾ teaspoon baking powder
¼ teaspoon salt

Cut onion into ¼-inch slices; separate into rings. Heat fat or oil (1 inch) in large skillet to 375°.

Beat remaining ingredients with rotary beater until smooth. Dip each onion ring in batter, letting excess drip into bowl.

Fry a few onion rings at a time in hot fat, turning once, until golden brown, about 2 minutes; drain. (Can be served immediately.) Cool thoroughly. Wrap, label and freeze.

■ **15 minutes before serving, heat oven to 350°.** Remove French Fried Onion Rings from freezer and unwrap; place on ungreased baking sheet. Heat 6 or 7 minutes.

*If using self-rising flour, omit baking powder and salt.

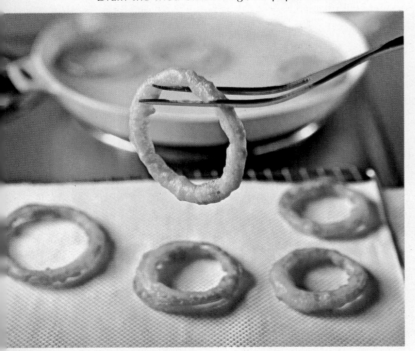

Vegetables with a Difference

You can vary the flavor of your vegetables with different seasonings.

Onions: Add a pinch of basil, cayenne pepper or celery seed.

Potatoes: Add a little bit of bay leaf, sage or poppy seed.

Green Beans: Sprinkle lightly with basil, dill, nutmeg or thyme.

Eggplant: Create an interesting flavor with garlic, curry powder, allspice or rosemary.

Corn: Add a little cayenne pepper, chili powder or celery seed.

Squash: Try oregano or rosemary.

TWICE BAKED POTATOES

Store no longer than 2 months. Makes enough for 4 servings.

4 large baking potatoes
  Shortening
⅓ to ½ cup milk
¼ cup butter or margarine, softened
½ teaspoon salt
  Dash pepper
  Shredded Cheddar cheese, if desired

Heat oven to 350°. Rub potatoes with shortening for softer skins. Prick several times with fork to allow steam to escape. Bake until potatoes are soft, 1¼ to 1½ hours.

Cut thin slice from top of each potato; scoop out inside, leaving a thin shell. Mash potato until no lumps remain. Add small amounts of milk, beating after each addition. (Amount of milk needed to make potato smooth and fluffy depends on kind of potatoes.) Add butter, salt and pepper; beat vigorously until potato is light and fluffy.

Fill potato shells with mashed potato; sprinkle cheese on top. (To serve immediately, see below.) Wrap, label and freeze.

■ **45 minutes before serving, heat oven to 400°.** Remove Twice Baked Potatoes from freezer and unwrap; place on ungreased baking sheet. Bake until centers of potatoes are hot, about 40 minutes. (Or, thaw potatoes uncovered at room temperature 1 hour 45 minutes; bake in 400° oven until golden brown, about 20 minutes.)

To Serve Immediately: Increase oven temperature to 400°. Place potatoes on ungreased baking sheet. Bake until golden, about 20 minutes.

GNOCCHI

Store no longer than 3 months. Makes enough for 4 servings.

2½ cups milk
1 cup white cornmeal
1 tablespoon butter or margarine
2 eggs, well beaten
¼ teaspoon salt
1 tablespoon butter or margarine
¼ to ½ cup grated Parmesan cheese

Butter baking pan, 8×8×2 inches. Heat milk in medium saucepan until small bubbles appear; remove from heat. Sprinkle cornmeal slowly into hot milk, stirring constantly. Cook over medium-high heat, stirring constantly, until very thick (spoon will stand upright in the Gnocchi), about 7 minutes.

Remove from heat. Mix in 1 tablespoon butter, the eggs and salt; beat until smooth. Spread in pan; cool. Refrigerate uncovered at least 2 hours. (Store no longer than 24 hours.)

Cut cornmeal mixture into sixteen 2-inch squares. Arrange squares in buttered baking dish, 10×6 inches, or ovenproof skillet; dot with 1 tablespoon butter and sprinkle cheese on top. (To serve immediately, see below.) Wrap, label and freeze.

■ **40 minutes before serving, remove Gnocchi from freezer and unwrap.** Bake uncovered in 425° oven until golden brown, about 35 minutes.

To Serve Immediately: Heat oven to 425°. Bake uncovered 10 to 12 minutes. Set oven control at broil and/or 550°. Broil Gnocchi with top 2 to 3 inches from heat until golden brown, about 2 minutes.

ASPARAGUS WITH CASHEWS

Makes enough for 3 or 4 servings.

1 package (10 ounces) frozen
  cut asparagus
¼ cup cashew nuts
2 tablespoons finely chopped
  onion
2 tablespoons butter or margarine

Cook asparagus as directed on package; drain. Cook and stir nuts and onion in butter until golden brown; toss with asparagus.

CLASSIC ASPARAGUS

Makes enough for 3 servings.

1 package (10 ounces) frozen
  asparagus spears
1 tablespoon butter or margarine
1 tablespoon light cream
¼ teaspoon salt
¼ teaspoon nutmeg
  Lemon wedges

Cook asparagus as directed on package; drain. Arrange asparagus in serving dish; top with butter, cream, salt and nutmeg. Serve with lemon wedges.

BUTTERED BLACKEYE ASPARAGUS

Makes enough for 8 servings.

Cook 2 packages (10 ounces each) frozen asparagus spears as directed on package; drain. Toss asparagus with ¼ cup soft butter or margarine and ¼ cup sliced pitted ripe olives until butter melts.

GREEN BEANS AND BAMBOO SHOOTS

Makes enough for 4 servings.

1 package (9 ounces) frozen cut
  green beans
1 tablespoon salad oil
½ cup water
¼ cup bamboo shoots, cut into
  ½-inch pieces or ¼ cup
  sliced water chestnuts
½ teaspoon salt
¼ teaspoon sugar
¼ teaspoon ginger

Rinse beans with small amount of running cold water to separate and remove ice crystals; drain. Cook and stir beans in oil 2 minutes. Stir in remaining ingredients. Heat until mixture boils; cook until beans are tender, 5 to 8 minutes.

GREEN BEANS IN SOUR CREAM

Makes enough for 3 or 4 servings.

1 package (10 ounces) frozen
  green beans
2 tablespoons finely chopped
  onion
2 tablespoons chopped pimiento
  Salt and pepper
½ cup dairy sour cream

Cook green beans as directed on package; drain and return to saucepan. Stir in onion, pimiento, salt and pepper; heat. Turn into serving dish; spoon sour cream on top.

SMOKY GREEN BEANS

Makes enough for 6 servings.

Cook 2 packages (9 ounces each) frozen cut green beans as directed on package; drain. Stir in 1 teaspoon smoky salt.

OVEN GREEN BEANS

Makes enough for 4 servings.

1 package (9 ounces) frozen
  cut green beans
½ teaspoon seasoned salt
¼ cup water
1 to 2 tablespoons butter or
  margarine

Heat oven to 425°. Place frozen beans in ungreased 1½-quart casserole. Sprinkle salt and water on beans; dot with butter. Cover tightly; bake 15 minutes. Separate beans with fork; cover and bake 15 minutes.

ITALIAN GREEN BEANS

Makes enough for 3 or 4 servings.

1 package (10 ounces) Italian
  green beans
1 small onion, thinly sliced
½ teaspoon salt
2 tablespoons oil and vinegar
  salad dressing

Cook green beans as directed on package except—stir in onion during last 2 minutes; drain. Toss green beans with salt and dressing.

CREOLE LIMA BEANS

Makes enough for 5 servings.

1 can (8 ounces) stewed
  tomatoes
1 package (10 ounces) frozen
  baby lima beans
⅔ cup thinly sliced celery
¾ teaspoon salt
⅛ teaspoon pepper

Heat tomatoes to boiling. Stir in remaining ingredients. Return to boiling; separate beans with fork. Reduce heat; cover tightly and simmer until beans are tender, 5 minutes.

BAKED LIMAS IN CREAM

Makes enough for 4 servings.

1 package (10 ounces) frozen baby lima beans
½ cup light cream (20%)
1 teaspoon salt
⅛ teaspoon pepper

Heat oven to 350° Place all ingredients in ungreased 1-quart casserole. Cover tightly; bake 30 minutes.

DILLY BROCCOLI

Makes enough for 3 or 4 servings.

1 package (10 ounces) frozen chopped broccoli
1 tablespoon butter or margarine
¾ teaspoon dill weed

Cook broccoli as directed on package; drain. Stir in butter and dill weed.

BROCCOLI WITH MUSTARD SAUCE

Makes enough for 3 servings.

1 package (10 ounces) frozen broccoli spears
1 tablespoon butter or margarine
1 tablespoon light cream
½ teaspoon dry mustard
1 teaspoon sugar
⅛ teaspoon pepper

Cook broccoli as directed on package; drain. Stir in butter. Turn into serving dish. Mix cream, mustard, sugar and pepper; pour on broccoli.

SAVORY BROCCOLI

Makes enough for 3 or 4 servings.

1 package (10 ounces) frozen chopped broccoli
1 tablespoon butter or margarine
⅛ teaspoon allspice

Cook broccoli as directed on package; drain. Stir in butter and allspice.

SWEET AND SOUR BRUSSELS SPROUTS

Makes enough for 3 or 4 servings.

1 package (10 ounces) frozen Brussels sprouts
1 tablespoon butter or margarine
1 teaspoon vinegar
1 teaspoon sugar
2 slices bacon, crisply fried and crumbled

Cook Brussels sprouts as directed on package; drain. Stir in butter, vinegar, sugar and bacon.

BRUSSELS SPROUTS À L'ORANGE

Makes enough for 3 or 4 servings.

1 package (10 ounces) frozen Brussels sprouts
3 thin orange slices, cut into wedges
1 tablespoon butter or margarine
1 tablespoon honey
⅛ teaspoon cloves

Cook Brussels sprouts as directed on package; drain. Stir in orange wedges, butter, honey and cloves.

CARROTS 'N GREEN ONIONS

Makes enough for 3 or 4 servings.

1 package (10 ounces) frozen carrots
1 tablespoon butter or margarine
2 green onions, sliced

Cook carrots as directed on package; drain. Stir in butter and onion.

Buttered Blackeye Asparagus (page 46)

Italian Green Beans (page 46)

Brussels Sprouts à l'Orange

Orange-glazed Carrots

Sweet Corn

Vegetable Medley

ORANGE-GLAZED CARROTS

Makes enough for 3 or 4 servings.
1 **package (10 ounces) frozen carrots**
1 **tablespoon butter or margarine**
1 **tablespoon orange marmalade**
2 **tablespoons chopped pecans**

Cook carrots as directed on package; drain. Stir in butter, orange marmalade and pecans.

VEGETABLE COMBINATION

Makes enough for 6 servings.
1 **package (10 ounces) frozen cauliflower**
1 **package (10 ounces) frozen chopped spinach**
1 **tablespoon butter or margarine**
1 **tablespoon lemon juice**

Cook cauliflower and spinach separately as directed on packages; drain. Toss cauliflower with spinach; stir in butter and lemon juice. Garnish with lemon slices.

CAULIFLOWER AND TOMATO

Makes enough for 4 or 5 servings.
1 **package (10 ounces) frozen cauliflower**
⅛ **teaspoon instant minced garlic**
1 **tablespoon butter or margarine**
½ **teaspoon salt**
1 **medium tomato, cut into eighths**
1 **tablespoon snipped parsley**
2 **tablespoons grated Parmesan cheese**

Cook cauliflower as directed on package; drain and return to saucepan. Add garlic, butter, salt and tomato. Cover tightly; simmer 2 to 3 minutes. Turn into serving dish; sprinkle parsley and cheese on top.

CHILI CORN

Makes enough for 3 or 4 servings.
1 **package (10 ounces) frozen whole kernel corn**
1 **tablespoon butter or margarine**
¼ **teaspoon chili powder**
¼ **cup sliced ripe olives**

Cook corn as directed on package; drain. Stir in butter, chili powder and olives.

SWEET CORN

Makes enough for 3 or 4 servings.
1 **package (10 ounces) frozen whole kernel corn**
1 **tablespoon butter or margarine**
1 **tablespoon maple-flavored syrup**

Cook corn as directed on package; drain. Stir in butter and syrup.

VEGETABLE MEDLEY

Makes enough for 6 or 7 servings.
1 **can (16 ounces) chop suey vegetables**
1 **package (10 ounces) frozen green peas**
2 **tablespoons butter or margarine**
1 **tablespoon soy sauce**

Drain chop suey vegetables; rinse with running cold water and drain. Cook peas as directed on package except—when peas and water are boiling, stir in chop suey vegetables. Reduce heat; cover tightly and simmer 5 minutes. Drain; stir in butter and soy sauce.

CRUNCHY PEAS

Makes enough for 3 or 4 servings.

1 package (10 ounces) frozen green peas
1 tablespoon butter or margarine
1 can (1¾ ounces) shoestring potatoes

Cook peas as directed on package; drain. Stir in butter and potatoes.

Substitution

½ cup canned French fried onions can be substituted for the potatoes.

CASSEROLED SPINACH

Makes enough for 6 servings.

2 packages (10 ounces each) frozen chopped spinach
1 teaspoon salt
⅛ teaspoon pepper
⅛ teaspoon instant minced garlic
2 teaspoons lemon juice
1 tablespoon flour
2 eggs

Heat oven to 350°. Cook spinach as directed on package except—simmer 3 minutes; drain. Beat remaining ingredients with hand beater in ungreased 1-quart casserole until very well mixed. Stir in spinach. Bake uncovered 25 minutes.

ZESTY SPINACH

Makes enough for 3 or 4 servings.

1 package (10 ounces) frozen leaf spinach
1 tablespoon butter or margarine
2 tablespoons milk
2 teaspoons horseradish

Cook spinach as directed on package; drain. Stir in butter, milk and horseradish.

VEGETABLE SAUCES

Store no longer than 4 months in the freezer (or 2 months in the refrigerator).

Seasoned Butter Pieces

Mix ½ cup butter or margarine softened, and ½ cup all-purpose flour. Stir in one of the following seasonings and 4 or 5 drops yellow food color:

¼ cup grated Parmesan cheese
2 teaspoons chili powder
1 teaspoon garlic powder
¼ cup soy sauce
2 teaspoons chopped parsley flakes
1 teaspoon dill weed
2 tablespoons grated lemon peel and 1 tablespoon lemon juice
2 tablespoons grated orange peel and 1 tablespoon orange juice

Drop mixture by level measuring tablespoonfuls onto waxed paper. Chill until firm, about 1 hour. Freeze or refrigerate in covered container or plastic bag.

Frozen Vegetable with Sauce

Cook 1 package (about 9 ounces) frozen vegetable, using ½ cup water as directed except —2 minutes before vegetable is done, add 2 Seasoned Butter Pieces. Cook 2 minutes; stir gently until sauce is smooth.

Canned Vegetable with Sauce

Drain liquid from 1 can (about 16 ounces) vegetable into saucepan. Heat liquid until it boils; boil until about ½ cup liquid remains. Add vegetable and 2 Seasoned Butter Pieces. Heat over medium heat until vegetable is hot and butter pieces melt. Stir gently until sauce is smooth.

Crunchy Peas

Zesty Spinach

Seasoned Butter Pieces (orange)

Breads

CHEESE SOUFFLÉ BREAD

Store no longer than 6 months. Makes 1 loaf.

 1 **package active dry yeast**
 ¼ **cup warm water (105 to 115°)**
 ¼ **cup lukewarm milk (scalded then cooled)**
 ⅓ **cup butter or margarine, softened**
 1 **egg**
 ½ **teaspoon salt**
 ¼ **teaspoon pepper**
 ⅔ **cup finely shredded Cheddar cheese**
 1½ **cups all-purpose flour***
 Soft butter or margarine

Dissolve yeast in warm water in large mixer bowl. Add milk, ⅓ cup butter, the egg, salt, pepper, cheese and ½ cup of the flour; mix on low speed, scraping bowl constantly, ½ minute. Beat on medium speed, scraping bowl occasionally, 2 minutes. Stir in remaining flour until dough is smooth. Scrape dough from side of bowl. Cover; let rise in warm place until double, about 30 minutes. (Dough is ready if impression remains when touched.)

Beat dough about 25 strokes. Spread evenly in greased 1-quart casserole. Cover; let rise until double, about 40 minutes.

Heat oven to 375°. Bake until loaf is brown and sounds hollow when tapped, 40 to 45 minutes. Immediately remove bread from casserole; place on wire rack. Brush top of bread with butter.

Cool 1 hour. Wrap in heavy-duty aluminum foil, label and freeze.

■ **4 hours before serving, remove Cheese Soufflé Bread from freezer and unwrap.** Thaw at room temperature at least 3½ hours. Rewrap loaf in foil; heat in 400° oven until warm, 30 minutes. To serve, cut into wedges with serrated knife.

*If using self-rising flour, omit salt.

PUMPERNICKEL RYE BREAD

Store no longer than 9 months. Makes 2 loaves.

 3 **packages active dry yeast**
 1½ **cups warm water (105 to 115°)**
 ½ **cup light molasses**
 1 **tablespoon plus 1 teaspoon salt**
 2 **tablespoons shortening**
 2 **tablespoons caraway seed**
 2¾ **cups rye flour**
 2¾ **to 3¼ cups all-purpose flour***
 Cornmeal

Dissolve yeast in warm water in large bowl. Mix in molasses, salt, shortening, caraway seed and rye flour; beat until smooth. Stir in enough white flour to make dough easy to handle.

Turn dough onto lightly floured board. Cover; let stand 10 to 15 minutes. Knead until smooth, 5 to 10 minutes. Place in greased bowl; turn greased side up. Cover; let rise in warm place until double, about 1 hour.

Punch down dough; round up, cover and let rise again until double, about 40 minutes.

Grease baking sheet; sprinkle cornmeal on greased sheet. Punch down dough; divide in half. Shape each half into round, slightly flat loaf. Place loaves in opposite corners of baking sheet. Cover; let rise 1 hour.

Heat oven to 375°. Bake 25 to 30 minutes. Cool. (Can be served immediately.)

Cool loaves 1½ hours. Wrap in heavy-duty aluminum foil, label and freeze.

■ **2 hours 30 minutes before serving, remove Pumpernickel Rye Bread from freezer.** Thaw in wrapper at room temperature.

*If using self-rising flour, omit salt.

BLUEBERRY COFFEE CAKE

*Store no longer than 3 months. Makes 2 cakes—
9 to 12 servings each.*

  4 cups all-purpose flour*
1½ cups sugar
  1 tablespoon plus 2 teaspoons
    baking powder
1½ teaspoons salt
  ½ cup shortening
1½ cups milk
  2 eggs
  4 cups fresh or frozen blueberries
    Topping (below)
    Confectioners' Glaze (below),
    if desired

Heat oven to 375°. Grease 2 layer pans, 9×1½
inches, or 2 baking pans, 9×9×2 inches. Mix
all ingredients except blueberries, Topping and
Confectioners' Glaze until moistened; beat
vigorously ½ minute. Carefully stir in blueberries. Spread half the batter in each pan;
sprinkle Topping on batter. Bake until wooden
pick inserted in center comes out clean, 45 to
50 minutes.

Cool slightly. Drizzle Confectioners' Glaze on
top. (Can be served immediately.) Cool thoroughly. Wrap, label and freeze.

■ **50 minutes before serving, remove Blueberry Coffee Cake from freezer and unwrap.** Heat uncovered in 350° oven until warm, 45 minutes.

TOPPING

Mix 1 cup sugar, ⅔ cup all-purpose flour, 1
teaspoon cinnamon and ½ cup soft butter.

CONFECTIONERS' GLAZE

Mix 2 cups confectioners' sugar, ¼ cup butter
or margarine, softened, and 1 teaspoon vanilla.
Stir in ⅓ to ½ cup water, about 2 tablespoons
at a time, until glaze is spreading consistency.

*If using self-rising flour, omit baking powder and salt.

BUTTERY STREUSEL COFFEE CAKE

*Store no longer than 3 months. Makes 2 cakes—
9 to 12 servings each.*

  3 cups all-purpose flour*
1½ cups sugar
  1 tablespoon plus 2 teaspoons
    baking powder
1½ teaspoons salt
  ½ cup shortening
1½ cups milk
  2 eggs
    Cinnamon-Nut Filling (below)
    Streusel Topping (below)
    Confectioners' Glaze (left), if desired

Heat oven to 375°. Grease 2 layer pans, 9×1½
inches, or 2 baking pans, 9×9×2 inches. Mix
all ingredients except Cinnamon-Nut Filling,
Streusel Topping and Confectioners' Glaze
until moistened; beat vigorously ½ minute.
Spread ⅓ of batter (about 1⅓ cups) in each
pan. Sprinkle half the Cinnamon-Nut Filling
on the batter in each pan; spread half the
remaining batter (about ⅔ cup) in each pan.
Sprinkle Streusel Topping on top. Bake until
wooden pick inserted in center comes out
clean, 30 to 35 minutes.

Cool slightly. Drizzle Confectioners' Glaze on
top. (Can be served immediately.) Cool thoroughly. Wrap, label and freeze.

■ **25 minutes before serving, remove Buttery Streusel
Coffee Cake from freezer and unwrap.** Heat uncovered in 350° oven until warm, about 20 minutes.

*If using self-rising flour, omit baking powder and salt.

CINNAMON-NUT FILLING

Mix ½ cup brown sugar (packed), ½ cup finely
chopped nuts and 2 teaspoons cinnamon.

STREUSEL TOPPING

Mix ½ cup all-purpose flour, 1 cup sugar and
½ cup firm butter until crumbly.

FRUITED LOAF

Store no longer than 9 months. Makes 2 coffee cakes.

Dough
 1 package active dry yeast
 ¾ cup warm water (105 to 115°)
 ½ cup sugar
 ½ teaspoon salt
 3 eggs
 1 egg yolk (reserve white)
 ½ cup butter or margarine, softened
 3½ cups all-purpose flour*
 ½ cup chopped blanched almonds
 ¼ cup cut-up citron
 ¼ cup cut-up candied cherries
 ¼ cup raisins
 1 tablespoon grated lemon peel
 ¼ cup plus 2 tablespoons soft butter

Icing (optional)
 1½ cups confectioners' sugar
 1½ tablespoons milk

Dissolve yeast in warm water in large mixer bowl. Add sugar, salt, eggs, egg yolk, ½ cup butter and 1½ cups of the flour; mix on low speed, scraping bowl constantly, ½ minute. Beat on medium speed, scraping bowl occasionally, about 10 minutes.

Stir in remaining flour, the almonds, citron, cherries, raisins and lemon peel. Scrape dough from side of bowl. Cover; let rise in warm place until double, 1½ to 2 hours.

Beat dough 25 strokes. Cover tightly; refrigerate at least 8 hours. Turn dough onto well-floured board; coat with flour. Divide dough in half; press each half into oval, about 10×7 inches. Spread 3 tablespoons butter on each oval. Fold in half lengthwise; press only folded edge firmly. Place on greased baking sheet. Beat reserved egg white slightly; beat in 1 tablespoon water. Brush loaves with beaten egg white. Let rise until double, 45 to 60 minutes.

Heat oven to 375°. Bake until golden brown, 20 to 25 minutes. Mix confectioners' sugar and milk until smooth. While loaves are warm, frost with Icing; if desired, decorate with almond halves, pieces of citron and cherry halves.

Cool 1 hour. (Can be served immediately.) If frosted and decorated, freeze uncovered 2 hours. Wrap, label and return to freezer.

■ **2 hours before serving, remove Fruited Loaf from freezer; thaw in wrapper at room temperature 1 hour.** Unwrap and thaw 1 hour. (Or, after first hour of thawing, loaf can be sliced and thawed on serving plate 30 minutes.)

*Do not use self-rising flour in this recipe.

Storage Time for Dairy Products at 0°

Butter, Margarine	3 months
Cheese	1½ to 4 months
Ice Cream	less than 1 month
Eggs (prepared)	9 months

Note: Do not freeze milk or cream.

Overwrap butter or margarine in freezer wrap, even if it is already in parchment or a carton.

Keep cheese in unopened first wrapping. Overwrap in freezer wrap. Before eating, thaw in refrigerator; use as soon as possible.

Ice cream keeps better when you overwrap the carton with freezer wrap. In an opened carton, smooth plastic wrap over surface of ice cream.

To freeze egg yolks, break yolks. For each cup of yolks, add either 1 teaspoon salt or 2 tablespoons sugar or 2 tablespoons corn syrup. Stir, but do not beat air in. To freeze egg whites, strain through sieve; do not add anything. To freeze eggs whole, break yolks; mix well with whites, but do not stir air in.

Pictured at right: Blueberry Coffee Cake (page 51), Fruited Loaf, Buttery Streusel Coffee Cake (page 51) and Citron-Anise Loaf (page 55)

Spread the dough with a filling (Apricot-Cherry Filling, page 55, is shown here) and roll up, starting from long side.

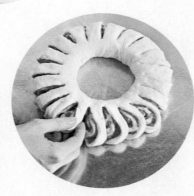

After shaping the roll into a ring, cut partway through at 1-inch intervals with scissors. Twist each section on its side.

Filled Rings: The unglazed ring is made with Date Filling (page 55), the glazed one with Apricot-Cherry Filling.

FILLED RINGS

Store no longer than 9 months. Makes 3 rings.

2 cups dairy sour cream
2 packages active dry yeast
½ cup warm water (105 to 115°)
¼ cup butter or margarine, softened
⅓ cup sugar
2 teaspoons salt
2 eggs
  About 6 cups all-purpose flour*
  Fillings (page 55)

Heat sour cream over low heat just until lukewarm. Dissolve yeast in warm water in large bowl. Mix in sour cream, butter, sugar, salt, eggs and 2 cups of the flour; beat until smooth. Stir in enough remaining flour to make dough easy to handle.

Turn dough onto well-floured board; knead until smooth, about 10 minutes. Place in greased bowl; turn greased side up. Cover; let rise in warm place until double, about 1 hour.

Heat oven to 375°. Punch down dough; divide into 3 parts. Roll each part into rectangle, 15×9 inches. Spread a different filling evenly on each rectangle. Roll up, beginning at long side. Pinch edge of dough into roll to seal securely. Stretch roll to make even.

With sealed edge down, shape into ring on lightly greased baking sheet. Pinch ends together. With scissors, make cuts ⅔ of the way through each ring at 1-inch intervals. Turn each section on its side. Bake until golden brown, 15 to 20 minutes. Cool. (Can be served immediately.) Freeze uncovered until firm, about 2 hours. Wrap in heavy-duty aluminum foil, label and return to freezer.

■ **40 minutes before serving, remove Filled Ring from freezer.** Heat wrapped ring in 350° oven 35 minutes. Or, thaw in wrapper at room temperature 2 hours. If desired, drizzle Glaze (page 55) on top.

*If using self-rising flour, omit salt.

FILLINGS

Date Filling (enough for 1 ring)
1 cup chopped dates
¼ cup sugar
⅓ cup water
⅓ cup coarsely chopped nuts

Cook dates, sugar and water over medium heat, stirring constantly, until thickened. Stir in nuts; cool.

Cinnamon-Raisin Filling (enough for 1 ring)
2 tablespoons butter or margarine
½ cup brown sugar (packed)
2 teaspoons cinnamon
½ cup raisins

Spread butter on rectangle; sprinkle sugar, cinnamon and raisins on top.

Apricot-Cherry Filling (enough for 1 ring)
½ cup finely chopped dried apricots
½ cup drained finely chopped
   maraschino cherries

Mix apricots and cherries.

GLAZE

Mix 2 cups confectioners' sugar, ¼ cup butter or margarine, softened, 1 teaspoon vanilla and enough water so glaze is proper consistency to drizzle on rings.

Fresh from the Freezer

With your freezer and a little planning ahead, you can serve fresh rolls and coffee cake at the crack of dawn. When you bake, overwrap sweet rolls individually; wrap 2 slices of coffee cake together. Unwrapped, the separated slices and the rolls will thaw out in a few minutes. Packed lunches, too, will taste fresh when sandwiches are made with frozen bread.

CITRON-ANISE LOAF

Store no longer than 9 months. Makes 2 loaves.

Dough
  2 packages active dry yeast
  ½ cup warm water (105 to 115°)
  ½ cup lukewarm milk (scalded
       then cooled)
  ½ cup sugar
  1 teaspoon salt
  2 eggs
  ½ cup butter or margarine, softened
4½ to 5 cups all-purpose flour*
  ½ cup raisins
  ½ cup cut-up citron
  1 tablespoon anise seed
  2 tablespoons pine nuts, if desired

Glaze
  1 egg
  1 tablespoon water

Dissolve yeast in warm water in large bowl. Mix in milk, sugar, salt, 2 eggs, the butter and 2½ cups of the flour; beat until smooth. Stir in fruit, anise seed, nuts and enough remaining flour to make dough easy to handle.

Turn dough onto lightly floured board; knead until smooth and elastic, about 5 minutes. Place in greased bowl; turn greased side up. Cover; let rise in warm place until double, 1½ to 2 hours.

Punch down dough; divide in half. Shape each half into round, slightly flat loaf. Place loaves in opposite corners of greased baking sheet. Cut a cross ½ inch deep on top of each loaf. Let rise until double, about 1 hour.

Heat oven to 350°. Mix 1 egg and 1 tablespoon water; brush on loaves. Bake 35 to 45 minutes. Cool. (Can be served immediately.)

Cool loaves 1 hour. Wrap in heavy-duty aluminum foil, label and freeze.

■ **2½ hours before serving, remove Citron-Anise Loaf from freezer.** Thaw in wrapper at room temperature. Can be warmed, if desired.

*If using self-rising flour, omit salt.

QUICK BUTTERMILK SWEET DOUGH

- 2 packages active dry yeast
- ½ cup warm water (105 to 115°)
- 1¼ cups buttermilk
- 2 eggs
- 5½ to 6 cups all-purpose flour*
- ½ cup butter or margarine, softened
- ½ cup sugar
- 2 teaspoons baking powder
- 2 teaspoons salt

Dissolve yeast in warm water in large mixer bowl. Add buttermilk, eggs, 2½ cups of the flour, the butter, sugar, baking powder and salt; mix on low speed, scraping bowl constantly, ½ minute. Beat on medium speed, scraping bowl occasionally, 2 minutes. Stir in enough remaining flour to make dough easy to handle. (Dough should remain soft and slightly sticky.)

Turn dough onto well-floured board; knead 5 minutes or about 200 turns. Shape dough immediately (no need to let rise) into desired rolls and coffee cakes. Cover; let rise in warm place until double, about 1 hour. Use for your choice of the recipes on pages 56 to 57.

*If using self-rising flour, omit baking powder and salt.

CINNAMON ROLLS

Store no longer than 9 months. Makes 12 rolls.

- ½ recipe Quick Buttermilk Sweet Dough (above)
- 1 tablespoon butter or margarine, softened
- ¼ cup sugar
- 1 teaspoon cinnamon
  Confectioners' Icing (right), if desired

Roll dough into rectangle, 12×7 inches. Spread butter on dough. Sprinkle sugar and cinnamon on rectangle. Roll up, beginning at long side. Pinch edge of dough into roll to seal securely. Stretch roll to make even; cut into 12 slices.

Place slices slightly apart in greased layer pan, 9×1½ inches. Let rise until double. Heat oven to 375°. Bake 25 minutes. Frost with Confectioners' Icing. (Can be served immediately.)

Cool rolls 1 hour. Freeze uncovered until completely frozen, at least 2 hours. Wrap in heavy-duty aluminum foil, label and return to freezer.

■ **50 minutes before serving, remove Cinnamon Rolls from freezer and place wrapped rolls on oven rack.** Heat in 350° oven until warm, about 45 minutes.

CONFECTIONERS' ICING

Mix ¾ cup confectioners' sugar, 1 tablespoon milk and ½ teaspoon vanilla until smooth.

FROSTED ORANGE ROLLS

Store no longer than 8 months. Makes 12 rolls.

- 3 tablespoons butter or margarine, softened
- 1 tablespoon grated orange peel
- 2 tablespoons orange juice
- 1½ cups confectioners' sugar
- ½ recipe Quick Buttermilk Sweet Dough (left)

Beat butter, orange peel, juice and confectioners' sugar until creamy and smooth. Roll dough into rectangle, 12×7 inches. Spread half the orange filling on dough. Roll up, beginning at long side. Pinch edge of dough into roll to seal securely. Stretch roll to make even; cut into 12 slices.

Place slices slightly apart in greased layer pan, 9×1½ inches. Let rise until double. Heat oven to 375°. Bake 25 to 30 minutes. Spread remaining filling on warm rolls. (Can be served immediately.)

Cool rolls 1 hour. Freeze uncovered until completely frozen, at least 2 hours. Wrap in heavy-duty aluminum foil, label and return to freezer.

■ **50 minutes before serving, remove Frosted Orange Rolls from freezer and place wrapped rolls on oven rack.** Heat in 350° oven until warm, about 45 minutes.

BUTTERSCOTCH-PECAN ROLLS

Store no longer than 8 months. Makes 15 rolls.

½ recipe Quick Buttermilk Sweet Dough
  (page 56)
2 tablespoons butter or margarine,
  softened
¼ cup granulated sugar
2 teaspoons cinnamon
½ cup butter or margarine
½ cup brown sugar (packed)
½ cup pecan halves

Roll dough into rectangle, 15×9 inches. Spread 2 tablespoons butter on dough. Mix granulated sugar and cinnamon; sprinkle on rectangle. Roll up, beginning at long side. Pinch edge of dough into roll to seal securely. Stretch roll to make even. Melt ½ cup butter in baking pan, 13×9×2 inches; sprinkle brown sugar and pecan halves on butter.

Cut roll into 15 slices. Place slices slightly apart in baking pan. Let rise until double. Heat oven to 375°. Bake 25 to 30 minutes. Immediately invert pan onto large tray. Let pan remain a minute so butterscotch drizzles down on rolls. (Can be served immediately.)

Cool rolls 1 hour. Freeze uncovered until completely frozen, at least 2 hours. Wrap in heavy-duty aluminum foil, label and return to freezer.

■ **30 minutes before serving, remove Butterscotch-Pecan Rolls from freezer and place wrapped rolls on oven rack.** Heat in 350° oven until warm, about 25 minutes.

FROSTED CHOCOLATE ROLLS

Store no longer than 9 months. Makes 12 rolls.

3 tablespoons cocoa
3 tablespoons butter or margarine,
  softened
2 tablespoons milk
1½ cups confectioners' sugar
½ recipe Quick Buttermilk Sweet Dough
  (page 56)

Beat cocoa, butter, milk and confectioners' sugar until creamy and smooth. Roll dough into rectangle, 12×7 inches. Spread half the chocolate filling on dough. Roll up, beginning at long side. Pinch edge of dough into roll to seal securely. Stretch roll to make even; cut into 12 slices.

Place slices slightly apart in greased layer pan, 9×1½ inches. Let rise until double. Heat oven to 375°. Bake 25 to 30 minutes. Spread remaining filling on warm rolls. (Can be served immediately.)

Cool rolls 1 hour. Freeze uncovered until completely frozen, at least 2 hours. Wrap in heavy-duty aluminum foil, label and return to freezer.

■ **50 minutes before serving, remove Frosted Chocolate Rolls from freezer and place wrapped rolls on oven rack.** Heat in 350° oven until warm, about 45 minutes.

HUNGARIAN COFFEE CAKE

Store no longer than 8 months. Makes 1 coffee cake.

Quick Buttermilk Sweet Dough (page 56)
¾ cup sugar
1 teaspoon cinnamon
½ cup finely chopped nuts
½ cup butter or margarine, melted

Shape 1½-inch pieces of dough into balls. Mix sugar, cinnamon and nuts. Dip balls in butter, then in sugar mixture. Place a single layer of balls so they just touch in well-greased 10-inch tube pan. (If pan has removable bottom, line with aluminum foil.) Top with another layer of balls. Let rise until double.

Heat oven to 375°. Bake 1 hour. (If coffee cake browns too quickly, cover with aluminum foil.) Loosen from pan. Invert pan onto serving plate so butter-sugar mixture can drizzle down over cake. (To serve immediately, break coffee cake apart with 2 forks.)

Cool 1 hour. Wrap in heavy-duty aluminum foil, label and freeze.

■ **8 to 12 hours before serving, remove Hungarian Coffee Cake from freezer; thaw in wrapper at room temperature.** Thirty-five minutes before serving, heat oven to 350°. Heat wrapped coffee cake on oven rack until warm, about 30 minutes.

FLAKY FILLED CRESCENTS

Store no longer than 12 months. Makes 40 crescents.

Dough

   1 **package active dry yeast**
   ½ **cup warm water (105 to 115°)**
   1 **cup lukewarm milk (scalded then**
      cooled)
   2 **tablespoons shortening**
   2 **tablespoons sugar**
   1 **teaspoon salt**
   1 **teaspoon grated lemon peel**
   2 **eggs**
4½ to 5 **cups all-purpose flour***

Filling

   1 **cup butter or margarine, softened**
     About ½ cup orange marmalade

Sugar Glaze

   3 **tablespoons sugar**
   1 **tablespoon water**

Dissolve yeast in ½ cup warm water in large bowl. Mix in milk, shortening, 2 tablespoons sugar, the salt, lemon peel, eggs and 2½ cups of the flour; beat until smooth. Stir in enough remaining flour to make dough easy to handle.

Turn dough onto lightly floured board; knead until smooth and elastic, about 5 minutes. Place in greased bowl; turn greased side up. Cover; let rise in warm place until double. Punch down dough. Cover; chill 1 hour.

Punch down dough again. Turn dough onto lightly floured board; roll into rectangle, 20×10 inches. Spread ⅓ cup butter on rectangle. Fold rectangle into 3 parts, one on top of the other, making 3 layers; roll out. Repeat 2 times, spreading ⅓ cup butter on rectangle each time. Divide dough in half; chill at least 1 hour. (Chill no longer than 18 hours.)

Shape half the dough at a time (keep other half chilled). Roll each half into rectangle, 20×10 inches. Cut lengthwise in half, then crosswise 5 times. Cut each square diagonally into 2 triangles. Spread ½ teaspoon marmalade on each triangle. Roll up, beginning at long side. Place rolls with points underneath on ungreased baking sheet; curve ends to form crescents. Chill 30 minutes.

Heat oven to 425°. Mix 3 tablespoons sugar and 1 tablespoon water; brush rolls with sugar-water mixture. Bake until golden brown and crisp, about 15 minutes. (Can be served immediately.) Cool; divide crescents among 4 pieces heavy-duty aluminum foil. Wrap, label and freeze.

■ **25 minutes before serving, heat oven to 350°.** Remove 1 package Flaky Filled Crescents from freezer; heat wrapped rolls on oven rack until warm, about 20 minutes.

*If using self-rising flour, omit salt.

Flavors for Frozen Rolls and Bread

Buttered rye bread is especially delicious when sprinkled with sesame seed. Cut slices crosswise into 4 strips. Broil 6 inches from heat until seeds are brown, 1½ to 2 minutes.

Brush brown-and-serve rolls with melted butter or margarine, then sprinkle with one of these: snipped chives; parsley flakes; dill weed; garlic salt; onion salt. Bake at 400° until golden brown, 10 to 12 minutes.

Spread cut surfaces of English muffins with soft butter or margarine, then sprinkle with garlic salt and grated Parmesan cheese. Broil 4 inches from heat until golden brown, 5 to 6 minutes.

Cut nut bread into ½-inch slices. Spread with soft butter or margarine. Bake at 400° until light brown, 6 to 8 minutes.

Brush brown-and-serve rolls with melted butter or margarine. Bake at 400° until golden brown, 10 to 12 minutes. Frost hot rolls with confectioners' sugar icing and serve warm.

HONEY HORNS

Store no longer than 9 months. Makes 3 dozen rolls.

Dough
  2 packages active dry yeast
  ½ cup warm water (105 to 115°)
  ½ cup lukewarm milk (scalded then
    cooled)
  ½ cup sugar
  1 teaspoon salt
  2 eggs
  ½ cup shortening or butter or
    margarine, softened
  3¾ to 4½ cups all-purpose flour*

Topping
  ¼ cup honey
  ⅓ cup sugar
  ¼ cup finely chopped nuts
  3 tablespoons butter or margarine
  ⅛ teaspoon cinnamon

Filling
  ½ cup sugar
  2 teaspoons cinnamon
  ¼ cup butter or margarine, melted

Dissolve yeast in warm water in large bowl. Mix in milk, ½ cup sugar, the salt, eggs, shortening and 2½ cups of the flour; beat until smooth. Stir in enough remaining flour to make dough easy to handle.

Turn dough onto lightly floured board; knead until smooth and elastic, about 5 minutes. Place in greased bowl; turn greased side up. Cover; let rise in warm place until double, about 1½ hours.

Heat Topping ingredients, stirring frequently, until mixture boils. Cool slightly. Mix ½ cup sugar and 2 teaspoons cinnamon; set aside. Punch down dough. Turn dough onto floured board; divide into 3 parts. Roll each part into 10-inch circle. Spread about 1 tablespoon of the melted butter and 2 tablespoons Topping on each circle; sprinkle about 3 tablespoons sugar-cinnamon mixture on top. Cut each circle into 12 wedges. Roll up, beginning at rounded edges. Place rolls with points underneath in spoke fashion in 3 greased layer pans, 8 or 9×1½ inches; curve ends to form crescents. Let rise in warm place until double, about 45 minutes.

Heat oven to 400°. Bake 10 minutes; remove rolls from oven and spread remaining Topping on top. Bake until golden brown, about 10 minutes. Immediately remove from pans; cool. Wrap in heavy-duty foil, label and freeze.

■ **35 minutes before serving, remove Honey Horns from freezer and place wrapped rolls on oven rack.** Heat in 350° oven until warm, about 30 minutes.

*If using self-rising flour, omit salt.

Break individual Honey Horns from the ring.

Each recipe makes 3 pans of rolls.

BROWN 'N SERVE ROLLS

Store no longer than 2 months. Makes 2 dozen rolls.

 1 package active dry yeast
¾ cup warm water (105 to 115°)
¾ cup lukewarm milk (scalded
   then cooled)
¼ cup sugar
2¼ teaspoons salt
¼ cup shortening
4½ cups all-purpose flour*

Dissolve yeast in warm water in large bowl. Mix in milk, sugar, salt, shortening and 2½ cups of the flour; beat until smooth. Stir in enough remaining flour to make dough easy to handle. Turn dough onto lightly floured board; knead until smooth and elastic, about 5 minutes. Place in greased bowl; turn greased side up. Cover; let rise in warm place until double, about 1½ hours.

Punch down dough; turn onto lightly floured board and divide into 24 pieces. Shape each piece into smooth ball. Place each ball in a greased muffin cup or place balls about 3 inches apart on greased baking sheet. Cover; let rise until almost double, about 45 minutes. Heat oven to 275°. Bake 20 to 30 minutes (do not allow rolls to brown). Remove from pans and cool at room temperature. Wrap, label and freeze.

■ **15 minutes before serving, heat oven to 400°.** Remove rolls from freezer and unwrap; place on ungreased baking sheet. Bake until brown and hot, 7 to 10 minutes.

Note: After rolls are cool, they may be wrapped and refrigerated. Store no longer than 8 days.

*If using self-rising flour, omit salt.

FREEZER FRENCH TOAST

Store no longer than 1 month. Makes enough for 8 servings.

 5 eggs
1¼ cups milk
1½ tablespoons sugar
½ teaspoon salt
16 slices white bread

Heat oven to 500°. Beat eggs, milk, sugar and salt until mixed. Dip bread slices in egg mixture; arrange on buttered baking sheets. Bake until underside is golden brown, about 5 minutes. Turn slices; bake until golden brown, about 2 minutes. (Can be served immediately.) Cool on wire racks. Place in a single layer on baking sheets. Freeze until hard, about 2 hours. Wrap, label and return to freezer.

■ **15 minutes before serving, heat oven to 375°.** Remove Freezer French Toast from freezer and unwrap; place on ungreased baking sheets. Heat until hot, 8 to 10 minutes. Or, small quantities can be heated in a toaster.

Freezer French Toast

Desserts

STRAWBERRY-RHUBARB COBBLER

Store no longer than 2 months. Makes enough for 9 servings.

Base

1 cup all-purpose flour*
¼ cup sugar
⅛ teaspoon baking powder
½ teaspoon salt
⅓ cup butter or margarine

Filling

2 cups fresh strawberries, halved
1 cup thinly sliced rhubarb
¾ cup sugar
3 tablespoons cornstarch
1 teaspoon cinnamon
1 tablespoon lemon juice
1 tablespoon butter or margarine

Heat oven to 400°. Grease baking pan, 9×9×2 inches. Mix flour, ¼ cup sugar, the baking powder and salt. Cut in ⅓ cup butter until mixture is crumbly; press evenly in bottom of pan. Bake until light brown, 8 to 10 minutes. Cool.

Arrange fruit on base. Mix ¾ cup sugar, the cornstarch and cinnamon. Sprinkle sugar mixture and lemon juice on fruit; dot with 1 tablespoon butter. Wrap, label and freeze.

■ **1 hour 15 minutes before serving, remove Strawberry-Rhubarb Cobbler from freezer and unwrap.** Bake uncovered in 400° oven until hot and bubbly throughout, about 40 minutes. Remove from oven; spoon Topping (below) on cobbler. Cool 30 minutes.

TOPPING

Mix 1 tablespoon sugar, 1 teaspoon vanilla and 1 cup dairy sour cream.

*If using self-rising flour, omit baking powder and salt.

FRUIT DESSERT FREEZE

Store no longer than 1 month. Makes enough for 12 servings.

1 package (15.4 ounces) creamy white frosting mix
2 cups whipping cream
1 large banana
1 can (8¼ ounces) crushed pineapple, drained
1 can (11 ounces) mandarin orange segments, drained
⅓ cup halved maraschino cherries, drained
⅓ cup cut-up dates
⅓ cup chopped pecans, if desired
2 tablespoons lemon juice

Chill frosting mix (dry) and whipping cream covered in small mixer bowl at least 1 hour. Beat until soft peaks form. Slice banana into frosting mixture; fold in remaining ingredients. Pour mixture into baking pan, 9×9×2 inches, or 2 refrigerator trays. Wrap, label and freeze. Freeze until firm, at least 4 hours. Remove from freezer 5 minutes before cutting.

ORANGE CHEESECAKE

Store no longer than 1 month. Makes enough for 9 to 12 servings.

Base

1½ cups graham cracker crumbs (about 18 crackers)
3 tablespoons sugar
¼ cup butter or margarine, melted

Topping

1 can (16.5 ounces) vanilla frosting
1 cup creamed cottage cheese
1 cup dairy sour cream
1 can (6 ounces) frozen orange juice concentrate, partially thawed

Mix graham cracker crumbs, sugar and butter. Reserve 3 tablespoons of the crumb mixture; press remaining mixture evenly in bottom of ungreased baking pan, 9×9×2 inches.

Beat Topping ingredients in large mixer bowl until mixed, about 2 minutes; pour on crust. Sprinkle reserved crumbs on top. Wrap, label and freeze. Freeze at least 8 hours.

STRAWBERRY ICE

Store no longer than 1 month. Makes enough for 8 to 10 servings.

1 package (3 ounces) strawberry-
  flavored gelatin
½ cup sugar
1½ cups boiling water
2 packages (10 ounces each) frozen sliced
  strawberries, partially thawed
¼ cup orange juice
¼ cup lemon juice

Stir gelatin and sugar in large bowl. Pour boiling water on gelatin mixture; stir until gelatin is dissolved. Stir in remaining ingredients.

Pour into 2 refrigerator trays. Freeze until mushy, about 1 hour. Remove from trays; beat until smooth. Return to trays. Wrap, label and freeze. Freeze until firm, at least 1 hour.

CHERRIES SUPREME

Store no longer than 1 month. Makes enough for 9 servings.

½ cup butter or margarine, softened
¼ cup brown sugar (packed)
1 cup all-purpose flour
½ cup chopped pecans
½ gallon vanilla ice cream, softened

Heat oven to 400°. Mix butter, sugar, flour and pecans; press evenly in bottom of ungreased baking pan, 9×9×2 inches. Bake until light brown, about 12 minutes. Crumble with spoon. Cool.

Reserve 1 cup of the crumbs; press remaining crumbs evenly in bottom of pan. Pack ice cream on crumbs. Sprinkle reserved crumbs on top. Wrap, label and freeze. Freeze until firm, at least 4 hours.

■ **Just before serving, heat 1 can (21 ounces) cherry pie filling, stirring occasionally.** Stir in 2 tablespoons rum flavoring if desired. Remove Cherries Supreme from freezer and unwrap. Cut into 3-inch squares. Spoon topping on each serving.

FROZEN MOLD GRENADINE

Store no longer than 4 weeks. Makes enough for 6 to 8 servings.

Sauce
¼ cup grenadine syrup
1 tablespoon orange-flavored liqueur

Ice-cream Mold
1 pint vanilla ice cream, slightly softened
¼ cup orange-flavored liqueur
¾ cup flaked coconut
2 tablespoons diced roasted almonds
2 teaspoons confectioners' sugar
½ cup chilled whipping cream

Mix grenadine syrup and 1 tablespoon liqueur; pour into 5-cup mold. Mix ice cream, ¼ cup liqueur, the coconut, almonds and sugar. Beat cream in chilled bowl until stiff. Fold whipped cream into ice-cream mixture; pour into mold. Cover, label and freeze.

■ **Remove Frozen Mold Grenadine from freezer; invert onto serving plate with a rim.** Dip a cloth in hot water; wring out and place over mold just a few minutes. Lift off mold. Spoon grenadine sauce on each serving.

Delightful Ice-cream Desserts

□ Warm 1 cup prepared mincemeat in ½ cup cranberry cocktail. Serve warm over vanilla ice cream.

□ Warm ½ cup honey with ½ cup apricot brandy. (This is especially delicious with coffee ice cream.)

□ Add 1 cup maple-flavored syrup to ½ cup whole cranberry sauce. Stir and warm; pour over ice cream.

□ Three ways to vary flavor: Into 1 quart vanilla ice cream, stir 2 teaspoons cinnamon; or ⅓ cup Nesselrode; or 1 tablespoon powdered instant coffee.

CRÊPES

Store no longer than 3 months. Makes 12 crêpes.

1½ cups all-purpose flour*
 1 tablespoon sugar
 ½ teaspoon baking powder
 ½ teaspoon salt
 2 cups milk
 2 eggs
 ½ teaspoon vanilla
 2 tablespoons butter or margarine, melted

Measure flour, sugar, baking powder and salt into bowl. Stir in remaining ingredients. Beat with rotary beater until smooth.

For each crêpe, lightly butter 8-inch skillet; heat over medium heat until butter is bubbly. Pour scant ¼ cup of the batter into skillet; rotate pan immediately until batter covers bottom. Cook until light brown; turn crêpe and brown on other side. Stack crêpes as you remove them from skillet. (To serve immediately, see below.) Cool; keep crêpes covered to prevent drying out. Make 2 stacks of 6 crêpes each, with waxed paper between crêpes. Wrap, label and freeze each stack.

■ **3 hours 10 minutes before serving, remove Crêpes from freezer. Have ready:** applesauce, currant jelly or raspberry jam. Thaw crêpes in wrapper at room temperature about 3 hours.

Heat oven to 325°. Spread applesauce, currant jelly or raspberry jam thinly on crêpes; roll up. Place in ungreased baking dish, 11½×7½×1½ inches. Heat uncovered 10 minutes. Sprinkle sugar on top.

To Serve Immediately: Spread applesauce, currant jelly or raspberry jam thinly on crêpes; roll up. Sprinkle sugar on top.

*If using self-rising flour, omit baking powder and salt.

CRÊPES SUZETTE

Store no longer than 3 months. Makes enough for 6 servings.

 Crêpes (left)
⅔ cup butter or margarine
¾ teaspoon grated orange peel
⅔ cup orange juice
¼ cup sugar

Prepare Crêpes. Stack so first baked side is down when removing from skillet. Cool; keep crêpes covered to prevent drying out.

Heat butter, orange peel, juice and sugar in 10-inch ovenproof skillet, stirring occasionally, until mixture boils. Boil and stir 1 minute. (To serve immediately, see below.) Remove from heat. To assemble Crêpes Suzette, fold crêpes in half, then in half again; place in hot orange sauce and turn once. Arrange crêpes around edge of skillet. Cool. Cover, label and freeze.

■ **65 minutes before serving, heat oven to 350°.**
Have ready: ⅓ cup brandy; ⅓ cup orange-flavored liqueur.

Remove Crêpes Suzette from freezer. Cover; bake 40 minutes. Uncover; bake until hot and bubbly, about 20 minutes.

Heat brandy and orange-flavored liqueur in small saucepan, but do not boil. Pour warm brandy mixture into center of skillet and ignite. Spoon flaming sauce on crêpes. Place 2 crêpes on each dessert plate; spoon sauce on crêpes.

To Serve Immediately: Have ready: ⅓ cup brandy; ⅓ cup orange-flavored liqueur.

Reduce heat; simmer uncovered. Heat brandy and orange-flavored liqueur in small saucepan, but do not boil. To assemble Crêpes Suzette, fold crêpes in half, then in half again; place in hot orange sauce and turn once. Arrange crêpes around edge of skillet. Pour warm brandy mixture into center of skillet and ignite. Spoon flaming sauce on crêpes. Place 2 crêpes on each dessert plate; spoon sauce on crêpes.

Shape meringue into 6-inch circles on a baking sheet covered with brown paper. If you first draw circles on the paper, it's easy to make the meringue layers uniform.

Frozen Torte

FROZEN TORTE

Store no longer than 1 month. Makes enough for 9 servings.

   4 egg whites
   ½ teaspoon cream of tartar
   1 cup sugar
   Mocha Filling (page 65)

Heat oven to 275°. Cover 2 baking sheets with brown paper. Beat egg whites and cream of tartar in large mixer bowl until foamy. Beat in sugar, 1 tablespoon at a time; beat until stiff and glossy. Do not underbeat.

Divide meringue into 3 parts. Place 1 part on 1 baking sheet; shape into 6-inch circle. Shape two 6-inch circles on second baking sheet. Bake 45 minutes. Turn off oven; leave meringue in oven with door closed 1 hour. Remove meringue from oven; cool away from draft.

Fill layers and frost top of torte with Mocha Filling. Decorate with chocolate curls. Freeze uncovered until filling on top is firm, at least 3 hours. (Can be served immediately. To cut, dip knife in hot water and wipe after cutting each slice.) Wrap, label and return to freezer.

■ **Remove Frozen Torte from freezer and unwrap.** To cut, dip knife in hot water and wipe after cutting each slice.

Note: This dessert mellows if frozen 1 week or longer.

Fill the baked and cooled meringue layers with Mocha Filling, using it to frost the top of the torte as well. Stack and decorate with chocolate curls before placing torte in the freezer.

MOCHA FILLING

2 packages (about 1½ ounces each)
  whipped topping mix
3 tablespoons cocoa
½ cup sugar
2 tablespoons powdered instant coffee

Prepare whipped topping mix as directed on package except—before beating, add cocoa, sugar and instant coffee.

BISCUIT TORTONI

Store no longer than 3 weeks. Makes enough for 8 servings.

⅔ cup cookie crumbs (vanilla
  wafers or macaroons)
¼ cup cut-up candied red cherries
½ cup chopped salted almonds
1 quart vanilla ice cream
  Red and green candied cherries

Line 8 muffin cups with paper baking cups. Mix cookie crumbs, cut-up cherries and almonds. Slightly soften ice cream; fold in crumb mixture. Divide ice-cream mixture among paper-lined muffin cups. Arrange red cherry half and slices of green cherry on each to resemble a flower. Freeze uncovered until firm. Wrap, label and return to freezer.

■ **At serving time, have ready:** 8 clusters seedless green grapes.

Place cups and grape clusters on tiered server.

PUMPKIN COOKIES

Store no longer than 9 months. Makes about 6 dozen cookies.

1½ cups brown sugar (packed)
 ½ cup shortening
 2 eggs
 1 can (16 ounces) pumpkin
2¾ cups all-purpose flour*
 3 teaspoons baking powder
 1 teaspoon cinnamon
 ½ teaspoon salt
 ½ teaspoon nutmeg
 ¼ teaspoon ginger
 1 cup raisins
 1 cup chopped pecans

Heat oven to 400°. Mix brown sugar, shortening, eggs and pumpkin. Stir in remaining ingredients.

Drop dough by teaspoonfuls about 2 inches apart onto ungreased baking sheet. Bake until light brown, 12 to 15 minutes. Remove immediately from baking sheet; cool. (Can be served immediately.) Wrap, label and freeze.

■ **20 minutes before serving, remove Pumpkin Cookies from freezer and unwrap.** Place on serving plate; thaw uncovered at room temperature.

*If using self-rising flour, omit baking powder and salt.

CHOCOLATE CHIP COOKIES

Store no longer than 6 months. Makes about 7 dozen cookies.

 ⅔ cup shortening
 ⅔ cup butter or margarine, softened
 1 cup granulated sugar
 1 cup brown sugar (packed)
 2 eggs
 2 teaspoons vanilla
 3 cups all-purpose flour*
 1 teaspoon soda
 1 teaspoon salt
 1 cup chopped nuts
 2 packages (6 ounces each) semisweet
     chocolate pieces

Heat oven to 375°. Mix shortening, butter, sugars, eggs and vanilla. Stir in the remaining ingredients.

Drop dough by rounded teaspoonfuls 2 inches apart onto ungreased baking sheet. Bake until light brown, 8 to 10 minutes. Cool slightly; remove from baking sheet. (Can be served immediately.) Wrap, label and freeze.

■ **20 minutes before serving, remove Chocolate Chip Cookies from freezer and unwrap.** Place on serving plate; thaw uncovered at room temperature.

*If using self-rising flour, omit soda and salt.

Top row, left to right: Quick Orange Cookies (page 67), Chocolate Oatmeal Cookies (page 68) and Pumpkin Cookies. Bottom row, left to right: Double Chocolate Drops (page 67), Soft Molasses Cookies (page 67) and Chocolate Chip Cookies.

DOUBLE CHOCOLATE DROPS

Store no longer than 2 months. Makes about 6 dozen cookies.

- ½ **cup butter or margarine, softened**
- 1 **cup sugar**
- 1 **egg**
- 2 **ounces melted unsweetened chocolate (cool)**
- ⅓ **cup buttermilk**
- 1 **teaspoon vanilla**
- 1¾ **cups all-purpose flour***
- ½ **teaspoon soda**
- ½ **teaspoon salt**
- 1 **cup chopped nuts**
- 1 **package (6 ounces) semisweet chocolate pieces**
  Chocolate Icing or Browned Butter Icing (below)

Mix butter, sugar, egg, chocolate, buttermilk and vanilla. Stir in flour, soda, salt, nuts and chocolate pieces. Cover; chill 1 hour.

Heat oven to 400°. Drop dough by rounded teaspoonfuls 2 inches apart onto ungreased baking sheet. Bake until almost no imprint remains when touched with finger, 8 to 10 minutes. Remove immediately from baking sheet; cool. Frost cookies. (Can be served immediately.) Wrap, label and freeze.

■ **20 minutes before serving, remove Double Chocolate Drops from freezer and unwrap.** Place on serving plate; thaw uncovered at room temperature.

CHOCOLATE ICING

Melt 2 ounces unsweetened chocolate and 2 tablespoons butter or margarine over low heat. Remove from heat; mix in 2 cups confectioners' sugar and about 3 tablespoons water until spreading consistency.

BROWNED BUTTER ICING

Heat ¼ cup butter or margarine over low heat until golden brown. Remove from heat; mix in 2 cups confectioners' sugar, 1 teaspoon vanilla and about 2 tablespoons light cream until spreading consistency.

*If using self-rising flour, omit soda and salt. If using quick-mixing flour, increase buttermilk to ½ cup.

SOFT MOLASSES COOKIES

Store no longer than 2 months. Makes about 6 dozen cookies.

- 1 **cup shortening**
- 1 **cup sugar**
- 1 **egg**
- ½ **cup molasses**
- ¾ **cup dairy sour cream**
- 3 **cups all-purpose flour***
- 2 **teaspoons soda**
- 1 **teaspoon salt**
- 1 **teaspoon ginger**
- 1 **teaspoon cinnamon**

Heat oven to 375°. Mix shortening, sugar, egg and molasses. Stir in remaining ingredients.

Drop dough by teaspoonfuls about 2 inches apart onto ungreased baking sheet. Bake about 8 minutes. Cool slightly; remove from baking sheet. While warm, cookies can be frosted with canned vanilla frosting; cool. (Can be served immediately.) Wrap, label and freeze.

■ **20 minutes before serving, remove Soft Molasses Cookies from freezer and unwrap.** Place on serving plate; thaw uncovered at room temperature.

*If using self-rising flour, omit soda and salt.

QUICK DATE DROPS

Store no longer than 2 months. Makes about 2½ dozen cookies.

- 1 **package (14 ounces) date bar mix**
- ¼ **cup hot water**
- 1 **egg**

Heat oven to 400°. Mix Date Mix and hot water. Mix in crumb mix and egg. Drop by rounded teaspoonfuls about 2 inches apart onto lightly greased baking sheet. Bake 8 to 10 minutes. Remove immediately from baking sheet; cool. (Can be served immediately.) Wrap, label and freeze.

■ **20 minutes before serving, remove Quick Date Drops from freezer and unwrap.** Place on serving plate; thaw uncovered at room temperature.

CHOCOLATE OATMEAL COOKIES

Store no longer than 2 months. Makes about 6 dozen cookies.

½ cup shortening
½ cup butter or margarine, softened
1½ cups sugar
1 egg
¼ cup water
1 teaspoon vanilla
1 cup all-purpose flour*
3 cups quick-cooking oats
⅓ cup cocoa
½ teaspoon soda
½ teaspoon salt
1 package (6 ounces) semisweet chocolate
pieces

Heat oven to 350°. Mix shortening, butter, sugar, egg, water and vanilla. Stir in remaining ingredients.

Drop dough by rounded teaspoonfuls 1 inch apart onto ungreased baking sheet. Bake until almost no imprint remains when touched with finger, 10 to 12 minutes. Remove immediately from baking sheet; cool. (Can be served immediately.) Wrap, label and freeze.

■ **20 minutes before serving, remove Chocolate Oatmeal Cookies from freezer and unwrap.** Place on serving plate; thaw uncovered at room temperature.

*If using self-rising flour, omit soda and salt.

FRUITED DROPS

Store no longer than 9 months. Makes about 7½ dozen cookies.

1½ cups raisins
1 cup water
¾ cup shortening
1½ cups sugar
2 eggs
3 cups all-purpose flour*
1½ teaspoons salt
1 teaspoon cinnamon
¾ teaspoon baking powder
¾ teaspoon soda
¼ teaspoon allspice
¼ teaspoon nutmeg
¾ cup chopped nuts
½ cup chopped maraschino cherries

Heat oven to 400°. Heat raisins and water, stirring occasionally, until water boils. Boil 5 minutes. Drain; reserve ⅓ cup liquid. Mix shortening, sugar, eggs and reserved liquid. Stir in remaining ingredients, including raisins.

Drop dough by rounded teaspoonfuls 2 inches apart onto ungreased baking sheet. Bake until light brown, 8 to 10 minutes. Remove immediately from baking sheet; cool. (Can be served immediately.) Wrap, label and freeze.

■ **20 minutes before serving, remove Fruited Drops from freezer and unwrap.** Place on serving plate; thaw uncovered at room temperature.

*If using self-rising flour, omit salt, baking powder and soda.

PEANUT BUTTER CHIPPERS

Store no longer than 9 months. Makes about 4 dozen cookies.

- **1 can (14 ounces) sweetened condensed milk**
- **½ cup creamy peanut butter**
- **2 cups crushed whole wheat flake cereal**
- **1 package (6 ounces) semisweet chocolate pieces**

Heat oven to 350°. Mix milk and peanut butter until smooth. Stir in cereal and chocolate pieces.

Drop dough by rounded teaspoonfuls about 2 inches apart onto ungreased baking sheet. Bake until light brown, 10 to 12 minutes. Remove immediately from baking sheet; cool. (Can be served immediately.) Wrap, label and freeze.

■ **20 minutes before serving, remove Peanut Butter Chippers from freezer and unwrap.** Place on serving plate; thaw uncovered at room temperature.

CHOCOLATE ALMOND CHIPS

Store no longer than 2 months. Makes about 4 dozen cookies.

- **1 cup butter or margarine, softened**
- **1 cup sugar**
- **1 egg**
- **½ teaspoon almond extract**
- **½ cup roasted diced almonds**
- **2 cups all-purpose flour**
- **2 squares (2 ounces) semisweet cooking chocolate, melted**

Heat oven to 325°. Grease baking pan, 13×9×2 inches. Mix all ingredients except chocolate; beat on lowest speed of mixer or by hand until dough forms. Spread in pan.

Bake until golden brown, 35 to 40 minutes. Drizzle with chocolate. Cool slightly; cut into 1-inch squares. Cool. (Can be served immediately.) Wrap, label and freeze.

■ **20 minutes before serving, remove Chocolate Almond Chips from freezer and unwrap.** Thaw uncovered at room temperature.

BROWNIES

Store frosted brownies no longer than 2 months, unfrosted brownies no longer than 3 months. Makes 32 cookies.

- **4 ounces unsweetened chocolate**
- **⅔ cup shortening**
- **2 cups sugar**
- **4 eggs**
- **1 teaspoon vanilla**
- **1¼ cups all-purpose flour***
- **1 teaspoon baking powder**
- **1 teaspoon salt**
- **1 cup chopped nuts**

Heat oven to 350°. Grease baking pan, 13×9×2 inches. Melt chocolate and shortening in large saucepan over low heat. Remove from heat. Mix in sugar, eggs and vanilla. Stir in remaining ingredients. Spread in pan.

Bake until brownies start to pull away from sides of pan, about 30 minutes. Do not overbake. Cool slightly. If desired, spread your favorite frosting on slightly cooled brownies. Cut into bars, about 2×1½ inches. Cool completely or until frosting is firm. (Can be served immediately.) Wrap, label and freeze.

■ **30 minutes before serving, remove Brownies from freezer and unwrap.** Place on serving plate; thaw uncovered at room temperature.

*If using self-rising flour, omit baking powder and salt.

MIX-QUICK BROWNIES

Store frosted brownies no longer than 2 months, unfrosted brownies no longer than 3 months. Makes 3 or 4 dozen cookies.

Bake fudgy or fudge cake brownies as directed on fudge brownie mix or fudge brownie mix supreme package. Cool. If desired, spread your favorite frosting on cooled brownies. When frosting is firm, cut into 1½-inch squares. Wrap, label and freeze.

■ **30 minutes before serving, remove Mix-Quick Brownies from freezer and unwrap.** Place on serving plate; thaw uncovered at room temperature.

SPICY TOFFEE TRIANGLES

Store no longer than 4 months. Makes 4 dozen cookies.

1 cup butter or margarine, softened
1 cup brown sugar (packed)
1 egg, separated
1 teaspoon vanilla
2 cups all-purpose flour*
¼ teaspoon salt
1 teaspoon cinnamon
1 cup chopped walnuts

Heat oven to 275°. Mix butter, sugar, egg yolk and vanilla. Stir in flour, salt and cinnamon. Spread evenly in ungreased jelly roll pan, 15½×10½×1 inch. Brush dough with unbeaten egg white. Sprinkle walnuts on top; press into dough. Bake 1 hour. While warm, cut into 2½-inch squares, then cut each square diagonally in half. Cool. (Can be served immediately.) Wrap, label and freeze.

■ **20 minutes before serving, remove Spicy Toffee Triangles from freezer and unwrap.** Place on serving plate; thaw uncovered at room temperature.

VARIATIONS

Hawaiian Spice Triangles: Substitute 1 teaspoon ginger for the cinnamon and ¼ cup chopped salted macadamia nuts and ¼ cup flaked coconut for the 1 cup chopped walnuts.

Greek Triangles: Substitute 1 teaspoon ground cardamom for the cinnamon and 1 can (5 ounces) diced roasted almonds for the 1 cup chopped walnuts.

Orange-Chocolate Triangles: Substitute ½ teaspoon cloves and 1 tablespoon grated orange peel for the cinnamon and 2 packages (6 ounces each) semisweet chocolate pieces for the 1 cup chopped walnuts.

*If using self-rising flour, omit salt.

Top row, left to right: Brownies (page 69), Apricot-Cherry Bars (page 71) and Hawaiian Spice Triangles. Bottom row, left to right: Spicy Toffee Triangles, Mix-quick Date Bars (page 71), Mixed Nut Bars (page 71) and Orange-Chocolate Triangles.

MIXED NUT BARS

Store no longer than 6 months. Refrigerate no longer than 2 weeks. Makes 4 dozen cookies.

Base
1 cup butter or margarine, softened
1 cup brown sugar (packed)
1 egg yolk
1 teaspoon vanilla
2 cups all-purpose flour*
¼ teaspoon salt

Topping
1 package (6 ounces) butterscotch pieces
½ cup light corn syrup
2 tablespoons butter or margarine
1 tablespoon water
1 can (13 ounces) salted mixed nuts

Heat oven to 350°. Mix 1 cup butter, the sugar, egg yolk and vanilla. Stir in flour and salt. Press evenly in bottom of ungreased baking pan, 13×9×2 inches. Bake until light brown, about 25 minutes. Cool.

Mix butterscotch pieces, corn syrup, 2 tablespoons butter and the water in saucepan. Cook over medium heat, stirring occasionally, until butterscotch pieces are melted; cool.

Spread butterscotch mixture on cooled base. Sprinkle nuts on top; gently press into topping. Chill until topping is firm, about 1 hour. Cut into 1½-inch squares. (Can be served immediately.) Wrap, label and freeze or cover and refrigerate.

■ **30 minutes before serving, remove Mixed Nut Bars from freezer and unwrap.** Place on serving plate; thaw uncovered at room temperature.

*Do not use self-rising flour in this recipe.

MIX-QUICK DATE BARS

Store no longer than 3 months. Makes 32 cookies.

Bake 1 package (14 ounces) date bar mix as directed; cool. Cut into bars, 2×1 inch. Wrap, label and freeze.

■ **30 minutes before serving, remove Mix-Quick Date Bars from freezer and unwrap.** Place on serving plate; thaw uncovered at room temperature.

APRICOT-CHERRY BARS

Store no longer than 3 months. Makes 2½ dozen cookies.

¼ cup water
2 eggs
¼ cup butter or margarine, softened
¼ cup brown sugar (packed)
1 package (18.5 ounces) yellow cake mix with pudding
½ cup drained chopped maraschino cherries
1 cup cut-up dried apricots
Confectioners' sugar

Heat oven to 375°. Grease and flour jelly roll pan, 15½×10½×1 inch. Beat water, eggs, butter, brown sugar and half the cake mix (dry) until smooth. Stir in remaining cake mix, the cherries and apricots.

Spread evenly in pan. Bake 20 to 25 minutes. Cool thoroughly. Sprinkle confectioners' sugar on top. Cut into bars, 3×1½ inches. (Can be served immediately.) Wrap, label and freeze.

■ **30 minutes before serving, remove Apricot-Cherry Bars from freezer and unwrap.** Place on serving plate; thaw uncovered at room temperature.

RUSSIAN TEACAKES

Store no longer than 6 months. Makes about 4 dozen cookies.

1 cup butter or margarine, softened
½ cup confectioners' sugar
1 teaspoon vanilla
2¼ cups all-purpose flour*
¼ teaspoon salt
¾ cup finely chopped nuts
Confectioners' sugar

Heat oven to 400°. Mix butter, ½ cup confectioners' sugar and the vanilla. Work in flour, salt and nuts until dough holds together. Shape dough into 1-inch balls; place on ungreased baking sheet.

Bake until set but not brown, 10 to 12 minutes. While warm, roll in confectioners' sugar. Cool. Roll in sugar again. Wrap, label and freeze.

■ **20 minutes before serving, remove Russian Teacakes from freezer and unwrap.** Place on serving plate; thaw uncovered at room temperature.

*Do not use self-rising flour in this recipe.

BRAZILIAN COFFEE COOKIES

Store no longer than 6 months. Makes about 4 dozen cookies.

⅓ cup shortening
½ cup brown sugar (packed)
½ cup granulated sugar
 1 egg
1½ teaspoons vanilla
 1 tablespoon milk
 2 cups all-purpose flour*
½ teaspoon salt
¼ teaspoon soda
¼ teaspoon baking powder
 2 tablespoons powdered instant coffee

Heat oven to 400°. Mix shortening, sugars, egg, vanilla and milk. Stir in remaining ingredients. Shape dough into 1-inch balls. (If dough is too soft, chill until easy to handle.) Place about 2 inches apart on ungreased baking sheet. Flatten balls with greased fork dipped in sugar (press only in one direction) or with greased bottom of glass dipped in sugar, until ⅛ inch thick. Bake until light brown, 8 to 10 minutes. Cool. (Can be served immediately.) Wrap, label and freeze.

■ **20 minutes before serving, remove Brazilian Coffee Cookies from freezer and unwrap.** Place on serving plate; thaw uncovered at room temperature.

*If using self-rising flour, omit salt, soda and baking powder.

Storehouse of Cookies

Thoroughly cool baked cookies before freezing them in an airtight container or freezer wrap. Unfrosted cookies store better than frosted cookies. Baked cookies thaw out quickly.

To store rolls of cookie dough, freezer-wrap and freeze. Frozen dough keeps 5 to 6 months. To bake: Slice the frozen dough with a sharp knife.

PECAN CRESCENTS

Store no longer than 3 months. Makes about 3 dozen cookies.

1 packet or 2 sticks pie crust mix
1 cup confectioners' sugar
1 cup ground or very finely chopped pecans
1 egg
1 teaspoon vanilla
  Confectioners' sugar

Heat oven to 350°. Mix pie crust mix (dry), 1 cup confectioners' sugar and the pecans. Stir in egg and vanilla; gather dough into ball. Turn dough onto lightly floured cloth-covered board; knead until smooth. Shape into ¾-inch balls. Shape balls into crescents on ungreased baking sheet. Bake until light brown, 10 to 15 minutes. While warm, roll in confectioners' sugar. Cool. Roll in sugar again. Wrap, label and freeze.

■ **20 minutes before serving, remove Pecan Crescents from freezer and unwrap.** Place on serving plate; thaw uncovered at room temperature.

CHINESE ALMOND COOKIES

Store no longer than 3 months. Makes about 3 dozen.

1 packet or 2 sticks pie crust mix
1 cup confectioners' sugar
1 cup ground or very finely chopped almonds
1 egg
3 teaspoons almond extract
  Granulated sugar
36 blanched whole almonds

Heat oven to 400°. Mix pie crust mix (dry), confectioners' sugar and almonds. Stir in egg and extract; gather dough into ball. Turn dough onto lightly floured cloth-covered board; knead until smooth. Shape into 1-inch balls; roll in granulated sugar. Flatten balls on ungreased baking sheet until ½ inch thick; gently press an almond in center of each cookie. Bake until edges are light brown, 8 to 10 minutes. Cool. Wrap, label and freeze.

■ **20 minutes before serving, remove Chinese Almond Cookies from freezer and unwrap.** Place on serving plate; thaw uncovered at room temperature.

DELUXE SUGAR COOKIES

Store no longer than 9 months. Makes about 5 dozen 2- to 2½-inch cookies.

  1 cup butter or margarine, softened
1½ cups confectioners' sugar
  1 egg
  1 teaspoon vanilla
  ½ teaspoon almond extract
2½ cups all-purpose flour*
  1 teaspoon soda
  1 teaspoon cream of tartar
   Granulated sugar

Mix butter, confectioners' sugar, egg, vanilla and almond extract. Stir in flour, soda and cream of tartar. Cover; chill 2 to 3 hours.

Heat oven to 375°. Divide dough in half. Turn one half onto lightly floured cloth-covered board; roll until 3/16 inch thick. Cut into desired shapes; sprinkle granulated sugar on cookies. Place on lightly greased baking sheet. Bake until light brown on edges, 7 to 8 minutes. Remove immediately from baking sheet; cool. (Can be served immediately.) Wrap, label and freeze.

■ **20 minutes before serving, remove Deluxe Sugar Cookies from freezer and unwrap.** Place on serving plate; thaw uncovered at room temperature.

*If using self-rising flour, omit soda and cream of tartar.

Sweet Treats from the Freezer

Stored at 0°, most candy stays fresh a year or more. Overwrap with freezer wrap. Marshmallows and chocolate-covered nuts also freeze well.

CINNAMON CRISPIES

Store no longer than 3 months. Makes about 2 dozen crispies.

Dough
  1 cup butter
1½ cups all-purpose flour*
  ½ cup dairy sour cream

Filling
  3 tablespoons sugar
  1 teaspoon cinnamon

Sugar Glaze
  3 tablespoons sugar
  1 tablespoon water

Cut butter into flour with pastry blender. Stir in sour cream until thoroughly mixed. Divide dough in half; wrap each. Chill 8 to 12 hours.

Mix 3 tablespoons sugar and the cinnamon. Turn half of dough onto sugared, well-floured cloth-covered board. Roll into rectangle, 20×7 inches. Sprinkle half the cinnamon-sugar on dough. Roll up tightly, beginning at narrow end; set aside. Roll other half of dough into rectangle, 20×7 inches. Sprinkle remaining cinnamon-sugar on dough. Place loose end of roll on narrow edge of rectangle; pinch edges to seal securely. Continue to roll up tightly; pinch edge of dough into roll to seal securely. Wrap and chill at least 1 hour. Store no longer than 48 hours.

Heat oven to 350°. Cut roll into ¼-inch slices; place slices 2 inches apart on ungreased baking sheet. Mix 3 tablespoons sugar and the water; brush on cookies. Bake until golden brown, 20 to 25 minutes; cool. (Can be served immediately.) Wrap in heavy-duty aluminum foil, label and freeze.

■ **25 minutes before serving, heat oven to 375°.** Remove Cinnamon Crispies from freezer and unwrap. Place on ungreased baking sheet; heat until hot, about 10 minutes.

*Self-rising flour can be used in this recipe. Baking time may be longer.

MIX-QUICK CAKES AND CUPCAKES

Store no longer than 1 month.

Bake 1 package (18.5 ounces) of any of the following cake mixes as directed for cakes or cupcakes:

Yellow cake mix with pudding
Devils food cake mix with pudding
White cake mix with pudding
Cherry chip cake mix with pudding
Sour cream chocolate cake mix with pudding
Sour cream white cake mix with pudding
Milk chocolate cake mix with pudding
Lemon cake mix with pudding
Banana cake mix with pudding

Cool cake on wire rack 1 hour. (Can be frosted and served immediately.) Place on ungreased baking sheet. Freeze uncovered 2 hours. Wrap in aluminum foil, label and return to freezer. (To insure a well-shaped cake, do not stack anything on top of layers during the freezer storage time. Pressure on top of cake causes wrapping to stick to cake.)

■ **1 hour 45 minutes before serving, remove Mix-Quick Cake or Cupcakes from freezer; thaw in wrapper at room temperature 45 minutes.** Remove wrapper carefully to prevent cake from sticking to wrapper; thaw cake uncovered at room temperature 1 hour. Frost and serve.

FROSTED MIX-QUICK CAKE

Store no longer than 2 months.

Prepare 1 package (14.3 or 15.4 ounces) of your favorite creamy-type frosting mix as directed. Frost cooled cake. (Can be served immediately.) Freeze uncovered 2 hours. Wrap (wooden picks are not necessary as frosting is set from preliminary freezing), label and return to freezer.

■ **2 hours 30 minutes before serving, remove Frosted Mix-Quick Cake from freezer and loosen wrapper.** Thaw at room temperature 2 hours. Cake can be sliced at this time although center will be somewhat frosty. Place on serving plates and thaw 30 minutes.

MIX-QUICK ANGEL FOOD CAKE

Store no longer than 6 months.

Bake 1 package (15 or 16 ounces) angel food cake mix as directed. Cool at least 1 hour. Remove from pan. Place cake on ungreased baking sheet. Freeze uncovered 1 hour. Wrap, label and return to freezer.

■ **About 2 hours before serving, remove Mix-Quick Angel Food Cake from freezer; thaw in wrapper at room temperature 45 minutes.** Remove wrapper carefully to prevent cake from sticking to wrapper; thaw cake uncovered at room temperature.

MIX-QUICK GERMAN CHOCOLATE CAKE

Store no longer than 2 months.

Bake 1 package (18.5 ounces) German chocolate cake mix as directed. Cool.

Prepare 1 package (9.9 ounces) coconut-pecan frosting mix as directed. Frost cake. (Can be served immediately.)

Freeze uncovered 2 hours. Wrap, label and return to freezer.

■ **About 1½ hours before serving, remove Mix-Quick German Chocolate Cake from freezer and loosen wrapper so that it does not touch frosting or cake.** Thaw at room temperature 1 hour. Cut cake into serving pieces. Place on serving plate and thaw 30 minutes.

For the Sake of Cake

Cakes do not freeze solid. To prevent crushing, keep your wrapped, frozen cake in a rigid container. It's smart to package cake in family portions or single pieces, which thaw out quickly and are nice for the lunchbox. To store cakes for as long as 4 to 6 months, leave them unfrosted.

OATMEAL SPICE CAKE

Store no longer than 2 months.

1½ cups all-purpose flour*
 1 cup quick-cooking oats
 1 cup brown sugar (packed)
 ½ cup granulated sugar
1½ teaspoons soda
 1 teaspoon cinnamon
 ½ teaspoon salt
 ½ teaspoon nutmeg
 ½ cup shortening
 1 cup water
 2 eggs (½ to ⅔ cup)
 2 tablespoons dark molasses
   Coconut Topping (below)

Heat oven to 350°. Grease and flour baking pan, 13×9×2 inches. Measure all ingredients except topping into large mixer bowl. Mix on low speed, scraping bowl constantly, ½ minute. Beat on high speed, scraping bowl occasionally, 3 minutes. Pour into pan.

Bake until wooden pick inserted in center comes out clean, 35 to 40 minutes; cool slightly. Spread topping on cake. Set oven control at broil and/or 550°. Place top of cake 3 inches from heat. Broil until topping is golden brown and bubbly, 2 to 3 minutes. (Can be served immediately.)

Cool cake 1 hour. Freeze uncovered 2 hours. Wrap, label and return to freezer.

■ **30 minutes before serving, remove Oatmeal Spice Cake from freezer and loosen wrapper.** Thaw at room temperature. (If plastic wrap has been used, place wooden picks at intervals to prevent wrapper from sticking to topping.)

COCONUT TOPPING

¼ cup butter or margarine, melted
⅔ cup brown sugar (packed)
½ cup flaked coconut
½ cup chopped pecans
 3 tablespoons light cream

Mix all ingredients.

*If using self-rising flour, omit soda and salt.

BUTTERY FREEZER CAKE

Store no longer than 1 month.

⅔ cup butter or margarine, softened
1¾ cups sugar
 2 eggs (⅓ to ½ cup)
1½ teaspoons vanilla
 3 cups cake flour or 2¾ cups all-purpose
   flour*
2½ teaspoons baking powder
 1 teaspoon salt
1¼ cups milk
   Buttery Frosting (below)

Heat oven to 350°. Grease and flour baking pan, 13×9×2 inches, or two 9-inch or three 8-inch round layer pans. Mix butter, sugar, eggs and vanilla in large mixer bowl until fluffy. Beat on high speed, scraping bowl occasionally, 5 minutes. On low speed, mix in flour, baking powder and salt alternately with milk. Pour into pan(s).

Bake until wooden pick inserted in center comes out clean, oblong 45 to 50 minutes, layers 30 to 35 minutes. Cool. Frost cake with Buttery Frosting. (Can be served immediately.)

Place wooden picks at intervals around top of cake to prevent wrapper from sticking to frosting. Wrap, label and freeze.

■ **2 hours before serving, remove Buttery Freezer Cake from freezer.** Thaw in wrapper at room temperature 1 hour. Remove wrapper; thaw cake uncovered 1 hour. (Or, after the first hour of thawing, cut cake into serving pieces. Place on serving plate and thaw 30 minutes.)

BUTTERY FROSTING

2⅔ cups confectioners' sugar
 ⅔ cup butter, softened
 2 ounces melted unsweetened
   chocolate (cool)
 ¾ teaspoon vanilla
 2 tablespoons milk

Beat sugar, butter, chocolate and vanilla in small mixer bowl on low speed. Gradually beat in milk until smooth and fluffy.

*If using self-rising flour, omit baking powder and salt.

Best Chocolate Cake can be frozen in the pan in which it was baked; just wrap it well, pan and all.

BEST CHOCOLATE CAKE

Store no longer than 1 month.

2 cups all-purpose flour* or cake flour
2 cups sugar
1 teaspoon soda
1 teaspoon salt
½ teaspoon baking powder
¾ cup water
¾ cup buttermilk
½ cup shortening
2 eggs (⅓ to ½ cup)
1 teaspoon vanilla
4 ounces melted unsweetened
   chocolate (cool)
   Fluffy White Frosting (right)

Heat oven to 350°. Grease and flour baking pan, 13×9×2 inches, or two 9-inch or three 8-inch round layer pans. Measure all ingredients except frosting into large mixer bowl. Mix on low speed, scraping bowl constantly, ½ minute. Beat on high speed, scraping bowl occasionally, 3 minutes. Pour into pan(s).

Bake until wooden pick inserted in center comes out clean, oblong 40 to 45 minutes, layers 30 to 35 minutes. Cool. Frost cake with frosting.

Place cake in cake box. Wrap box, label and freeze. (Frosting will remain soft.)

■ **2 hours before serving, remove Best Chocolate Cake from freezer.** Thaw in box at room temperature 1 hour. Remove cake from box; thaw uncovered 1 hour. (Or, after the first hour of thawing, cut cake into serving pieces. Place on serving plate and thaw 30 minutes.)

FLUFFY WHITE FROSTING

½ cup sugar
¼ cup light corn syrup
2 tablespoons water
2 egg whites (¼ cup)
1 teaspoon vanilla

Mix sugar, corn syrup and water in small saucepan. Cover tightly; heat over medium heat until mixture boils vigorously. Uncover; boil rapidly, without stirring, to 242° on candy thermometer (or until small amount of mixture spins a 6- to 8-inch thread when dropped from spoon).

While mixture boils, beat egg whites until stiff peaks form. Pour hot syrup very slowly in a thin stream into the beaten egg whites, beating constantly on medium speed. Beat on high speed until stiff peaks form, adding vanilla during last minute of beating.

*If using self-rising flour, omit soda, salt and baking powder.

PASTRY

One-crust Pie
One 8- or 9-inch
1 cup all-purpose flour*
½ teaspoon salt
⅓ cup plus 1 tablespoon shortening or
    ⅓ cup lard
2 to 3 tablespoons cold water

Two 8- or 9-inch
2 cups all-purpose flour*
1 teaspoon salt
⅔ cup plus 2 tablespoons shortening or
    ⅔ cup lard
    4 to 5 tablespoons cold water

Two-crust Pie
One 8- or 9-inch
 2 cups all-purpose flour*
 1 teaspoon salt
 ⅔ cup plus 2 tablespoons shortening or
    ⅔ cup lard
    4 to 5 tablespoons cold water

Two 8- or 9-inch
    4 cups all-purpose flour*
    2 teaspoons salt
1½ cups shortening or 1⅓ cups lard
 ⅔ cup cold water

Measure flour and salt into mixing bowl. Cut in shortening thoroughly. Sprinkle water, 1 tablespoon at a time, on flour-shortening mixture, mixing with fork until all flour is moistened and dough almost cleans side of bowl (1 to 2 teaspoons water can be added if needed). Gather dough into ball; turn onto lightly floured cloth-covered board and shape into flattened round. (For 2 One-crust Pies or Two-crust Pie, divide in half and shape into 2 flattened rounds. For 2 Two-crust Pies, divide into 4 parts.) Roll dough with floured stockinet-covered rolling pin 2 inches larger than inverted pie pan. Fold pastry in half, then in half again; unfold and ease into pan.

For One-crust Pie, trim overhanging edge of pastry 1 inch from rim of pan. Fold and roll pastry under, even with pan; flute. Fill and bake as directed in recipe. For Baked Pie Shell, prick bottom and side thoroughly with fork. Bake in 475° oven 8 to 10 minutes.

For Two-crust Pie, turn desired filling into pastry-lined pie pan. Trim overhanging edge of pastry ½ inch from rim of pan. Roll second round of dough. Fold in half, then in half again; cut slits so steam can escape. Place over filling and unfold. Trim overhanging edge of pastry 1 inch from rim of pan. Fold and roll top edge under lower edge, pressing on rim to seal securely; flute. Cover edge of pastry with 2- to 3-inch strip of aluminum foil to prevent excessive browning. Bake as directed in recipe. Remove foil 15 minutes before pie is done.

*If using self-rising flour, omit salt. Pastry made with self-rising flour differs in flavor and texture.

Short of Pie Pans?

If you don't want to tie up your pie pans in the freezer, do this. Line pan with an aluminum foil circle, cut 3 inches larger than the pan. Press foil smoothly into the pan. Proceed as directed in recipe. Freeze pie, and when it is completely frozen, grasp the foil extensions and lift foil and pie from the pan. Overwrap with freezer wrap. Place pie in box or container.

Because frozen pies are bulky, they take up a great deal of freezer space. Solution: Package your own special pie fillings in frozen-food containers. When ready to use, partially thaw in container. Add non-freezable ingredients and pour into pastry-lined pie pans.

FROZEN PASTRY CIRCLES

Store no longer than 2 months.

Use *one* of the following:

**Pastry for Two 8- or 9-inch
Two-crust Pies (page 77)**
**4 sticks or 2 packets pie crust mix
(one 22-ounce-size package or two 11-
ounce-size packages)**

Prepare pastry as directed for 2 Two-crust Pies. Divide into 4 parts. Roll each part 2 inches larger all around than inverted 8- or 9-inch pie pan.

Stack circles, with waxed paper between, on ungreased baking sheet. Freeze uncovered 1 hour. Wrap stack, label and return to freezer. To prevent breaking, store on flat surface.

■ **Baked Pie Shell or One-crust Baked Pie: 35 minutes before needed, remove 1 Frozen Pastry Circle from freezer; place on pie pan.** Thaw uncovered at room temperature until soft, about 20 minutes. Heat oven to 475°. Ease pastry gently into pan. Trim overhanging edge of pastry 1 inch from rim of pan. Fold and roll pastry under, even with pan; flute. (For One-crust Baked Pie, proceed as directed in recipe.) For Baked Pie Shell, prick bottom and side thoroughly with fork. Bake until light brown, 8 to 10 minutes.

■ **Two-crust Pie: 25 minutes before needed, remove 2 Frozen Pastry Circles from freezer; place one on pie pan and one on flat surface. Have ready:** filling.

Thaw uncovered at room temperature until soft, about 20 minutes. Heat oven to temperature designated in recipe. Ease pastry gently into pan. Trim overhanging edge of pastry ½ inch from rim of pan. Pour filling into pastry-lined pie pan. Fold second circle in half, then in half again; cut slits so steam can escape. Place over filling and unfold. Trim overhanging edge of pastry 1 inch from rim of pan. Fold and roll top edge under lower edge, pressing on rim to seal securely; flute. Bake as directed.

FRESH APPLE PIES

Store no longer than 6 months. Makes 2 pies.

**Pastry for Two 9-inch Two-crust Pies
(page 77)**

Filling for **1** pie
¾ cup sugar
¼ cup all-purpose flour
½ teaspoon nutmeg
½ teaspoon cinnamon
  Dash salt
**6 cups thinly sliced pared tart apples
(about 6 medium)**
2 tablespoons butter or margarine

Heat oven to 425°. Prepare pastry. Mix sugar, flour, nutmeg, cinnamon and salt; toss with apples. Turn into pastry-lined pie pan; dot with butter. Repeat for second pie. Cover with top crusts which have slits cut in them; seal securely and flute. Cover edges of pastry with 2- to 3-inch strips of aluminum foil to prevent excessive browning; remove foil 15 minutes before pies are done. Bake until crusts are brown and juice begins to bubble through slits in crusts, 40 to 50 minutes. Cool. (Can be served immediately.)

Cool pies until barely warm, about 2 hours. Freeze uncovered until completely frozen, at least 3 hours. (If you prefer to remove pies from pans for storage, freeze 6 hours. See Note.) Wrap, label and return to freezer.

■ **1 hour 40 minutes before serving, remove Fresh Apple Pie(s) from freezer and unwrap.** (Replace in pan if you have frozen out of pan.) Thaw at room temperature 1 hour. Heat in 375° oven on lowest rack position 35 to 40 minutes.

Note: If you prefer, line pie pans with aluminum foil circles cut 3 inches larger all around than inverted pie pans. After pies are completely frozen, gently lift pies from pans with foil extensions.

FRESH PEAR PIES

Store no longer than 6 months. Makes 2 pies.

**Pastry for Two 9-inch Two-crust Pies
  (page 77)**

Filling for **1** pie
½ cup sugar
⅓ cup all-purpose flour
½ teaspoon mace, if desired
4 cups sliced pared fresh pears
  (about 7 medium)
1 tablespoon lemon juice
2 tablespoons butter or margarine

Heat oven to 425°. Prepare pastry. Mix sugar, flour and mace; toss with pears. Turn into pastry-lined pie pan; sprinkle lemon juice on pears and dot with butter. Repeat for second pie. Cover with top crusts which have slits cut in them; seal securely and flute. Cover edges of pastry with 2- to 3-inch strips of aluminum foil to prevent excessive browning; remove foil 15 minutes before pies are done. Bake until crusts are brown and juice begins to bubble through slits in crusts, 40 to 50 minutes. Cool. (Can be served immediately.)

Cool pies until barely warm, about 2 hours. Freeze uncovered until completely frozen, at least 3 hours. (If you prefer to remove pies from pans for storage, freeze 6 hours. See Note.) Wrap, label and return to freezer.

■ **1 hour 40 minutes before serving, remove Fresh Pear Pie(s) from freezer and unwrap.** (Replace in pan if you have frozen out of pan.) Thaw at room temperature 1 hour. Heat in 375° oven on lowest rack position 35 to 40 minutes.

Note: If you prefer, line pie pans with aluminum foil circles cut 3 inches larger all around than inverted pie pans. After pies are completely frozen, gently lift pies from pans with foil extensions.

CRANBERRY-APPLE PIES

Store no longer than 6 months. Makes 2 pies.

**Pastry for Two 9-inch Two-crust Pies
  (page 77)**

Filling for **1** pie
1¾ cups sugar
¼ cup all-purpose flour
3 cups sliced pared tart apples (2 to 3
  medium)
2 cups fresh cranberries
2 tablespoons butter or margarine

Heat oven to 425°. Prepare pastry. Mix sugar and flour. In pastry-lined pie pan, alternate layers of apples, cranberries and sugar mixture, beginning and ending with apples; dot with butter. Repeat for second pie. Cover with top crusts which have slits cut in them; seal securely and flute. Cover edges with 2- to 3-inch strips of aluminum foil to prevent excessive browning; remove foil 15 minutes before pies are done. Bake until crusts are brown, 40 to 50 minutes. Cool. (Can be served immediately.)

Cool pies until barely warm, 2 hours. Freeze uncovered until completely frozen, at least 3 hours. (If you prefer to remove pies from pans for storage, freeze 6 hours. See Note.) Wrap, label and return to freezer.

■ **1 hour 40 minutes before serving, remove Cranberry-Apple Pie(s) from freezer and unwrap.** (Replace in pan if you have frozen out of pan.) Thaw at room temperature 1 hour. Heat in 375° oven on lowest rack position 35 to 40 minutes.

Note: If you prefer, line pie pans with aluminum foil circles cut 3 inches larger all around than inverted pie pans. After pies are completely frozen, gently lift pies from pans with foil extensions.

Chill the lemon mixture for the chiffon pie filling in the refrigerator or in a bowl of ice and water until it forms soft mounds when dropped from a spoon.

Lemon Chiffon Pie and Pumpkin Chiffon Pie

LEMON CHIFFON PIE

Store no longer than 1 month.

9-inch Baked Pie Shell (Pastry for One
8- or 9-inch One-crust Pie—page 77)
½ cup sugar
1 envelope unflavored gelatin
4 eggs, separated
⅔ cup water
⅓ cup lemon juice
1 tablespoon grated lemon peel
½ teaspoon cream of tartar
½ cup sugar

Bake pie shell. Mix ½ cup sugar and the gelatin in small saucepan. Beat egg yolks, water and lemon juice; stir into sugar mixture. Cook over medium heat, stirring constantly, just until mixture boils. Stir in peel. Place pan in bowl of ice and water or chill in refrigerator, stirring occasionally, until mixture mounds slightly when dropped from spoon.

Beat egg whites and cream of tartar in large mixer bowl until foamy. Beat in ½ cup sugar, 1 tablespoon at a time; beat until stiff and glossy. Do not underbeat. Fold lemon mixture into meringue; pile into baked pie shell. (To serve today, chill until set, at least 3 hours.)

Freeze uncovered 1½ hours. Place wooden picks at intervals around top of pie to prevent wrapper from sticking to pie. Wrap, label and return to freezer.

■ **1 hour 30 minutes before serving, remove Lemon Chiffon Pie from freezer.** Thaw in wrapper in refrigerator.

VARIATION
Lime Chiffon Pie: Substitute lime juice for the lemon juice and grated lime peel for the lemon peel. Add a few drops green food color to intensify color.

Insert wooden picks around the top of the completed pie, then wrap it for freezing. The picks prevent the wrapper from sticking to the pie.

PUMPKIN CHIFFON PIES

Store no longer than 2 months. Makes 2 pies.

**Two Baked Pie Shells (Pastry for Two 8-
or 9-inch One-crust Pies—page 77)**
1 cup brown sugar (packed)
1 tablespoon plus 1 teaspoon unflavored
gelatin
½ teaspoon salt
½ teaspoon ginger
½ teaspoon cinnamon
½ teaspoon nutmeg
1 can (16 ounces) pumpkin
4 eggs, separated
⅔ cup milk
½ teaspoon cream of tartar
⅔ cup granulated sugar

Bake pie shells. Mix brown sugar, gelatin, salt, ginger, cinnamon and nutmeg in medium saucepan. Beat pumpkin, egg yolks and milk; stir into brown sugar mixture. Cook over medium heat, stirring constantly, just until mixture boils. Place pan in bowl of ice and water or chill in refrigerator, stirring occasionally, until mixture mounds slightly when dropped from spoon.

Beat egg whites and cream of tartar in large mixer bowl until foamy. Beat in granulated sugar, 1 tablespoon at a time; beat until stiff and glossy. Do not underbeat. Fold pumpkin mixture into meringue; pile into baked pie shells (3 cups filling for each pie). Garnish with whipped cream if desired. (To serve today, chill until set, at least 3 hours.)

Freeze uncovered 1½ hours. Place wooden picks at intervals around top of pie to prevent wrapper from sticking to pie. Wrap, label and return to freezer.

■ **1 hour 30 minutes before serving, remove Pumpkin Chiffon Pie(s) from freezer.** Thaw in wrapper in refrigerator.

CHOCOLATE PIE DELUXE

Store no longer than 2 months.

Graham Cracker Crust (below)
16 large marshmallows or 1½ cups miniature marshmallows
½ cup milk
3 bars (4 ounces each) milk chocolate
1 envelope (about 1½ ounces) whipped topping mix or 1 cup chilled whipping cream

Prepare crust. (If you want to remove pie from pan after freezing, line pie pan before pressing in crumbs with aluminum foil circle cut 3 inches larger all around than inverted pie pan.) Heat marshmallows, milk and chocolate over medium heat, stirring constantly, just until marshmallows and chocolate melt. Chill until thickened.

Prepare whipped topping mix as directed on package. (If using whipping cream, beat in chilled bowl until stiff.) Stir marshmallow mixture; fold into whipped topping. Pour into crust. (To serve today, chill until set, at least 8 hours.)

Freeze uncovered until pie is completely frozen, about 3 hours. Gently lift pie from pan with foil extension. Wrap, label and return to freezer.

■ **30 minutes before serving, remove Chocolate Pie Deluxe from freezer.** (Unwrap and replace in pan if you have frozen out of the pan. Rewrap.) Thaw in wrapper at room temperature. If desired, garnish with toasted slivered almonds.

GRAHAM CRACKER CRUST

Heat oven to 350°. Mix 1½ cups graham cracker crumbs (about 20 crackers), 3 tablespoons sugar and ⅓ cup butter or margarine, melted. Press mixture firmly and evenly against bottom and side of 9-inch pie pan. Bake 10 minutes.

After freezing 6 hours, lift pie from pan, using foil extensions.

PECAN PIES

Store no longer than 1 month. Makes 2 pies.

Pastry for Two 9-inch One-crust Pies (page 77)
6 eggs
1⅓ cups sugar
1 teaspoon salt
⅔ cup butter or margarine, melted
2 cups dark or light corn syrup
2 cups pecan halves or broken pecans

Heat oven to 375°. Prepare pastry. Beat eggs, sugar, salt, butter and syrup with rotary beater. Sprinkle 1 cup pecans evenly in each pastry-lined pie pan. Slowly pour 2⅓ cups filling on pecans in each pan. Bake until filling is set, 40 to 50 minutes. Cool. (Can be served immediately.)

Cool pies 2 hours. Freeze uncovered at least 3 hours. (If you prefer to remove pies from pans for storage, freeze 6 hours. See page 77.) Wrap, label and return to freezer.

■ **20 minutes before serving, remove Pecan Pie(s) from freezer and unwrap.** (Replace in pan if you have frozen out of pan.) Thaw in refrigerator 20 minutes to allow pastry to soften. (Filling is ready for cutting directly from freezer.)

Special Freezer Helps

Plan, Buy and **Use** are the key words for making the most efficient use of your freezer. The more frozen food you keep in stock and use, the more you benefit from owning a freezer.

Plan: Mark your packages with the date that ends the recommended storage period. The way you arrange your food in the freezer can help you to use it in good time, too. Instead of dividing it into meat, vegetables and desserts, you could assign separate freezer areas for food to be used this month, next month, etc. Alternatively, keep a running inventory, storing your packages in the order of "expiration" dates.

Before you set out to restock your freezer, check your calendar for the entertaining you will do in the next month or so. Then plan your purchases to take care of your normal needs, of entertaining, and of some unforeseen circumstances, too.

Buy: With a freezer, you can enjoy the best foods at the lowest prices all the time—if you take advantage of your supermarket's "specials" and of the food that costs less because it is in season. Make sure that the food you buy is in top condition. You may want to prepare a freezer recipe with the food you bought, or package it in smaller portions. Whatever you do with it, get the food into your freezer as soon as you can.

Use: It pays you handsome dividends to label packages accurately before freezing. Labeling directions are on page 85. Every freezer recipe in this book carries its own storage instructions. When you want to freeze food prepared from other recipes, consult the general freezing directions on pages 88 through 90.

Now that the exciting possibility exists, consider the electronic oven—a real complement to your freezer, since it's ideal for frozen food. Frozen food can be defrosted in minutes in the electronic oven. One small note of caution: follow the manufacturer's directions meticulously. You'll find that you need to make changes from your normal packaging and timing procedures.

Happy Freezing!

COOL QUICKLY

Have you noticed how the freezer recipes tell you to cool the food quickly after cooking? The less time this food spends at temperatures between 45° and 140°, the better. If you allow foods to remain at these temperatures for more than 3 or 4 hours, they may not be safe to eat. Remember that in these recipes this time span includes all the time the food remains in this temperature range. So speed the cooling process!

Hot foods can be placed right in the refrigerator provided they don't raise the refrigerator temperature above 45°. A large quantity of hot food should be cooled in a big bowl (or a sink) filled with cold water and ice that almost reach the top of the food container. Replace ice as it melts; freeze the food as soon as it is cool.

WRAP

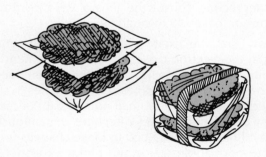

If food is to maintain its high quality in the freezer, it must be stored in wraps or containers which are moisture- and vapor-proof. The containers and wrapping materials that you buy should be designed for the purpose for which you use them. Some are made for the freezer, others for the refrigerator. It's important to use the right type and the right size, so check their labels. When you wrap, press out the air—and wrap tightly. Close packages with tape.

Special tips on wrapping and storage: For easy separation, place freezer wrap between individual patties, chops and small steaks; or wrap them individually and freeze before putting them into a freezer bag. Protect fragile foods with a box; place the freezer-wrapped food in the box, or overwrap the box. Since food expands in freezing, make sure a container has enough room for expansion. When you have to freeze a mixture of solid and liquid food in a container which is too large, fill the space between the food and the lid with crumpled freezer wrap.

There are casseroles now on the market designed to go directly from freezer to oven. Why not splurge a bit and buy some of these?

LABEL

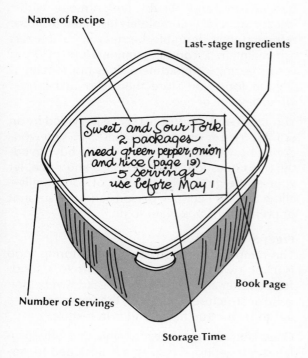

Name of Recipe

Last-stage Ingredients

Sweet and Sour Pork
2 packages
need green pepper, onion
and rice (page 19)
5 servings
use before May 1

Number of Servings

Book Page

Storage Time

Did you ever look into your freezer and wonder what you'd put into one of the packages or containers there? It's better not to rely on your memory, especially if you make good use of your freezer and keep it well stocked. Label your packages before you put them in the freezer.

What you will need are labels, a grease pencil or a felt-tipped pen, and freezer tape. Keep these handy with your packaging materials so you won't be tempted to smuggle an unlabeled package into the freezer.

Here's the information you'll need to include: **Name of Recipe:** Copy its exact title from the cookbook. If you have more than one package from the same recipe, note that on the label.

Last-stage Ingredients: If your recipe calls for additional ingredients after you take the food from the freezer, note this on the label.

Book Page: Copy the number of the page on which your recipe appears. You'll need to refer to that page again later for the instructions which follow the ■ and the **boldface type.**

Number of Servings: Write down the number of servings your package contains. (You'll find the number of servings each recipe provides printed below its title.) Our calculations are based on average servings. If there are hearty eaters in your family, take that into account. Just write down how many servings the package will provide for your hungry crew.

Storage Time: Look at the recommended storage time for your recipe—it's given directly under the title. Now figure out when your package should be used; put that date on your label.

If you leave your package in the freezer beyond the recommended storage time (see pages 88 to 90), your food won't spoil—but it may begin to lose some of its flavor, moisture or texture.

Your Own Recipes and Other Foods: Label them with the same type of information as you put on your Do-Ahead packages. When you freeze meat, note its weight. For your own recipes, write down and keep your own instructions for reheating or last-stage ingredients.

...AND FREEZE

Freezer Types

When it comes to buying a freezer, you will find that you have a choice of three basic types: the refrigerator with a freezer unit; the upright freezer—with shelves from top to bottom; and the freezer chest—with baskets and dividers.

If you are short of floor space or you don't need a great deal of freezer space, the refrigerator-freezer may be your best bet. In a refrigerator-freezer, the storage capacity of your freezer will be between 2 and 10 cubic feet. A model with a freezer unit that is completely insulated from the refrigerator is desirable because such freezers can maintain a constant temperature of 0°. If your freezing compartment does not remain at 0°, the food you store there should be used within a week or two.

You may need the freezer space provided by an upright freezer or a freezer chest. Are you wondering how big a freezer you should buy? In addition to questions of floor space and price, let yourself be guided by the size of your family—allow 5 cubic feet per person—and the amount of preplanning you want to do.

Freezer Temperature

The temperature for freezing and storing food is 0° or lower. At a low temperature (0°), foods freeze faster and there is less breakdown in their cellular structure. Therefore, the foods are more apt to retain true flavor and firm texture.

Chest and upright freezers (and the fully-insulated refrigerator-freezers) are designed to stay at a constant 0° temperature. Be sure the control setting of your freezer is correct—use a freezer thermometer.

Food Freezing

At any one time, freeze only as much food as you can place against a freezing surface. The faster your food freezes, the better it retains flavor and texture. For fast freezing, food packages should be in direct contact with a freezing surface, at least 1 inch apart so the air can circulate. (Once the food is frozen solid, you can stack packages.)

When you want to freeze food in large quantities, guard against a rise of temperature in your freezer. Reduce your freezer temperature to −10° or lower about 24 hours before you put a large amount of unfrozen food into your freezer. This way, your food will be frozen solid in 10 to 12 hours.

It's important that you know exactly what temperature is maintained in your freezer—especially when you're freezing foods. We strongly recommend that you buy a freezer thermometer. Check the thermometer often, and make sure that your freezer actually maintains a temperature of 0° or lower.

Defrosting and Cleaning

Above all, read the manufacturer's instructions carefully.

Unless you have a self-defrosting freezer, defrost it as soon as you see thick frost. Transfer your frozen food to the refrigerator. If necessary, pile frozen foods into a laundry basket and cover with newspapers or a blanket. To speed the defrosting, have an electric fan blow into the freezer, or place pans of warm water in the freezer. Wash with a solution of 3 tablespoons soda to 1 quart water, or with a mild detergent solution. Dry thoroughly before resetting temperature control.

Emergencies

In case of power failure or mechanical defect, *keep the freezer closed*. In a full freezer that is kept at 0°, little or no thawing will take place within the first 12 to 20 hours.

If your freezer might be out of commission for more than a day and you are storing a lot of food, you will want to take action. You can take the contents of your freezer to a frozen food locker. Or you can buy dry ice. Wear heavy gloves when you handle dry ice. Lay cardboard over the packages in your freezer, and place the dry ice on the cardboard; do not place it directly on the packages. A 50-pound block of dry ice will prevent foods from thawing for 2 to 3 days.

GENERAL RECOMMENDATIONS FOR FREEZER STORAGE

Let this 3-page section of general instructions be your guide when you want to freeze food prepared from your own recipes—or purchased products. There's no need to consult these pages when you freeze recipes from this book. Each Do-Ahead recipe has its own specific storage instructions—these have been thoroughly tested.

Appetizers

Storage Time: 1 to 2 months

Recommendations: It is best to freeze hors d'oeuvres and pastry before baking.
Deep-fried appetizers—such as the Chili Cheese Fries on page 41—can be frozen after frying and then reheated in the oven.

Meat, Poultry, Fish

Storage Times: See pages 9, 19, 23, 24 and 30.

Recommendations: Freeze fresh meat, poultry and fish as promptly as possible. One way to freeze cleaned fish is in a waterproof container; cover the fish with water and freeze.

If you thaw meat, poultry or fish before cooking, start cooking them while they are still chilled. Frozen roasts require $1/3$ to $1/2$ more than their normal cooking time. For small roasts, the additional cooking time will be closer to $1/3$, for large roasts, closer to $1/2$.

Cooked meat in sauce and leftover roasts freeze very well, as a rule; if possible, they should be slightly undercooked before freezing.

Cooked dishes can be taken from the freezer and heated without thawing. Heat in the oven (use the instructions for Swiss Steak, page 14, as a guide), or place in a skillet and add a little water (see the Pepper Steak instructions, page 13).

We don't recommend that you freeze fried meat, poultry or fish, since these fried foods will often develop a rancid or warmed-over flavor. Sometimes, however, fried foods can be frozen. Take a look at the recipes for Sweet and Sour Pork (page 19), Fried Chicken (page 29), and Batter-fried Fish (page 30). Note that their recommended storage times are very short.

Main Dishes

Storage Time: About 3 months

Recommendations: In adapting your own recipe to freezer storage, find a Do-Ahead recipe that closely resembles your own. Base the preparations for freezing, the storage time, heating and completing of your recipe on the instructions for the Do-Ahead recipe. Check through the Do-Ahead recipes for ingredients that are added just before serving, and observe the same procedure; those ingredients do not freeze well. In preparing your main dish, work according to the food temperature rules on page 84, and remember to reheat your dish quickly.

Fruits and Vegetables

Storage Times:

Citrus Fruits . . . . 3 to 4 months
Other Fruits . . . . 1 year
Vegetables . . . . 1 year

Recommendations: Let your produce man advise you on the varieties that freeze best; new varieties—developed specifically for freezing—will be available before long. Freeze fruit and vegetables at the peak of their ripeness. For good freezing instructions, check the booklet that came with your freezer, the United States Department of Agriculture or a local university.

Breads

Storage Times:

Quick Breads . . . . 2 to 3 months
Yeast Breads . . . . 9 months

Recommendations: Bake breads before freezing; breads baked after freezing will be smaller and tougher. Overwrap the bread you buy if it is to stay in the freezer for more than one week. To thaw at room temperature, keep breads wrapped—at least in the beginning. To thaw and heat breads in the oven, set oven at 350°; heating time will vary with size. For quick thawing, freeze rolls or nut bread or coffee cake slices individually wrapped. Check the recipes on pages 50 to 60 for standard instructions for thawing or heating bread or coffee cakes.

freeze uncovered till firm

unfrosted freeze 4 to 6 months

Cakes
Storage Times:

Frosted .1 to 2 months
Unfrosted . . . . .4 to 6 months

Recommendations: Freeze frosted cakes without wrapping; freezer wrap them as soon as they are firm. To prevent crushing, place cake in box; overwrap box. Frostings that freeze well (not all of them do) are given in recipes in this book. Confectioners' sugar and fudge frostings freeze particularly well.

most cookies can be frozen 9 to 12 months

Cookies
Storage Times:

Frosted .2 to 3 months
Unfrosted . . . . .9 to 12 months

Recommendations: Nearly all cookies—baked or unbaked—can be frozen. For specific storage times, look through the recipes on pages 66 to 73. When you freeze several cookie varieties in the same container, the least storable cookie should set the storage time. Freeze frosted cookies uncovered until they are firm; then wrap. For additional freezing suggestions, see the notes on page 72.

yes

no!

Pies and Pastry
Storage Times:

Chiffon Pies . . . . .1 month
Other Pies . . . . .4 months
Pastry . . . . .4 months

Recommendations: To prevent soggy crusts, bake pies before freezing. Empty pie shells can be frozen unbaked; then they should *not* be thawed before baking. Do not try to freeze custard or cream pies or pies with a meringue topping. To thaw chiffon pies, leave them wrapped in the refrigerator for 1½ hours. Thawing and heating directions for double-crust pies appear in recipes on pages 78 and 79. To heat a pie that is in a pan made of aluminum foil, place a baking sheet under the pie pan for browning.

Your Refrigerator: Short-Term Planning

Your Refrigerator: Short-Term Planning

Your refrigerator is an old friend, one you probably take for granted. But it can serve as one of the best kitchen helpers you could have. In the following pages, you'll find recipes for food you can prepare ahead of time and store in the refrigerator. Some of these recipes can be prepared one day ahead; others—for foods that will keep longer, such as salads, yeast rolls and cookies—can wait in your refrigerator for 2 days or more.

Before serving time, look up the serving instructions which follow this symbol—■; they are in **boldface type** toward the end of the recipe. If you store your prepared food in an ovenproof pan or baking dish, you'll be able to transfer it directly from the refrigerator to the oven.

Your refrigerator—which should be set at 40° or lower—is less effective than your freezer in stopping all bacterial activity. We therefore recommend the following safeguards:

1 Buy fresh food of top quality.

2 As soon as you get home from the grocery store, put foods that require cold storage in your refrigerator.

3 Prepare the food you bring home as soon as you can, and be sure that everything which comes in contact with it is spotless.

4 Refrigerate the food you prepare as soon as possible. Hot foods may be immediately placed in the refrigerator provided the food does not raise the refrigerator's temperature above 45°. With large quantities, place the container of hot food in a large bowl or a basin filled with cold water and ice. This cooling mixture of ice and water should almost reach the top of your food container. Renew the ice as it melts; refrigerate food as soon as possible.

5 Be sure to serve the food within the recommended storage period. This information is listed at the top of every recipe.

Pictured on the preceding page:
Marinated Roast Beef (page 97)

Meats and Main Dishes

STROGANOFF HAMBURGERS

Store no longer than 48 hours. Makes enough for 8 sandwiches.

Base
1 **pound ground beef**
3 **tablespoons instant chopped onion**

Sauce
⅓ **cup chili sauce**
2 **tablespoons flour**
1 **tablespoon prepared mustard**
½ **teaspoon salt**
¼ **teaspoon pepper**

Cook and stir meat and onion until meat is brown. Spoon off fat. Stir in Sauce ingredients; simmer uncovered about 5 minutes. Cover and refrigerate.

■ **About 10 minutes before serving, have ready:** 1 cup dairy sour cream; 8 hamburger buns, split and toasted; 8 slices tomato; lettuce leaves.

Stir sour cream into hamburger mixture; heat until hot. Serve in buns with tomato slices and lettuce.

ROAST BEEF HASH

Store no longer than 48 hours. Makes enough for 3 or 4 servings.

2 **cups finely chopped cooked beef**
2 **cups finely chopped cooked potato**
2 **tablespoons grated onion**
¼ **cup beef gravy**
1 **teaspoon salt**

Mix all ingredients; spread in ungreased 8-inch foil pie pan or layer cake pan, 8×1½ inches. Cover and refrigerate.

■ **25 minutes before serving, heat oven to 400°.** Bake Roast Beef Hash uncovered until hot, about 20 minutes.

MEAT LOAF AND GRAVY DUET

Store no longer than 24 hours. Makes enough for 6 to 8 servings.

2 **pounds ground beef**
1 **envelope (about 1½ ounces) onion soup mix**
1 **can (10¾ ounces) condensed cream of mushroom soup**

Place 24×18-inch piece of heavy-duty aluminum foil in baking pan, 9×9×2 inches. Mix meat and onion soup mix; turn onto foil and shape into loaf. Spread mushroom soup on loaf. Fold foil loosely over meat. Bake in 350° oven 1 hour. (To serve immediately, bake 20 minutes longer.) Cool quickly. Spoon off fat, re-wrap and refrigerate.

■ **About 45 minutes before serving, cook Meat Loaf and Gravy Duet in 350° oven until done.**

POCKET STEW

Store no longer than 24 hours. Makes enough for 4 servings.

1½ **pounds ground beef**
4 **slices Bermuda or Spanish onion**
4 **cooked pared medium potatoes**
4 **medium carrots, cut into julienne strips**
1½ **teaspoons salt**
⅛ **teaspoon pepper**

Shape meat into 4 patties, each about 3 inches in diameter and 1 inch thick. Place patties on 25×18-inch piece of heavy-duty aluminum foil. Top each patty with an onion slice and a potato. Arrange carrots *around* meat. Season with salt and pepper. Fold foil over potatoes and carrots, seal foil securely and refrigerate.

■ **About 55 minutes before serving, place Pocket Stew on ungreased baking sheet.** Bake in 400° oven until carrots are tender, about 45 minutes.

Note: If you wish to serve individual portions, divide ingredients among 4 foil packets.

STUFFED GREEN PEPPERS

Store no longer than 24 hours. Makes enough for 6 servings.

Peppers
6 large green peppers
5 cups water
1 teaspoon salt

Filling
1 pound ground beef
2 tablespoons chopped onion
1 teaspoon salt
⅛ teaspoon garlic salt
1 cup cooked rice
1 can (15 ounces) tomato sauce

Cut thin slice from stem end of each pepper. Remove seeds and membranes. Heat water and 1 teaspoon salt until water boils. Cook peppers in boiling water 5 minutes; drain.

Cook and stir meat and onion in medium skillet until onion is tender. Spoon off fat. Stir in salt, garlic salt, rice and 1 cup of the tomato sauce; heat until hot.

Heat oven to 350°. Lightly stuff each pepper with ½ cup meat mixture. Stand peppers upright in ungreased baking dish, 8×8×2 inches. Reserve ⅓ cup tomato sauce; pour remaining sauce on peppers. (To serve immediately, see below.) Cover tightly; bake 30 minutes. Refrigerate peppers and reserved tomato sauce.

■ **45 minutes before serving, heat oven to 350°.** Pour reserved tomato sauce on peppers. Bake uncovered 35 minutes.

To Serve Immediately: Cover tightly; bake 45 minutes. Pour reserved tomato sauce on peppers. Bake uncovered 15 minutes.

CHOW MEIN CASSEROLE

Store no longer than 24 hours. Makes enough for 4 or 5 servings.

1 pound ground beef
¾ cup chopped celery
3 tablespoons instant minced onion
½ cup uncooked converted rice
½ teaspoon salt
1 can (10½ ounces) condensed chicken with rice soup
1 can (4 ounces) mushroom stems and pieces, drained
2 tablespoons soy sauce
1 tablespoon brown sugar
1 teaspoon butter or margarine

Cook and stir meat, celery and onion until meat is brown. (To serve immediately, see below.) Spoon off fat. Stir in remaining ingredients. Pour into greased 2-quart casserole. Cover and refrigerate.

■ **1½ hours before serving, stir 1¼ cups boiling water into casserole.** Cover tightly; bake in 350° oven 30 minutes. Stir casserole; bake uncovered 50 minutes.

To Serve Immediately: While browning meat, pour 1¼ cups boiling water on rice and salt in greased 2-quart casserole and cover. Stir meat mixture into rice; bake covered in 350° oven 30 minutes. Stir casserole; bake uncovered 30 minutes.

To Store Meat and Poultry

Wrap loosely. For 1 or 2 days, meat and poultry can stay in their original wrap. Place them in the coldest part of your refrigerator.

Recommended Storage Time:
1 to 2 days: Ground beef, chicken, turkey, giblets, liver, cooked meat.

2 to 4 days: Roasts, steaks, chops, ham, frankfurters, cold cuts.

7 days: Bacon.

SPINACH MEAT ROLL

Store no longer than 24 hours. Makes enough for 8 servings.

Filling
- **1 package (10 ounces) frozen leaf spinach**

Meat Mixture
- **2 pounds ground beef**
- **2 eggs**
- **¼ cup catsup**
- **¼ cup milk**
- **¾ cup soft bread crumbs (about 1 slice bread)**
- **½ teaspoon salt**
- **¼ teaspoon pepper**
- **¼ teaspoon oregano**

Filling
- **1 teaspoon salt**
- **1 package (3 ounces) smoked sliced ham**

Thaw frozen spinach quickly by rinsing spinach with running hot water to separate and remove ice crystals; drain. Mix Meat Mixture ingredients. On 18×15-inch piece of aluminum foil, pat meat mixture into rectangle, 12×10 inches.

Arrange spinach evenly on meat mixture, leaving ½-inch margin around edges. Sprinkle the 1 teaspoon salt on spinach; arrange ham on top. Carefully roll up meat, beginning at narrow end and using foil to lift meat. Press edges and ends of roll to seal. Place on rack in ungreased baking pan, 13×9×2 inches. (To serve immediately, see below.) Cover with plastic wrap and refrigerate.

■ **1 hour 35 minutes before serving, have ready:** 3 slices mozzarella cheese, cut diagonally into halves.

Bake Spinach Meat Roll uncovered in 350° oven 1½ hours. Overlap cheese triangles on roll; bake just until cheese begins to melt, about 5 minutes. (Center of meat roll may be slightly pink due to ham.) Nice served with chili sauce.

To Serve Immediately: Have ready: 3 slices mozzarella cheese, cut diagonally into halves.

Bake Spinach Meat Roll uncovered in 350° oven 1 hour 15 minutes. Overlap cheese triangles on roll; bake just until cheese begins to melt, about 5 minutes.

Roll up the meat and filling, using foil to lift.

Overlap the cheese triangles on top of the baked roll.

Spinach Meat Roll

CABBAGE PATCH STEW

Store no longer than 48 hours. Makes enough for 4 to 6 servings.

- **1 pound ground beef**
- **2 medium onions, thinly sliced**
- **1½ cups coarsely chopped cabbage**
- **½ cup diced celery**
- **1 can (16 ounces) tomatoes**
- **1½ teaspoons garlic salt**
- **1 teaspoon salt**
- **1 teaspoon marjoram**
- **⅛ teaspoon pepper**

Cook and stir meat in Dutch oven until light brown. Spoon off fat. Add onion, cabbage and celery; cook and stir until vegetables are light brown. Stir in tomatoes and seasonings. Cover tightly; simmer 15 minutes. (To serve immediately, see below.) Cool quickly. Cover and refrigerate.

■ **30 minutes before serving, have ready:** 1 can (15½ ounces) kidney beans; instant mashed potato puffs (enough for 4 servings).

Stir in beans (with liquid); heat until mixture boils. Simmer uncovered 15 to 20 minutes. Prepare potato puffs as directed on package. Top stew with potatoes.

To Serve Immediately: Have ready: 1 can (15½ ounces) kidney beans; instant mashed potato puffs (enough for 4 servings).

Stir in beans (with liquid); heat until mixture boils. Simmer uncovered 15 to 20 minutes. Prepare potato puffs as directed on package. Top stew with potatoes.

Pour marinade on beef in plastic bag. Place bag in shallow dish and refrigerate.

Marinated Roast Beef

MARINATED ROAST BEEF

Store no longer than 24 hours. Makes enough for 12 to 14 servings.

Meat
3- to 4-pound beef tip roast

Marinade
**1 bottle (12 ounces) beer or 1½ cups
  apple cider**
⅓ cup salad oil
1 teaspoon salt
¼ teaspoon garlic powder
¼ teaspoon pepper

Pierce meat about 20 times with fork. Place meat in plastic bag or shallow baking dish. Mix 1 cup of the beer and remaining Marinade ingredients; pour on meat. (Reserve remaining beer.) Fasten bag securely or cover dish with plastic wrap. Refrigerate meat, turning occasionally, at least 12 hours.

■ **About 2 hours before serving, place Marinated Roast Beef fat side up on rack in open shallow roasting pan or baking dish. Have ready: 1 loaf (1 pound) French bread, cut into 1-inch slices.**

Insert meat thermometer so tip is in center of thickest part of meat and does not rest in fat. Roast in 325° oven until thermometer registers 160°, about 2 hours.

Place meat on warm platter. Remove drippings from pan, leaving brown particles. Return ¼ cup drippings to pan. Stir in 1 cup water, the reserved ½ cup beer and 1½ teaspoons salt. Heat until mixture boils. Place thin slices of beef on slices of French bread; top with juices.

Add water and beer to drippings from the roast; scrape brown particles from pan.

STEAK CONTINENTAL

Store no longer than 24 hours. Makes enough for 4 to 6 servings.

Meat
2-pound beef round steak, ¾ inch thick

Marinade
3 tablespoons soy sauce
1 tablespoon salad oil
1 tablespoon tomato paste
1 teaspoon salt
½ teaspoon pepper
½ teaspoon oregano
⅛ teaspoon instant minced garlic

Place meat on large piece of plastic wrap. Mix Marinade ingredients; brush both sides of meat with marinade. Fold wrap over meat and seal securely. Refrigerate at least 5 hours. (Flavor improves with longer storage.)

■ **About 15 minutes before serving, set oven control at broil and/or 550°.** Broil Steak Continental with top 3 inches from heat until rare, 5 to 6 minutes on each side, or until medium, 7 to 8 minutes on each side. Cut into ⅛-inch slices.

Tender Treatment

Cuts such as beef round steak, beef tip steak, beef flank steak, pork blade steak or pork arm steak need to be tenderized before they can be broiled. A marinade will tenderize these cuts; it will also add flavor (which these meats lack because they have so little fat).

After meat has been broiled, cut it diagonally across the grain into thin slices. Use a very sharp knife.

Marinades are ideal for tenderizing somewhat tough roasts, too (see pages 97, 102 and 105).

OLD-FASHIONED BEEF STEW

Store no longer than 48 hours. Makes enough for 6 servings.

Meat
½ cup all-purpose flour*
1 teaspoon salt
¼ teaspoon pepper
2 pounds beef stew meat, cut into 1-inch pieces
2 tablespoons shortening
6 cups water

Vegetables
3 medium potatoes, pared and cut into 1-inch cubes
1 medium turnip, cut into 1-inch cubes
4 carrots, cut into 1-inch slices
1 green pepper, cut into strips
1 cup sliced celery (1-inch pieces)
1 medium onion, diced (about ½ cup)

Seasonings
1 tablespoon salt
2 beef bouillon cubes
1 bay leaf

Mix flour, 1 teaspoon salt and the pepper. Coat meat with flour mixture. Melt shortening in large skillet. Brown meat thoroughly.

Add water; heat until water boils. Reduce heat Cover tightly; simmer 2 hours. Stir in vegetables and seasonings. Cover and simmer until vegetables are tender, about 30 minutes.

If desired, thicken stew. Shake 1 cup water and 2 to 4 tablespoons flour in covered jar; stir slowly into stew. Heat, stirring constantly, until stew boils. Boil and stir 1 minute. (Can be served immediately.) Cover and refrigerate.

■ **15 minutes before serving, heat Old-fashioned Beef Stew over medium-high heat.**

VARIATION

Chicken Stew: Substitute 3- to 4-pound stewing chicken, cut up, for the stew meat and chicken bouillon cubes for the beef bouillon cubes. Increase first cooking period to 2½ hours; skim fat from broth before adding vegetables.

*If using self-rising flour, decrease 1 teaspoon salt to ½ teaspoon.

PORK AND SQUASH IN FOIL

Store no longer than 24 hours.

For each serving:
1 pork chop, 1 inch thick
⅛ teaspoon salt
Dash pepper
½ acorn squash
1 tablespoon brown sugar
1 tablespoon honey
1 tablespoon butter or margarine

Trim excess fat carefully from meat. Place chop on 18×12-inch piece of heavy-duty aluminum foil. Season with salt and pepper.

Fill hollow of squash with brown sugar, honey and butter; place squash cut side up on chop. Fold foil over squash and seal securely. Place foil package on baking sheet. Bake in 400° oven 45 minutes. (To serve immediately, bake until meat is done and squash is tender, about 15 minutes longer.) Refrigerate.

■ **About 1 hour before serving, bake in 400° oven until meat is done and squash is tender.**

Note: If preparing more than 1 chop, be sure to wrap each individually. This separate packaging is especially convenient for serving 1 portion at a time—when family members are eating at different times, for instance. Or for a person eating alone.

SPARERIBS AND SAUERKRAUT

Store no longer than 24 hours. Makes enough for 4 servings.

1 can (29 ounces) sauerkraut
¼ cup brown sugar (packed)
2 unpared apples, cut into eighths
3 to 4 pounds spareribs, cut into serving pieces

Mix sauerkraut (with liquid), sugar and apple pieces in open shallow roasting pan; top with spareribs, meaty side up. Cover tightly; bake in 325° oven 1 hour. Uncover; bake 30 minutes. (To serve immediately, spoon off fat and bake until done, about 20 minutes.) Cool quickly. Cover and refrigerate.

■ **About 30 minutes before serving, spoon off fat from Spareribs and Sauerkraut. Bake uncovered in 325° oven until done.**

SPICY PORK STEAKS

Store no longer than 24 hours. Makes enough for 3 or 4 servings.

Meat
1¾ to 2 pounds pork steaks, ¾ inch thick

Marinade
½ cup orange juice
3 tablespoons brown sugar
3 tablespoons vinegar
1 teaspoon salt
½ teaspoon dry mustard
¼ teaspoon ginger
2 tablespoons catsup

Place meat in plastic bag or shallow glass dish. Mix Marinade ingredients; pour on meat. Fasten bag securely or cover dish with plastic wrap. Refrigerate at least 8 hours.

■ **About 1 hour before serving, remove Spicy Pork Steaks from marinade; reserve marinade.** Place meat in open shallow roasting pan or baking dish. Bake uncovered in 350° oven 15 minutes; pour ¼ cup of reserved marinade on meat. Bake 30 minutes; turn meat and pour on another ¼ cup marinade. Bake until tender, about 15 minutes.

SWEET AND SOUR PORK

Store no longer than 24 hours. Makes enough for 5 or 6 servings.

Sweet and Sour Pork (page 19)
2 medium green peppers, cut into 1-inch pieces
1 medium onion, cut into ½-inch pieces
4 cups hot cooked rice

Prepare Sweet and Sour Pork as directed except—refrigerate 1 package pork cubes and 1 container sauce.

Heat pork cubes on ungreased baking sheet in 400° oven until hot, about 7 minutes. Heat ¼ cup water and the sauce in large saucepan until mixture boils. Stir in green pepper and onion; cover tightly and simmer 5 minutes. Just before serving, stir pork cubes into sauce. Serve on rice.

PORK TENDERLOIN BAKE

Store no longer than 48 hours. Makes enough for 6 servings.

Meat
2 pork tenderloins (10 to 12 ounces each)

Marinade
1 can (13¼ ounces) crushed pineapple, drained (reserve ¼ cup syrup)
¼ cup dry sherry or apple juice
2 tablespoons soy sauce
2 tablespoons chili sauce
¼ teaspoon red food color
1 teaspoon salt
2 cloves garlic, crushed
1 green onion, cut into thick slices
2 slices gingerroot, smashed

Glaze
1 cup honey

Place meat in plastic bag or shallow glass dish. Mix pineapple and reserved syrup with remaining ingredients except honey; pour on meat. Fasten bag securely or cover dish with plastic wrap. Refrigerate meat, turning occasionally, at least 2 hours.

■ **About 1½ hours before serving, remove Pork Tenderloin Bake from marinade; reserve marinade.** Place meat on rack in open shallow baking pan or dish. Roast in 325° oven 30 minutes. Mix reserved marinade and honey; pour on meat. Bake until done, 30 to 60 minutes. Cut meat diagonally across grain into ¼-inch slices.

Apricot Ham Buffet can be served hot, as pictured, as well as cold.

APRICOT HAM BUFFET

Store no longer than 24 hours. Makes 15 to 18 servings.

5- to 7-pound fully cooked boneless ham
1 tablespoon prepared mustard
1 jar (12 ounces) apricot preserves
1 can (30 ounces) apricot halves, drained
  Whole cloves

Place meat fat side up on rack in open shallow roasting pan. Insert meat thermometer so tip is in center of thickest part of meat and does not rest in fat. Roast in 325° oven 1 hour 45 minutes. Heat mustard and apricot preserves in small saucepan over low heat until preserves are melted; keep warm.

Remove meat from oven. Trim excess fat carefully from meat; brush meat evenly with half the apricot glaze. Bake until thermometer registers 130°, about 20 minutes. Remove meat from oven. Fasten apricots on meat with whole cloves. Carefully brush top with remaining warm apricot glaze. Bake 10 minutes. (Can be served immediately.) Cover and refrigerate.

■ **About 10 minutes before serving, place ham on platter.** Serve cold.

Pour the marinade over the meat, cover and refrigerate, turning occasionally.

The tip of the meat thermometer should be in the center of the thickest part of the meat.

Luau Roast—a patio feast

LUAU ROAST

Store no longer than 24 hours. Makes enough for 10 servings.

Meat
4-pound pork boneless blade Boston roast

Marinade
½ **cup pineapple juice**
½ **cup salad oil**
½ **cup dark corn syrup**
¼ **cup lime juice**
1 **small clove garlic, crushed**
2 **tablespoons brown sugar**
1 **tablespoon prepared mustard**
1 **tablespoon soy sauce**
2 **teaspoons salt**
1 **teaspoon ground coriander**
½ **teaspoon ginger**

Trim excess fat carefully from meat. Place meat in glass bowl, plastic bag or shallow baking dish. Mix Marinade ingredients; pour on meat. Fasten bag securely or cover dish with plastic wrap. Refrigerate meat, turning occasionally, at least 8 hours.

■ **About 2½ hours before serving, remove Luau Roast from marinade; reserve marinade.** Place meat fat side up on rack in open shallow baking pan or dish. Insert meat thermometer so tip is in center of thickest part of meat and does not rest in fat. Roast in 325° oven, basting occasionally with reserved marinade, until thermometer registers 170°, about 2½ hours.

BAKED HAM WITH SPINACH STUFFING

Store no longer than 24 hours. Makes enough for 4 to 6 servings.

Filling
1 package (10 ounces) frozen chopped spinach
¼ cup diced celery
1 can (4 ounces) mushroom stems and pieces, drained
2 tablespoons chopped onion
2 tablespoons salad oil
¼ teaspoon salt
⅛ teaspoon pepper

Meat
2 fully cooked ham slices, ½ inch thick (about 1½ pounds)
1 tablespoon butter or margarine, melted

Cook spinach as directed on package; drain. Cook and stir celery, mushroom and onion in oil until celery is tender. Stir in spinach, salt and pepper.

Place 1 slice meat in ungreased shallow baking dish. Spread spinach mixture on meat; top with second slice and brush top with butter. Cover with aluminum foil and refrigerate.

■ **65 minutes before serving, have ready:** 1 envelope (1½ ounces) white sauce mix; 1 tablespoon horseradish, well drained; 1 tablespoon prepared mustard; ⅛ teaspoon nutmeg.

Bake ham covered in 325° oven 30 minutes. To make Horseradish Sauce, prepare white sauce mix as directed on package. Stir in horseradish, mustard and nutmeg. Uncover meat; bake 30 minutes. Serve with Horseradish Sauce.

POTATO DOGS

Store no longer than 24 hours. Makes enough for 5 servings.

Instant mashed potato puffs (enough for 4 servings)
2 tablespoons parsley flakes
2 tablespoons instant chopped onion
1 teaspoon prepared mustard
1 pound frankfurters (about 10)

Prepare potato puffs as directed on package. Stir in parsley, onion and mustard. Cut frankfurters lengthwise, being careful not to cut completely through. Arrange cut side up on ungreased baking sheet; spread potato mixture on frankfurters. (To serve immediately, see below.) Cover with plastic wrap and refrigerate.

■ **About 10 minutes before serving, set oven control at broil and/or 550°.** Broil Potato Dogs with tops 5 inches from heat until potatoes are golden brown, 8 to 10 minutes. Garnish with cherry tomatoes or tomato wedges.

To Serve Immediately: Set oven control at broil and/or 550°. Broil frankfurters with tops 5 inches from heat until potatoes are golden brown, 5 to 8 minutes. Garnish with cherry tomatoes or tomato wedges.

LASAGNE

Store no longer than 24 hours. Makes enough for 8 to 10 servings.

Prepare Lasagne as directed on page 20 except —cover and refrigerate instead of freezing. One hour 5 minutes before serving, heat oven to 350°. Remove Lasagne from refrigerator and unwrap. Bake uncovered until hot and bubbly, 55 to 60 minutes.

BAKED SAUSAGE RING

Store no longer than 24 hours. Makes enough for 8 servings.

   2 pounds bulk pork sausage
   2 eggs, beaten
1½ cups dry bread crumbs
   ¼ cup parsley flakes
   1 tablespoon instant minced onion

Heat oven to 350°. Lightly grease 6-cup ring mold. Mix all ingredients. Press into mold. Bake uncovered 20 minutes. Spoon off fat. Cover and refrigerate immediately.

■ **About 40 minutes before serving, have ready:** ¾ cup applesauce; 2 teaspoons vinegar or lemon juice; ½ teaspoon horseradish.

Bake Baked Sausage Ring uncovered in 350° oven 25 to 30 minutes. After ring has baked 15 minutes, heat applesauce, vinegar and horseradish.

Remove Baked Sausage Ring from oven; pour off fat. Turn onto warm platter; top with applesauce mixture. Very pretty garnished with orange-slice twists and parsley.

To Store Cheese

Store soft cheeses (such as Camembert, cream cheese and cottage cheese) tightly covered. Cottage cheese keeps for 3 to 5 days; other soft cheeses keep for 2 weeks.

Harder cheeses (such as Swiss, Cheddar or Parmesan) will keep for several months. Store them unopened in their original wrappers. After opening, wrap them tightly with foil or plastic wrap.

LAYERED HAM DINNER

Store no longer than 24 hours. Makes enough for 4 to 6 servings.

Base
1 package (9 ounces) frozen cut green beans

Sauce
1 can (10¾ ounces) condensed cream of celery soup
¼ cup mayonnaise
1 tablespoon prepared mustard

Base and Topping
2 packages (3 or 4 ounces each) thinly sliced cooked ham
1 cup shredded Cheddar cheese
¼ cup dry bread crumbs

Rinse beans with small amount of running cold water to separate and remove ice crystals; drain. Place beans in ungreased 1½-quart casserole.

Mix soup, mayonnaise and mustard; spoon half the sauce on beans. Top with meat; spoon remaining sauce on meat. Sprinkle cheese and crumbs on sauce. (To serve immediately, see below.) Cover and refrigerate.

■ **50 minutes before serving, heat oven to 350°.** Bake Layered Ham Dinner uncovered until hot and bubbly, about 40 minutes.

To Serve Immediately: Bake uncovered in 350° oven until hot and bubbly, about 25 minutes.

LEG O' LAMB BARBECUE

Store no longer than 24 hours. Makes enough for 6 to 8 servings.

4- to 5-pound leg of lamb
2 small cloves garlic, peeled and slivered
½ cup red wine vinegar
⅓ cup salad oil
⅓ cup brown sugar (packed)
2 tablespoons tarragon leaves
1 teaspoon salt
2 green onions (with tops), cut into 2-inch slices
1 can (8 ounces) tomato sauce

Cut 4 or 5 small slits in meat with tip of sharp knife; insert garlic slivers in slits. Place meat in large plastic bag or shallow glass dish. Mix remaining ingredients except tomato sauce; pour on meat. Fasten bag securely or cover dish with plastic wrap. Refrigerate meat, turning occasionally, at least 8 hours.

■ **About 3 hours before serving, remove meat from marinade; reserve marinade.** Place meat fat side up on rack in open shallow roasting pan or baking dish. Insert meat thermometer so tip is in center of thickest part of meat and does not touch bone or rest in fat. Roast in 325° oven 2 hours. Mix reserved marinade and tomato sauce. Remove meat from oven; brush meat with some of the tomato glaze. Bake, brushing several times with remaining glaze, until thermometer registers 175 to 180°, about 30 minutes. Remove garlic slivers before serving.

HEARTY LAMB SHANKS

Store no longer than 24 hours. Makes enough for 4 servings.

4 lamb shanks (about 12 ounces each)
1½ cups buttermilk
2 tablespoons instant minced onion
1 teaspoon salt
¾ teaspoon ginger
¾ teaspoon ground coriander
½ teaspoon celery seed
½ teaspoon pepper

Arrange meat in ungreased baking dish, 11½ × 7½ × 1½ inches. Mix remaining ingredients; pour on meat. Cover and refrigerate, turning meat occasionally, at least 8 hours.

■ **About 2½ hours before serving, heat oven to 350°.** Bake Hearty Lamb Shanks covered 2 hours. Uncover; bake until tender, about 30 minutes.

ORIENTAL VEAL CASSEROLE

Store no longer than 24 hours. Makes enough for 5 or 6 servings.

1 pound boneless veal,* cut into 1-inch cubes
  Flour
2 tablespoons shortening
1½ cups sliced celery
2 small onions, chopped
1 can (10¾ ounces) condensed cream of chicken soup
1 can (10¾ ounces) condensed cream of mushroom soup
1 soup can water
2 to 3 tablespoons soy sauce
½ cup uncooked regular rice

Heat oven to 325°. Coat meat with flour. Melt shortening in large skillet. Brown meat in shortening. Stir in remaining ingredients.

Pour into ungreased 3-quart casserole. Cover tightly; bake 1 hour. (To serve immediately, bake 30 minutes longer.) Cover and refrigerate immediately.

■ **1 hour before serving, heat oven to 325°.** Bake Oriental Veal Casserole uncovered 50 minutes. If desired, sprinkle chopped cashews on top and serve with soy sauce.

*1 pound lean pork shoulder, cut into 1-inch cubes, can be substituted for the veal.

MEXICALI CHICKEN

Store no longer than 24 hours. Makes enough for 4 or 5 servings.

Chicken
2 tablespoons salad oil
2½- to 3-pound broiler-fryer chicken, cut up

Sauce
1 bottle (7 ounces) spicy sauce for tacos
½ cup water
1 teaspoon salt
½ teaspoon oregano
¼ teaspoon instant minced garlic
¼ cup instant minced onion

Topping
2 cups shredded Cheddar cheese (about 8 ounces)

Heat oil in large skillet or electric frypan. Brown chicken in oil over medium heat about 15 minutes. Spoon off fat. Mix Sauce ingredients; pour on chicken. Reduce heat; cover tightly and simmer until chicken is done, about 30 minutes.

Place chicken in ungreased baking pan, 9×9×2 inches, or ovenproof serving dish. Sprinkle cheese on top. Cover and refrigerate.

■ **40 minutes before serving, heat oven to 400°.** Bake Mexicali Chicken covered 10 minutes. Uncover; bake 20 minutes.

Note: If spicy sauce for tacos is not available, mix 1 can (8 ounces) tomato sauce, 1 teaspoon chili powder, 5 drops red pepper sauce and 2 tablespoons vinegar or lemon juice. Omit water.

To Store Stuffing

When you get poultry ready the day before you cook it, refrigerate the stuffing ingredients (not mixed) separately from the bird. Stuff the bird just before you cook it. With leftovers, too, remove the stuffing from the bird and refrigerate meat and stuffing separately. Use leftovers within 2 or 3 days.

SKILLET COQ AU VIN

Store no longer than 24 hours. Makes enough for 4 servings.

Meat and Vegetables
½ cup all-purpose flour*
1 teaspoon salt
¼ teaspoon pepper
3- to 3½-pound broiler-fryer chicken, cut up
6 slices bacon
6 small onions
½ pound mushrooms, sliced

Bouquet Garni
½ teaspoon thyme leaves
1 bay leaf
2 large sprigs parsley

Carrots and Broth
4 carrots, halved
1 teaspoon instant chicken bouillon
1 cup hot water
1 cup red Burgundy
1 clove garlic, crushed
½ teaspoon salt

Mix flour, 1 teaspoon salt and the pepper; coat chicken with flour mixture. Cook bacon in large skillet until crisp; remove bacon from skillet and drain. Brown chicken in bacon fat over medium heat.

Push chicken to one side of skillet. Cook and stir onions and mushroom in other side of skillet until mushroom is tender, about 5 minutes. Drain off fat.

To prepare Bouquet Garni: Tie thyme leaves, bay leaf and parsley in cheesecloth or place in tea ball.

Crumble bacon; stir in bacon, Bouquet Garni and remaining ingredients.

Cover tightly; simmer until done, about 1 hour. Remove Bouquet Garni. Spoon off fat. (Can be served immediately.) Cover and refrigerate.

■ **About 20 minutes before serving, spoon off fat.** Heat Skillet Coq au Vin until mixture boils. Cover and simmer 10 minutes. Garnish each bowl with sprig of parsley.

*If using self-rising flour, decrease 1 teaspoon salt to ½ teaspoon.

JAMBALAYA

Store no longer than 24 hours. Makes enough for 6 or 7 servings.

**2½- to 3-pound broiler-fryer chicken,
    cut up**
 3 teaspoons salt
 ¼ teaspoon pepper
 8 pork sausage links
 **2 cans (16 ounces each) stewed
    tomatoes**
 1 large clove garlic, minced
 ¼ teaspoon thyme
 **⅛ to ¼ teaspoon cayenne red
    pepper**

Place chicken in Dutch oven. Add enough water to cover chicken. Season with salt and pepper. Heat until water boils. Reduce heat; cover tightly and simmer 45 minutes.

Remove chicken from broth; set aside. Strain broth; reserve 2 cups. Brown sausage in large pan or Dutch oven. Spoon off fat; reserve 2 tablespoons. Return reserved fat to pan. Add chicken; stir in reserved broth and remaining ingredients. (To serve immediately, see below.) Cover and refrigerate.

■ **About 35 minutes before serving, have ready:** 1 cup uncooked regular rice; snipped parsley.

Heat Jambalaya until mixture boils; stir in rice. Cover and simmer 25 minutes. Serve in large bowl; sprinkle parsley on top.

To Serve Immediately: Have ready: 1 cup uncooked regular rice; snipped parsley.

Heat Jambalaya until mixture boils; stir in rice. Cover and simmer 25 minutes. Serve in large bowl; sprinkle parsley on top.

CHICKEN CASSEROLE

Store no longer than 24 hours. Makes enough for 6 servings.

Base

**1 package (10 ounces) frozen
chopped broccoli**

Sauce

**¼ cup butter or margarine
¼ cup all-purpose flour
1½ teaspoons salt
¼ teaspoon pepper
½ teaspoon lemon pepper
1 cup chicken broth
2 cups milk**

Base

**7 ounces spaghetti, cooked and drained
2 cups cut-up cooked chicken or turkey
1 can (3 ounces) sliced mushrooms,
drained
½ cup sliced ripe olives
½ cup dry bread crumbs
1 tablespoon butter or margarine, melted**

Rinse frozen broccoli with small amount of running cold water to separate and remove ice crystals; drain. Melt ¼ cup butter in large saucepan over low heat. Stir in flour and seasonings. Cook over low heat, stirring constantly, until mixture is smooth and bubbly.

Remove from heat; stir in broth and milk. Heat, stirring constantly, until sauce boils. Boil and stir 1 minute. Stir in spaghetti, chicken, broccoli, mushrooms and olives.

Pour into ungreased baking dish, 8×8×2 inches. Toss crumbs in melted butter; sprinkle crumbs on top. (Can be baked immediately.) Cover and refrigerate.

■ **About 1½ hours before serving, heat oven to 350°.** Bake Chicken Casserole covered 45 minutes. Uncover; bake until hot and bubbly, about 25 minutes.

TURKEY DIVAN

Store no longer than 24 hours. Makes enough for 5 servings.

Base

**2 packages (10 ounces each)
frozen broccoli spears**

Sauce

**¼ cup butter or margarine
¼ cup all-purpose flour
1½ cups chicken broth***
**2 tablespoons sherry, if desired
⅛ teaspoon nutmeg
½ cup whipping cream, whipped
½ cup grated Parmesan cheese**

Base and Topping

**5 large slices cooked turkey or chicken
breast (about ¾ pound)
½ cup grated Parmesan cheese**

Cook broccoli as directed on package except— simmer only 3 minutes; drain. Melt butter in medium saucepan over low heat. Stir in flour. Cook over low heat, stirring constantly, until smooth and bubbly. Remove from heat; stir in chicken broth. Heat until sauce boils. Boil and stir 1 minute. Remove from heat; stir in sherry and nutmeg. Gently fold in whipped cream and ½ cup cheese.

Arrange broccoli in ungreased baking dish, 11½×7½×1½ inches; top with turkey. Pour sauce on meat. Sprinkle ½ cup cheese on top. (To serve immediately, see below.) Cover and refrigerate.

■ **About 55 minutes before serving, heat oven to 350°.** Bake Turkey Divan uncovered until hot, about 45 minutes.

To Serve Immediately: Set oven control at broil and/or 550°. Broil with top of dish 3 to 5 inches from heat until cheese is golden brown.

*Chicken broth can be made by dissolving 2 chicken bouillon cubes or 2 teaspoons instant chicken bouillon in 1½ cups boiling water, or use canned chicken broth.

FISH BAKE

Store no longer than 24 hours. Makes enough for 6 servings.

  2 **pounds fresh or frozen cod, pike, pollack**
    or flounder fillets
  ¼ **cup all-purpose flour**
  2 **teaspoons salt**
  ¼ **teaspoon pepper**
  1 **teaspoon dill weed**
  1 **cup milk**
  2 **cups croutons**
  ¼ **cup butter or margarine, melted**

If fish is frozen, thaw. Heat oven to 350°. Cut fish into serving pieces. Mix flour, salt and pepper. Coat fish with flour mixture. Arrange fish in single layer in ungreased baking dish, 13½×9×2 inches. Sprinkle dill weed on fish; pour milk on top. Bake uncovered 45 minutes. Toss croutons with butter; sprinkle on fish. (To serve immediately, bake 10 minutes longer.) Cover and refrigerate.

■ **40 minutes before serving, heat oven to 350°.** Bake Fish Bake uncovered 30 minutes. Garnish with lemon slices and parsley.

For Best Results

Thaw frozen fish in its original wrapping under cold running water. Measure other ingredients while fish thaws. Combine it with other ingredients while still chilled. Work quickly; refrigerate immediately. Clean fresh-caught fish at once. Refrigerate or put on ice immediately.

PIKE FIESTA

Store no longer than 24 hours. Makes enough for 2 or 3 servings.

  1 **pound fresh or frozen walleye pike fillets**
  1½ **teaspoons salt**
  ¼ **teaspoon pepper**
  1 **small onion, thinly sliced**
  1 **tomato, peeled and cut into**
    ½-inch slices
  1 **tablespoon lime juice**
  1 **tablespoon salad oil**
  1 **tablespoon snipped parsley**
  8 **pitted ripe olives**

If fish is frozen, thaw. Arrange fish in ungreased baking dish, 8×8×2 inches. Season with salt and pepper. Cover fish with onion and tomato slices; sprinkle lime juice, salad oil and parsley on onion and tomato. Top with olives. (Can be baked immediately.) Cover and refrigerate.

■ **About 55 minutes before serving, heat oven to 375°.** Bake Pike Fiesta covered 30 minutes. Uncover; bake until fish flakes easily with fork, about 15 minutes. Garnish with lime wedges.

SOY HALIBUT STEAKS

Store no longer than 48 hours. Makes enough for 4 to 6 servings.

  2 **pounds fresh or frozen halibut**
    steaks (about 6)
  3 **tablespoons soy sauce**
  1 **teaspoon ginger**
  ½ **teaspoon garlic powder**
  2 **teaspoons sugar**
  1 **teaspoon grated lemon peel**
  ¼ **cup fresh lemon juice**
  ¼ **cup water**

If fish is frozen, thaw. Arrange fish in single layer in shallow dish. Mix remaining ingredients; pour on steaks. Cover and refrigerate.

■ **About 20 minutes before serving, set oven control at broil and/or 550°.** Arrange Soy Halibut Steaks on broiler rack; reserve marinade for basting. Broil steaks with tops about 3 inches from heat until brown, 4 to 6 minutes. Brush with reserved sauce; turn and brush again. Broil until fish flakes easily with fork, 4 to 6 minutes. Garnish with parsley and lemon slices, if desired.

SHRIMP INTERNATIONALE

Store no longer than 24 hours. Makes enough for 5 or 6 servings.

Base
12 ounces frozen cleaned raw shrimp

Marinade
½ cup creamy Italian salad dressing
1 tablespoon soy sauce
1 teaspoon parsley flakes

Vegetables and Seasoning
2 tablespoons salad oil
1 medium onion, diced
¼ cup chopped green pepper
¼ pound fresh mushrooms, trimmed and sliced, or 1 can (2 ounces) mushroom stems and pieces, drained
1 tablespoon soy sauce

Base
2 cups cooked rice
1 can (8¼ ounces) crushed pineapple, drained

Rinse frozen shrimp with running cold water to remove ice glaze. Place shrimp on 18×12-inch piece of heavy-duty aluminum foil. Mix salad dressing, 1 tablespoon soy sauce and the parsley flakes; pour on shrimp. Wrap shrimp securely in the foil and refrigerate.

Heat oil in large skillet or electric frypan. Cook and stir onion, green pepper and mushroom in oil until onion is tender. Remove from heat; stir in 1 tablespoon soy sauce, the rice and pineapple. Place mixture in ungreased 1-quart casserole. (To serve immediately, see right.) Cover and refrigerate.

■ **55 minutes before serving, have ready:** cabbage leaves; ⅓ cup slivered almonds; lime wedges.

Bake rice mixture covered in 375° oven 15 minutes; place foil package of shrimp on baking sheet in oven. Bake until rice is hot and shrimp are tender, about 30 minutes.

Line salad bowl with cabbage leaves. Stir almonds into rice mixture; spoon into bowl. Top with shrimp and sauce; garnish with lime wedges.

To Serve Immediately: Have ready: cabbage leaves; ⅓ cup slivered almonds; lime wedges.

Bake foil package of shrimp on baking sheet and rice mixture covered in 375° oven 25 minutes.

Line salad bowl with cabbage leaves. Stir almonds into rice mixture; spoon into bowl. Top with shrimp and sauce; garnish with lime wedges.

HOT SHRIMP AND MACARONI SALAD

Store no longer than 24 hours. Makes enough for 4 to 6 servings.

1 package (7.25 ounces) macaroni and cheese
1 can (4½ ounces) shrimp, rinsed and drained
½ cup chopped celery
¼ cup chopped gherkins
2 hard-cooked eggs, chopped

Cook macaroni and cheese as directed on package. Stir in remaining ingredients. (To serve immediately, heat, stirring occasionally.) Cover and refrigerate.

■ **About 15 minutes before serving, stir in ¼ cup water.** Cover Hot Shrimp and Macaroni Salad tightly; heat over medium heat, stirring occasionally, until hot, about 12 minutes.

About Quantities

Shrimp: 2 cans (4½ ounces each) medium shrimp = 1 package (12 ounces) frozen cleaned shrimp.

To Make 2 Cups of Cooked Rice: Bring ⅔ cup regular rice, ½ teaspoon salt and 1⅓ cups water to a boil, stirring occasionally. Reduce heat; cook tightly covered for 14 minutes. Remove from heat; fluff with fork. Cover and let stand for 5 to 10 minutes.

BAKED AVOCADO-CRABMEAT SALADS

Store no longer than 24 hours. Makes enough for 6 servings.

Salad
- **1 can (7½ ounces) crabmeat, drained and cartilage removed**
- **2 hard-cooked eggs, chopped**
- **¼ cup finely chopped sweet pickle or pickle relish**
- **⅓ cup salad dressing or dairy sour cream**
- **¼ teaspoon salt**
- **⅛ teaspoon red pepper sauce**

Base and Topping
- **3 ripe avocados**
- **½ cup shredded Swiss cheese**

Mix all ingredients except avocados and cheese. Cut unpeeled avocados lengthwise into halves; remove pits. Place avocados cut side up in ungreased baking dish, 9×9×2 inches. Fill each half with ⅓ cup crabmeat salad; sprinkle cheese on salad. (Can be baked immediately.) Cover with plastic wrap and refrigerate.

■ **30 minutes before serving, heat oven to 400°.** Bake salads uncovered until hot and bubbly, about 20 minutes.

Baked Avocado-Crabmeat Salad

CRAB SHELLS

Store no longer than 24 hours. Makes enough for 8 servings.

Filling
- **1 can (6½ ounces) crabmeat, drained and cartilage removed**
- **2 tablespoons chopped pimiento**
- **1 hard-cooked egg, chopped**
- **1 tablespoon chopped onion**
- **⅓ cup chopped celery**
- **½ teaspoon salt**
- **⅓ cup mayonnaise**

Pastry
- **2 cups all-purpose flour***
- **1 teaspoon salt**
- **⅔ cup plus 2 tablespoons shortening**
- **4 to 5 tablespoons cold water**

Mix Filling ingredients. Refrigerate. Prepare Pastry: Measure flour and 1 teaspoon salt into bowl. Cut in shortening thoroughly. Sprinkle in water, 1 tablespoon at a time, mixing until all flour is moistened and dough almost cleans side of bowl (1 to 2 teaspoons water can be added if needed). Gather dough into a ball; divide in half.

Roll each half into 11-inch circle and cut into eight 4-inch circles. Place 2 tablespoons crabmeat mixture on each of 8 pastry circles. Moisten edge with water; cover with a remaining circle. Press edge with tines of fork to seal securely. Fit Crab Shells into ungreased baking shells; prick top crusts several times. Place shells on baking sheet. (To serve immediately, bake uncovered in 425° oven 20 to 25 minutes.) Cover with plastic wrap and refrigerate.

■ **40 minutes before serving, heat oven to 425°.** Bake Crab Shells uncovered 30 minutes. Turn each baked Crab Shell over in baking shell so lines will show on the pastry.

*If using self-rising flour, omit salt from Pastry. Pastry made with self-rising flour differs in flavor and texture.

Spoon half the flaked salmon onto the cucumber slices.

Jellied Salmon Loaf

JELLIED SALMON LOAF

Store no longer than 24 hours. Makes enough for 8 servings.

Gelatin
  2 **envelopes unflavored gelatin**
  ½ **cup cold water**
1½ **cups boiling water**
  ¼ **cup lemon juice**
  1 **tablespoon vinegar**
  2 **teaspoons salt**

Base
  1 **cup chopped celery**
  ½ **medium cucumber, chopped**
  ½ **medium cucumber, thinly sliced**
  2 **cans (16 ounces each) red salmon, drained, flaked and boned**

Sauce
  ¾ **cup dairy sour cream**
  ½ **green pepper, finely chopped**
  2 **teaspoons snipped parsley**
  2 **teaspoons snipped chives**
  ½ **teaspoon salt**
    Dash pepper

Sprinkle gelatin on cold water to soften. Stir boiling water gradually into gelatin; stir until gelatin is dissolved. Mix in lemon juice, vinegar and salt; cool.

In another bowl, mix celery and chopped cucumber. Arrange cucumber slices in bottom of loaf pan, 9×5×3 inches. Layer half the salmon, the cucumber-celery mixture and remaining salmon on slices.

Pour gelatin on salmon. Chill until set. Mix Sauce ingredients. Cover and refrigerate.

■ **Just before serving, loosen Jellied Salmon Loaf from mold; invert onto serving plate.** Garnish as you wish. Serve sauce with salad.

Loosen the salmon loaf around the edges; dip the pan into hot water to unmold.

TUNA MACARONI SALAD

Store no longer than 48 hours. Makes enough for 4 servings.

Base
1 cup elbow macaroni, cooked and drained
1 can (9¼ ounces) tuna, drained
2 tablespoons chopped red onion
1 to 2 tablespoons chopped radish
½ cup chopped green pepper

Dressing
½ cup mayonnaise
½ teaspoon dry mustard
½ teaspoon salt
¼ teaspoon pepper
1 tablespoon lemon juice

Mix Base ingredients. Mix Dressing ingredients; pour dressing on macaroni mixture and toss. Cover and chill at least 3 hours. (Can be served immediately.)

■ **Just before serving, line large bowl with greens or place lettuce cups on plate. Fill with Tuna Macaroni Salad.**

CREAMY TUNA CHEESE MOLD

Store no longer than 48 hours. Makes enough for 4 servings.

1 envelope unflavored gelatin
⅓ cup cold water
½ cup boiling water
¾ cup diced celery
¼ cup minced onion
¼ cup chopped green pepper
1 can (9¼ ounces) tuna, drained
½ teaspoon salt
½ teaspoon lemon pepper
½ cup shredded sharp Cheddar cheese
⅓ cup mayonnaise
1 teaspoon lemon juice

Sprinkle gelatin on cold water to soften. Stir boiling water gradually into gelatin; stir until gelatin is dissolved. Mix in remaining ingredients. Pour salad into 4-cup mold. Cover and chill until firm. (Can be served immediately.)

■ **Just before serving, loosen Creamy Tuna Cheese Mold from mold; invert onto serving plate.**

TUNA CASSEROLE

Store no longer than 24 hours. Makes enough for 4 to 6 servings.

Sauce
- 1 envelope (1½ to 2 ounces) white sauce mix
- 1 tablespoon peanut butter

Base
- 1 cup elbow macaroni, cooked and drained
- 2 cans (6½ ounces each) tuna, drained
- 1 can (4 ounces) mushroom stems and pieces
- ¼ cup chopped green pepper
- ½ cup sliced pitted ripe olives
- 1 to 1½ teaspoons seasoned salt
- ¼ teaspoon oregano
- ¼ teaspoon pepper

Topping
- 1 cup shredded Cheddar cheese (about 4 ounces)

Prepare 1 cup medium white sauce as directed on sauce mix package. Stir in peanut butter. Mix in macaroni, tuna, mushrooms (with liquid) and remaining ingredients except cheese. Pour into ungreased 1½-quart casserole. Sprinkle cheese on top. (To serve immediately, bake uncovered in 350° oven 30 minutes.) Cover and refrigerate.

■ **50 minutes before serving, heat oven to 350°.** Bake Tuna Casserole covered 30 minutes. Uncover; bake 10 minutes.

"Just Enough" Macaroni

To Make 1 Cup of Cooked Elbow Macaroni: Drop ½ cup elbow macaroni and ½ teaspoon salt into 1½ cups of rapidly boiling water. Bring water to a rapid boil once more. Cook for 3 minutes, stirring constantly. Cover pan tightly and remove from heat. Let the pan stand covered for 10 minutes. Drain. Rinse macaroni with cold water.

BAKED BEANS

Store no longer than 5 days. Makes enough for 6 to 8 servings.

- 1 pound dried navy or pea beans (about 2 cups)
- ¼ pound salt pork (without rind)
- 1 medium onion, sliced
- ¼ cup brown sugar (packed)
- 3 tablespoons molasses
- ¼ teaspoon dry mustard
- ⅛ teaspoon pepper

Place beans in large saucepan. Add enough water to cover beans. Heat until water boils. Boil 2 minutes. Remove from heat; cover and set aside 1 hour. To keep beans covered with water, add small amount of water if necessary. Simmer uncovered until tender, about 1 hour. (Do not boil or beans will burst.) Drain beans; reserve liquid.

Heat oven to 300°. Cut salt pork into several pieces; layer salt pork, beans and onion in ungreased 2-quart bean pot or casserole. Mix 1 cup of the reserved liquid, the sugar, molasses, mustard and pepper; pour on beans. Add enough of the remaining reserved liquid (or water) to almost cover beans. Cover tightly; bake, stirring occasionally, 2 hours. Uncover; bake 1½ hours. Cool slightly. Cover and refrigerate.

■ **15 minutes before serving, place 1 can (8 ounces) tomato sauce and Baked Beans in large skillet.** Cook over medium heat, stirring occasionally, until bubbly, about 15 minutes.

LIMA-MEATBALL STEW

Store no longer than 24 hours. Makes enough for 6 servings.

 1 **cup dried large lima beans**
4½ **cups water**
 ½ **cup water**
 3 **tablespoons flour**
 1 **can (16 ounces) whole tomatoes**
 1 **cup sliced celery**
 3 **medium carrots, cut into 2-inch pieces**
 ½ **cup chopped onion**
 1 **tablespoon salt**
 ¼ **teaspoon pepper**
 1 **bay leaf**
 1 **container frozen Mini Meatballs (page 10)**

Heat beans and 4½ cups water to boiling in Dutch oven. Boil uncovered 2 minutes. Remove from heat; cover and set aside 1 hour. Do not drain.

Heat oven to 375°. Mix ½ cup water and the flour; stir into beans. Heat, stirring occasionally, until mixture boils and thickens. Stir in vegetables, salt, pepper and bay leaf. Heat until mixture boils. Cover tightly; bake 1½ hours. Add frozen meatballs. (To serve immediately, cover and bake until meatballs are hot, about 1 hour.) Cover and refrigerate.

■ **40 minutes before serving, heat oven to 375°.** Bake Lima-Meatball Stew covered until meatballs are hot, about 30 minutes.

Tomorrow's Sandwiches

When you make sandwiches the night before, always butter bread right to edges, so other fillings won't soak in. Wrap whole sandwich in plastic bag or wrap. Close tightly. Wrap greens and tomato slices separately. A few tasty combinations: sliced beef and sliced radishes on English muffins; lunch meat and sliced olives on corn muffins.

HEARTY SANDWICH LOAF

Store no longer than 24 hours. Makes enough for 6 servings.

Bread
 1 **loaf (1 pound) unsliced white bread (about 8 inches long)**

Butter Mixture
 ½ **cup soft butter or margarine**
 3 **tablespoons instant minced onion**
 3 **tablespoons prepared mustard**
 1 **tablespoon poppy seed**
 1 **tablespoon lemon juice**
   Dash cayenne red pepper

Filling
 6 **slices Swiss cheese**
 6 **thin slices luncheon meat**

Carefully trim crust from top of bread. Make 5 diagonal cuts at equal intervals from top of loaf almost to bottom. Mix butter, onion, mustard, poppy seed, lemon juice and cayenne red pepper. Reserve 3 tablespoons butter mixture. Spread remaining butter mixture into cuts.

Place 1 cheese slice and 1 meat slice in each of 4 cuts; alternate 2 slices cheese and 2 slices meat in last cut. Spread reserved butter mixture on top and sides of loaf. (To serve immediately, see below.) Wrap in heavy-duty aluminum foil and refrigerate.

■ **1 hour before serving, heat oven to 350°.** Place wrapped Hearty Sandwich Loaf on ungreased baking sheet; open foil. Bake 30 minutes. Cover loaf with foil; bake until hot, about 20 minutes. To serve, slice through each diagonal cut between meat slice and bread.

To Serve Immediately: Place loaf on lightly greased baking sheet. Bake in 350° oven 15 minutes. Cover loaf with foil; bake 10 minutes.

SPICY CHEESE PIE

Store no longer than 24 hours. Makes enough for 4 to 6 servings.

Pastry
1 cup all-purpose flour*
½ teaspoon salt
⅓ cup plus 1 tablespoon shortening
2 to 3 tablespoons cold water

Egg and Cheese Mixture
4 eggs
¼ cup milk
½ cup diced salami
½ cup diced pepperoni
2 cups shredded mozzarella cheese (about 8 ounces)
½ teaspoon basil
½ teaspoon oregano
¼ teaspoon pepper

Tomato Sauce
2 tablespoons chopped onion
2 tablespoons chopped green pepper
1 tablespoon butter or margarine
1 can (8 ounces) tomato sauce
1 teaspoon salt
¼ teaspoon pepper

Prepare Pastry: Measure flour and ½ teaspoon salt into bowl. Cut in shortening thoroughly. Sprinkle in water, 1 tablespoon at a time, mixing until all flour is moistened and dough almost cleans side of bowl (1 to 2 teaspoons water can be added if needed). Gather dough into a ball. Roll into circle 2 inches larger than inverted 8-inch pie pan on lightly floured cloth-covered board. Fold pastry in half, then in half again; place in pan with point in center and unfold. Trim overhanging edge of pastry 1 inch from rim of pan. Fold and roll pastry under, even with pan; flute. Cover pastry-lined pie pan with plastic wrap and refrigerate.

Mix Egg and Cheese Mixture ingredients. Cover and refrigerate.

Cook and stir onion and green pepper in butter until onion is tender. Stir in tomato sauce, 1 teaspoon salt and ¼ teaspoon pepper. Cover saucepan and refrigerate.

■ **About 50 minutes before serving, place pastry-lined pie pan on oven rack.** Pour egg and cheese mixture into pie pan. Bake in 425° oven until light brown, 35 to 40 minutes. Let stand 5 minutes before cutting. After pie has baked 25 minutes, heat Tomato Sauce. Spoon sauce on wedges of pie.

*If using self-rising flour, omit salt from Pastry. Pastry made with self-rising flour differs in flavor and texture.

EGGS FLORENTINE CASSEROLE

Store no longer than 24 hours. Makes enough for 4 to 6 servings.

Base
2 packages (10 ounces each) frozen chopped spinach
2 tablespoons minced onion
2 tablespoons lemon juice
½ cup shredded Cheddar cheese
8 hard-cooked eggs, sliced

Sauce
3 tablespoons butter or margarine
3 tablespoons flour
½ teaspoon salt
½ teaspoon dry mustard
¼ teaspoon pepper
2¼ cups milk

Topping
½ cup dry bread crumbs
1 tablespoon butter or margarine, melted

Cook spinach as directed on package; drain. Stir in onion and lemon juice. Spread spinach in ungreased baking dish, 8×8×2 inches. Sprinkle cheese on spinach; top with egg slices.

Melt 3 tablespoons butter in saucepan over low heat. Stir in flour and seasonings. Cook over low heat, stirring constantly, until smooth and bubbly. Remove from heat; stir in milk. Heat, stirring constantly, until Sauce boils. Boil and stir 1 minute. Pour on eggs.

Toss crumbs with melted butter; sprinkle crumbs on sauce. (To serve immediately, heat oven to 400°; bake uncovered 20 minutes.) Cover and refrigerate.

■ **40 minutes before serving, heat oven to 400°.** Bake Eggs Florentine Casserole uncovered 30 minutes.

QUICHE LORRAINE

Store no longer than 24 hours. Makes enough for 6 main-dish servings (8 appetizer servings).

Pastry
  1 cup all-purpose flour*
  ½ teaspoon salt
  ⅓ cup plus 1 tablespoon shortening
  2 to 3 tablespoons cold water

Base
  12 slices bacon (about ½ pound), crisply fried and crumbled
  1 cup shredded natural Swiss cheese (4 ounces)
  ⅓ cup minced onion

Egg Mixture
  4 eggs
  2 cups half-and-half
  ¾ teaspoon salt
  ¼ teaspoon sugar
  ⅛ teaspoon cayenne red pepper

Pour the egg mixture into the pie pan on the oven rack.

Bake the quiche until a knife inserted 1 inch from the edge comes out clean.

Prepare Pastry: Measure flour and ½ teaspoon salt into bowl. Cut in shortening thoroughly. Sprinkle in water, 1 tablespoon at a time, mixing until all flour is moistened and dough almost cleans side of bowl (1 to 2 teaspoons water can be added if needed). Gather dough into a ball. Roll into circle 2 inches larger than inverted 9-inch pie pan on lightly floured cloth-covered board. Fold pastry in half then in half again; place in pan with point in center and unfold. Trim overhanging edge of pastry 1 inch from rim of pan. Fold and roll pastry under, even with pan; flute.

Sprinkle bacon, cheese and onion in pastry-lined pie pan. Cover with plastic wrap and refrigerate. Beat eggs slightly; beat in remaining ingredients. Cover and refrigerate.

■ **1 hour before serving, place pastry-lined pie pan on oven rack.** Stir egg mixture and pour into pie pan. Bake in 425° oven 15 minutes. Reduce oven temperature to 300°; bake until knife inserted 1 inch from edge comes out clean, about 30 minutes longer. Let stand 10 minutes before cutting.

*If using self-rising flour, omit salt from Pastry. Pastry made with self-rising flour differs in flavor and texture.

Quiche Lorraine

Appetizers

BEEF TERIYAKI KABOBS

Store no longer than 48 hours.

1 pound beef sirloin steak or beef round
  steak, 1¼ inches thick
¼ cup soy sauce
¼ cup water
2 tablespoons honey
¼ teaspoon garlic salt
¼ teaspoon allspice
⅛ teaspoon ginger

Trim fat and bone from meat; cut meat into
1¼-inch strips. Cut each strip into ¼-inch pieces.
Mix remaining ingredients; pour on meat in
glass bowl. Cover and refrigerate at least 1 hour.

■ **20 minutes before serving, set oven control at
broil and/or 550°. Have ready:** 2 bunches green
onions. Trim green tops from onions; cut onions
into 1-inch pieces. Reserve marinade; alternate
3 pieces meat and 2 pieces onion on each
skewer.

Broil kabobs with tops 3 to 4 inches from heat,
brushing occasionally with reserved marinade,
3 to 4 minutes on each side. To serve, spoon
small amount reserved marinade on meat.

Note: 1 pound white chicken meat, cut into
1×1×¼-inch pieces, can be substituted for
meat.

To Charcoal-grill: Cook kabobs on hibachi over
hot coals, turning frequently, 10 to 15 minutes.
Use a hibachi in a ventilated place—a fireplace
with the draft open, near an open window or
outdoors. Judge hot coals with a grill thermometer or hold your hand, palm toward the
heat, near the grid. If you have to withdraw
your hand in less than three seconds, the coals
are hot (about 400°).

DEVILED EGGS

Store no longer than 24 hours. Makes enough for 6 servings.

- **6 hard-cooked eggs**
- **½ teaspoon salt**
- **½ teaspoon dry mustard**
- **¼ teaspoon pepper**
- **3 tablespoons salad dressing, vinegar or light cream (20%)**

Cut peeled eggs lengthwise into halves. Slip out yolks; mash with fork. Mix in seasonings and salad dressing. Fill whites with egg yolk mixture, heaping it lightly. Arrange on large serving plate. (Can be served immediately.) Cover plate with plastic wrap and refrigerate.

VARIATIONS

Catsup-flavored Deviled Eggs: Decrease salt to ¼ teaspoon and substitute ¼ cup plus 1 tablespoon catsup for the salad dressing.

Deviled Eggs with Olives: Decrease salt to ¼ teaspoon, omit dry mustard and mix ¼ cup finely minced ripe olives and ⅛ teaspoon curry powder into egg yolk mixture.

Zesty Deviled Eggs: Decrease salt to ¼ teaspoon and mix one of the following into the egg yolk mixture:

- ½ cup finely shredded process American cheese
- 2 tablespoons snipped parsley
- 1 teaspoon horseradish

To Store Eggs

Refrigerate eggs right after you buy them. Use them within a week.

Leftover egg whites will keep in the refrigerator in a covered jar 7 to 10 days. Cover leftover yolks with water and store in a covered jar for 2 to 3 days.

MARINATED SHRIMP

Store no longer than 1 week.

- **1½ teaspoons salt**
- **1 package (12 ounces) frozen cleaned raw shrimp**
- **1 cup oil and vinegar salad dressing**
- **1 bay leaf, crushed**

Heat 2 cups water and the salt to boiling. Add shrimp; heat until water boils. Cook until shrimp are tender, 1 to 2 minutes; rinse quickly with running cold water to cool.

Mix shrimp, salad dressing and bay leaf. Cover and refrigerate at least 2 hours. (Can be served immediately.)

Note: Two cans (4½ ounces each) medium shrimp, rinsed and drained, can be substituted for the cleaned raw shrimp.

SPICED PEACHES

Store no longer than 8 days. Makes 1 quart.

- **1 can (29 ounces) peach halves, drained**
- **1½ cups honey**
- **½ cup vinegar**
- **3 three-inch cinnamon sticks**
- **3 whole cloves**

Place peach halves in 1-quart jar. Heat remaining ingredients until syrup boils. Pour on peaches; cool. Cover and refrigerate at least 8 hours.

VARIATIONS

Spiced Apricots: Substitute 1 can (30 ounces) apricot halves, drained, for the peach halves.

Spiced Pears: Substitute 1 can (29 ounces) pear halves, drained, for the peach halves; ½ to 1 teaspoon red or green food color can be added to sauce. Pears will be fully colored in 12 hours.

Spiced Pineapple: Substitute 1 can (30 ounces) pineapple chunks, drained, for the peach halves.

CUCUMBER SOUP

Store no longer than 48 hours. Makes enough for 6 servings.

  2 medium cucumbers
  ¼ cup buttermilk
  1 teaspoon salt
  ⅛ teaspoon pepper
  1 teaspoon instant minced onion
1¼ cups buttermilk

Pare one of the cucumbers; cut both cucumbers into ¾-inch slices. Reserve six of the unpared slices for garnish; wrap in plastic wrap and refrigerate.

Pour ¼ cup buttermilk into blender; add half the cucumber slices. Beat on high speed until smooth. Add remaining cucumber slices, the salt, pepper and onion. Beat until smooth, about 1 minute. Stir in remaining buttermilk. Cover and refrigerate at least 2 hours. (Can be served immediately.)

■ **At serving time, garnish each serving of Cucumber Soup with a reserved cucumber slice.**

RUBY CONSOMMÉ

Store no longer than 4 days. Makes enough for 8 servings.

2 cans (10½ ounces each) beef
  consommé
1 cup tomato juice
1 cup water

Mix consommé, tomato juice and water; heat through. (Can be served immediately.) Cover and refrigerate.

■ **At serving time, heat Ruby Consommé or serve cold.** Garnish with cucumber or radish slices, if desired.

BORSCH

Store no longer than 24 hours. Makes enough for 4 servings.

1 can (10½ ounces) condensed beef broth
    (bouillon)*
1 can (16 ounces) shoestring beets
1 cup shredded cabbage
2 tablespoons minced onion
1 teaspoon sugar
1 teaspoon lemon juice

Heat broth, beets (with liquid), cabbage, onion and sugar until mixture boils. Reduce heat; simmer uncovered 5 minutes. Stir in lemon juice. Cover and chill. (Can be served immediately.)

■ **At serving time, top each serving of Borsch with a spoonful of dairy sour cream.**

*Beef broth can be made by dissolving 2 beef bouillon cubes or 2 teaspoons instant beef bouillon in 1¼ cups boiling water.

VICHYSSOISE

Store no longer than 3 days. Makes enough for 8 servings (½ cup each).

  1 small onion, grated
  3 chicken bouillon cubes
  1 cup water
  ¼ teaspoon salt
  ½ cup milk
1¼ cups instant mashed potato puffs
1½ cups milk

Heat onion, bouillon cubes, water and salt in large saucepan until mixture boils. Reduce heat; cover tightly and simmer 10 minutes. Remove from heat; stir in ½ cup milk. Mix in potato puffs with fork; beat until fluffy. Stir in 1½ cups milk gradually; heat just until soup boils. Cover and chill thoroughly.

■ **5 minutes before serving, have ready:** 1 cup light cream (20%); snipped chives or watercress.

Stir cream into soup with fork; beat vigorously. Serve in small cups or bowls; sprinkle snipped chives on top.

GOLDENROD EGG DIP

Store no longer than 48 hours. Makes 2 cups.

 6 **hard-cooked eggs, finely chopped**
⅓ **cup mayonnaise or salad dressing**
 2 **tablespoons pickle relish**
 1 **tablespoon butter or margarine, softened**
 2 **teaspoons lemon juice**
 1 **teaspoon prepared mustard**
 1 **teaspoon salt**
½ **teaspoon instant minced onion**
¼ **teaspoon red pepper sauce**
⅛ **teaspoon pepper**

Mix all ingredients. Cover and refrigerate. Chill at least 2 hours. (Can be served immediately.) Stir before serving.

PIQUANT DIP

Store no longer than 48 hours. Makes 2 cups.

Mix 2 cups dairy sour cream and 1 envelope (about .7 ounce) of your favorite salad dressing mix (Parmesan, garlic-cheese or blue cheese) or 1 envelope (about 1½ ounces) spaghetti sauce mix. Cover and refrigerate. Chill at least 1 hour. (Can be served immediately.) Stir before serving.

DILL WEED DIP

Store no longer than 3 days. Makes about 1½ cups.

 1 **cup dairy sour cream**
½ **cup mayonnaise or salad dressing**
 1 **tablespoon dill weed**
 1 **teaspoon seasoned salt**

Mix all ingredients. Cover and refrigerate. Chill at least 1 hour. (Can be served immediately.)

TEMPTING TUNA DIP

Store no longer than 24 hours. Makes 2 cups.

 1 **package (3 ounces) cream cheese, softened**
 1 **cup dairy sour cream**
 1 **can (6½ ounces) tuna, drained and flaked**
¼ **cup chopped stuffed olives**
 2 **tablespoons snipped chives**
 2 **teaspoons horseradish**
 1 **teaspoon Worcestershire sauce**
¼ **teaspoon salt**

Mix cream cheese and sour cream until smooth. Stir in remaining ingredients. Cover and refrigerate. Chill at least 2 hours. (Can be served immediately.) Stir before serving.

BAVARIAN DIP

Store no longer than 48 hours. Makes about 1 cup.

 3 **tablespoons liverwurst**
 1 **cup dairy sour cream**
 2 **tablespoons sweet pickle relish**

Mash liverwurst with fork. Mix in sour cream gradually until smooth. Stir in pickle relish. Cover and refrigerate. Chill at least 1 hour. (Can be served immediately.)

GARLIC CHEESE DIP

Store no longer than 5 days. Makes about 2½ cups.

 2 **cups creamed cottage cheese**
 1 **medium clove garlic, crushed**
⅓ **cup chopped olives**
 1 **tablespoon milk**

Mix all ingredients. Cover and refrigerate. Chill at least 3 hours. (Can be served immediately.) Stir before serving.

NEAPOLITAN DIP

Store no longer than 3 days. Makes about 1 cup.

  2 **tablespoons milk**
  2 **packages (3 ounces each) cream cheese,**
    softened
  2 **tablespoons chili sauce**
  2 **tablespoons grated Parmesan cheese**
  ½ **teaspoon oregano leaves**
  1 **teaspoon horseradish**

Stir milk gradually into cream cheese. Mix in remaining ingredients. Cover and refrigerate. Chill at least 1 hour. (Can be served immediately.) Stir before serving.

LIVERWURST SPREAD

Store no longer than 48 hours. Makes about 1½ cups.

  ½ **pound liverwurst**
  1 **tablespoon sweet pickle relish**
  ¼ **cup mayonnaise or salad dressing**
  1 **tablespoon catsup**
  1 **teaspoon prepared mustard**
    Dash Worcestershire sauce

Mash liverwurst with fork; mix in remaining ingredients. Press plastic wrap onto surface of spread and refrigerate. Chill at least 3 hours. (Can be served immediately.)

■ **Serve Liverwurst Spread with rye crackers, pumpernickel or other thinly sliced dark bread.**

CHEESE APPLE

Store no longer than 5 days.

  1 **jar (5 ounces) pasteurized process sharp**
    American cheese spread
  1 **jar (5 ounces) pasteurized Neufchâtel and**
    blue cheese spread
  1 **package (3 ounces) cream cheese, softened**
    Garlic salt
    Worcestershire sauce
    Paprika

Beat all ingredients except paprika in small mixer bowl on low speed just until smooth. Cover and chill at least 8 hours. (Can be served immediately.)

■ **Just before serving, shape cheese mixture into ball.** Sprinkle paprika on piece of waxed paper; roll cheese ball in paprika to coat. Mold ball into apple shape by making small depression for stem end. If you like, insert a clove and a small leaf. Serve with crackers or snacks.

SALMON PARTY BALL

Store no longer than 4 days. Makes enough for about 12 servings (3 cups).

  1 **package (8 ounces) cream cheese,**
    softened
  1 **can (16 ounces) salmon, drained**
    and flaked
  1 **tablespoon lemon juice**
  1 **tablespoon grated onion**
  ¼ **teaspoon liquid smoke**
  ¼ **teaspoon salt**

Mix all ingredients. Cover and chill at least 8 hours.

■ **At serving time, have ready:** ½ cup chopped walnuts or pecans; 3 tablespoons snipped parsley; crackers.

Mix nuts and parsley. Shape salmon mixture into ball; roll in nut mixture. Serve with crackers.

Salads

COTTAGE-LIME SALAD

Store no longer than 3 days. Makes enough for 10 servings.

- **3 cups boiling water**
- **2 packages (3 ounces each) lime-flavored gelatin**
- **1 cup pineapple juice**
- **1 teaspoon vinegar**
- **½ teaspoon salt**
- **2 cups creamed cottage cheese**
- **1 teaspoon minced onion**
- **1 teaspoon minced green pepper**
- **½ cup coarsely chopped cucumber**
- **½ cup coarsely chopped celery**

Pour boiling water on gelatin in large bowl; stir until gelatin is dissolved. Stir in pineapple juice, vinegar and salt. Pour 1 cup of gelatin mixture into 8-cup ring mold. Chill until firm.

While bottom layer chills, chill remaining mixture until thickened slightly but not set; beat with rotary beater until light and fluffy. Mix in remaining ingredients; pour on gelatin layer in mold. Chill until firm; cover. (Can be served immediately.)

CRUNCHY CARROT-PINEAPPLE SALAD

Store no longer than 48 hours. Makes enough for 8 servings.

- **1 can (8¼ ounces) crushed pineapple**
- **½ cup water**
- **1 package (3 ounces) orange-flavored gelatin**
- **1 cup miniature marshmallows**
- **½ cup diced celery**
- **½ cup shredded carrot**
- **⅓ cup chopped nuts**
- **½ cup frozen whipped topping (thawed)**
- **½ cup mayonnaise or salad dressing**

Heat pineapple (with syrup) and water until mixture boils. Pour boiling mixture on gelatin in bowl; stir until gelatin is dissolved. Chill until thickened slightly but not set. Mix in remaining ingredients including pineapple; pour into 4-cup mold or 8 individual molds. Chill until firm; cover. (Can be served immediately.)

■ **5 minutes before serving, unmold Crunchy Carrot-Pineapple Salad and garnish with salad greens.**

Note: This recipe can be doubled.

Tips for Molded Salads

To determine the size of a mold, fill it with water; then pour the water into a large measuring cup. Some molds may be marked: 2 cups=1 pint; 4 cups= 1 quart.

When a recipe specifies that gelatin should be "thickened slightly," it means that the gelatin should be just about the consistency of liquid egg whites. If you want to speed up the thickening process, you can place the gelatin mixture in a bowl of ice and water. Remove the mixture from the ice-filled bowl just when it starts to thicken. If the gelatin has become too set, soften it over hot water.

Pour the orange mixture over the slightly-thickened raspberry layer in the mold. A lime layer comes next.

Unmold by wrapping a hot, damp towel carefully around the mold. Lift off the mold.

Ribbon Mold

RIBBON MOLD

Store no longer than 3 days. Makes enough for 9 to 12 servings.

Raspberry Layer
1 **cup boiling water**
1 **package (3 ounces) raspberry-flavored gelatin**
1 **package (10 ounces) frozen raspberries**

Orange Layer
1 **cup boiling water**
1 **package (3 ounces) orange-flavored gelatin**
1 **package (8 ounces) cream cheese, softened**
1 **can (11 ounces) mandarin orange segments**

Lime Layer
1 **cup boiling water**
1 **package (3 ounces) lime-flavored gelatin**
1 **can (8¼ ounces) crushed pineapple**

Raspberry Layer: Pour boiling water on raspberry-flavored gelatin in large bowl; stir until gelatin is dissolved. Stir in frozen raspberries. Chill until thickened slightly but not set; pour into 8-cup mold or 9×9×2-inch baking pan. Chill until almost firm.

Orange Layer: Pour boiling water on orange-flavored gelatin in large bowl; stir until gelatin is dissolved; stir gradually into cream cheese. Chill until thickened slightly but not set. Mix in orange segments (with syrup); pour evenly on raspberry layer. Chill until almost firm.

Lime Layer: Pour boiling water on lime-flavored gelatin in large bowl; stir until gelatin is dissolved. Stir in pineapple (with syrup). Chill until thickened slightly but not set; pour evenly on orange layer. Chill until firm; cover. (Can be served immediately.)

■ **At serving time, unmold Ribbon Mold or cut into pieces.**

CRANBERRY FRUIT MOLD

Store no longer than 3 days. Makes enough for 6 to 8 servings.

¾ **cup boiling water**
1 **package (3 ounces) raspberry-flavored**
  gelatin
1 **can (8¼ ounces) seedless grapes**
1 **can (8½ ounces) pineapple tidbits**
1 **can (16 ounces) whole cranberry sauce**
½ **cup nuts, coarsely chopped**

Pour boiling water on gelatin in large bowl; stir until gelatin is dissolved. Stir in grapes (with syrup), pineapple tidbits (with syrup) and cranberry sauce. Chill until thickened slightly but not set.

Stir in nuts. Pour mixture into 5-cup mold or 8 to 10 individual molds. Chill until firm; cover. (Can be served immediately.) Serve with your favorite fruit salad dressing.

CREAMY CUCUMBER SALAD

Store no longer than 24 hours. Makes enough for 6 to 8 servings.

5 **medium cucumbers**
¾ **cup boiling water**
1 **package (3 ounces) lime-flavored**
  gelatin
3 **tablespoons vinegar**
1 **teaspoon onion juice**
½ **cup mayonnaise or salad dressing**
½ **cup dairy sour cream**

Pare cucumbers; shred and drain thoroughly. Measure 2 cups. Pour boiling water on gelatin in large bowl; stir until gelatin is dissolved. Stir in vinegar, onion juice, mayonnaise, sour cream and cucumber; pour into 4- or 5-cup mold. Chill in refrigerator until firm; cover. (Can be served immediately.)

■ **At serving time, unmold Creamy Cucumber Salad onto crisp salad greens; garnish as desired.**

Note: Drain shredded cucumber in sieve, pressing out liquid with spoon.

GOLDEN APRICOT MOLD

Store no longer than 5 days. Makes enough for 8 servings.

1 **can (30 ounces) apricot halves, drained**
  (reserve syrup)
¼ **cup vinegar**
1 **teaspoon whole cloves**
4-inch **stick cinnamon**
1 **package (3 ounces) orange-flavored**
  gelatin

Cut apricot halves into fourths; place in 4-cup mold or 8 individual molds. Heat reserved syrup, vinegar and spices until mixture boils. Reduce heat; simmer uncovered 10 minutes. Remove spices. Add enough hot water to hot syrup mixture to measure 2 cups. Pour on gelatin in bowl; stir until gelatin is dissolved. Pour gelatin mixture on apricots. Chill until firm; cover. (Can be served immediately.)

■ **5 minutes before serving, unmold 4-cup mold onto salad greens or individual molds onto slices of jellied cranberry sauce.**

BEET AND HORSERADISH MOLD

Store no longer than 3 days. Makes enough for 6 to 8 servings.

1 **cup boiling water**
1 **package (3 ounces) lemon-flavored**
  gelatin
1 **can (16 ounces) diced beets, drained**
  (reserve 1 cup liquid)
¾ **cup chopped celery**
2 **tablespoons chopped green onion**
2 **tablespoons cream-style horseradish**

Pour boiling water on gelatin in large bowl; stir until gelatin is dissolved. Stir in reserved beet liquid, the beets, celery, onion and horseradish. Chill until thickened slightly but not set; pour into 4-cup mold or 6 to 8 individual molds. Chill until firm; cover. (Can be served immediately.)

■ **At serving time, unmold Beet and Horseradish Mold on salad greens and serve with mayonnaise.**

MACARONI FRUIT SALAD

Store no longer than 24 hours. Makes enough for 4 to 6 servings.

1½ cups uncooked macaroni rings
 1 tablespoon cornstarch
 1 tablespoon sugar
 1 can (30 ounces) fruit cocktail, drained
    (reserve ½ cup syrup)
 2 tablespoons lemon juice
 1 cup frozen whipped topping (thawed)
 ¼ cup maraschino cherries, cut into halves

Cook macaroni rings as directed on package; drain. Mix cornstarch and sugar in saucepan. Gradually stir in reserved fruit cocktail syrup and the lemon juice. Cook over medium heat, stirring constantly, until mixture thickens and boils. Boil and stir 1 minute; stir into hot macaroni rings. Cover and chill at least 4 hours.

Fold whipped topping, fruit cocktail and cherries into macaroni rings. (Can be served immediately.) Cover and refrigerate.

■ **At serving time, stir Macaroni Fruit Salad.** If desired, serve on greens.

BRIGHT BEAN SALAD

Store no longer than 24 hours. Makes enough for 4 servings.

 1 medium carrot
 1 can (16 ounces) French-style green
    beans, drained
 2 tablespoons chopped onion
 ⅛ teaspoon salt
 3 tablespoons oil and vinegar salad dressing

Cut carrot into 1-inch lengths; chop in blender, watching carefully. (Or carrot can be finely chopped by hand.) Mix all ingredients. Cover and refrigerate at least 4 hours. (Can be served immediately.)

Note: 1 package (9 ounces) frozen French-style green beans, cooked and drained, can be substituted for the canned beans.

FRUIT 'N CHEESE SLAW

Store no longer than 48 hours. Makes enough for 6 to 8 servings.

 4 cups shredded cabbage (about ½ head)
 ⅓ cup crumbled blue cheese (about 2
    ounces)
 ½ cup dairy sour cream
 ¼ cup salad dressing or mayonnaise
 ½ teaspoon seasoned salt

Toss cabbage and cheese. Mix sour cream, salad dressing and salt. Pour mixture on cabbage mixture and toss. (To serve immediately, see below.) Cover and refrigerate.

■ **10 minutes before serving, have ready:** 1 or 2 apples. Cut unpared apples into slices (2 cups), then cut into narrow strips. Toss with cabbage mixture.

Note: To chop or crumble blue cheese, freeze first. It is easier to handle and remains in separate pieces.

To Serve Immediately: Cut 1 or 2 unpared apples into slices (2 cups), then cut into narrow strips. Toss with cabbage mixture.

BRUSSELS AND CARROT SALAD

Store no longer than 48 hours. Makes enough for 6 to 8 servings.

 ½ cup oil and vinegar salad dressing
 1 package (10 ounces) frozen Brussels
    sprouts
 1 can (16 ounces) sliced carrots, drained

Heat salad dressing and Brussels sprouts in covered saucepan until dressing boils. Reduce heat; simmer covered 8 minutes. Add carrots; cook until Brussels sprouts are tender. Turn into serving dish. Cover and refrigerate at least 6 hours; stir occasionally. (Can be served immediately.)

MARINATED CUCUMBER SALAD

Store no longer than 48 hours. Makes enough for 4 to 6 servings.

- **1 medium cucumber**
- **1 small onion**
- **½ cup vinegar**
- **½ cup water**
- **2 tablespoons sugar**
- **¼ teaspoon salt**

Run tines of fork lengthwise down side of unpared cucumber. Thinly slice cucumber and onion into glass bowl. Mix vinegar, water, sugar and salt; pour on cucumber and onion slices. Cover and refrigerate at least 2 hours. (Can be served immediately.)

■ **At serving time, have ready:** crisp salad greens. Drain vegetables. Serve on salad greens.

ITALIAN MUSHROOM-BEAN SALAD

Store no longer than 24 hours. Makes enough for 4 or 5 servings.

- **1 package (10 ounces) frozen baby lima beans**
- **8 mushrooms, trimmed and sliced**
- **4 green onions, chopped**
- **2 tablespoons snipped parsley**
- **½ teaspoon salt**
- **½ teaspoon oregano**
- **¼ cup oil and vinegar salad dressing**

Cook lima beans as directed on package; drain. Mix beans and remaining ingredients. Cover and refrigerate at least 4 hours. (Can be served immediately.)

■ **At serving time, pimiento strips or a twisted orange slice add a colorful garnish.**

Marinated Cucumber Salad, Brussels and Carrot Salad (page 126) and Italian Mushroom-Bean Salad

Cook almonds and sugar together until the sugar melts and coats the almonds.

Mandarin Salad

TOMATO MARINADE

Store no longer than 48 hours. Makes enough for 6 to 8 servings.

**8 to 12 tomato slices, ¾ inch thick, or
  peeled small tomatoes**
1 cup olive oil or salad oil
⅓ cup wine vinegar
2 teaspoons oregano leaves
1 teaspoon salt
½ teaspoon pepper
½ teaspoon dry mustard
**2 cloves garlic, crushed
  Minced green onion
  Snipped parsley**

Arrange tomatoes in baking dish, 8×8×2 inches. Shake oil, vinegar, oregano leaves, salt, pepper, mustard and garlic in tightly covered jar; pour on tomatoes. Sprinkle onion and parsley on tomatoes. Cover and refrigerate at least 3 hours; spoon dressing on tomatoes occasionally. (Can be served immediately.)

■ **At serving time, have ready:** crisp lettuce leaves. Arrange Tomato Marinade on lettuce; drizzle some of the dressing on top.

Note: Tomato Marinade is pictured on page 16 as an accompaniment to Braised Beef on Rice.

Add mandarin oranges and dressing to the greens, fasten the bag and shake.

MANDARIN SALAD

Store no longer than 24 hours. Makes enough for 4 to 6 servings.

Dressing
½ teaspoon salt
   Dash pepper
2 tablespoons sugar
2 tablespoons vinegar
¼ cup salad oil
   Dash red pepper sauce
1 tablespoon snipped parsley

Salad
¼ cup sliced almonds
1 tablespoon plus 1 teaspoon sugar
¼ head lettuce
¼ head romaine
1 cup chopped celery
2 green onions (with tops), thinly sliced

Shake Dressing ingredients in tightly covered jar; refrigerate.

Cook almonds and 1 tablespoon plus 1 teaspoon sugar over low heat, stirring constantly, until sugar is melted and almonds are coated. Cool and break apart. Store at room temperature.

Tear lettuce and romaine into bite-size pieces (about 4 cups). Place greens in plastic bag; add celery and onion. (To serve immediately, see below.) Fasten bag securely and refrigerate.

■ **5 minutes before serving, pour dressing into bag; add 1 can (11 ounces) mandarin orange segments, drained.** Fasten bag securely and shake until greens and oranges are well coated. Add almonds and shake.

To Serve Immediately: Do not refrigerate Dressing or Salad ingredients.

Vegetables

HERB BARLEY CASSEROLE

Store no longer than 24 hours. Makes enough for 4 to 6 servings.

¾ cup uncooked barley
1 medium onion, thinly sliced
1 tablespoon instant beef bouillon
1 tablespoon butter or margarine
¼ teaspoon rosemary leaves
2 cups boiling water

Heat oven to 400°. Mix all ingredients in ungreased 1½-quart casserole. Cover tightly; bake 45 minutes. (To serve immediately, continue baking until liquid is absorbed and barley is tender, about 15 minutes.) Cover and refrigerate.

■ **35 minutes before serving, heat oven to 400°.** Stir ½ cup water into Herb Barley Casserole. Cover tightly; bake until barley is tender, about 30 minutes.

TRADITIONAL SWEET-SOUR RED CABBAGE

Store no longer than 48 hours. Makes enough for 6 servings.

4 slices bacon
¼ cup brown sugar (packed)
2 tablespoons flour
1 teaspoon salt
⅛ teaspoon pepper
½ cup water
¼ cup vinegar
5 cups shredded red cabbage (about 1 medium head)
1 small onion, sliced

Fry bacon in large skillet until crisp. Remove bacon; pour off all but 1 tablespoon fat. Stir sugar, flour, salt and pepper into fat until smooth. Stir in remaining ingredients.

Cover tightly; heat until mixture boils. Reduce heat; cook, stirring occasionally, 25 to 30 minutes. Crumble bacon on top. (Can be served immediately.) Cover and refrigerate.

■ **15 minutes before serving, heat Traditional Sweet-Sour Red Cabbage covered over medium heat, stirring occasionally, until hot.**

Green Salad Tips

Select crisp fresh greens; avoid those with rusty-looking tips. Wash and drain greens thoroughly. Store in refrigerator in plastic bag or in vegetable crisper; use within a week.

To make a do-ahead green salad, break up washed and dried greens 24 hours before you want to serve the salad. Store greens in a plastic bag. Just before serving, add salad dressing to bag, close and shake until greens are coated. Chopped green pepper, carrots or zucchini add interest to a salad—they can be stored with the torn greens.

SWEET CARROT STICKS

Store no longer than 48 hours. Makes enough for 6 servings.

8 to 10 large carrots
2 tablespoons butter or margarine
½ teaspoon salt
Dash pepper

Heat oven to 400°. Cut each carrot lengthwise into 4 parts; place on double thickness heavy-duty aluminum foil. Dot with butter and sprinkle salt and pepper on top. Wrap carrots securely in the foil. Bake 1 hour. (To serve immediately, see below.) Refrigerate.

■ **35 minutes before serving, heat oven to 400°.** Have ready: ¼ cup brown sugar (packed).

Bake carrots 25 minutes. Sprinkle sugar on carrots (heat of carrots will melt sugar).

To Serve Immediately: Have ready: ¼ cup brown sugar (packed).

Bake 10 minutes longer. Sprinkle sugar on carrots.

VARIATION

Herb-seasoned Carrots: Sprinkle carrots lightly with dill weed or thyme leaves before wrapping; omit brown sugar.

GOLDEN SQUASH BAKE

Store no longer than 24 hours. Makes enough for 6 to 8 servings.

6 cups cut-up pared Hubbard squash
2 tablespoons butter or margarine
1 cup dairy sour cream
½ cup finely chopped onion
1 teaspoon salt
¼ teaspoon pepper

Place squash in saucepan with small amount of boiling salted water (½ teaspoon salt to 1 cup water). Cover tightly and cook until tender, about 15 minutes. Drain squash thoroughly. Mash squash; stir in remaining ingredients. Mound mixture into ungreased 1-quart casserole. Cover and refrigerate.

■ **50 minutes before serving, heat oven to 350°.** Bake Golden Squash Bake uncovered until heated through, about 45 minutes.

About Vegetables

Most vegetables (except root vegetables) should be refrigerated to help preserve freshness and nutrients. Store cleaned vegetables in crisper or plastic bags.

If you buy green peas or limas in the pod, store them in the refrigerator that way. Use within 2 days.

Carrots without tops stay fresh longer than those with tops.

Sweet potatoes, winter squash, eggplant, rutabagas and onions should be stored at about 60°—not in refrigerator.

CELERY BAKE

Store no longer than 24 hours. Makes enough for 4 to 6 servings.

4 cups ¼ inch diagonally sliced celery
1 jar (2 ounces) sliced pimiento, drained and chopped
1 can (8 ounces) water chestnuts, drained and sliced
1 can (10¾ ounces) condensed cream of chicken soup or condensed cream soup of your choice
¼ cup water
½ teaspoon salt

Cook celery in 1 inch boiling salted water (½ teaspoon salt to 1 cup water) in tightly covered saucepan 5 minutes; drain. Mix all ingredients in ungreased 1½-quart casserole. (Can be baked immediately.) Cover and refrigerate.

■ **55 minutes before serving, heat oven to 350°.** Cover and bake Celery Bake until hot, 45 minutes. Stir before serving; garnish with salted nuts.

MASHED RUTABAGAS WITH GREEN PEAS

Store no longer than 24 hours. Makes enough for 4 to 6 servings.

1 large or 2 medium rutabagas (about 2 pounds)
Instant mashed potato puffs (enough for 2 servings)
½ teaspoon salt
Dash pepper

Cut rutabaga into ½-inch cubes or 2-inch pieces. Heat 1 inch salted water (½ teaspoon salt to 1 cup water) until water boils. Add rutabaga. Cover tightly; heat until water boils. Cook until tender, 15 to 20 minutes; drain.

Prepare potato puffs as directed on package for 2 servings except—omit milk and butter. Combine rutabaga and potato. Add salt and pepper; mash. Spoon rutabaga mixture into ungreased 1-quart casserole. (To serve immediately, cook 1 package [10 ounces] frozen green peas as directed on package; drain. Make indentation in center of rutabaga mixture; fill with peas.) Cover and refrigerate.

■ **50 minutes before serving, heat oven to 350°. Have ready:** 1 package (10 ounces) frozen green peas.

Heat rutabaga mixture covered 40 minutes. Cook peas as directed on package; drain. Make indentation in center of rutabaga mixture; fill with peas.

POTATO PATTIES

Store no longer than 3 days. Makes enough for 4 to 6 patties.

Prepare instant mashed potato puffs as directed on package for 4 servings except—decrease water to 1 cup; use ⅓ cup milk and add ½ teaspoon instant minced onion. Shape potato into patties; coat with flour. Cover and refrigerate.

■ **10 minutes before serving, cook Potato Patties in butter over medium heat until golden brown, about 3 minutes per side.**

GOLDEN BAKED POTATOES

Store no longer than 24 hours. Makes enough for 4 to 6 servings.

½ cup cornflake crumbs
1 teaspoon salt
4 to 6 medium potatoes, pared
2 tablespoons butter or margarine, melted

Heat oven to 375°. Mix cornflake crumbs and salt. Brush potatoes with butter, then coat with crumbs. Arrange in ungreased baking pan, 9×9×2 inches. Bake uncovered 1 hour. (To serve immediately, bake until potatoes are tender, 15 minutes longer.) Cover and refrigerate.

■ **35 minutes before serving, heat oven to 375°.** Bake Golden Baked Potatoes uncovered until tender, 25 minutes.

ELEGANT HASH BROWNS

Store no longer than 24 hours. Makes enough for 4 to 6 servings.

1 package (6 ounces) hash brown potatoes with onions
½ cup chopped green onion
1 cup shredded sharp Cheddar cheese (about 4 ounces)
½ teaspoon salt
3 tablespoons butter or margarine

Cover potato with boiling water; let stand 5 minutes. Drain thoroughly. Layer ½ each of potato, onion and cheese in ungreased baking dish, 8×8×2 inches, or shallow 8-inch baking dish. Season with half the salt; dot with half the butter. Repeat with remaining ingredients. (To serve immediately, bake covered in 350° oven 20 minutes. Uncover; bake 10 minutes.) Cover with aluminum foil; refrigerate.

■ **45 minutes before serving, heat oven to 350°.** Bake Elegant Hash Browns covered 20 minutes. Uncover; bake until cheese is melted and potato is golden brown, 15 minutes.

Pictured at right, top to bottom: Elegant Hash Browns, Golden Baked Potatoes and Caramel-glazed Sweet Potatoes (page 134)

CHEESE POTATOES

Store no longer than 48 hours. Makes enough for 6 to 8 servings.

Prepare instant mashed potato puffs as directed on package for 8 servings except—omit butter. After stirring in potato puffs, stir in 1 jar (5 ounces) pasteurized process sharp American cheese spread or flavored pasteurized Neufchâtel cheese spread (the latter is now available with a wide variety of added flavor sparkers, i.e., pineapple, pimiento, relish).

Turn potato into ungreased 1½-quart casserole. (To serve immediately, bake uncovered in 350° oven until hot, 15 to 20 minutes.) Cover and refrigerate.

■ **About 45 minutes before serving, heat oven to 350°.** Bake Cheese Potatoes uncovered until hot, 40 minutes.

CRISPY POTATOES

Store no longer than 24 hours. Makes enough for 4 to 6 servings.

Cook 4 to 6 unpared medium potatoes in 1 inch boiling salted water (½ teaspoon salt to 1 cup water) in tightly covered saucepan until tender, 30 to 35 minutes; drain. Cool.

Heat fat or oil (1 inch) to 375°. Peel potatoes; cut into 4 pieces. Fry in hot fat, turning once, until golden brown, 5 to 7 minutes; drain. (Can be served immediately. Season with salt.) Cover and refrigerate.

■ **25 minutes before serving, heat oven to 400°.** Heat Crispy Potatoes on ungreased baking sheet 15 minutes. Season with salt.

LEMONY POTATOES

Store no longer than 24 hours. Makes enough for 4 to 6 servings.

**4 large potatoes, pared and cut into
  ½-inch cubes (about 4 cups)**
¼ cup butter or margarine, melted
2 teaspoons salt
1 teaspoon grated lemon peel
¼ teaspoon nutmeg
¼ teaspoon coarsely ground pepper
3 tablespoons lemon juice
1 green onion (with top), chopped

Cook potato in 1 inch boiling salted water (½ teaspoon salt to 1 cup water) in tightly covered saucepan just until tender; drain. Mix remaining ingredients; toss with potato. Spoon on 20×14-inch piece of double thickness heavy-duty aluminum foil. Wrap potato securely in the foil. (To serve immediately, let stand at room temperature 1 hour. Bake in 350° oven 20 minutes.) Refrigerate.

■ **50 minutes before serving, heat oven to 350°.** Bake Lemony Potatoes 40 minutes.

CARAMEL-GLAZED SWEET POTATOES

Store no longer than 48 hours. Makes enough for 4 servings.

**1 can (17 ounces) vacuum-pack sweet
  potatoes**
½ teaspoon salt
⅓ cup caramel ice-cream topping

Mash sweet potatoes and salt. Mound in ungreased 1-quart casserole; drizzle with caramel topping. (To serve immediately, see below.) Cover and refrigerate.

■ **45 minutes before serving, heat oven to 350°.** Heat Caramel-glazed Sweet Potatoes uncovered until hot, 40 minutes.

To Serve Immediately: Heat oven to 350°. Heat uncovered until hot, 30 minutes.

Breads

CINNAMON-APPLE TOAST

Store no longer than 24 hours. Makes enough for 6 servings.

½ **cup sugar**
¾ **teaspoon cinnamon**
2 **tablespoons soft butter or margarine**
6 **slices bread, toasted**
1 **jar (16½ ounces) chunky applesauce**
⅓ **cup raisins**

Butter baking pan, 13×9×2 inches. Mix sugar and cinnamon; sprinkle 2 tablespoons cinnamon-sugar into pan. Spread butter on toast; arrange buttered side up in pan. Sprinkle 2 tablespoons cinnamon-sugar on toast. Mix applesauce and raisins; spread on toast. Sprinkle remaining cinnamon-sugar on applesauce. Cover and refrigerate.

■ **45 minutes before serving, heat oven to 350°.** Bake Cinnamon-Apple Toast uncovered 35 minutes.

FRIED CORNMEAL MUSH

Store no longer than 2 weeks. Makes enough for 9 servings.

1 **cup cornmeal**
1 **cup cold water**
3 **cups boiling water**
1 **teaspoon salt**

Grease loaf pan, 9×5×3 or 8½×4½×2 inches. Mix cornmeal and cold water in saucepan. Stir in boiling water and salt. Cook, stirring constantly, until mixture thickens and boils. Cover tightly; cook over low heat 10 minutes. Spoon cornmeal mush into pan. Cover and refrigerate.

■ **About 10 minutes before serving, invert pan to unmold cornmeal mush. Have ready:** 2 tablespoons butter or margarine; flour; syrup or jelly.

Cut loaf into ½-inch slices. Melt butter in large skillet. Coat slices with flour; brown on each side in skillet. Serve hot with syrup and, if desired, with bacon, ham or sausage.

To Store Fruits

Fruits will not ripen in the refrigerator. Once ripe, however, most of them stay at their best when refrigerated. Try to use them up soon, since they are fragile.

Berries should be refrigerated whole, and cleaned just before serving. Use within 1 or 2 days.

Wrap ripe pineapples tightly to prevent their odor from permeating other refrigerated foods.

Canned fruits can be stored in the already-opened (but covered) can in the refrigerator.

Orange juice can be kept covered in the refrigerator for several days with little loss of Vitamin C.

CONTINENTAL BRUNCH TOAST

Store no longer than 24 hours. Makes enough for 6 or 7 servings.

½ **loaf (1-pound size) French bread**
3 **eggs**
⅓ **cup granulated sugar**
½ **teaspoon cinnamon**
 Dash salt
1½ **cups milk**
2 **tablespoons raisins**
2 **tablespoons brown sugar**

Butter baking pan, 9×9×2 inches. Into pan, tear bread into 1- to 1½-inch pieces, each with a little crust (about 8 cups). Beat eggs, granulated sugar, cinnamon and salt; stir in milk and raisins. Pour egg mixture on bread pieces; sprinkle brown sugar on top. (To serve immediately, see below.) Cover and refrigerate.

■ **1 hour 10 minutes before serving, heat oven to 325°.** Bake Continental Brunch Toast uncovered until crust is golden brown, about 1 hour. Serve warm.

Note: For 8 to 10 servings, double amounts of all ingredients except French bread. Bake in buttered baking pan, 13×9×2 inches.

To Serve Immediately: Heat oven to 325°. Bake uncovered until crust is golden brown, 50 to 55 minutes. Serve warm.

RAISED FLAPJACKS

Store no longer than 24 hours. Makes about twenty 4-inch pancakes.

1 **package active dry yeast**
¼ **cup warm water (105 to 115°)**
1 **egg**
1⅓ **cups milk**
2 **cups buttermilk baking mix**

Dissolve yeast in warm water in large bowl. Add remaining ingredients; beat with rotary beater until smooth. Cover and refrigerate at least 8 hours. (Can be cooked immediately.)

■ **20 minutes before serving, heat griddle.** (Grease if necessary.) Cook Raised Flapjacks, turning when bubbles break.

BISCUIT FAN TANS

Store no longer than 24 hours. Makes enough for 6 biscuits.

2 **cups buttermilk baking mix**
½ **cup cold water**
¼ **cup butter or margarine, softened**

Mix baking mix and water until soft dough forms. Turn dough onto floured cloth-covered board; smooth gently into a ball. Knead 5 times. Roll dough until ¼ inch thick.

Spread half the butter on half the dough; fold in half. Spread remaining butter on half the dough; fold in half again. Roll dough until ½ inch thick. Cut with floured 2-inch cutter. Place 2 biscuits on sides in each ungreased muffin cup. (To serve immediately, bake in 450° oven about 10 minutes.) Cover and refrigerate.

■ **20 minutes before serving, heat oven to 450°.** Bake Biscuit Fan Tans 13 to 15 minutes.

CHEESE BREAD

Store no longer than 24 hours.

1 **egg**
1½ **cups milk**
3¾ **cups buttermilk baking mix**
1 **cup shredded sharp Cheddar cheese (about 4 ounces)**

Heat oven to 350°. Grease loaf pan, 9×5×3 inches. Beat egg in large mixer bowl. Add remaining ingredients; beat on medium speed ½ minute. Pour batter into pan. Bake 1 hour. Cool. (Can be served immediately.) Wrap and refrigerate.

■ **25 minutes before serving, heat oven to 375°.** Place wrapped Cheese Bread on oven rack; heat 15 minutes. Cut into ½-inch slices.

PUMPKIN BREAD

Store no longer than 10 days.

⅔ cup shortening
2⅔ cups sugar
 4 eggs
 1 can (16 ounces) pumpkin
⅔ cup water
3⅓ cups all-purpose flour*
 2 teaspoons soda
1½ teaspoons salt
½ teaspoon baking powder
 1 teaspoon cinnamon
 1 teaspoon cloves
⅔ cup coarsely chopped nuts
⅔ cup raisins

Heat oven to 350°. Grease two 9×5×3-inch loaf pans or three 8½×4½×2½-inch loaf pans. Beat shortening and sugar in large bowl until fluffy. Stir in eggs, pumpkin and water. Mix in flour, soda, salt, baking powder, cinnamon and cloves. Stir in nuts and raisins. Pour batter into pans.

Bake until wooden pick inserted in center comes out clean, about 1 hour 10 minutes. Cool completely. (Can be served immediately.) Wrap and refrigerate.

*If using self-rising flour, omit soda, salt and baking powder.

Bread Ahead

Normally, bread is stored in its own wrapper at room temperature. But in hot weather store in wrapper in refrigerator to protect against mold.

Here's a simple do-ahead garlic bread: Cut a 1-pound loaf of French bread into 1-inch slices. Spread with mixture of ½ cup soft butter and ¼ teaspoon garlic powder. Reassemble loaf; wrap with 28x18-inch piece of heavy-duty foil. Store up to 24 hours in refrigerator. Heat in 350° oven 15 to 20 minutes.

BUTTERSCOTCH BISCUITS

Store no longer than 24 hours. Makes about 12 biscuits.

½ cup butter or margarine, melted
½ cup brown sugar (packed)
⅓ cup pecan halves
 Cinnamon
 Biscuit dough (enough for 10 biscuits)

Grease 12 medium muffin cups (2½ inches in diameter). Place 2 teaspoons butter, 2 teaspoons sugar and 2 or 3 pecan halves in each muffin cup; sprinkle cinnamon on top.

Prepare dough as directed on buttermilk baking mix package except—spoon dough on mixture in cups. (Can be baked immediately in 425° oven 15 minutes.) Cover and refrigerate.

■ **25 minutes before serving, heat oven to 425°.** Bake Butterscotch Biscuits uncovered 18 minutes. Immediately invert pan onto large tray. Let pan remain a minute so butterscotch drizzles down on biscuits.

CORN POCKET ROLLS

Store no longer than 8 hours. Makes 10 rolls.

1½ cups all-purpose flour
½ cup cornmeal
 3 teaspoons baking powder
½ teaspoon salt
 2 tablespoons sugar
 1 egg, beaten
¾ cup dairy sour cream
 1 tablespoon soft butter or margarine

Mix dry ingredients. Blend egg and sour cream and stir into dry ingredients. Turn dough onto lightly floured board; roll ⅜ inch thick. Cut with 3-inch biscuit cutter. Brush butter on circles. Fold circles in half, pressing folded edges, and place on ungreased baking sheet. (To serve immediately, bake in 375° oven until golden brown, 12 to 15 minutes.) Cover and refrigerate.

■ **20 minutes before serving, heat oven to 375°.** Bake Corn Pocket Rolls until golden brown, about 15 minutes.

SHOOFLY COFFEE CAKE

Store no longer than 5 days.

Batter
- ¾ cup butter or margarine, softened
- 1 cup granulated sugar
- 3 eggs
- 1½ teaspoons vanilla
- ½ cup light molasses
- 3 cups all-purpose flour*
- 1½ teaspoons baking powder
- 2 teaspoons soda
- ¼ teaspoon salt
- 1⅓ cups dairy sour cream

Filling
- ½ cup brown sugar (packed)
- ½ cup finely chopped nuts
- 1½ teaspoons cinnamon

Heat oven to 350°. Grease tube pan, 10×4 inches, or 2 loaf pans, 9×5×3 inches. Measure butter, granulated sugar, eggs, vanilla and molasses into large mixer bowl. Beat on medium speed 2 minutes or by hand 300 vigorous strokes. Mix in flour, baking powder, soda and salt alternately with sour cream.

Mix Filling ingredients.

For tube pan, spread ⅓ of batter (about 2 cups) in pan. Sprinkle ⅓ of filling (about 6 tablespoons) on batter. Repeat 2 times. For loaf pans, spread ¼ of batter (about 1½ cups) in each pan. Sprinkle ¼ of filling (about 5 tablespoons) on batter in each pan. Repeat.

Bake until wooden pick inserted in center(s) comes out clean, 55 to 60 minutes. Cool slightly before removing from pan(s). Cool thoroughly. (Can be served immediately.) Cover with plastic wrap and refrigerate.

*If using self-rising flour, decrease soda to 1 teaspoon; omit baking powder and salt.

BLUEBERRY-OATMEAL BREAD

Store no longer than 1 week.

- 1 package (13.5 ounces) wild blueberry muffin mix
- 1 egg
- ¾ cup milk
- ½ cup rolled oats
- ½ cup chopped nuts

Heat oven to 350°. Grease bottom of loaf pan, 9×5×3 or 8½×4½×2½ inches. Drain and rinse blueberries. Mix egg and milk. Stir in muffin mix, oats and nuts. Fold in blueberries; pour into pan.

Bake until wooden pick inserted in center comes out clean, 9-inch 40 to 45 minutes, 8-inch 50 to 55 minutes. Cool slightly before removing from pan. Cool thoroughly. (Can be served immediately.) Wrap and refrigerate.

FRUIT AND NUT BREAD

Store no longer than 4 days.

- 3 cups buttermilk baking mix
- ⅔ cup sugar
- ⅓ cup all-purpose flour*
- 1 egg
- 1 cup orange juice
- 1 cup chopped dried fruit (apricots, peaches, dates, raisins or figs)
- ¾ cup chopped nuts

Heat oven to 350°. Grease loaf pan, 9×5×3 inches. Mix baking mix, sugar, flour, egg and orange juice; beat vigorously ½ minute. Stir in fruit and nuts. Pour batter into pan.

Bake until wooden pick inserted in center comes out clean, 55 to 60 minutes. Cool slightly before removing from pan. Cool thoroughly. (Can be served immediately.) Wrap and refrigerate.

*Do not use self-rising flour in this recipe.

POTATO REFRIGERATOR DOUGH

Store in refrigerator at 45° or below no longer than 5 days.

1 package active dry yeast
1½ cups warm water (105 to 115°)
⅔ cup sugar
1½ teaspoons salt
⅔ cup shortening
2 eggs
1 cup lukewarm mashed potatoes
7 to 7½ cups all-purpose flour*

Dissolve yeast in warm water. Mix in sugar, salt, shortening, eggs, potatoes and 4 cups of the flour. Beat until smooth. Stir in enough remaining flour to make dough easy to handle.

Turn dough onto lightly floured board; knead until smooth and elastic, about 5 minutes. Place in greased bowl; turn greased side up. Cover bowl tightly; refrigerate at least 8 hours.

■ **2 to 2½ hours before serving, punch down dough; divide into 3 parts.** Use for your choice of 3 of the following recipes on pages 139 to 140: Parker House Rolls; Orange Butterhorn Rolls; Four-leaf Clover Rolls; Apricot Cream Cake; Cinnamon Braid; Rich Nut Roll.

**If using self-rising flour, omit salt.*

PARKER HOUSE ROLLS
Makes 13 rolls.

Roll 1 part dough (left) into rectangle, 15×10 inches, about ¼ inch thick. Cut into 3-inch circles; fold so top half overlaps slightly. Pinch edges together. Place close together in greased pan, 9×9×2 inches. Brush with butter. Let rise until double, about 1½ hours. Heat oven to 400°. Bake until brown, about 20 minutes.

ORANGE BUTTERHORN ROLLS
Makes 24 rolls.

Divide 1 part dough (left) in half; roll each half into 10-inch circle. Spread 2 tablespoons Orange Glaze (below) on outside of circle, leaving a 2-inch circle in the center without glaze. Cut into 12 wedges. Roll up, beginning at rounded edge. Place rolls with point underneath on greased baking sheet. Let rise until double, about 1½ hours. Heat oven to 400°. Bake until light brown, 10 to 15 minutes. Spread remaining glaze on hot rolls.

Orange Glaze: Mix 2 tablespoons soft butter or margarine, 1 tablespoon grated orange peel, 1 tablespoon orange juice and 1½ cups confectioners' sugar until smooth and spreading consistency. If necessary, stir in 1 to 2 teaspoons additional orange juice.

Parker House Rolls

Orange Butterhorn Rolls

Four-leaf Clover Rolls (page 140)

Apricot Cream Cake

Cinnamon Braid

Rich Nut Roll

FOUR-LEAF CLOVER ROLLS

Makes 16 rolls.

Shape pieces of 1 part Potato Refrigerator Dough (page 139) into 2-inch balls. Place each ball in greased muffin cup. Snip each ball in half, then in half in opposite direction with scissors. Brush with butter. Let rise until double, about 1½ hours. Heat oven to 400°. Bake until brown, about 15 minutes.

APRICOT CREAM CAKE

Makes 16 servings.

Roll 1 part Potato Refrigerator Dough (page 139) into 15-inch circle; place over greased 9-inch ring mold. Fit dough into ring mold (outer edge of circle will come to rim of mold). Spoon Cream Cheese Filling (below) on dough. Lap edge of circle over filling; seal to inside ring of dough. Cut a cross in dough which covers the center of mold. Fold each triangle formed back over ring and pinch each point to the dough to seal securely. Let rise until double, about 1½ hours. Heat oven to 350°. Bake 30 minutes.

Remove Apricot Cream Cake from pan; place top side up on serving plate. Heat ½ cup apricot jam until melted; spoon on ring. Sift 1 tablespoon confectioners' sugar on top.

Cream Cheese Filling: Beat 1 package (8 ounces) cream cheese, softened, and ¼ cup sugar until light and fluffy. Stir in 3 tablespoons flour, 1 egg yolk, ½ teaspoon grated lemon peel and 1 tablespoon lemon juice.

CINNAMON BRAID

Divide 1 part Potato Refrigerator Dough (page 139) into 3 parts; roll each part into strand, 15 inches long. Mix 2 tablespoons sugar and 1 teaspoon cinnamon. Roll each strand in sugar-cinnamon mixture. Place strands close together and braid gently and loosely. Seal ends securely and tuck under. Place in greased loaf pan, 9×5×3 inches. Brush braid with . milk; sprinkle remaining sugar-cinnamon mixture on top. Let rise until double, about 1½ hours. Heat oven to 375°. Bake until loaf sounds hollow when tapped, about 30 minutes.

RICH NUT ROLL

Roll 1 part Potato Refrigerator Dough (page 139) into rectangle, 12×10 inches. Spread Nut Filling (below) to within ½ inch of edge. Roll up tightly; beginning at long side. Pinch edge of dough into roll to seal securely. Stretch roll to make even. Place on greased baking sheet; seal ends securely. Let rise until double, about 1½ hours. Heat oven to 350°. Beat 1 egg white slightly; brush roll with beaten egg white. Sprinkle 2 tablespoons chopped nuts on top. Bake 40 minutes. While warm, drizzle mixture of ¼ cup confectioners' sugar and 1 tablespoon light cream on top.

Nut Filling: Beat 1 egg white until stiff. Fold in 1 tablespoon flour, ½ cup brown sugar (packed) and ½ cup finely chopped nuts.

Desserts

BAKED APPLES

Store no longer than 24 hours.

Core baking apples (e.g., Rome Beauty, Starr, Jersey Red, Winesap, Northern Spy, Golden Delicious or Greening). Pare 1-inch strip of skin around middle of each apple or upper half of each to prevent skin from splitting.

Heat oven to 375°. Place apples upright in ungreased baking dish. Fill center of each apple with 1 to 2 tablespoons granulated or brown sugar, 1 teaspoon butter or margarine and ⅛ teaspoon cinnamon. Pour water (¼ inch) into baking dish.

Spooning syrup in pan on apples several times during baking, bake 30 minutes. Cool 30 minutes. Cover and refrigerate.

■ **35 minutes before serving, heat oven to 350°.** Bake Baked Apples uncovered until hot, about 25 minutes.

STRAWBERRY CREAM

Store no longer than 24 hours. Makes enough for 6 servings.

½ cup confectioners' sugar
1 quart strawberries, hulled
1 envelope (about 1½ ounces) whipped topping mix
3 or 4 tablespoons orange-flavored liqueur

Sprinkle sugar on strawberries; stir gently. Cover and refrigerate at least 2 hours.

Prepare whipped topping mix as directed on package. Gradually stir in liqueur. Fold in strawberries. (Can be served immediately.) Cover and refrigerate.

APPLE CRISP

Store no longer than 48 hours. Makes enough for 4 servings.

Butter Crunch
¼ cup butter or margarine
2 tablespoons brown sugar (packed)
½ cup all-purpose flour*
¼ cup chopped pecans, walnuts or coconut

Apple Mixture
1 can (21 ounces) apple pie filling
1 teaspoon lemon juice
½ teaspoon cinnamon
1 or 2 drops aromatic bitters, if desired

Heat oven to 400°. Mix Butter Crunch ingredients with hands. Spread in ungreased baking pan, 8×8×2 inches. Bake until light brown, about 15 minutes. Stir with spoon; cool.

Mix remaining ingredients. Place apple mixture in ungreased 9-inch pie pan or baking dish, 8×8×2 inches. Sprinkle the Butter Crunch evenly on top. (To serve immediately, bake uncovered in 450° oven until golden brown and bubbly, about 10 minutes.) Cover and refrigerate.

■ **30 minutes before serving, heat oven to 450°.** Bake Apple Crisp uncovered until golden brown and bubbly, about 20 minutes. Delicious topped with ice cream.

*Do not use self-rising flour in this recipe.

CHERRY-CHERRY

Store no longer than 48 hours. Makes enough for 5 servings.

1 cup boiling water
1 package (3 ounces) cherry-flavored gelatin
4 to 6 ice cubes
1 carton (8 ounces) cherry-flavored yogurt
Frozen whipped topping (thawed)

Pour boiling water on gelatin in bowl; stir until gelatin is dissolved. Stir in ice cubes until gelatin thickens; remove any remaining ice cubes.

Beat in yogurt with rotary beater until smooth. Pour into individual serving dishes, glasses or molds; refrigerate at least 45 minutes. (Can be served immediately.) Serve with a dollop of whipped topping. Try toasted almonds or toasted coconut for a crunchy garnish.

Note: Please your own personal preference with other flavor combinations. Try strawberry-flavored gelatin and strawberry-flavored yogurt; raspberry-flavored gelatin and raspberry-flavored yogurt; orange-flavored gelatin and orange-flavored yogurt.

Whipping Cream

□ Cream can be kept in the refrigerator 3 to 5 days.

□ Remember that whipping causes cream to double in quantity.

□ Before whipping, add 2 tablespoons granulated or confectioners' sugar for every ½ cup of cream.

□ If it is to whip well, cream must have at least 35% butterfat. To whip, chill cream, bowl and beaters thoroughly. Beat with electric mixer just until stiff. (Overbeaten cream will separate.)

APRICOT SOUFFLÉ

Store no longer than 24 hours. Makes enough for 6 to 8 servings.

1 can (29 ounces) apricot halves, drained (reserve syrup)
2 envelopes unflavored gelatin
1 can (17.5 ounces) vanilla pudding
1 cup chilled whipping cream

Extend depth of 5-cup soufflé dish by securing 4-inch band of double thickness aluminum foil around top.

Pour ⅔ of the reserved apricot syrup into blender; sprinkle gelatin on syrup. Heat remaining apricot syrup until syrup boils; pour into blender. Blend on low speed until gelatin is dissolved, about ½ minute. Add apricot halves; blend on high speed until apricots are pureed, about 1 minute. Fold pudding into apricot mixture.

Beat whipping cream in chilled bowl until stiff; fold into apricot-pudding mixture. Pour into soufflé dish. Cover with plastic wrap and chill until firm, about 4 hours. (Can be served immediately.) Especially pretty with a garnish of maraschino cherries and frozen whipped topping.

MAPLE BROWNIE DESSERT

Store no longer than 48 hours. Makes enough for 9 servings.

1 package (15.5 ounces) fudge brownie mix
1 cup chilled whipping cream
¼ cup confectioners' sugar
1 teaspoon maple flavoring
9 walnut halves

Prepare Cake-like Brownies as directed on package except—bake 30 minutes. Cool thoroughly.

Beat whipping cream, sugar and maple flavoring in chilled bowl until stiff. Spread whipped cream on brownies; top with walnut halves. Cover and refrigerate at least 2 hours. (Can be served immediately.)

■ **At serving time, cut Maple Brownie Dessert into squares.**

MAZARINE TORTE

Store no longer than 24 hours. Makes enough for 10 servings.

Dough

1⅓ cups all-purpose flour*
1 teaspoon baking powder
⅓ cup sugar
½ cup butter or margarine, softened
1 egg

Filling

½ cup raspberry jam
½ cup butter or margarine, softened
⅔ cup sugar
1 cup blanched almonds, ground or finely chopped
½ teaspoon almond extract
2 eggs

Frosting

½ cup confectioners' sugar
2 teaspoons lemon juice

Spread raspberry jam over the dough, then spoon the almond mixture on top of the jam.

Cover torte with plastic wrap before you refrigerate it. (Wooden picks help to keep wrap from touching the top.)

Grease layer pan, 9×1½ inches. (For ease in removing torte from pan, use a pan with removable bottom.) Mix Dough ingredients; press evenly on bottom and side of pan. Spread ¼ cup of the jam on dough; chill.

Heat oven to 350°. Beat ½ cup butter and ⅔ cup sugar; stir in the almonds and extract. Add 2 eggs, one at a time, beating well after each addition; spoon on jam. Bake 50 minutes. Cool. Remove from pan.

Mix confectioners' sugar and lemon juice until smooth. Spread remaining ¼ cup jam on top; drizzle Frosting on jam. (Can be served immediately.) Insert wooden picks at intervals around top to hold wrap away from the filling. Wrap and refrigerate.

■ **30 minutes before serving, cut Mazarine Torte into pieces and let stand at room temperature.**

*If using self-rising flour, omit baking powder.

Mazarine Torte

Melt the granulated sugar in a saucepan, then quickly coat a pie pan with the caramelized sugar. Pour the pumpkin mixture into the coated pan.

Pumpkin Flan

PUMPKIN FLAN

Store no longer than 24 hours. Makes enough for 10 to 12 servings.

    Spice Cake (page 145)
 ¾ **cup granulated sugar**
 1 **can (16 ounces) pumpkin**
 1 **cup light cream (20%)**
 2 **eggs**
 ½ **cup brown sugar (packed)**
 3 **to 4 tablespoons light rum**

Bake Spice Cake. Melt granulated sugar in saucepan, stirring constantly, until an even amber color. Remove from heat; pour quickly into 9-inch pie pan. Coat bottom and side of pan by tipping pan quickly in all directions.

Heat oven to 350°. Beat remaining ingredients until smooth. Pour into sugar-glazed pie pan. Place in pan of hot water (½ to ¾ inch). Bake until knife inserted halfway between center and edge comes out clean, about 70 minutes. Cool.

Run knife around edge of pumpkin custard to loosen. Invert cake on custard. Invert serving plate on cake and turn upright so custard is top layer. (To serve immediately, see below.) Refrigerate.

■ **At serving time, have ready:** frozen whipped topping (thawed).

Decorate top of Pumpkin Flan and cover space between cake and custard with whipped topping in decorators' tube.

To Serve Immediately: Have ready: frozen whipped topping (thawed).

Decorate top of flan and cover space between cake and custard with whipped topping in decorators' tube.

Using whipped topping in a decorators' tube, decorate the top of the flan and cover the space where the cake and custard meet.

SPICE CAKE

1⅓ cups all-purpose flour*
¾ cup sugar
⅓ cup shortening
⅔ cup milk
1 egg
1¼ teaspoons baking powder
½ teaspoon salt
1½ teaspoons pumpkin pie spice
¾ teaspoon vanilla

Heat oven to 350°. Grease and flour layer pan, 9×1½ inches. Measure all ingredients into large mixer bowl; beat on low speed ½ minute. Beat on medium speed, scraping bowl frequently, 3 minutes. Pour into pan. Bake until wooden pick inserted in center comes out clean, 35 to 40 minutes. Cool.

Note: The Spice Cake can be baked in an 8-inch round layer pan. Bake pumpkin custard in an 8-inch pie pan and 2 individual custard cups.

*If using self-rising flour, omit baking powder and salt.

To Make a Decorating Cone

Cut a 15-inch square of heavy paper or parchment into 2 triangles. Grasping edges with the thumb and forefinger, twist to form a cone (with point at center of longest side). Fold down top edges and fasten cone with transparent tape. Snip off a small opening at point or insert a metal tip into cone. (We used a star tip for this dessert.) Fill cone about half full. Fold top over. Press out whipped cream with one hand near top of cone. Use other hand to guide tip.

TRIFLE

Store no longer than 24 hours. Makes enough for 6 to 8 servings.

1 package (18.5 ounces) yellow cake mix
4 teaspoons sherry
1 package (16 ounces) frozen strawberry halves, thawed
1 can (17.5 ounces) vanilla pudding
1 envelope (about 1½ ounces) whipped topping mix
2 tablespoons toasted slivered almonds

Bake cake in baking pan, 13×9×2 inches, as directed on package. Cool. Cut cake crosswise in half. Wrap, label and freeze one half for future use.

Cut remaining cake half into 8 pieces; split each piece horizontally. Arrange half the pieces in 2-quart glass serving bowl, cutting pieces to fit shape of bowl. Sprinkle 2 teaspoons of the sherry on cake pieces in bowl. Pour half the strawberries on cake pieces; spread half the pudding (1 cup) on strawberries. Repeat with remaining cake pieces, sherry, strawberries and pudding.

Prepare whipped topping mix as directed on package; spread on trifle. Sprinkle almonds on top. Cover and refrigerate at least 1 hour. (Can be served immediately.)

Special Tips

☐ Strawberries or other frozen fruits may be thawed quickly by putting the wrapped package in a bowl under cool running water.

☐ Toasted and/or chopped nuts may be stored in the refrigerator. The best type of container for them is a tightly covered jar.

WHIPPED CHERRY TORTE

Store no longer than 3 days. Makes enough for 8 to 10 servings.

Filling
1 package (7.2 ounces) fluffy white frosting mix
2 cups whipping cream

Torte Layers
1 packet or 2 sticks pie crust mix
1 cup confectioners' sugar
1 cup ground or finely chopped pecans
1 egg
1 teaspoon vanilla
Granulated sugar

Filling
¼ cup cherry-flavored liqueur
5 to 6 drops red food color
12 maraschino cherries, chopped and drained

Chill frosting mix (dry) and whipping cream covered in small mixer bowl at least 1 hour.

Heat oven to 450°. Mix pie crust mix, confectioners' sugar and pecans; stir in egg and vanilla. Gather dough into ball. Turn dough onto lightly floured cloth-covered board; knead until smooth. Divide into 6 parts. Roll each part into 7-inch circle; place on ungreased baking sheet. Prick circles with fork; sprinkle granulated sugar on each one. Bake until golden brown, 6 to 8 minutes. Cool on wire racks.

Stir frosting mixture and beat until stiff. Gradually beat in liqueur. Stir in food color; fold in cherries. Stack circles, filling layers with about ½ cup frosting mixture. Frost stack with remaining frosting mixture. Cover torte with plastic wrap or aluminum foil tent; refrigerate at least 8 hours. (Can be served immediately.)

CHOCOLATE SOUFFLÉ

Store no longer than 6 hours. Makes enough for 6 servings.

⅓ cup sugar
¼ cup all-purpose flour
⅓ cup cocoa
1 cup milk
3 egg yolks
2 tablespoons butter or margarine, softened
1 teaspoon vanilla
4 egg whites
¼ teaspoon cream of tartar
⅛ teaspoon salt
3 tablespoons sugar

Mix ⅓ cup sugar, the flour and cocoa in small saucepan. Gradually stir in milk. Heat, stirring constantly, until mixture boils. Remove from heat. Beat yolks in medium bowl with fork. Beat in about ⅓ of cocoa mixture. Gradually stir in remaining cocoa mixture. Stir in butter and vanilla. Cool slightly. Butter and sugar 6-cup soufflé dish.

Beat egg whites, cream of tartar and salt in large mixer bowl until foamy. Beat in 3 tablespoons sugar, 1 tablespoon at a time, just until stiff peaks form. Stir about ¼ of egg whites into chocolate mixture. Fold in remaining whites. Pour carefully into dish. (Can be baked immediately.) Cover and refrigerate.

■ **1 hour 20 minutes before serving, place oven rack in lowest position.** Heat oven to 350°. Make 4-inch band of triple thickness aluminum foil 2 inches longer than circumference of dish. Butter one side of foil band and sprinkle sugar on butter. Extend depth of dish by securing foil band buttered side in around outside edge of dish. Place dish in baking pan, 9×9×2 inches, on oven rack; pour very hot water (1 inch) into pan. Bake 1¼ hours. If desired, serve with Best Sauce (below).

BEST SAUCE

Beat ½ cup confectioners' sugar and ½ cup soft butter in small saucepan until smooth and creamy. Beat ½ cup chilled whipping cream in chilled bowl until stiff. Fold whipped cream into sugar-butter mixture. Heat, stirring occasionally, until sauce boils. Serve immediately.

RICH CHOCOLATE BAKE

Store no longer than 24 hours. Makes enough for 4 servings.

⅔ cup semisweet chocolate pieces
1 cup half-and-half
2 eggs
3 tablespoons sugar
  Dash salt
1½ tablespoons rum, if desired

Heat oven to 350°. Heat chocolate pieces and half-and-half, stirring constantly, until chocolate is melted and mixture is smooth. Cool slightly. Beat remaining ingredients; stir gradually into chocolate mixture. Pour into 4 ungreased 6-ounce custard cups or 4 or 5 ovenproof pot de crème cups.

Place cups in baking pan on oven rack. Pour boiling water into pan to within ½ inch of tops of cups. Bake 20 minutes. Cool slightly. Cover and chill at least 4 hours.

CHOCOLATE REFRIGERATED DESSERT

Store no longer than 4 days. Makes 10 to 12 servings.

½ large angel food cake
1 package (6 ounces) semisweet chocolate pieces
4 eggs
1 package (about 1½ ounces) whipped topping mix
1 teaspoon vanilla
¾ cup chopped nuts

Tear cake into small pieces. Place half of cake pieces in baking dish, 13½×9×2 inches. In top of double boiler over hot water, melt chocolate pieces. Cool. Beat eggs until thick and lemon colored. Stir in chocolate.

Prepare whipped topping mix as directed on package. Fold in chocolate mixture, vanilla and nuts. Pour half of chocolate mixture on cake pieces in baking dish. Cover with remaining cake pieces; pour remaining chocolate mixture on top. Cover and refrigerate at least 12 hours. (Can be served immediately.)

COMPANY CHEESECAKE

Store no longer than 10 days. Makes enough for 9 to 12 servings.

Crust
1¼ cups graham cracker crumbs (about
    15 crackers)
2 tablespoons sugar
3 tablespoons butter or margarine, melted

Filling
2 packages (8 ounces each) plus
    1 package (3 ounces) cream cheese,
    softened
1 cup sugar
2 teaspoons grated lemon peel
¼ teaspoon vanilla
3 eggs

Topping
2 cups dairy sour cream
¼ cup sugar
1 teaspoon vanilla

Heat oven to 350°. Mix graham cracker crumbs and 2 tablespoons sugar. Stir in butter. Press mixture evenly in bottom of ungreased 9-inch springform pan or in baking pan, 9×9×2 inches. Bake 10 minutes. Cool.

Reduce oven temperature to 300°. Beat cream cheese in large mixer bowl. Gradually beat in 1 cup sugar; beat until fluffy. Add lemon peel and ¼ teaspoon vanilla. Beat in eggs, one at a time; pour on crumb mixture.

Bake until center is firm, about 1 hour. Cool 10 minutes. Mix Topping ingredients; spread on hot cheesecake. Bake 10 minutes. Chill uncovered until cold, about 2 hours. (Can be served immediately.) Cover and refrigerate.

■ **At serving time, loosen edge of Company Cheese-cake with knife before removing from pan.**

CANDY COOKIES

Store no longer than 5 days. Makes about 4 dozen cookies.

2 cups sugar
¼ cup cocoa
½ cup milk
½ cup butter or margarine
½ cup peanut butter
2 cups quick-cooking oats
2 teaspoons vanilla
½ cup chopped nuts

Heat sugar, cocoa, milk and butter in large saucepan, stirring occasionally, until mixture boils. Boil 1 minute. Remove from heat; immediately stir in remaining ingredients. Drop mixture by teaspoonfuls onto waxed paper. (Cookies will spread very thin.) Let stand until firm, about 40 minutes. (Can be served immediately.) Remove from waxed paper; place in covered container and refrigerate.

ALMOND DROPS

Store no longer than 8 days. Makes 7 dozen candies.

1 can (16.5 ounces) vanilla frosting
¾ teaspoon almond extract
½ teaspoon vanilla
½ cup slivered almonds, toasted

Mix all ingredients; drop by level teaspoonfuls onto waxed paper-covered baking sheet. Chill until set, about 4 hours. (Can be served immediately.) Remove from waxed paper; place in covered container and refrigerate.

Versatile Cookie Mix: Peanut Butter Cookies, Spice Cookies and Banana Cookies

VERSATILE COOKIE MIX

Store no longer than 10 weeks. Makes 9 to 10 cups cookie mix.

   4 cups all-purpose flour*
1¼ cups granulated sugar
1¼ cups brown sugar (packed)
   3 teaspoons baking powder
1½ teaspoons salt
1½ cups shortening

Mix flour, sugars, baking powder and salt in large bowl. Cut in shortening with pastry blender or with electric mixer on medium speed until mixture looks like coarse meal. Do not overmix.

Measure desired amounts of cookie mix into jars or plastic containers: 2 cups for 2 dozen Peanut Butter Cookies; 2½ cups each for 3 dozen Banana Cookies and 2½ dozen Spice Cookies. (Can be baked immediately.) Seal tightly, label and refrigerate.

■ **30 minutes before serving, prepare one of the cookie recipes at right.**

Note: Do not use butter or margarine. If dough is dry, stir in 1 to 2 teaspoons cream.

*If using self-rising flour, omit baking powder and salt.

PEANUT BUTTER COOKIES

Heat oven to 375°. Mix 2 cups cookie mix, ½ cup chunky peanut butter, 1 egg and 1 teaspoon vanilla. Shape dough by teaspoonfuls into balls. Place about 2 inches apart on ungreased baking sheet; flatten with tines of fork dipped in flour. Bake until light brown, 10 to 12 minutes. (2 dozen cookies.)

BANANA COOKIES

Heat oven to 375°. Mix 2½ cups cookie mix, ½ cup mashed ripe banana, 1 teaspoon vanilla, 1 egg and ½ cup chopped nuts. Drop dough by rounded teaspoonfuls 2 inches apart onto ungreased baking sheet. Bake until light brown, 12 to 15 minutes. (3 dozen cookies.)

SPICE COOKIES

Heat oven to 375°. Mix 2½ cups cookie mix, 1 egg, ½ teaspoon cinnamon, ½ teaspoon lemon extract, ½ cup raisins and ½ cup chopped nuts. Drop dough by rounded teaspoonfuls 2 inches apart onto ungreased baking sheet. Bake until light brown, 12 to 15 minutes. (2½ dozen cookies.)

DATE-NUT PINWHEELS

Store no longer than 6 weeks. Makes about 5 dozen cookies.

- ¾ pound pitted dates, chopped
- ⅓ cup granulated sugar
- ⅓ cup water
- ½ cup chopped nuts
- ½ cup shortening (half butter or margarine, softened)
- 1 cup brown sugar (packed)
- 1 egg
- ½ teaspoon vanilla
- 1¾ cups all-purpose flour*
- ¼ teaspoon salt

Cook dates, granulated sugar and water in saucepan, stirring constantly, until thickened slightly. Remove from heat; stir in nuts. Cool.

Mix shortening, brown sugar, egg and vanilla until smooth. Stir in flour and salt; divide dough in half. Roll each half on waxed paper into rectangle about 11×7 inches; spread half the date-nut filling on each rectangle. Roll up tightly, beginning at long side. Pinch edge to dough to seal securely. Wrap and chill at least 4 hours. (Can be baked immediately.)

■ **15 minutes before serving, heat oven to 400°.** Cut rolls into ¼-inch slices; place 1 inch apart on ungreased baking sheet. Bake until light brown, about 10 minutes. Remove immediately from baking sheet.

VARIATIONS

Caramel-Nut Cookies: Omit date-nut filling. Stir in 1 cup finely chopped nuts with the flour. Shape dough into rolls, 2 inches in diameter; wrap and chill at least 4 hours.

Orange-Pecan Cookies: Omit date-nut filling. Mix in 1 tablespoon grated orange peel with the shortening; stir in ½ cup chopped pecans with the flour. Shape dough into rolls, 2 inches in diameter; wrap and chill at least 4 hours.

*If using self-rising flour, omit salt.

Pictured at left: The rolls of cookie dough make Date-Nut Pinwheels, Almond-Molasses Toppers (page 152), Brownie Refrigerator Cookies (page 152) and Candied Fruit Cookies (page 152).

NEAPOLITAN COOKIES

Store no longer than 6 weeks. Makes about 6½ dozen cookies.

- 1 cup butter or margarine, softened
- ½ cup sugar
- 1 egg
- 1 teaspoon vanilla
- 2¼ cups all-purpose flour*
- ½ teaspoon salt
- 1 ounce melted unsweetened chocolate (cool)
- ¼ cup chopped walnuts
- 2 tablespoons finely chopped maraschino cherries

Mix butter, sugar, egg and vanilla. Stir in flour and salt. Divide dough into 3 parts. Leave 1 part plain; mix chocolate and walnuts into 1 part and cherries into remaining part. Line loaf pan, 9×5×3 inches, with aluminum foil. Spread plain dough evenly in bottom of pan. Top with a layer each of chocolate and cherry dough. Chill at least 2 hours. Remove dough with foil from pan. (Can be baked immediately.) Wrap and refrigerate.

■ **20 minutes before serving, heat oven to 375°.** Cut dough into ¼-inch slices; cut each slice crosswise in half. Place 1 inch apart on ungreased baking sheet. Bake until light brown, about 10 minutes. Remove immediately from baking sheet.

*Do not use self-rising flour in this recipe.

BROWNIE REFRIGERATOR COOKIES

Store no longer than 4 weeks. Makes about 4 dozen cookies.

  1 package (15.5 ounces) fudge
    brownie mix
  1 egg
  ½ cup finely chopped walnuts

Mix brownie mix (dry), egg and walnuts with hands. (If necessary, add about 1 teaspoon water.) Shape into roll, 2 inches in diameter. Wrap and chill at least 4 hours. (Can be baked immediately.)

■ **15 minutes before serving, heat oven to 375°.** Cut roll into ⅛-inch slices; place on ungreased baking sheet. Bake until set, about 5 minutes. Cool slightly; remove from baking sheet.

VARIATION

Cherry Refrigerator Cookies: Add ¼ cup drained chopped maraschino cherries.

CANDIED FRUIT COOKIES

Store no longer than 6 weeks. Makes about 6 dozen cookies.

  1 cup butter or margarine, softened
  1 cup confectioners' sugar
  1 egg
  2¼ cups all-purpose flour*
  ¼ teaspoon cream of tartar
  ½ cup chopped pecans
  ½ cup chopped mixed candied fruit
  1 cup candied whole cherries

Mix butter, sugar and egg. Stir in remaining ingredients. Divide dough in half; shape each half into roll, 1½ inches in diameter. Wrap and chill at least 4 hours. (Can be baked immediately.) (Rolls of cookies can also be frozen if you prefer. Thaw before slicing.)

■ **About 15 minutes before serving, heat oven to 375°.** Cut rolls into ⅛-inch slices; place 1 inch apart on ungreased baking sheet. Bake about 8 minutes. Remove immediately from baking sheet.

*Self-rising flour can be used in this recipe.

ALMOND-MOLASSES TOPPERS

Store no longer than 6 weeks. Makes about 3½ dozen cookies.

  ½ cup butter or margarine, softened
  2 tablespoons molasses
  ½ teaspoon vanilla
  ¼ cup confectioners' sugar
  1 cup all-purpose flour*
  ¼ teaspoon soda
  ⅓ cup butter or margarine, softened
  1 cup confectioners' sugar
  1 cup finely chopped almonds

Mix ½ cup butter, the molasses, vanilla, ¼ cup confectioners' sugar, the flour and soda until soft dough forms. Divide dough in half; shape each half into roll, 6 inches long. Wrap and chill in refrigerator at least 4 hours. (Can be baked immediately.)

Mix ⅓ cup butter, 1 cup confectioners' sugar and the almonds. Divide mixture in half; shape each half into roll, 6 inches long. Wrap and chill at least 4 hours.

■ **20 minutes before serving, heat oven to 350°.** Cut rolls into ¼-inch slices. Place molasses slices 1 inch apart on ungreased baking sheet; top each with almond slice. Bake until delicate brown, 10 to 12 minutes. Remove immediately from baking sheet.

*If using self-rising flour, omit soda.

Easy-to-Cut Cookies

For nicely shaped refrigerator cookies:
☐ Be sure dough has been thoroughly mixed and shaped into *firm* rolls.

☐ Use a sharp, thin-bladed knife. Make slices all the same size so that they will bake in the same length of time.

QUICK REFRIGERATOR COOKIES

Store no longer than 10 weeks. Makes about 8 dozen cookies.

**1 package (15.4 ounces) creamy white
   frosting mix
2 cups all-purpose flour*
1 cup butter or margarine, softened
½ cup chopped pecans**

Measure 1½ cups of the frosting mix (dry) into large bowl; reserve remaining frosting mix. Mix in flour, butter and pecans with hands. Divide dough in half; shape each half into roll, about 1½ inches in diameter and 7½ inches long. Wrap and chill at least 4 hours. (Can be baked immediately.)

■ **20 minutes before serving, heat oven to 400°.
Have ready:** reserved frosting mix; 1½ tablespoons butter or margarine, softened; 2 tablespoons hot water.

Cut rolls into ⅛-inch slices; place 1 inch apart on ungreased baking sheet. Bake 4 to 6 minutes. Cool slightly; remove from baking sheet.

Mix butter, water and reserved frosting mix. (If necessary, stir in 1 to 2 teaspoons water.) Frost cookies. (Enough frosting for about 4 dozen cookies; leave remainder unfrosted.)

*Do not use self-rising flour in this recipe.

ORANGE PECAN LOAF

Store no longer than 4 days.

Heat oven to 350°. Grease and flour 2 loaf pans, 9×5×3 inches. Prepare orange cake mix with pudding (18.5 ounces) as directed on package except – use 2 tablespoons less water and add ½ cup chopped pecans. Pour into pans.

Bake until loaves pull away from sides of pans and spring back when touched lightly in center, 35 to 40 minutes. Cool thoroughly. (Can be served immediately.) Wrap and refrigerate.

PUMPKIN CAKE

Store no longer than 1 week.

**1 package (18.5 ounces) yellow cake mix
   with pudding
2 eggs
¼ cup water
2 teaspoons soda
½ can (16-ounce size) pumpkin
   (about 1 cup)
2 teaspoons pumpkin pie spice**

Heat oven to 350°. Grease and flour 12-cup cast aluminum bundt cake pan or baking pan, 13×9×2 inches. Stir all ingredients in large mixer bowl. Beat on medium speed 2 minutes. Pour batter into pan. Bake until cake pulls away from side of pan and springs back when touched lightly in center, bundt cake pan 40 to 45 minutes, 13×9×2-inch pan 35 to 40 minutes. Cool 10 minutes; remove from pan. Cool; wrap and refrigerate.

ALMOND TORTE

Store no longer than 24 hours.

Bake a devils food cake mix with pudding (18.5 ounces) in 2 layer pans, 8 or 9×1½ inches, as directed on package. Cool. Split to make 4 layers.

Prepare Almond Whipped Cream Filling (below). Fill layers and frost top of torte, using ¼ of the filling (about 1 cup) for each layer. Sprinkle chocolate shot around top edge of torte. Decorate with blanched almonds. Chill at least 4 hours. (Can be served immediately.) Insert wooden picks at intervals on top and side of torte to prevent wrap from touching filling. Wrap and refrigerate.

■ **35 minutes before serving, remove torte from refrigerator and unwrap.** Cut Almond Torte and let stand at room temperature.

ALMOND WHIPPED CREAM FILLING
**2 envelopes (about 1½ ounces each)
   whipped topping mix
1 cup milk
1½ teaspoons almond extract
½ cup confectioners' sugar**

Mix whipped topping mix, milk and extract in bowl. Gradually beat in sugar; beat until stiff.

FRUIT SALAD PIE

Store no longer than 24 hours.

Pastry for 9-inch Two-crust Pie (page 77)
2 tablespoons soft butter or margarine
1 medium banana
2 cans (17 ounces each) fruits for salad, drained
1 can (16 ounces) mandarin orange segments, drained
⅓ cup honey
2 tablespoons granulated ascorbic acid mixture
3 tablespoons quick-cooking tapioca
¼ teaspoon salt
¼ teaspoon allspice

Prepare pastry. Spread butter on pastry in pie pan. Slice banana into bowl; add fruits for salad and orange segments. Pour honey on fruits; toss until fruits are coated. Mix ascorbic acid mixture, tapioca, salt and allspice; stir into fruit mixture. Turn fruit mixture into pie pan; cover with top crust. Do not cut slits in top crust. Seal edge; flute. (To serve immediately, see below.) Refrigerate.

■ **1 hour before serving, heat oven to 425°.** Cut slits in top crust. Cover edge with 2- to 3-inch strip of aluminum foil to prevent excessive browning; remove foil 15 minutes before pie is done. Bake until crust is brown, 45 to 55 minutes. Cool slightly.

To Serve Immediately: Heat oven to 425°. Cut slits in top crust. Cover edge with 2- to 3-inch strip of aluminum foil; remove after pie has baked 25 minutes. Bake until crust is brown, 40 to 50 minutes. Cool slightly.

STRAWBERRY MINUTE PIE

Store no longer than 48 hours.

8- inch Baked Pie Shell (page 77)
1 cup boiling water
1 package (3 ounces) strawberry-flavored gelatin
1 package (16 ounces) frozen sliced strawberries

Bake pie shell. Pour boiling water on gelatin in bowl; stir until gelatin is dissolved. Add frozen strawberries; stir to break berries apart. When mixture is partially set, pour into baked pie shell. Chill until set, about 2 hours. (Can be served immediately.) If desired, serve with frozen whipped topping.

VANILLA CREAM PIE

Store no longer than 48 hours.

9- inch Baked Pie Shell (page 77)
⅔ cup sugar
¼ cup cornstarch
½ teaspoon salt
3 cups milk
4 egg yolks, slightly beaten
2 tablespoons butter or margarine, softened
1 tablespoon plus 1 teaspoon vanilla

Bake pie shell. Mix sugar, cornstarch and salt in saucepan. Beat milk and egg yolks; stir gradually into sugar mixture. Cook over medium heat, stirring constantly, until mixture thickens and boils. Boil and stir 1 minute. Remove from heat; stir in butter and vanilla. Pour immediately into baked pie shell. Immediately press plastic wrap onto filling. Chill at least 2 hours. (Can be served immediately.) If desired, serve with sweetened whipped cream.

VARIATIONS

Chocolate Cream Pie: Increase sugar to 1½ cups and cornstarch to ⅓ cup. Omit butter and stir in 2 ounces melted unsweetened chocolate with the vanilla.

Coconut Cream Pie: Decrease vanilla to 2 teaspoons and stir in ¾ cup flaked coconut. Sprinkle ¼ cup flaked coconut on whipped cream if desired.

EGGNOG PIE

Store no longer than 48 hours.

9- inch Baked Pie Shell (page 77)
1 envelope (about 1½ ounces) whipped
    topping mix
1 teaspoon rum flavoring
½ teaspoon nutmeg
¼ teaspoon ginger
1 can (17.5 ounces) vanilla pudding

Bake pie shell. Prepare topping mix as directed on package except—omit vanilla; stir in rum flavoring, nutmeg and ginger. Fold pudding into whipped topping; pour into pie shell. Chill until set, at least 4 hours. (Can be served immediately.)

STRAWBERRY CHIFFON PIE

Store no longer than 48 hours.

9- inch Baked Pie Shell (page 77)
¼ cup sugar
1 envelope unflavored gelatin
1 package (10 ounces) frozen strawberry
    halves, thawed
3 egg whites
¼ teaspoon cream of tartar
⅓ cup sugar
½ cup chilled whipping cream

Bake pie shell. Mix ¼ cup sugar and the gelatin in saucepan; stir in strawberries. Cook over medium heat, stirring constantly, just until mixture boils. Place pan in bowl of ice and water or chill in refrigerator, stirring occasionally, until mixture mounds slightly when dropped from spoon.

Beat egg whites and cream of tartar until foamy. Beat in ⅓ cup sugar, 1 tablespoon at a time; beat until stiff and glossy. Do not underbeat. Fold strawberry mixture into meringue. Beat cream in chilled bowl until stiff; fold into strawberry meringue. Pile into baked pie shell. Chill until set, at least 3 hours. (Can be served immediately.)

Note: For ease in cutting pie, dip knife into hot water.

LEMON CHIFFON PIE

Store no longer than 48 hours.

9- inch Baked Pie Shell (page 77)
½ cup sugar
1 envelope unflavored gelatin
4 eggs, separated
⅔ cup water
⅓ cup lemon juice
1 tablespoon grated lemon peel
½ teaspoon cream of tartar
½ cup sugar

Bake pie shell. Mix ½ cup sugar and the gelatin in small saucepan. Beat egg yolks, water and lemon juice; stir into sugar mixture. Cook over medium heat, stirring constantly, just until mixture boils. Stir in peel. Place pan in bowl of ice and water or chill in refrigerator, stirring occasionally, until mixture mounds slightly when dropped from spoon.

Beat egg whites and cream of tartar until foamy. Beat in ½ cup sugar, 1 tablespoon at a time; beat until stiff and glossy. Do not underbeat. Fold lemon mixture into meringue. Pile into baked pie shell. Chill until set, at least 3 hours. (Can be served immediately.)

Note: For ease in cutting pie, dip knife into hot water.

For Great Chiffon Pies

☐ Look at the photo on page 80 to determine when gelatin "mounds slightly."

☐ Separate eggs while they are cold; then let whites come to room temperature (they'll beat up faster and to a larger volume). Be sure there is no yolk in the white.

☐ Fold thickened gelatin mixture into meringue carefully but thoroughly. Use a rubber scraper, cutting down through the mixture. Slide scraper across the bottom of the bowl and up the side.

Index